SRA ART Connections

Arts Education for the 21st Century

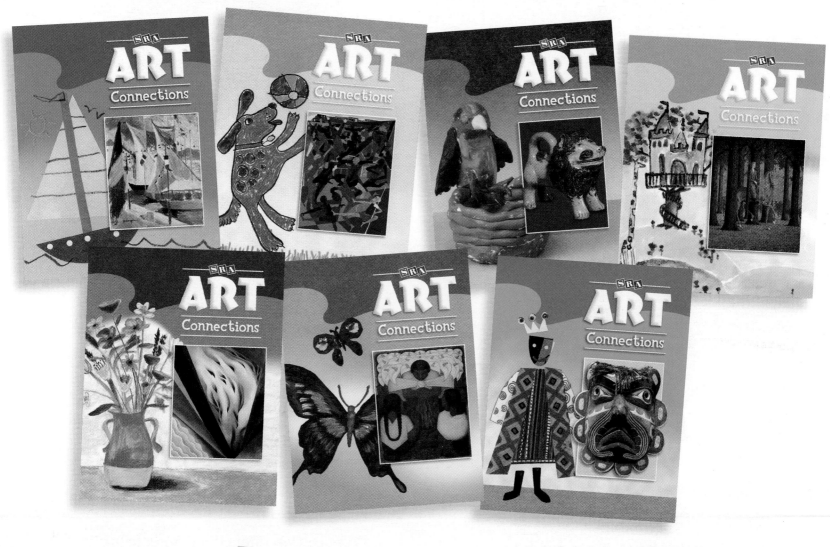

Culture

Personal Expression

Creativity

History

Beauty

Critical Thinking

Art encourages different ways of learning, knowing, and communicating.

i

All the Resources you Need for Great Art Teaching!

Art Connections provides everything teachers need to offer meaningful art education.

Student Edition K-6

Comprehensive student materials in two formats:

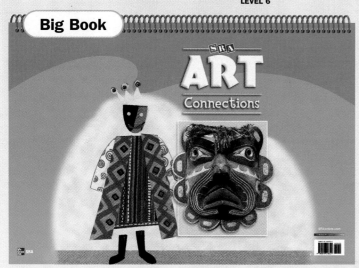

Student Edition

LEVEL 6

Big Book

LEVEL 6

Teacher Edition

Everything classroom and art teachers need to teach art effectively

TEACHER EDITION

LEVEL 4

- Complete lesson plans to teach
  - elements and principles of art
  - art history and culture
  - art criticism
  - art production
- Art background
- Cross-curricular connections
- Program resources guide

Technology Components

e-Presentation for students and teachers

LEVEL K

e-Presentation offers the complete Student Edition as a presentation tool for teachers, complete with multimedia experiences, assessments, teacher materials, and a gallery of all artworks in the entire program.

This electronic gallery allows immediate access to all the artwork in the *Art Connections* program.

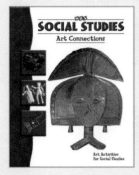 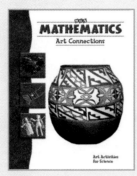  

Cross-Curricular Art Connections include practical art projects for the classroom to help meet subject-area guidelines in

- Social Studies
- Mathematics
- Language Arts and Reading
- Science

LEVEL 3

Reading and Writing Test Preparation that reinforces art content

LEVEL 1

Home and After-School Connections for every unit, in English and Spanish

Professional Development Guide for both classroom teachers and art specialists

LEVEL 5

Assessment with tests in English and Spanish for every lesson

Art Around the World CD-ROM includes 150 works of art from the *Art Around the World Collection,* representing a variety of thought-provoking perspectives and activities.

The National Museum of Women in the Arts Collection CD-ROM dynamically explores the 200-print collection to introduce students to key women artists.

Connections

Enrich students' lives with exposure to the great masters and cultures of the world.

Fine-Art Resources

Transparencies Overhead transparency study prints for all lesson artwork allow for up-close examination.

LEVEL 5

Large Prints for each unit provide exemplary artwork to develop unit concepts.

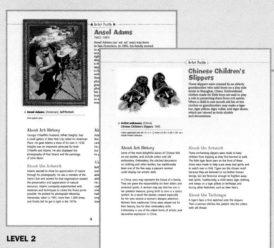

Ansel Adams
1902–1984

Chinese Children's Slippers

LEVEL 2

LEVEL 1

Artist Profiles Pictures, background information, and profiles for every artist in the program provide valuable historical and cultural information at your fingertips.

Literature and Art Videos and DVD develop art connections to literature.

The Polar Express

Art Around the World 150-print resource explores the art of the world's cultures.

iv

Elements and Principles of Art Teaching Resources

Artsource® Performing Arts Resource Package (Video and DVD) integrates the performing arts of dance, music, and theatre.

LEVEL 3

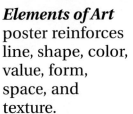

The National Museum of Women in the Arts Collection This 200-print resource provides famous artwork from famous women artists.

Elements of Art poster reinforces line, shape, color, value, form, space, and texture.

Principles of Art poster develops concepts of rhythm, balance, movement, harmony, variety, emphasis, and unity.

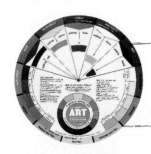

Use the *Color Wheel* to explore color concepts.

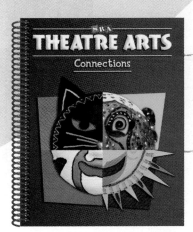

Theatre Arts Connections is a complete dramatic arts program that ties to *Art Connections*.

LEVEL 4

Flash Cards provide a quick review of the elements and principles of art.

v

SRA ART
Connections

Build a foundation in the elements and principles of art.

36 Lessons at every grade level develop the elements and principles of art in six-lesson units.

◀ Rembrandt van Rijn.
Portrait of Rembrandt.

▶ Frida Kahlo.
Frida y Diego Rivera.

LEVEL 6

Unit Openers introduce students to unit concepts and master artists.

Unit 5

Space, Proportion, and Distortion

Artists use accurate proportions to realistically depict people and objects.

Copley painted this realistic portrait of the Pepperrell family in 1778. The Pepperrell family lived in New England until about the time of the American Revolution, when they moved to England. At about the same time, Sir William Pepperrell lost most of his wealth. Notice that Copley used correct proportions to make the painting realistic.

▲ John Singleton Copley.
(American).
Sir William Pepperrell and His Family. 1778.

Oil on canvas. 90 × 108 inches (228.6 × 274.32 cm). North Carolina Museum of Art, Raleigh, North Carolina.

154 Unit 5

Artists use space in paintings to give the appearance of depth on a flat surface.

▶ How do you think John Singleton Copley created space in *Sir William Pepperrell and His Family?*
▶ Which objects in the painting look closer to you? Which objects look farther away?

Artists use accurate **proportions** to show people or things realistically.

▶ Do you think the people in Copley's painting look like they have been painted with accurate proportions? Explain.

In This Unit you will learn about different ways that artists show size and placement. Here are the topics you will study:
▶ Foreground, middle ground, and background
▶ Perspective techniques
▶ Point of view
▶ Face proportion
▶ Body proportions
▶ Distortion

Master Artist Profile

John Singleton Copley
(1738–1815)

John Singleton Copley was a popular portrait painter during the eighteenth century. When he was seventeen years old he created a portrait of George Washington. In his attempt to capture details and to make his subjects appear natural, Copley sometimes required fifteen or sixteen sittings for a single portrait. Copley moved to England during the American Revolution and did not return to America.

Unit 5 **155**

LEVEL 4

Unit Wrap-Ups review concepts, explore Art Museums or Art Careers and allow students to experience Artsource® connections to dance, theatre, and music.

Wrapping Up Unit 5
Space, Proportion, and Distortion

▲ Jacob Lawrence. (American). *Study for the Munich Olympic Games Poster.* 1971.

Gouache on paper. 35 × 27 inches (90.17 × 68.58 cm). Seattle Art Museum, Seattle, Washington.

180 Unit 5

Wrapping Up Unit 5
Space, Proportion, and Distortion, continued
Show What You Know

VISIT A MUSEUM
The Smithsonian

Art Criticism Critical Thinking

Describe What do you see?
During this step you will collect information about the subject of the work.
▶ How many people do you see? What kinds of facial expressions do they have?
▶ What are the people doing? What are they wearing?
▶ What is the setting?

Analyze How is this work organized?
Think about how the artist used the elements and principles of art.
▶ Which people or objects look closest to you? Which look farthest away?
▶ What is in the foreground, the middle ground, and the background?
▶ Where do you see a part of someone's body that overlaps and covers part of another person or object?
▶ What is the point of view of this painting?
▶ Where do you see distortion?

Interpret What is the artist trying to say?
Use the clues you discovered during your analysis to find the message the artist is trying to show.
▶ Which runner do you think will win the race? Why?
▶ What is the mood of this painting?
▶ What sounds would you hear if you could go into the painting?

Decide What do you think about the work?
Use all the information you have gathered to decide whether this is a successful work of art.
▶ Is the work successful because it is realistic, because it is well-organized, or because it has a strong message?

Unit 5 **181**

Space and Proportion in Music

...orn in Cuba. ...ld he moved to ...ard harp music. ...from his friend ...master harpist. ...but eventually ...fe to the harp.

...make a simple

...nd. Vibration is ...nsation caused in ...of air. You can hear ...a string tightly ...ck the string.

...tch rubber bands ...re that rubber ...cknesses.

...if you get ...ls. The thickness, ...e strings will

...thicknesses of ...igher or lower

▲ Ortiz. "Joropo Azul."

Art Criticism

Describe Describe how you made your instrument.
Analyze What did you do to get a higher or lower tone or pitch?
Interpret What did you feel as you created an instrument and heard the sounds it made?
Decide Were you able to get a satisfying musical sound from your simple instrument?

Unit 5 **183**

LEVEL 4

Integrate the four disciplines of art into every lesson for well-rounded exposure to all the dimensions of art.

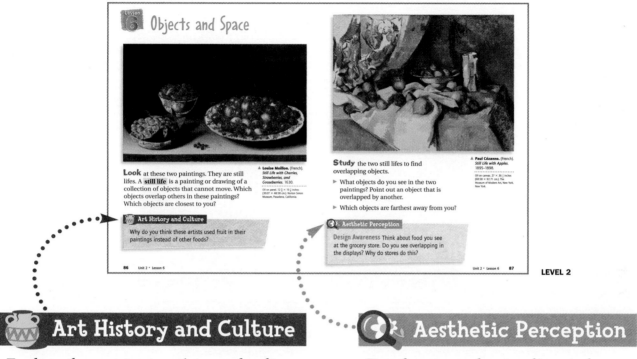

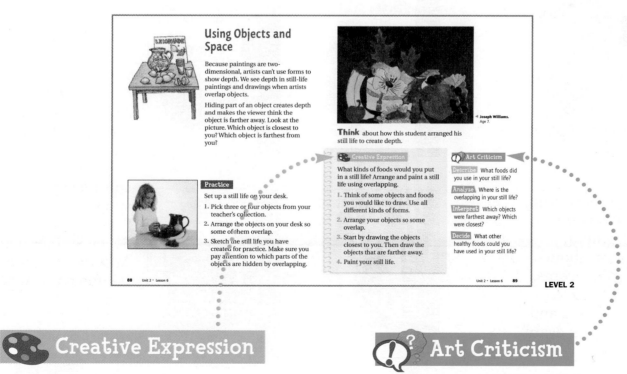

Art History and Culture

Explore the great art, artists, and cultures of the world.

Aesthetic Perception

Develop an understanding and appreciation for art.

Creative Expression

Encounter a broad range of art media in a variety of hands-on art activities that give students an avenue for self-expression and self-esteem.

Art Criticism

Enrich critical-thinking skills as students learn about the elements and principles of art by examining their own and others' artwork.

Add dimension to all subjects with meaningful art connections.

Connect Art to Mathematics, Social Studies, Science, Language Arts and Reading.

LEVEL 1

History
Develop historical understanding as students explore art history and culture in every lesson.

LEVEL 2

Reading and Writing Test Preparation
Use art content, information about artists, art concepts, and art history to practice reading and writing skills in every unit.

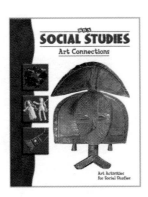

Cross-Curricular Art Connections
These books provide a wealth of exciting art activities designed specifically to support subject-area studies in Science, Mathematics, Social Studies, Language Arts and Reading as they reinforce art concepts.

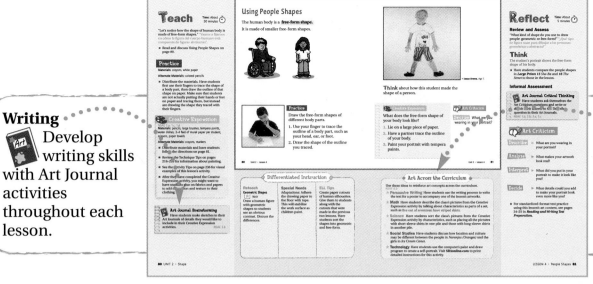

Writing

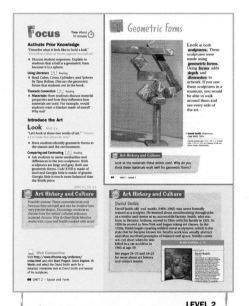

Develop writing skills with Art Journal activities throughout each lesson.

Cross-Curricular Ideas

Show students how artwork and concepts relate to science, mathematics, social studies, reading/language arts, and technology in every lesson.

Cross-Curricular Integration

Integrate language arts and reading, math, science, and social studies concepts naturally as students work through each art lesson.

Vocabulary Development

Key vocabulary terms are highlighted, defined, and reviewed to develop the language of art.

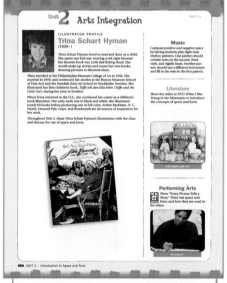

Literature Integration

Integrate literature with Illustrator Profiles and Literature and Art video experiences at the beginning of every unit.

Research has shown that incorporating the arts into core curriculum areas in a way that actively involves students in the learning process produces "significant positive effects on student achievement, motivation, and engagement in learning, and notable changes in classroom practices" ("Different Ways of Knowing: 1991-94 National Longitudinal Study Final Report" in Schools, Communities, and the Arts: A Research Compendium).

Integrate all the Performing Arts for a complete Art education.

Expose children to music, dance, and theatre as they explore the visual arts.

Music

LEVEL 2

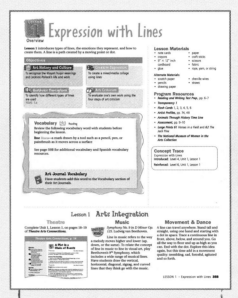

LEVEL 5

 Music Connections in every Unit Opener translate the visual arts elements and principles into music.

 Music Experiences in every lesson from Macmillan/McGraw-Hill's *Spotlight on Music* expand creativity and develop music appreciation.

 Artsource® music performances on video and DVD explore the elements and principles of art through the performing arts.

LEVEL 4

 Artsource® LEVEL 3
dance performances on
video and DVD explore
the elements and
principles of art through
the performing arts.

 Artsource® LEVEL 5
theatre performances on
video and DVD explore
the elements and
principles of art through
the performing arts.

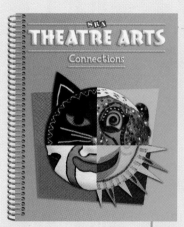

LEVEL 3

Theatre Arts Connections for
grades K–6
lessons explore
the elements
and principles of
theatre arts as
students develop
the elements
and principles of
visual arts.

Case studies have indicated that
students perceive "that the arts
facilitate their personal and social
development." It also appears that to
gain the full benefit of arts education,
students should be exposed to all of the
arts, including fine arts, dance,
theatre, and music ("Arts Education in
Secondary School: Effects and
Effectiveness" in <u>Critical Links</u>, p. 76).

National Standards for Arts Education

Content Standard #1:

Understanding and applying media, techniques, and processes

The Creative Expression activity in every lesson of *Art Connections* develops understanding and experience with a wide variety of media, techniques, and processes. Practice activities in every lesson focus specifically on techniques.

Content Standard #2:

Using knowledge of structures and functions

Art Connections develops the elements and principles of art in every grade level, K–6. Units and lessons are organized to explore the elements and principles in exemplary art and then to practice techniques and create works of art that employ specific structures and functions of art.

Content Standard #3:

Choosing and evaluating a range of subject matter, symbols, and ideas

Art Connections introduces students to subject matter and symbols at the beginning of every grade level and then uses that knowledge throughout every lesson in the Aesthetic Perception questions and Creative Expression activities as students explore content to develop meaning in artwork.

Ali M. Forbes. Age 7.

Jasmine Krasel. Age 9.

Briana Kittle. Age 6.

Content Standard #4:

Understanding the visual arts in relation to history and cultures

Every lesson in *Art Connections* has a specific objective related to the understanding of art history and culture. These objectives are met as students analyze and interpret exemplary artwork and develop their own artwork.

Content Standard #5:

Reflecting upon and assessing the characteristics and merits of one's own work and the work of others

The four steps of art criticism are explored in every lesson throughout the program as students analyze their own artwork and the work of others.

Content Standard #6:

Making connections between visual arts and other disciplines

Theatre, Dance, and Music are integrated into every unit of *Art Connections*. The elements and principles of visual art are translated into Dance, Theater, and Music through the Artsource® lessons and experiences. In addition, *Theatre Arts Connections* lessons and Music connections throughout the program develop a comprehensive understanding of the connections between visual arts and the performing arts.

Cross-curricular connections are built into every lesson through teaching strategies and ideas that integrate language arts and reading, math, science, and social studies concepts. Art Projects for each of the different subject areas are also included in the program.

Let the experts bring the best practices to your classroom.

Rosalind Ragans, Ph.D., Senior Author

Artist, Associate Professor Emerita

Georgia Southern University

Authors

Willis "Bing" Davis

Artist, Art Consultant

Associate Professor Emeritus,

Central State University, Ohio

Tina Farrell

Assisstant Superintendant, Curriculum and Instruction

Clear Creek Independent School District, Texas

Jane Rhoades Hudak, Ph.D.

Professor of Art

Georgia Southern University

Gloria McCoy

Former President, Texas Art Education Association

K–12 Art Director

Spring Branch Independent School District, Texas

Bunyan Morris

Art Teacher

Effingham County School System

Springfield, Georgia

Nan Yoshida

Art Education Consultant

Los Angeles, California

Contributors

Jackie Ellet

Elementary Art Teacher

Duncan Creek Elementary School

Georgia

Artsource® Music, Dance, and Theatre Lessons

Education Division

The Music Center of Los Angeles County

National Museum of Women in the Arts Collection

National Museum of Women in the Arts

Washington, D.C.

Your Fine-Arts Partner for K–12 Art, Theatre, Dance and Music

McGraw-Hill offers textbook programs to build, support, and extend an enriching fine-arts curriculum from kindergarten through high school.

**Senior Author
Rosalind Ragans**

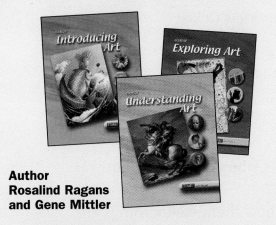

**Author
Rosalind Ragans
and Gene Mittler**

**Author
Rosalind Ragans**

Start with Art SRA

SRA/McGraw-Hill presents *Art Connections* for Grades K–6. *Art Connections* builds the foundations of the elements and principles of art across the grade levels as the program integrates art history and culture, aesthetic perception, creative expression in art production, and art criticism into every lesson.

Art Connections also develops strong cross-curricular connections and integrates the arts with literature, *Theatre Arts Connections* lessons, *Artsource*® experiences, and integrated music selections from Macmillan/McGraw-Hill's *Spotlight on Music*.

Integrate with Art Glencoe

Glencoe/McGraw-Hill offers comprehensive middle and high school art programs that encourage students to make art a part of their lifelong learning. All Glencoe art programs interweave the elements and principles of art to help students build perceptual skills, promote creative expression, explore historical and cultural heritage, and evaluate artwork.

- Introduce students to the many themes artists express.
- Explore the media, techniques, and processes of art.
- Understand the historical and cultural contexts of art.

ArtTalk offers high school students opportunities to perceive, create, appreciate, and evaluate art as it develops the elements and principles of art.

Motivate with Music Macmillan McGraw-Hill

Macmillan/McGraw-Hill's *Spotlight on Music* offers an exiting and comprehensive exposure to music foundations and appreciation.

Sing with Style Glencoe

Glencoe/McGraw-Hill introduces *Experiencing Choral Music* for Grades 6–12. This multilevel choral music program includes instruction in the basic skills of vocal production and music literacy, and provides expertly recorded music selections in many different styles and from various periods of history.

Connections

Getting Started
The very basics...

Here are some tips for Getting Started with Art Connections.

Before School Begins

1. Explore the components you have (student materials, **Overhead Transparencies**, **Large Prints**, and so on). Consider uses and alternative uses for each of the components.

2. Plan your year.
   - Consider how often you meet with students.
   - Decide how many lessons you can present.
   - Examine your curriculum requirements.
   - Select the lessons that best meet your curriculum requirements.

3. Organize art materials.
   - Identify the *Creative Expression* activities you will have students develop.
   - Determine how you will budget materials to last the entire year.
   - Compile a list of materials and order them.
   - Arrange classroom space to store materials.

4. Arrange classroom space to create and store student artwork.

The First Day of School

1. Give an overview of your expectations, objectives, and what you want students to accomplish.

2. Introduce the artroom to students. Show them where things are kept.

3. Establish and communicate:
   - rules for behavior.
   - rules for handling art materials.
   - rules for cleaning up.

4. Begin the **Art Connections** introductory lessons, including *What Is Art?*, *About Art Criticism*, *About Aesthetic Perception*, and *About Art History and Culture*.

Planning a Lesson

1. Review the lesson in the *Teacher's Edition,* including lesson objectives, in-text questions, *Practice*, and *Creative Expression* activities.

2. Assemble program components, such as **Transparencies, Large Prints,** and the **Big Book**.

3. Make any copies of activities or assessments that will be needed for the lesson.

4. Assemble art materials.

5. Determine how you will assess the lesson.

TEACHER'S EDITION

SRA ART Connections

Level 3

Authors

Rosalind Ragans, Ph.D., Senior Author

Willis "Bing" Davis   Jane Rhoades Hudak, Ph.D.   Bunyan Morris

Tina Farrell   Gloria McCoy   Nan Yoshida

Contributing Author

Jackie Ellett

Education Division
The Music Center of Los Angeles County

Columbus, OH

The **McGraw·Hill** Companies

Authors

Senior Author
Dr. Rosalind Ragans, Ph.D.
Associate Professor Emerita
Georgia Southern University

Willis "Bing" Davis
Associate Professor Emeritus
Central State University - Ohio
President & Founder of SHANGO:
The Center for the Study of
African American
Art & Culture

Tina Farrell
Assistant Superintendent,
Curriculum and Instruction
Clear Creek Independent School
District,
League City, Texas

Jane Rhoades Hudak, Ph.D.
Professor of Art
Georgia Southern University

Gloria McCoy
Former President,
Texas Art Education Association
Spring Branch Independent
School District, Texas

Bunyan Morris
Art Teacher
Effingham County School System,
Springfield, Georgia

Nan Yoshida
Art Education Consultant
Retired Art Supervisor,
Los Angeles Unified School
District
Los Angeles, California

Photo Credit **Cover,** René Magritte, *The Blank Signature*
(Carte Blance). Gift of Mr. and Mrs. Paul Mellon, Image
©2003 Board of Trustees, National Gallery of Art,
Washington, DC. ©Artist Rights Society (ARS), New
York/ADAGP, Paris.

SRAonline.com

 SRA

Send all inquiries to:
SRA/McGraw-Hill
8787 Orion Place
Columbus, OH 43240-4027

Printed in the United States of America.

ISBN 0-07-600393-0

3 4 5 6 7 8 9 BCM 10 09 08 07 06

The **McGraw·Hill** Companies

Contributors

Contributing Author
Jackie Ellett
Elementary Art Teacher
Duncan Creek Elementary School
Hoschton, Georgia

Artsource® Music, Dance, Theatre Lessons
Mark Slavkin, Vice President
for Education
The Music Center of Los Angeles County
Michael Solomon, Managing Director
Music Center Education Division
Melinda Williams, Concept Originator and
Project Director
Susan Cambigue-Tracey, Project Coordinator
and Writer
Madeleine Dahm, Movement and Dance
Connection Writer
Keith Wyffels, Staff Assistance
Maureen Erbe, Logo Design

Music Connections
Kathy Mitchell
Music Teacher
Eagan, Minnesota

More about Aesthetics
Richard W. Burrows, Executive Director
Institute for Arts Education
San Diego, California

Art History
Gene A. Mittler, Ph.D.
Professor Emeritus
Texas Tech University

Resources for Students with Disabilities
Mandy Yeager
Ph. D. Candidate
The University of North Texas
Denton, Texas

Brain-Based Learning in the Arts
Jamye Ivey
K-12 Art Supervisor
Dougherty County School System, Georgia

Safe Use of Art Materials
Mary Ann Boykin
Director, The Art School for Children and
Young Adults
University of Houston—Clear Lake
Houston, Texas

Integrating the Four Art Forms
Susan Cambigue-Tracey
The Music Center of Los Angeles County

Using Writing to Enhance Your Art Curriculum
Mary Lazzari, EdS
Elementary Art Teacher
Clarke County School District
Athens, Georgia

Museum Education
Marilyn J. S. Goodman
Director of Education
Solomon R. Guggenheim Museum
New York, New York

Displaying Student Artwork
Jackie Ellett
Duncan Creek Elementary School
Hoschton, Georgia

Student Activities

Cassie Appleby
Glen Oaks Elementary School
McKinney, Texas

Maureen Banks
Kester Magnet School
Van Nuys, California

Christina Barnes
Webb Bridge Middle School
Alpharetta, Georgia

Beth Benning
Willis Jepson Middle School
Vacaville, California

Chad Buice
Craig Elementary School
Snellville, Georgia

Beverly Broughton
Gwinn Oaks Elementary School
Snellville, Georgia

Missy Burgess
Jefferson Elementary School
Jefferson, Georgia

Marcy Cincotta-Smith
Benefield Elementary School
Lawrenceville, Georgia

Joanne Cox
Kittredge Magnet School
Atlanta, Georgia

Carolyn Y. Craine
McCracken County Schools
Mayfield, Kentucky

Jackie Ellett
Duncan Creek Elementary School
Hoschton, Georgia

Tracie Flynn
Home School
Rushville, Indiana

Phyllis Glenn
Malcom Bridge Elementary
Bogart, Georgia

Dallas Gillespie
Dacula Middle School
Dacula, Georgia

Dr. Donald Gruber
Clinton Junior High School
Clinton, Illinois

Karen Heid
Rock Springs Elementary School
Lawrenceville, Georgia

Alisa Hyde
Southwest Elementary
Savannah, Georgia

Kie Johnson
Oconee Primary School
Watkinsville, Georgia

Sallie Keith, NBCT
West Side Magnet School
LaGrange, Georgia

Letha Kelly
Grayson Elementary School
Grayson, Georgia

Diane Kimiera
Amestoy Elementary School
Gardena, California

Desiree LaOrange
Barkley Elementary School
Fort Campbell, Kentucky

Deborah Lackey-Wilson
Roswell North Elementary
Roswell, Georgia

Dawn Laird
Goforth Elementary School
Clear Creek, Texas

Mary Lazzari
Timothy Road Elementary School
Athens, Georgia

Michelle Leonard
Webb Bridge Middle School
Alpharetta, Georgia

Lynn Ludlam
Spring Branch ISD
Houston, Texas

Mark Mitchell
Fort Daniel Elementary School
Dacula, Georgia

Martha Moore
Freeman's Mill Elementary School
Dacula, Georgia

Connie Niedenthal
Rushville Elementary
Rushville, Indiana

Barbara Patisaul
Oconee County Elementary School
Watkinsville, Georgia

Elizabeth Paulos-Krasle
Social Circle Elementary
Social Circle, Georgia

Jane Pinneau
Rocky Branch Elementary School
Watkinsville, Georgia

Marilyn Polin
Cutler Ridge Middle School
Miami, Florida

Michael Ramsey
Graves County Schools
Paducah, Kentucky

Rosemarie Sells
Social Circle Elementary
Social Circle, Georgia

Jean Neelen Siegel
Baldwin School
California

Debra Smith
McIntosh County School System
Darien, Georgia

Patricia Spencer
Harmony Elementary School
Buford, Georgia

Melanie Stokes
Smiley Elementary School
Ludowici, Georgia

Rosanne Stutts
Davidson Fine Arts School
Augusta, Georgia

Fran Sullivan
South Jackson Elementary School
Athens, Georgia

Kathy Valentine
Home School
Burkburnett, Texas

Debi West
Rock Springs Elementary School
Lawrenceville, Georgia

Sherry White
Bauerschlog Elementary School
League City, Texas

Patricia Wiesen
Cutler Ridge Middle School
Miami, Florida

Deayna Woodruff
Loveland Middle School
Loveland, Ohio

Gil Young
Beverly Hills Middle School
Beverly Hills, California

Larry A. Young
Dacula Elementary School
Dacula, Georgia

Table of Contents

◀ **Pablo Picasso.**
Mother and Child.

Unit 1 Line and Shape

➟ indicates Core Lessons   **5**

Reading Comprehension Skills and Strategies

➊ Vocabulary, Using Literature, Comparing and Contrasting

➋ Vocabulary, Thematic Connection: Imagination, Comparing and Contrasting

➌ Vocabulary, Using Literature, Comparing and Contrasting

➍ Vocabulary, Using Literature, Comparing and Contrasting

➎ Vocabulary, Using Literature, Comparing and Contrasting

➏ Vocabulary, Using Literature, Comparing and Contrasting

◄ **Edgar Degas.**
*Little Dancer,
Aged Fourteen.*

Unit 2 Space and Form

6

➥ **indicates Core Lessons**

Reading Comprehension Skills and Strategies

➊ Vocabulary, Using Literature, Comparing and Contrasting

➋ Vocabulary, Thematic Connection: Storytelling, Comparing and Contrasting

➌ Vocabulary, Using Literature, Comparing and Contrasting

➍ Vocabulary, Using Literature, Comparing and Contrasting

➎ Vocabulary, Thematic Connection: Sharing Stories, Comparing and Contrasting

➏ Vocabulary, Using Literature, Comparing and Contrasting

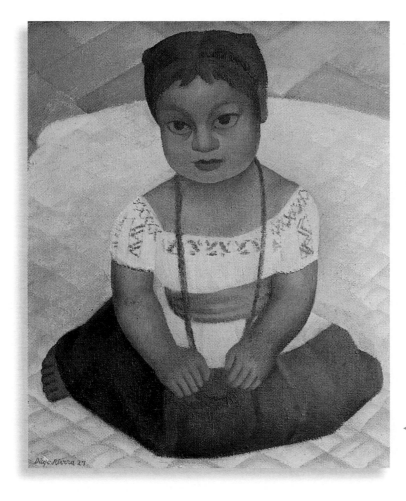

◄ **Diego Rivera.**
*Kneeling Child on
Yellow Background.*

Unit 3 Color and Value

➠ indicates Core Lessons   **7**

Reading Comprehension Skills and Strategies

❶ Vocabulary, Using Literature, Comparing and
Contrasting

❷ Vocabulary, Using Literature, Comparing and
Contrasting

❸ Vocabulary, Using Literature, Comparing and
Contrasting

❹ Vocabulary, Using Literature, Main Idea and
Details

❺ Vocabulary, Using Literature, Comparing and
Contrasting

❻ Vocabulary, Using Literature, Main Idea and
Details

▲ **Audrey Flack.**
Strawberry Tart Supreme.

Unit 4 Texture and Balance

8

➤ **indicates Core Lessons**

Reading Comprehension Skills and Strategies

❶ Vocabulary, Thematic Connection: Storytelling, Comparing and Contrasting
❷ Vocabulary, Using Literature, Comparing and Contrasting

❸ Vocabulary, Using Literature, Comparing and Contrasting
❹ Vocabulary, Using Literature, Comparing and Contrasting

❺ Vocabulary, Using Literature, Comparing and Contrasting
❻ Vocabulary, Using Literature, Comparing and Contrasting

◀ **John James Audubon.**
Great Blue Heron.

Unit 5 Pattern, Rhythm, and Movement

➡ indicates Core Lessons   9

Reading Comprehension Skills and Strategies

➊ Vocabulary, Using Literature, Drawing Conclusions
➋ Vocabulary, Comparing and Contrasting

➌ Vocabulary, Using Literature
➍ Vocabulary, Using Literature, Summarizing

➎ Vocabulary, Using Literature, Comparing and Contrasting
➏ Vocabulary, Using Literature, Comparing and Contrasting

◀ **Fredric Remington.**
Mountain Man.

Unit 6 Harmony, Variety, Emphasis, and Unity

10   ➥ indicates Core Lessons

Reading Comprehension Skills and Strategies

➊ Vocabulary, Comparing and Contrasting
➋ Vocabulary, Summarizing
➌ Vocabulary, Main Idea and Details
➍ Vocabulary, Comparing and Contrasting
➎ Vocabulary, Summarizing
➏ Vocabulary, Comparing and Contrasting

Technique Tips

Activity Tips

Overview

The purpose of these pages is to open students' minds to the idea that visual arts include many components and take many forms. The arts satisfy the human needs for display, celebration, personal expression, and communication. We use the visual arts to enhance our innermost feelings and to communicate ideas. Art is made by people. Even people who are not professional artists can enjoy the creative process.

Activating Prior Knowledge

■ Ask students what they think art is. Encourage creative, divergent thinking. In visual art, there are many answers to a question.

Questions to Discuss

■ Have students look at the images on pages 12 and 13 and name the things that are visual art. Then ask the following questions.

► Which of these things could you hold in your hands?

► Which one could you walk inside?

► Which ones would you hang on a wall?

► Which ones could you wear?

■ Encourage students to think about things they have at home that fit the categories on these pages. The building they live in is architecture. They have dishes and other containers. Many of them have things hanging on the walls to enhance their visual environments. A few may have sculpture in the home. Many will have seen sculpture in and around public buildings.

What Is Art?

Art is . . .

Painting is color applied to a flat surface.

▲ **Edward Hopper.** (American). *Early Sunday Morning.* 1930.
Oil on canvas. $35\frac{3}{16} \times 60\frac{1}{4}$ inches (89.4 × 153 cm.). Whitney Museum of American Art, New York, New York.

Drawing is the process of making art with lines.

▲ **Pablo Picasso.** (Spanish). *Mother and Child.* 1922.
Oil on canvas. 40 × 32 inches (100 × 81 cm.). The Baltimore Museum of Art, Baltimore, Maryland.

Sculpture is art that fills up space.

▲ **Kiawak Ashoona.** (Inuit). *Seal Hunter.*
Serpentine. Home and Away Gallery, Kennebunkport, Maine.

Architecture is the art of designing and constructing buildings.

▲ **Artist Unknown.** (Roman), *Maison Carée.*
1st century B.C.
Nîmes, France.

Printmaking is the process of transferring an original image from one prepared surface to another.

◄ **Maria Sibylla Merian.** (German). *Plate 2 (from "Dissertation in Insect Generations and Metamorphosis in Surinam").* 1719.
Hand-colored engraving on paper. 18 × 13¾ inches (45.72 × 34.93 cm.). National Museum of Women in the Arts, Washington, D.C.

Photography is a technique of capturing an image of light on film.

▲ **Ansel Adams.** (American). *Early Sunday Morning, Merced River, Yosemite Valley, CA.* c. 1950, printed c. 1978.
9⅝ × 12⅞ inches (24.45 × 32.70 cm.). Museum of Modern Art, New York, New York.

Art is made by people

Pottery is an object made from clay.

▲ **Artist Unknown.** (China). *Covered Jar.* 1522–1566.
Porcelain painted with underglaze cobalt blue and overglaze enamels. 18½ inches high, 15¾ inches in diameter. (7 cm. high, 6 cm. in diameter). Asia Society of New York, New York.

A mask is a covering for the face to be used in ceremonies and other events.

◄ **Artist Unknown.** (Ivory Coast). *Senufo Face Mask.* Nineteenth to twentieth century.
Wood, horn, fiber, cloth, feather, metal. 14½ inches tall (35.56 cm.). The Metropolitan Museum of Art, New York, New York.

▶ to communicate ideas.

▶ to express feelings.

▶ to give us well-designed objects.

What Is Art?   **13**

Using the Credit Line

The credit line is a list of important facts about the work of art that appears below or next to the work. For example, you can help students understand the size of an artwork and how it relates to their own size. Most credit lines contain the following information.

- Name of the artist.

- Title of the work. This always appears in italics. If the word *detail* follows the title, it means that the image is part of a larger work of art.

- Year the work was created. A *c* before the date indicates that the piece was made around the year given.

- Medium used by the artist.

- Size of the work. The first number is the height, the second is the width, and a third number indicates depth for three-dimensional works.

- Location of the work. This tells the museum, gallery, or collection in which the work is housed.

Art Studios, Galleries, and Museums

Works of art are created in ***studios.*** A studio is an artist's workplace, much like a classroom is a studio for students. Almost everything an artist needs to create an artwork will be found in his or her studio. It is possible for people to visit artist studios, but an invitation from the artist is usually required.

Art galleries are private businesses where art dealers display and sell works of art. Art galleries are typically open to the public and the works of art may be viewed even if the patrons do not intend to buy anything.

A ***museum*** is a public or private building where valuable and important works of art are cared for and displayed for the public to view. *Curators* are people who supervise the museum and organize exhibitions. *Docents* are special tour directors who help explain the art to visitors.

Overview

These pages introduce students to the three components that define a work of art: the subject, the composition, and the content.

Subject

The subject is the image that the viewer can easily identify in a work of art. The subject may be one person or many people. It may be a thing. It can be an event, such as a party. In recent years, some artists have chosen to create nonobjective art. This is art that has no recognizable subject matter, such as *The Voice of the City of New York Interpreted/The Great White Way Leaving the Subway (White Way I)*. In this work of art, the elements of art become the subject.

Composition

The composition is the way the principles of art are used to organize the elements of art. Notice how Henry Moore has organized line, form, and texture in space to create the feeling that we are looking at a seated family.

Content

The content is the message the work communicates to the viewer. The message may be an idea, such as family unity, or an emotion or feeling, such as joy or loneliness. If the work of art is functional, such as *Easy Chair*, then the function is the meaning. Does the work of art look like it could perform the function it is supposed to?

What Is Art?

Every work of art has three parts.

Subject

The subject is the object you can recognize in the artwork. If a work has no objects, the elements of art are the subject.

Composition

The composition is how the elements and principles are organized in the artwork.

Content

The content is the message or meaning of the artwork. When the work of art is functional, then the function of the work is the meaning.

▶ In which work of art do you think the subject matter is very important?

▶ In which artwork do you think composition is most important?

▶ Which work seems to have the strongest message? Explain.

▶ Which artwork's meaning relates to its function?

▲ **Lorenzo Scott.** (American). *Ballet Dancers.*

Oil on canvas. 50 × 30 inches (127 × 76.2 cm.). Collection of Ann and Ted Oliver.

◀ **Joseph Stella.** (American). *The Voice of the City of New York Interpreted/ The Great White Way Leaving the Subway (White Way I).* c. 1920–22.

Oil and tempera on canvas. 88½ × 54 inches (224.79 × 137.16 cm.). The Newark Museum, Newark, New Jersey.

▲ **Henry Moore.** (British). *Family Group.* 1948–1949.

Bronze (cast 1950), 59¼ × 46½ × 29⅞ inches (150.5 × 118.1 × 75.88 cm.). Museum of Modern Art, New York, New York.

▲ **Caleb Gardner.** (American). *Easy Chair.* 1758.

Walnut, maple, and hand stitched upholstery. 46⅜ × 32⅜ × 25⅞ inches (117.8 × 82.2 × 65.7 cm.). The Metropolitan Museum of Art, New York, New York.

What Is Art? **15**

Activating Prior Knowledge

▪ Ask students what is the first thing they look for when they look at a work of art. Students may say they look at color, size, or what it's about. Some may say they look for the feeling or message they get from it. Give students time to explore this question. It will provide a good context for the discussion on these pages.

Questions to Discuss

▪ Read with students the text on page 14 and look at the images on page 15. Share with them some of the information above. Encourage students to think about their responses during the Activating Prior Knowledge discussion as they look at these images and think about the information you have shared with them.

▶ Read the questions on page 14, and discuss the answers. The subject matter is important in *Ballet Dancers* and *Family Group.* Composition is most important in *The Voice of the City of New York Interpreted/The Great White Way Leaving the Subway (White Way I).* *Easy Chair* is the work in which the meaning relates to its function. Most students will think that *Ballet Dancers* and *Family Group* have the strongest message. However, it is important to point out that the function of a work is an important message *(Easy Chair)* and that nonobjective work such as *The Voice of the City of New York Interpreted/The Great White Way Leaving the Subway (White Way I)* is communicating through the elements and principles of art.

Overview

In art, *subject* means something an artist has depicted or represented in an artwork. For example, the subject matter of Paul Cézanne's still life is fruit. Some subject matter, like the objects in Cézanne's still life, are easy to identify. Others are more difficult because the artwork may be symbolic or nonobjective. Artists create works of art on a variety of subjects: the natural world, literature, religion, the constructed world, history, and so on. These pages deal with several of the most common subject-matter topics—people, objects, everyday life, stories, things outside, colors and shapes, and things that have a deeper meaning.

Talk with students about each subject-matter topic description below. Encourage them to look for examples of different subject matter in the lessons. By helping them to look at each subject in greater detail and by asking thoughtful questions, your students will begin to develop an understanding for differences among subject matter in art.

Still Life

Artists create works of art that show a variety of objects. Traditional still lifes are bowls, vases, bottles, pitchers, fruit, flowers, food on a table, and/or musical instruments (among other things) that are artfully arranged.

▶ **Question:** What are the objects in this still life?

Subject Matter

Artists make art about many subjects. *Subject matter* is the content of an artist's work. For example, the subject of a painting can be a vase of flowers or a self-portrait. This subject matter is easy to see. The subject matter is harder to understand when the artwork stands for something beyond itself. Look at the artwork on these pages. Notice the different kinds of subject matter.

Still Life

▲ **Paul Cézanne.** (French). *Still Life with Apples. 1895–1898.*
Oil on canvas. 27 × 36½ inches (68.58 × 92.71 cm.). The Museum of Modern Art, New York, New York.

Landscape

▲ **Claude Monet.** (French). *Japanese Bridge over a Pool of Water Lilies.* 1899.
Oil on canvas. $36\frac{1}{2} \times 29$ inches (93 × 74 cm.). The Metropolitan Museum of Art, New York, New York.

Landscape

This area includes the natural world—plants, animals, or other things outside. The suffix *scape* means "a view of." For example, a *cityscape* is buildings and city life in an artwork. A *seascape* is a scene of the sea.

▶ **Question:** What objects do you see in this landscape?

Genre

In art, the term *genre* is used to indicate subjects that have to do with ordinary people engaged in everyday activities.

▶ **Question:** What everyday activities are these people doing?

Genre

▲ **Jacob Lawrence.** (American). *Street Scene (Boy with Kite)*. 1962.
Egg tempera on hardboard. $23\frac{7}{8}$ × 30 inches (60.64 × 76.2 cm.). Conservation Center of the Institute of Fine Arts, New York, New York.

Nonobjective

▲ **Joseph Stella.** (American). *The Voice of the City of New York Interpreted/The Great White Way Leaving the Subway (White Way I).* c. 1920–22.
Oil and tempera on canvas. 88½ × 54 inches (224.79 × 137.16 cm.). The Newark Museum, Newark, New Jersey.

Nonobjective

Sometimes artwork is nonobjective. It does not have an identifiable subject matter—no familiar subjects are shown. People respond to the way the artwork has been organized and designed. Nonobjective art focuses specifically on the elements and principles of art: line, shape, color, and so on.

▶ **Question:** The artwork does not use a subject we can identify. What are some of the lines, shapes, and colors you see in this picture?

Portrait

This category includes portraits, self-portraits, and group portraits. Portraits are one of the oldest subjects in art history. An artist tries to present an accurate depiction and other aspects of a person's character in a portrait.

▶ **Question:** What do you think the artist is telling us about this person?

Portrait

▲ **Diego Rivera.** (Mexican). *Kneeling Child on Yellow Background.* 1927.
Oil on canvas. 25½ × 21 inches (65 × 53 cm.). San Francisco Museum of Modern Art, San Francisco, California.

A Story Shown as Symbols

▲ **Artist Unknown.** (English). *The Five Senses: Hearing. (Detail.)* c. 1650–1675.
White satin embroidered in petit point and enriched with seed pearls and coral. The Metropolitan Museum of Art, New York.

Stories

A story is an account of an incident from a real person's life, a historic event, or from a myth, legend, or other piece of symbolic literature.

▶ **Question:** This antique needle-crafted artwork tells a story about one of the five senses. Which sense does it depict?

Overview

Each language has its own system of words and rules of grammar. To learn a new language, you need to learn new words and a new set of rules for putting the words together. The language of visual art also has its own system. The words of the language are the **elements** of art. They are the basic visual symbols in the language of art. Just as there are basic kinds of words such as nouns, verbs, adjectives, and adverbs, there are basic kinds of art elements. These are line, shape, color, value, space, form, and texture. These elements are the visual building blocks that the artist puts together to create a work of art. No matter what materials are used, the artwork will contain all of the visual elements. Sometimes one element will be more important than the others.

Visual images are organized according to rules. In language, these are the rules of grammar. In visual art, the rules for organizing the elements of art are called the **principles** of art. These principles include pattern, rhythm, balance, emphasis, harmony, variety, and unity.

Activating Prior Knowledge

- Ask students what they think of when they hear each of the following words: *line, shape, color.* Encourage them to look around the classroom for examples.

Questions to Discuss

- Have students examine the images on pages 22 and 23. Ask them what they can tell about each photo. What stands out in each image? How does each image help explain the element or principle?

Elements of Art

Art is a language. The words of the language are the elements of art.

Line

Shape

Form

Space

Color

Value

Texture

Principles of Art

Artists organize their works using the principles of art.

Pattern

Rhythm

Balance

Emphasis

Harmony

Variety

Unity

What Is Art? **23**

The Language of Art

The elements and principles of art are the concepts or ideas that artists use to organize their artwork. Artists use a variety of media and materials to make art. *Media* are types of art such as photography, watercolor, and so on. *Materials* are the things used to make the art, such as markers, paint, paper, clay, fabric, wood, metal, or glass.

There are specific techniques and processes that artists use to manipulate the materials. For example, the proper way to hold a brush to create a thin line with watercolor paint is a specific technique unique to watercolor painting. The process of creating a finished watercolor painting consists of many interwoven steps such as thinking about what to paint, sketching several ideas, deciding which elements and principles will enhance the work, choosing the best sketch, deciding which watercolor techniques to use, and finally producing the finished work.

Special techniques and procedures are used with each material. You will need to learn different techniques and follow different procedures for modeling clay than you will for creating paper sculpture. Drawing with crayons requires different techniques and procedures from drawing with oil pastels or chalk. Using the computer to make original art requires that you learn how to use specific computer hardware and software.

Overview

 Art History and Culture

Art history is the record of art from the past to the present. By looking at art from the past, we learn what the people who lived before us were like—their feelings and beliefs, clothes, food, houses, and how they viewed the world around them.

Questions to Discuss:

Knowledge

▶ Who created the artwork?

▶ When was the artwork created?

▶ What is the artwork's title?

▶ Have you ever seen an artwork like this? Where?

Comprehension

▶ Is this artwork useful? How is it used?

▶ Compare this artwork with another artwork from a similar time period. How are the works of art alike and different?

▶ What interests you most about this artwork?

▶ What is the major theme of this artwork?

Application

▶ What types of materials were used to create this artwork?

▶ Demonstrate how the artwork was created.

▶ Explain how this artwork could have a different use today.

Analysis

▶ What are the main elements in this artwork?

▶ Compare this painting with another painting in this book. How are they alike? How are they different?

▶ What does this artwork mean?

About Art

▲ **Horace Pippin.** (American). *Victorian Parlor II.*
1945. Oil on canvas. $25\frac{1}{4} \times 30$ inches (64.1 × 76.2 cm.). The Metropolitan Museum of Art, New York.

 **Art History and Culture**

Look at the artwork.
▶ What people or objects do you see?
▶ Do they look like people and objects you see around you today? Explain.

Look at the caption.
▶ When was the artwork created?
▶ What can you learn about the artist?

Learn more.
▶ Do some research to find out more about the artist, the artwork, and the time period.

Synthesis
▶ How many titles can you create for this artwork? Name them.
▶ Name a person you would like to give this artwork to as a gift. Why?
▶ Imagine that two people in this room are having a conversation. What would they say to each other? Why?

Evaluation
▶ Do you think this artwork is interesting? Why?
▶ Summarize this artwork's unique qualities.

What to Do
▪ Have students research to find out information about the life and times of Horace Pippin. Students may write a biography of the artist or dress up as the artist and tell the artist's story to classmates.

▪ Have students research Pippin and another artist who lived at the same time. Students should research information about the media, styles, techniques, and procedures the artists used. Have pairs of students role-play a discussion between the two artists about media, style, and personal beliefs about art.

▪ Have students work in groups to act out this painting. They should write a script for what happened before, during, and after the moment shown in the painting.

Overview

Aesthetic Perception

Aesthetic perception encourages students to make choices rather than give "right answers." By understanding the process of aesthetic perception, students can see something from a new perspective and ultimately realize that art is all around them.

 Journal writing is an integral part of aesthetic perception. It is an ongoing record of what a student does, notices, and thinks. Journals track the evolution of thoughts and experiences over time. Through this recorded journey, the student has the ability to reflect on where one has been and where one is going. Writing thoughts, reactions, perceptions, new information, and questions intensifies each student's life experiences.

Guidelines for Aesthetic Perception

Students like to know what is important about a work of art and what was important to the artist. They are fascinated with information, questions, and descriptions. There are some guiding principles in the development of aesthetic perception at this level that can profoundly influence teaching practice.

1. All aesthetic perception actively involves the learner.

2. All aesthetic perception involves reflection.

3. The works of art have substance. Their tools and a working vocabulary are vital to empower the learner.

4. Aesthetic perception is a process based upon examination of the artist's choices and the choices in response made by the viewer.

5. All responses are valid. Right and wrong are irrelevant issues when viewing works of art.

6. All works of art relate to each other, and each relates to all other areas of life.

About Art

▲ **Horace Pippin.** (American). *Victorian Parlor II.* 1945.

Oil on canvas. 25¼ × 30 inches (64.1 × 76.2 cm.). The Metropolitan Museum of Art, New York.

◉ Aesthetic Perception

Look

▶ Look at the work of art. What sounds and smells are in this work of art?

▶ What happened just before and just after in this work of art?

Look Inside

▶ Describe the rest of this house. What is in each room?

▶ Tell or write a story about this work of art with a beginning, a middle, and an end.

▶ How would it feel to sit in one of those chairs?

Look Outside

▶ How is this like or different from your own life?

▶ What does the artist want you to know or think about in this work of art?

▶ What will you remember about this work?

Questions to Discuss

▶ What is happening in this work of art?

▶ What is this work of art about?

▶ What is your favorite part of this work of art?

▶ What is most important in this artwork?

▶ What happened just before and just after in this work of art?

▶ If you were in this work of art, what would you be doing?

▶ What have you learned about the work of art?

▶ What does the artist want you to know or think about in this work of art?

▶ How do you feel about the work of art? What does it make you feel?

▶ What will you remember about this work of art?

▶ Has this work of art changed your thinking?

Things to Do

▪ Draw yourself into the work of art.

▪ Draw what you can't see in the work of art.

▪ Act out or show the story in the work of art.

▪ Collect objects that are similar to the objects in the work of art and make aesthetic judgments about them.

▪ Role-play an interview with the artist about how the work of art was made.

Overview

Art criticism is an organized system for looking at and talking about art. The purpose of art criticism is to get the viewer involved in a perception process that delays judgment until all aspects of the image have been studied. Learning art criticism also gives each viewer the confidence to discuss a work of art without worrying what other people might think.

Describe What do I see?

During this step, the viewer lists all the obvious things in the artwork. Objectivity is important. For example, you do not know from looking at *Victorian Parlor II* that it is a room used by two people. All you can say is that you see a room with furniture.

Questions to Discuss

► List and describe everything you see in the artwork. Answers may include: There is a green rug with a design. There is a round, brown pedestal table with a lace doily and a large vase filled with flowers. On each side of the table is a black chair. Each chair has doilies to protect the head and arm areas. There is a brown footstool at the foot of each chair and a basket of yarn on the floor (and so on).

Analyze How is the work organized?

During this step the viewer examines how the elements and principles of art are used in the artwork.

Questions to Discuss

► Describe the elements of art you see. Answers may include: **Line**—There are horizontal lines where the floor meets the wall, on the wall, and in the rug. **Shape**—The tabletops, bookcase, lamp, doilies, and picture frames are geometric. The chairs, vase, flowers, leaves, and pitchers are free-form shapes (and so on).

► How has the artist used the principles of design? Answers may include: **Balance**—The painting has formal balance, but it is not symmetrical. **Emphasis**—The area of emphasis is the center with the table and vase that are larger than the other objects, and the two matching black chairs (and so on).

About Art

▲ **Horace Pippin.** (American). *Victorian Parlor II.* 1945.

Oil on canvas. 25¼ × 30 inches (64.1 × 76.2 cm.). The Metropolitan Museum of Art, New York.

 **Art Criticism**

Describe

► List everything you see in this painting.

Analyze

► How has the artist used line, shape, color, value, space, and texture?

► How has the artist used rhythm, balance, and variety to organize this painting?

Interpret

► What is the artist telling you about the people who live in this room?

Decide

► Have you ever seen another artwork like this?

► Is it successful because it is realistic?

► Is it successful because it is well-organized?

► Is it successful because you have strong feelings when you study it?

More About Aesthetic Judging

You can use art criticism to make aesthetic judgments about functional objects such as cars or shoes. Follow the first two steps (**Describe** and **Analyze**) as described. During **Interpret,** consider the purpose of the object as its meaning. (Does a pitcher look like it will pour liquid without spilling?) As you **Decide,** consider whether the object works when it is used. (If a chair is not comfortable to sit in, it is not functioning properly and is not successful as a chair.)

Interpret **What is the artist saying to me?**

During interpretation, viewers will make inferences about the message in the work of art. Each interpretation can be different because each is based upon the feelings and life experiences of the viewer.

Questions to Discuss

► What do I think about this artwork?

► What is the artist trying to tell us about this room? This is a living room from a time before electricity. There is no cord for the lamp and no evidence of modern technology.

► Who lives here? What are they like? Answers will vary. They may be elderly because there is no sign of children. They are very neat. The large bouquet suggests that they like to garden.

Decide

This is when the viewer decides whether or not the work is successful. There are two levels of judgment to be made. The first is personal: do you like the work?

The second level is also subjective, but it uses aesthetic theories to help the viewer decide whether the work is successful. More than one theory may be used to judge a work.

■ Some critics think that the most important thing about a work of art is the realistic presentation of the subject matter. This aesthetic theory is called **imitationalism** or **realism.**

■ Other critics think that composition is the most important fact in a work of art. This aesthetic theory, called **formalism** or **composition,** emphasizes the design qualities and the arrangement of the elements of art by using the principles of art.

■ Some critics claim that no object should be considered art if it fails to arouse an emotional response in the viewer. **Emotionalism** or **expressionism** is a theory concerned with the content or the meaning of the work of art.

Questions to Discuss

► Have you seen any works of art in this book that look similar to the style of this artist?

► Which aesthetic theories would you use to judge the success of this work? Even though objects have been simplified, it is still fairly realistic. The artist has used approximate symmetry to organize the work and has balanced harmony and variety to create unity. The painting evokes curiosity about the residents of this room.

Overview

Creative Expression

The creative process, like the writing process or the scientific method, is an organized approach to creative problem solving that can be used by professional artists and students alike. Throughout *Art Connections,* the Creative Expression activities are presented as problems to be solved. Remind students of the steps in the creative process as they work on the activities.

Get an idea.

■ Inspiration can come from many places. In the *Art Connections* Creative Expression activities, the idea comes from the activity instructions. Professional artists may get ideas from a client who has commissioned a piece of art from nature, from a historical event, from everyday life, or from the available media and materials.

■ Try the following to help students when they have trouble getting an idea.

1. As a class, brainstorm about where to get ideas for artwork: works by other artists, personal experiences, stories students have read, and so on.

2. Encourage students to write ideas in the Ideas section of their Art Journals. Remind students that they can make notes for ideas anytime, not just in art class.

3. Pair students who are having trouble thinking of ideas with students who have many ideas. One student can model getting ideas for the other student.

Plan your work.

■ Once students have an idea, they must decide the best way to execute that idea. Would a two-dimensional or three-dimensional artwork best convey the idea that students are trying to show? Should students use watercolor or pencil?

Make a sketch.

■ Just like professional writers, professional artists do not make a perfect work on the first try. They may make several sketches, evaluate those sketches, and revise them before deciding on a final vision for the artwork.

■ Encourage students to make sketches in the Ideas section of their Art Journals.

▲ **Horace Pippin.** (American). *Victorian Parlor II.* 1945.
Oil on canvas. $25\frac{1}{4} \times 30$ inches (64.1 $\times$ 76.2 cm.). The Metropolitan Museum of Art, New York.

Creative Expression

**How does an artist create art?
You can follow the same steps
to create your own art.**

1. Get an idea.
▶ Inspiration comes from many places. Look around you.

2. Plan your work.
▶ Decide what media you want to use. What materials will you need?

3. Make a sketch.
▶ Think about how you want your artwork to look. Sketch several ideas. Then choose the best idea.

4. Use the media.
▶ Make an artwork based on your best idea. You can practice using the materials first.

5. Share your final work.

Use the media.
■ In this stage of the creative process, students make their artwork based on their plans. Encourage students to practice using unfamiliar media, and to try out new techniques on a small practice piece before using those techniques on their artwork.

■ Even during this stage of the process, students may get new ideas. Encourage them to be flexible.

Share your final work.
■ Art is meant to be shared with and viewed by others. Encourage students to share their artwork with family or friends, display it in the classroom, or display it in the school display area. This is also a good time for students to self-evaluate their work using the four steps of art criticism.

More About Art Journals
■ Art Journals are a wonderful way to work through ideas. At the beginning of the school year, help students set up an Art Journal. This can be a spiral notebook or a three-ring binder with pages for writing and sketching. The Art Journal will be divided into sections for Concepts, Ideas, Critical Thinking (Art Criticism), Vocabulary, and Research (at Level 6 only).

1. Encourage students to use the Concepts section of their journals for summarizing unit and lesson concepts, writing questions they have, and listing other things they want to learn.

2. Students can use the Ideas section of their Art Journals for brainstorming, organizing, planning, and sketching. Remind students that they can write ideas in their journals any time; they do not need to wait until a designated time in art class.

3. Students can use the Critical Thinking section of their journals to self-evaluate their work using the four steps of Art Criticism. In *Art Connections* students are asked to self-evaluate after each Creative Expression activity. This can be a valuable tool to help students review art concepts and get ideas for their next work.

4. Encourage students to use the Vocabulary section of their Art Journals to record unfamiliar words, summarize or explain definitions, and so on. Developing vocabulary is an important step in being able to think about and communicate about art.

Overview

Elementary teachers are responsible for the safety of their students. Specific guidelines have been established by the Center for Safety in the Arts, and these guidelines should be followed to ensure that both students and teachers use art materials safely. Following are some general tips for using art materials safely. For more detailed information, see "Safe Use of Art Materials" on page T12 of this book.

Safe Art Materials

- Use only water-soluble AP- or CP-designated markers. Never use permanent or scented markers.

- Use only dustless chalk.

- Make sure that crayons have the AP or CP label to ensure that they do not contain lead.

- When using tempera paint, use only liquid tempera, not powdered tempera. Do not use any spray paints or fixatives.

- Use only water-soluble printers' inks.

- Use pencils to carve into soft surfaces for printing blocks. Do not use mat knives or other sharp instruments.

- Do not allow young children to use sharp scissors; blunt points are safe.

- Do not use rubber cement unless it bears the AP or CP label. Do not use solvent-based glues.

Safety

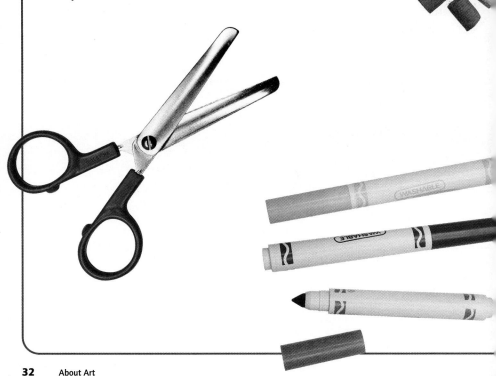

- ▶ Use art materials only on your artwork.
- ▶ Keep art materials out of your mouth, eyes and ears.
- ▶ Use scissors carefully. Keep your fingers away from the blades.
- ▶ Wash your hands after using the art materials.
- ▶ Wear an art shirt or smock to protect your clothes.

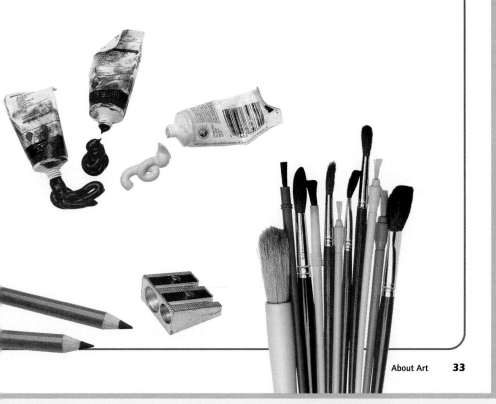

- ▶ Use only art materials with a "nontoxic" label.
- ▶ Keep fingers clear when using a stapler.
- ▶ Be careful not to breathe chalk or clay dust.
- ▶ Return art materials to their proper storage place.
- ▶ Always follow your teacher's directions when using art materials.

General Safety Precautions for Art

- Read the labels on all materials used in the art room. Look carefully for the AP/CP labels. If these are not present, be suspicious. Imported art materials should be looked upon with extreme caution. Other countries have not developed the rigid safety codes adopted by the United States.

- Do not accept or use old art materials that may have been left in the school or donated by some well-meaning adult. If the materials do not bear the current safety codes, toss them out.

- Never allow food or drink in the room where art activities are being conducted. Dust and even fibers float freely in the air and can readily contaminate food or drink.

- Practice cleanliness. Have children wash their hands thoroughly with soap after using art materials.

- Use absolutely no permanent markers or solvent-based materials in the art room. If a material stains the clothes or hands and does not clean up with simple soap and water, it is not appropriate or safe for young children to use.

- Use plastic containers for washing paintbrushes; glass is dangerous in the hands of young children.

- Paper cutters should not be used by elementary school children. The paper cutter should be kept out of the students' reach, and left in a locked position always with the blade turned to the wall.

- Do not use commercial dyes around children; use vegetable or natural dyes (flowers, teas, onion skins).

- Do not allow children in a room where a kiln is firing; both the heat and the fumes are dangerous.

	Lesson Title	Suggested Pacing	Creative Expression Activity
Lesson 1	Expressive Lines	65 minutes	Draw a weather scene
Lesson 2	Line Variations	65 minutes	Installation Art in shoebox
Lesson 3	Shapes	65 minutes	Paint a still life
Lesson 4	Complex Geometric Shapes	65 minutes	Create a geometric design
Lesson 5	Shapes in Architecture	65 minutes	Draw a building
Lesson 6	Shapes of People	65 minutes	Make a portrait
ART SOURCE ARTSOURCE	Space and Form in Dance	35 minutes	Create a short dance

Materials	Program Resources	Fine Art Resources	Literature Resources
white drawing paper, construction paper, colored markers, sketch paper, pencils	*Assessment,* pp. 9–10 *Home and After School Connections* *Flash Cards,* 1 and 4 *Reading and Writing Test Preparation,* pp. 6–7	*Transparency,* 1 *Artist Profiles,* pp. 35, 41 *Large Prints,* 37, 38 *Animals Time Line* *Art Around The World*	*A River Ran Wild* by Lynne Cherry
shoe box, watercolor paints, large and small paintbrushes, containers of water, newspaper, paper towels, pencils, sketch paper	*Assessment,* pp. 11–12 *Flash Cards,* 2 and 3 *Reading and Writing Test Preparation,* pp. 8–9	*Transparency,* 2 *Artist Profiles,* pp. 8, 30 *Large Prints,* 37, 38 *Animals Time Line* *Women in the Arts*	*Best Friends* by Loretta Krupinski
white construction paper, liquid tempera paints, still-life objects, paintbrushes of various sizes, containers of water, oil pastels, paper plates, paper towels, newspaper	*Assessment,* pp. 13–14 *Flash Cards,* 7 and 17 *Reading and Writing Test Preparation,* pp. 10–11	*Transparency,* 3 *Artist Profiles,* pp. 19, 56 *Large Prints,* 37, 38 *Animals Time Line* *Women in the Arts*	*Birds, Nests and Eggs* by Mel Boring
pencils, black construction paper, colored construction paper, scissors, sketch paper, glue, pencils	*Assessment,* pp. 15–16 *Flash Cards,* 7 and 16 *Reading and Writing Test Preparation,* pp. 12–13	*Transparency,* 4 *Artist Profiles,* pp. 65, 72 *Large Prints,* 37, 38 *Animals Time Line* *Art Around The World*	*Mowing* by Jessie Haas
white paper, pencils, colored construction paper, black felt-tip pens, markers	*Assessment,* pp. 17–18 *Flash Cards,* 10 and 11 *Reading and Writing Test Preparation,* pp. 14–15	*Transparency,* 5 *Artist Profiles,* pp. 10, 25 *Large Prints,* 37, 38 *Animals Time Line* *Art Around The World*	*Wild in the City* by Janet Thornhill
paper, pencils, colored construction paper, oil pastels, dustless chalk	*Assessment,* pp. 19–20 *Flash Cards,* 8 and 16 *Reading and Writing Test Preparation,* pp. 16–17	*Transparency,* 6 *Artist Profiles,* pp. 11, 22 *Large Prints,* 37, 38 *Animals Time Line* *Art Around The World*	*Tell Me a Story, Mama* by Angela Johnson
			Eagle Dance and *Hoop Dance* by American Indian Dance Theatre

Unit Overview

1 Line and Shape

Lesson 1: Lines include vertical, horizontal, diagonal, zigzag, and curved lines, with each type having certain expressive qualities.

Lesson 2: Line variations are different ways in which lines vary in appearance.

Lesson 3: Complex geometric shapes and **free-form shapes** are flat, two-dimensional shapes.

Lesson 4: Complex geometric shapes are made by combining simple geometric shapes.

Lesson 5: Shapes in architecture are both geometric and free-form shapes.

Lesson 6: Shapes occur in nature, in buildings, and in furniture.

Introduce Unit Concepts

"Artists use the elements of line and shape in creating all kinds of art." "Los artistas usan los elementos de la línea y la figura para crear todo tipo de arte".

Lines
- Have students suggest words that come to mind when you say phrases that include the word *line*, for example, *fishing line, telephone line,* and *wait in line.*

- Ask students to draw lines in the air with their fingers. Have students describe the kind of line each one created, for example, straight, bent, curved, or wiggly.

Shapes
- Review shapes by asking students to name as many kinds of shapes as they can think of.

- Ask students to each draw the main shape of an object seen anywhere in the classroom. Have students identify the objects drawn by their classmates.

Cross-Curricular Projects
- See the *Language Arts and Reading, Mathematics, Science,* and *Social Studies Art Connections* books for activities that further develop line concepts.

34 UNIT 1 • Line and Shape

Line and Shape

Unit 1

◄ **Pablo Picasso.** (Spanish). *Mother and Child.* 1922.
Oil on canvas. 40 × 32 inches (100 × 81 cm.). The Baltimore Museum of Art, Baltimore, Maryland.

Artists use line and shape to create all types of art.

In this artwork, Picasso used simple lines and shapes to show the feelings between a mother and child.

34 Unit 1

Fine Art Prints
Display **Large Prints 37** *Broadway* and **38** *The Cow with the Subtile Nose.* Refer to the prints throughout the unit as students learn about lines and shapes.

Large Print 37

Large Print 38

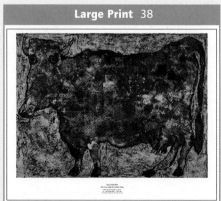

Artists use a variety of **lines** to outline objects and show details.

▶ Which lines outline the objects in *Mother and Child*?

▶ How do lines show detail in the mother's hair? Where else do you see lines that show detail?

Artists also use **geometric shapes** and **free-form** shapes.

▶ What main shape did Picasso use to draw the mother and child? What kind of shapes are the leaves?

▶ What complex geometric shapes did Picasso use for the child's right foot?

In This Unit you will learn to use different kinds of lines. You will study:
▶ Kinds of Lines
▶ Line Variations
▶ Geometric and Free-Form Shapes

Pablo Picasso
(1881–1973)

Pablo Picasso was born in Malaga, Spain. One day his father came home to a surprise—his son had finished a portrait. After examining the work, Picasso's father gave his art supplies to the boy. The work was so magnificent, the father vowed to never paint again himself. Picasso was eight.

Picasso went to Paris in 1904 and met many artists and writers. He became a creative leader. He was a painter, a sculptor, a printmaker, and a ceramicist. Picasso is most famous for developing the style of cubism.

Unit 1   **35**

Examine the Artwork

"Let's look closely at the painting." *"Vamos a observar detalladamente la pintura".*

■ Have students look at Pablo Picasso's *Mother and Child*. Ask them to describe what they see in the painting. Encourage students to think about the relationship between the mother and child.

■ Have students answer the questions on page 35 about the lines and shapes used in *Mother and Child*.

▶ The curved lines move around the outside edges of the objects to outline them.

▶ The curved lines show the mother's hair is wavy. The lines on either side of her part change direction at the point where they disappear below the area that is pulled back. Lines also show detail in the leaves.

▶ The main shape of the mother and child together is triangular. The leaves are free-form shapes.

▶ The bottom of the child's foot is a parallelogram.

Unit Pretest

T Display *Transparency 43* as a pretest. Answers: 1.B, 2.A, 3.C, 4.C, 5.B

Home Connection

■ See *Home and After-School Connections* for family newsletters and activities for this unit.

Art History and Culture

Pablo Picasso

Pablo Picasso (pä blo pē käs´ sō)(1881–1973) learned to draw before he could talk. In his teens he could draw with photographic accuracy. An innovator of many artistic styles, Picasso was a prolific artist. He studied at art schools in both La Coruña and Barcelona. He became famous for his role in the development of cubism. At age 14, Picasso completed the one-month qualifying examination for the Academy of Fine Arts in Barcelona in one day. He produced an estimated 50,000 works during his lifetime. Picasso was 91 when he died on April 8, 1973, in Mougins, France.

See pages 24–25 and 16–21 for more about art history and subject matter.

Artist Profiles, p. 45

◀ Artist Profile ▶
Pablo Picasso
1881–1973

Pablo Picasso (pä´ blō pi kä´ sō) was born in Málaga, Spain. He did poorly in school but his father, an art teacher, taught him to draw and paint. Picasso learned quickly. When he was only 14 had a painting accepted for an exhibition. Picasso moved to Paris, France when he was 18. At the time he was very poor. Thieves stole what little he had, yet they left his now valuable drawings. In time the outgoing Picasso made many friends. Among them were the American writers Ernest Hemingway and Gertrude Stein and the Russian composer Igor Stravinsky. Picasso painted at night and slept late most mornings. He worked hard his entire life. He completed 200 paintings the year he turned 90.

NSAE 3a

ILLUSTRATOR PROFILE
Floyd Cooper

Growing up in Tulsa, Oklahoma, Floyd Cooper was a tireless artist from the age of three, when he drew his first picture on a piece of discarded plasterboard. Cooper went on to earn a college degree in fine art, then found employment as an illustrator with a greeting card company in Missouri.

Feeling restricted in his work, Cooper moved to New York to explore other career opportunities. When he was given the chance to illustrate a children's picture book (*Grandpa's Face*, 1988), Cooper knew he'd found his niche. Reviewers agreed, and Cooper has received praise for his work ever since; his illustrations are consistently described as "rich," "warm," and "sensitive."

Cooper achieves soft, glowing colors in his oil wash paintings using what he calls a "subtractive process." He begins by painting a board with oil paint, then he strategically erases some of the paint to create a picture. Cooper enjoys demonstrating this technique for children as a means of showing that there are different ways to approach common tasks.

Throughout Unit 1 share Cooper's illustrations with the class to discuss the use of lines in his works of art. Which parts of the illustrations show expressive lines? Which parts show geometric and free-form shapes?

Music

Line in music refers to the way a melody moves. *Shapes* also pertains to melodic contour. Have students sing a song and show the movement of the melody with their hands.

Literature

Show the video or DVD *Old Henry* to introduce the concepts of line and shape. Pause the video and have students describe lines and shape.

Literature and Art

Dance

 Show "Eagle Dance." Point out lines and shape as he dances in the video.

Artsource®

Lesson 1 Overview

Expressive Lines

Lesson 1 introduces different kinds of lines and their expressive qualities. Artists use different kinds of lines to create moods and feelings.

Objectives

 Art History and Culture

To identify and compare the use of expressive lines in landscape paintings

 Creative Expression

To plan and create a weather scene using lines to express a feeling or mood

 **Aesthetic Perception**

To identify the five different kinds of lines and their expressive qualities

 Art Criticism

To evaluate own work using the four steps of art criticism

Vocabulary Reading

Review the following vocabulary words with students before beginning the lesson.

line **línea**—a mark drawn by a tool such as pencil, pen, or paintbrush as it moves across a surface

vertical lines **líneas verticales**—lines that move straight up and down

See page 59B for additional vocabulary and Spanish vocabulary resources.

 Art Journal: Vocabulary

Have students add these words to the Vocabulary section of their Art Journals.

Lesson Materials

- 12" × 18" white drawing paper
- 12" × 18" construction paper
- colored markers
- sketch paper
- pencils

Alternate Materials:
- pencils
- crayons
- oil paints or oil pastels

Program Resources

- *Reading and Writing Test Prep.,* pp. 6–7
- *Transparency 1*
- *Flash Cards 1* and *4*
- *Artist Profiles,* pp. 35, 41
- *Animals Through History Time Line*
- *Assessment,* pp. 9–10
- *Large Prints 37* Broadway and *38 The Cow with the Subtile Nose*
- *Art Around the World Collection*

Concept Trace
Expressive Lines
Introduced: Level 2, Unit 1, Lesson 3
Reinforced: Level 4, Unit 1, Lesson 1

Lesson 1 Arts Integration

Theatre

Complete Unit 1, Lesson 1 on page 18–19 of ***Theatre Arts Connections.***

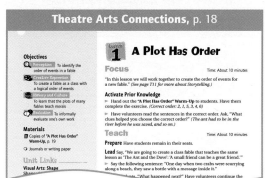

Music

SPOTLIGHT ON MUSIC *My Favorite Things.* Rogers and Hammerstein.

Line in music refers to the way a melody moves higher and lower (up, down, or the same). To relate the concept of line in music to line in visual art, play *My Favorite Things* from *The Sound of Music.* Have students draw the vertical, horizontal, diagonal, zigzag, and curved lines that they think go with the music.

Performing Arts

Students walk freely in the space to the beat of a drum or music. Direct their attention to the pathway they are making (probably curved), and ask them to exaggerate it. Now ask students to walk in straight lines, turning sharply every four counts. How does this effect energy? Now try walking in a spiral pattern. Does this increase the speed of the walk?

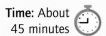ocus

Time: About 45 minutes

Activate Prior Knowledge

"Think about lines you see outside in nature."

"Piensen acerca de las líneas que pueden observar en la naturaleza".

■ Discuss student responses. Have students use their arms to demonstrate lines formed by a winding road, running water, tall grass blowing in the wind, and lightning during a rainstorm.

Using Literature [★] Reading

■ Read *A River Ran Wild* by Lynne Cherry. Have students discuss the use of expressive lines in the book.

Thematic Connection [★] Science

■ **Weather:** Have students use the scenery of the artwork as the basis for a discussion about changes that occur in weather, seasons, or geographic environments.

Introduce the Art

Look

"Let's take a close look at the two paintings."

"Vamos a observar detalladamente las dos pinturas".

Comparing and Contrasting [★] Reading

■ Have students describe the subject matter in each painting.

■ Have students list the similarities and differences of the two paintings. Both are outdoor scenes, both include wooded areas, and both include different kinds of lines. The horizontal direction of the lines in Monet's painting creates a feeling of calm or peace. The curved and diagonal lines in Lismer's painting illustrate strong winds with force and steadiness.

NSAE 3a

Art History and Culture

Monet's painting uses vertical lines to express a quiet mood, and Lismer uses diagonal lines to express a sense of excitement.

Web Connection

Visit **www.webpages.marshall.edu/~smith82/ monet.html** to view more of Claude Monet's artwork.

Expressive Lines

◀ **Claude Monet.** (French). *Japanese Bridge over a Pool of Water Lilies.* 1899.

Oil on canvas. 36 ½ × 29 inches (93 × 74 cm). Metropolitan Museum of Art, New York, New York.

Look at the landscape paintings on these pages. Both artists used lines to express different kinds of weather. Compare the moods of the two paintings.

Art History and Culture

How did the two artists show different moods in nature? How did they use lines to express a mood?

Art History and Culture

Claude Monet

Claude Monet (klöd mô nā) (1840–1926) did not want to become a painter. However, painter Eugene Boudin saw talent in Monet's exaggerated drawings and encouraged him to paint. Although artists generally painted in studios at that time, Boudin urged Monet to paint outdoors. It was there that Monet learned to capture his first impressions on canvas. Monet realized that the colors of a subject change as the day progresses. He recorded these impressions during a long, productive life. His greatest wish was to "mingle more closely with nature."

See pages 24–25 and 16–21 for more about art history and subject matter.

Artist Profiles, p. 41

Artist Profile

Claude Monet
1840–1926

Claude Monet (klöd mô nā) did not want to be a painter as a young man in France. He was already well paid for drawing caricatures of tourists. Painter Eugene Boudin saw talent in Monet's exaggerated drawings and encouraged him to paint. Although artists were "supposed" to paint in studios, Boudin urged Monet to paint outside in the open air. There Monet learned to capture his first impressions on canvas. He recorded these impressions during a long and productive life. His greatest wish was to "mingle more closely with nature."

▲ **Arthur Lismer.** (Canadian).
September Gale, Georgian Bay.
1921.
••••••••••••••••••••••••••••••
Oil on canvas. 48 × 64 ¼ inches (122 × 163 cm). National Gallery of Canada, Ottawa, Ontario, Canada.

Study both landscape paintings.

▶ Find the vertical lines.

▶ Find the horizontal lines.

▶ Identify the diagonal lines.

▶ Where are the curved lines in each painting?

▶ Find the lines that zigzag.

 Aesthetic Perception

Seeing Like an Artist Look outside your classroom windows. Look for things such as trees, leaves, and grass. Find lines similar to those in the landscape paintings.

Art History and Culture

Arthur Lismer

Arthur Lismer (är thər lis´mər) (1885–1969) was born in Sheffield, England. By the age of 26, Lismer found that many British artists were migrating to Canada. Friends wrote to Lismer and told him about their many successes there. There were great prospects in the commercial arts industry in Canada at that time, so in 1911 Lismer left his desk job and boarded a ship to Canada.

Many of Lismer's paintings depict the Canadian landscape. He portrayed the land by using impressionist colors and a romantic sense of form and natural rhythm. Lismer later became part of a group known as the Group of Seven.

See pages 24–25 and 16–21 for more about art history and subject matter.

Artist Profiles, p. 35

◆ Artist Profile ◆

Arthur Lismer
1885–1969

Although Arthur Lismer (är´ thər lis´mər) was born in England he is generally considered a Canadian artist. He studied art in England and Belgium and then moved to Canada in 1911 to take a job as a commercial artist. Outgoing and outspoken, Lismer helped form the Group of Seven. This group of young artists painted the Canadian landscape they loved so much. They also encouraged each other to experiment with painting styles and held exhibitions together. Lismer taught art and served as the principal of art schools in Quebec and Nova Scotia. In addition, he set up children's art centers at the Art Gallery of Toronto and the Montreal Museum of Fine Arts.

Study

▶ Vertical lines: *September Gale, Georgian Bay:* The tree and the grass have vertical lines. *Japanese Bridge over a Pool of Water Lilies:* The grass, the bridge and the trees all have vertical lines.

▶ Horizontal lines: *Japanese Bridge over a Pool of Water Lilies:* The water lilies have horizontal lines. *September Gale, Georgian Bay:* The landforms are horizontal.

▶ Diagonal lines: *Japanese Bridge over a Pool of Water Lilies:* The grass has diagonal lines. *September Gale, Georgian Bay:* The waves, as well as the grass and rocks, have diagonal lines.

▶ Curved lines: *Japanese Bridge over a Pool of Water Lilies:* Curved lines illustrate the shape of the bridge. *September Gale, Georgian Bay:* Curved lines are used in the tree, waves, and sky.

▶ Zigzag lines: *September Gale, Georgian Bay:* Zigzag lines in the water create a sense of forcefulness of the water.

■ For more examples of art from Europe, see the *Art Around the World Collection.*

 Art Journal

Encourage students to write their own explanation of expressive lines in the Concepts section of their Art Journals. What else do they want to know?

Aesthetic Perception

National Standards for Arts Education in Visual Arts (NSAE) 2a, c

Seeing Like an Artist Have students discuss the objects in the neighborhood around the school and describe the types of lines they are made of. Students will likely identify trees, grass, and leaves as containing the different types of lines. Have students identify lines similar to those found in the paintings.

Developing Visual Literacy Discuss the meaning that each artist might have been trying to convey. Invite students to discuss what they think of after looking at the two pieces of art. For example, do they think of a bright, sunny day or of a cold, dreary day?

Web Connection
Visit **www.tomthomson.org** to find out more about Arthur Lismer and the Group of Seven.

Teach

Time: About 45 minutes

"How can you use lines to show different kinds of weather?" "¿Cómo se pueden usar las lineas para mostrar diferentes tipos de clima?"

- Have students read and discuss the five different kinds of lines and the expressive qualities of each kind on page 38.

Practice

Materials: 12" × 18" white paper, markers

Alternate Materials: pencils

- Distribute the materials and have students follow the directions on page 38 for using lines to illustrate each of the weather conditions.

 Creative Expression

Materials: 12" × 18" white construction paper, colored markers, sketch paper, pencils

Alternate Materials: pencils, crayons, oil paints or oil pastels

- Distribute materials and have students follow the directions on page 39.
- Review the Activity Tips on page 232 for visual examples.

Art Journal: Brainstorming

Have students brainstorm a variety of weather conditions and the different moods that they create. Have students make rough sketches in their Art Journals and experiment with different kinds of lines. Review the names of the types of lines and their expressive qualities and discuss how these lines can be drawn in the Creative Expression activity.

Using Lines

Lines are marks drawn by a tool such as a pencil, pen, or paintbrush as it moves across a surface. There are five different kinds of lines. Each one can make you feel a certain way.

 Vertical lines move straight up and down. They make things look tall, steady, and calm.

 Horizontal lines move straight across from side to side. They give a feeling of calm peace.

 Diagonal lines are slanted. They look as if they are falling or rising. They make things look active.

 Zigzag lines are diagonal lines that connect. They give a feeling of excitement.

Curved lines bend and change direction slowly. They give a feeling of graceful movement.

Practice

Use different kinds of lines to create a weather chart. Use white paper and markers.

1. Fold a sheet of paper into six equal boxes. Each box will show a different weather condition that occurs in nature, such as strong wind, rainstorm, or blizzard. Write the name of one of the weather conditions at the bottom of each box.

2. Use different kinds of lines like the ones above to draw the weather condition written at the bottom of each box.

Differentiated Instruction

Reteach

Have students look around the classroom to find objects that contain an example of each of the five types of lines. Ask students to identify the objects and name the types of lines that they contain. Have students use pencils, crayons, paints, and/or oil pastels to make an expressive weather scene.

Special Needs

To reinforce the objectives of this lesson, have students look outside and describe the current weather conditions. Using a demonstration board, have students draw the types of lines they see outside, then begin the lesson activity.

ELL Tips

Students will need to know the definitions of the five different kinds of lines to be able to participate in the comparison of the two paintings. You may wish to make a chart of the types of lines for students to use as a reference.

NSAE 4b

◀ **Anna Boynton.**
Age 8.

Think about the mood this student artist created in her weather scene.

 Creative Expression

How do different kinds of weather make you feel? Draw a weather scene that causes you to have a certain feeling.

1. Think about the different kinds of weather where you live. What mood does each create?

2. Select the type of weather condition you would like to draw. Make a rough sketch to plan the scene. Experiment with different kinds of lines. Decide which lines will best express the mood you wish to create.

3. Draw your scene. Be sure to use the right kinds of lines to create a calm or active feeling.

Art Criticism

Describe List the different kinds of lines you used in your scene.

Analyze Did you create a calm or an active scene? Did you use lines to express this feeling?

Interpret If you were to change the lines, how would the mood or feeling change?

Decide If you could draw this scene again, how would you change it?

Unit 1 • Lesson 1 **39**

Time: About 45 minutes

Review and Assess

"How can you create moods with curved, straight, zigzag, horizontal, and diagonal lines?" "¿Qué ánimos pueden crear con líneas rectas, curvas, en zigzag y diagonales?"

Think

The artist used a variety of lines to create a weather scene in her work of art.

■ Use **Large Prints 37** *Broadway* and **38** *The Cow with the Subtle Nose* to have students compare the expressive qualities of their lines to those of the works of art in this lesson.

Informal Assessment

Art Journal: Critical Thinking
Have students answer the four art criticism questions—Describe, Analyze, Interpret, and Decide—in their Art Journals. In small groups, have students discuss the use of lines in their drawings.

■ For standardized-format test practice using this lesson's art content, see pages 6–7 in **Reading and Writing Test Preparation**.

● Art Across the Curriculum ●

Use these simple ideas to reinforce art concepts across the curriculum.

★ **Narrative Writing** Have students each create a travel advertisement for the place depicted in *September Gale, Georgian Bay* or *Water Lilies and Japanese Bridge*.

★ **Math** Have students look at the classroom clock. Ask them to identify vertical, horizontal, diagonal, and curved lines on the clock.

★ **Science Connection** Show students photographs of various constellations. Have them imagine lines that connect the stars and identify the shapes that they form.

★ **Social Studies** Ask students to discuss ways in which people can help protect natural environments.

★ **Technology** Have students use the paintbrush feature in the computer's paint program to create a weather scene that conveys a certain mood or feeling. Visit **SRAonline.com** to print detailed instructions for this activity.

Expressive Lines

 For the Art Specialist

Time: About 45 minutes

Focus

Use *Transparency 1* and *Large Prints 37 Broadway* and *38 The Cow with the Subtle Nose* to discuss how artists use lines to create moods or feelings. Look at the lines in the artwork. Point out lines that make you feel calm. Use your finger to trace over lines that are energetic, or that make you feel like they are moving. Does the picture have more calm lines or more energetic lines? How does the picture make you feel?

Teach

Have students follow the directions and use a combination of pencils, crayons, paints, and/or oil pastels to make a winter landscape.

Reflect

Have students evaluate their artwork using the four steps of art criticism. Encourage them to find expressive lines throughout the classroom.

Alternate Activity

Materials:
- 12" × 18" manilla paper
- crayons
- thinned white tempera paint
- paintbrushes

1. Have students draw a winter landscape using a variety of lines. Students should use heavy pressure with the crayons to color in all parts of the drawing, including the sky and the background.

2. When the drawing is completely colored, students can paint thinned white paint over the drawing, using overlapping vertical strokes. The crayon will resist the white paint and look like snow falling on a winter landscape.

Research in Art Education

Some studies have shown that there is "a significant association between arts study (that includes visual arts) and standardized measures of creative thinking" ("Does Studying the Arts Engender Creative Thinking? Evidence for Near but Not Far Transfer" in *Critical Links,* p. 82). Students who study the arts tend to score higher on drawing-based creativity tests than on verbal creativity tests. As they learn about lines and their expressive qualities, encourage students to think of other ways lines can express moods or feelings in paintings.

Assessment

Use the following rubric to evaluate the artwork students make in the Creative Expression activity and to assess students' understanding of different kinds of lines and their expressive qualities.

Have students complete page 9 or 10 in their *Assessment* books.

	Art History and Culture	Aesthetic Perception	Creative Expression	Art Criticism
3 POINTS	The student demonstrates knowledge of the lives and work of Monet and Lismer.	The student accurately identifies the five different kinds of lines and their expressive qualities.	The student effectively plans and creates a weather scene using lines to express a feeling or mood.	The student evaluates his or her own work using the four steps of art criticism.
2 POINTS	The student demonstrates weak or incomplete knowledge of the lives and work of Monet and Lismer.	The student shows emerging awareness of the five different kinds of lines and their expressive qualities but cannot consistently identify them.	The student shows some awareness of how to plan and create a weather scene using lines to express a feeling or mood.	The student attempts to evaluate his or her own work but shows an incomplete understanding of evaluation criteria.
1 POINT	The student cannot demonstrate knowledge of the lives and work of Monet or Lismer.	The student cannot identify the five different kinds of lines or their expressive qualities.	The student shows no understanding of how to plan or create a weather scene using lines to express a feeling or mood.	The student makes no attempt to evaluate his or her own artwork.

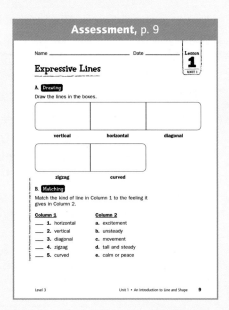

Assessment, p. 9

Name _____ Date _____ **Lesson 1** UNIT 1

Expressive Lines

A. Drawing
Draw the lines in the boxes.

vertical	horizontal	diagonal

zigzag	curved

B. Matching
Match the kind of line in Column 1 to the feeling it gives in Column 2.

Column 1	Column 2
___ 1. horizontal	a. excitement
___ 2. vertical	b. unsteady
___ 3. diagonal	c. movement
___ 4. zigzag	d. tall and steady
___ 5. curved	e. calm or peace

Level 3   Unit 1 • An Introduction to Line and Shape   9

Line Variations

Lesson 2 introduces line variations. Artists change lines in a variety of ways to make their works of art more interesting.

Objectives

 Art History and Culture

To identify and compare line variations in nonobjective and abstract paintings

 Creative Expression

To plan and create installation art using a variety of lines

 Aesthetic Perception

To identify ways in which lines can vary in appearance

Art Criticism

To evaluate own work using the four steps of art criticism

Vocabulary ⭐ Reading

Review the following vocabulary word with students before beginning the lesson.

line variations *variación lineal*—short or long, thick or thin, rough or smooth, and broken or solid lines

See page 59B for additional vocabulary and Spanish vocabulary resources.

 Art Journal: Vocabulary

Have students add this word to the Vocabulary section of their Art Journals.

Lesson Materials

- crayons
- watercolor paints
- large and small paintbrushes
- containers of water
- newspaper
- paper towels
- pencils
- sketch paper
- shoe boxes (one for each student)
- colored markers

Alternate Materials:
- pencils
- broad-tip and thin-tip markers

Program Resources

- *Reading and Writing Test Prep.*, pp. 8–9
- *Transparency 2*
- *Flash Cards 2* and *3*
- *Artist Profiles*, pp. 8, 30
- *Animals Through History Time Line*
- *Assessment*, pp. 11–12
- *Large Prints 37* Broadway and *38* The Cow with the Subtile Nose
- *The National Museum of Women in the Arts Collection*

Concept Trace

Line Variations

Introduced: Level 2, Unit 1, Lesson 2

Reinforced: Level 4, Unit 1, Lesson 2

Lesson 2 Arts Integration

Theatre

Complete Unit 1, Lesson 2 on pages 20–21 of *Theatre Arts Connections.*

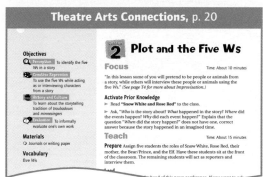

Music

William Tell Overture. Gioacchino Rossini.

To reinforce line variety, play Rossini's *William Tell Overture* as students complete the Practice activity. Have them draw long, short, thick, thin, rough, smooth, broken, or solid lines in response to the music.

Performing Arts

Have each student divide a sheet of paper into 4 quarters and number them 1–4. Students will write their names (cursively) different ways in each section. Have them take each section and translate it into large movement. Movements should be continuous but contain curves that change direction, such as loops, under curves, arcs, dots and slashes.

Focus

Time: About 45 minutes

Activate Prior Knowledge

"Think about the lines in a tree. How do the lines in the trunk of a tree look different from lines in its branches?" "Piensen en las líneas de un árbol. ¿En qué se diferencian las líneas en el tronco del árbol de las líneas de sus ramas?"

- Discuss student responses and how the lines are different widths.

Using Literature Reading

- Read *Best Friends* by Loretta Krupinski. Discuss the use of line variations in the book.

Thematic Connection Reading

- **Imagination:** Have students imagine what Borofsky and Kandinsky were trying to portray in their works of art.

Introduce the Art

Look

"Let's take a look at the two paintings." "Vamos a observar detalladamente las dos pinturas".

Comparing and Contrasting Reading

- Have students describe the subject matter in each painting. Both pieces include a variety of lines to make them more interesting. *Improvisation No. 27* is considered a nonobjective painting; there are no recognizable objects in the painting. *Big Ears* is an abstract painting. The face in the painting can be identified; however, it does not represent what an actual face looks like.

NSAE 2a, c

Art History and Culture

Kandinsky's painting has no recognizable objects. Borofsky's painting has a face, but it does not represent an actual face.

 Web Connection

Visit **www.russianavantgard.com/** to view more Russian art as well as more of Wassily Kandinsky's paintings.

Line Variations

▲ **Wassily Kandinsky.** (Russian). *Improvisation No. 27.* 1912.

Oil paint. 47 3/8 × 55 1/4 inches (120 × 140.34 cm). Metropolitan Museum of Art, New York, New York.

Look at the artwork on these pages. Both artists used lines; however, the two pieces of art are very different. Kandinsky used lines as part of the subject, and Borofsky used lines to create a giant face.

Art History and Culture

Both artists used a variety of lines. What is the difference between the two works of art?

Art History and Culture

Wassily Kandinsky

Wassily Kandinsky (va sēl´ ē kan din´ skē) (1866–1944) was born in Moscow and gave up a career in law to study painting in Munich, Germany. After looking at one of his paintings resting on its side, he discovered the beauty of colors and shapes. As a result, he became the first artist to abandon recognizable reality and create non-objective paintings. From around 1910, Kandinsky's transition to abstract painting became apparent. The figural elements in his work were reduced, and finally, they disappeared completely. Like a musician, Kandinsky titled his works *impressions*, *compositions*, or *improvisations*.

See pages 24–25 and 16–21 for more about art history and subject matter.

Artist Profiles, p. 30

● Artist Profile ●

Wassily Kandinsky
1866–1944

Wassily Kandinsky (va sēl´ ē kan din´ skē) first tried painting as a teenager in his native Russia. Even then he felt that each color had a mysterious life of its own. He was still drawn to colors and painting while he studied law and economics in college, but he believed that art was "a luxury forbidden to a Russian." In time, he moved to Germany, studied art, and began his career. Throughout his life Kandinsky moved back and forth between Russia and Germany. In 1933 he settled in France after Nazi storm troopers labeled his painting style "degenerate."

Study both works of art to find a variety of lines.

▶ Find lines that are long and lines that are short.

▶ Find lines that are thick and lines that are thin.

▶ Do you see any lines that look rough? Where are they? Find the lines that look smooth.

▶ Where do you see lines that move in different directions?

🔍 Aesthetic Perception

Seeing Like an Artist Look around your classroom. Find lines like those you saw in the paintings.

 ### Art History and Culture

Jonathan Borofsky

At an early age, Jonathan Borofsky (jon´ əthən bô rôf´ skē) (1942–) was encouraged by his parents to become an artist. Throughout much of his childhood, he took painting lessons. In 1964 he received a fine arts degree from Carnegie-Mellon University in Pittsburgh, Pennsylvania, and in 1966 he received an MFA from Yale University. Many of Borofsky's works were inspired by his dreams. He would deliberately wake up and record his dreams through a combination of words and spontaneous drawings. He recreated some of the images in his dreams in his artwork. Many of Borofsky's monuments and sculptures are on display from Seattle, Washington, to Tokyo, Japan.

See pages 24–25 and 16–21 for more about art history and subject matter.

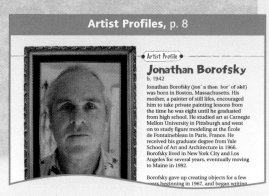

Artist Profiles, p. 8

Artist Profile
Jonathan Borofsky
b. 1942

Jonathan Borofsky (jon´ a than bor´ of skē) was born in Boston, Massachusetts. His mother, a painter of still lifes, encouraged him to take private painting lessons from the time he was eight until he graduated from high school. He studied art at Carnegie Mellon University in Pittsburgh and went on to study figure modeling at the École de Fontainebleau in Paris, France. He received his graduate degree from Yale School of Art and Architecture in 1966. Borofsky lived in New York City and Los Angeles for several years, eventually moving to Maine in 1992.

Borofsky gave up creating objects for a few years beginning in 1967, and began writing...

Study

▶ Long and short lines: *Big Ears:* Long lines outline the face and the short lines represent the mouth, nose, and squiggly lines surrounding the face. *Improvisation No. 27:* The long lines run across the bottom starting in the middle left section of the painting. The short lines start at the middle right section of the painting.

▶ Thick and thin lines: *Big Ears*: There are thick lines around the eyes, ears, and nose; thin lines make up the inner eyes and shading around the face. *Improvisation No. 27*: There are thick and thin lines at the bottom of the painting and in the upper-right side.

▶ Rough and smooth lines: *Improvisation No. 27*: There are rough red lines in the central yellow area and smooth lines in the upper right-hand corner.

■ For more examples of abstract art, see **The National Museum of Women in the Arts Collection.**

📓 Art Journal: Writing

Encourage students to write their own explanations of line variations in the Concepts section of their Art Journals. What else do they want to know?

🔍 Aesthetic Perception

Seeing Like an Artist Have students identify objects in the classroom that have line variations such as thick or thin, long or short, broken or solid, or smooth or rough lines; for example, the lines where the walls of the room meet may be thick or thin lines.

Developing Visual Literacy Have students discuss what each artist was trying to convey. Have them think about the titles of the works of art and try to interpret each artist's reason for giving the artwork that name.

💻 Web Connection

Visit **www.borofsky.com** to learn more about Jonathan Borofsky and his other works of art.

Teach

Time: About 45 minutes

"How can you use crayons in different ways to create line variations?" *"¿Cómo se pueden usar de diferentes maneras los creyones para crear variaciones lineales?"*

■ Have students read and discuss the ways to create variations in lines on page 42.

Practice

Materials: 9" × 12" white paper, crayons

Alternate Materials: pencils

■ Distribute the materials and have students follow the directions on page 42 for illustrating line variations.

■ Encourage students to experiment with the crayons and to fill the page with a variety of lines.

Creative Expression

Materials: watercolor paints, large and small paintbrushes, containers of water, newspaper, paper towels, pencils, sketch paper, shoe box

Alternate Materials: broad-tip and thin-tip markers

■ Distribute the materials and have students follow the directions on page 43.

■ Review ways to create line variations.

■ Review the Activity Tips on page 232 for visual examples of techniques.

Art Journal: Brainstorming

Have students brainstorm a variety of places they would like to visit and write their ideas in their Art Journals. Students can look through travel brochures, magazines, and books for ideas. Then have students plan how they will show their weather scenes in the Creative Expression activity.

Using a Variety of Lines

Artists can change lines in many ways to make them look different. You saw **line variety** in *Improvisation No. 27* and *Self Portrait with Big Ears*.

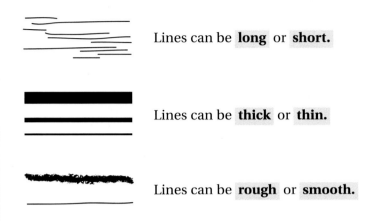

Lines can be **long** or **short.**

Lines can be **thick** or **thin.**

Lines can be **rough** or **smooth.**

Lines can be **broken** or **solid.**

Practice

1. Draw a variety of lines. Use white paper and crayons.

2. Use crayons to make as many different kinds of lines as you can on a sheet of paper.

3. Now use your crayon in different ways to make rough, smooth, thick, and thin lines.

Differentiated Instruction

Reteach	Special Needs	ELL Tips
Create flash cards showing the different kinds of lines. Have students use the flash cards to review line variations.	For students who have difficulty grasping small paintbrushes, tape or rubber band a foam rubber cylinder around the brush for the student to grasp.	Some students may need your support to discuss their works of art. Instead of asking them to describe, analyze, interpret, and decide on their own, ask them specific questions that will allow responses such as pointing or saying *yes* or *no*. For example, you might say, "Find lines that make your painting appear to be peaceful."

◀ **Alayna McCormack.** Age 8.

Think about the types of lines this student used to decorate a room.

Creative Expression

What kind of a face would you use to decorate a room? Draw a room and then draw a face on it.

1. Think about a room you would like to decorate. Is it your classroom, your bedroom, or some other room?

2. Draw the room showing the floor, walls, and furniture inside a shoebox.

3. Make some sketches of the kind of face that you would like to see in that room. Select your favorite idea.

4. Using a variety of lines, draw the face in your picture of the room. Use black markers to complete the drawing.

Art Criticism

Describe Describe the room you decided to decorate.

Analyze List the different kinds of lines you used in your painting.

Interpret How did the face you chose to paint affect the mood of the room?

Decide Did you successfully use a variety of lines to paint the face in the picture of your room?

Reflect
Time: About 45 minutes

Review and Assess

"What are some ways you can vary the texture, curve, and width of lines?" "¿Cuáles son algunas formas de variar la textura, la curva y el ancho de las líneas?"

Think

The artist used horizontal, long and short, thick and thin, and solid and broken lines to decorate her room.

■ Use *Large Prints 37* Broadway and *38 The Cow with the Subtile Nose* to have students identify line variations.

Informal Assessment

Art Journal: Critical Thinking

Have students answer the four art criticism questions—Describe, Analyze, Interpret, and Decide—in their Art Journals. In small groups, have students discuss the use of lines in their artwork.

■ For standardized-format test practice using this lesson's art content, see pages 8–9 in *Reading and Writing Test Preparation.*

Art Across the Curriculum

Use these simple ideas to reinforce art concepts across the curriculum.

★ **Narrative Writing** Have students look at Kandinsky's *Improvisation No. 27* and each write a short story about what they think the picture is describing.

★ **Math** Have students look at both paintings and estimate the lengths of some of the lines used in them.

★ **Science** Have students discuss the directions of the lines in the paintings. Then have them discuss how these lines compare to lines on objects found in natural environments, such as forests and bodies of water.

★ **Social Studies** Have students look at the letters of the alphabet in the headlines, captions, and text of a newspaper and study the line variations in the letters.

★ **Technology** Have students use the paintbrush tool in the computer's paint program to create different kinds of lines. Visit **SRAonline.com** to print detailed instructions for this activity.

Line Variations

Wrap-Up

 For the Art Specialist

Time: About 45 minutes

Focus

Use **Transparency 2** and **Large Prints 37** *Broadway* and **38** *The Cow with the Subtile Nose* to select a line in the painting and follow it with your finger. What happens to the line as you follow it? Does the line change from thick to thin? Does it change from light to dark, or rough to smooth? Why do you think the artist would change the way a line looks?

Teach

Have students follow the directions and use oil pastels or crayons to create a landscape with a variety of lines.

Reflect

Have students evaluate their artwork using the four steps of art criticism. Encourage them to locate a variety of lines in the classroom.

Alternate Activity

Materials:
- 12" × 18" construction paper in a variety of colors
- oil pastels or crayons
- scissors
- white glue or glue stick

1. Talk with students about the three parts of a landscape. Tell them they will select three sheets of construction paper, one sheet for each part of their landscape.

2. Have them cut a horizontal, wavy, or zigzag line, starting about 3" or 4" from the top of the paper. This line will represent hills or mountains and will be the middle ground of their landscape.

3. The last paper will be used as the foreground of the landscape.

4. Students may use construction paper scraps to cut out trees, plants, buildings, and people to add to their landscapes.

Research
in Art Education

There is a link between "arts education and creative thinking, academic self-concept, and school climate" ("Learning in and Through the Arts: The Question of Transfer" in *Critical Links*, p. 66). Students in schools with quality arts programs tend to use more creativity, take more risks, and view themselves as academically competent. As students learn to identify ways that lines can vary, have them think about other forms of art that involve line variations.

Assessment

Use the following rubric to evaluate the artwork students make in the Creative Expression activity and to assess students' understanding of the ways in which lines can vary in appearance.

Have students complete page 11 or 12 in their **Assessment** books.

Art History and Culture	Aesthetic Perception	Creative Expression	Art Criticism
3 POINTS The student demonstrates knowledge of the lives and work of Kandinsky and Borofsky.	The student accurately identifies the ways in which lines vary in appearance.	The student effectively plans and creates a landscape painting using a variety of lines.	The student evaluates his or her own work using the four steps of art criticism.
2 POINTS The student demonstrates weak or incomplete knowledge of the lives and work of Kandinsky and Borofsky.	The student shows emerging awareness of the ways in which lines vary in appearance.	The student shows some awareness of how to plan and create a landscape painting using a variety of lines.	The student attempts to evaluate his or her own work using the four steps of art criticism.
1 POINT The student cannot demonstrate knowledge of the lives and work of Kandinsky or Borofsky.	The student cannot identify the ways in which lines vary in appearance.	The student shows no understanding of how to plan and create a landscape painting using a variety of lines.	The student makes no attempt to evaluate his or her own work.

Assessment, p. 11

Name _____ Date _____

Lesson **2** UNIT 1

Line Variations

A. Drawing
Draw the lines in the boxes.

short lines	thin lines	rough lines

wide lines	lines that move in different directions	lines that curve a lot

B. Short Answer
Give three examples of lines found in nature.
1. _____
2. _____
3. _____

C. Writing
Look at *Improvisation No. 27* by Wassily Kandinsky. Describe how the artist used a variety of lines in his painting.

Level 3   Unit 1 • An Introduction to Line and Shape   **11**

Lesson 3 Overview — Shapes

Lesson 3 introduces simple geometric shapes and free-form shapes and how artists use lines to create shapes.

Objectives

 Art History and Culture

To identify and compare the use of simple geometric shapes and free-form shapes in still lifes

 Creative Expression

To plan and create a still-life painting using simple geometric and free-form shapes

 **Aesthetic Perception**

To identify simple geometric shapes and free-form shapes in works of art

 Art Criticism

To evaluate own work using the four steps of art criticism

Vocabulary ⭐ Reading

Review the following vocabulary words with students before beginning the lesson.

free-form shapes *figuras abstractas*—shapes that are uneven and are not regular

geometric shapes *figuras geométricas*—shapes, such as circles, squares, triangles, ovals, and rectangles, that can be defined using mathematical formulas

See page 59B for additional vocabulary and Spanish vocabulary resources.

 Art Journal: Vocabulary

Have students add these words to the Vocabulary section of their Art Journals.

Lesson Materials

- 12" × 18" white construction paper
- liquid tempera paints
- still-life objects
- paintbrushes of various sizes
- containers of water
- oil pastels
- paper plates
- paper towels
- newspaper

Alternate Materials:
- watercolor paints

Program Resources

- *Reading and Writing Test Prep.*, pp. 10–11
- *Transparency 3*
- *Flash Cards 7* and *17*
- *Artist Profiles*, pp. 19, 56
- *Animals Through History Time Line*
- *Assessment and Test Prep*, pp. 13–14
- *Large Prints 37* Broadway and *38* The Cow with the Subtile Nose
- *The National Museum of Women in the Arts Collection*

Concept Trace

Shapes
Introduced: Level 3, Unit 1, Lesson 3
Reinforced: Level 4, Unit 2, Lesson 1

Lesson 3 Arts Integration

Theatre

Complete Unit 1, Lesson 3 on pages 22–23 of *Theatre Arts Connections*.

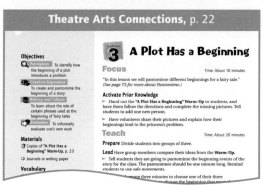

Theatre Arts Connections, p. 22

Music

Circus Music from *The Red Pony*. Aaron Copland.

In music, shape can pertain to the contour of the higher/lower movement of a melodic line. Play Copland's *Circus Music* as students complete the Practice activity in which they create geometric and free-form shapes. Discuss the shapes students create that fit with the music.

Performing Arts

Have students form a large circle. They will work in the center of the circle three at a time. #1 enters and forms a free-form shape using curved lines, #2 enters and creates a free-form shape using diagonal lines, #3 enters and creates a free-form shape using straight lines. Now all three take eight counts to change their shape in some way, finding a new level, size, or direction to face.

Focus

Time: About 45 minutes

Activate Prior Knowledge

"Think about the lines you use when you write your name. Which letters have lines that come around and close?" *"Piensen en las líneas que usan al escribir sus nombres ¿Qué letras tienen líneas que dan la vuelta y se cierran?"*

- Discuss student responses and how shapes vary in size.

Using Literature Reading

- Read *Birds, Nests, and Eggs* by Mel Boring. Discuss the use of shapes in the book.

Thematic Connection Science

- **Food/Nutrition:** Have students discuss different types of climates. Have them decide what type of climate(s) the fruit in the paintings needs to grow.

Introduce the Art

Look

"Let's look closely at the two paintings." *"Vamos a observar detalladamente las dos pinturas".*

Comparing and Contrasting Reading

- Have students describe the subject matter in each work of art. *Yellow Pad* and *Composition* are both still-life paintings. *Yellow Pad* depicts a floral arrangement with a pen and pad, fruit, and a Chinese checkers game. *Composition* is filled with different kinds of fruit.

- Have students make a list of the similarities and differences in the two paintings. Both still lifes contain fruit. Both contain the color red, and bright and dark colors. *Composition* contains many oval and circular shapes, while *Yellow Pad* contains a variety of triangles, squares, ovals, and free-form shapes.

NSAE 3a

Art History and Culture

Possible answer: Both still lifes contain fruit however Fish's painting uses geometric and free-form shapes and Vytlacil uses more oval and circular shapes.

 Web Connection

Visit **www.artnet.com** to learn more about Janet Fish and her other works of art.

Lesson 3 # Shapes

Look at the paintings on these pages. Both artists used lines to create various shapes in their paintings.

▲ **Janet Fish.** (American). *Yellow Pad.* 1997.

Oil on canvas. 36 × 90 inches (91 × 229 cm.). Columbus Museum, Columbus, Georgia.

 Art History and Culture

Do the paintings appear to be the same style?

Art History and Culture

Janet Fish

Janet Fish (jan´ ət fish) (1938–   ) was born in Boston, Massachusetts. She studied sculpture and printmaking at Smith College and Skowhegan Summer School. In 1963 Fish became one of the first women artists to receive her MFA from Yale University. Although Fish earned two degrees in fine arts from Yale University, she struggled to find work. For a while, she supported herself by painting bars of soap for a department store. Her lively still lifes have since become greatly admired. She has taught at art schools across the nation.

See pages 24–25 and 16–21 for more about art history and subject matter.

Artist Profiles, p. 19

Artist Profile

Janet Fish
b. 1938

Janet Fish (jan´ ət fish) earned two degrees in fine arts from Yale University but struggled to find work. For a while, she supported herself by painting bars of soap for a department store. Since then her large, lively still lifes have become much admired. Fish has taught at art schools across the nation. She now spends half her time in New York and half in Vermont.

◀ **Vaclav Vytlacil.**
(American).
Composition. 1931.
Oil on canvas. 28 $\frac{7}{8}$ × 39 $\frac{3}{8}$
inches (73.15 × 99 cm.).
Norton Museum of Art,
West Palm Beach, Florida.

Study both still-life paintings to find the following shapes.

▶ Find as many round shapes as you can.

▶ Find the square shapes.

▶ Where are the triangles?

▶ Are there any oval shapes? Where?

▶ Locate the free-form shapes.

🔍 Aesthetic Perception

Seeing Like an Artist Think about different shapes or look outside to find them in your environment.

🏺 Art History and Culture

Vaclav Vytlacil

Vaclav Vytlacil (vä klev vət´ la sil) (1892–1984) born in New York City in 1892 to Czechoslovakian immigrants. In 1906 he studied at the Art Institute of Chicago. In 1913, on a scholarship from the Art Student League, he went back to New York City and studied under painter John C. Johansen. Vytlacil's first teaching position, at the Minneapolis School of Art, lasted from 1916 to 1921. He eventually settled in Munich, Germany, where he enrolled in the Royal Academy of Art. In 1924 he helped organize the Hoffman Summer School on the island of Capri. Vytlacil married in 1927 in Florence, Italy, and eventually returned to the United States to study at the University of California, Berkeley.

See pages 24–25 and 16–21 for more about art history and subject matter.

Artist Profiles, p. 56

◀ Artist Profile ▶
Vaclav Vytlacil
1892-1984
Although he was born in New York, Vaclav Vytlacil (vä klev vət´ la sil) grew up in the Midwest. He took classes at the Art Institute of Chicago as a child and moved back to New York City in 1913 to attend the Art Students League. After saving some money, Vytlacil traveled and studied art in Europe. In Munich he met Hans Hofmann, a painter who became his mentor. Vytlacil left Europe to give a series of lectures at the University of California at Berkeley before joining the faculty of the Art Students League. After spending more time abroad, Vytlacil helped found the American Abstract Artists and taught at a variety of schools, including Queens College in New

Study

▶ Round shapes: *Yellow Pad*: the bowl, the Chinese checkers board, and the marbles; *Composition:* the fruit and the bowl

▶ Square shapes: *Yellow Pad*: the notepad and pencils

▶ Triangles: *Yellow Pad*: the Chinese checkers board and the design on tablecloth

▶ Ovals: *Yellow Pad*: the walnuts and vase; *Composition*: the bowl, the grapes, and the apples

▶ Free-form shapes: *Yellow Pad*: the flowers and the tablecloth: *Composition*: the grapes

■ For more examples of still lifes, see ***The National Museum of Women in the Arts Collection.***

📔 Art Journal: Writing

Encourage students to write their own explanations of shapes in the Concepts section of their Art Journals. What else do they want to know about shapes?

🔍 Aesthetic Perception

NSAE 3a

Seeing like an Artist Have students identify and discuss objects in the environment that contain different shapes, such as those in the paintings. Many flowers and leaves are examples of free-form shapes.

Developing Visual Literacy Have students discuss *Yellow Pad* and *Composition* and describe the details of each painting. Why do students think the artists used different styles?

💻 Web Connection

Visit **provincetownartistregistry.com/V/ vytlacil_vaclav.html** to learn more about Vaclav Vytlacil.

**each**

Time: About 30 minutes

"Look around the room and find objects that have geometric and free—form shapes."

"Observen alrededor del salón y busquen objetos que tengan figuras geométricas y abstractas".

- Have students read and discuss simple geometric and free-form shapes on page 46.

Practice

Materials: 9" × 12" paper, crayons

Alternate Materials: pencils

- Have students illustrate shapes by tracing the outside edges of objects with a crayon or pencil.

Creative Expression

Materials: 12" × 18" white construction paper, liquid tempera or watercolor paints, still-life objects, paintbrushes of various sizes, containers of water, oil pastels, paper plates, paper towels, newspaper

Alternate Materials: watercolors

- Distribute the materials and have students follow the directions on page 47.

- Review the Activity Tips on page 233 for visual examples.

Art Journal: Brainstorming

Have students brainstorm ideas for objects of various sizes to use in a still-life arrangement. Have them list their ideas in their Art Journals. Then have then discuss how they could arrange these objects in the Creative Expression activity.

Using Shapes

Everything has a **shape.** Shapes are flat, two-dimensional areas that are geometric or free-form.

Here are some simple **geometric** shapes.

circle   square   triangle   oval   rectangle

Free-form shapes are uneven and irregular. They can look many different ways.

Lines can be used to outline all these shapes.

Practice

Outline geometric and free-form shapes.

1. Find three geometric and three free-form shapes in your classroom.

2. In the air, use your index finger to trace the outline of each object. Close one eye as you trace. Now trace the outside edge of a shape on paper, using a crayon or pencil.

Differentiated Instruction

Reteach

Have students draw a variety of simple geometric and free-form shapes and write the names of the shapes next to them.

Special Needs

Students with visual or motor impairments may benefit from having their paper stabilized by tape as they create their painting.

ELL Tips

Students may benefit from working with partners during the Creative Expression activity. Partners can plan and discuss the artwork they plan to create. If possible, have students who speak same native language work together.

◀ **Natalie Hardison.** Age 8.

Think about the shapes you see in this student artist's still life.

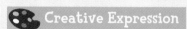 Creative Expression

What are some of the shapes you see in the objects around you? Paint a still-life picture using lines to make shapes.

1. Arrange five objects of different shapes and sizes in a variety of ways. Select the best arrangement.

2. Which object captures your attention most? Outline the shape of that object on your paper. In the same way, add the shapes of the other objects.

3. Begin to fill your shapes with different colors. Use one color at a time in several places on your picture. Continue to do this until your paper is filled with color.

Art Criticism

Describe What objects did you use in your still life?

Analyze What geometric shapes did you use in your painting? What free-form shapes did you use?

Interpret Give your still life an expressive title.

Decide If you could paint this scene again, what would you do differently?

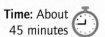 eflect

Time: About 45 minutes

Review and Assess

"How you can create moods with curved, straight, zigzag, and diagonal lines?" "¿Qué ánimos pueden crear con líneas rectas, curvas, en zigzag y diagonales?"

Think

The artist used various sizes of geometric shapes in her still life.

■ Use **Large Prints 37** *Broadway* and **38** *The Cow with the Subtile Nose* to have students compare the expressive quality of their lines with the works in this lesson.

Informal Assessment

Art Journal: Critical Thinking

Have students answer the four art criticism questions—Describe, Analyze, Interpret, and Decide—in their Art Journals. In small groups, have students discuss the use of lines in their drawings.

■ For standardized-format test practice using this lesson's art content, see pages 10–11 in *Reading and Writing Test Preparation.*

Art Across the Curriculum

Use these simple ideas to reinforce art concepts across the curriculum.

★ **Narrative Writing** Have students draw different sizes of shapes, such as squares, triangles, ovals, and circles. Have students write words inside of each shape that could be used to describe the shape.

★ **Math** Have students sort a list of objects according to their geometric shapes.

★ **Science** Have students look at a map of the United States. Ask students to think about the areas in the United States where the types of flowers and fruit in the paintings are grown.

★ **Social Studies** Have students look at Yellow Pad by Janet Fish. Have them list five objects in the painting and decide where the artist might have found them.

★ **Technology** Have students use the draw tool on the computer to draw geometric and free-form shapes. Visit **SRAonline.com** to print detailed instructions for this activity.

NSAE 1d

Shapes

Extra! For the Art Specialist

Time: About 45 minutes

Focus

Use *Transparency 3* and *Large Print 37 Broadway* to discuss how lines can create shapes. Have students look for basic geometric shapes in the artwork. How many circles and ovals can they see? Are there any square or triangular shapes in the artwork? Are the geometric shapes repeated in other objects in the artwork?

Teach

Have students follow the directions to complete their still lifes. Have them use the oil pastels to outline their still lifes and fill in the shapes by smearing different colors.

Reflect

Have students evaluate their artwork using the four steps of art criticism. Encourage them to locate and describe other areas in the classroom where they see geometric and free-form shapes.

Alternate Activity

Materials:
- 12" × 18" colored construction paper
- 9" × 12" colored construction paper
- oil pastels
- still-life arrangement
- 6" × 9" colored construction paper
- scissors
- white glue

1. Ask students to examine the still life, looking for the basic geometric shapes that can be found in each of the objects.

2. Have students select a sheet of 12" × 18" construction paper to use as the background for their still life, and two or three sheets of 9" × 12" construction paper to use for the larger shapes in their still life.

3. Students will cut shapes from the construction paper to represent the objects in the still life, overlapping the shapes where appropriate.

4. Students may use oil pastels to add details and shading to the still life objects.

Research in Art Education

There is a link between "arts education and creative thinking, academic self-concept, and school climate" ("Learning In and Through the Arts: The Question of Transfer" in *Critical Links,* p. 66). Students in schools with quality arts programs tend to use more creativity, take more risks, and view themselves as academically competent. As students learn about geometric and free-form shapes, discuss other types of art in which artists use these shapes.

Assessment

Use the following rubric to evaluate the artwork students make in the Creative Expression activity and to assess students' understanding of geometric and free-form shapes.

Have students complete page 13 or 14 in their *Assessment* books.

	Art History and Culture	Aesthetic Perception	Creative Expression	Art Criticism
3 POINTS	The student demonstrates knowledge of the lives and work of Fish and Vytlacil.	The student accurately identifies simple geometric and free-form shapes.	The student effectively plans and creates a still-life painting using a variety of geometric and free-form shapes.	The student evaluates his or her own work using the four steps of art criticism.
2 POINTS	The student demonstrates weak or incomplete understanding of the lives and works of Fish and Vytlacil.	The student shows emerging awareness of simple geometric and free-form shapes.	The student shows some awareness of how to plan and create a still-life painting using a variety of geometric and free-form shapes.	The student attempts to evaluate his or her own work using the four steps of art criticism.
1 POINT	The student demonstrates no knowledge of the lives and work of Fish or Vytlacil.	The student shows no awareness of simple geometric and free-form shapes.	The student shows no understanding of how to plan and create a still-life painting using a variety of geometric and free-form shapes.	The student makes no attempt to evaluate his or her own work.

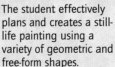

Assessment, p. 13

Name _____ Date _____

Shapes
Lesson 3 UNIT 1

A. Drawing
Draw an example of each shape.

circle   square   triangle

oval   rectangle   free-form

B. Identifying
Circle the geometric shapes below. Underline the free-form shapes.

Level 3   Unit 1 • An Introduction to Line and Shape   13

Complex Geometric Shapes

Lesson 4 introduces complex geometric shapes and how they are used to create designs.

Objectives

 Art History and Culture

To identify and compare the cultural purposes of different types of works of art

 Creative Expression

To plan and design a robot using complex geometric and free-form shapes

 Aesthetic Perception

To identify the use of complex geometric shapes in works of art

 Art Criticism

To evaluate own work using the four steps of art criticism

Vocabulary Reading

Review the following vocabulary word with the students before beginning the lesson.

complex geometric shapes figuras geométricas complejas— shapes formed by combining simple geometric shapes

See page 59B for additional vocabulary and Spanish vocabulary resources.

 Art Journal: Vocabulary

Have students add this word to the Vocabulary section of their Art Journals.

Lesson Materials

- pencils
- 12" × 18" black construction paper
- 9" × 12" colored construction paper
- scissors
- sketch paper
- glue
- pencils

Alternate Materials:
- crayons or markers
- wrapping paper, wallpaper, or fabric

Program Resources

- *Reading and Writing Test Prep.*, pp. 12–13
- *Transparency 4*
- *Flash Cards 7* and *16*
- *Artist Profiles*, pp. 65, 72
- *Animals Through History Time Line*
- *Assessment*, pp. 15–16
- *Large Prints 37* Broadway and *38* The Cow with the Subtile Nose
- *Art Around the World Collection*

Concept Trace
Complex Geometric Shapes
Introduced: Level 3, Unit 1, Lesson 4

Reinforced: Level 4, Unit 2, Lesson 1

Lesson 4 Arts Integration

Theatre

Complete Unit 1, Lesson 4 on pages 24–25 of *Theatre Arts Connections.*

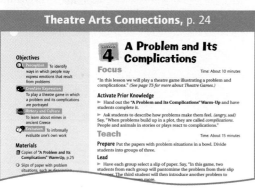

Music

 Minuet from Eine Kleine Nachtmusik. Wolfgang Amadeus Mozart.

Complex geometric shapes like diamonds, pentagons, and octagons are made by combining simple geometric shapes. In music, complex compositions are made by combining instruments, simple notes, and melodies. Play Mozart's Minuet as students complete the Practice activity. Discuss the different instruments and melodies they hear in the composition.

Performing Arts

Using elastic or string, students will create a series of geometric shapes working in groups of eight or ten. Measure and manipulate the elastic or string to create diamonds, pentagons, hexagons, and other geometric shapes, with a person representing each corner.

Activate Prior Knowledge

"Imagine you are riding in a car that slowly comes to a stop. What is the shape of the stop sign on the corner?" "Imagínense que van en un carro que se detiene lentamente. ¿Cuál es la forma de la señal de alto en la esquina?"

■ Discuss students' responses, and then draw an octagon on the board. Have students identify the simple geometric shapes that form the octagon.

Using Literature [★] Reading

■ Read *Mowing* by Jessie Haas. Discuss the use of complex geometric shapes in the book.

Thematic Connection [★] Reading

■ **Shapes:** Have students think about shapes they see every day in their community. Have them discuss buildings where they have noticed these shapes.

NSAE 4a

Introduce the Art

Look

"Let's take a look at the two works of art." "Vamos a observar detalladamente las dos obras de arte".

Comparing and Contrasting [★] Reading

■ Have students list the similarities and differences in *Double Saddlebag* and *Mihrab*. Both works of art are functional, have formal balance, and are decorated with complex geometric shapes. *Mihrab* is divided into many areas of shapes and patterns, whereas the saddlebag has shapes in a single area.

 Art History and Culture

Possible answer: Answers will vary. Students may say because the shapes worked best with what the artist was trying to portray.

 Web Connection

Visit **www.dia.org/collections/aonwc/ nativeamericanart/nativeamericanart.html** to find out more about Native American art.

Look at the artwork on these pages. *Double Saddlebag* was created in North America by a member of the Sioux in 1875. *Mihrab* (the focal area in an Islamic house of worship) was created in Iran about 500 years earlier and is decorated with colorful tiles. Both pieces are decorated with complex geometric shapes.

◀ **Artist unknown.** (Native American, Sioux). *Double Saddlebag.* 1875.
•••••••••••••••••••••••••••••••••
Buckskin, canvas, glass beads, sinew, and wool. 45 × 13 inches (113.7 × 33 cm.). Detroit Institute of Arts, Detroit, Michigan.

 Art History and Culture

These works were created by artists from different cultures. Why do you think they used similar shapes?

48 Unit 1 • Lesson 4

 Art History and Culture

Double Saddlebag

A member of the Sioux tribe created *Double Saddlebag*. The saddlebag is decorated with colorful glass "seed" beads that were brought to the tribe by traders around 1840. *Double Saddlebag* is made of a variety of material, including buckskin, canvas, glass beads, sinew, and wool.

See pages 24–25 and 16–21 for more about art history and subject matter.

Artist Profiles, p. 65

‹ Artist Profile ›

Double Saddlebag

The Sioux were native to the northern plains of North America, including land now known as Minnesota, the Dakotas, and Nebraska. They hunted their food and followed migrating herds of buffalo across the plains. During the mid-1800s, settlers and gold seekers killed many buffalo on the Sioux hunting reservations. Although groups led by Sitting Bull and Crazy Horse fought back, the Sioux eventually lost their freedom to choose where they lived. Now about half of the existing Sioux live on reservations. The others live in cities across the United States, where many work to preserve Sioux traditions and crafts.

Artist unknown (Native American, Sioux).

Study both works of art and find complex geometric shapes.

▶ Find the shapes that have six sides.

▶ Point to the large diamond shapes in *Double Saddlebag.* Look closely to find smaller diamond shapes in *Mihrab.*

▶ Where do you see some star shapes?

▶ Look at the large shapes in *Double Saddlebag.* What simple geometric shapes are used to make them?

▲ **Artist unknown.** (Iran). *Mihrab.* 1354.
Faience mosaic of glazed terra cotta cut and embedded in plaster. 11 feet 3 inches × 7 feet 6 inches (3.4 × 2.3 meters). Metropolitan Museum of Art, New York, New York.

🔍 Aesthetic Perception

Design Awareness Notice the shapes of things you see every day, such as the buildings in your neighborhood. What shapes do you see in the spaces around them?

🏺 Art History and Culture

Mihrab

Mihrab is a niche in the interior wall of a mosque, which is a house of worship for Muslims. *Mihrab* is large enough to accommodate one standing person. It indicates the direction of Mecca, a city in Saudi Arabia that is a pilgrimage site because it is the birthplace of Mohammed, the founder of Islam. *Mihrab* is a symbolic architectural structure. *Mihrab* is a faience mosaic of glazed clay tiles cut and imbedded in plaster.

See pages 24–25 and 16–21 for more about art history and subject matter.

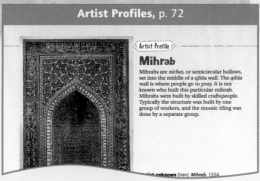

Artist Profiles, p. 72

◁ Artist Profile ▷

Mihrab

Mihrabs are *niches,* or semicircular hollows, set into the middle of a *qibla* wall. The *qibla* wall is where people go to pray. It is not known who built this particular mihrab. Mihrabs were built by skilled craftspeople. Typically the structure was built by one group of workers, and the mosaic tiling was done by a separate group.

Artist unknown (Iran). *Mihrab.* 1354.

Study

▶ Hexagons: *Mihrab:* There are hexagonal shapes in the area above the central horizontal line and in the rectangular area above the arch.

▶ Diamonds: *Saddlebag:* There are diamond shapes on both sides of the central axis. *Mihrab:* There are small diamond shapes in the thin bands that frame the dome and rectangular area on the outside surface.

▶ Stars: *Mihrab:* There are star shapes inside the domed, hollow area.

▶ Complex geometric shapes: *Saddlebag:* Squares, rectangles, and triangles are used to make the complex geometric shapes.

■ For more examples of art from the Middle East see the ***Art Around the World Collection.***

📓 Art Journal: Writing

Encourage students to write their own explanation of complex geometric shapes in the Concepts section of their Art Journals. What else do they want to know about complex geometric shapes?

🔍 Aesthetic Perception

Seeing Like an Artist Discuss with students buildings they see every day and ask them to describe the complex geometric shapes in the buildings. Have students explain the complex geometric shapes they see in the classroom.

Developing Visual Literacy Discuss with students what life may have been like when *Double Saddlebag* and *Mihrab* were created. Ask students how long they think it took each artist to create the work of art. Have them also suggest what tools may have been used by the artists to create their works of art.

💻 Web Connection

Visit **www.metmuseum.org/** to find out more about Iranian art.

Teach

"How can you make complex geometric shapes?" "¿Cómo pueden hacer figuras geométricas complejas?"

■ Have students read and discuss how complex geometric shapes are made up from simple geometric shapes on page 50.

Practice

Materials: 12" × 18" paper, pencils

Alternate Materials: crayons or markers

■ Distribute the materials and have students follow the directions on page 50.

■ Make sure to explain how to fold the paper into six sections.

Creative Expression

Materials: 12" × 18" black construction paper, 9" × 12" colored construction paper, scissors, glue, sketch paper, pencils

Alternate Materials: wrapping paper, wallpaper, or fabric

■ Distribute the materials and have students follow the directions on page 51.

■ Review the Activity Tips on page 233 for visual examples.

Art Journal: Brainstorming

Have students brainstorm ideas for creating designs and list their ideas in their Art Journals. Demonstrate how simple geometric shapes can be combined to create complex geometric shapes. Then have students plan their designs for the Creative Expression activity.

Using Complex Geometric Shapes

Complex geometric shapes are made by combining simple geometric shapes such as triangles, squares, and rectangles. You found examples of complex geometric shapes in the two pieces of art.

diamond

pentagon

trapezoid

hexagon

parallelogram

octagon

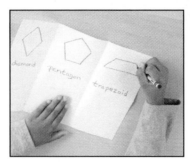

Practice

Use a pencil to draw complex geometric shapes.

1. Fold a sheet of paper into six equal boxes. Print the name of a complex geometric shape at the bottom of each box.

2. Draw one complex geometric shape in each box.

Differentiated Instruction

Reteach
Have students look around the classroom and point to the complex geometric shapes they see. Have students illustrate different textures for their designs by using a combination of materials.

Special Needs
A display board with names and pictures of complex geometric shapes will assist students with disabilities in successfully naming and using these shapes during the lesson activity.

ELL Tips
Students will benefit from an introduction to the words that name complex geometric shapes during examination of the works of art. Verbalize the name of the diamond shape as you point to it.

Think about the geometric shapes in this student artist's design.

◀ **Julian Anguiano.**
Age 8.

 Creative Expression

How can you use geometric shapes to create a design? Make your design by using complex geometric shapes.

1. Imagine a design you can create with complex geometric shapes.

2. Use your imagination to make a design using simple and complex geometric shapes.

3. Use your scrap paper to design a frame or border for your art.

Art Criticism

Describe Describe the design you created.

Analyze Name the simple and complex geometric shapes you used.

Interpret Give your design a name.

Decide If you could create this design again, what would you do differently?

 Time: About 45 minutes

Review and Assess

"What are some common designs in your surroundings that include complex geometric shapes made of simple geometric shapes?" "¿Cuáles son algunos diseños comunes que ven en sus alrededores que poseen figuras geométricas simples para crear figuras geométricas complejas hechas de figuras geométricas simples?

Think

The artist used several complex geometric shapes in creating his design.

- Use *Large Prints 37 Broadway* and *38 The Cow with the Subtile Nose* to have students compare their complex geometric shapes with the works of art in this lesson.

Informal Assessment

Art Journal: Critical Thinking

Have students answer the four art criticism questions—Describe, Analyze, Interpret, and Decide—in their Art Journals. In small groups, have students discuss the use of complex geometric shapes in their collages.

- For standardized-format test practice using this lesson's art content, see pages 12–13 in *Reading and Writing Test Preparation.*

Art Across the Curriculum

Use these simple ideas to reinforce art concepts across the curriculum.

★ **Narrative Writing** Have students draw the shapes of different road signs they have seen while riding in an automobile. Underneath each shape they draw, students should write the name of the shape.

★ **Math** Have students look down the right and left sides of *Double Saddlebag*, and name the complex geometric shapes they see.

★ **Science** Have students each draw a picture of a snowflake. Make sure that they use geometric shapes in their drawings. Discuss with students the shapes they decided to use in their drawings.

★ **Social Studies Connection** Have students draw shapes they see in a local newspaper. Have them describe how the complex geometric shapes were used.

★ **Technology** Have students use the paint program on the computer to draw four complex geometric shapes. Have them use different tools to create their shapes. Visit **SRAonline.com** to print detailed instructions for this activity.

Lesson 4 Wrap-Up

Complex Geometric Shapes

Extra! For the Art Specialist

 Time: About 45 minutes

Focus

Use **Transparency 4** and **Large Prints 37** *Broadway* and **38** *The Cow with the Subtile Nose* to discuss the ways in which artists use complex geometric shapes. Have students identify complex geometric shapes.

Teach

Have students follow the directions to complete their radial design.

Reflect

Have students evaluate their artwork using the four steps of art criticism.

Alternate Activity

Materials:
• 8" squares of white drawing paper
• 6" × 9" sheets of colored tissue paper
• scissors
• thinned white glue
• paintbrushes

1. Have students divide the white paper into quarters, then match opposite corners together to fold the paper into triangles.

2. Students will fold one sheet of tissue paper in half three times, then cut one large complex geometric shape, producing eight identical shapes. Repeat the process with two other sheets of tissue paper.

3. Students will glue one complex geometric shape at a time on each of the fold lines to form a radial design. Shapes may be overlapped to create a more interesting design.

Research in Art Education

Some studies have shown that there is "a significant association between arts study (that includes visual arts) and standardized measures of creative thinking" ("Does Studying the Arts Engender Creative Thinking? Evidence for Near but Not Far Transfer" in *Critical Links*, p. 82). Students who study the arts tend to score higher on drawing-based creativity tests than on verbal creativity tests. As they learn about complex geometric shapes, encourage students to observe how many buildings in their city or town are made of complex geometric shapes.

Assessment

Use the following rubric to evaluate the artwork students make in the Creative Expression activity and to assess students' understanding complex geometric shapes.

Have students complete page 15 or 16 in their *Assessment* books.

	Art History and Culture	Aesthetic Perception	Creative Expression	Art Criticism
3 POINTS	The student demonstrates knowledge of the cultural purposes of both works of art.	The student accurately identifies the use of complex geometric shapes.	The student effectively plans and designs a robot using complex geometric shapes.	The student evaluates his or her own work using the four steps of art criticism.
2 POINTS	The student demonstrates weak or incomplete knowledge of the cultural purposes of the works of art.	The student shows emerging awareness of the use of complex geometric shapes.	The student shows some awareness of how to plan and design a robot using complex geometric shapes.	The student attempts to evaluate his or her own work using the four steps of art criticism.
1 POINT	The student demonstrates no knowledge of the cultural purposes of either work of art.	The student demonstrates no awareness of the use of complex geometric shapes.	The student shows no understanding of how to plan and design a robot using complex geometric shapes.	The student makes no attempt to evaluate his or her own work.

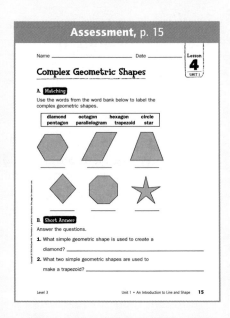

Shapes in Architecture

Lesson 5 introduces simple geometric and free-form shapes that are found in architecture. Architects use geometric and free-form shapes to design buildings.

Objectives

Art History and Culture
To identify and compare the use of geometric and free-form shapes in paintings of different types of buildings

Creative Expression
To draw a building from observation using geometric and free-form shapes

Aesthetic Perception
To identify geometric and free-form shapes in architecture

Art Criticism
To evaluate own work using the four steps of art criticism

Vocabulary Reading

Review the following vocabulary words with students before beginning the lesson.

architect *arquitecto*—an artist who designs and draws plans for cities, buildings, and bridges, and generally supervises the construction of them

architecture *arquitectura*—the art form of designing and planning the construction of buildings or other structures

See page 59B for additional vocabulary and Spanish vocabulary resources.

Art Journal: Vocabulary
Have students add these words to the Vocabulary section of their Art Journals.

Lesson Materials
- 9" × 12" white paper
- pencils
- 12" × 18" colored construction paper
- black felt-tip pens
- markers

Alternate Materials:
- markers
- dustless chalk and oil pastels

Program Resources
- *Reading and Writing Test Prep.*, pp. 14–15
- *Transparency 5*
- *Flash Cards 10* and *11*
- *Artist Profiles*, pp. 10, 25
- *Animals Through History Time Line*
- *Assessment*, pp. 17–18
- *Large Prints 37* Broadway and *38* The Cow with the Subtile Nose
- *Art Around the World Collection*

Concept Trace
Shapes in Architecture
Introduced: Level 3, Unit 1, Lesson 5

Reinforced: Level 5, Unit 2, Lesson 6

Lesson 5 Arts Integration

Theatre

Complete Unit 1, Lesson 5 on pages 26–27 of **Theatre Arts Connections.**

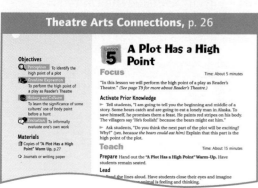

Music

Have to Have a Habitat. Bill Oliver.

Play Bill Oliver's *Have to Have a Habitat* to and discuss the need for buildings and habitats for people and animals to provide shelter from the elements. Discuss the lines and shapes in architecture that make buildings solid, long-lasting structures.

Performing Arts

Discuss and study the following structures: dome, coliseum, skyscraper. Call out one structure at a time. In small groups students will simultaneously (without talking) create the structure within ten counts. Each group will remember their designs and sequence them using eight counts to form each design and hold each for four counts.

Focus

Time: About 45 minutes

Activate Prior Knowledge

"Think about the doors and windows in your home. What shapes are they? What shape is the roof of your home?" "Piensen en las puertas y ventanas de sus casas. ¿Qué formas tienen? ¿De qué forma es el techo?"

- Discuss students' responses regarding shapes in architecture.

Using Literature ☆ Reading

- Read *Wild in the City* by Janet Thornhill. Discuss the use of shapes in architecture in the book.

Thematic Connection ☆ Social Studies

- **Buildings:** Encourage students to look outside and discuss the geometric and free-form shapes they see that have been created by nature.

Introduce the Art

Look

"Let's take a close look at the two works of art." "Vamos a observar detalladamente las dos obras de arte".

Comparing and Contrasting ☆ Reading

- Have students describe the subject matter of *The City* and *The Clock Tower in the Piazza San Marco*. They both are cityscapes.

- Have students list the similarities and differences in the two works of art. Both are outdoor scenes, include buildings, and show sunlight. *The City* is a colored painting that includes several buildings with many windows. *The Clock Tower in the Piazza San Marco* is a painting that also includes color and contains many rectangles, circles, and half-circle forms.

🏺 Art History and Culture

Possible answer: Students may say buildings look different and they look as though they are from different cultures.

💻 Web Connection

Visit **www.pbs.org/wgbh/nova/pyramid/** to learn more about buildings from other cultures that include geometric shapes.

 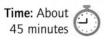

Look at the artwork on these pages. Both works of art show geometric shapes being used for windows and other objects on the building.

▲ **Edward Hopper.** (American). *The City.* 1927.
· ·
Oil on canvas. 28 × 36 inches (71 × 91 cm.). University of Arizona Museum of Art, Tucson, Arizona.

🏺 Art History and Culture

Do the buildings in the paintings appear to be created during the same time period?

Art History and Culture

Edward Hopper

Edward Hopper (ed´ wərd hä pər) (1882–1967) trained under Robert Henri. Hopper painted landscapes and cityscapes to express the world around him. Many of Hopper's paintings were based on urban and village life, and they expressed loneliness, emptiness, and stagnation. His paintings are generally without action, and many of the people in his paintings show little expression. Hopper gained a reputation as the artist who gave visual form to the loneliness and boredom of life in a big city. Outside the United States, his work made its mark by appearing in several Alfred Hitchcock films as well as other films.

See pages 24–25 and 16–21 for more about art history and subject matter.

Artist Profiles, p. 25

◆ Artist Profile ◆

Edward Hopper
1882-1967

Edward Hopper (ed´ wərd hä´ pər) was born in Nyack, New York. He attended the New York School of Art and made three trips to Europe to study art. He worked as an illustrator in New York City and eventually opened a studio in Greenwich Village. Hopper married another painter, Josephine Nivison, who helped arrange his first exhibition. They spent their summers on an island off the Maine coast, on Cape Cod, and at other East Coast locations. These spots became the settings of many of Hopper's paintings.

Study both pieces of artwork to find the following shapes.

▶ Point to all the square shapes you see.

▶ Where are the rectangles?

▶ Find the triangles.

▶ Do you see any circles?

▶ Find some free-form shapes.

▲ **Giovanni Antonio Canal.** (Italian). *The Clock Tower in the Piazza San Marco.* c. 1730.

Oil on canvas. 20 ½ × 27 ⅜ inches (52 × 71 cm.). Nelson Atkins Museum, Kansas City, Missouri.

🔍 Aesthetic Perception

Design Awareness Go outside your classroom and look at the buildings in the neighborhood. Look for geometric and free-form shapes.

🏺 Art History and Culture

Giovanni Antonio Canal (Canaletto)

Giovanni Antonio Canal (jō van´nē an tō´nē ō ka nəl´) (1697–1768) was the most famous view painter of the eighteenth century. His father, who was also an artist, was instrumental in Canal's training. By 1723 he was painting dramatic and picturesque views of Venice. He soon discovered that mass production of celebrated sights for tourists paid better than the individual painting of masterpieces. Then Canal began to streamline his technique by training his studio assistants to paint bright pictures based on many of his drawings.

For the remainder of his life, he lived and painted in Venice.

See pages 24–25 and 16–21 for more about art history and subject matter.

Artist Profiles, p. 10

▸ Artist Profile ◂
Canaletto
1697-1768

Giovanni Antonio Canal, known as Canaletto (ka na´lät tō), was born in Venice, Italy. He first began to paint with his father, who was a painter of theatre scenery. Canaletto traveled to Rome in 1719 and may have studied with painters of classical ruins. He began to paint dramatic city views of festivals and ceremonies for which he became very famous. Travelers from England often bought his paintings as souvenirs of their trips. Canaletto eventually moved to England and painted there for ten years. He then returned to Venice and continued to work for the remainder of his life.

Study

▶ Squares: many of the windows on the buildings in *The City* and *The Clock Tower in the Piazza San Marco.*

▶ Rectangles: the windows and the buildings in *The City* and *The Clock Tower in the Piazza San Marco.*

▶ Triangles: the tops of the buildings in *The City* and *The Clock Tower in the Piazza San Marco.*

▶ Circles: the clock, part of the design on the building with the clock in *The Clock Tower in the Piazza San Marco*; part of the structure of the building closest to the viewer in *The City.*

▶ Free-form shapes: the clouds and people's clothing in *The Clock Tower in the Piazza San Marco.*

■ For more examples of art from North America, see *The Art Around the World Collection.*

📓 Art Journal: Writing

Encourage students to write their own explanations of shapes in architecture in the Concepts section of their Art Journals. What else do they want to know?

🔍 Aesthetic Perception

Seeing Like an Artist Discuss neighborhood buildings with students. Buildings usually contain a variety of geometric and free-form shapes. Windows and rooftop, for example, often include rectangles, squares, and triangles.

Developing Visual Literacy Discuss what the artists were trying to convey in the scenes of each painting. One painting shows a city with many people, while the other shows a city with almost no people at all. Does the number of people in each painting have something to do with the time of day that the artist portrayed?

💻 Web Connection

Visit www.ibiblio.org/wm/paint/auth/hopper/ to find more information about Edward Hopper and his other works of art.

 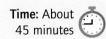

Teach

Time: About 45 minutes

"How can you use shapes to draw a building?" "¿Cómo pueden usar las figuras para dibujar un edificio?"

- Have students read and discuss simple and complex geometric shapes, as well as free-form shapes, on page 54.

Practice

Materials: 9" × 12" white paper, pencils

Alternate Materials: markers

- Distribute the materials and have students follow the directions on page 54.

Creative Expression

Materials: 12" × 18" construction paper, black felt-tip pens, markers

Alternate Materials: dustless chalk and oil pastels

- Distribute materials and have students follow the directions on page 55.
- Review the Activity Tips on page 234 for visual examples.

 Art Journal: Brainstorming
Have students observe the school building and identify the various shapes they see. Then have them select an area of the building they would like to draw for the Creative Expression activity.

Shapes in Architecture

Architecture is the art of designing and planning buildings. You saw examples of architecture in the artwork on the previous pages. An **architect** is the person who plans and designs buildings. Architects use **geometric** and **free-form shapes** in their designs.

Practice
Use a pencil to illustrate geometric and free-form shapes in architecture.

1. On a sheet of paper, use your pencil to draw a building using various shapes.
2. Use your imagination to add smaller geometric and free-form shapes to create the roof, windows, and doors.

Differentiated Instruction

Reteach
Have students find at least three examples of architecture in a book. Ask them to draw and list all the geometric and free-form shapes they see.

Special Needs
Provide visual prompts in the form of pre-cut geometric shapes for students with disabilities as they complete the lesson activity.

ELL Tips
Some students may be hesitant to answer the open-ended questions in this lesson. Provide support by describing, analyzing, and interpreting the elements in their drawings yourself, or by inviting other students to do so. Encourage students to point to elements in their drawings as you describe them.

◄ **Edwin Vasquez.**
Age 8.

Think about the parts of this student's drawing that have free-form shapes and geometric shapes.

 Creative Expression

In the world around you, what kinds of buildings are designed with geometric and free-form shapes? Draw a building using geometric and free-form shapes.

1. Walk outside and choose an area of your school building that you would like to draw.

2. Point out all the geometric shapes you see. Then look for the free-form shapes.

3. Draw the area of the school building you selected. Make sure you include all the geometric and free-form shapes you see.

Art Criticism

Describe Describe the shapes you used in your drawing.

Analyze Where did you place free-form shapes in your drawing? Why?

Interpret How could you completely change the appearance of the building with different shapes?

Decide Does your drawing look like your school? If not, what needs to be changed to improve your drawing?

Reflect

Review and Assess

"What geometric and free-form shapes are used to design roofs, windows, and doors?
"¿Qué figuras geométricas y abstactas se usan para diseñar techos, ventanas y puertas?"

Think

The artist used various free-form and geometric shapes in designing his building.

- Use *Large Prints 37 Broadway* and *38 The Cow with the Subtile Nose* to have students compare different geometric and free-form shapes.

Informal Assessment

Art Journal: Critical Thinking
Have students answer the four art criticism questions—Describe, Analyze, Interpret, and Decide—in their Art Journals. In small groups, have students discuss the use of geometric and free-form shapes in their drawings.

- For standardized-format test practice using this lesson's art content, see pages 14–15 in *Reading and Writing Test Preparation.*

❖ Art Across the Curriculum ❖

Use these simple ideas to reinforce art concepts across the curriculum.

★ **Narrative Writing** Have students each write a simile to create a word picture of a skyscraper.

★ **Math** Have students count how many geometric shapes they see on the buildings in *The City.*

★ **Science** Have students look at *The Clock Tower in the Piazza San Marco* and decide what objects use electricity to operate.

★ **Social Studies** Have students think about and discuss ways in which climate can be a factor in the design of buildings. Have students give examples of buildings they know of that may have been designed a certain way because of the climate in which they are located.

★ **Technology** Have students use the paint tool on the computer to draw a building using geometric and free-form shapes. **SRAonline.com** to print detailed instructions for this activity.

Lesson 5

Wrap-Up

Shapes in Architecture

Extra! For the Art Specialist

Time: About 45 minutes

Focus

Use *Transparency 5* and *Large Prints 37 Broadway* and *38 The Cow with the Subtile Nose*. Look at the buildings in the artworks. What is the largest geometric shape? Do you see any circles and triangles? Are there any free-form shapes? How would the buildings look different if they were mostly free-form shapes instead of geometric shapes, or vice versa?

Teach

Have students follow the directions to complete a collograph.

Reflect

Have students evaluate their artwork using the four steps of art criticism. Encourage them to locate and describe other areas of free-form and geometric shapes in the classroom.

Alternate Activity

Materials:

- 9" × 12" sheets of tagboard or oaktag (manila folders)
- 6" × 9" sheets of tagboard or oaktag
- scissors
- white glue
- brayers
- printing ink
- 12" × 18" white and colored paper for printing

1. Explain to students they are going to make a collograph plate of a building using geometric and free-form shapes.

2. Students will cut their building shape from a 6" × 9" piece of tagboard and glue it to the 9" × 12" background sheet of tagboard. Students will cut the roof, windows, and doors from other 6" × 9" pieces of tagboard.

3. After the collograph plates have dried, students will roll printing ink onto the plates with brayers, place the 12" × 18" paper over the inked plates and rub the back of the paper to produce a print.

Research in Art Education

Research has indicated that one important outcome of integrating arts into other curriculum areas is an increased level of classroom discussions and more time spent on problem solving. The level of teacher dedication and experience seems to influence these outcomes ("Different Ways of Knowing: 1991–94 National Longitudinal Study Final Report" in *Schools, Communities, and the Arts: A Research Compendium*). As students learn about geometric and free-form shapes in architecture, encourage students to be aware of noticing these shapes in other buildings.

Assessment

 Use the following rubric to evaluate the artwork students make in the Creative Expression activity and to assess students' understanding of shapes in architecture.

	Art History and Culture	Aesthetic Perception	Creative Expression	Art Criticism
3 POINTS	The student demonstrates knowledge of the lives and cultures of Canale and Hopper.	The student accurately identifies the use of geometric and free-form shapes in architecture.	The student effectively draws a building from observation using geometric and free-form shapes.	The student evaluates his or her own work using the four steps of art criticism.
2 POINTS	The student demonstrates weak or incomplete knowledge of the lives and cultures of Canale and Hopper.	The student shows emerging awareness of the use of geometric and free-form shapes in architecture.	The student shows some awareness of how to draw a building from observation using geometric and free-form shapes.	The student attempts to evaluate his or her own work using the four steps of art criticism.
1 POINT	The student demonstrates no knowledge of the lives and cultures of either Canale or Hopper.	The student cannot identify the use of geometric and free-form shapes in architecture.	The student shows no understanding of how to draw a building from observation using geometric and free-form shapes.	The student makes no attempt to evaluate his or her own work.

Have students complete page 17 or 18 in their *Assessment* books.

Assessment, p. 17

Name _____ Date _____ **Lesson 5 UNIT 1**

Shapes in Architecture

A. Short Answer
Answer the question.
What is an architect? _____

B. Drawing
Design and draw a house. Include the following:
1. Five different simple geometric shapes
2. Two complex geometric shapes
3. One free-form shape

C. Writing
Look at the house you drew. Write a paragraph that describes how the different shapes were used.

Level 3   Unit 1 • An Introduction to Line and Shape   **17**

Lesson 6 Overview

Shapes of People

Lesson 6 introduces simple geometric and free-form shapes that make up people and objects in art and the environment. Artists use geometric and free-form shapes in portraits.

Objectives

Art History and Culture

To identify and compare the use of geometric and free-form shapes in eighteenth- and twentieth-century portraits

Creative Expression

To draw a portrait using geometric and free-form shapes

Aesthetic Perception

To identify the use of geometric and free-form shapes that make up people and objects in works of art and the environment

Art Criticism

To evaluate own work using the four steps of art criticism

Vocabulary ⭐ Reading

Review the following vocabulary word with students before beginning the lesson.

portrait *retrato*—a painting, drawing, or photograph of a person

See page 59B for additional vocabulary and Spanish vocabulary resources.

Art Journal: Vocabulary

Have students add this word to the Vocabulary section of their Art Journals.

Lesson Materials
- 8½" × 11" paper
- pencils
- 12" × 18" colored construction paper
- oil pastels
- dustless chalk

Alternate Materials:
- liquid tempera paints

Program Resources
- *Reading and Writing Test Prep.*, pp. 16–17
- *Transparency 6*
- *Flash Cards 8* and *16*
- *Artist Profiles*, pp. 11, 22
- *Animals Through History Time Line*
- *Assessment*, pp. 19–20
- *Large Prints 37* Broadway and *38* The Cow with the Subtile Nose
- *Art Around the World Collection*

Concept Trace
Shapes in Architecture
Introduced: Level 3, Unit 1, Lesson 6
Reinforced: Level 4, Unit 2, Lesson 1

Lesson 6 Arts Integration

Theatre

Complete Unit 1, Lesson 6 on pages 28–33 of *Theatre Arts Connections.*

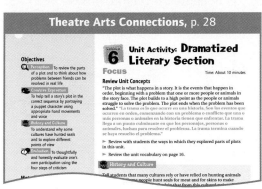

Music

Consider Yourself. Lionel Bart.

Play *Consider Yourself* as students complete the Practice activity. Discuss the different types of shapes of people in society.

Performing Arts

Have students work with a partner. The first person takes a neutral standing position and closes their eyes. The partner then traces (without touching) the outline of their shape. Students work slowly, with focus and concentration, identifying the straight lines and curves that make up the outline, or contour, of the human form.

Shapes of People

ocus

Time: About 45 minutes

Activate Prior Knowledge

"Think about masks. What shapes are used on masks for the eyes, nose, and mouth?"
"Piensen en máscaras. ¿Qué figuras se usan en las máscaras para los ojos, la nariz y la boca?"

■ Discuss students' responses and how faces are made up of different shapes.

Using Literature ⭐ Reading

■ Read *Tell Me a Story, Mama* by Angela Johnson. Discuss the use of shapes of people in the book.

Thematic Connection ⭐ Social Studies

■ **Our Country and its People:** Encourage students to discuss what life may have been like during the times in which *The Blue Boy* was painted.

Introduce the Art

Look

"Let's look at the two works of art." "Vamos a observer detalladamente las dos obras de arte".

Comparing and Contrasting ⭐ Reading

■ Have students make a list of similarities and differences in the two works of art. Both are realistic portraits whose subjects are in formal poses. *Silas Johnson* is an indoor painting, while the *The Blue Boy* is an outdoor painting. The lighting in *Silas Johnson* is even, while the lighting in *The Blue Boy* shows the boy emerging from a darker background. The trees in the background of *The Blue Boy* create the sense of deep space, whereas *Silas Johnson* conveys a sense of shallow space.

 Art History and Culture

Possible answer: Answers will vary. Students may say because camera's had not been invented.

 Web Connection

Visit **www.wrhs.org/** to learn more about Allen E. Cole and his other works of art.

▲ **Allen E. Cole.** (American). *Silas Johnson.* 1920.

Western Reserve Historical Society, Cleveland, Ohio.

Look at the portraits on these two pages. A portrait is a picture of a person. Allen E. Cole used a camera to take the photograph of Silas Johnson in the 1920s. About 150 years earlier, *The Blue Boy* was painted by Thomas Gainsborough. Both portraits show geometric and free-form shapes.

 Art History and Culture

Why do you think Thomas Gainsborough didn't take a photograph of his subject?

Art History and Culture

Allen E. Cole

Allen E. Cole (ă lən kōl) (1884–1970) was born in Kearnsville, West Virginia. After graduating from Storer College, he worked as a railroad porter and waiter before moving to Cleveland, Ohio. There he met Joseph Opet, who was the manager of the Frank Moor studios. Opet introduced Cole to various aspects of photography in exchange for Cole's doing odd jobs and cleaning. In 1922 Cole opened a home studio, which was close to churches, business establishments, and residences. He became Cleveland's first professional African American photographer.

See pages 24–25 and 16–21 for more about art history and subject matter.

 **Artist Profiles**, p. 11

┌ Artist Profile ┐
Allen E. Cole
1884–1970
Allen Cole (al' an kōl) was an American photographer known for his pictures of people and places during the Great Depression. Cole did not plan to be a photographer. After high school and college he worked as a railroad porter, a real estate developer, and a waiter. After being injured in a train accident, Cole met Joseph Opet, a studio manager in Cleveland, Ohio, who introduced him to photography. He opened his first studio in his home in 1922.

Study both portraits to find geometric and free-form shapes.

▶ Find the circles.

▶ Point to the rectangles you see.

▶ Are there any triangles?

▶ Find the free-form shapes.

▶ Where are the oval shapes?

◀ **Thomas Gainsborough.** (English). *Jonathan Buttall: The Blue Boy.* c. 1770.

Oil on canvas. 70 ⅝ × 48 ¾ inches (180 × 124 cm.). The Huntington Library, San Marino, California.

Aesthetic Perception

Seeing Like an Artist Look at your face in a mirror or think about the shape of your face. Use your index finger to trace the shape of your face. Name the shapes you traced.

Study

▶ Circles: There are circular shapes in the wicker chair in *Silas Johnson*.

▶ Rectangles: There are rectangular shapes on the boy's jacket in *The Blue Boy*

▶ Triangles: *Silas Johnson*: The man's arm on the left side is bent into the shape of a triangle. *The Blue Boy*: the bottom portion of the jacket

▶ Free-forms: *Silas Johnson*: The man is a free-form shape; *The Blue Boy*: The boy and the background are free-form shapes.

▶ Ovals: *Silas Johnson*: The man's eyes and head are oval shaped; *The Blue Boy*: The boy's face and eyes are oval shaped.

■ For more examples of art from Europe, see the *Art Around the World Collection.*

Art Journal: Writing

Encourage students to write their own explanations of shapes of people in the Concepts section of their Art Journals. What else do they want to know?

Aesthetic Perception

Seeing Like an Artist Discuss with students the ways in which their faces are shaped. Have them look in a mirror, place their index fingers on the mirror or on their faces, and trace all the shapes that their faces contain. Have students name the shapes they traced.

Developing Visual Literacy Have students imagine and describe what type of families the people in the works of art came from.

Art History and Culture

Thomas Gainsborough

Thomas Gainsborough (to´ məs gānz´ bər ə)(1727–1788) Thomas Gainsborough was an English painter of portraits, landscapes and pictures. He was born at Sudbury, Soffolk, and went to London in about 1740. In 1752 he started up as a portrait painter which mainly consisted of painting heads of individuals. In 1768 he was chosen to be a foundation member of the Royal Academy, and in 1774 Gainsborough moved to London permanently.

Painting portraits was considered Gainsborough's profession, while painting landscapes was what he preferred. He painted many landscape drawings and later became a favorite painter of the royal family.

See pages 24–25 and 16–21 for more about art history and subject matter.

Artist Profiles, p. 22

● Artist Profile ●

Thomas Gainsborough
1727–1788

British artist Thomas Gainsborough was born in Sudbury, Suffolk, in 1727. When he was about thirteen years old, Gainsborough went to London to study art. After finishing his education, he worked as a portrait artist in the town of Ipswich and later in Bath. In 1768, Gainsborough was elected a foundation member of the Royal Academy. He relocated permanently to London in 1774, where he focused on cultivating his luminous personal painting style. So exquisite and captivating were his portraits that he quickly became a sought after and respected artist throughout London's high society set, and he was a favorite painter of

Web Connection

Visit **www.kfki.hu/~arthp/html/g/gainsbor/** to find out more about Thomas Gainsborough's life and work.

Teach

"What shapes do you see in objects in the classroom?" *"¿Que figuras ven en los objetos en el salón de clases?"*

■ Discuss student answers in reference to the different types of shapes.

Practice

Materials: 8½" × 11" white paper, pencils

■ Distribute the materials and have students follow the directions on page 58 for drawing the shapes of an object in the classroom.

Creative Expression

Materials: 12" × 18" colored construction paper, oil pastels, dustless chalk

Alternate Materials: liquid tempera paints

■ Distribute the materials and have students follow the directions on page 59.

■ Review the Activity Tips on page 234 for visual examples.

Art Journal: Planning

Have students brainstorm different shapes of faces and list their ideas in their Art Journals. Have students make rough sketches in their Art Journals and decide how they will draw the portraits for the Creative Expression activity.

Using Shapes

Shapes are all around us. You have already seen different shapes in the landscape paintings on pages 36 and 37. **Free-form shapes** can be found in nature. Puddles, clouds, and flowers are examples of free-form shapes. People also are free-form shapes.

Geometric shapes are usually found in objects that are made by people. Buildings, furniture, and road signs are some examples of geometric shapes.

Most objects have one primary shape. Some objects are made of many smaller shapes.

Practice

Use a pencil to draw the shapes of an object.

1. Choose an object from your classroom to draw. Find the smaller geometric or free-form shapes in it.

2. On a sheet of paper, draw the object by putting together the smaller shapes you see.

Differentiated Instruction

Reteach
Have students look through their books to find another portrait. Ask them to read the title of the work and identify the geometric and free-form shapes they see in it.

Special Needs
To ensure success in this lesson activity, begin by asking students to name and air trace the shapes found in the model and props.

ELL Tips
Students will benefit from visual support to understand the lesson concepts. Use the works of art from previous lessons as visual support. Point to the geometric and free-form shapes in the works of art as you name them.

◄ **Carolina Monsure.**
Age 8.

Think about the geometric shapes in this student artist's portrait.

 Creative Expression

What are the shapes of the faces of some people you know? Draw a portrait using geometric and free-form shapes.

1. Ask a classmate to be your model. Select some objects from the classroom to use as props. Have your model use these props as they pose for you.

2. Look carefully at your model. Find the geometric and free-form shapes.

3. Use chalk to draw your model and the props. Use lines to create the geometric and free-form shapes you see. Fill the shapes with oil pastels.

Art Criticism

Describe What are you wearing in your portrait? What props did you use?

Analyze Where did you use geometric shapes? Where did you use free-form shapes?

Interpret Give your portrait a title. Then, invite your model to give the portrait a title.

Decide Did your portrait turn out as you had hoped? If you were to re-create your portrait, how would you improve it?

Reflect
Time: About 45 minutes

Review and Assess

"What are the most common geometric and free-form shapes used to draw a portrait?"
"¿Cuáles son las figuras geométricas y abstractas más communes que se utilizan para hacer un retrato?"

Think

The artist used different kinds of geometric shapes in her portrait.

- Use *Large Prints 37* Broadway and *38 The Cow with the Subtle Nose* to have students compare shapes used in portraits to those used in the prints.

Informal Assessment

Art Journal: Critical Thinking
Have students answer the four art criticism questions—Describe, Analyze, Interpret, and Decide—in their Art Journals. Have students discuss in small groups the use of geometric and free-form shapes in their drawings.

- For standardized-format test practice using this lesson's art content, see page 16–17 in *Reading and Writing Test Preparation.*

Art Across the Curriculum

Use these simple ideas to reinforce art concepts across the curriculum.

★ **Narrative Writing** Have students look at the portraits and choose a person they would like to interview. Have students write questions that they would ask.

★ **Math** Have students ask five different classmates how many of them have had a portrait painted of them.

★ **Science** Place a blank sheet of paper under a light. Have students place their hand under the sheet of paper. Ask students to describe what they see.

★ **Social Studies** Discuss with students the time in which *The Blue Boy* was painted.

★ **Technology** Have students draw a portrait using paintbrush tools on the computer. Make sure they use geometric and free-form shapes. Visit **SRAonline.com** to print detailed instructions for this activity.

Using Shapes

Extra! For the Art Specialist

Time: About 45 minutes

Focus

Use *Transparency 6* and *Large Prints 37 Broadway* and *38 The Cow with the Subtile Nose*. What types of shapes make up their bodies? Are there more geometric shapes or freeform shapes in their faces and bodies?

Teach

Have students follow the directions to complete their self-portrait collage.

Reflect

Have students evaluate their art using the four steps of art criticism. Encourage them to locate and describe other areas where they see shapes being used in the classroom.

Alternate Activity

Materials:

- 12" × 18" colored construction paper
- 9" × 12" construction paper in a variety of beiges, tans, and browns
- construction paper scraps
- wallpaper pieces (optional)
- pencils
- scissors
- glue or glue sticks

1. Explain to students that they will make a self-portrait collage. Have them select construction paper that is closest to their own skin color.

2. After the head shape is glued to the background paper, students can also cut out a neck and ears from the skin-colored paper.

3. Students will observe the geometric and free-form shapes of their eyes, eyebrows, noses, and mouths, and cut the shapes from construction paper scraps. Use wallpaper pieces or construction paper to create clothes.

Research in Art Education

Research has indicated that one important outcome of integrating arts into other curriculum areas is an increased level of classroom discussions and more time spent on problem solving. The level of teacher dedication and experience seems to influence these outcomes ("Different Ways of Knowing: 1991–94 National Longitudinal Study Final Report" in *Schools, Communities, and the Arts: A Research Compendium*). As students learn about geometric and free-form shapes in portraits, encourage them to look for geometric and free-form shapes in books and magazines.

Assessment

Use the following rubric to evaluate the artwork students make in the Creative Expression activity and to assess students' understanding of geometric and free-form shapes in portraits.

Have students complete pages 19–20 in their *Assessment* books.

	Art History and Culture	Aesthetic Perception	Creative Expression	Art Criticism
3 POINTS	The student demonstrates knowledge of the lives and cultures of Cole and Gainsborough.	The student accurately identifies geometric and free-form shapes that up people and objects in art and the environment.	The student effectively draws a portrait using geometric and free-form shapes.	The student evaluates his or her own work using the four steps of art criticism.
2 POINTS	The student demonstrates weak or incomplete understanding of the lives and cultures of Cole and Gainsborough.	The student shows emerging awareness of the geometric and free-form shapes that make up people and objects in art and the environment.	The student shows some awareness of how to draw a portrait using geometric and free-form shapes.	The student attempts to evaluate his or her own work using the four steps of art criticism.
1 POINT	The student demonstrates no knowledge of the lives and cultures of Cole or Gainsborough.	The student cannot identify geometric and free-form shapes that make up people and objects in art and the environment.	The student shows no understanding of how to draw a portrait using geometric and free-form shapes.	The student makes no attempt to evaluate his or her own work.

Assessment, p. 19

Name _____ Date _____

Lesson 6 UNIT 1

Shapes

A. Drawing

Draw three different objects found in nature that have free-form shapes.

B. Short Answer

Answer the questions.
Name three different objects made by people that have geometric shapes.

1. _____
2. _____
3. _____

Look around your classroom. Name two objects that have geometric shapes.

1. _____
2. _____
3. _____

Level 3   Unit 1 • An Introduction to Line and Shape   **19**

architect—an artist who is designs and drawing up plans for cities, buildings, and bridges, and generally supervising the construction of them. **arquitecto**—un artista que diseña y traza planos para las ciudades, los edificios y los puentes, y que generalmente supervisa su construcción

architecture—the art form of designing and planning construction of buildings, or other structures for people. **arquitectura**—la forma artística de diseñar y planificar la construcción de edificios u otras estructuras para las personas

complex geometric shapes—shapes formed by combining simple geometric shapes. **figuras geométricas complejas**—figuras formadas al combinar figuras geométricas simples

curved—lines that bend and change direction slowly **curva**—líneas que se doblan y cambian lentamente de dirección

diagonal—lines that are slanted **diagonal**—líneas inclinadas

free-form—shapes that are uneven and are not regular **abstracta**—figuras que son irregulares

free-form shapes—shapes that are uneven and irregular, not geometric **figuras abstractas**—figuras que son irregulares y no geométricas

geometric—shapes that can be defined using mathematical formulas **geométrica**—figuras que se pueden definir usando fórmulas matemáticas

geometric shapes—math shapes, such as circles, triangles, rectangles, or squares **figuras geométricas**—figuras matemáticas, como los círculos, los triángulos, los rectángulos o los cuadrados

horizontal—lines that move straight across from side to side **horizontal**—líneas que se mueven de lado a lado

line—a mark drawn by a tool such as pencil, pen, or paintbrush as it moves across a surface **línea**—una marca que se traza con un instrumento como un lápiz, una pluma o un pincel al desplazarlo por una superficie

line variety—short or long, thick or thin, rough or smooth, and broken or solid **variedad lineal**—corta o larga, gruesa o fina, áspera o suave, y entrecortada o continua

portrait—a picture of a person **retrato**—una ilustración de una persona

shapes—flat, two-dimensional areas that are either geometric or free-form figures **figuras**—áreas planas y bidimensionales que son geométricas o abstractas

vertical—lines that move straight up and down **vertical**—líneas que se mueven hacia arriba y hacia abajo

zigzag—diagonal lines that connect **en zigzag**—líneas diagonales que se conectan

---

Vocabulary Practice

T Display Transparency 37 to review unit vocabulary words.

Words in Context ⭐ Vocabulary

Explain to students that when they understand the meaning of a word, they will be able to identify the word being used correctly in a sentence. Have them choose two words from the vocabulary list and write a sentence using the word in a different meaning.

Dictionary Entries ⭐ Vocabulary

Have students look up the word *shape* in a dictionary. Ask them if the dictionary entry gives the similar or different definition than the **Student Edition.** Explain the differences.

Visualization Strategies ⭐ Vocabulary

Point out to students that many words begin with the same two letters. Have students write the word *diagonal*. Have students write as many words as they can using the letters *di*.

Wrapping Up Unit 1
Line and Shape

Wrapping Up Unit 1

Line and Shape

▲ **Jacob Lawrence.** (American.)
Builders No. 1. 1971.
Gouache on paper. 30 × 22 inches (76.2 × 55.9 cm).
Birmingham Museum of Art, Birmingham, Alabama.

 Art Criticism

Critical Thinking Art criticism is an organized system for looking at and talking about art. You can criticize art without being an expert. The purpose of art criticism is to get the viewer involved in a perception process that delays judgment until all aspects of the artwork have been studied.

■ See pages 28–29 for more about art criticism.

Describe

► Ask students to describe what the credit line says about this painting. Possible answers: It was painted by Jacob Lawrence in 1971. The title of the painting is *Builders No. 1.* It was painted with gouache, an opaque watercolor paint on paper, and it is 30 inches tall and 22 inches wide. It is at the Birmingham Museum of Art in Birmingham, Alabama.

► Have the students describe the man and the setting. Possible answers: This is an adult, African American man. He is bald and wearing a loose blue shirt and blue pants. In front of the man is a blue table covered with carpentry tools. Behind him is a set of gray shelves with tools on every shelf.

Analyze

► Ask students to tell where they see vertical, horizontal, and diagonal lines. Possible answers: The brown wide lines on the side of the cabinet are vertical. Three nails on the table are sitting vertically on their heads. The top of the cabinet and the front of the shelves are horizontal lines. The man's neck, arms, fingers, and legs are all diagonal in direction. The edges of his clothes and a band across his chest are light blue diagonal lines. The sides of the table and the sides of the shelves are diagonal.

60   Unit 1

Art History and Culture

Jacob Lawrence

Jacob Lawrence's (jā´ kəp lô´ rens) most famous work is a series of 60 paintings called *The Migration of the Negro.* The paintings tell a story that begins at a train station in the South and ends at a station in the North. The scenes he chose to paint focus on the struggle of leaving one life for another and the search for freedom and dignity.

Artist Profiles, p. 33

◆ Artist Profile ◆

Jacob Lawrence
1917–2000

Jacob Lawrence (jā´ kəb lär´ ənz) had parents who met on their migration to the North. His father was born in South Carolina, and his mother in Virginia. Lawrence was born in Atlantic City, New Jersey, in 1917. The family finally settled in Harlem in 1929 at the end of the Harlem Renaissance. Because his mother worked all day, she enrolled Lawrence in the Harlem Art Workshop after school to keep him out of trouble. He had many excellent teachers there, including Charles Alston. Lawrence won a scholarship to the American Artists School. He taught at New York's Pratt Institute from 1958 to 1965. From 1970, he taught at the University of Washington in Seattle, where he also served as head of the

 **Art Criticism** Critical Thinking

Describe What do you see?

During this step you will collect information about the subject of the work.

▶ What does the credit line tell you about this painting?

▶ Describe the man and the setting.

Analyze How is this work organized?

Think about how the artist has used the elements and principles of art.

▶ Where do you see vertical, horizontal, and diagonal lines?

▶ Where do you see curves?

▶ Where do you see free-form and geometric shapes?

Interpret What is the artist trying to say?

Use the clues you discovered during your analysis to find the message the artist is trying to show.

▶ Is this a calm picture or a busy picture? How do the lines and shapes affect the look of this work?

▶ Do you think the man likes what he is doing?

Decide What do you think about the work?

Use all the information you have gathered to decide whether this is a successful work of art.

▶ Is this painting successful because it is realistic, because it is well organized, or because it has a strong message? Explain.

Aesthetic Perception

Seeing Like an Artist Have students find tools at their homes like the tools found in *Builders No. 1*. Have them decide if the tools they find at home are similar or different from those found in the painting. Explain.

Describe ▶ List and describe how many different tools you find in the painting.

Analyze ▶ Where do you see outlining shapes?

Interpret ▶ Do you think this man is working for someone else, or is he making this boat part for himself? Explain your answer.

Decide ▶ How would you paint the picture differently. What shapes and colors would you use?

▶ Ask students where they see curves. Possible answers: The two major curves in the painting are the red boat rib that the man is holding and the man's back. Several tools such as the hammers and the C-clamps have parts that are curved.

▶ Do they notice any free-form or geometric shapes? Possible answers: The man, hammerheads, and chisel handles are free-form shapes. The pink boat rib is a free-form shape. Most of the other shapes in the painting are geometric, but many of them are partially hidden so it may be difficult to identify them.

Interpret

▶ Ask students if this a calm or busy picture. How do the lines and shapes affect the look of this work? Answers may vary. The shelves are calm, stable vertical and horizontal lines. Every other shape and line has either curves or diagonal edges. Most students will say this makes this work a very busy looking work.

▶ Does it look like the man likes what he is doing? Answers will vary. The man looks like he is smiling. He is leaning toward the work, and the curve of his back balances the curve of the boat rib. He seems to be intensely involved with his work. Everything in the picture relates to the work he is doing. Most will say he likes what he is doing.

Decide

▶ Ask students if this painting is successful because it is realistic, well-organized, or because it has a strong message. Explain. Answers will vary. Most will choose the message. Both realism and composition are possible answers. Some may choose all three theories.

Art Journal: Writing

Have students write answers to Aesthetic Perception in their Art Journals.

"Artists use different kinds of lines and shapes to create all types of art." "Los artistas usan diferentes tipos de líneas y figuras para crear todo tipo de arte".

T Review unit vocabulary with students using *Transparency 37.*

Art Journal: Writing
Have students answer the questions on page 62 in their Art Journals or on a separate sheet of paper. Answers 1. B, 2. A, 3. C, 4. B, 5. C

T For further assessment, have students complete the unit test on *Transparency 43.*

CAREERS IN ART
Advertisers

► Encourage students to discuss different kinds of advertisements and commercials. Ask them to give examples of advertisements they like or dislike and to explain why they feel that way.

Show What You Know

Answer these questions on a separate sheet of paper.

❶ Lines that make things look tall and calm are called _____.
  A. curved
  B. vertical
  C. horizontal

❷ Lines that cause a feeling of excitement are _____.
  A. zigzag
  B. curvy
  C. squiggly

❸ Shapes that are uneven and not regular are called _____.
  A. complex
  B. circles
  C. free-form shapes

❹ Shapes that are made by combining simple geometric shapes are called _____.
  A. diamonds
  B. complex geometric shapes
  C. horizontal lines

❺ The art of designing and planning buildings is called _____.
  A. art designer
  B. planner
  C. architecture

CAREERS IN ART
Advertisers

Have you ever seen a commercial? Commercials are created by advertisers.

Art Directors develop and design advertising campaigns based on market research. The research tells them at what type of audience to aim their advertisements. Then they apply their creative ideas and imagination to find original ways to execute their advertisements.

Layout Artists create the visual aspects of advertising in magazine and newspaper ads, television commercials, and product packaging. They prepare artwork samples for people who plan advertising campaigns.

▲ **Layout Artist**

Unit Assessment Options

 Aesthetic Perception

Practice Have student choose three concepts from page 62 and have them find examples of each in the classroom

 Creative Expression

Student Portfolio Have students review all the works of art they have created during this unit and select the pieces they wish to keep in their portfolios.

 Art Criticism

Activity Have students select an artwork from this unit and study it using the four steps of art criticism. (See pages 28–29 for more information about Art Criticism.) Have students work alone or in pairs and present their findings orally or in writing.

Line and Shape

Native Americans observed animals to learn from them. The eagle represents wisdom, strength, and vision. They believe that eagles are messengers between man and the creator. Dancers mime the movements of this creature to honor it. They form different body shapes and create straight, diagonal, and curved lines as they dance.

What to Do Create an original eagle dance.

The "Eagle Dance" is sacred to all Native American tribes. The dances show the life of the eagle. Many tribes believe that the eagle can take messages from humans to the world beyond. Think of these ideas as you create your dance.

1. Study pictures of eagles perched on limbs, soaring, and diving. Make these positions with your body.

2. Make a list of actions done by the eagle. Pick one or two actions and express them with movement. Think about the kinds of lines you are creating.

3. Create a simple dance about the eagle. Select three action words from your list. Dance each action for eight counts. End in either a swooping or perched eagle shape.

4. Perform your dance in a group.

▲ American Indian Dance Theatre.

Art Criticism

Describe Describe the way you made your three eagle shapes.

Analyze Explain how you made your eagle movements show two different actions.

Interpret How does your dance express the strength, wisdom, and vision of the eagle?

Decide How well did you show what an eagle is like? How did you use shape and line in your body?

Unit 1　**63**

Art History and Culture

Native American Dance

Dance and music serve as a framework to which Native American philosophy and tradition are attached. Hanay Geiogamah developed a system for categorizing Native American dance: seasonal/functional; spriritual/ceremonial; and celebrational/bravura. He researches and collects traditional dances from many of the 430 tribes in the United States, maintaining their original intent.

Space and Form in Dance

Objective: To create the actions, positions, and qualities of eagles using line and shape

Materials: American Indian Dance Theatre
Video: *Eagle Dance* and *Hoop Dance*

Focus

Time: 5 minutes

■ Discuss the information on page 62.

Art History and Culture

■ Have students view pictures of eagles and list ideas describing their qualities and actions so that they can use them as inspiration for their eagle dances.

Teach

Time: 20 minutes

Aesthetic Perception

■ Direct students to look at pictures of eagles and describe their actions and shapes.

■ Have students use the words and pictures to inspire individual interpretations.

Creative Expression

■ Ask students to create a short dance that depicts the eagle in different actions, such as soaring, gliding, diving, perching, or carrying prey.

■ Have several perform their dances simultaneously. Comment positively on their interpretations.

Reflect

Time: 10 minutes

Art Criticism

■ Have students answer the four art criticism questions on page 63 orally or in writing.

■ Did students effectively create eagle dances using action words, lines, and shapes?

Unit 2 Planning Guide

	Lesson Title	Suggested Pacing	Creative Expression Activity
Lesson 1	Positive and Negative Space	65 minutes	Create a two-dimensional paper mask.
Lesson 2	Creating Depth	65 minutes	Draw an outdoor scene.
Lesson 3	Overlapping	65 minutes	Create a drawing using overlapping.
Lesson 4	Form	65 minutes	Create an animal sculpture.
Lesson 5	Relief Sculpture	65 minutes	Make a relief sculpture.
Lesson 6	Three-Dimensional Art to Wear	65 minutes	Create a necklace.
ARTSOURCE	Space and Form in Animation	35 minutes	Create a story that is portrayed in a four-frame storyboard.

Materials	Program Resources	Fine Art Resources	Literature Resources
colored construction paper, glue, pencil or chalk to draw mask, scissors	*Assessment,* pp. 21–22 *Home and After-School Connections* *Art Around The World* *Reading and Writing Test Preparation,* pp. 18–19	*Transparency,* 7 *Artist Profiles,* pp. 78, 81 *Large Prints,* 39, 40 *Flash Cards,* 20 *Animals Through History Time Line*	*Frederick* by Leo Leonni
white construction paper, pencils, set of watercolor paints, brushes of various sizes, containers of water, sketch paper, tape, paper towels	*Assessment,* pp. 23–24 *Art Around The World Collection* *Reading and Writing Test Preparation,* pp. 20–21	*Transparency,* 8 *Artist Profiles,* pp. 55, 83 *Large Prints,* 39, 40 *Animals Through History Time Line*	*Farewell to Shady Glade* by Bill Peet
white construction paper, pencils, sketch paper	*Assessment,* pp. 25–26 *Art Around The World Collection* *Reading and Writing Test Preparation,* pp. 22–23	*Transparency,* 9 *Artist Profiles,* pp. 26, 38 *Large Prints,* 39, 40 *Animals Through History Time Line*	*Saturday Sancocho* by Leyla Torres
various found objects (paper towel rolls, small cardboard boxes, bottle caps, yarn, felt), tissue paper, white glue, markers	*Assessment,* pp. 27–28 *The National Museum of Women in the Arts* *Reading and Writing Test Preparation,* pp. 24–25	*Transparency,* 10 *Artist Profiles,* pp. 14, 34 *Large Prints,* 39, 40 *Animals Through History Time Line*	*Our Money* by Bornemann Spies
clay, rolling pins, muslin, cardboard frame, pencils, paper clips, various textured objects, sketch paper, tape, containers of water, slip brushes	*Assessment,* pp. 29–30 *Art Around The World Collection* *Reading and Writing Test Preparation,* pp. 26–27	*Transparency,* 11 *Artist Profiles,* pp. 68, 76 *Large Prints,* 40 *Animals Through History Time Line*	*Our Money* by Bornemann Spies
cardboard, scissors, glue, low-relief objects, aluminum foil, yarn, hole punch	*Assessment,* pp. 31–32 *Art Around The World Collection* *Reading and Writing Test Preparation,* pp. 28–29	*Transparency,* 12 *Artist Profiles,* pp. 73, 74 *Large Prints,* 40 *Animals Through History Time Line*	*Fire Talking* by Patricia Polacco
Every Picture Tells a Story by John Ramirez. Paper, pencils or markers			

Unit Overview

2 Space and Form

Lesson 1 **Positive and negative space** is the emptiness or area between, around, above, below, or within objects.

Lesson 2 **Creating depth** occurs when some objects seem to be very close and others seem to be far away.

Lesson 3 **Overlapping** occurs when one object covers part of a second object.

Lesson 4 **Form** is the element of art that is three-dimensional and encloses space.

Lesson 5 **Relief sculpture** is three-dimensional artwork made from a variety of materials.

Lesson 6 **Jewelry** is three-dimensional artwork that is made for people to wear.

Introduce Unit Concepts

"Artists use the elements of space and form in creating all kinds of art." "Los artistas usan los elementos de espacio y forma para crear todo tipo de arte".

Positive and Negative Space
- Have students brainstorm different meanings of the word *space,* for example, stars, planets, and parking.

Form
- Have students name different geometric and free-form shapes. Discuss how a form is like a shape because it has height and width, but it also has depth. Forms are three-dimensional.

- Ask students to list various objects in their desks that are geometric forms.

Cross-Curricular Projects
- See the *Language Arts and Reading, Mathematics, Science,* and *Social Studies Art Connections* books for activities that further develop line concepts.

National Standards for Arts Education in Visual Arts (NSAE) 2.a; 3.a

---

Space and Form

Artists use space and form to make all kinds of artwork.

Degas was the first to show the realistic form of a young ballet dancer. Look at her face. You can see how she is straining to hold her pose. He was also the first to add real fabric and ribbon to a bronze sculpture.

◄ **Edgar Degas.** (French). *Little Dancer, Aged Fourteen.* 1881.
....
Wax, bronze, tulle skirt, satin hair ribbon, wood base. 39 inches (99 cm.). The Metropolitan Museum of Art, New York, New York.

Fine Arts Prints

Display *Large Prints 39 The Oregon Trail* and *40 Vaquero.* Refer to the prints throughout the unit as students learn about space and form.

Large Print 39

Large Print 40

Artists create space in works of art that are two-dimensional and three-dimensional.

▶ Which parts of *Little Dancer, Aged Fourteen* are behind or partly covered by other parts?

▶ Describe the area around the sculpture.

Artists create form in three-dimensional work.

▶ Which areas of the sculpture are raised?

▶ Which parts appear to be farther back?

▶ If you walked around to the back of this sculpture, how do you think the girl's head would look on the other side?

In This Unit you will learn about and practice techniques to create the appearance of space on a flat surface. You will also learn about three-dimensional forms. Here are topics you will study:
▶ Space
▶ Depth
▶ Overlapping
▶ Form
▶ Sculpture

Edgar Degas

(1834–1917)

Edgar Degas was born the son of a banker in Paris, France. As a child Degas took drawing lessons and developed his artistic ability. His study of Japanese art led him to experiment with different visual angles. He was best known for his pictures of ballet dancers, café life, and horseracing scenes. His style, subject matter, and ability set him apart from other impressionist artists. Degas was not well known to the public, and his true artistic stature did not become evident until after his death.

Unit 2   **65**

Examine the Artwork

"Let's look closely at the sculpture." "Vamos a observar detalladamente la escultura".

■ Have students look at Edgar Degas' *Little Dancer, Aged Fourteen*. Ask them to describe what they see. Have students answer the questions about space and form on page 65.

▶ The girl's arms and hands are behind her body.

▶ There is empty space through the legs and all around the sculpture.

▶ Details of the girl's features and the pleats of the skirt are raised.

▶ The left foot and arms are farther back.

▶ On the back of the girl's head is her hair.

Unit Pretest

T Display *Transparency 44* as pretest. Answers: 1. B, 2. C, 3. A, 4. A, 5. B

Home Connection

■ See *Home and After School Connections* for family newsletters and activities for this unit.

Art History and Culture

Edgar Degas   NSAE 4.a; 4.b; 4.c; 5.a; 5.b

Edgar Degas (ed´ gər də gä´) (1834–1917) was born in Paris, France. As a young boy he had dreams of becoming an artist. Degas' inspiration to create came from his passion for the Parisian life with its theaters, dancehalls, circuses, and ballets. Degas' artwork has never been classified in a particular category simply because of his ability to paint as a classicist, impressionist, and realist, which placed him in a class of his own. It is estimated that Edgar Degas made approximately 1500 paintings, pastels, prints, and drawings of dancers.

See pages 24–25 and 16–21 for more about art history and subject matter.

Artist Profiles, p. 15

◀ Artist Profile ▶
Edgar Degas
1834-1917
Edgar Degas (ed´ gir´ dä ga´) was born in Paris, France, to a wealthy family. He studied law for a short time before discovering his interest in painting. Degas studied briefly at the École des Beaux-Arts in Paris around 1855. He worked at an artist's studio and traveled widely to study art. His early work showed a concern with classical painting, in subject matter as well as composition. His themes always dealt with people and city life, especially dancers at the theater. After 1909, Degas turned to sculpture due to failing eyesight. He left many wax models of dancers and horses that were cast in bronze after his death.

ILLUSTRATOR PROFILE
Trina Schart Hyman
(1939–)

Trina Schart Hyman loved to read and draw as a child. She spent one full year wearing a red cape because her favorite book was *Little Red Riding Hood*. She would make up stories and create her own books, drawing pictures to illustrate them.

Trina enrolled at the Philadelphia Museum College of Art in 1956. She married in 1959, and continued her studies at the Boston Museum School of Fine Arts and the Swedish State Art School in Stockholm, Sweden. She illustrated her first children's book, *Toffe och den lilla bilen (Toffe and the Little Car)*, during her time in Sweden.

When Trina returned to the U.S., she continued her career as a children's book illustrator. Her early work was in black and white; she illustrated nearly 60 books before producing one in full color. Arthur Rackham, N. C. Wyeth, Howard Pyle, Goya, and Rembrandt are all sources of inspiration for her work.

Throughout Unit 2, share Trina Schart Hyman's illustrations with the class and discuss the use of space and form.

Music
Compare positive and negative space by having students play eight-beat rhythm patterns. One pattern should contain rests on the second, third, sixth, and eighth beats. Another pattern should use a different instrument and fill in the rests in the first pattern.

Literature
Show the video or DVD *When I Was Young in the Mountains* to introduce the concepts of space and form.

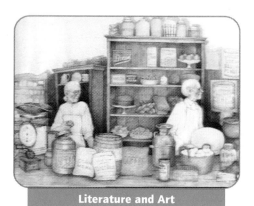
Literature and Art

Performing Arts
 Show "Every Picture Tells a Story." Point out space and form and how they are used in the video.

Artsource®

Positive and Negative Space

Lesson 1 introduces the use of positive and negative space in artwork.

Objectives

Art History and Culture

To compare folk art from ancient Peru and modern Poland and its use of positive and negative space

Creative Expression

To create a two-dimensional paper mask using positive and negative space

Aesthetic Perception

To identify and explore positive and negative space

Art Criticism

To evaluate own work using the four steps of art criticism

Vocabulary ⭐ Vocabulary

Review the following vocabulary with students before beginning the lesson.

appliqué *aplicación*—decoration made from cloth cutouts

positive spaces *espacios positivos*—shapes or forms in two- and three-dimensional art

negative spaces *espacios negativos*—empty spaces surrounding shapes and forms

See page 89B for additional vocabulary and Spanish vocabulary resources.

Art Journal

Have students add these words to the Vocabulary section of their Art Journals.

Lesson Materials

- 9" × 12" light-colored construction paper
- half sheets of dark-colored construction paper (full sheets folded vertically and cut)
- glue
- pencil or chalk to draw mask
- scissors
- crayons

Program Resources

- *Reading and Writing Test Prep.,* pp. 18–19
- *Transparency 7*
- *Flash Card* 20
- *Artist Profiles,* pp. 78, 81
- *Animals Through History Time Line*
- *Assessment,* pp. 21–22
- *Large Prints 39* The Oregon Trail and *40* Vaquero
- *Art Around The World Collection*

Concept Trace

Space and Form

Introduced: Level 2, Unit 5, Lesson 3

Reinforced: Level 4, Unit 4, Lesson 3

Lesson 1 Arts Integration NSAE 6.a

Theatre

Complete Unit 2, Lesson 1, on pages 36–37 of *Theatre Arts Connections.*

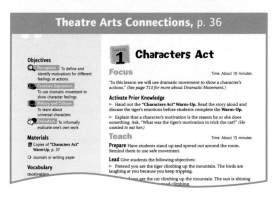

Music

Negative space in music is silence, or "rests." It can also be the time of silence before and after a piece of music is performed. That frame of silence sets music apart from ordinary sounds. Another place there can be silence is between pieces in a suite, movements in a symphony, or sections of a song. Listen to *Circus Music* from *The Red Pony* by Aaron Copeland. During the breaks in this piece you can imagine the performer taking a bow.

Movement & Dance

In small groups, students form architectural structures that reveal positive and negative space. Each building must show the inside and outside of the structure and all the primary details.

Example: Floors, walls, roof, windows, door frames. As each group presents their idea, the rest of the class will identify the positive and negative spaces.

ocus

Time: About 10 minutes

Activate Prior Knowledge

"Why is a parking space sometimes hard to find?" "¿Por qué a veces es difícil conseguir un lugar para estacionar?"

Using Literature ⭐ Reading

- Read *Frederick* by Leo Lionni. Have students discuss the use of positive and negative space in the book.

Thematic Connection ⭐ Reading

- **Cultural Diversity:** Encourage students to discuss the different cultures of each artwork and how they may differ. Discuss the colors that were used. Do the colors have anything to do with where the artwork was made?

Introduce the Art

Look NSAE 3.a

"Let's take a close look at the two works of art." "Vamos a observar detalladamente las dos obras de arte".

Comparing and Contrasting ⭐ Reading

- Have students list the similarities and differences in the works of art. Both pieces depict objects from nature, balance symmetrically, and use free-form shapes. *Sleeveless Shirt* is a functional object made from fabric; it focuses on a single motif. *Tree of Life* is a decorative piece made from paper; it focuses on a variety of motifs.

🏺 Art History and Culture

Possible answer: This shows that Incans wove designs into the fabric on the clothes they wore. It also shows that Polish people liked to make designs by cutting paper.
NSAE 4.a; 4.b; 4.c; 5.a; 5.b

💻 Web Connection

View **www.cybersleuthkids.com/sleuth/History/ Ancient_Civilizations/Incas/index1.htm** to find out more about Peruvian and Inca history.

66 UNIT 2 • Space and Form

 Lesson 1

Positive and Negative Space

◄ Artist Unknown. Coastal Inca (Peru). *Sleeveless Shirt (two cats).* c. 1438–1532.
....
Wool and cotton. The Metropolitan Museum of Art, Nelson Rockefeller Collection, New York, New York.

Look at the artwork on these pages. *Sleeveless shirt (two cats)* is an **appliqué,** or decoration made from cutouts. The cotton cloth shapes were sewn onto a woolen background. *Tree of Life* is a paper cutout. Positive and negative spaces bring out the design in both works.

🏺 Art History and Culture

Look at these two works of art and how they were created. What do these works tell you about the crafts produced by Incan and Polish people?

66 Unit 2 • Lesson 1

🏺 Art History and Culture

Peru NSAE 4.a; 4.b; 4.c; 5.a; 5.b

Sleeveless Shirt was created in Peru during a time when the Inca controlled the Andes. Every citizen was employed, and the emperor was the absolute ruler. The Inca were skilled artists and craftspeople; the huge stones (up to 200 tons) that the Inca used to construct buildings were so perfectly carved that they fit together without mortar.

Sleeveless Shirt is an iconographic, which means that pictures or symbols represent a real-life object. *Sleeveless Shirt* is wool and cotton fabric appliqué. In appliqué pieces, fabric shapes attach to a fabric background.

See pages 24–25 and 16–21 for more about art history and subject matter.

Artist Profiles, p. 78

Artist Profile

Sleeveless Shirt (Two Cats)

It is not known who crafted this sleeveless shirt. Most likely, it was made by a skilled weaver who worked during the time of the Incas before the Spanish arrived in the mid-1500s.

◄ Artist unknown. (Coastal Incan). (Peru).
Sleeveless Shirt (Two Cats). c. 1438–1532.

Study both works of art to find examples of positive and negative space.

▶ What objects do you see in each work? What colors are they?

▶ What colors are the negative spaces around the objects in each work?

▶ How do the empty spaces in both works of art help make the objects stand out?

◀ **Stanistawa Bakula.** (Polish). *Tree of Life.* 1962.
....
Cut paper. 12 $\frac{3}{8}$ × 7 $\frac{1}{2}$ inches (31 × 19 cm.). Museum of International Folk Art, Santa Fe, New Mexico.

 Aesthetic Perception

Design Awareness Notice how the negative space around clouds changes as the clouds are moved by the wind.

Study NSAE 1.b; 2.a; 2.b; 3.a; 5.c

▶ Positive space: black cats in *Sleeveless Shirt;* black tree, birds, and roosters in *Tree of Life.*

▶ Negative space: red-orange areas in *Sleeveless Shirt,* including the cats' eyes and mouths; white areas in *Tree of Life.*

▶ Empty space: The lighter background in each piece makes the darker objects stand out.

■ For more examples of art from Latin America, see the ***Art Around the World Collection.***

Art Journal

Encourage students to write explanations of positive and negative space in the Concepts section of their Art Journals. What else do they want to see?

Aesthetic Perception

Design Awareness Have students observe the clouds in the sky. Discuss how the negative space around the clouds changes as the clouds are moved by the wind.

Developing Visual Literacy Discuss what each artwork "says." What meaning was the artist trying to convey? Invite students to share any personal experiences that contribute to their understanding of the works of art. For example, have students had cats or birds as pets?

Art History and Culture

Polish Paper Cut Outs

Tree of Life is an example of a Polish folk art called *wycinanki* (vee-chin-on-kee). Early wycinanki were made by workers to decorate the walls of their cottages, and were inspired by the tapestries seen in more affluent homes. The themes of the paper cutouts involved things seen in everyday life, especially animals. *Tree of Life* was created in Poland during the 1960s when, due to poor economic conditions and oppressive Soviet presence, the people were often at odds with the Polish Communist government. Like *Sleeveless Shirt, Tree of Life* is iconographic.

See pages 24–25 and 16–21 for more about art history and subject matter.

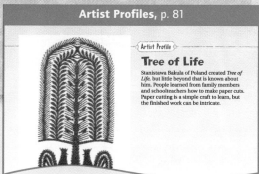

Artist Profiles, p. 81

⟨ Artist Profile ⟩

Tree of Life

Stanistawa Bakula of Poland created *Tree of Life,* but little beyond that is known about him. People learned from family members and schoolteachers how to make paper cuts. Paper cutting is a simple craft to learn, but the finished work can be intricate.

Web Connection

Visit **www.moifa.org** to learn about New Mexico's Museum of International Folk Art. Have students share their ideas about works they view online.

Teach

"How can you use shapes to show positive and negative spaces?" "¿Cómo pueden usar figuras para mostrar espacios positivos y negativos?"

■ Discuss positive and negative space on page 68.

Practice

Materials: 9" × 12" paper, crayons

Alternate materials: oil pastels

■ Distribute the materials and have students follow the directions on page 68.

Creative Expression

Materials: 9" × 12" light-colored construction paper, half sheets of dark-colored construction paper (full sheets folded vertically and cut), glue, pencil or chalk to draw mask, scissors

■ Ask students if they have ever worn a mask. How did it make them feel?

■ Distribute the materials and have students follow the directions on page 69.

■ Be sure to have students start at the center on the left side of the construction paper. It will have one half of a face—one eye, half of a nose, and half of a mouth.

■ Encourage students to keep their mask designs simple by drawing big shapes for the eyes, nose, and mouth.

■ Review the Activity Tips on page 235 for visual examples of techniques if needed.

■ Review the Technique Tips on pages 220–221 for information about using scissors and glue.

Art Journal: Brainstorming

Have students brainstorm ideas for animals and other items found in nature and list their ideas in their Art Journals. Then have students select three or four items and plan how they will show those items in their paper cutting.

Using Positive and Negative Space

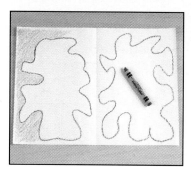

In a work of art, the area that shapes and objects fill is called **positive space.** The empty space is called **negative space.**

Negative space can be just as important as positive space. Negative space affects the way shapes and objects look. What objects do you see in the pictures to the left? Can you tell which areas are positive space and which are negative space?

Practice

Create a design with positive and negative space. Use crayons.

1. Fold a piece of paper into two equal parts. Draw a large free-form shape on the outside of each half.

2. Use crayons to color the negative spaces only.

3. Open the paper. How do the negative spaces help you see the shapes that you drew?

Differentiated Instruction

Reteach
Have students look through the *Student Edition* or *Large Prints* to find three works of art that use positive and negative space. Ask them to describe what they find.

Special Needs
Students who have difficulty cutting may benefit from the use of adaptive scissors for this lesson activity.

ELL Tips
Students may be hesitant to answer interpretive questions about their artwork. You may wish to phrase questions as an either/or choice so the vocabulary needed to answer the question is contained in the question itself.

Think about how the student artist created positive and negative space in her print.

◄ **Palmira Caloncit.**
Age 8.

 Creative Expression

What shapes do you find interesting? Create a two-dimensional paper mask.

1. Study *Sleeveless Shirt* and *Tree of Life*.

2. Choose a light color, full-size sheet of construction paper. Choose a contrasting color for the half sheet.

3. Lay the half sheet on top of the left side of the full sheet of construction paper.

4. When all pieces are positioned in the correct location, glue them into place.

 Art Criticism

Describe List the steps you followed to make your mask.

Analyze Identify the positive and negative space.

Interpret What kind of expression does your mask have?

Decide Does your mask have positive and negative space with both sides mirroring each other?

 **Reflect** Time: About 5 minutes

Review and Assess

"How you would explain the differences between positive and negative space?"
"¿Cómo explicarían la diferencia entre espacio positivo y espacio negativo?"

Think

The artist created negative space by cutting out parts of the paper. Positive space is what remains.

■ Use *Large Prints 39 The Oregon Trail* and *40 Vaquero* to have students identify positive and negative space in this lesson.

Informal Assessment
NSAE 1.b; 2.a; 2.b; 3.a; 5.c

Art Journal: Critical Thinking
Have students answer the four art criticism questions—Describe, Analyze, Interpret, and Decide—orally or in writing. Discuss the use of lines in their drawings. (You might also have students discuss each other's work in a group session.)

■ For standardized-format test practice using this lesson's art content, see pages 18–19 in *Reading and Writing Test Preparation.*

Art Across the Curriculum

Use these simple ideas to reinforce art concepts across the curriculum.

★ **Poetry Writing** Have students sit in an interesting position. Have them write about the positive space they are creating.

★ **Math** Have students look at *Tree of Life* and add the total amount of animal figures they see in the artwork.

★ **Science** Have students discuss how heating and cooling objects can cause changes like artists manipulating positive and negative space. What would happen if you placed a pan of water on the stove to heat it?

★ **Social Studies** Discuss with students how leaders use power in positive and negative ways.

★ **Technology** Have students use the paint tool to draw a free-form shape. Then have them copy and flip the shape. Use the fill tool to make the background black. Visit **SRAonline.com** for detailed instructions for this activity.

NSAE 1.b; 6.b

For the Art Specialist

Time: About 45 minutes

Focus

Use *Transparency 7* and *Large Prints 39 The Oregon Trail* and *40 Vaquero* to demonstrate how an artist uses positive and negative space in art. Have students study the artwork and point out the positive and negative space. How did the artist treat the negative space? How do the positive and negative spaces fit together? Is one type of space more important than the other? Explain.

Teach

After students complete their initial stencil print, encourage them to add another color, using a smaller stencil to change the look of the print. How did the relationship of positive and negative space change?

Reflect

Have students evaluate their art using the four steps of art criticism. Encourage them to locate and describe areas in the classroom where they see positive and negative space.

Alternate Activity

Materials:
- 6" × 9" pieces of white drawing paper
- pencils
- colored markers
- block letter stencils (optional)

1. Students will draw two large, block-letter initials on the white drawing paper, either freehand or using stencils.

2. Students will fill in the positive space of their drawing with patterns and the negative space with solid colors.

3. To teach color schemes, students could fill in the block letters (positive space) with warm colors and the negative space with cool colors.

Research in Art Education

"There is more to learning about art than learning to do it. Most people wil not actually seek to make art in their lifetime, but all of us have daily contact with visual stimuli that deliberately (in package design, fashion, or good building) or accidentally (a pattern of leaves on snow or an unexpected bright color against a faded doorway) appeal to our aesthetic sense and offer a bit of visual order in the bustle of the everyday" (Elizabeth Vallance. "Criticism as Subject Matter in Schools and in Art Museums." *Journal of Aesthetic Education* 22 (4). (1988): 69–81).

Assessment
Use the following rubric to evaluate the artwork students make in the Creative Expression activity and to assess students' understanding of positive and negative space.

Have students complete page 21 or 22 in their *Assessment* books.

	Art History and Culture	Aesthetic Perception	Creative Expression	Art Criticism
3 POINTS	The student is able to compare folk art from ancient Peru and modern Poland and their use of positive and negative space.	The student accurately identifies positive and negative space.	The student effectively designs a mask using positive and negative space.	The student evaluates his or her own work using the four steps of art criticism.
2 POINTS	The student attempts to compare folk art from ancient Peru and modern Poland and their use of positive and negative space.	The student shows emerging awareness of positive and negative space.	The student shows some awareness of how to effectively design a mask using positive and negative space.	The student attempts to evaluate his or her own work using the four steps of art criticism.
1 POINT	The student cannot identify folk art from ancient Peru and modern Poland and their use of positive and negative space.	The student cannot identify positive and negative space.	The student shows no understanding of how to create a mask using positive and negative space.	The student does not attempt to evaluate his or her own work.

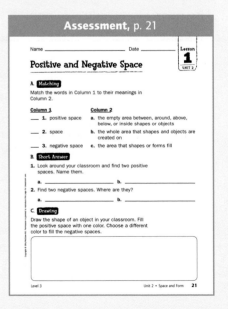

Lesson 2 · Creating Depth

Overview

Lesson 2 introduces how artists create depth by size and placement of objects in artwork.

Objectives

 Art History and Culture

To discuss the artwork *Washington's Headquarters 1780*

 Creative Expression

To plan and create a real or imaginary scene with a foreground and background that illustrate depth

 Aesthetic Perception

To identify how artists create depth by the size and placement of objects

Art Criticism

To evaluate own work using the four steps of art criticism

Vocabulary ⭐ Vocabulary

Review the following vocabulary words with students before beginning the lesson.

foreground primer plano—the part of the picture that appears closest to the viewer

background fondo—the part of the picture that seems to be the farthest from the viewer

See page 89B for additional vocabulary and Spanish vocabulary resources.

 Art Journal: Critical Thinking

Have students add these words to the Vocabulary section of their Art Journals.

Lesson Materials

- 9" × 12" construction paper
- colored pencils
- 12" × 18" white construction paper
- pencils
- set of watercolor paints
- brushes of various sizes
- containers of water
- sketch paper
- tape
- paper towels

Alternate Materials:
- oil pastels
- crayons

Program Resources
- *Reading and Writing Test Prep.*, pp. 20–21
- *Transparency 8*
- *Artist Profiles*, pp. 55, 83
- *Animals Through History Time Line*
- *Assessment*, pp. 23–24
- *Large Prints 39* The Oregon Trail and *40* Vaquero
- *Art Around the World Collection*

Concept Trace
Creating Depth
Introduced: Level 2, Unit 2, Lesson 5

Reinforced: Level 4, Unit 5, Lesson 1

Lesson 2 Arts Integration NSAE 6.a

Theatre

Complete Unit 2, Lesson 2 on pages 38–39 of *Theatre Arts Connections.*

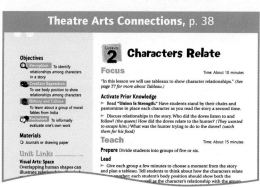

Theatre Arts Connections, p. 38

Music

 Soft music can seem farther away than loud music. Listen to *Byldo* from *Pictures at an Exhibition* by Modest Mussorgsky. This portrayal of an ox cart gets louder gradually and seems to be approaching the listener. Besides just playing the melody louder on the English horn, what other means are used to add volume?

Movement & Dance

Artists work with foreground and background, which can be related in dance to exploring the different areas of a stage. The farthest point from the audience is called *upstage*; the closest point is *downstage*. The center is called *center stage*. Have students sit as an audience. Select four students at a time to work in the space. Identify each stage area. As each area is called out, the students place themselves where they think they should be.

Focus

Time: About 10 minutes

Activate Prior Knowledge

"Suppose you are looking out your bedroom window. Why do even large-size objects in the distance all fit within the window frame?"

"Vamos a suponer que se asoman por la ventana de su habitación. ¿Por qué hasta los objetos grandes en la distancia caben dentro del marco de la ventana?"

■ Discuss student responses. Point out that the farther away objects are, the smaller they look.

Using Literature ⭐ Reading

■ Read *Farewell to Shady Glade* by Bill Peet. Have students discuss the use of depth in the book.

Thematic Connection ⭐ Reading

■ **Storytelling:** Both works of art seem to be about something. Have students talk about what kind of story the artist may have been trying to tell.

Introduce the Art

Look

"Let's take a look at the two works of art."
"Vamos a observar las dos obras de arte".

Comparing and Contrasting ⭐ Reading

■ Have students make a list of similarities and differences in the two works of art. Both works of art are outdoor scenes; both are realistic in style and show depth. *Washington's Headquarters 1780* has many colors and includes a great number of people, as well as a wide variety of objects. *Mortlake Terrace* displays neutral colors and illustrates only a few objects.

Art History and Culture

Possible answers: The painting was inspired by the United States Centennial, which was celebrated in 1876.

Web Connection

Visit **www.nmaa.si.edu** to learn more about the National Museum of American Art. Have students view works online and share their ideas.

70 UNIT 2 • Space and Form

Lesson 2 — Creating Depth

Look at the artwork on these pages. Both artists show depth by making the objects in the foreground larger and the objects in the background smaller.

▲ **Artist Unknown.** (United States). *Washington's Headquarters 1780.* c. 1876.
Mixed-media. 21 ¼ × 28 inches (54 × 71 cm). Smithsonian American Art Museum, Washington, D.C.

Art History and Culture

What time in American History does the painting *Washington's Headquarters* tell about?

70 Unit 2 • Lesson 2

Art History and Culture

Washington's Headquarters 1780

Washington's Headquarters 1780 was created in the late 1800s, a time when Americans began to place greater importance on the arts and develop a strong interest in realism. *Washington's Headquarters 1780* was inspired by the United States Centennial, which was celebrated in 1876, the year that the artwork was completed. A theme of patriotism is apparent. *Washington's Headquarters 1780* is a mixed media collage.

See pages 24–25 and 16–21 for more about art history and subject matter.

Artist Profiles, p. 83

Washington's Headquarters

Washington's Headquarters was made sometime after 1876. Even though the work has no exact date, an estimate is possible because many of the images in the work have been cut out of Currier and Ives prints that were made after 1875.

▲ **Artist unknown.** (United States). *Washington's Headquarters 1780.* c. 1876.

Study both paintings to see how the artists create depth by making objects seem near or far away.

▶ Find the objects that seem to be closest.

▶ Which objects seem to be farthest away?

▶ Which objects can you see most clearly?

▶ Draw a line with your finger between the front and back scenes. Do the objects in the front and the back look like they are the same size?

▲ **Joseph Mallord William Turner.** (English). *Mortlake Terrace.* 1826.
••••••••••••••••••••••••••
Oil on canvas. 36 $\frac{1}{4}$ × 48 $\frac{1}{8}$ inches (92 × 122 cm). National Gallery of Art, Washington, D.C.

Aesthetic Perception

Design Awareness What looks smaller, the objects closer to you or the objects farther away?

Art History and Culture

Joseph Mallord William Turner

Joseph Mallord William Turner (jō′ sef ma′ lərd wil′ yəm tûr′ nər) (1775–1851) was born in London, England. At 13 he was making drawings at home and exhibiting them in his father's shop window for sale. By the time he was 18, he had his own art studio where people were eager to buy his paintings. Venice was the inspiration of many of Turner's paintings. Wherever he visited, he studied the effects of sea and sky in every kind of weather. Turner is regarded as one of the founders of English watercolor and landscape painting.

See pages 24–25 and 16–21 for more about art history and subject matter.

 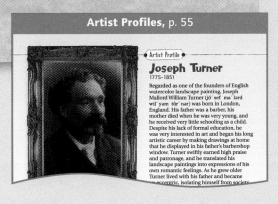

Artist Profiles, p. 55

◆ Artist Profile ◆

Joseph Turner
1775–1851

Regarded as one of the founders of English watercolor landscape painting, Joseph Mallord William Turner (jō′ sef ma′ lərd wil′ yəm tûr′ nər) was born in London, England. His father was a barber, his mother died when he was very young, and he received very little schooling as a child. Despite his lack of formal education, he was very interested in art and began his long artistic career by making drawings at home that he displayed in his father's barbershop window. Turner swiftly earned high praise and patronage, and he translated his landscape paintings into expressions of his own romantic feelings. As he grew older Turner lived with his father and became eccentric, isolating himself from society.

Study   NSAE 1.b; 2.a; 2.b; 3.a

▶ Foreground: *Mortlake Terrace:* the dog, tree, and sailboats.

▶ Background: In *Washington's Headquarters 1780,* the mountains are the farthest objects. *Mortlake Terrace:* the tree line in the background as well as the small house

▶ The objects in the foreground can be seen most clearly.

▶ Size: *Washington's Headquarters 1780* and *Mortlake Terrace:* In each scene, the objects in the front are larger than the objects in the back.

■ For more examples of art from Europe, see the *Art Around the World Collection.*

 Art Journal: Writing
Encourage students to write explanations of creating depth in the Concepts section of their Art Journals. What else do they want to know?

Aesthetic Perception

Seeing Like an Artist Have students look out into the neighborhood. Ask them which objects look smaller, the things closest to them or the objects farthest away? Artists create depth by painting objects to appear close or far away.

Developing Visual Literacy Have students discuss which objects appear to be close or far away. What are the artists trying to convey in their paintings? Invite students to share any personal experiences that contribute to their understanding of the works of art.

NSAE 2.a,b

Web Connection
Visit **www.ibiblio.org/wm/paint/auth/turner/** to find more about Joseph Mallord William Turner. Have students share their ideas about his work.

# Teach

"How can you create a sense of depth?"
"¿Cómo pueden crear una sensación de profundidad?"

- Read and discuss depth, foreground, and background found on page 72.

Practice

Materials: 9" × 12" construction paper, colored pencils

Alternate Materials: crayons

- Distribute the materials and have students follow the directions on page 72 to show foreground and background.

Creative Expression

Materials: 12" × 18" white construction paper, pencils, set of watercolor paints, brushes of various sizes, containers of water, sketch paper, tape, and paper towels

- Distribute materials and have students follow the directions on page 73.
- Review procedures for working with watercolor paint in Technique Tips on page 219.
- Review the Activity Tips on page 235 for visual examples of techniques.
- Create a class exhibition of finished works. Have students share their ideas about the exhibition.

Art Journal: Brainstorming
Have students brainstorm a variety of places they might visit to see animals. Have students write the places they would see animals in their Art Journals. Then have them decide how they will show depth using animals for the Creative Expression activity.

Creating Depth

Depth in artwork is created when some objects seem to be very close and others seem to be far away.

Just like in real life, objects in artwork that are larger seem to be closer. Objects that are smaller seem to be farther away. Also, objects in artwork that have clear, sharp edges and many details seem closer. Objects that have fuzzy edges and little detail seem farther away.

Foreground is the part of the picture plane that appears closest to the viewer. The foreground is usually at the bottom of the picture plane.

Background is the part of the picture plane that seems to be farthest from the viewer. It is usually located at the top of the picture plane.

Practice

Draw objects in the **foreground** and in the **background.**

1. Near the bottom of your paper, draw a large animal or object.

2. Draw the same animal or object near the top of your paper, but make it much smaller.

Differentiated Instruction

Reteach
Have students look through the book to find three works of art that create the illusion of depth. Ask them to list the title of each work and describe the techniques the artists used to create a sense of depth.

Special Needs
Activate the prior knowledge of students with disabilities by giving them three different sized cutouts of the same animal. Have students place these on a pre-drawn scene located on a teacher display board. Ask students to identify the position of each animal.

ELL Tips
Students may find it difficult to follow a class discussion without additional visual clues. Use the illustrations provided in the *Student Edition* to demonstrate what you are talking about or to paraphrase a student response.

Katie Waters.
Age 9.

Think about how the student artist showed depth in her drawing.

 Creative Expression

What does your favorite outdoor place look like? Draw it using a variety of lines.

1. Think about a place where there are lots of animals.
2. Make a rough sketch of the animals and other objects you want in your scene. Show depth by drawing animals and objects larger in the foreground and smaller in the background.
3. Fill your scene with color.

Art Criticism

Describe Name the animals and objects you put in your picture.

Analyze What did you put in the background?

Interpret What title would you give your drawing?

Decide Were you able to create a feeling of depth in your work?

Unit 2 • Lesson 2   **73**

 **R** **eflect**   **Time:** About 5 minutes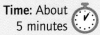

Review and Assess

"How do artists create a feeling of depth in a drawing or painting?" "¿Cómo crean los artistas una sensación de profundidad en un dibujo o una pintura?"

Think

The artist created an illusion of depth by drawing objects larger and smaller.

- Use *Large Prints 39 The Oregon Trail* and *40 Vaquero* to have students compare the techniques used to create the illusion of depth in the prints and in the works in this lesson.

Informal Assessment
NSAE 1.b; 2.a; 2.b; 3.a; 5.c

Art Journal: Critical Thinking
Have students answer the four art criticism questions—Describe, Analyze, Interpret, and Decide—in their Art Journals. In small groups, have students discuss the ways in which they created depth in their works of art.

- For standardized-format test practice using this lesson's art content, see pages 20–21 in *Reading and Writing Test Preparation.*

Art Across the Curriculum

Use these simple ideas to reinforce art concepts across the curriculum.

★ **Narrative Writing** When used in a news story, the term *in depth* means that a report is clear and thorough. Have students imagine they are news reporters and choose a topic to write about.

★ **Math** Have students create depth by drawing five to six different geometrical and free-form shapes.

★ **Science** Objects can be made to appear near or far away by the way an artist places them in a picture. The direction and speed of objects can be changed by pushing or pulling them. Have students think about objects that are pushed or pulled.

★ **Social Studies** Have students discuss and write down important things they notice in *Washington Headquarters 1780.*

★ **Technology** Have students use the paint tool to create a scene showing plants that are close and far away. Visit **SRAonline.com** for detailed instructions for this activity.

NSAE 4.b; 6.b

Creating Depth

Extra! For the Art Specialist

Time: About 45 minutes

Focus

Use **Transparency 8** and **Large Prints 39** *The Oregon Trail* and **40** *Vaquero* to demonstrate how artists create depth by making objects appear close or far away. Direct students' attention to two objects in the artwork. Ask them which one seems to be farther away from the viewer. Ask students to explain what the artist did to make the object appear that way. What else could the artist do to make something appear to be farther away?

Teach

Have students follow the directions to complete their pictures. Would the depth of the art change if the artist made the objects larger?

Reflect

Have students evaluate their art using the four steps of art criticism. Encourage them to locate and describe areas in the classroom where they might find depth.

Alternate Activity

Materials:
- 12" × 18" manila paper
- crayons

1. Have students think of their favorite team-sports activity, either a team they play on or a professional sport they like to watch. Have students visualize where the sport is played, how many players are on each team, and what kind of uniforms they wear.

2. Students will begin their pictures by drawing larger players closest to the bottom of the page. As the other players are added, they will be drawn a little smaller and moved up the picture plane.

3. After the players are drawn, students will draw the horizon line above the middle of the paper and add details to complete their drawings.

Research in Art Education

"It seems without a doubt that children do, indeed, respond to and are able to talk about art in meaningful ways" (Anderson, Tom. "Talking About Art with Children: From Theory to Practice." *Art Education* 39(1). (1986): 5–8).

Assessment

Use the following rubric to evaluate the artwork students make in the Creative Expression activity and to assess students' understanding of how artists create depth by the size and placement of objects.

	Art History and Culture	Aesthetic Perception	Creative Expression	Art Criticism
3 POINTS	The student demonstrates knowledge of the art and life of Joseph Mallord William Turner.	The student accurately identifies how artists create depth by the size and placement of objects.	The student effectively plans and creates an imaginary scene with a foreground and a background that illustrates depth.	The student evaluates his or her own work using the four steps of art criticism.
2 POINTS	The student demonstrates some understanding of the art and life of Joseph Mallord William Turner.	The student shows emerging awareness of how artists create depth by the size and placement of objects.	The student shows some awareness of planning and creating an imaginary scene with a foreground and a background that illustrates depth.	The student attempts to evaluate his or her own work using the four steps of art criticism.
1 POINT	The student demonstrates no knowledge of the art and life of Joseph Mallord William Turner.	The student cannot identify how artists create depth.	The student shows no understanding of how to plan and create an imaginary scene with a foreground and a background that illustrates depth.	The student makes no attempt to evaluate his or her own work.

Have students complete page 23 or 24 in their **Assessment** books.

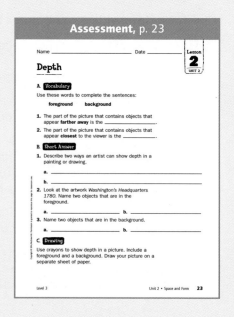

Assessment, p. 23

Name _____ Date _____

Lesson **2** UNIT 2

Depth

A Vocabulary
Use these words to complete the sentences:
foreground   background

1. The part of the picture that contains objects that appear **farther away** is the _____
2. The part of the picture that contains objects that appear **closest** to the viewer is the _____

B Short Answer
1. Describe two ways an artist can show depth in a painting or drawing.
   a. _____
   b. _____
2. Look at the artwork *Washington's Headquarters 1780*. Name two objects that are in the foreground.
   a. _____   b. _____
3. Name two objects that are in the background.
   a. _____   b. _____

C Drawing
Use crayons to show depth in a picture. Include a foreground and a background. Draw your picture on a separate sheet of paper.

Level 3   Unit 2 • Space and Form   **23**

Overlapping

Lesson 3 introduces how artists create the illusion of depth by overlapping objects.

Objectives

 Art History and Culture

To compare works by artists from different cultures

 Creative Expression

To plan and create a drawing that shows depth by overlapping

 Aesthetic Perception

To describe how artists create the illusion of depth by overlapping objects

 Art Criticism

To evaluate own work using the four steps of art criticism

Vocabulary Vocabulary

Review the following vocabulary words with students before beginning the lesson.

overlap superponer—the placement of one object over another so that part of the second object is hidden

depth profundidad—the appearance of distance of flat surface

See page 89B for additional vocabulary and Spanish vocabulary resources.

 ### Art Journal

Have students add these words to the Vocabulary section of their Art Journals.

Lesson Materials

- 9" × 12" paper
- pencils or crayons
- 12" × 18" white construction paper
- pencils
- sketch paper

Alternate Materials:
- fine-line black felt-tip markers

Program Resources

- *Reading and Writing Test Prep.*, pp. 22–23
- *Transparency 9*
- *Artist Profiles*, pp. 26, 38
- *Animals Through History Time Line*
- *Assessment*, pp. 25–26
- *Large Prints 39* The Oregon Trail and *40* Vaquero
- *Art Around the World*

Concept Trace
Overlapping
Introduced: Level 2, Unit 2, Lesson 6

Reinforced: Level 4, Unit 5, Lesson 2

Lesson 3 Arts Integration NSAE 6.a

Theatre

Complete Unit 2, Lesson 3 on pages 40–41 of *Theatre Arts Connections.*

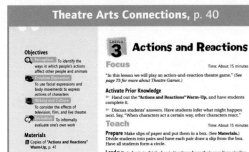

Theatre Arts Connections, p. 40

Music

 Singing a round, or canon, illustrates overlapping in music. A more complex example of this is a fugue. Listen to Purcell's *Variations and Fugue on a Theme* by Benjamin Britten. Each variation is played by a different section of the orchestra, leading to a grand fugue where each introduction of the melody is played by each section.

Movement & Dance

Students walk freely in the space to the beat of the drum. When the drum stops, students take four counts to create a shape that connects to two or three people closest to them. Emphasize shapes that overlap other shapes on different levels, reaching over, under, around, and through each other. Repeat the sequence several times. Each time, students find new people to connect with and explore new variations of shape.

Focus

Time: About 10 minutes

Activate Prior Knowledge

"Suppose you are sitting in a movie theater. Why can't you see the entire person in front of you?" *"Vamos a suponer que están sentados en un cine. ¿Por qué no pueden ver completamente a la persona en frente de ustedes?"*

Using Literature ⭐ Reading

■ Read *Saturday Sancocho* by Leyla Torres. Have students discuss the use of overlapping in the book.

Thematic Connection ⭐ Science

■ **Weather/Seasons:** Have students talk about the weather in the artwork. Which artwork appears to be set in a warmer climate? Which artwork could be in a colder climate? Discuss the reasons for each.

Introduce the Art

Look

"Let's take close look at the two paintings." *"Vamos a observar detalladamente las dos pinturas".*

Comparing and Contrasting ⭐ Reading

■ Have students list the similarities and differences in the two paintings. Both paintings are outdoor scenes, realistic in style, and show depth. Jean-Gilles's painting has many colors, includes people and houses, and is a spring or summertime scene. Mangold's painting has limited colors, illustrates only trees, and is a winter scene.

🏺 Art History and Culture

Joseph Jean-Gilles overlaps objects to show the great diversity in the lush landscape. He has studied the trees and plants of Haiti and arranges them in precise patterns.

💻 Web Connection

Visit **www.alexanderandbonin.com/artists/ mangold.html** to learn more about Sylvia Plimack Mangold. Have students share their ideas about her work.

Overlapping

Look at the landscape paintings on these pages. In *Haitian Landscape,* Joseph-Jean Gilles created a landscape of a farming community by overlapping houses, trees, and gardens. In *The Locust Trees with Maple,* Sylvia Plimack Mangold added a sense of depth by painting branches that cover each other. This makes the trees in front look closer to the viewer.

▲ **Sylvia Plimack Mangold.** (American). *The Locust Trees with Maple.* 1990.

Oil on linen. Brooke Alexander Gallery, New York, New York.

🏺 Art History and Culture

Artists paint scenes from the environment where they live.

🏺 Art History and Culture

Sylvia Plimack Mangold

Sylvia Plimack Mangold (sil´ vē ə pli´ mak man´ gold) (1938–) was born in New York City. She attended several art schools and earned a degree in fine arts from Yale University. In 1974 she had her first show. Her work has been much admired ever since. Mangold paints daily and relies on images in her immediate environment as sources of inspiration—the floors and walls of her studio and the landscape of the Hudson River Valley. Her work does not fit easily into a category. Many of her realistic paintings still have an abstract quality.

Mangold has taught at the School of Visual Arts in New York City. She is married to artist Robert Mangold, and they have two sons.

See pages 24–25 and 16–21 for more about art history and subject and subject matter.

Artist Profiles, p. 38

◆ Artist Profile ◆

Sylvia Plimack Mangold
b. 1938

Sylvia Plimack Mangold (sil´ vē ə pli´ mak man´ gōld) was born in New York City. She attended several art schools and earned a degree in fine arts from Yale University. In 1974, she had her first show, and her work has been much admired ever since. Mangold taught at the School of Visual Arts in New York City. She is married to artist Robert Mangold, and they have two sons. She lives on a 150-acre farm in Washingtonville, New York.

Study both paintings to see how overlapping creates a feeling of depth.

▶ Find objects in each painting that overlap.

▶ Which branches in *The Locust Trees with Maple* look closer to you? Which look farther away?

▶ What objects cover parts of the houses in *Haitian Landscape?* What objects do the houses cover?

▶ Describe the objects in *Haitian Landscape* that look closest to you. Which look farthest away?

▲ **Joseph Jean-Gilles.**
(Haitian). *Haitian Landscape.* 1973.
....
Oil on canvas. 30 × 48 inches (76 × 122 cm.). Art Museum of the Americas, Organization of American States, Washington, D.C.

 Aesthetic Perception

Design Awareness Look out a window and find examples of objects that overlap.

Art History and Culture

Joseph Jean-Gilles

Joseph Jean-Gilles (zhoˊ zəf zhän zhēl) (1943–   ) lives in Florida, but his native land of Haiti is never far from his mind. He studied art at Centre d'Art in Port Au Prince, Haiti, and he has been painting scenes of his homeland ever since. Jean-Gilles is considered a professional primitive painter like French painter Rousseau. He has gained skills that take him beyond a spontaneous recording of what he sees or imagines to a carefully planned sophisticated portrayal of his ideas.

Jean-Gilles has had a number of exhibitions in New York and Washington, D.C., as well as Haiti. One his paintings hangs permanently in New York's Museum of Modern Art.

See pages 24–25 and 16–21 for more about art history and subject matter.

Artist Profiles, p. 26

◆ Artist Profile ◆

Joseph Jean-Gilles
b. 1943

Born in Haiti, Joseph Jean-Gilles (zhōˊ zaf zhän gil lēˊ) now lives in Florida, but his native land is never far from his mind. He studied art at Centre d'Art in Port-au-Prince, Haiti, until 1967, and has been painting scenes of his homeland ever since. Jean-Gilles has had a number of exhibitions in New York and Washington, D.C., as well as in Haiti. His paintings hang in museums including New York's Museum of Modern Art and the Art Museum of the Americanas in Port-au-Prince.

▶ Overlapping: *Haitian Landscape:* The trees in front overlap the hills in the middle ground. Grass and bushes overlap the houses. The houses overlap the hills behind them. *The Locust Trees with Maple:* The branches of the trees overlap.

▶ In *The Locust Trees with Maple:* the branches that overlap look closest. The branches that are overlapped look farther away.

▶ Objects that cover houses: plants and hills Objects that houses cover: brown hills

▶ Closest: *Haitian Landscape:* the plants and hills at the bottom of the artwork. Farthest: *Haitian Landscape:* the trees and hills at the top of the artwork

■ For more examples of art from Latin America, see the *Art Around the World Collection.*

Art Journal: Writing

Encourage students to write explanations of overlapping in the Concepts section of their Art Journals. What else do they want to know?

Aesthetic Perception

Design Awareness Discuss the outdoors with students, and have them look out the window to find examples of objects that overlap. Many trees and shrubs have branches that overlap. Students may notice buildings or hills that overlap. These all provide good examples of overlapping.

Developing Visual Literacy Have students discuss the art. Encourage them to ask questions about why the artist created the painting. Invite students to discuss any insights they have about the artwork.

Web Connection

View www.discoverhaiti.com/history_summary.htm to learn more about Haitian history and culture.

Teach

Time: About 45 minutes

"How can you draw shapes that overlap?"
"¿Cómo pueden trazar figuras que se superponen?"

- Discuss how to overlap shapes to create depth. Emphasize that an object in the foreground may partially conceal an object in the background.

Practice

Materials: 12" × 12" paper, pencils or crayons

Alternate Materials: markers

- Distribute the materials and have students follow the directions on page 76.

Creative Expression

Materials: 12" × 18" white construction paper, pencils, sketch paper

Alternate Materials: black, fine-line, felt-tip markers

- Distribute the materials and have students follow the directions on page 77.

- Review the Activity Tips on page 236 for visual examples of techniques.

- Review the Technique Tips on page 214 for information about using pencils.

Art Journal: Brainstorming

Have students brainstorm different parts of a tree. Review overlapping as a technique for creating depth in an artwork and list their ideas in their Art Journals. Then have students plan how they will show their drawing in the Creative Expression activity.

Creating Overlapping

Overlapping occurs when one object covers part of a second object. Overlapping makes the object in front seem closer to the viewer.

When objects overlap, they create depth, or the appearance of distance, on a flat surface. The object in front appears to be closer to the viewer, and the second object seems to be farther away.

Practice

Draw shapes that overlap. Use pencil or crayon.

1. Create a feeling of depth in a design by overlapping geometric shapes.

2. Draw one large shape. Then draw a second shape so that part of it is hidden behind the large shape.

3. Add other shapes.

Differentiated Instruction

Reteach

Have students look outside and find five objects that overlap other objects. Ask them to list the objects in front and the objects they overlap.

Special Needs

Point out for students the positive and negative shapes that exist in their compositions. This not only activates prior knowledge from Lesson 1, but it also is a useful drawing technique.

ELL Tips

For the first step of drawing overlapping trees and branches, you may wish to create a chart as students share their ideas about trees. Write the different parts of a tree and draw a quick sketch. Model how to draw a rough sketch; then show how to use it to create the final drawing.

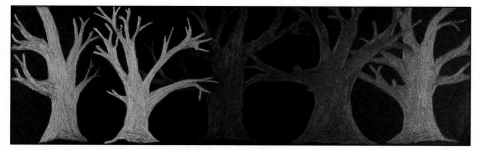

▲ **Darries Robinson.**
Age 9.

Think about how the student artist created a
sense of depth by overlapping branches.

Creative Expression

How do the trees look when you are
walking toward them? Create a drawing of
overlapping trees and branches.

1. Think about the different parts of a
   tree. How do the brances look? Sketch
   some, using different kinds of lines.
2. Draw some trees, making each tree's
   branches and leaves overlap to create a
   feeling of depth.
3. Fill your page, and touch all edges of
   the paper with your lines and shapes.

Art Criticism

Describe What kind of trees
did you draw?

Analyze How did
overlapping help create a
feeling of depth?

Interpret How would your
drawing change if the trees did
not overlap?

Decide How is your drawing
like the paintings shown in the
lesson? How is it different?

Art Across the Curriculum

Use these simple ideas to reinforce art concepts across the curriculum.

★ **Narrative Writing** Ask students to write some words and phrases
  that describe a tree or that tell what they like about trees. Then have
  them use the ideas to write a poem.

★ **Math** Have students study both paintings and decide which has
  more geometric shapes.

★ **Science** Discuss what happens to plants and animals during each
  season. On a sheet of paper, have students choose a plant or an
  animal and draw what it looks like during each season.

★ **Social Studies** Have students analyze *Haitian Landscape*. Have
  them think about ways the lives of the Haitians shown in the picture
  may be different from theirs.

★ **Technology** Have students use the paint tool to create a scene
  using overlapping to show objects that are close and far away. Visit
  SRAonline.com for detailed instructions for this activity.

NSAE 4.a; 5.b; 6b

Reflect
**Time: About
5 minutes**

Review and Assess

"What have you learned about the use of
overlapping in a painting or drawing?"
"¿Qué han aprendido acerca del uso de la
superposición en una pintura o un dibujo?"

Think

The student artist created a feeling of depth
by overlapping branches.

■ Use *Large Prints 39* The Oregon Trail and
  40 Vaquero to have students compare how
  the print and the works in this lesson use
  overlapping.

Informal Assessment
NSAE 1.b; 2.a; 2.b; 3.a; 5.c

Art Journal: Critical Thinking
Have students answer the four art
criticism questions—Describe, Analyze,
Interpret, and Decide—in their Art
Journals. Discuss the use of overlapping in
their drawings.

■ For standardized-format test practice
  using this lesson's art content, see
  pages 22–23 in *Reading and Writing
  Test Preparation.*

Lesson 3 Wrap-Up

Overlapping

Extra! For the Art Specialist

Time: About 45 minutes

Focus

Use *Transparency 9* and *Large Prints 39 The Oregon Trail* and *40 Vaquero* to discuss how overlapping makes some objects seem close and others far away. Have students look for objects in the painting that overlap another object or appear to be in front of or behind something else. Ask students why the artist would overlap objects when they could be depicted side by side. Do students think the artwork would be as interesting if none of the objects overlapped each other?

Teach

Have students follow the directions to complete their landscape paintings. How does overlapping enhance the landscape?

Reflect

Have students evaluate their art using the four steps of art criticism. Encourage them to describe pictures or paintings in the classroom that show examples of overlapping.

Alternate Activity

Materials:
- 12" × 18" manila paper
- tempera paints
- paintbrushes
- 9" × 12" colored construction paper
- scissors
- white glue or glue sticks

1. Students will paint the backgrounds of their landscapes with tempera paint and put them up to dry.

2. Have students cut out three or more objects that could be placed in a landscape (i.e., barn, fence, trees, and a variety of animals for a farm landscape).

3. After the backgrounds dry, students will attach their cut-out objects to the backgrounds, being sure to overlap at least two objects.

Research in Art Education

"Children respond to art in a holistic manner; their reactions are immediate, subjective, and rarely go beyond the 'like/don't like' stage . . . It takes a sensitive teacher to help educate the vision of the child so that appreciation may occur" (Hurwitz, Al, and Stanley Medeja. *The Joyous Vision*. New Jersey: Prentice Hall, 1997).

Assessment
Use the following rubric to evaluate the artwork students make in the Creative Expression activity and to assess students' understanding of overlapping.

Have students complete page 25 or 26 in their *Assessment* books.

	Art History and Culture	Aesthetic Perception	Creative Expression	Art Criticism
3 POINTS	The student identifies and compares works by artists from different cultures.	The student accurately identifies how artists create the illusion of depth by overlapping objects.	The student effectively plans and creates a drawing that shows depth through overlapping.	The student evaluates his or her own work using the four steps of art criticism.
2 POINTS	The student's comparison is weak or incomplete.	The student shows emerging awareness of how artists create the illusion of depth by overlapping objects.	The student shows some awareness of how to plan and create a drawing that shows depth through overlapping.	The student attempts to evaluate his or her own work using the four steps of art criticism.
1 POINT	The student cannot identify or compare the different works of art.	The student cannot identify how artists create the illusion of depth.	The student shows no understanding of how to plan and create a drawing that shows depth through overlapping.	The student does not attempt to evaluate his or her own work.

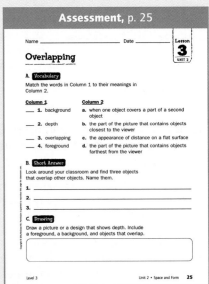

Form

Lesson 4 introduces how artists use three-dimensional forms to create sculptures.

Objectives

 Art History and Culture

To describe the lives and artwork of Niki de Saint Phalle and Fernand Léger

Creative Expression

To create a three-dimensional animal form using collected objects

 Aesthetic Perception

To identify three-dimensional forms used by artists

Art Criticism

To evaluate own work using the four steps of art criticism

Vocabulary ⭐ Vocabulary

Review the following vocabulary words with the students before beginning the lesson.

three-dimensional *tridimensional*—something that can be measured by height, width, and depth

sculpture *escultura*—three-dimensional work of art created by carving, welding, casting, or modeling materials together.

See page 89B for additional vocabulary and Spanish vocabulary resources.

Art Journal: Vocabulary

Have students add these words to the Vocabulary section of their Art Journals.

Lesson Materials

- various found objects (paper towel, small cardboard boxes, bottle caps, yarn, and felt)
- tissue paper
- glue
- markers

Program Resources

- *Reading and Writing Test Prep.*, pp. 24–25
- *Transparency 10*
- *Artist Profiles*, pp. 14, 34
- *Animals Through History Time Line*
- *Assessment*, pp. 27–28
- *Large Prints 39* The Oregon Trail and *40* Vaquero
- *The National Museum of Women in the Arts Collection*

Concept Trace
Form
Introduced: Level 2, Unit 2, Lesson 3
Reinforced: Level 4, Unit 1, Lesson 1

Lesson 4 Arts Integration NSAE 6.a

Theatre

Complete Unit 2, Lesson 4, on pages 24–25 of *Theatre Arts Connections.*

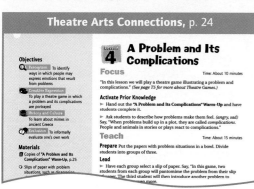

Theatre Arts Connections, p. 24

Music

 Form in music pertains to how sections are repeated or contrasted. Listen to *Russian Sailors Dance* from *The Red Poppy* by Reinhold Gliere. This piece consists of variations on the *A* theme. Being aware there is an introduction and coda, keep track of the repeats of *A* on the board while you listen. What happens in the music so you don't tire of the same melody repeated so many times?

Movement & Dance

Volume in dance can be shown by the relationship of the dancer to space—how the dancer moves through space, takes up space, and also gathers and forms it. Ask each student to create volume with their arms by taking, gathering, shaping, and forming the space around them. Work on different levels and face a variety of directions.

 **Focus**

Time: About 10 minutes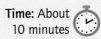

Activate Prior Knowledge

"Think about three-dimensional geometric shapes that you see in buildings."

"Piensen acerca de las figuras geómetricas tridimensionales que ven en los edificios".

Using Literature ⭐ Reading

■ Read *Our Money* by Bornemann Spies. Have students discuss the use of forms in the book.

Thematic Connection ⭐ Reading

■ **Colors:** Encourage students to discuss the different colors they see. Do they see any primary colors or intermediate colors?

Introduce the Art

Look

"Let's take a look at the two sculptures."

"Vamos a observar detalladamente las dos esculturas".

Comparing and Contrasting ⭐ Reading

■ Have students make a list of similarities. Both objects are nonobjective in style, use basic free-form, three-dimensional forms, and have appendages that radiate from the central point. *The Walking Flower* is a relatively smaller monument made from clay. *The Sun God* is a 14-foot bird placed atop a 15-foot concrete arch made of polyester, fiberglass, and steel.

NSAE 3.a

 Art History and Culture

Fernand Léger used three-dimensional forms to create sculptures. His wartime experiences contributed to his interest in social themes and machine art.

Web Connection

Visit **www.kids.albrightknox.org** to find out more about Fernand Léger.

 Form

Look at the sculptures on these pages. *The Walking Flower* is a clay sculpture. The *Sun God* is a sculpture made from polyester. Form is an important element in both sculptures.

◀ **Fernand Leger.** (French). *The Walking Flower.* 1951.

Ceramic. 26 $\frac{1}{2}$ × 20 $\frac{1}{2}$ × 15 inches (67 × 50 × 38 cm.). Albright-Knox Art Gallery, Buffalo, New York.

 Art History and Culture

Artists use three-dimensional forms to create sculptures.

 Art History and Culture

Fernand Léger

Fernand Léger (fer nän´ lā zhā´) (1881–1955) was born in Argentan, Normandy. Like other cubists, Léger looked at his subjects from several angles and combined angles in the same picture. For example, he might show the top, bottom, and sides of a subject in one painting. To do this, cubists broke a subject into surfaces or "planes." To some people, cubist paintings seem to be cubes or boxes falling through space.

Toward the end of Léger's career, his art became increasingly abstract and geometric.

See pages 24–25 and 16–21 for more about art history and the subject matter.

Artist Profiles, p. 34

◆ Artist Profile ◆

Fernand Léger
1881-1955

Fernand Léger (fer nän´ lä zhä´) was the son of French peasants, but his art strayed far from the rural countryside. He spent his life exploring the modern industrial world from an artist's point of view. Perhaps his early training in an architect's office encouraged his fascination with what came to be known as "machine art." Léger combined the cubist painting style with images from the industrial world. The people in his pictures, broken into flat planes, seem more like robots than humans.

◄ **Niki de Saint Phalle.**
(French). *Sun God.*
. . . .
Polyester. 14 inches tall (36 cm.).
Stuart Collection of Sculpture at the
University of California San Diego,
San Diego, California.

Study both sculptures to find the following forms.

▶ Find a form that has a circle or a shape of a circle painted on it.

▶ Locate forms that look like triangles.

▶ Find free-form shapes in these sculptures.

 Aesthetic Perception

Design Awareness Look around your classroom. Find objects that have forms like the ones you found in the artwork.

Unit 2 • Lesson 4   **79**

Study   NSAE 1.b; 2.a; 2.b; 3.a

▶ Sphere: *The Walking Flower:* The red form in the center of the sculpture has a shape like a circle. *Sun God:* The center section of the sculpture has circular shapes.

▶ Triangular Forms: *Sun God:* The crown on the head has triangular shapes.

▶ Free Forms: *The Walking Flower:* The entire sculpture is free-form.

■ For more examples of narrative art, see ***The National Museum of Women in the Arts Collection.***

Art Journal: Writing
Encourage students to write explanations of form in the Concepts section of their Art Journals. What else do they want to know about forms?

Aesthetic Perception

Seeing Like an Artist Discuss objects found around the classroom. Students may notice many shapes on the walls and in other places that are similar to the artwork. Have them point out circular, free-form, and triangular shapes.

Developing Visual Literacy Have students discuss what each artwork "says." What do they believe the artist was trying to portray by creating the artwork? Invite students to share any insights they may have that will contribute to their understanding of the artwork.
NSAE 2.c

Art History and Culture

Niki de Saint Phalle

Niki de Saint Phalle (niˊ kē də san fäl) (1930–2002) was best recognized for her oversized figures of women's bodies called the Nana series. Many of these sculptures explored ancient feminine deities and displayed vivid colors and exaggerated body forms. Her intention was to try and change and revalue the woman's body. Painting was often a form of therapy for Saint Phalle. She later worked on monuments, theatre, and movie making. *Sun God* was her first artwork displayed in the United States.

See pages 24–25 and 16–21 for more about art history and the subject matter.

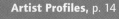
Artist Profiles, p. 14

◄ Artist Profile ►
Niki de Saint Phalle
1930-2002
Niki de Saint Phalle (niˊ kē da san fäl) was born Catherine Marie-Agnes in France, and moved to Connecticut with her family in 1933. They spent their summers in France, and her career was influenced by living in two cultures. As a child in New York, the artist often questioned authority and was transferred to different schools. After she graduated in 1948, de Saint Phalle moved to Paris and traveled throughout Europe where she was impressed with the idea that cathedrals were created by the collaboration of many artists. In 1960, she began her friendship and artistic partnership with Jean Tingueley, whom she married in 1971.

Web Connection
Visit www.nikidesaintphalle.com/biography.html to find out more about Niki de Saint Phalle. Have students share their ideas about her work.

LESSON 4 • Form   **79**

 **Teach**

Time: About 45 minutes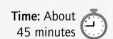

"How can you create a three-dimensional form with a two-dimensional sheet of paper?" "¿Cómo pueden crear una forma tridimensional con una hoja de papel bidimensional?"

- Discuss techniques for manipulating paper.

Practice

Materials: 9" × 12" paper

Alternate Materials: brown craft paper

- Distribute the materials and have students follow the directions on page 80.

Creative Expression

Materials: various found objects (paper towel rolls, small cardboard boxes, bottle caps, yarn, and felt), tissue paper, glue, markers

- Distribute the materials and have students follow the directions on page 81.
- Review the Technique Tips on page 221 for visual examples of using glue.
- Review the Activity Tips on page 236 for visual examples of creating forms.
  NSAE 1.d
- Create a class exhibition of finished works. Have students share their ideas about the exhibition.

Art Journal: Brainstorming

Have students brainstorm ideas for their paper sculptures and draw them in their Art Journals.

Using Form

Shapes and forms are similar. They both can be geometric or free-form. But they are different, too. **Shapes** are flat and are **two-dimensional.** They can be measured in only two ways: height and width.

Forms are not flat. They are **three-dimensional** and can be measured in three ways: height, width, and depth.

Below are five basic forms. You saw them in the sculptures in this lesson. Which shapes do these forms remind you of?

sphere   cone   pyramid   cylinder   free-for

Sculpture is three-dimensional art. The form of the sculpture is the positive space. The negative space is the area all around the sculpture.

Practice

Use a sheet of paper to make a form. It w have three dimensions.

1. Tear a sheet of paper in several place without tearing it completely apart.

2. Fold, bend, curl, and twist the paper make a form. Notice that it has three dimensions: height, width and depth.

Differentiated Instruction

Reteach

Have students look around the room and identify an object for each of the basic forms. Have them list the basic forms with the corresponding objects.

Special Needs

To help students understand the difference between shapes and forms during the lesson activity, have them create a wire or chenille stick version of their sculpture. Note how the two sculptures vary.

ELL Tips

Students may have difficulty following oral directions without some kind of visual support. Consider modeling the steps in creating the sculpture with the whole class. To review, write the steps on the chalkboard along with a quick sketch before asking students to complete the activity.

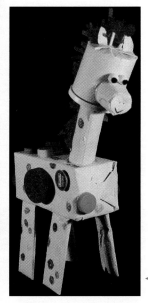

Think about how the sculpture appears to be three-dimensional.

 Avery Terry.
Age 8.

Creative Expression

What objects around you have three dimensions? Create a three-dimensional paper sculpture.

1. Have you ever seen a sculpture shaped like an animal form?

2. Notice the sculptures *The Walking Flower* and *Sun God*. What are the similarities and differences?

3. Find objects outdoors to be used to create an animal.

4. Use a rectangular box or juice can for the body. Use pieces of cardboard for the legs. You can draw texture on your animal sculpture.

Art Criticism

Describe What are the different materials you used to make your sculpture?

Analyze Point to the three dimensions in your sculpture. Identify the positive and negative spaces.

Interpret What does your sculpture make you think of?

Decide Why did you choose the animal form you used for the sculpture?

Unit 2 • Lesson 4   **81**

Reflect

Review and Assess

"What have you learned about the way artists use forms to create art?" "¿Qué han aprendido acerca de las maneras en que los artistas usan las formas para crear arte?"

Think

The sculpture has three dimensions: height, width, and depth.

- Use **Large Prints 39** *The Oregon Trail* and **40** *Vaquero* to have students compare the complex geometric shapes to the works in this lesson.

Informal Assessment

Art Journal: Critical Thinking
Have students answer the four art criticism questions—Describe, Analyze, Interpret, and Decide—in their Art Journals. In small groups, have students discuss the use of forms in their sculptures.
NSAE 5.c

- For standardized-format test practice using this lesson's art content, see pages 24–25 in *Reading and Writing Test Preparation.*

Art Across the Curriculum

Use these simple ideas to reinforce art concepts across the curriculum.

★ **Narrative** Explain to students that forms and shapes are similar. Have students look up words that are similar in the dictionary and write short sentences for each.

★ **Math** Have students count the number of three-dimensional objects in their book bags.

★ **Science** A mobile is a form. It moves with the air around it. Ask students to determine different objects that are powered by the wind.

★ **Social Studies** Explain to students that a mobile has the freedom to move with the air around it. Have students write a definition of *freedom*. Then have them write examples of things they are free to do.

★ **Technology** Have students use the paint tool to create a three-dimensional sculpture. Visit **SRAonline.com** for detailed instructions for this activity.

NSAE 6.b

Lesson 4 — Form

Wrap-Up

Extra! For the Art Specialist

Time: About 45 minutes

Focus

Use *Transparency 10* and *Large Prints 39 The Oregon Trail* and *40 Vaquero* to demonstrate how artists use three-dimensional forms to create sculptures. Guide students to look closely at the artwork to see the basic forms in its composition. Have students point out spheres, cubes, cylinders, cones, and/or pyramids that make up the artwork. What materials do you think the artist used to make this artwork?

Teach

Have students follow the directions to complete the design on their playground. What kind of forms did they decide to use in their designs?

Reflect

Have students evaluate their art using the four steps of art criticism. Have them describe two- and three-dimensional objects around the room.

Alternate Activity

Materials:
- 11" × 14" pieces of posterboard, one per group of 3 or 4 students
- 9" × 12" pieces of colored construction paper
- 6" × 9" pieces of colored construction paper
- scissors
- craft tacky glue
- wooden craft sticks, chenille sticks, etc.

1. Have students think about their favorite pieces of playground equipment (parallel bars, slides, swings, and so on).

2. Tell students they are going to design their own ideal playground and construct a model of it.

3. Divide students into groups of three or four to construct their playgrounds.

Research in Art Education

"The elementary classroom offers an environment that can foster creativity, independence, self-awareness, self-expression, and an understanding of the visual world. Education through art can provide opportunities for exploring one's creativity, for communicating ideas, and enabling students to express themselves through the use of materials, processes, and tools" (Andra Nyman, "Cultural Content, Identity, and Program Development: Approaches to Art Education for Elementary Educators," in *Contemporary Issues in Art Education,* edited by Y. Gaudelius and P. Spiers, 61–69. New Jersey: Prentice Hall, 2002).

NSAE 1.d

Assessment

Use the following rubric to evaluate the artwork students make in the Creative Expression activity and to assess students' understanding of three-dimensional forms.

Have students complete page 27 or 28 in their *Assessment* books.

	Art History and Culture	Aesthetic Perception	Creative Expression	Art Criticism
3 POINTS	The student demonstrates knowledge of the lives and artwork of Fernand Léger and Niki de Saint Phalle.	The student accurately identifies the use of three-dimensional forms used by artists.	The student effectively plans and creates a three-dimensional animal form using collected objects.	The student evaluates his or her own work using the four steps of art criticism.
2 POINTS	The student cannot identify the cultural purpose of the lives and artwork of Fernand Léger and Niki de Saint Phalle.	The student shows emerging awareness of three-dimensional forms used by artists.	The student shows some ability to plan and create a three-dimensional animal form using collected objects.	The student attempts to evaluate his or her own work using the four steps of art criticism.
1 POINT	The student demonstrates no understanding of the lives and artwork of Fernand Léger and Niki de Saint Phalle.	The student shows no awareness of three-dimensional forms used by artists.	The student shows no understanding of how to plan and create a three-dimensional animal form using collected objects.	The student does not attempt to evaluate his or her own work.

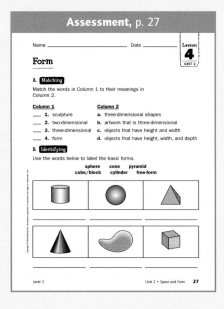

Assessment, p. 27

Name _____ Date _____

Form — Lesson 4 UNIT 2

A. Matching
Match the words in Column 1 to their meanings in Column 2.

Column 1
___ 1. sculpture
___ 2. two-dimensional
___ 3. three-dimensional
___ 4. form

Column 2
a. three-dimensional shapes
b. artwork that is three-dimensional
c. objects that have height and width
d. objects that have height, width, and depth

B. Identifying
Use the words below to label the basic forms.

sphere   cone   pyramid
cube/block   cylinder   free-form

Level 3 — Unit 2 • Space and Form   **27**

Lesson 5

Overview

Relief Sculpture

Lesson 5 introduces sculptures by making raised forms on flat surfaces.

Objectives

Art History and Culture

To compare works by artists from different cultures

Creative Expression

To plan and create a ceramic relief tile

Aesthetic Perception

To identify the difference between relief and freestanding sculpture

Art Criticism

To evaluate own work using the four steps of art criticism

Vocabulary ⭐ Vocabulary

Review the following vocabulary words with students before beginning the lesson.

freestanding *autoestable*—a three-dimensional work of art surrounded by negative space

relief sculpture *escultura en relieve*—a work of art in which forms project from a flat surface

See page 89B for additional vocabulary and Spanish vocabulary resources.

Art Journal: Vocabulary

Have students add these words to the Vocabulary section of their Art Journals.

Lesson Materials
- 9" × 12" paper
- glue
- yarn
- clay about the size of a baseball for each student
- rolling pins or thick dowel sticks
- muslin
- 6" × 9" cardboard frame
- pencils
- paper clips
- various textured objects
- sketch paper
- tape
- containers of water and slip
- slip brushes

Alternate Materials:
- glue and foil relief

Program Resources
- *Reading and Writing Test Prep.*, pp. 26–27
- *Transparency 11*
- *Artist Profiles*, pp. 68, 76
- *Animals Through History Time Line*
- *Assessment*, pp. 29–30
- *Large Prints 39* The Oregon Trail and *40* Vaquero
- *Art Around the World Collection*

Concept Trace
Relief Sculpture
Introduced: Level 2, Unit 2, Lesson 2

Reinforced: Level 4, Unit 2, Lesson 2

Lesson 5 Arts Integration NSAE 6.a

Theatre

Complete Unit 2, Lesson 5, on pages 26–27 of *Theatre Arts Connections.*

Theatre Arts Connections, p. 26

Objectives

Lesson 5 A Plot Has a High Point

Focus   Time: About 5 minutes

"In this lesson we will perform the high point of a play as Reader's Theatre." *(See page T9 for more about Reader's Theatre.)*

Activate Prior Knowledge

➤ Tell students, "I am going to tell you the beginning and middle of a story. Some bears catch and are going to eat a lonely man in Alaska. To save himself, he promises them a feast. He paints red stripes on his body. The villagers say 'He's foolish' because the bears might eat him."

➤ Ask students, "Do you think the next part of the plot will be exciting? Why?" *(yes, because the bears could eat him)* Explain that this part is the high point of the plot.

Teach   Time: About 15 minutes

Prepare Hand out the "A Plot Has a High Point" Warm-Up. Have students remain seated.

Lead

Read the lines aloud. Have students close their eyes and imagine animal is feeling and thinking.

Music

SPOTLIGHT on MUSIC Solo work can interact with its accompaniment from hardly at all to the extent it almost seems like a duet. Listen to *What a Wonderful World* by George Weiss and Bob Thiele, performed by Louis Armstrong. When he sings, does he blend in with the background accompaniment, or does his voice stand out as clearly as a relief sculpture?

Movement & Dance

Have half of the class create a strong unified wall across the classroom. The second half of the class will show the idea of *relief.* One at a time, the students will enter, each person will decorate the wall by attaching or placing themselves to it, so they are sticking out of the wall. Include different levels, and geometric and free-form shapes.

Focus

Time: About 10 minutes

Activate Prior Knowledge

"Imagine you are holding a quarter in your hand. How does the surface of the coin feel?"

"Vamos a imaginar que ustedes sostienen una moneda de 25¢ en sus manos. ¿Cómo se siente la superficie de la moneda?"

■ Discuss students' responses. Point out that coins have raised surfaces.

Using Literature ⭐ Reading

■ Read *Our Money* by Bornemann Spies. Have students discuss the use of relief sculptures in the book.

Thematic Connection ⭐ Reading

■ **Sharing Stories:** Have students imagine they are the person in *Hunting Scene on Handle from a large bowl,* and then write a short story. Have them create dialogue for their character.

Introduce the Art

Look

"Let's take a look at the two sculptures."

"Vamos a observar detalladamente las dos esculturas".

Comparing and Contrasting ⭐ Reading

■ Have students describe the subject matter in each sculpture. Both have areas raised from a flat surface, the center of interest in the middle and both include human form. *Presentation of Captives to a Maya Ruler* includes several figures and has areas of high and low relief. *Hunting Scene on a handle from a large bowl* has a flat background with several figures in low relief.

🏺 Art History and Culture

Mayan relief carvings were usually made from stone. *Presentation of Captives to a Maya Ruler* was made from limestone and found near the Usumacinta River Valley.

 Web Connection

Visit **www.mayankids.com/mkintro.htm** to learn more about Mayan history and culture.

Relief Sculpture

◀ **Artist Unknown.** (Mayan). *Presentation of Captives to a Maya Ruler.* c. 785.

Limestone with traces of paint. 45 $\frac{3}{8}$ × 35 inches (114 × 89 cm). Kimbell Art Museum, Fort Worth, Texas.

Look at the artwork on these two pages. Both seem to have freestanding figures. *Presentation of Captives to a Maya Ruler* is a limestone relief sculpture which was created around A.D. 783. *Roman Hunting Scene* is also a relief sculpture that was created around the second century.

🏺 Art History and Culture

Artists create relief sculptures by making raised forms on flat surfaces. Reliefs are often used for decoration.

🏺 Art History and Culture

Presentation of Captives to a Maya Ruler

It is unclear exactly where this relief was located. *Presentation of Captives to a Maya Ruler* was created in the late classic period between A.D. 700 and A.D. 900. It may have been a wall panel inside a building or a lintel over an entrance. Lintels like this were frequently used to record important domestic events. The Mayan glyphs have been translated. This inscription tells about the capture of a lord named Balam-Ahau by another lord, Ah Chac Max, that occurred in A.D. 783.

See pages 24–25 and 16–21 for more about art history and subject matter.

Artist Profiles, p. 76

Artist Profile

Presentation of Captives to a Maya Ruler

The Mayan people—founders of a vast, powerful, and ancient kingdom—have historically lived throughout an enormous geographic area of what is today Mexico and Central America. Historians can date evidence of the Mayan culture back to 700 B.C. Mayan civilization had a complex written language, sophisticated methods of producing crops, accurate calendars and other methods of keeping time, and an impressive knowledge of astronomy.

Artist unknown. (Mayan). *Presentation of*

▲ **Artist Unknown.**
(Roman). *Hunting
Scene on Handle from
a large bowl.* Second
century or later.

Silver. 5 × 14 3/8 × 35 inches
(13 × 38 × 89 cm.). The
Metropolitan Museum of Art,
New York, New York.

Study both works of art to find the following areas
of relief.

▶ Find the areas that appear to be raised. Trace
   them with your finger.

▶ Where are the flat areas?

▶ Which relief seems to be the highest?

▶ In which work do the figures seem most realistic?

 Aesthetic Perception

Design Awareness Look closely at both sides of a coin.
Which areas are raised? Why do you think the background
is empty?

Art History and Culture

Hunting Scene on Handle from a large bowl

Hunting Scene on Handle from a large bowl is a form of ancient
Roman art. Roman art was influenced by many things, including
the countries the Romans ruled such as Greece, Egypt, and Africa.
Romans had many different art forms that usually displayed the
power of an important person such as an emperor, a god, a
goddess, or common people. Romans used four styles for
displaying their art. One style used realistic-looking scenes that
looked like a view through a window. Roman sculpture was used to
decorate public and private
buildings, and much of it was
used as official propaganda.

See pages 24–25 and 16–21
for more about art history
and subject matter.

Artist Profiles, p. 68

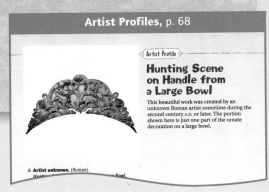

◇ Artist Profile ◇

**Hunting Scene
on Handle from
a Large Bowl**

This beautiful work was created by an
unknown Roman artist sometime during the
second century A.D. or later. The portion
shown here is just one part of the ornate
decoration on a large bowl.

▲ Artist unknown. (Roman).
Hunting ...

NSAE 1.b; 2.a; 2.b; 3.a
Study

▶ Relief: The figures, trees, animals, and
   people in *Presentation of Captives to a
   Maya Ruler* are raised in relief. The people,
   curtains, and glyphs in *Hunting Scene on
   a Handle from a large bowl* are raised in
   relief.

▶ Flat: *Presentation of Captives to a Maya
   Ruler* and *Hunting Scene on a Handle from
   a large bowl*: all the areas surrounding the
   people are flat.

▶ Answers will vary.

▶ Lifelike Figures: The figures in *Presentation
   of Captives to a Maya Ruler* and *Hunting
   Scene on a Handle from a large bowl* have
   figures that seem lifelike.

■ For more examples of art from Latin
   America, see the **Art Around the World
   Collection.**

Art Journal: Writing

Encourage students to write
explanations of relief sculpture in the
Concepts section of their Art Journals.
What else do they want to know about
relief sculptures?

Aesthetic Perception

Design Awareness Discuss with students
what coins look like. Have them look closely
at both sides of coins. Explain to students
that coins are excellent examples of areas
that are raised, similar to relief sculptures.
Ask students for any ideas as to why the
background of the coin is empty.

Developing Visual Literacy Have students
discuss what each artwork says. What do
they believe the artist was trying to convey?
Invite students to share any personal
information or experiences that contribute
to their understanding of the artwork.

NSAE 5.a

Web Connection

Visit **www.dia.org/collections/ancient/rome/
rome.html** to learn more about ancient Roman art.

Teach

Time: About 45 minutes

"How can you use yarn to create areas of relief?" "¿Cómo pueden usar hilo para crear áreas de relieve?"

- Discuss information on the use of yarn to create relief sculpture on page 84.

Practice

Materials: 9" × 12" paper, glue, yarn

- Distribute materials and have students follow the directions on page 84 for creating relief.

Creative Expression

Materials: clay about the size of a baseball for each student, rolling pins or thick dowel sticks, muslin, 6" × 9" cardboard frame, pencils, paper clips, various textured objects, sketch paper, tape, containers of water and slip, slip brushes

Alternate Materials: glue and foil relief

- Distribute the materials and have students follow the directions on page 85.
- Review the Technique Tips on page 226 for information about working with clay.
- Review the Activity Tips on page 237 for visual examples of creating a relief sculpture.

NSAE 1.d

Art Journal: Brainstorming

Have students brainstorm ideas for things they want to show in their self-portrait, and then write the ideas in their Art Journals. Have students plan how they will show their relief sculpture in the Creative Expression activity.

relief sculpture

free standing sculpture

Creating Relief Sculpture

Artwork in which forms stand out from a flat surface is called **relief sculpture.**

Most three-dimensional sculptures are **freestanding.** They have empty, negative space all around them. Relief sculptures, however, are not freestanding. The background in a relief sculpture is flat, and the positive areas are raised.

Coins are one example of relief that we see every day. What other examples can you think of?

Practice

Write your name in relief. Use glue and yarn.

1. Make a design with thick lines of yarn glued onto a piece of paper.
2. Allow the glue to dry for a few hours.

Differentiated Instruction

Reteach

Have students look outside and find five examples of relief. Ask them to list their examples and describe the areas of relief they found.

Special Needs

Students with disabilities learn best when information is presented in multiple ways. Have actual examples of relief sculpture for students to feel as they begin this lesson.

ELL Tips

You may wish to use the self-portraits of students to review or introduce vocabulary about body parts. Depending on the students' level of English proficiency, you may wish to introduce the more finely detailed vocabulary for body parts, such as *eyelashes, forehead, wrist,* and so on.

Think about how this student's relief sculpture is different from one that is freestanding.

Creative Expression

What would you like to show in a self-portrait? Create a self-portrait in relief tile.

1. Describe what is happening in both of the relief works. Do some of the areas appear to stick out more than others?

2. If you could make a relief sculpture that told a story about you, what would you put on the relief?

3. Roll out a slab of clay and create a relief of objects or a picture of a person who is important to you.

4. With a pencil draw the design into the clay. Press lightly so as not to cut through the clay.

Art Criticism

Describe What shapes did you use? What elements in the tile make it a relief?

Analyze Which areas are in relief? What are a few facts about the artwork?

Interpret What words would you use to describe your self-portrait? How would the work change if there were no raised areas?

Decide What do you like best about your relief? Why?

Unit 2 • Lesson 5   **85**

Review and Assess

"What do you know about relief sculpture?"
"¿Qué saben acerca de la escultura en relieve?"

Think

This student artist's sculpture was created on a flat surface. A freestanding sculpture is surrounded by negative space.

■ Use **Large Print 40** *Vaquero* to have students compare areas of relief.

Informal Assessment

Art Journal: Critical Thinking

Have students answer the four art criticism questions—Describe, Analyze, Interpret, and Decide—in their Art Journals. In small groups, have students discuss the areas of relief in their self-portrait tiles.
NSAE 5.b

■ For standardized-format test practice using this lesson's art content, see pages 24–25 in *Reading and Writing Test Preparation*.

Art Across the Curriculum

Use these simple ideas to reinforce art concepts across the curriculum.

★ **Narrative Writing** Have students look at the relief tile portraits they made and write some words that tell a little about who they are.

★ **Math** Have students guess how many hours it may have taken to create *Presentation of Captives to a Maya Ruler.*

★ **Science** *Hunting Scene on a Handle* shows people who appear to be muscular. Have students hold a book in each hand, raising and lowering the books from their shoulders. Do this five times and discuss what they felt.

★ **Social Studies** During the period of *Presentation of Captives to a Maya Ruler*, the method of communicating was often to write on the walls. List some methods of communication that we use today.

★ **Technology** Have students create a three-dimensional relief sculpture using the paint tool. Visit **SRAonline.com** for detailed instructions for this activity.

NSAE 6.b

Lesson 5 — Relief Sculpture
Wrap-Up

Extra! For the Art Specialist
Time: About 45 minutes

Focus

Use *Transparency 11* and *Large Print 40 Vaquero*. Have students compare areas of relief. Explain to students that a relief is an artwork that is raised from the background. Ask students if the artwork is a high relief, where the figures are almost completely raised from the background, or a low relief, where the design is only slightly raised from the background. Do the students think the artwork seems to tell a story? If so, what do they think it is about?

Teach

Have students follow the directions to complete their low relief sculptures.

Reflect

Have students evaluate their art using the four steps of art criticism. Encourage them to locate and describe other relief in objects around the classroom.

Alternate Activity

Materials:
- 5" × 7" pieces of posterboard
- 4" × 6" pieces of posterboard
- posterboard scraps
- pencils and erasers
- scissors, glue
- thinned white glue
- paintbrushes
- 7" × 9" pieces of aluminum foil
- dark shoe polish in applicator bottles
- facial tissues

1. Tell students they will make low relief sculptures of an insect.

2. Have students draw their insects on the 4" × 6" pieces of posterboard. Students will cut out their insects and glue them onto the 5" × 7" pieces of posterboard.

3. Students will brush a coat of the thinned glue over their insects and the background posterboard. Next they will lay a sheet of foil over their reliefs and smooth the foil, working from the center to smooth out any air bubbles. Students will carefully fold extra foil to the back of the relief.

4. Students will apply shoe polish to the foil, using a tissue to rub off excess polish.

Research in Art Education

Research has shown that "learning happens best when kids have fun, and the arts are fun for kids." It is important to remember that the arts can act "as catalysts for learning other subject areas across the curriculum," but they are also valuable in their own right ("Arts Literacy for Business," in *The Vision for Arts Education in the 21st Century*).

Assessment

Use the following rubric to evaluate the artwork students make in the Creative Expression activity and to assess students' understanding of the differences between relief and freestanding sculpture.

	Art History and Culture	Aesthetic Perception	Creative Expression	Art Criticism
3 POINTS	The student effectively compares works of art by artists from different cultures.	The student accurately identifies the difference between relief and freestanding sculptures.	The student effectively plans and creates a ceramic relief tile.	The student evaluates his or her own work using the four steps of art criticism.
2 POINTS	The student demonstrates some ability to compare works of art by artists from different cultures.	The student shows emerging awareness of the difference between relief and freestanding sculptures.	The student shows some awareness of how to plan and create a ceramic relief tile.	The student attempts to evaluate his or her own work using the four steps of art criticism.
1 POINT	The student cannot compare works of art by artists from different cultures.	The student cannot identify relief and freestanding sculptures.	The student shows no understanding of how to plan and create a ceramic relief tile.	The student does not attempt to evaluate his or her own work.

Have students complete page 29 or 30 in their *Assessment* books.

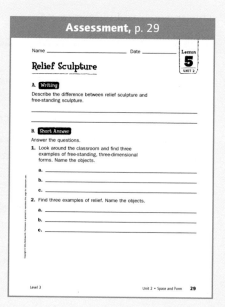

Assessment, p. 29

Name _____ Date _____
Relief Sculpture — Lesson 5 UNIT 2

A. Writing
Describe the difference between relief sculpture and free-standing sculpture.

B. Short Answer
Answer the questions.
1. Look around the classroom and find three examples of free-standing, three-dimensional forms. Name the objects.
   a. _____
   b. _____
   c. _____
2. Find three examples of relief. Name the objects.
   a. _____
   b. _____
   c. _____

Level 3 — Unit 2 • Space and Form **29**

Lesson 6 Overview

Three-Dimensional Art to Wear

Lesson 6 introduces jewelry, which is three-dimensional artwork that is made for people to wear.

Objectives

 Art History and Culture

To demonstrate knowledge about jewelry from two cultures

 Creative Expression

To plan and create a medallion in relief

 Aesthetic Perception

To identify three-dimensional forms in jewelry

 Art Criticism

To evaluate own work using the four steps of art criticism

Vocabulary Vocabulary

Review the following vocabulary words with students before beginning the lesson.

jeweler *joyero*—an artist who designs and creates jewelry

jewelry *joyas*—three-dimensional ornaments such as rings, bracelets, and earrings

See page 89B for additional vocabulary and Spanish vocabulary resources.

 Art Journal: Vocabulary

Have students add these words to the Vocabulary section of their Art Journals.

Lesson Materials

- assorted low-relief objects, such as paper clips, cardboard, toothpicks, buttons, and pasta, 8" × 8" heavy-duty aluminum foil
- 4" × 4" cardboard
- scissors, glue
- 6" × 6" heavy-duty aluminum foil
- pieces of yarn (about 24")
- hole punch

Alternate Materials:
- objects found in nature
- wood or pasta

Program Resources

- *Reading and Writing Test Prep.*, pp. 28–29
- *Transparency 12*
- *Artist Profiles*, pp. 73, 74
- *Animals Through History Time Line*
- *Assessment*, pp. 31–32
- *Large Prints 39* The Oregon Trail and *40* Vaquero
- *Art Around the World Collection*

Concept Trace

Three-Dimensional Art to Wear

Introduced: Level 2, Unit 2, Lesson 2

Reinforced: Level 4, Unit 4, Lesson 1

Lesson 6 Arts Integration NSAE 6.a

Theatre

Complete Unit 2, Lesson 6, on pages 28–33 of *Theatre Arts Connections.*

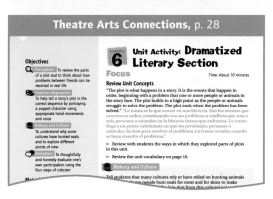

Music

 As we hear more music from other cultures, we learn there are certain songs to accompany celebrations and daily tasks. Listen to *Dragon Dance.* During a parade of a dragon in China on holidays, a group of people make boisterous music to drive away evil spirits and provide good luck for the new year.

Movement & Dance

Jewelry used as musical instruments is a universal idea and can be seen in many cultures around the world. In Africa, China, Persia, and India, for example, dancers attach bells and shakers to their ankles, wrists, waists, and hips. Their movements help create rhythmic sound and the bells, jewels, and beads also serve to decorate their bodies. Attach small bells to elastic, place them on the wrists or ankles, and explore moving rhythmically with them.

Focus

Time: About 10 minutes

Activate Prior Knowledge

"Think about the different kinds of jewelry you have seen people wear for decoration. Can you name some? Can you describe how the jewelry looks?" "Piensen acerca de los diferentes tipos de joyas que hayan visto que las personas usan como decoración. ¿Pueden nombrar algunas? ¿Pueden describer cómo son?"

Using Literature ⭐ Reading

- Read *Fire Talking* by Patricia Polacco. Have students discuss the use of three-dimensional art in the book.

Thematic Connection ⭐ Reading

Shapes: Encourage students to discuss the shapes they recognize in the jewelry. Have students tell you whether they see any geometrical or free-form shapes.

Introduce the Art

"Let's look at the two works of art." "Vamos a observar detalladamente las dos obras de arte".

Compare and Contrast

- Have students make a list of similarities and differences in the two jewelry pieces. Both use round shapes and formal balance. *Necklace* is meant to be worn around the neck. *Côte d'Ivoire*, which is also a necklace, is to be worn by the chief of a clan. *Côte d'Ivoire* is made of disc-shaped and rectangular beads. The beads usually symbolize objects that have hidden meanings.

NSAE 2.c

 ## Art History and Culture

Necklace was made by an unknown Berber artist in the Rif region of Morocco. Berber silversmiths are primarily male and Jewish.

🖥 **Web Connection**

Visit **www.afro.com/children/discover/morocco/morocco.html** to learn more about the Moroccan history and culture.

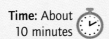 **Lesson 6**

Three-Dimensional Art to Wear

Look at the necklace from Morocco and the necklace from the Ivory Coast. They are both forms of three-dimensional art. These pieces of jewelry also have raised areas and were made from a variety of materials.

▲ **Artist unknown.** (Morocco). *Necklace.* Twentieth century.

Beads and silver alloy.
14 inches long (35.5 cm.).
Private collection.

 Art History and Culture

A jeweler creates decorative, three-dimensional forms to wear.

 Art History and Culture

Morocco

Necklace was made by an unknown Berber artist in the Rif region of Morocco. The Berbers of North Africa live in the rugged Atlas, Rif, and Kabylia mountains and in the arid lands at the edge of the Saharan Desert. Berber silversmiths are primarily male and Jewish. *Necklace* was made with a variety of materials, including coral beads and stones. It was created in a land where the people are mainly farmers or belong to nomadic tribes. Women wear veils to cover their faces and do not mix with men in the open-air markets.

See pages 24–25 and 16–21 for more about art history and subject matter.

Artist Profiles, p. 73

▷ **Artist Profile** ▷

Necklace

This necklace was made by an unknown Berber artist in the Rif region of Morocco. The Berbers of North Africa live in the rugged Atlas, Rif, and Kabylia Mountains and the arid lands at the edge of the Sahara Desert. Berbers create art that is more Islamic than African in nature. As late as the fifteenth century, Jewish goldsmiths and silversmiths fleeing the Spanish Inquisition settled in northern Africa and introduced the jewelry-making techniques that are still used in the region.

▲ **Artist unknown.** (Morocco). *Necklace.* Twentieth century.

◀ **Artist Unknown.**
(Ivory Coast). *Cote
d' Ivoire.*
Gold. c. 1900
....
118 ½ inches (300 cm.).
Museum of Fine Arts,
Houston, Texas.

Study both works of art.

▶ Find areas where the designs are raised.

▶ What do you think the necklaces will sound
like when worn?

▶ Find the free-form shapes.

▶ Where are the round shapes?

Aesthetic Perception

Seeing Like an Artist Look around your classroom. Is
anyone wearing jewelry? What color is it?

Art History and Culture

Ivory Coast (Côte d'Ivoire)

The gold necklace from the Ivory Coast comes from the Baule clan
and was worn by a Baule chief. Baule necklaces can be easily
distinguished from other African clans by their circular and
rectangular beads. Some of the beads are called *srala*, or bamboo
door. The bamboo door is said to symbolize the chief. Disc-shaped
beads represent a form of marriage payment for the man to obtain
his bride. The man presented the beads to her family, who in turn
provided part of the family treasure to be handed down from one
generation to the next.

See pages 24–25 and 16–21
for more about art history
and subject matter.

Artist Profiles, p. 74

◈ Artist Profile ◈

Necklace

The artist, or goldsmith, who created this
necklace was a member of the Baule culture
of Côte d'Ivoire, formerly called the Ivory
Coast, West Africa. The Baule people are
one of the largest ethnic groups in the
country of Côte d'Ivoire, numbering more
than one million individuals, and they have
maintained their cultural traditions to the
present day. The culture of the Baule people
is influenced by their belief that every
person lived in a spirit world before being
born, and thus everyone is influenced in
this life by spirits and the supernatural.
The majority of Baule people live in small
fishing or farming villages.

◀ **Artist unknown.** (Ivory Coast).
Cote d' Ivoire. c. 1900.

Study NSAE 1.b; 2.a; 2.b; 3.a

▶ Raised designs: *Necklace:* Rectangular
pieces with raised designs are found
throughout the necklace. *Côte d'Ivoire* also
has raised pieces on the circular and
rectangular shapes.

▶ Sound: *Necklace:* It will jingle when worn.

▶ Some of the designs on the discs are free-
form shapes.

▶ Many of the discs are circles and some of
the beads are spheres.

■ For more examples of art from Africa, see
the *Art Around the World Collection.*

Art Journal: Writing
Encourage students to write
explanations of three-dimensional art in
the Concepts section of their Art Journals.
What else do they want to know about
three-dimensional art?

Aesthetic Perception

Design Awareness Discuss with students
different types of jewelry. Have students look
around the classroom to see if anyone is
wearing jewelry. Ask them to describe the
color and the materials of which it is made.
Many materials can be used to create
jewelry, including gold, bronze, silver, and
aluminum. Ask students to describe any
other materials that are used to create and
design jewelry.

Developing Visual Literacy Discuss what each
work of art "says." What meaning was the
artist trying to convey? Invite students to
share any personal information that
contributes to their understanding of the
works of art.
NSAE 2.c

Web Connection
Visit **www.hcjb.org/kidsweb/kids&countries/
morocco.htm** to learn more about the Ivory Coast's
history and culture.

Teach

Time: About 45 minutes

"How can you create areas of relief on a flat surface?" "¿Cómo pueden crear áreas de relieve sobre una superficie plana?"

- Discuss the use of objects to create a foil relief.

Practice

Materials: assorted low-relief objects such as paper clips, yarn, toothpicks, buttons, pasta, and cardboard, 8" × 8" heavy-duty aluminum foil

Alternate Materials: objects found in nature

- Distribute materials and have students follow the directions on page 88 for demonstrating areas of relief.

Creative Expression

Materials: 4" × 4" cardboard, scissors, assorted low-relief objects, 6" × 6" heavy-duty aluminum foil, pieces of yarn or ribbon (about 24")

Alternate Materials: wood or pasta

- Ask students if they have ever worn jewelry for an occasion. Did wearing jewelry make the occasion seem more special?

- Distribute the materials and have students follow the directions on page 89.

- Review the Technique Tips on page 228 for using aluminum foil.

- Review the Activity Tips on page 237 for creating three-dimensional art.

NSAE 1.d

Art Journal: Brainstorming

Have students brainstorm ideas to create areas of relief and write those ideas in their Art Journals. Then have students plan how they will show relief in the Creative Expression activity.

Designing and Making Jewelry

A piece of **jewelry** is three-dimensional artwork that is made for people to wear. A **jeweler** is an artist who designs and makes jewelry. The art of making jewelry has been around for about 4000 years. Rings and necklaces are forms of jewelry. Can you think of any other forms?

Varieties of materials are used to make jewelry. Gold, silver, and gemstones are used most often. Jewelry can also be made with wood, glass, leather, beads, and paper. Can you think of any other materials that are used to make jewelry?

Practice

Use a found object and foil to practice making a foil relief.

1. Place foil on top of an object such as a button to get the feel of stretching foil gently. Start in the middle and use your fingers to gently press and smooth the foil across the flat surface and over the ridges.

2. Remove the foil from the object and you will have the object's impression.

Differentiated Instruction

Reteach

Have students look around the classroom to find five areas of relief. Ask them to list the objects and describe the relief areas.

Special Needs

Help foster students' awareness of others by giving them the option of creating their medallion for a family member or friend.

ELL Tips

Hands-on projects provide a lot of support for students. To maximize language and learning, encourage all your students to talk about what they are doing. You may wish to pair or group students while they work to ensure that everyone has a chance to talk about their artwork.

◀ **Ashley Blake.**
Age 9.

Think about what makes a medallion a relief.

 Creative Expression

What type of jewelry would you like to wear? Create a medallion.

1. Think about small objects that have interesting shapes.

2. Cut a piece of cardboard into a geometric shape. Arrange objects on top of the cardboard in different ways. Glue your favorite arrangement to the cardboard.

3. When dry, cover the surface with foil.

4. Punch a hole at the top of your design. Pass a piece of yarn or ribbon through the hole, and tie the ends to make a necklace.

Art Criticism

Describe What objects did you use to create the raised areas of the relief?

Analyze What kind of shapes did you use to create your relief work?

Interpret When would you wear a medallion?

Decide If you could create another medallion, what would you change?

Reflect

 Time: About 5 minutes

Review and Assess

■ "How can you use three-dimensional design to create jewelry?" "¿Cómo pueden usar un diseño tridimensional para crear joyas?"

Think

The student used an object with round shapes to create relief.

■ Have students look for jewelry in *Large Print 40 Vaquero.*

Informal Assessment
NSAE 1.b; 2.a; 3.a; 5.c

Art Journal: Critical Thinking
Have students answer the four art criticism questions—Describe, Analyze, Interpret, and Decide—in their Art Journals. In small groups, have students discuss the use of relief in their medallions.

■ For standardized-format test practice using this lesson's art content, see pages 28–29 in *Reading and Writing Test Preparation.*

Art Across the Curriculum

Use these simple ideas to reinforce art concepts across the curriculum.

★ **Narrative Writing** Have students write a short story about what they think it would be like to live in Morocco.

★ **Math** The necklace from the Ivory Coast is a valuable piece of jewelry. Have students imagine they receive $5 a week for an allowance. Have them decide how they will spend it and how much of it they will save.

★ **Science** Explain to students that some artists use pieces from old jewelry to create new jewelry. Have students list some items that can be recycled, then make another list of what could be made from the recycled things.

★ **Social Studies** Have students locate the Ivory Coast on a map.

★ **Technology** Have students use the paint tool to design and create a medallion in relief. Students can include squares, rectangles, triangles, and free-form shapes in the medallion. Visit **SRAonline.com** for detailed instructions for this activity.

Three-Dimensional Art to Wear

Extra! For the Art Specialist

Time: About 45 minutes

Focus

Use *Transparency 12* and discuss types of body adornment with students. Ask students why people wear jewelry and what some purposes of jewelry are.

Teach

Have students follow the directions to complete their necklaces.

Reflect

Have students evaluate their art using the four steps of art criticism. Encourage students to discuss the type of jewelry they or their classmates are wearing.

Alternate Activity

Materials:
- low-fire clay rolled into 3" diameter balls, two per student
- tools for working with clay
- pieces of plastic to work clay on
- thick spaghetti strands, two or three per student
- waxed dental floss, 24" per student
- watercolors (optional)

1. Tell students they will make clay beads and medallions to string on a necklace.

2. Flatten a ball of clay to make a medallion. Make a hole at the top. Decorate the medallion.

3. Use the second ball of clay to make a pinch pot to hold the beads and medallion for firing. The beads can be fired while strung on the spaghetti strands, which will dissolve in the kiln.

4. After the beads and medallions are fired, string them on the waxed dental floss. The beads may be painted with watercolors, if desired.

Research in Art Education

"At a time when development of thinking skills is particularly important the presence of a program that fosters flexibility, promotes a tolerance for ambiguity, encourages risk taking and depends upon the exercise of judgment outside the sphere of rules is an especially valuable resource" (Eisner, Elliot W. *The Arts and the Creation of Mind*. New Haven: Yale Univ. Press, 2002).

Assessment

Use the following rubric to evaluate the artwork students make in the Creative Expression activity and to assess students' understanding of three-dimensional forms of jewelry.

Have students complete page 31 or 32 in their *Assessment* books.

	Art History and Culture	Aesthetic Perception	Creative Expression	Art Criticism
3 POINTS	The student demonstrates knowledge about jewelry from the two cultures.	The student accurately identifies three-dimensional forms in jewelry.	The student effectively plans and creates a medallion in relief.	The student evaluates his or her own work using the four steps of art criticism.
2 POINTS	The student demonstrates some understanding about jewelry from the two cultures.	The student shows emerging awareness of three-dimensional forms in jewelry.	The student shows some ability to plan and create a medallion in relief.	The student attempts to evaluate his or her own work using the four steps of art criticism.
1 POINT	The student cannot identify jewelry from the two cultures.	The student cannot identify three-dimensional forms in jewelry.	The student shows no understanding of how to plan and create a medallion in relief.	The student does not attempt to evaluate his or her own work.

Assessment, p. 31

Name _____ Date _____

Lesson 6 UNIT 2

Three Dimensional Art to Wear

A Vocabulary
Use the words below to complete the sentences.
jeweler   forms   jewelry

1. An artist who designs and makes jewelry is called a _____.
2. Rings and necklaces are _____ of jewelry.
3. Three-dimensional art that is made for people to wear as decoration is called _____.

B Short Answer
Name five examples of jewelry that is worn by people.
1. _____
2. _____
3. _____
4. _____
5. _____

C Writing
Look at the necklace. Name and describe the shapes and materials used by the artist.
_____
_____
_____

Level 3   Unit 2 • Space and Form   **31**

appliqué—decoration made from cloth cutouts **aplicación**—decoración hecha de cortes de tela

background—the part of the picture that appears to be the farthest from the viewer **fondo**—la parte de la pintura que parece ser más lejano del espectador

depth—the appearance of distance on a flat surface **profundidad**—el sentimiento de distancia en una superficie plana

foreground—the part of the picture that appears closest to the viewer **frente**—la parte de la pintura que aparece más cerca al espectador

form—the element of art that is three-dimensional and encloses space **forma**—el elemento del arte que es tridimensional y encierra espacio

freestanding—a three-dimensional work of art surrounded by negative space **autoestable**—obra de arte tridimensional rodeada de espacio negativo

jeweler—an artist who designs and creates jewelry **joyero**—un artista que disená y crea joyas

jewelry—three-dimensional ornaments such as rings, bracelets, and earrings **joyas**—ornamentos tridimensional como anillos, brazaletes y pendientes

negative spaces—empty spaces surrounding shapes and forms **espacios negativos**—espacios vacíos rodeando figuras y formas

overlap—the placement of one object over another so that part of the second object is hidden **superponer**—la colocación de un objeto sobre otro para que parte del segundo objeto esté escondido

positive spaces—shapes or forms in two- and three-dimensional art **espacios positivos**—figuras y formas en arte bi- y tri- dimensional

relief sculpture—a work of art in which forms project from a flat surface **escultura en relieve**—obra de arte en que formas se proyectan desde una superficie plana

sculpture—three-dimensional work of art created out of wood, stone, metal, or clay by carving, welding, casting, or modeling **escultura**—obra de arte tridimensional creada de madera, piedra, metal o arcilla mediante al tallar, soldar, fundir o modelar

three-dimensional—something that can be measured by height, width, and depth **tridimensional**—algo que puede ser medido por altura, ancho y profundidad

Vocabulary Practice

T Display *Transparency 38* to review unit vocabulary words.

Answering Questions ⭐ Vocabulary
Ask students questions using the vocabulary words. Encourage students to use the vocabulary words in their answers. For example: Is the playground slide a three-dimensional object? Yes, the slide is three-dimensional because it has height, width, and depth.

Definitions: Demonstrate Meanings ⭐ Vocabulary
Display *Large Prints 39* *The Oregon Trail* and *40* *Vaquero*. Have volunteers select a vocabulary word, such as *negative space*, and explain how it is shown in the works of art.

Other References ⭐ Vocabulary
Allow students to find out more about the vocabulary words by using various resources such as electronic encyclopedias, the Internet, and dictionaries.

Space and Form

▲ **Rene Magritte.** (Belgian). *The Blank Signature (Carte Blance).* 1965.
. . . .
Oil on canvas. 32 × 25 ⅛ inches (81 × 64 cm.).
National Gallery of Art, Washington, D.C.

 ## Art Criticism

Critical Thinking Art criticism is an organized system for looking at and talking about art. You can criticize art without being an expert. The purpose of art criticism is to get the viewer involved in a perception process that delays judgment until all aspects of the artwork have been studied.

See pages 28–29 for more about art criticism.

Describe

▶ Ask students to describe what the credit line says about the painting. Possible answers: Rene Magritte painted this work. The title is *The Blank Signature.* It was painted in 1965. It was painted with oil paint on canvas. It is 32" × 25 ⅝". It is at the National Gallery of Art in Washington, D.C.

▶ Have students describe the woman and what she is doing. Possible answers: The woman is riding a horse. She is wearing a riding suit, jacket, long skirt, hat, white turtleneck sweater, white gloves, and black boots. She holds a riding crop in one hand and the reins in the other hand.

▶ What is the setting? Possible answers: The horse and rider are passing through a forest.

Analyze

▶ Ask students where they see positive shapes and negative spaces. Possible answers: The horse, rider, and the trees are positive shapes. The light green spaces between the trees are negative spaces.

▶ Have the students discuss what objects are in the foreground and background. Possible answers: The grass is in the foreground. The trees, rider, and horse are in the middle ground. The faded area of greens, blues, and light violets is in the background.

▶ How does the artist use size and detail to show depth? Possible answers: The trees that are closer are painted larger. Trees

 ## Art History and Culture

René Magritte

René Magritte (rə nē´ mə grēt´) (1898–1967) was born in Belgium and trained as a painter at Brussels Academy. He made his living for a time designing wallpaper and drawing fashion advertisements. He is best known for his surrealist paintings. Many of his paintings have a dreamlike, unnatural element to them with objects appearing in unusual places. His art looks like riddles but is there to challenge our ready acceptance of art and reality. In his last year Magritte began to make sculptures of some of his painted images. Much of his work is spread around the world.

Artist Profiles, p. 37

Artist Profile
René Magritte
1898–1967
René Magritte (rə nē´ mə grēt´) was born in Belgium at the end of the nineteenth century. After studying art in Brussels, he worked briefly in a wallpaper factory. The influence of his time at this factory is sometimes evident in his patterned paintings. Magritte had a mischievous attitude, and displayed an avant-garde, poetic energy. He directed this energy into numerous creations and was honored with retrospective exhibitions in both Europe and the United States.

 **Art Criticism** Critical Thinking

Describe What do you see?

▶ What does the credit line tell you about the painting?

▶ Describe the woman and what she is doing.

▶ What is the setting?

Analyze How is this work organized?

▶ Where do you see positive shapes and negative spaces?

▶ What is in the foreground, middle ground, and background?

▶ Which objects seem to be closest, and which are farthest away?

▶ How did the artist use size and detail to show depth?

▶ What unusual trick has the artist played with space?

Interpret What is the artist trying to say?

▶ How does the artist's use of space and shape affect the look of this work?

▶ What do you think is happening in this painting? Write a brief paragraph explaining this image.

Decide What do you think about the work?

▶ Is this painting successful because it is realistic, because it is well-organized, or because it has a strong message? Explain.

Unit 2   **91**

Aesthetic Perception

Critical Thinking Ask students if they have ever played in a grove of trees.

Describe
▶ Describe who you were with and what you were doing.

Analyze
▶ Where were the positive and negative spaces in the trees?

Interpret
▶ What did it feel like to be in the grove?

Decide
▶ Decide if you would rather be alone or with a group of friends.

that are farther away are painted smaller. The trees in the foreground and middle ground show details such as bark, branches, and individual leaves. The trees in the background are a mass of paint dabs.

▶ Ask students to describe what unusual trick the artist played with space. Possible answers: In one place, part of the horse and rider is not visible. The small tree behind the woman begins behind the large tree behind the horse, and then weaves forward to overlap in front of the woman and the horse.

Interpret

▶ Ask students how the artists use of space and shape affect the look of this work. Possible answers: Some will say it looks weird because things move back and forth in space illogically. The realistic style of painting makes this more unusual. Everything is painted to show accuracy and depth, yet the tricks with space are unrealistic.

▶ Have students describe what is happening in the painting and have them explain by writing a brief explanation of the image. Answers will vary. Science fiction, fantasy, or a dream story is possible. Anything that explains the invisible shape and the interweaving of shapes is acceptable.

Decide

▶ Ask students if this painting is successful because it is realistic, well-organized, or because it has a strong message. Explain. Possible answers: In this work most students will say the strong message because of the surrealism. But realism and organization are also acceptable if explained properly.

Art Journal: Writing
Have students write answers to Aesthetic Perception in their Art Journals.

"Artists show depth and use the technique of overlapping to create space in paintings and drawings. They show three-dimensional forms in sculpture." *"Los artistas muestran profundidad y usan la técnica de superposición para crear espacio en las pinturas y los dibujos. Ellos muestran formas tridimensionales en sus esculturas".*

T Review the unit vocabulary with students using *Transparency 38.*

Art Journal: Writing

Have students answer the questions on page 92 in their Art Journals or on a separate sheet of paper. Answers: 1. B, 2. C, 3. A, 4. C, 5. A

T For further assessment, have students complete the unit test on *Transparency 44.*

CAREERS IN ART
Architecture

► Ask students if they have a park, playground, or community center in their neighborhood or city. Have them discuss the different aspects they enjoy most about these recreational areas.

► Have students list items found in their ideal playground. Allow them to share their answers.

► Encourage interested students to find out more about a career as a city planner. Have them share their findings with the class.

"Art is a method of opening up areas of feeling rather than merely an illustration of an object." —Francis Bacon

---

Show What You Know

Answer these questions on a separate sheet of paper.

❶ The area that shapes and forms fill is _____.
   A. negative space
   B. positive space
   C. relief sculpture

❷ Three-dimensional shapes are called _____.
   A. jewelry
   B. positive space
   C. forms

❸ The part of an artwork that appears farthest away is the _____.
   A. background
   B. foreground
   C. relief

❹ _____ is when one object covers part of another object.
   A. Relief
   B. Freestanding
   C. Overlapping

❺ The area between and around an object is _____.
   A. negative space
   B. relief
   C. form

92   Unit 2

Unit Assessment Options

 Aesthetic Perception

Practice Have students select two concepts from the Show What You Know section on page 92 and then find examples of each concept in the classroom.

 Creative Expression

Student Portfolio Have students review all the artwork they have created during this unit and select the pieces they wish to keep in their portfolios. Have students share their portfolios with classmates and identify each other's use of space and form.

Art Criticism

Activity Have students select an artwork from this unit and study it using the four steps of art criticism. (See pages 28–29 for more information about art criticism.) Have students work alone or in pairs, and present their findings aloud or in writing.

CAREERS IN ART
Architecture

Look around your neighborhood. What do the buildings look like? there parks? These things were designed to look the way they d

Architects design buildings fro houses to sports stadiums. Architects must think about how building will be used as well as it should look.

Landscape architects design green spaces. They must think al how the shapes and colors of different plants will look togethe

City planners think about wha kinds of housing, parking, and p people will need.

▲ Architect

Space and Form in Animation

John Ramirez is an animator and storyboard artist. His video "Every Picture Tells a Story" shows how he works with a team to make animated films. He studies space and form in photographs to know how to draw scenes in his storyboards.

What to Do Tell a short story in a four-frame comic strip.

Comic strips are a simple form of storyboarding. They have four frames in which to tell a simple story. The style of art and the layout of the frames are important. They help show the story from beginning to end.

1. Think of a simple story. Your story should have characters and a beginning, a middle, and an end.
2. Sketch out four scenes that will show action in the story.
3. Use overlapping to create depth in your scenes. Name your characters. Add dialogue and a title.
4. Share your comic strip with friends. Ask them if they understand the story.

▲ John Ramirez and Paul Tracey. "Every Picture Tells a Story."

 Art Criticism

Describe Describe the scenes you chose to show your story.

Analyze How did you choose the four scenes that would best tell your story?

Interpret How did you create depth in your drawings?

Decide Was there something you wanted in your story but couldn't quite achieve?

Unit 2 **93**

 **Art History and Culture**

About Storyboarding

John Ramirez has been an animator and storyboard artist for both Walt Disney and Warner Brothers Feature Animation. As a storyboard artist he pitches the story line and describes the characters to the other members of the creative team. *Every Picture Tells a Story* shows the process of taking an idea, developing it into a story sequence with a creative team, and storyboarding it.

Space and Form in Animation

Objective: To create a story that is portrayed in a four-frame storyboard

Materials: *Every Picture Tells a Story* by John Ramirez, storyboard artist. Running time: 10:07 paper, pencils or markers

Focus

Time: 5 minutes

■ Discuss the information on page 93.

 Art History and Culture

■ Have students brainstorm ideas for a short story or joke that can be illustrated in four scenes of a storyboard or comic strip.

Teach

Time: About 20 minutes

 Aesthetic Perception

■ Explain to students about storyboards and their function.

Creative Expression

■ Direct students to think of a short original story or joke.

■ Ask them to think of four scenes that could portray the idea. Sketch the ideas before drawing them.

■ Ask them to have a clear idea of characters and sequence.

■ Have them share and give positive feedback.

Close

Time: About 10 minutes

 Art Criticism

■ Have students answer the four art criticism questions on page 93 aloud or in writing.

■ Did students effectively create four-frame storyboards?

Unit 3 Planning Guide

	Lesson Title	Suggested Pacing	Creative Expression Activity
Lesson 1	**Looking at Color**	65 minutes	Use color to express a mood.
Lesson 2	**Intermediate Colors**	65 minutes	Create a color wheel.
Lesson 3	**Color Wheel**	65 minutes	Create a color wheel amusement ride.
Lesson 4	**Cool Colors**	65 minutes	Create a paper sculpture.
Lesson 5	**Warm Colors**	65 minutes	Make an imaginative painting.
Lesson 6	**Color Contrasts**	65 minutes	Create a group mural.
ART SOURCE	**Color and Value in Theatre**	35 minutes	Design costumes and sets.

Materials	Program Resources	Fine Art Resources	Literature Resources
white paper, markers in assorted colors, liquid tempera paints, paper towels, paintbrushes, water dishes, paper plates, newspapers, prism	*Assessment*, pp. 33–34 *Home After School Connections* *Art Around The World* *Reading and Writing Test Preparation*, pp. 30–31	*Transparency*, 13 *Artist Profiles*, pp. 23, 52 *Large Prints*, 41, 42 *Flash Cards*, 7–10 *Animals Through History Time Line*	*The Worry Stone* by Marianna Dengler
white construction paper, liquid tempera paints, paper plates for palettes, brushes, containers of water, paper towels, glue, newspaper, color wheel, paper plate	*Assessment*, pp. 35–36 *Women in the Arts Collection* *Reading and Writing Test Preparation*, pp. 32–33	*Transparency*, 14 *Artist Profiles*, pp. 59, 67 *Large Prints*, 41, 42 *Flash Card*, 16 *Animals Through History Time Line*	*The Great Kapok Tree* by Lynne Cherry
construction paper, poster board, scissors, glue, sketch paper, markers	*Assessment*, pp. 37–38 *Women in the Arts Collection* *Reading and Writing Test Preparation*, pp. 34–35	*Transparency*, 15 *Artist Profiles*, pp. 28, 47 *Large Prints*, 41, 42 *Flash Card*, 19 *Animals Through History Time Line*	*Sylvester and the Magic Pebble* by William Steig
construction paper, scissors, tape or glue, oil pastels, sketch paper, pencils, markers	*Assessment*, pp. 39–40 *Art Around The World Collection* *Reading and Writing Test Preparation*, pp. 36–37	*Transparency*, 16 *Artist Profiles*, pp. 6, 54 *Large Prints*, 41, 42 *Flash Card*, 15 *Animals Through History Time Line*	*Snowflake Bentley* by Jacqueline Briggs Martin
white construction paper, oil pastels, watercolor paints, brushes of various sizes, containers of water, sketch paper, pencils, tape, paper towels	*Assessment*, pp. 41–42 *Women in the Arts Collection* *Reading and Writing Test Preparation*, pp. 38–39	*Transparency*, 17 *Artist Profiles*, pp. 31, 44 *Large Prints*, 41, 42 *Flash Card*, 17 *Animals Through History Time Line*	*How I Spent My Summer Vacation* by Mark Teague
mural paper for every team, liquid tempera paints, large brushes, construction paper, oil pastels, glue, paper towels, palettes, water containers, newspaper	*Assessment*, pp. 43–44 *Art Around the World Collection* *Reading and Writing Test Preparation*, pp. 40–41	*Transparency*, 18 *Artist Profiles*, pp. 58, 64 *Large Prints*, 41, 42 *Animals Through History Time Line*	*The Mountain That Loved a Bird* by Alice McLerran
The Story of Babar, the Little Elephant, picture books, paper, paints or markers			

3 Color and Value

Lesson 1: Primary colors cannot be made by mixing other colors, while **secondary colors** are made by mixing two primary colors. **Value** is the lightness or darkness of a color.

Lesson 2: Intermediate colors are made by mixing a primary color with a secondary color.

Lesson 3: The color wheel is the color spectrum bent into a circle.

Lesson 4: Cool colors suggest a feeling of calmness.

Lesson 5: Warm colors suggest a feeling of warmth.

Lesson 6: Color contrasts are created when warm and cool colors are placed side by side.

Introduce Unit Concepts

"Artists use the elements of color and value in creating all kinds of art." "Los artistas usan los elements del color y valor para crear todo tipo de arte".

Color
- Ask students to survey at least twenty people of different ages to learn their favorite colors. Have students determine the most popular color and report it to the class.

- Have students select a color and make a list of nouns, adjectives, and adverbs that are associated with that particular color. Ask students to write a poem about the color by connecting words from their lists.

Value
- Have students suggest words that come to mind when you say the word *value*. Possible answers might include *worth*, *respect*, and *ideals*.

- Turn off the lights in the classroom and shine a flashlight on different objects in the room. Discuss how the color of each object looks in bright light and in dim light.

Color and Value

 Diego Rivera. (Mexican). *Kneeling Child on Yellow Background.* 1927.

Oil on canvas. 25 ½ × 21 inches (65 × 53 cm.). San Francisco Museum of Modern Art, San Francisco, California.

Artists use color and value to make their artwork special.

Diego Rivera was inspired by ancient Mexican sculpture forms. This painting shows a portrait of a young Mexican girl. It was made by mixing together different colors.

94 Unit 3

Fine Art Prints

Display **Large Prints 41** *Firebirds* and **42** *Noreaster.* Refer to the prints throughout the unit as students learn about color and value.

Large Print 41

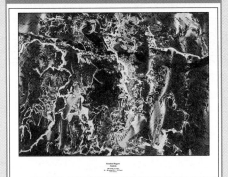

Large Print 42

Artists use color to create a certain feeling or emotion in art.

▶ What colors do you see in *Kneeling Child on Yellow Background*?

▶ What do the colors make you think of?

Some artists use different **values** of a color to show the highlights and shadows of an object.

▶ Where did Rivera use light and dark color values on the young girl's face?

▶ Where else do you see light and dark values of a color?

In This Unit you will learn about colors and the moods they create. You will practice mixing and using colors.

Here are the topics you will study:
▶ Primary and Secondary Colors
▶ Value
▶ Intermediate Colors
▶ Color Wheel
▶ Warm and Cool Colors
▶ Color Contrast

Self-Portrait

Diego Rivera
(1886–1957)

Diego Rivera was born in Mexico. As a young boy, he loved to draw and paint. When he grew up, Rivera became famous for creating large murals on the sides of buildings and on walls. His murals show people in their struggle for a better life. These murals can be seen today in Mexico and the United States.

Unit 3   **95**

Examine the Artwork

"Let's look closely at the painting." "Vamos a observar detalladamente la pintura".

■ Have students look at Rivera's painting *Kneeling Child on Yellow Background*. Ask them to describe what they see in the painting. Have students answer the questions about color and value on page 95.

▶ Secondary colors: The little girl's skirt is violet and her waistband is orange. Warm colors: the yellow mat and orange tile floor. The colors remind the viewer of the sun.

▶ Value: The flesh color of the young girl's face is darker under her chin and lighter down the middle of her nose. The violet color in the skirt is darker inside the folds and lighter at the top of each fold.

Unit Pretest

T Display *Transparency 45* as pretest. Answers: 1. B, 2. B, 3. C, 4. A, 5. C

Home Connection

■ See *Home and After-School Connections* for family newsletters and activities for this unit.

Art History and Culture   NSAE 4.a, 4.b, 4.c, 5.a, 5.b

Diego Rivera

Diego Rivera (dē ā´gō rē bā´rä) (1886–1957) was one of the most productive Mexican artists of his time. He attended art school in Mexico but did not stay long. His first exhibition of paintings, in 1907, allowed him to study in Europe. There he studied the work of modern artists, including Klee, Cézanne, and Picasso. Rivera wanted to create art that could be enjoyed by ordinary people. For this reason Rivera focused on simple designs and interesting subjects. Public murals were ideal for him because many people could see his art.

See pages 24–25 and 16–21 for more about art history and subject matter.

Artist Profiles, p. 50

◆ Artist Profile ◆
Diego Rivera
1886-1957
Diego Rivera (dē ā´ gō rē bā´ rä) was one of the most productive Mexican artists. He attended art school in Mexico but did not stay long. His first exhibition of paintings in 1907 won him a scholarship to Europe. There he studied the work of modern artists. After returning from a second trip to Europe in 1911, he became Mexico's leading mural painter. Rivera was a large man with strong opinions. His great love for his people and his country showed in his art. Crowds gathered to watch him paint his large murals on public walls. His third wife was the famous painter Frida Kahlo. They often fought and separated, but they always supported each other's artistic efforts.

ILLUSTRATOR PROFILE
Ezra Jack Keats
(1916–1983)

Ezra Jack Keats began his life as Jacob Ezra Katz, the third child of Polish immigrants living in Brooklyn, New York. Keats was interested in art as a young child, a pursuit that his mother encouraged but his father seemed to support begrudgingly. Concerned that an artist's life would be one of hardship, Keats's father cautioned his son against becoming an artist, but he was secretly very proud of his son's talent.

Upon his father's death, Keats worked to help support his family. He had earned several scholarships to art school, but felt obligated to take a job. In 1937 he became a mural painter for the Works Progress Administration. Subsequent jobs included work as a comic book illustrator and as a designer of camouflage patterns for the Army.

Keats began illustrating children's books in 1954 and published his first work, *My Dog Is Lost*, in 1960 as both author and illustrator. Over the next couple of years, Keats developed a young, black character named Peter who was based on photos that Keats had seen in *Life* magazine. Keats, who had kept the pictures of the boy for more than 20 years, said, "I just loved looking at him. This was the child who would be the hero of my book." Indeed, Keats's very first book about Peter, *The Snowy Day*, was awarded the Caldecott Medal in 1963.

While studying Unit 3, share Ezra Jack Keats's illustrations with the class and discuss the use of color and value in his works of art. Ask students to identify primary, secondary, and intermediate colors. How did Keats use warm and cool colors? Have students study value by finding light and dark colors in Keat's illustrations.

Music

Color in music refers to the distinctive tone qualities, or *timbre*, of different instruments and voices. *Value*, while not a musical term, has a parallel in music: the ability of performers to create subtle differences in tone that are sometimes characterized as "warm" or "cool."

Literature

Watch the video or DVD *Diego* to learn about Diego Rivera. Look to see how he used primary, secondary, warm, and cool colors.

Literature and Art

Performing Arts

 Show *The Story of Babar the Little Elephant*. Design costumes and sets using colors from the book illustrations.

Artsource®

Lesson 1
Overview

Looking at Color

Lesson 1 introduces the primary and secondary colors, as well as value. The primary colors are red, blue, and yellow. The secondary colors are green, orange, and violet. Value is the lightness or darkness of a color.

Objectives

Art History and Culture

To demonstrate knowledge of the lives and art of Russell and Held

NSAE 4.a, 4.b, 4.c

Creative Expression

To plan and create an illustration of a special occasion using colors to express a mood or emotion

NSAE 1.c, 1.d

Aesthetic Perception

To identify the primary and secondary colors, as well as tints and shades, in works of art and in the environment

NSAE 2.a, 2.b, 2.c

Art Criticism

To evaluate own work using the four steps of art criticism

NSAE 5.a, 5.b, 5.c

Vocabulary ⭐ Vocabulary

Review the following vocabulary words with students before beginning the lesson.

primary colors colores primarios—red, yellow, and blue, which cannot be made by mixing other colors

secondary colors colores secundarios—green, orange, and violet, which are each made by mixing two primary colors together

See page 119B for additional vocabulary and Spanish vocabulary resources.

Art Journal: Vocabulary

Have students add these words to the Vocabulary section of their Art Journals.

Lesson Materials

- 12" × 18" white paper
- markers in assorted colors
- liquid tempera paints
- paper towels
- paintbrushes
- water dishes
- paper plates
- newspapers
- paper cut into strips
- pencils
- shoe boxes
- prism

Alternate Materials:
- oil pastels or colored pencils

Program Resources
- *Reading and Writing Test Prep.,* pp. 30–31
- *Transparency 13*
- *Flash Cards 7–10*
- *Artist Profiles,* pp. 23, 52
- *Assessment,* pp. 33–34
- *Large Prints 41* Firebirds and *42* Noreaster
- *Art Around the World Collection*

Concept Trace
Color and Value

Introduced: Level K, Unit 3, Lessons 1–6

Reinforced: Level 4, Unit 3, Lessons 1–6

Lesson 1 Arts Integration

Theatre

Complete Unit 3, Lesson 1, on pages 54–55 of *Theatre Arts Connections.*

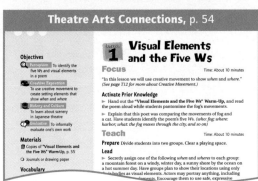

Theatre Arts Connections, p. 54

Music

Musical instruments are grouped into four families. The two that use vibrating air streams are Woodwinds and Brass. Percussion instruments produce sound by striking or shaking, and String instruments produce sound by plucking, bowing, or striking the strings to make them vibrate. Listen to *Das Wandern* from the album "Schubert Die Schone Mullerin", by Franz Schubert. What families can you distinguish?

Movement and Dance

Give each student a colored scarf or strip of crepe paper in either a primary or secondary color. Arrange the students in a large circle with the primary colors (red, yellow, blue) on one side of the circle and the secondary colors (orange, green, violet) on the other side. Call out two primary colors. These students move into the center of the circle and take eight counts to dance with and around each other, and then they return. Repeat with secondary colors.

LESSON 1 • Looking at Color **95B**

Focus

Time: About 10 minutes

Activate Prior Knowledge

"What colors do you see in the springtime?"
"¿Qué colores ven en la primavera?"

- Discuss students' responses. Have students identify the colors they name as primary or secondary colors.

Using Literature ⭐ Reading

- Read *The Worry Stone* by Marianna Dengler. Use the illustrations to discuss primary and secondary colors and value.

Thematic Connection ⭐ Language Arts

- **Games:** Encourage students to study *Piero's Piazza* and to imagine what the artist was trying to describe in this painting. Ask students to write a short story that includes a game for which they could use the shapes in the painting.

Introduce the Art NSAE 3.a

Look

"Let's take a close look at the two artworks."
"Vamos a observar de cerca estas dos obras de arte".

- Have students describe the subject matter in each painting.

Comparing and Contrasting ⭐ Reading

- Have students list the similarities and differences between the two works of art. Both pieces show depth of space and use a variety of colors. *Boy's Day* is a landscape, while *Piero's Piazza* is abstract.

 ### Art History and Culture

Possible answer: The bright colors give the works a festive mood.

Tell students that Boys' Day is a Japanese festival that celebrates children. Carp-like streamers are flown for each son in a family. There is also a Girls' Day.

Web Connection

Visit the Honolulu Academy of Arts online at **honoluluacademy.org**.

96 UNIT 3 • Color and Value

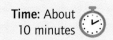 **Lesson 1**

Looking at Color

◄ **Shirley Ximena Hopper Rus...**
(American). *Boys' Day*. 1935.
Oil on canvas. 29 ⅝ × 24 ⅝ inches (76 × 63.5 cm.). Honolulu Academy of Art, Honolulu, Hawaii.

Look at Shirley Russell's *Boy's Day*. It about a holiday celebrated by flying flags and colorful streamers. *Piero's Piazza* painted by Al Held is an abstract painting. It is a tribut to a late fifteenth-century artist by the name of Piero della Francesca. Both artis use color to show the mood of the events they painted.

 ### Art History and Culture

Look at the different colors in these two artworks. How did the artists use color to express different feelings or moods in the works of art?

96 Unit 3 • Lesson 1

 ### Art History and Culture NSAE 4.a, 4.b, 4.c, 5.a, 5.b

Shirley Russell

Shirley Russell (shŭr lē rus′ əl) (1886–1985) was born in California and studied art in college. She also studied art in Paris from 1927–1928 and 1937–1938 to build her creative skills. After her husband died, Russell moved to Hawaii and taught art at the high-school level for twenty-three years. Like many Hawaiian artists, Russell painted still lifes and landscapes of the scenery around her. Her work has been exhibited not only in Hawaii, but also in Los Angeles, San Francisco, Cincinnati, New York, Baltimore, and France.

See pages 16–21 and 24–25 for more about subject matter and art history.

Artist Profiles, p. 52

Artist Profile
Shirley Russell
1886–1985
Shirley Russell (shŭr′ lē′ rə′ sal) was born in California and studied art in college at Stanford University. The turning point in her career was a trip to Hawaii with her son after her husband died in 1921. Russell returned to Hawaii in 1923 and began a 23-year teaching career. Russell also studied art in Paris to build her creative skills from 1927 to 1928 and from 1937 to 1938. Her work has been exhibited not only in Hawaii, but also in Los Angeles, San Francisco, Cincinnati, New York City, and Baltimore. Her last show was held when she was 93.

Study both paintings to find the following colors.

▶ Find the primary colors—red, yellow, and blue.

▶ Point to the secondary colors—orange, green, and violet.

▶ Where are the light colors? The dark colors?

▲ **Al Held.** (American). *Piero's Piazza.* 1982.
....
Acrylic on canvas. 96 ½ × 143 ⅞ inches (244 × 366 cm). Albright-Knox Art Gallery, Buffalo, New York.

Aesthetic Perception

Seeing Like an Artist Look in a magazine. Find the same colors that you saw in the paintings.

Art History and Culture
NSAE 4.a, 4.b, 4.c, 5.a, 5.b

Al Held

Al Held (al held) (1928–   ) was born in Brooklyn, New York, and grew up in the Bronx during the Great Depression. His family experienced difficult financial times when he was young, but Held found a way to attend the Art Students League from 1948 to 1949 and later the Academie de la Grande Chaumiere in Paris. He settled in New York after his schooling and became known for his experiments in geometric form and line. From 1962 to 1978 Held was a member of the art faculty of Yale University and later moved to a studio near Woodstock, New York, where he lives today.

See pages 24–25 and 16–21 for more about art history and subject matter.

Artist Profiles, p. 23

Artist Profile
Al Held
b. 1928

Al Held (al held) was born in Brooklyn, New York, and grew up in the Bronx during the Great Depression. His family experienced difficult financial times, but Held found a way to attend the Art Students League from 1948 to 1949 and later the Academie de la Grande Chaumiere in Paris. He settled in New York and became known for his experiments in geometric form and line. From 1962 to 1978, Held was a member of the art faculty of Yale University and later moved to a studio near Woodstock, New York, where he lives today.

Study
NSAE 1.b, 2.a, 2.b, 3.a, 5.c

▶ **Primary colors:** In *Boy's Day* the flag designs are red and blue. The fish kites are red. *Piero's Piazza:* The left edge is red and there are red, yellow, and blue lines throughout the artwork.

▶ **Secondary colors:** In *Boy's Day* the earth in the foreground is orange, and the grass in the middle ground is green. The trees in the background, on the left-hand side, are violet.

▶ **Light colors:** In *Boy's Day* the areas in direct sunlight are painted with light colors. *Piero's Piazza:* the yellow at the bottom and the lighter green color in the middle of the painting

▶ **Dark colors:** *Boy's Day:* The buildings, fence, and tall bushes on the left side are dark. The ground in the foreground is dark. *Piero's Piazza:* The right background has dark shades of red. The middle floor area has dark blue.

■ For more examples of art from North America, see the ***Art Around the World Collection.***

Art Journal: Writing
Encourage students to define and illustrate tints and shades in the Concepts section of their Art Journals. What else do they want to know about tints and shades?

Aesthetic Perception
NSAE 2.a, 2.b, 3.a
Seeing Like an Artist Provide magazines for the students to browse. Ask students to cut out areas of color that match the colors in the fine art.
NSAE 4.a, 4.b, 4.c
Developing Visual Literacy Invite students to share any personal experiences that contribute to their understanding the works of art. For example, what kinds of celebrations have they attended? Were there any decorations like the flags and streamers in *Boy's Day?*

Web Connection
Visit the Albright-Knox Art Gallery online at http://www.albrightknox.org/index.html.

Teach

Time: About 45 minutes

"What questions can you create about color?"
"¿Qué preguntas sobre el color pueden crear?"

- Discuss the definitions of *primary* and *secondary colors* and *value* on page 98.

Practice
NSAE 1.a, 1.d

Materials: paper cut into strips, pencils, shoe boxes

- Distribute the materials and have students follow the directions on page 98.

- Randomly choose someone from another team to decide whether the answer is correct.

- Award 2 points for each correct answer.

NSAE 1.a, 1.c, 1.d, 2.c, 3.b

Creative Expression

Materials: 12" × 18" white paper, prism, markers in assorted colors, liquid tempera paints, paper towels, paintbrushes, water dishes, paper plates, newspapers

Alternate Materials: oil pastels or colored pencils

- Use the prism to show students how light can be separated into colors.

- Review the Activity Tips on page 238 for visual examples of techniques.

Art Journal: Brainstorming

Have students discuss their favorite colors and what kind of mood or feelings they think of for each color. What life experiences do they associate with these colors? Have them write their ideas in their Art Journals. Then have them choose one event to draw.

Using Colors

Colors are used to express different moods or feelings in works of art. **Hue** is another word for *color*. The three **primary colors** are red, yellow, and blue. They cannot be made by mixing colors.

The **secondary colors** are made by mixing two primary colors.

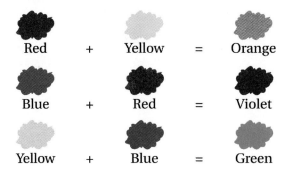

Red + Yellow = Orange

Blue + Red = Violet

Yellow + Blue = Green

Value is the lightness or darkness of a color. Adding white makes a color lighter. Adding black makes a color darker. When the value of a color is lighter, it is called a **tint.** When the value of a color is darker, it is called a **shade.**

Practice

Hold a "Color Bee."

1. Divide into four teams. Think up color questions based on the above information.

2. Write each question on a piece of paper. Fold the papers and put them into a question box.

3. Take turns pulling questions from the box and answering them.

Differentiated Instruction

Reteach

Have students look through the **Student Edition** to find three works of art that incorporate the spectrum of colors as well as tints and shades. Ask students to list the title of each work and describe the colors they find.

Special Needs

As an introduction to this activity, provide paintings or pictures of different events for the students to study. Ask students to identify the event, the colors used, and the mood or feelings portrayed in each picture.

ELL Tips

When discussing special occasions, take a moment to quickly sketch important elements of these celebrations. Pair English-language learners with fluent English-speaking peers to discuss special occasions or events.

◄ **Domenique Chery.** Age 8.

Think about how this student artist created mood in her artwork.

 Creative Expression

What colors do you like? Draw a picture of a special event using colors that show the feeling of that event.

1. Think of ways that you, your family, and friends celebrate special events. Choose one event for your drawing. What colors will you need to include? What colors will you use to show the mood of this event?

2. Draw the event or occasion with colored markers on white construction paper.

3. Fill your paper with color.

Art Criticism

Describe What special event did you draw? Describe the people and objects. Point to the tints and shades.

Analyze Name the colors you used. Did you use some colors for special effects?

Interpret What is the mood of your event?

Decide If you could make this drawing again, how would you improve it?

Reflect

Time: About 10 minutes

Review and Assess

"How can you use color to create a certain feeling in a work of art?" "¿Cómo pueden usar el color para crear un sentimiento especial en un obra de arte?"

Think

NSAE 1.b, 2.a, 2.b

The student artist created a happy, celebratory mood in her artwork by using bright colors.

■ Use *Large Prints 41 Firebirds* and *42 Noreaster* to have students identify and compare primary and secondary colors.

NSAE 1.b, 2.a, 2.b, 3.a, 5.c

Informal Assessment

Art Journal: Critical Thinking

Have students answer the four art criticism questions—Describe, Analyze, Interpret, and Decide—in their Art Journals. In small groups, have students discuss the use of color in their art.

■ For standardized-format test practice using this lesson's art content, see pages 30–31 in *Reading and Writing Test Preparation.*

■ Collect and display other works by Al Held. Have students identify the main idea and mood in these works. Discuss how Held's use of color contributes to the mood.

Art Across the Curriculum

Use these simple ideas to reinforce art concepts across the curriculum

★ **Personal Writing** Explain to students that some color words have two meanings. For example, *violet* can name a color or flower. Have students think of other color words that have two meanings.

★ **Math** Have students list some of the shapes they see in the painting *Piero's Piazza.*

★ **Science** Identify characteristics among species that allow each to survive, including camouflage. Compare the colors of animals and insects to their environment.

★ **Social Studies** Point out to students that in *Boy's Day,* the artist used bright colors to paint decorations for a holiday celebration. Have students think of holidays celebrated around the world and identify colors associated with them.

★ **Technology** Have students use the paint tool to create a picture of a celebration using color to show a mood. Visit **SRAonline.com** to print out detailed instructions for this activity.

NSAE 6.b

Lesson 1 Wrap-Up

Color and Value

NSAE 1.a, 1.b, 1.c, 1.d, 2.a, 2.b, 2.c, 3.b

Extra! For the Art Specialist

Time: About 45 minutes

Focus

Have students point out primary and secondary colors in the art on **Large Prints 41** *Firebirds* and **42** *Noreaster*. Ask students to describe how the artists used color to emphasize important parts. Discuss how the repetition of colors unifies each artwork, or gives it a sense of rhythm. Ask students to explain how an artist's use of color can affect the mood of an artwork.

Teach

Have students create a drawing using colors that illustrate a particular mood.

Reflect

Have students use the four steps of art criticism to evaluate their work. Did they effectively use color to illustrate a mood in their drawing? Create a class exhibition. Have students identify the main idea of the works of art.

Alternate Activity

Materials:
- 12" × 18" manila paper
- multicolor packs of crayons (at least 64 colors per pack)

1. Ask students to think of something that makes them experience an emotion, or mood. For example, playing with their dog or cat might make them feel happy, or doing homework might make them feel grouchy.

2. Students select several colors they feel will illustrate their mood and create a drawing about the event using a limited palette of only those colors.

Research in Art Education

Education in the arts aids in "developing worthy citizens, people who enjoy intellectual and emotional control, people with skill and initiative, and people who are aware of their world" (Gaitskell, C.D., and Al Hurwitz. *Children and Their Art: Methods for the Elementary School.* Toronto: Harcourt, 1970).

Assessment

Use the following rubric to evaluate the artwork students make in the Creative Expression activity and to assess students' understanding of primary and secondary colors and value as created by tints and shades.

Have students complete page 33 or 34 in their *Assessment* books.

	Art History and Culture	Aesthetic Perception	Creative Expression	Art Criticism
3 POINTS	The student demonstrates knowledge of the lives and art of Russell and Held.	The student accurately identifies the primary and secondary colors and tints and shades in works of art and in the environment.	The student effectively plans and creates an illustration of a special occasion using color to express a mood or an emotion.	The student evaluates own work using the four steps of art criticism.
2 POINTS	The student shows emerging awareness of the lives and art of Russell and Held.	The student shows emerging awareness of the primary and secondary colors and tints and shades in works of art and in the environment.	The student shows some awareness of how to plan and create an illustration of a special occasion using color to express a mood or an emotion.	The student attempts to evaluate own work but shows an incomplete understanding of evaluation criteria.
1 POINT	The student does not demonstrate knowledge of the lives and art of Russell and Held.	The student cannot identify primary and secondary colors or tints and shades in works of art or in the environment.	The student shows no awareness of how to plan and create an illustration of a special occasion using color to express a mood or an emotion.	The student makes no attempt to evaluate own artwork.

Assessment, p. 33

Name _____ Date _____

Lesson 1 UNIT 3

Looking at Color

A. Matching
Match the words in Column 1 to their meanings in Column 2.

Column 1
___ 1. tint
___ 2. secondary colors
___ 3. hue
___ 4. value
___ 5. shade
___ 6. primary colors

Column 2
a. the lightness or darkness of a color
b. a color + black
c. red, yellow, and blue
d. another name for color
e. a color + white
f. orange, green, and violet

B. Coloring
Use your primary-colored crayons to create the three secondary colors in the boxes below.

Level 3

Unit 3 • Color and Value **33**

Lesson 2 Intermediate Colors

 Overview

Lesson 2 introduces intermediate colors and how colors can express ideas. Intermediate colors are made by mixing a primary color with a secondary color.

 Objectives

 Art History and Culture

To identify how artists from diverse cultures use intermediate colors in works of art
NSAE 4.a, 4.b, 4.c

 Creative Expression

To design and make a creative color wheel based on a geometric or free-form shape NSAE 1.c, 1.d

Aesthetic Perception

To identify the intermediate colors in art and in the environment

NSAE 2.a, 2.b, 2.c

 Art Criticism

To evaluate own work using the four steps of art criticism

NSAE 5.a, 5.b, 5.c

Vocabulary ⭐ Vocabulary

Review the following vocabulary words with students before beginning the lesson.

intermediate colors colores intermedios —colors that are made by mixing a primary color with a secondary color

See page 119B for additional vocabulary and Spanish vocabulary resources.

 Art Journal: Vocabulary

Have students add these words to the Vocabulary section of their Art Journals.

Lesson Materials
- color wheel
- sketch paper
- tag board
- 9" × 12" or larger white drawing paper
- pencils
- tempera paints in both primary and secondary colors
- paintbrushes
- water containers
- newspapers
- mixing trays
- paper towels
- 9" × 12" paper folded into six boxes
- magazines
- glue

Program Resources
- *Reading and Writing Test Prep.*, pp. 32–33
- *Transparency 14*
- *Flash Card 16*
- *Artist Profiles*, pp. 59, 67
- *Assessment*, pp. 35–36
- *Large Prints 41* Firebirds and *42* Noreaster
- *The National Museum of Women in the Arts Collection*

Concept Trace
Intermediate Colors
Introduced: Level 3, Unit 3, Lesson 2

Reinforced: Level 4, Unit 3, Lesson 1

Lesson 2 Arts Integration

Theatre
Complete Unit 3, Lesson 2, on pages 56–57 of *Theatre Arts Connections.*

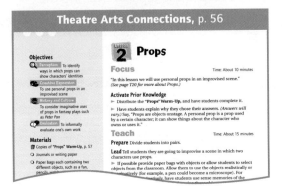

Theatre Arts Connections, p. 56

Music
SPOTLIGHT ON MUSIC Listen to *East St. Louis Toodle-o* from *The Very Best of Duke Ellington,* by Duke Ellington. The melody is passed from one tone color to another. Does it make you think of warm or cool colors? Do you hear a change of intensity when the color changes?

Movement and Dance
Divide students into pairs. Assign one student to represent a primary color and the other an intermediate color: red/orange, yellow/orange, yellow/green, blue/green, blue/violet, red/violet. The primary person creates a movement that depicts the color for four counts. The intermediate person creates a movement that is similar to the primary color, but has differences. Now combine both ideas.

Focus

Time: About 10 minutes

Activate Prior Knowledge

"Think about the colors you see in a bouquet of flowers. Can you describe them?" *"Piensen en los colores que verían en un ramo de flores. ¿Los pueden describir?"*

Using Literature ⭐ Reading

■ Read *The Great Kapok Tree* by Lynne Cherry. Ask students to identify intermediate colors in the illustrations.

Thematic Connection ⭐ Social Studies

■ **Cultural Diversity:** Share the Art History and Culture information with students. Compare the significance of cloth in ancient Peru to our use of cloth.

Introduce the Art

Look NSAE 3.a

"Let's take a close look at the two works of art." *"Vamos a observar detalladamente las dos obras de arte".*

Comparing and Contrasting ⭐ Reading

■ Have students make a list of similarities and differences between the works of art. Both incorporate a variety of shapes and images and have an intermediate-colored, red-orange color scheme. Wiley's artwork is two-dimensional, is not utilitarian, and shows a broad spectrum of colors.

 Art History and Culture

An alpaca is a domesticated mammal that is raised for its wool. Alpacas look similar to llamas and come from the same family, called *camelids*. The wool from alpacas is considered one of the finest and most luxurious natural fibers.

Web Connection

Visit **www.culturefocus.com/peru.htm** to learn more about the culture of Peru.

Intermediate Colors

Look at the two works of art on these pages. Both artists used intermediate colors in their works of art.

▲ **Artist Unknown.** (Peru). *Hat: Birds and Geometric Patterns.* 700–1000 A.D.

Alpaca and cotton. 4½ × 5 inches (11 × 13 cm). The Seattle Art Museum, Seattle, Washington.

 Art History and Culture

Hat is woven from Alpaca wool. This wool makes a very fine woven cloth. Alpacas are raised in many countries, including the United States and Australia.

 Art History and Culture NSAE 4.a, 4.b, 4.c, 5.a, 5.b

Ancient Peruvian Textiles

Hat was woven at a time in Peru when the Incas created varied and sophisticated textiles, and cloth held great value. Peruvian textiles are outstanding for the diversity of weaving techniques and their amazing colors. The cloth quality signified social, political, and religious status and was often used as a means of exchange. *Hat* is an example of the Andean textiles that were preserved in the dry desert south of Lima, Peru. This hat may have once adorned an ancient mummy. It was woven with cotton and alpaca, which is the wool from alpaca sheep.

See pages 24–25 and 16–21 for more about art history and subject matter.

Artist Profiles, p. 67

⌐Artist Profile⌐

Hat: Birds and Geometric Patterns

In the region now known as Peru, in the Andes Mountains of South America, the Incan empire slowly replaced an even older culture, the Wari. The ancient Incan empire had no coins or dollar bills. Handwoven cloth and clothing had so much value that they were was often used in place of money. The Incas also had another use for clothing. Like the ancient Egyptians, they wanted to preserve the bodies of people who had died. They often wrapped the dead in clothing and placed hats on their heads. Some ancient mummies have been found wrapped in dozens of layers of handwoven cloth.

Study both works of art to find the intermediate colors.

▶ Find the yellow-orange hues. Where are the red-orange hues?

▶ What other intermediate colors can you find?

▲ **William T. Wiley.**
(American). *Remedial Archaeology and the Like.* 1986.

100 × 165 inches (254 × 419 cm.). Acrylic and graphite on canvas. Birmingham Museum of Art, Birmingham, Alabama.

 Aesthetic Perception

Seeing Like an Artist Look through this unit. Find more examples of the colors you saw in the art on these pages.

Study
NSAE 1.b, 2.a, 2.b, 3.a, 5.c

▶ Yellow-orange: In *Hat*, the bird shape in the black area at the bottom is yellow-orange.

Red-orange: In *Hat*, the tassels at the top are red-orange.

▶ Yellow-green: In Wiley's painting, there is yellow-green to the right of the triangular shape in the center of the artwork.

Red-violet: In Wiley's painting, there is red-violet in the area above the sun image.

Blue-violet: In Wiley's painting, there is blue-violet in the area to the right of the hat, near the center.

■ For more examples of utilitarian art, see *The National Museum of Women in the Arts Collection.*

Art Journal: Writing
Have students browse through the pages of the Student Edition to look for other examples of intermediate colors.

 Aesthetic Perception

NSAE 2.a, 2.b, 3.a
Seeing Like an Artist Have students write an explanation of how intermediate colors are made and draw illustrations to go with it.
NSAE 4.a, 4.b, 4.c
Developing Visual Literacy Study the hat from Peru. Ask students to compare and contrast this hat to hats they have worn. Encourage them to speculate why the artist designed the hat this way.

Art History and Culture
NSAE 4.a, 4.b, 4.c, 5.a, 5.b

William T. Wiley

William T. Wiley (wil´ yəm w ī´ lē) (1937–) has spent most of his life in California. He earned two degrees from the San Francisco Art Institute and has taught at art schools and universities across the nation. In 1967 Wiley made an important discovery: he realized that he could create art in any way he wanted and did not have to worry about pleasing critics. Wiley now has his own style, which focuses on objects and borrows from surrealism by placing these objects in unexpected settings. His style is a form of abstract art that combines common objects and personal symbols.

See pages 24–25 and 16–21 for more about art history and subject matter.

Artist Profiles, p. 59

◀ Artist Profile ▶
William T. Wiley
b. 1937

William T. Wiley (wil´ yəm wī´ lē) was born in Indiana, but has lived mostly in California. He earned two degrees from the San Francisco Art Institute. He has taught at art schools and universities across the nation, but he says that his students have taught him more than he has taught them. Wiley is married and has a son.

Web Connection
Visit the Birmingham Museum of Art online at **www.artsbma.org/index.htm**.

Teach

Time: About 45 minutes

"How many examples of intermediate colors can you find in the classroom?" "¿Cuántos ejemplos de colores intermedios pueden hallar en el salón de clases?"

- Discuss how intermediate colors are made on page 102.

Practice
NSAE 1.a, 1.d

Materials: 9" × 12" paper folded into six boxes, magazines, glue

Alternate Materials: paper scraps

- Distribute the materials and have students follow the directions on page 102 for finding intermediate colors.

Creative Expression
NSAE 1.a, 1.c, 1.d, 2.c, 3.b

Materials: color wheel, sketchbooks or sketch paper, tag board, 9" × 12" or larger white drawing or construction paper, pencils, tempera paints in both primary and secondary colors, paint brushes, water containers, newspapers, mixing tray or paper plate, paper towels

Alternate Materials: watercolor paints

- Distribute materials and have students follow the directions on page 103.
- Review the Technique Tips for working with tempera paints on page 218.

Art Journal: Brainstorming
Have students brainstorm ideas for mixing intermediate colors.

Using Intermediate Colors

Intermediate colors are made by mixing a **primary color** and a **secondary color.** There are six intermediate colors—red-orange, yellow-orange, yellow-green, blue-green, blue-violet, and red-orange.

A **color wheel** is an artist's way of organizing these 12 colors.

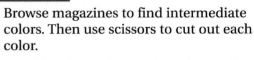

Practice

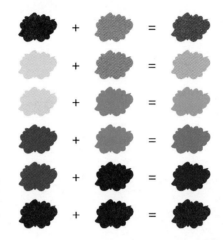

Browse magazines to find intermediate colors. Then use scissors to cut out each color.

1. Fold a sheet of paper into six equal boxes. Write the name of one intermediate color in each box.

2. Glue each example from the magazines into the correct box.

Differentiated Instruction

Reteach
Have students look around the classroom and find six objects with intermediate colors. Ask students to list the objects and name the intermediate colors of each object.

Special Needs
Students with cognitive disabilities may experience more success in this project if given the opportunity to mix colors during a guided teacher demonstration.

ELL Tips
During the Creative Expression activity, model the steps with your own color wheel as you give directions to the class. English-language learners will achieve greater comprehension of the vocabulary and process if they follow visual clues in addition to oral directions.

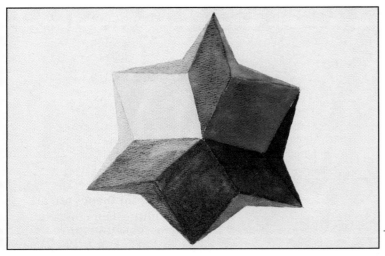

◄ **Alex Bryan.**
Age 9.

Think about what colors you like. Which colors do you like that are bright or dark? What colors do you like that can create a mood?

 Creative Expression

Design your own unique color wheel using primary, secondary, and intermediate colors.

1. The colors must be in the correct order.

2. Use primary paint colors to mix secondary and intermediate colors.

3. The wheel does not have to be round, or even a circle.

4. Plan and decide a way to indicate the difference between primary, secondary, and intermediate colors.

 Art Criticism

Describe What step did you follow to make your unique color wheel?

Analyze Name the primary, secondary, and intermediate colors in the color wheel.

Interpret Do any of the intermediate colors make you feel a certain way or put you in a particular mood?

Decide Which of the intermediate colors look the best? Which would you recreate? Why?

Unit 3 • Lesson 2   **103**

Reflect

Time: About 10 minutes

Review and Assess

"How do the intermediate colors make you feel?" "¿Cómo les hacen sentir los colores intermedios?"

Think
NSAE 1.b, 2.a, 2.b

Answers may vary; however, students might say that the bright colors like yellow and orange make them happy or think happy thoughts and that the dark colors like green and blue make them feel sad or think sad thoughts.

■ Use **Large Prints 41** *Firebirds* and **42** *Noreaster* to have students identify and compare intermediate colors.

NSAE 1.b, 2.a, 2.b, 3.a, 5.c

Informal Assessment

Art Journal: Critical Thinking
Have students answer the four art criticism questions—Describe, Analyze, Interpret, and Decide—in their Art Journals. Discuss the intermediate colors students mixed for their samples.

■ For standardized-format test practice using this lesson's art content, see pages 32–33 in **Reading and Writing Test Preparation.**

Art Across the Curriculum

Use these simple ideas to reinforce art concepts across the curriculum

★ **Narrative Writing** Have students write an alternate ending to *The Great Kapok Tree* by Lynne Cherry.

★ **Math** Look at page 102 and discuss why it makes sense to show the colors as addition math sentences.

★ **Science** Study *Hat* and two other objects to determine what kind of materials they are made of.

★ **Social Studies** Compare and contrast the United States with Peru.

★ **Technology** Have students use intermediate colors in a paint program to create a drawing of a hat. Visit **SRAonline.com** to print detailed instructions for this activity.

NSAE 6.b

Intermediate Colors

NSAE 1.a, 1.b, 1.c, 1.d, 2.a, 2.b, 2.c, 3.b

Extra! For the Art Specialist

Time: About 45 minutes

Focus

Have students point out intermediate colors in the art on *Large Prints 41 Firebirds* and *42 Noreaster*. Ask students to point out examples of a color being repeated. Have students explain why they think the artist repeated the colors.

Teach

Have students create a color wheel based on a theme.

Reflect

Have students use the four steps of art criticism to evaluate their work. Did they effectively create a color wheel based on a theme?

Alternate Activity

Materials:
- 9" × 12" sheets of tagboard
- 12" × 18" white drawing paper
- red, yellow, and blue tempera paint
- paint palettes
- paintbrushes
- water containers
- pencils
- scissors
- glue sticks

1. Tell students they will create a color wheel based on a theme of their choice.

2. Have students fold the 12" × 18" paper in half two times horizontally and three times vertically, totaling twelve spaces. Fill each space with a color from the color wheel; first primary colors, then mix to create secondary colors. Mix the primary and secondary colors to make intermediate colors.

3. Have students sketch shapes from their theme on the tagboard. Students will cut out the shapes and glue them in correct color wheel order onto a second sheet of white paper to form their thematic color wheels.

Research in Art Education

"Just as culture shapes art, art shapes culture. Our convictions, our technology, and our imagination shape our images, and our images, in turn, shape our perception of the world" (Eisner, Elliot. *The Role of Disciplined-Based Art Education in America's Schools.* The Getty Center for Arts Education in the Arts, 1987).

Assessment

Use the following rubric to evaluate the artwork students make in the Creative Expression activity and to assess students' understanding of intermediate colors.

Have students complete page 35 or 36 in their *Assessment* books.

	Art History and Culture	Aesthetic Perception	Creative Expression	Art Criticism
3 POINTS	The student demonstrates knowledge of how artists from diverse cultures use intermediate colors in works of art.	The student accurately identifies intermediate colors in art and in the environment.	The student effectively designed and created a color wheel based on a geometric or free-form shape.	The student evaluates his or her work using the four steps of art criticism.
2 POINTS	The student's knowledge of how artists from diverse cultures use intermediate colors in works of art is weak or incomplete.	The student shows emerging awareness of intermediate colors in art and in the environment.	The student shows emerging awareness of how to design and create a color wheel based on a geometric or free-form shape.	The student attempts to evaluate his or her work using the four steps of art criticism but shows an incomplete understanding of evaluation criteria.
1 POINT	The student cannot demonstrate knowledge of how artists from diverse cultures use intermediate colors in works of art.	The student cannot identify intermediate colors in art and in the environment.	The student shows no understanding of how to design and create a color wheel based on a geometric or free-form shape.	The student makes no attempt to evaluate his or her artwork.

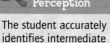

Assessment, p. 35

Name _____ Date _____

Intermediate Colors

Lesson 2 UNIT 3

A. Coloring
Use colored pencils or crayons to create each of the intermediate colors listed in the boxes below.

| yellow-orange | blue-green | red-violet |
| blue-violet | red-orange | yellow-green |

B. Short Answer
Look around your classroom to find three intermediate colors. Write the names of the objects that contain those colors.

1. _____
2. _____
3. _____

C. Writing
Look at the artwork *Remedial Archaeology and the Like* by William T. Wiley. Describe how the artist used a variety of colors in his painting.

_____
_____
_____

Level 3   Unit 3 • Color and Value   **35**

Lesson 3 Overview

Color Wheel

Lesson 3 introduces the specific arrangement of colors in the color wheel.

Objectives

Art History and Culture

To demonstrate knowledge of the lives and art of Man Ray and Calvin Jones

NSAE 4.a, 4.b, 4.c

Creative Expression

To create a color-wheel carnival ride

NSAE 1.c, 1.d

Aesthetic Perception

To identify the specific arrangement of colors on the color wheel

NSAE 2.a, 2.b, 2.c

Art Criticism

To evaluate own work using the four steps of art criticism

NSAE 5.a, 5.b, 5.c

Vocabulary ⭐ Vocabulary

Review the following vocabulary words with students before beginning the lesson.

color spectrum *colores del espectro*—the range of colors that come from light

color wheel *círculo cromático*—a tool for organizing colors that shows the color spectrum bent into a circle

See page 119B for additional vocabulary and Spanish vocabulary resources.

Art Journal: Vocabulary

Have students add these words to the Vocabulary section of their Art Journals.

Lesson Materials

- 8½" × 11" white paper
- crayons
- construction paper
- posterboard
- scissors
- glue
- sketch paper
- markers

Alternate Materials:
- magazines

Program Resources

- *Reading and Writing Test Prep.,* pp. 34–35
- *Transparency 15*
- *Flash Card 19*
- *Artist Profiles,* pp. 28, 47
- *Assessment,* pp. 37–38
- *Large Prints 41* Firebirds and *42* Noreaster
- *The National Museum of Women in the Arts Collection*

Concept Trace
Color Wheel

Introduced: Level 1, Unit 3, Lesson 1

Reinforced: Level 4, Unit 3, Lesson 1

Lesson 3 Arts Integration

Theatre

Complete Unit 3, Lesson 3, on pages 58–59 of *Theatre Arts Connections.*

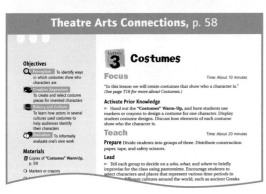

Theatre Arts Connections, p. 58

Music

SPOTLIGHT on MUSIC

The colors of the orchestra can be heard in traditional ways in classical orchestra music. Modern, contemporary composers have used new ways of combining instruments to create different colors. Listen to *Estancia Battel Suite Op. 8a First Movement "Los trabadores agricolas"* by Alberto Ginnestera. Do you hear any interesting combinations of instruments?

Movement and Dance

The colors in the color wheel echo the order of colors seen in a rainbow and also tell us how colors act when they are mixed together. With twelve students at a time, create the different levels of the color wheel. Give each student a piece of paper in a color from the color wheel: three primary colors (high level), three secondary colors (low level) and six intermediate colors (medium level). Have students arrange themselves in the order of the color wheel.

Focus

Time: About 10 minutes

Activate Prior Knowledge

"What colors do you see in a rainbow? See if you can name them in the order in which they appear." "¿Qué colores ve usted en un arco iris? Vea si usted los puede denominar en el orden en la que ellos aparecen".

■ Discuss students' responses and how the spectral colors appear in a specific order (red, orange, yellow, green, blue, and violet).

Using Literature ⭐ Reading

■ Read *Sylvester and the Magic Pebble* by William Steig. Have students find all the colors of the color wheel in the illustrations.

Thematic Connection ⭐ Science

■ **Weather/Seasons:** Observe and record information about the weather, including the colors visible in the sky.

Introduce the Art

Look

"Let's take a close look at the two works of art." "Vamos a observar de cerca estas dos obras de arte".

Comparing and Contrasting ⭐ Reading

Have students compare and contrast the two works of art. Both works include objects found in nature and incorporate the spectral colors and intermediate colors. *Brilliant as the Sun Upon the World* depicts images of animals, while *La Fortune* has no images of animals. It is a two-dimensional painting and shows a smooth visual texture.

🏺 Art History and Culture

Possible answers: Elephant, leopards, sun, and colorful fabric.

💻 **Web Connection**

Man Ray created art during the Dada Movement. Visit **www.lib.uiowa.edu/dada/** to learn more.

La Fortune / Man Ray 1938

Look at the works of art on these pages. Both artists have used spectral colors. *La Fortune* was painted by Man Ray in 1938. About the same time, Calvin Jones created *Brilliant as the Sun Upon the World*.

▲ **Man Ray.** (American). *La Fortune*. 1938.

Oil on canvas. 24 × 29 inches (61 × 74 cm.). Whitney Museum of Art, New York, New York.

🏺 Art History and Culture

Jones's painting contains many symbols and patterns of Africa. How many can you identify?

🏺 Art History and Culture

NSAE 4.a, 4.b, 4.c, 5.a, 5.b

Man Ray

Man Ray (man rā) (1890–1976) was born Emanuel Rabinovitch in Philadelphia. After studying architecture and engineering, he turned to painting and married a French painter. To support himself, Ray took photographs of friends' paintings and of French celebrities. In 1917 Ray combined photography and painting by placing objects on photographically sensitive paper and exposing it to light. He called the resulting images "Rayographs," which are patterns of shadows and tones rather than photographs. Ray himself purposely tried to paint not only unlike other artists, but even unlike how he painted his own earlier works.

See pages 16–21 and 24–25 for more about subject matter and art history.

Artist Profiles, p. 47

Artist Profile

Man Ray
1890-1976

Man Ray (man rā) was born in Philadelphia. His given name was Emanuel Rabinovitch. After studying architecture and engineering, he turned to painting. Ray moved to Paris in 1920, and to support himself, he took photographs of friends' paintings and of French celebrities. In time, Ray combined photography and painting by placing objects on photosensitive paper. He called the resulting image a *Rayograph*. A Rayograph was a pattern of shadows and tones rather than a photograph. Ray and his wife moved back and forth between Paris and the United States several times. He continued to paint and try new techniques until his death at age 86.

Study the colors used in both works of art.

▶ Find the primary colors.

▶ Where are the secondary colors?

▶ Which artist used intermediate colors?

▲ **Calvin Jones.**
(American). *Brilliant as the Sun Upon the World.* c. 1950.
....
Private Collection.

Aesthetic Perception

Seeing Like an Artist Look around to see how many colors of the spectrum you can find.

Study NSAE 1.b, 2.a, 2.b, 3.a, 5.c

▶ Primary colors: In *Brilliant as the Sun Upon the World,* the image of the cat, in the lower left-hand corner, is on a red background and is bordered with yellow and blue.

▶ Secondary colors: In *La Fortune,* there are orange, green, and violet clouds in the sky.

▶ Intermediate colors: In *Brilliant as the Sun Upon the World,* intermediate colors can be found in the various fabric pieces incorporated into the design.

■ For more examples of abstract art, see *The National Museum of Women in the Arts Collection.*

Art Journal: Writing
Have students write a detailed description of a rainbow, including the spectral colors in the correct order.

Aesthetic Perception

NSAE 2.a, 2.b, 3.a
Seeing Like an Artist Encourage students to observe their surroundings and identify as many colors of the spectrum as they can find.
NSAE 4.a, 4.b, 4.c
Developing Visual Literacy Discuss what each artwork "says." What meaning was each artist trying to convey? What might have been the artists' inspiration for creating these works of art?

Art History and Culture NSAE 4.a, 4.b, 4.c, 5.a, 5.b

Calvin Jones

Born in Illinois, Calvin Jones (kal' vin jōnz) (1934–   ) began exhibiting his work while he was still in elementary school in Chicago. After graduation from high school, he received a full scholarship to the Art Institute of Chicago, where he studied drawing, painting, and illustration. Jones worked for 17 years as an illustrator and graphic designer. He won many awards for his work before deciding to paint fulltime. Since then, he has gained widespread recognition for his ability to share the African American experience through modern art.

See pages 24–25 and 16–21 for more about art history and subject matter.

Artist Profiles, p. 28

Artist Profile
Calvin Jones
b. 1934

Born in Illinois, Calvin Jones (kal' vin jōnz) began exhibiting his work while he was still in elementary school in Chicago. After graduation from high school, he received a full scholarship to the Art Institute of Chicago, where he studied drawing, painting, and illustration. Jones worked for 17 years as an illustrator and graphic designer. He won many awards for his work before deciding to paint full-time. Since then, he has gained widespread recognition for his ability to share the African American experience through modern art.

Web Connection

To find out more about the Art Institute of Chicago visit **www.artic.edu/**.

Teach

Time: About 45 minutes

"Let's create a color chart." *"Vamos a crear un cuadro del color".*

- Identify the spectral and intermediate colors on page 106.

Practice   NSAE 1.a, 1.d

Materials: $8\frac{1}{2}$" × 11" white drawing paper, crayons

Alternate Materials: magazines

- Distribute the materials and have students follow the directions on page 106.

Creative Expression

NSAE 1.a, 1.c, 1.d, 2.c, 3.b

Materials: construction paper, posterboard, scissors, glue, sketch paper, markers

Alternate Materials: paints and poster board

- Review the order or placement of the spectral and intermediate colors on the color wheel.
- Distribute the materials and have students follow the directions on page 107.
- Review the Activity Tips on page 239 for visual examples of techniques.

Art Journal: Brainstorming

Have students brainstorm ideas for making color-wheel carnival rides in their Art Journals. Then have them choose their favorite ride. Why is this ride their favorite? What do students think this says about their personality?

Using a Color Wheel

The range of colors that comes from light is called the **color spectrum.** Rainbows are the most famous display of this spectrum in nature. The spectrum that artists use is bent into the shape of a circle. It is called a color wheel.

The color wheel includes the six spectral colors and six intermediate colors. Like the colors in the spectrum, these colors are always placed in the same order, no matter which way you turn the wheel.

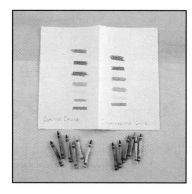

Practice

Use crayons to create a color chart.

1. Divide a sheet of paper in half. Label one side "Spectral Colors" and the other side "Intermediate Colors".
2. Use crayons to show the colors in spectral order on each side.

Differentiated Instruction

Reteach
Have students look through the **Student Edition** to find a work of art that incorporates all the spectral and intermediate colors. Ask students to write the title of the work and, in the order in which they appear on the color wheel, list the colors and where they are found in the work.

Special Needs
Some students with learning disabilities may need a more challenging assignment. Allow these students the chance to create a three-dimensional ride using paper and tape or glue.

ELL Tips
Some students may be reluctant to discuss their artwork. Write the descriptions that other students share on chart paper to familiarize them with the vocabulary they need. Draw a quick sketch to illustrate each concept.

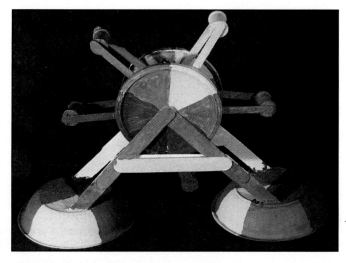

◀ **Savannah Valentine.** Age 8.

Think about this student's amusement ride. What colors did she use?

 Creative Expression

What is your favorite amusement ride? Create an amusement ride for the Rainbow Park using the color wheel.

1. Think about an amusement ride you can make using all the colors from a color wheel in order.

2. Be creative. Remember that the colors have to follow the order of the color wheel.

Art Criticism

Describe What kind of ride did you create?

Analyze How did you organize your colors?

Interpret Give your ride a name.

Decide Did you make an interesting ride?

Reflect

Time: About 10 minutes

Review and Assess

■ How would you describe your color-wheel ride? "¿Cómo describiría su aparato de atracciones con el círculo cromático que crearon?"

■ Display *Large Prints 41 Firebirds* and *42 Noreaster.* Ask students to point out colors from the color wheel in the fine art.

Think
NSAE 1.b, 2.a, 2.b

This student used spectral colors in her sculpture.

Informal Assessment
NSAE 1.b, 2.a, 2.b, 3.a, 5.c

Art Journal: Critical Thinking
Have students answer the four art criticism questions—Describe, Analyze, Interpret, and Decide—in their Art Journals. Discuss the arrangement of color in their color-wheel rides.

■ For standardized-format test practice using this lesson's art content, see pages 34–35 in *Reading and Writing Test Preparation.*

■ Collect and display works of art by various twentieth-century artists. Have students identify the main idea in the works. How do these artists use color?

Art Across the Curriculum

Use these simple ideas to reinforce art concepts across the curriculum

★ **Persuasive Writing** Explain to students that the artist of *La Fortune* always wanted a billiard table in the country. Have students think about something they have always wanted and write a persuasive speech convincing their guardians to get it for them.

★ **Math** Have students write math story problems based on what they see in *La Fortune.*

★ **Science** Study the relationship of the sun to Earth, both mentioned in the art title *Brilliant as the Sun Upon the World.*

★ **Social Studies** Learn about time zones, noting how they are always in the same order, like colors in the color wheel.

★ **Technology** Have students use a paint program to draw a color wheel. Visit **SRAonline.com** to print detailed instructions for this activity.

NSAE 6.b

Color Wheel

NSAE 1.a, 1.b, 1.c, 1.d, 2.a, 2.b, 2.c, 3.b

Extra! For the Art Specialist

Time: About 45 minutes

Focus

Use *Transparency 15* and *Large Prints 41 Firebirds* and *42 Noreaster*. Have students point out areas where the artists changed the value (lightness and darkness) of the colors. Ask students how the variations in colors and values help their eyes move around the composition. Assist students with the discussion of how the colors are arranged to help our eyes move around the picture.

Teach

Have students create tints and shades and use these to make a mosaic. Have students select one of the colors on the color wheel to mix tints and shades of that color.

Reflect

Have students use the four steps of art criticism to evaluate their work. Did they effectively create tints and shades of a color?

Alternate Activity

Materials:
- 12" × 18" manila paper
- 9" × 12" white drawing paper
- tempera paint
- paintbrushes
- water containers
- scissors
- white glue or glue sticks
- pencils

1. Students fold the manila paper in half twice vertically and once horizontally to create eight sections.

2. Give students two tablespoons of their selected color in their paint palette, plus black and white paint.

3. Have students paint the first section of their paper with the color they selected. Each section on the top row of the paper will be painted with the color plus white to make different tints of the color.

4. Each section of the bottom row of the paper will be painted with the color and black to make different shades.

5. When the paper is dry, students can cut squares from the different colors to make a mosaic.

Research in Art Education

Researchers have noted "substantial and significant differences in achievement and in important attitudes and behaviors between youth highly involved in the arts . . . and those with little or no arts engagement" ("Involvement in the Arts and Human Development: General Involvement and Intensive Involvement in Music and Theater Arts" in *Champions of Change*, p. 2). This applies to both economically advantaged and disadvantaged students.

Assessment

Use the following rubric to evaluate the artwork students make in the Creative Expression activity and to assess students' understanding of the color wheel.

Have students complete page 37 or 38 in their *Assessment* books.

	Art History and Culture	Aesthetic Perception	Creative Expression	Art Criticism
3 POINTS	The student demonstrates knowledge of the lives and art of Man Ray and Calvin Jones.	The student accurately identifies the specific arrangement of colors in the color wheel.	The student effectively creates a color-wheel ride.	The student evaluates his or her work using the four steps of art criticism.
2 POINTS	The student shows emerging awareness of the lives and art of Man Ray and Calvin Jones.	The student shows emerging awareness of the arrangement of colors in the color wheel.	The student shows some awareness of how to create a color-wheel ride.	The student attempts to evaluate his or her work but shows an incomplete understanding of evaluation criteria.
1 POINT	The student does not demonstrate knowledge of the lives and art of Man Ray and Calvin Jones.	The student cannot identify the arrangement of colors in the color wheel.	The student shows no understanding of how to create a color-wheel ride.	The student makes no attempt to evaluate his or her artwork.

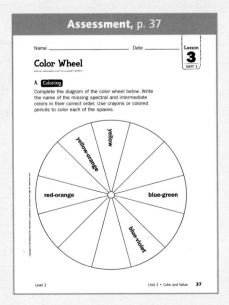

Assessment, p. 37

Name _____ Date _____

Lesson **3** UNIT 3

Color Wheel

A. Coloring

Complete the diagram of the color wheel below. Write the name of the missing spectral and intermediate colors in their correct order. Use crayons or colored pencils to color each of the spaces.

yellow
yellow-orange
red-orange
blue-green
blue-violet

Level 3   Unit 3 • Color and Value **37**

Lesson 4 Cool Colors

Overview

Lesson 4 introduces cool colors (blue, green, and violet) and their expressive qualities. Artists use cool colors to suggest calm emotions.

Objectives

 Art History and Culture

To demonstrate knowledge of the lives and art of Wayne Thiebaud and Milton Avery NSAE 4.a; 4.b; 4.c

 Creative Expression

To plan and create a three-dimensional sculpture using cool colors NSAE 1.c; 1.d

Aesthetic Perception

To identify the cool colors and their expressive qualities NSAE 2.a; 2.b; 2.c

Art Criticism

To evaluate own work using four steps of art criticism NSAE 5.a; 5.b; 5.c

Vocabulary Vocabulary

Review the following vocabulary word with the students before beginning the lesson.

cool colors colores frescos o fríos—colors that create a sense of calm or coolness: blue, green, and violet

See page 119B for additional Spanish vocabulary resources.

 Art Journal: Vocabulary

Have students add this word to the Vocabulary section of their Art Journals.

Lesson Materials

- 9" × 12" construction paper in cool colors
- scissors
- tape
- glue
- oil pastels in cool colors
- sketch paper
- pencils
- markers
- white paper
- crayons

Alternate Materials:
- wood scraps
- liquid tempera paints

Program Resources

- *Reading and Writing Test Prep.*, pp. 36–37
- *Transparency 16*
- *Flash Card 15*
- *Artist Profiles*, pp. 6, 54
- *Animals Through History Time Line*
- *Assessment*, pp. 39–40
- *Large Prints 41 Firebirds* and *42 Noreaster*
- *Art Around the World Collection*

Concept Trace
Cool Colors
Introduced: Level 2, Unit 3, Lesson 3
Reinforced: Level 4, Unit 3, Lesson 6

Lesson 4 Arts Integration

Theatre

Complete Unit 3, Lesson 4, on pages 60–61 of *Theatre Arts Connections.*

Theatre Arts Connections, p. 60

Music

 Listen to *Berceuse* by Gunild Keetman. What tone colors has Ms. Keetman used in this lullaby? What other qualities does the music have that would suggest a calm atmosphere?

Movement and Dance

Brainstorm a list of cool color objects found in nature. For example: grass, water, ice, icicle, snow, rain, polar bear, and moon. Call out each of the objects you listed and have students move for eight counts expressing the cool quality and energy of each.

Focus

Time: About 10 minutes

Activate Prior Knowledge

"Think about things in nature that feel cool. What colors are these objects?" *"Piensen en cosas de la naturaleza que sean frías. ¿De qué color son estas cosas?"*

Using Literature ⭐ Reading

- Read *Snowflake Bentley* by Jacqueline Briggs Martin, illustrated by Mary Azarian. Discuss the use of cool colors in the illustrations.

Thematic Connection ⭐ Social Studies

- **Jobs:** Have students discuss different kinds of jobs found in big cities.

Introduce the Art

Look NSAE 3.a

"Look at the two works of art." *"Observen detalladamente las dos obras de arte".*

Main Idea and Details ⭐ Reading

- Have students describe the subject matter in each artwork. Both paintings illustrate depth and feature cool colors. *Lighted City* is made up of mainly vertical and diagonal lines, while *Sea Grasses and Blue Sea* is mainly made up of horizontal lines. *Lighted City* uses large and small objects to create depth.

Art History and Culture

Possible answers: One work is a city street and the other is a deserted beach. Both works have a quiet feeling because of the cool colors.

Point out to students that both of these works were painted in the twentieth century. How are the styles of the works similar? Possible answer: Simplified shapes.

Web Connection

Visit **www.artnet.com/ag/fulltextsearch.asp?searchstring=wayne+thiebaud** to view more works of art by Wayne Thiebaud.

Cool Colors

Look at both works of art. They were created by twentieth-century artists. Milton Avery believed aesthetic composition should dominate his work. Wayne Thiebaud was concerned with realism. Both artists emphasized the use of cool colors in these paintings.

◄ **Wayne Thiebaud.** (American). *Lighted City.* 1987.

Gouache and charcoal on paper. 29 × 20 inches (74 × 51 cm.). Private Collection.

Art History and Culture

Look at these two works of art that show different outdoor scenes. How did the two artists use cool colors to suggest a calm emotion or feeling?

Art History and Culture NSAE 4.a; 4.b; 4.c; 5.a; 5.b

Wayne Thiebaud

Wayne Thiebaud (wān tē′ bō) (1920–) is considered a leading figure in modern American art. Born in Mesa, Arizona, Thiebaud began his artistic career as a cartoonist and commercial artist. While serving in the Army Air Corps., he developed the character Aleck for a comic strip called *Wingtips*. Many of Thiebaud's favorite themes include large-scale, isolated figures.

Lighted City is a gouache and charcoal on paper. A gouache is a method of painting using watercolors.

See pages 24–25 and 16–21 for more about art history and subject matter.

Artist Profiles, p. 54

• Artist Profile •

Wayne Thiebaud
b. 1920

Wayne Thiebaud (wān tē′ bō), one of California's most famous contemporary painters, has earned as many awards for excellence in teaching as he has for his painting and printmaking. He became interested in drawing in high school and later worked as a freelance cartoonist and illustrator. He continued his artwork during his military service in the U.S. Air Force during World War II. He drew cartoons for the military base newspaper. In 1949 Thiebaud decided to become a painter. His first one-person show in New York City was praised by the critics. At that time his subjects were mass-produced consumer goods, particularly junk food, and he was mistakenly classified with the pop artists.

▲ **Milton Avery.** (American).
Sea Grasses and Blue Sea.
1958.

Oil on canvas. 60 ⅛ × 6 ⅜ inches (152.4
× 15.24 cm.). The Museum of Modern
Art, New York, New York.

Study both works of art to find the following cool colors.

▶ Find the different kinds of blue.

▶ Find the intermediate colors blue-green and blue-violet.

▶ How do the cool colors affect the mood of each painting?

🔍 Aesthetic Perception

Seeing Like an Artist Look through magazines to find pictures of blue, green, and violet objects in nature. Write down what you see.

🏺 Art History and Culture

NSAE 4.a; 4.b; 4.c; 5.a; 5.b

Milton Avery

Milton Avery (mil´ tən ā´ və rē) (1893–1964), an American painter, was born in New York but grew up in Connecticut. Around 1905, Avery attended both the Connecticut League of Art Students in Hartford, Connecticut, and later the School of the Art Society in Hartford. He developed his own unique style that combined elements of American impressionism with abstract, simplified shapes similar to the style of Matisse. Often he would paint all day long in his New York studio, sometimes creating five or six paintings or studies in a day, establishing himself as a dedicated "color field" painter. He spent 50 years of his life painting, and created thousands of works of art.

See pages 24–25 and 16–21 for more about art history and subject matter.

Artist Profiles, p. 6

◆ Artist Profile ◆
Milton Avery
1893–1964
Milton Avery (mil´ tan ā´ va rē) was born in New York but grew up in Connecticut. He loved to paint and travel, and he also loved nature, landscapes, and color. Around 1905, Avery attended both the Connecticut League of Art Students in Hartford, Connecticut, and later the School of the Art Society in Hartford. Often he would paint all day long in his New York studio, sometimes creating five or six paintings or studies in a day. He established himself as a dedicated color field painter. He spent 50 years of his life painting, and created thousands of works of art.

Study

▶ Blue: In *Lighted City,* blue is found in the buildings and on the streets. In *Sea Grasses and Blue Sea,* the light shapes in the right upper triangle.

▶ Blue-Green: In *Sea Grasses and Blue Sea,* a light value of blue-green is in the lower left triangle. The strip across the top representing sky is blue-green.

Blue-Violet: In *Lighted City,* blue-violet appears in the buildings, the streets, and the shadows. In *Sea Grasses and Blue Sea,* the darker blue in the upper triangle is blue-violet.

▶ Mood: *Lighted City* has a mood of busyness. In *Sea Grasses and Blue Sea,* the blues create quiet moods in both pictures.

■ For more examples of art from North America, see the *Art Around the World* collection.

📓 Art Journal: Writing

Encourage students to write explanations of cool colors in the Concepts section of their Art Journals. What else do they want to know about cool colors?

🔍 Aesthetic Perception

NSAE 2.a; 2.b; 3.a

Seeing Like an Artist Have students look through magazines to find examples of blue, green, and violet objects. Ask the students what things they see. The may notice objects like grass, water or fruit. Explain that artists will use cool colors to suggest a calm or emotion feeling.

NSAE 4.a; 4.b; 4.c

Developing Visual Literacy Have students discuss the objects they find and what the colors cause them to think about. For example looking at blue water may cause them to think a cold swim at the lake. Invite students to share personal experiences of how colors have affected their moods.

💻 Web Connection

Visit **www.moma.org** to learn more about The Museum of Modern Art, New York, New York.

Teach

"How can you create a drawing using cool colors?" "¿Cómo pueden crear un dibujo usando colores frescos?"

■ Discuss the definition of *cool colors* and ways to mix the cool intermediate colors on page 110.

Practice NSAE 1.a; 1.d

Materials: 9" x 12" white paper; blue, green, and violet crayons

Alternate Materials: colored pencils

■ Distribute the materials and have students follow the directions on page 110.

Creative Expression

NSAE 1.a; 1.c; 1.d; 2.c; 3.b
Materials: 9" × 12" construction paper in cool colors, scissors, tape or glue, oil pastels in cool colors, sketch paper, pencils, markers

Alternate Materials: wood scraps, liquid tempera paints

■ Distribute the materials and have students follow the directions on page 111.

■ Review the Activity Tips on page 239 for visual examples if needed.

Art Journal: Brainstorming

Have students brainstorm ideas for creating different environments. Have them review the cool spectral and intermediate colors using the color wheel from their Art Journals. Have students decide how they will show their environments in the Creative Expression activity.

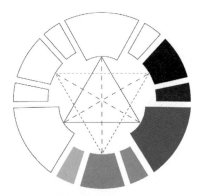

Using Cool Colors

Blue, green, and violet are considered **cool colors.** They can remind us of cool objects such as grass, water, and ice. Yellow-green, green, blue-green, blue, violet, and blue-violet are colors that are related, like members of a family. You can find them on a color wheel to see what they have in common.

Practice

Create a drawing using cool colors. Use crayons and white paper.

1. Write these words on a sheet of paper: *ocean, sky, grapes, grass, leaves,* and *lettuce.*

2. On the same sheet of paper, create a drawing that includes each of the objects listed above. Use the correct cool colors to color the objects.

Differentiated Instruction

Reteach
Have students look through the *Student Edition* to find three works of art that use cool colors. Ask students to list the title of each work and describe the cool colors they find.

Special Needs
Have visual prompts such as color wheels and posters of cool color schemes found in art and advertising for students to examine as they begin this activity.

ELL Tips
Pair English-language learners with more fluent English-speaking peers to look through magazines to find blue, green, and violet things in nature. Use this as an opportunity for students to learn new vocabulary in a low-risk way.

◄ **Jenna Mooney.**
Age 8.

Think about a name for this student artist's sculpture that ties its cool colors with the environment.

 Creative Expression

Where in your environment do you see cool colors? Design a sculpture of an environment using cool colors.

1. Think of ideas dealing with your environment, such as an animal habitat or a playground in the year 3001. Choose an idea and then sketch a few things you would find there.

2. Select several pieces of cool-colored paper. Choose one piece for the base. Outline objects you want in your environment on the other sheets of paper and cut them out. Add detail with oil pastels in cool colors. Attach the objects to your base.

Art Criticism

Describe Describe your environment. What objects did you use? How did you decide where to place them?

Analyze Which cool colors did you use?

Interpret How did using only cool colors affect the mood of your environment?

Decide If you could redo your sculpture, what would you do? What colors would you add?

 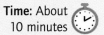

Reflect

Time: About 10 minutes

Review and Assess

"What feelings or moods do cool colors express?" "¿Qué sentimientos o ánimos expresan los colores frescos?"

Think
NSAE 1.b; 2.a; 2.b

The artist might name the work of art *Purple Playground.*

■ Use *Large Prints 42 Noreaster* to have students compare the uses of cool colors.
NSAE 1.b; 2.a; 2.b; 3.a; 5.c

Informal Assessment

Art Journal: Critical Thinking

Have students answer the four art criticism questions—Describe, Analyze, Interpret, and Decide—in their Art Journals. In small groups, have students discuss the expressive effects of cool colors in their sculptural environments.

■ For standardized-format test practice using this lesson's art content, see pages 36–37 in *Reading and Writing Test Preparation.*

■ Create a class exhibition. Have students identify the main idea in the works of art. Discuss the use of cool colors in the works.

Art Across the Curriculum

Use these simple ideas to reinforce art concepts across the curriculum

★ **Personal Writing** Explain to students how the title of *Lighted City* is considered a play on words. The painting does really show light. Have students draw a picture and give it a name that is a play on words. For example the student may draw a plate with food on it and call it a *square meal.*

★ **Math** Have students estimate the amount of time it took to paint *Sea Grasses and Blue Sea.*

★ **Science** Have students discuss and name the different bodies of water located in their community.

★ **Social Studies** Ask students to discuss the differences between an urban and rural community. Ask them to list which *Lighted City* appears to be, urban or rural?

★ **Technology** Have students use the paint program to create a drawing using cool colors. Visit **SRAonline.com** to print detailed instructions for this activity.

NSAE 6.b

Cool Colors

Wrap-Up

Extra! For the Art Specialist

NSAE 1.a; 1.b; 1.c; 1.d; 2.a; 2.b; 2.c; 3.b

Time: About 45 minutes

Focus

Use *Transparency 16* and *Large Print 42 Noreaster* to discuss the use of cool colors. Have students point out the cool colors in the artwork. How does the artist's use of these colors make you feel when you look at the artwork? How would the painting be different if the artist had used warm colors instead of cool colors?

Teach

Have students follow the directions to complete their drawings of a flower garden.

Reflect

Have students evaluate their works of art using the four steps of art criticism. Encourage them to locate more colors in the classroom and school building.

Alternate Activity

Materials:
- 9" × 12" white drawing paper
- oil pastels (only cool colors)
- watercolors (only cool colors)
- paint brushes
- water containers

1. Explain to students they will be drawing an up-close view of a flower garden using only cool colors.

2. Students will fill their papers with different types of flowers drawn with oil pastels in cool colors.

3. When the space on the papers is filled with flower shapes, students will paint the flowers with watercolors, again using only cool colors.

Research in Art Education

"Enriched and stimulated in art classes by a teacher's varied and challenging motivations, children learn to see more, sense more, and recall more . . . Some people, however, think that anything a child draws paints, or constructs is art . . . It may indeed be a child's visual statement, but it is not necessarily a quality work of art. To have quality, it must, as much as possible, be expressed in the language, structure, and form of art" (Wachowiak, Frank, and Robert Clements, *Emphasis Art: A Qualitative Art Program for Elementary and Middle Schools* (7th ed.) New York: Longman, 2001).

Assessment

Use the following rubric to evaluate the artwork students make in the Creative Expression activity and to assess students' understanding of cool colors.

Have students complete page 39 or 40 in their *Assessment* books.

	Art History and Culture	Aesthetic Perception	Creative Expression	Art Criticism
3 POINTS	The student demonstrates knowledge of the lives and art of Wayne Thiebaud and Milton Avery.	The student accurately identifies cool colors and their expressive qualities.	The student effectively plans and creates a three-dimensional sculpture using cool colors.	The student evaluates his or her work using the four steps of art criticism.
2 POINTS	The student shows emerging awareness of the lives and art of Wayne Thiebaud and Milton Avery.	The student shows emerging awareness of cool colors and their expressive qualities.	The student shows some awareness of how to plan and create a three-dimensional sculpture using cool colors.	The student attempts to evaluate his or her work but shows an incomplete understanding of evaluation criteria.
1 POINT	The student does not demonstrate knowledge of the lives and art of Wayne Thiebaud and Milton Avery.	The student cannot identify cool colors or their expressive qualities.	The student shows no understanding of how to plan and create a three-dimensional sculpture using cool colors.	The student makes no attempt to evaluate his or her artwork.

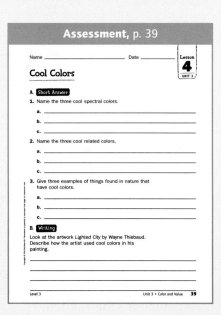

Assessment, p. 39

Name _____ Date _____

Lesson 4 UNIT 3

Cool Colors

A. Short Answer
1. Name the three cool spectral colors.
   a. _____
   b. _____
   c. _____
2. Name the three cool related colors.
   a. _____
   b. _____
   c. _____
3. Give three examples of things found in nature that have cool colors.
   a. _____
   b. _____
   c. _____

B. Writing
Look at the artwork *Lighted City* by Wayne Thiebaud. Describe how the artist used cool colors in his painting.

_____
_____
_____

Level 3   Unit 3 • Color and Value   39

Warm Colors

Lesson 5 introduces warm colors (red, orange, and yellow) and their expressive qualities.

Objectives

 Art History and Culture

To demonstrate knowledge of the lives and art of Paul Klee and Georgia O'Keeffe NSAE 4.a; 4.b; 4.c

 Creative Expression

To plan and create an imaginary landscape painting using warm colors NSAE 1.c; 1.d

 Aesthetic Perception

To identify warm colors and their expressive qualities in art and in the environment NSAE 2.a; 2.b; 2.c

 Art Criticism

To use the four steps of art criticism to evaluate own work NSAE 5.a; 5.b; 5.c

Vocabulary ⭐ Vocabulary

Review the following vocabulary words with students before beginning the lesson.

batik batik—the method of using wax and dye on fabric to create a picture or design

warm colors colores cálidos —colors that give a feeling of warmth: red, orange, and yellow

See page 119B for additional vocabulary and Spanish resources.

 Art Journal: Vocabulary

Have students add these words to the Vocabulary section of their Art Journals.

Lesson Materials

- 12" × 18" white construction paper
- oil pastels
- watercolor paints
- paintbrushes of various sizes
- containers of water
- sketch paper
- pencils
- tape
- paper towels
- 9" × 12" paper

Alternate Materials:
- dustless chalk

Program Resources

- *Reading and Writing Test Prep.,* pp. 38–39
- *Transparency*
- *Flash Cards 17*
- *Artist Profiles,* pp. 31, 44
- *Assessment,* pp. 41–42
- *Large Prints 41 Firebirds* and *42 Noreaster*
- *The National Museum of Women in the Arts Collection*

Concept Trace

Warm Colors

Introduced: Level 2, Unit 3, Lesson 2

Reinforced: Level 4, Unit 3, Lesson 6

Lesson 5 Arts Integration

Theatre

Complete Unit 3, Lesson 5, on pages 62–63 of *Theatre Arts Connections.*

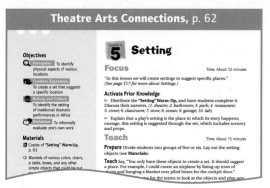

Music

Listen to *Humming Chorus* from *Madame Butterfly*, by Giacomo Puccini. This music was used in the opera when Madame Butterfly was waiting for a loved one. What emotions do you think she was having at this time? What instruments did the composer choose to portray her patience and faith?

Movement and Dance

Brainstorm a list of warm color objects found in nature. For example: sun, fire, lightning, light bulb, candle, and fireworks. Call out each of the objects you listed and have students move for eight counts expressing the warm quality and energy of each.

 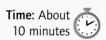

Focus

Time: About 10 minutes

Activate Prior Knowledge

"Think about things in nature that feel hot. What colors are these objects?" *"Piensen en cosas de la naturaleza que sean calientes. ¿De qué color son estas cosas?"*

- Discuss student's responses and how reds, oranges, and yellows create a feeling of warmth.

Using Literature ⭐ Reading

- Read *How I Spent My Summer Vacation* by Mark Teague. Ask students to identify warm colors in the illustrations.

Thematic Connection ⭐ Social Studies

- Plants: Have students discuss places they have visited and seen colorful flower garderns.

Introduce the Art

Look NSAE 3.a

"Let's look closely at the two works of art." *"Vamos a observar detalladamente las dos obras de arte".*

Comparing and Contrasting ⭐ Reading

- Have students describe the subject matter in each artwork. *Rotes Haus* is iconographic and *Red Canna* is an abstract painting.

- Have students list the similarities and differences between the two works of art. *Rotes Haus* illustrates shallow space, displays the subject as the center of interest, and uses warm colors. *Rotes Haus* displays large, simple geometric shapes. *Red Canna* is an abstract painting that illustrates a giant-sized flower and uses free-form shapes. Horizontal and vertical lines make *Rotes Haus* appear to be calm, while *Red Canna* has curved lines that could convey a sense of movement.

Art History and Culture

Answers may vary: *Red Canna* is based on observations of the red canna flower. *Rotes Haus* is an imaginary image.

 Web Connection

Visit **www.tumbletales.com/masters/index.html** to learn more about Paul Klee.

112 UNIT 3 • Color and Value

Lesson 5

Warm Colors

▲ **Paul Klee.** (Swiss). *Rotes Haus.* 1929.

Oil on canvas mounted on cardboard. 10 × 10 ⅞ inches (25 × 28 cm.). San Francisco Museum of Modern Art, San Francisco, California.

Look at the works of art on these two pages. *Rotes Haus* means "red house." Georgia O'Keeffe created *Red Canna*, which means "red flower," around 1925. Both artists used warm colors in their artwork.

 Art History and Culture

Which work of art is strictly imaginary, and which one is based on observation?

112 Unit 3 • Lesson 5

 Art History and Culture NSAE 4.a; 4.b; 4.c; 5.a; 5.b

Paul Klee

Paul Klee (paul klā) (1879–1940) was born into a musical Swiss family. His family hoped he also would become a musician. At age five, his grandmother gave him his first box of pencils. He thought of himself as an artist from then on, but he still kept an interest in music. Klee believed that childlike drawings were the most creative and original. He used line and color to imitate the simplicity of children's artwork. Klee lived in Munich, Germany, during a time Hitler banned jazz from the airwaves and confiscated art.

See pages 24–25 and 16–21 for more about art history and subject matter.

 **Artist Profiles, p. 31**

Artist Profile

Paul Klee
1879–1940

Paul Klee (paul klā) was born into a musical Swiss family. His family hoped he also would become a musician. At age five his grandmother gave him his first box of pencils. He thought of himself as an artist from then on, but he continued to have an interest in music. Klee played his violin for an hour nearly every morning of his life. He married a pianist. As an adult Klee still drew in a childlike way. Klee believed that childlike drawings were the most creative and original. He was not trying to share his ideas through his work. He just wanted to explore his imagination. Klee could use either hand proficiently when painting.

◀ **Georgia O' Keeffe.** (American).
Red Canna. 1925-1928.
....
Oil on canvas. 36 × 30 inches (91 × 76 cm.).
University of Arizona Museum of Art, Tucson,
Arizona.

Study both works of art to find the following
warm colors.

▶ Find the spectral hues red, orange, and yellow.

▶ Where are the intermediate hues red-orange and
yellow-orange?

▶ How would you describe the mood or feeling of
each piece?

Aesthetic Perception

Seeing Like an Artist Look at what your classmates are
wearing. Find examples of warm hues like those you saw in
the artwork.

Study
NSAE 1.b; 2.a; 2.b; 3.a; 5.c

▶ Red, orange, and yellow: *Red Canna* has
warm colors throughout.

▶ Red-orange and yellow-orange: *Red Canna*
has these colors throughout.

▶ Mood: *Rotes Haus* and *Red Canna* both
convey a sense of warmth.

■ For more examples of abstract art see ***The
National Museum of Women in the Arts
Collection.***

Art Journal: Writing
Encourage students to write
explanations of warm colors in the
Concepts section of their Art Journals.
What else do they want to know about
warm colors?

Aesthetic Perception

NSAE 2.a; 2.b; 3.a
Design Awareness Discuss with students
some places in nature where they might find
warm colors.
NSAE 4.a; 4.b; 4.c
Developing Visual Literacy Discuss each
artwork and what it conveys. What meanings
are the artists trying to convey? Invite
students to discuss any personal experiences
that contribute to their understanding of the
works of art.

Art History and Culture

NSAE 4.a; 4.b; 4.c; 5.a; 5.b

Georgia O'Keeffe

Georgia O'Keeffe (jôr´jə ō kēf´) (1887–1986) was born in Sun Prairie,
Wisconsin. At the age of ten, she began taking private art lessons,
but what she enjoyed most was experimenting with art at home.
By the age of thirteen, O'Keeffe had decided to become an artist.
She trained under experts and won many prizes for her art. For
years, she challenged the art world with her unique vision. She
eventually became famous for her spectacular, larger-than-life
paintings of such natural objects as flowers, animal skulls, and
shells. She loved nature,
especially the desert of New
Mexico, where she spent the
last half of her life.

See pages 24–25 and 16–21
for more about art history
and subject matter.

Artist Profiles, p. 44

▶ Artist Profile ▶

Georgia O'Keeffe
1887-1986
Georgia O'Keeffe (jôr´ jə ō kēf´) was born
in Sun Prairie, Wisconsin. At the age of ten
she began taking private art lessons, but
the thing she liked most was experimenting
with art at home. By 13, she had decided to
become an artist. She trained under experts
and won many prizes for her art. For years
she challenged the art world with her
unique vision. She eventually became
famous for her spectacular, larger-than-life
paintings of natural objects, including
flowers, animal skulls, and shells. She loved
nature, especially the desert of New Mexico,
where she spent the last half of her life.
O'Keeffe was married to the famous
American photographer Alfred Stieglitz
and appears in many of his photographs.

Web Connection
Visit **www.okeeffemuseum.org/indexflash.php** to
learn more about Georgia O'Keeffe.

Teach

Time: About 45 minutes

"How can you create a variety of warm colors?" "¿Cómo pueden crear una variedad de colores cálidos?"

■ Discuss the definition of *warm colors* and ways to mix the intermediate warm colors on page 114.

Practice NSAE 1.a; 1.d

Materials: 9" × 12" paper folded into three boxes, watercolor paints, paintbrushes, containers of water

Alternate Materials: crayons

■ Distribute the materials and have students follow the directions on page 114.

NSAE 1.a; 1.c; 1.d; 2.c; 3.b

Creative Expression

Materials: 12" × 18" white construction paper, oil pastels, watercolor paints, paintbrushes of various sizes, containers of water, sketch paper, pencils, tape, paper towels

Alternate Materials: dustless chalk

■ Distribute the materials and have students follow the directions on page 115.

■ Review the Activity Tips on page 240 for visual examples if needed.

Art Journal: Brainstorming

Have students brainstorm ways to include three unrelated items as part of a painting in their Art Journals. Then have students select three or four items and plan how they will use warm colors in their paintings for the Creative Expression activity.

Using Warm Colors

Warm colors are the **spectral colors** yellow, orange, and red that give a sense of warmth in a work of art. They can be found opposite the cool colors on the color wheel.

Red-violet, red, red-orange, orange, yellow-orange, and yellow are warm colors that are related. They remind many people of warm or hot things like fire and the sun.

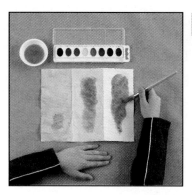

Practice

Mix a variety of warm colors. Use watercolor paints, brushes, and white paper.

1. Fold your sheet of paper into three equal parts. Paint the first box red, the middle box orange, and the last box yellow.

2. While the paint is still wet, add different amounts of violet to the red box, then mix.

3. In the same way, add and mix red in the orange box, and orange in the yellow box.

114   Unit 3 • Lesson 5

Differentiated Instruction

Reteach
Have students identify objects in the classroom that have each of the warm spectral and intermediate colors. Ask students to list the objects and the warm color of each object.

Special Needs
To reinforce project objectives of using warm colors in an imaginary scene, show students the work of surrealist artist Rene Magritte.

ELL Tips
Bring three unrelated objects and demonstrate how you will use these to create a fantasy landscape. As you demonstrate, talk about what you're doing. Then pair English-language learners with more peers, and invite them to talk about the objects in the landscape that each student will paint.

◀ **Michael Powell.**
Age 8.

Think about what makes this student artwork imaginary.

 Creative Expression

What colors in your environment give you a feeling of warmth? Create an imaginative painting using warm colors.

1. Use your imagination to create a fantasy landscape that includes three unrelated items such as a matchstick, a bowling pin, and a pair of sunglasses. Make a rough sketch of your idea.

2. Use lines to draw your idea on a sheet of white paper with warm-colored oil pastels.

3. Mix a variety of warm values with watercolor paint. Paint your scene. Remember that the values will get lighter as you add more water to your paint.

Art Criticism

Describe What objects did you include in your imaginative painting?

Analyze Name the warm colors you used in your landscape.

Interpret How did using only warm colors affect the mood of your imaginative painting? How would adding cool colors change the mood?

Decide If you could do this artwork over again, how would you improve it?

Reflect

Review and Assess

"What have you learned about the way artists use warm colors? "¿Qué han aprendido acerca de la manera en que los artistas usan los colores cálidos?"

Think
NSAE 1.b; 2.a; 2.b

The huge clock, matches, and centipede that the student artist included to make this work appear to be imaginary.

■ Use *Large Print 41 Firebirds* to have students identify uses of warm colors.

NSAE 1.b; 2.a; 2.b; 3.a; 5.c

Informal Assessment

Art Journal: Critical Thinking
Have students answer the four art criticism question—Describe, Analyze, Interpret, and Decide—in their Art Journals. In small groups, have students discuss the use of warm colors in their imaginary landscapes.

■ For standardized-format test practice using this lessons art content, see pages 38–39 in *Reading and Writing Test Preparation.*

Art Across the Curriculum

Use these simple ideas to reinforce art concepts across the curriculum

★ **Expository Writing** Paul Klee painted during a time when the Germans freedom was taken away. Have students use an encyclopedia find out more about two other important leaders during World War II and write a paragraph about them.

★ **Math** Have students look at *Rotes Haus* and list three shapes they see in the painting.

★ **Science** Have students write the names of different states where warm colors could be used to describe the weather conditions.

★ **Social Studies** Have students find out one important fact about the state of Wisconsin where Georgia O'Keeffe was born. Have them write a sentence about their findings.

★ **Technology** Have students use the paint program to create a drawing using warm colors. Visit **SRAonline.com** to print detailed instructions for this activity.

NSAE 6.b

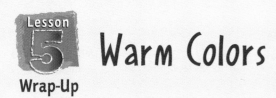

Warm Colors

Extra! **For the Art Specialist**
NSAE 1.a; 1.b; 1.c; 1.d; 2.a; 2.b; 2.c; 3.b

Time: About 45 minutes

Focus

Use *Transparency 17* and *Large Print 41* to demonstrate how artists use warm colors. Have students point out how warm colors are used in the artwork. How do the warm colors make the students feel? Discuss how the warm and cool colors are used differently in the background and foreground of the artwork (or in the positive and negative space of the artwork).

Teach

Have students follow the directions to complete their paintings using warm colors.

Reflect

Have students evaluate their works of art using the four steps of art criticism. Encourage them to locate other areas in the classroom where they see warm colors.

Alternate Activity

Materials:
- 12" × 18" white drawing or watercolor paper
- black permanent fine tip markers
- watercolor paints (only warm colors)
- paint brushes
- water containers

1. Talk with students about different points of view in a drawing or painting. Ask them to imagine they are very small, about the size of a bug. How would the grass, flowers, and insects look to them if they were the size of an ant?

2. Have students use black permanent markers to make a drawing from a bug's eye view of a garden.

3. Students will paint their drawings with a watercolor wash using warm colors.

Research in Art Education

"The arts help student develop their abilities to appreciate and interpret art of other cultures and to learn about people of the past through exposure to reproductions, to art works in museums and galleries, or through discussions about contemporary artists and art works" (Andrea Nyman, "Cultural Content, Identity, and Program Development: Approaches to Art Education for Elementary Educators," in *Contemporary Issues in Art Education,* edited by Y. Gaudelius and P. Speirs, 61–69. New Jersey: Prentice Hall, 2002).

Assessment

Use the following rubric to evaluate the artwork students make in the Creative Expression activity and to assess students' understanding of warm colors and their expressive qualities.

	Art History and Culture	Aesthetic Perception	Creative Expression	Art Criticism
3 POINTS	The student demonstrates knowledge of the lives and art of Paul Klee and Georgia O'Keeffe.	The student accurately identifies warm colors and their expressive qualities in art and in the environment.	The student effectively plans and creates an imaginary landscape painting using a variety of warm colors.	The student evaluates his or her work using the four steps of art criticism.
2 POINTS	The student shows emerging awareness of the lives and art of Paul Klee and Georgia O'Keeffe.	The student shows emerging awareness of warm colors and their expressive qualities in art and in the environment.	The student shows some awareness of how to plan and create an imaginary landscape painting using a variety of warm colors.	The student attempts to evaluate his or her work but shows an incomplete understanding of evaluation criteria.
1 POINT	The student does not demonstrate knowledge of the lives and art of Paul Klee and Georgia O'Keeffe.	The student cannot identify warm colors or their expressive qualities in art or in the environment.	The student shows no understanding of how to plan and create an imaginary painting using a variety of warm colors.	The student makes no attempt to evaluate his or her artwork.

Have students complete page 41 or 42 in their *Assessment* books.

Assessment, p. 41

Name _____ Date _____ Lesson **5** UNIT 3

Warm Colors

A. Coloring
Use crayons to color each of the boxes below with the warm spectral colors.

B. Short Answer
1. Name the three warm related colors.
   a. _____
   b. _____
   c. _____
2. Name three objects found in nature that have warm colors.
   a. _____
   b. _____
   c. _____

C. Writing
Look at the artwork *Red Canna* by Georgia O'Keeffe. Describe how the artist used warm colors in this abstract painting.
_____
_____

Level 3   Unit 3 • Color and Value   41

Lesson 6 Color Contrasts

Overview

Lesson 6 introduces the uses of color contrasts in artwork to make objects and subjects stand out.

Objectives

Art History and Culture

To identify the similarities and differences in works of art from different cultures NSAE 4.a; 4.b; 4.c

Creative Expression

To design a mural using color contrasts

NSAE 1.c; 1.d

Aesthetic Perception

To identify contrasting colors in art and in the environment
NSAE 2.a; 2.b; 2.c

Art Criticism

To use the four steps of art criticism to evaluate own work

NSAE 5.a; 5.b; 5.c

Vocabulary Vocabulary

Review the following vocabulary words with students before beginning the lesson.

contrast *contraste*—a difference between two things in an artwork

warm colors *colores cálidos*—spectral colors that give the feeling of warmth: red, orange, and yellow.

See page 119B for additional Spanish vocabulary resources.

Art Journal: Vocabulary

Have students add these words to the Vocabulary section of their Art Journals.

Lesson Materials

- large sheets of mural paper
- liquid tempera paints
- large paintbrushes
- 12" × 18" construction paper in warm colors
- oil pastels
- glue
- scissors
- paper towels
- palettes
- containers of water
- newspapers

Alternate Materials:
- construction paper of warm and cool colors

Program Resources

- *Reading and Writing Test Prep.,* pp. 40–41
- *Transparency 18*
- *Artist Profiles,* pp. 58, 64
- *Assessment,* pp. 43–44
- *Large Prints 41 Firebirds* and *42 Noreaster*
- *Art Around the World Collection*

Concept Trace

Color Contrasts

Introduced: Level 2, Unit 5, Lesson 4

Reinforced: Level 4, Unit 3, Lesson 3

Lesson 6 Arts Integration

Theatre

Complete Unit 3, Lesson 6, on pages 64–69 of *Theatre Arts Connections.*

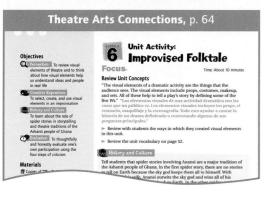

Music

 The contrast of tone colors in music keep our interest and also help us to identify the form. Listen to *Hornpipe* from *Water Music Suite* by George Frederic Handel. The strings introduce a melody that is repeated by the oboe and bassoon from what different orchestral family?

Movement and Dance

Using the movement technique of call and response, students work with a partner to explore cool and warm colors in movement. Student #1 moves for four beats using cool, smooth, fluid energy and then freezes. Student #2 moves for four counts using warm, bursting, explosive energy and then freezes. Repeat this pattern four times, encouraging students to find new ways to move with their color quality.

Focus

Activate Prior Knowledge

"Think about flowers growing outside. Why do the flowers attract your attention before you notice the leaves? "Piensen en las flores que crecen al aire libre. ¿Por qué las flores les llaman la atención antes de que noten las hojas?"

Using Literature [★] Reading

■ Read *The Mountain That Loved a Bird* by Alice McLerran, illustrated by Eric Carle. Have students study the illustrations and identify examples of contrast.

Thematic Connection [★] Social Studies

■ **Animals:** Have students discuss what kinds of animals they would place on a jar if they were creating one.

Introduce the Art

Look NSAE 3.a

"Let's look closely at the two works of art."
"Vamos a observar detalladamente las dos obras de arte".

Main Ideas and Details [★] Reading

■ Have students describe the subject matter in each artwork. Both are landscapes.

■ Have students make a list of similarities and differences between the two works of art. Both works illustrate underwater scenes, incorporate carp, and are realistic in style. *Pistia Kew* is a two-dimensional painting that shows a bird's-eye view, while *Covered Jar* is a three-dimensional form that can be viewed from different sides.

 Art History and Culture

Idelle Weber's focus on color and form is shown in *Pistia Kew*. Her attention to detail and realism cause the viewer to wonder if her painting is actually a photograph.

 Web Connection

Visit **www.idelleweber.com** to learn more about Idelle Weber.

116 UNIT 3 • Color and Value

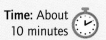 **Lesson 6**

Color Contrast

◀ **Idelle Weber.** (America Pistia Kew. 1989.
....
Oil on linen. 58 × 59 inches (14´ × 150 cm.). Schmidt Bingham Gallery, New York, New York.

Look at the artwork on these pages. *Pistia Kew* was painted by Idelle Weber in 1989. *Covered Jar* was created in China about 400 years ago. Both works show a contrast of warm and cool colors.

 Art History and Culture

Idelle Weber is best known for painting realistic objects seen in everyday environments.

116 Unit 3 • Lesson 6

Art History and Culture

NSAE 4.a; 4.b; 4.c; 5.a; 5.b

Idelle Weber

Idelle Weber (i´ del web´ ər) (1932–) was born in Chicago. She earned degrees in art at the University of California in Los Angeles. Weber's style is so realistic that her paintings look like photographs. Photo-realists usually take photographs of their subjects, then paint from these photographs and copy details with great accuracy. Weber and other photo-realists use a slide projector to project a photograph directly onto canvas. Then they paint using the photograph as the guide. Weber began painting as a realist in the 1950s. She teaches art at the college level.

See pages 24–25 and 16–21 for more about art history and subject matter.

Artist Profiles, p. 58

◆ Artist Profile ◆

Idelle Weber
b. 1932

Born in Chicago, Idelle Weber (i del we´ bar) grew up in Wilmette, Illinois, and Los Angeles, California. Drawing was her passion from an early age, and at the age of eight she became the youngest student to attend the Chouinard Art Institute of Los Angeles. Weber then moved to New York and painted images of city life in an abstract style. She was always fascinated with how things worked and were made and was very interested in depicting the lifestyles and objects she encountered while living in New York City.

◀ **Artist Unknown.**
(China). *Covered Jar.*
1522-1566.
....
Porcelain painted with underglaze
cobalt blue and overglaze enamels.
18 ½ inches high, 15 ¾ inches in
diameter (46.99 cm. high, 40 cm. in
diameter). Asia Society of New York,
New York.

Study both works of art to find the contrast
between warm and cool colors.

▶ Find all the cool colors. Are they placed near
each other?

▶ Locate all the warm colors.

 Aesthetic Perception

Seeing Like an Artist Look around your classroom and find
examples of cool colors that are near warm colors.

Art History and Culture

NSAE 4.a; 4.b; 4.c; 5.a; 5.b

Ming Dynasty Pottery

This covered jar was likely made by a professional artist trained in
the craft of pottery during the Ming dynasty. The term *dynasty*
refers to a series of rulers who come from the same family and rule
a country for a long time. The Ming dynasty ruled China from 1368
to 1644. Many great works of art, such as porcelain and silk items,
were produced during this time. These items were exported by boat
to faraway places like Africa and Europe.

See pages 24–25 and 16–21 for more about art history and subject
matter.

Artist Profiles, p. 64

⟨ Artist Profile ⟩

Covered Jar

This covered jar was probably made by a
professional artist trained in the craft of
pottery. Many excellent potters lived in
China during the Ming dynasty. They
produced many beautiful jars like this one.

◀ Artist unknown. (China). *Covered Jar.*
1522-1566.
Porcelain painted with underglaze cobalt blue and overglaze enamels.

NSAE 1.b; 2.a; 2.b; 3.a; 5.c

Study

▶ Cool Colors: In *Pistia Kew*, the water (blue)
and the leaves (green, yellow-green, and
blue-green) have cool colors. They are
placed near each other in the painting.

▶ Warm Colors: In *Covered Jar*, the carp
(orange, red-orange, and yellow-orange)
have warm colors. They are placed apart
from each other on the jar, which has the
most warm colors.

Color Contrast: In *Pistia Kew*, the
red-orange color of the fish attracts the
viewer's attention first because the fish
are placed in a background of cool colors.

■ For more examples of Asian art, see the
Art Around the World Collection.

Art Journal: Writing

Encourage students to write their
own explanations of color contrast in the
Concepts section of their Art Journals.
What else do they want to know about
color contrast?

Aesthetic Perception

NSAE 2.a; 2.b; 3.a
Seeing Like an Artist Discuss with students
how colors contrast. Have them look for
areas throughout the classroom or school
building where they see cool colors near
warm colors. Explain that artists use contrast
in their works of art to make colors and
subjects stand out.
NSAE 4.a; 4.b; 4.c
Developing Visual Literacy Have students
discuss the objects they found where colors
contrast. Ask them to describe the areas that
stand out to them.

Web Connection

Visit **www.historyforkids.org/learn/china/art/
ming.htm** to learn more about the Ming Dynasty.

each **Time:** About 45 minutes

"How can you create contrasts with warm and cool colors? *¿Cómo pueden crear contraste con colores cálidos y frescos?*"

■ Discuss the definition of contrast on page 118.

Practice NSAE 1.a; 1.d

Materials: 9" × 12" white paper, oil pastels

Alternate Materials: crayons

■ Distribute the materials and have students follow the directions on page 118.

Creative Expression

NSAE 1.a; 1.c; 1.d; 2.c; 3.b
Materials: large sheet of mural paper for every team, large paintbrushes, 12" × 18" construction paper in warm colors, oil pastels, glue, scissors, pencils, paper towels, palettes, containers of water, newspapers

Alternate Materials: construction paper of warm and cool colors

■ Distribute the materials and have students follow the directions on page 119.

■ Review the Activity Tips on page 240 for visual examples of techniques if needed.

Art Journal: Brainstorming

Have students brainstorm ideas for underwater plants, animals, and objects that they could use in a mural in their Art Journals. Then have students review warm and cool colors and techniques for creating color contrasts for the Creative Expression activity.

Using Color Contrast

Artists use **contrast** in order to show differences between two things.

The **warm colors** red, orange, and yellow come forward and attract your attention first. So do their related intermediate colors. The **cool colors** blue, green, and violet—and their related intermediate colors—seem to move away from you.

When warm colors are placed next to cool colors, a contrast is created.

Practice

Illustrate color contrast. Use oil pastels and white paper.

1. On a sheet of paper, place cool colors next to warm colors.

2. Mix the intermediate colors by blending the primary and secondary colors. Fill your paper with color contrasts.

Differentiated Instruction

Reteach

Have students look through the *Student Edition* to find three different works of art that illustrate color contrasts. Ask students to list the title of each work and identify the areas where color contrasts occur.

Special Needs

Show examples of color contrast as seen in posters, wrapping paper, wallpaper samples, or even clothes. Students will benefit from seeing the relationship between warm and cool colors in an array of materials.

ELL Tips

The group mural project is an especially supportive way for English-language learners to feel like productive members of the class. Prepare all students to appreciate each individual's strengths and weaknesses, especially as these pertain to language development.

Think about how the mood of this student's art would change if the background contained warm colors and the creatures were made using cool colors.

◀ **Aaron Ragans.** Age 8.

 Creative Expression

What warm-colored objects would you find in an underwater environment? Create a group mural contrasting warm and cool colors.

1. In a small group, make a list of underwater creatures. Draw the creatures on sheets of warm-colored construction paper. Use warm-colored oil pastels to add color and detail.

2. As a team, paint an underwater scene on a large sheet of paper. Mix cool colors to create water and plant life.

3. When the paint is dry, arrange and glue the sea creatures in place.

Art Criticism

Describe Describe the creatures your group created.

Analyze Which cool colors did you use in your mural? Which warm colors did you use?

Interpret How did the mood or feeling of your mural change when you added the warm-colored sea creatures to the background?

Decide If you could do this mural again, what would you do differently?

 **Reflect** Time: About 45 minutes

Review and Assess

What have you learned about color contrast?
"¿Qué han aprendido acerca del contraste de colores?"

Think   NSAE 1.b; 2.a; 2.b

The student artist used cool colors in the painting. The scene would have had a sense of warmth had the artist chosen warm colors.

■ Use *Large Prints 41 Firebirds* and *42 Noreaster* to have students identify color contrasts. Have students look through the *Student Edition* to find other examples of contrasting colors.
NSAE 1.b; 2.a; 2.b; 3.a; 5.c

Informal Assessment

Art Journal: Critical Thinking

Have students answer the four art criticism questions—Describe, Analyze, Interpret, and Decide—in their Art Journals. In small groups, have students discuss the use of color contrasts in their murals.

■ For standardized-format test practice using this lesson's art content, see pages 40–41 in *Reading and Writing Test Preparation.*

Art Across the Curriculum

Use these simple ideas to reinforce art concepts across the curriculum

★ **Descriptive Writing** Have students write a description of *Covered Jar*, including information about the contrasting colors.

★ **Math** Observe and record temperatures for several U.S. cities for a week. Study the contrasts in temperatures and discuss reasons for the differences.

★ **Science** Observe objects closely using a magnifying glass. Study the fine art with the magnifying glass. What new details do you notice?

★ **Social Studies** Study how Marco Polo set up trade with China, the origin of *Covered Jar*.

★ **Technology** Have students use a paint program to create a drawing that show contrast. Visit **SRAonline.com** to print detailed instructions for this activity.

NSAE 6.b

Extra! For the Art Specialist
NSAE 1.a; 1.b; 1.c; 1.d; 2.a; 2.b; 2.c; 3.b

Time: About 45 minutes

Focus
Use **Transparency 18** and **Large Prints 41** *Firebirds* and **42** *Noreaster* to demonstrate how colors contrast. Discuss with students how color can be used to create emphasis. Have them note changes in value (lightness and darkness of a color). Ask students if the artist used color to emphasize certain parts of the artwork. If so, explain how.

Teach
Have students follow the directions for creating a paper collage.

Reflect
Have students evaluate their own works of art using the four steps of art criticism. Encourage them to locate and describe other areas of contrasting colors in the classroom.

Alternate Activity

Materials:
- 9" × 12" white drawing paper or white posterboard, one per student
- tissue paper in warm and cool colors
- pencils
- scissors
- thinned white glue
- old paintbrushes

1. Tell students they will be making a landscape using tissue paper collage.

2. Students will use cool colors of tissue paper torn into 1" pieces for the background of their landscape. Have them lightly draw a horizon line about halfway up their paper. Brush the thinned glue mixture on a small section of the background, then carefully place the tissue paper on top. Paint over the tissue paper with another layer of the glue mixture to seal.

3. Students will use pieces of warm colors of tissue paper to make the foreground. They can cut or tear trees, plants, or landforms to complete their landscapes.

Research
in Art Education

Research continues to try and answer the questions of if and how the arts impacts student learning in other subject areas. Some researchers suggest that the relationship between the arts and other subject areas "may not be as unidirectional—from the arts to other disciplines—as other studies have implied. Rather, the relationship may be more dynamic and interactive" ("Learning in and Through the Arts: Curriculum Implications" in *Champions of Change*, p. 43).

Assessment
Use the following rubric to evaluate the artwork students make in the Creative Expression activity and to assess students' understanding of color contrast.

Have students complete page 43 or 44 in their *Assessment* books.

	Art History and Culture	Aesthetic Perception	Creative Expression	Art Criticism
3 POINTS	The student demonstrates and identifies the similarities and differences in the artwork from different cultures.	The student accurately identifies contrasting colors in art and in the environment.	The student effectively designs a mural using color contrast.	The student evaluates his or her work using the four steps of art criticism.
2 POINTS	The student's understanding of the differences in the artwork from different cultures is weak or incomplete.	The student shows emerging awareness of contrasting colors in art and in the environment.	The student shows some awareness of how to design a mural using color contrast.	The student attempts to evaluate his or her work using the four steps of art criticism.
1 POINT	The student does not display understanding of the differences in the artwork from different cultures.	The student cannot identify contrasting colors in art or in the environment.	The student shows no understanding of how to design a mural using color contrast.	The student makes no attempt to evaluate his or her work.

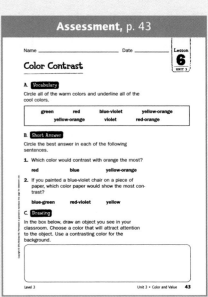

Assessment, p. 43

Unit 3 Vocabulary Review

batik—the method of using wax and dye on fabric to create a picture or design batik—el método de usar cera y tintura en una tela para crear una pintura o diseño

color spectrum—the range of colors that comes from light colores del espectro—el campo de colores que vienen de la luz

color wheel—a tool for organizing colors that shows the spectrum bent into a circle círculo cromático—una manera de organizar los colores que demuestran el espectro doblado en un círculo

contrast—the difference between two things in a work of art contraste—la diferencia entre dos cosas en una obra de arte

cool colors—spectral colors that give a feeling of coolness: blue, green, and violet colores frescos—colores del espectro que dan una sensación de fresco: azul, verde y violeta

hue—another name for *color* matiz—otro nombre para color

intermediate colors—colors made by mixing a primary color with a secondary color colores intermedios—colores hecho mediante la mezcla de un color primario con un color secundario

primary colors—red, yellow, and blue. Cannot be made by mixing other colors colores primarios—rojo, amarillo y azul. Que no se pueden hacer mezclando otros colores

secondary colors—colors that can be made by mixing together two primary colors colores secundarios—colores que son hechos mezclando dos colores primarios juntos

shade—the dark value of a color sombra—el valor oscuro de un color

tint—the light value of a color tono o tinte—el valor claro de un color

value—the lightness or darkness of a color valor—la claridad u oscuridad de un color

warm colors—spectral colors that give a feeling of warmth: red, orange, and yellow colores cálidos—colores del espectro que dan una sensación de calor: rojo, anaranjado y amarillo

Vocabulary Practice

T Display *Transparency 39* to review unit vocabulary words.

Categorizing/Classifying ⭐ Vocabulary
Have students classify the unit vocabulary words according to their parts of speech.

Dictionary Entries ⭐ Vocabulary
Have students find the word origins of the unit vocabulary words.

Definitions: Demonstrate Meanings ⭐ Vocabulary
Have volunteers act out a description of a unit vocabulary word.

Wrapping Up Unit 3
Color and Value

 Art Criticism

Critical Thinking Art criticism is an organized system for looking at and talking about art. You can criticize art without being an expert. The purpose of art criticism is to get the viewer involved in a perception process that delays judgment until all aspects of the artwork have been studied.

See pages 28–29 for more about art criticism.

Describe

▶ Ask students to describe what the credit line tells about the painting called *Display Rows*. Possible Answers: The credit line states that the artist is Wayne Thiebaud. The title is *Display Rows*. It was painted in 1989 with watercolor paints. The size is 11" × 9." The painting is located at the Campbell-Thiebaud Gallery in San Francisco, California.

▶ Ask them to describe what objects they see. Possible answers: The painting shows cakes, cookies and other foods lined up in five rows on a shiny surface.

Analyze

▶ Have students explain where they see primary colors. Possible answers: Red is visible in the wide layers on the second cake in the front row, on the top of the round cake with the white star in the second row, and on the cherry in row four. Yellow is on the top of the second cake in the first row, in the two middle cakes in row four, in the last cake in the back row. There is a touch of yellow on every dessert. Blue is on the stand in the foreground and in the shadows between the desserts,

▶ Where do they see secondary colors? Point them out. Possible answers: Green: The desserts in the front row on the left have green areas. The first cake in row two has a green curved line. In the back row, there is a green triangle. Violet: In the front row,

▲ **Wayne Thiebaud.** (American). *Display Rows.* 1989.
Watercolor. 11 × 9 inches (28 × 23 cm.). Private Collection.

Art History and Culture   NSAE 4.a; 4.b; 4.c; 5.a; 5.b

Wayne Thiebaud

Wayne Thiebaud (wān tē´ bō)(1920–), one of California's most famous contemporary painters, has earned as many awards for excellence in teaching as he has for his painting and printmaking. He became interested in drawing in high school and later worked as a freelance cartoonist and illustrator. Thiebaud continued with his art during military service in the United States Army Air Corps. during World War II by drawing cartoons for the military base newspaper.

In 1949 he decided to become a painter. His primary interest was to organize realistic subject matter in abstract compositions.

Artist Profiles, p. 54

Artist Profile

Wayne Thiebaud
b. 1920

Wayne Thiebaud (wān tē´ bō), one of California's most famous contemporary painters, has earned as many awards for excellence in teaching as he has for his painting and printmaking. He became interested in drawing in high school and later worked as a freelance cartoonist and illustrator. He continued his artwork during his military service in the U.S. Air Force during World War II. He drew cartoons for the military base newspaper. In 1949 Thiebaud decided to become a painter. His first one-person show in New York City was praised by the critics. At that time his subjects were mass-produced consumer goods, particularly junk food, and he was mistakenly classified with the pop artists

Describe **What do you see?**

During this step you will collect information about the subject of the work.

▶ What does the credit line tell you about the painting?

▶ What objects do you see?

Analyze **How is this work organized?**

Think about how the artist has used the elements and principles of art.

▶ Where do you see primary colors?

▶ What secondary colors do you see? Point them out.

Interpret **What is the artist trying to say?**

Use the clues you discovered during your analysis to find the message the artist is trying to show.

▶ What is out of the ordinary in this painting?

▶ Imagine that you are the manager of a store that sells these goodies. Write an advertisement for the local paper that will make people want to come.

Decide **What do you think about the work?**

Use all the information you have gathered to decide whether this is a successful work of art.

▶ Is this painting successful because it is realistic, because it is well organized, or because if has a strong message. Explain your answer.

Unit 3 **121**

 Aesthetic Perception

Seeing Like an Artist Have students find pictures in magazines that show pastries and desserts. Have them name specific places they could find these items.

Describe ▶ List and describe all the primary and secondary colors you find in the painting.

Analyze ▶ Name at least three intermediate colors in the painting.

Interpret ▶ Where do you see light and dark values? Do you see any warm and cool colors that contrast?

Decide ▶ Do you like the artwork? Why or why not?

the shadows on the sides of the desserts are violet. The first cake in row four has a layer of violet. In the second row the first dessert has a round violet shape. Orange: the first cake in the third row has an orange top.

Interpret

▶ **Have them explain what is out of the ordinary in this painting.** Answers will vary. Some will notice that all the foods are sitting on a shiny surface without plates or any other protective materials. They may also notice that the pieces of food are all different. When you see them in a display case all the same kinds of foods are usually together. Finally, some may realize that these are not normal food colors. The colors are very bright spectral colors.

▶ **Have students imagine that they are the manager of the store that sells these goodies.** They will write an advertisement for the local paper that will make people want to come. Use your imagination to invent a name for the store and to describe the items you have for sale. Answers will vary.

Decide

▶ **Ask students if this painting is successful because it is realistic, because it is well organized, or because it has a strong message? Explain your answer.** Answers will vary. Most will refer to the artist's organization of color. Some may refer to realism. Others may talk about a strong message about food.

Art Journal: Writing
Have students write answers to Aesthetic Perception in their Art Journals.

"Artists use primary, secondary, and intermediate colors to express feelings or moods in all kinds of art. Adding black or white to colors creates different values."

"Los artistas usan los colores primarios, secundarios e intermedios para expresar un sentimiento o un ánimo en todo tipo de arte. Cuando se agrega negro o blanco a los colores, se crean diferentes valores ".

T Review unit vocabulary with students using *Transparency 39*.

Art Journal: Writing

Have students answer the questions on page 122 in their Art Journals or on a separate sheet of paper. Answers: 1. C, 2. B, 3. C, 4. C, 5. B

T For further assessment, have students complete the unit test on *Transparency 45.*

VISIT A Museum

► The art collection at the Museum of Fine Arts in Houston is the largest and most outstanding in the Southwest. Renaissance, baroque, impressionist, post-impressionist, and African gold art highlight the museum's collection. In addition, a wide variety of programs and classes in the fine arts are offered for adults and children.

"The business of the artist is to tell his audience the secrets of their own hearts."

—Robin George Collingwood

Show What You Know

Answer these questions on a separate sheet of paper.

❶ These colors are considered pure colors. _____
  A. secondary colors
  B. tricolor
  C. primary colors

❷ The lightness or darkness of a color is called _____.
  A. color
  B. value
  C. shade

❸ This tool is used to organize the twelve colors. _____
  A. organizing tool
  B. circle of colors
  C. color wheel

❹ Yellow-green and blue-green are colors that remind us of cool things. These color are called _____.
  A. warm colors
  B. chill colors
  C. cool colors

❺ Which word is used to show differences between two things?
  _____
  A. comparing
  B. contrast
  C. difference

The Museum of Fine Arts in Houston, Texas, is the largest art museum in the Southwest. Its collection contains over 27,000 works of art. There you can see examples of styles of art from different periods in history. There is also a large collection of American decorative arts including furniture, paintings, metals, ceramics, glass, and textiles. If you visit the museum, you can walk in the sculpture garden and see sculpture created by many nineteenth- and twentieth-century artists.

Unit Assessment Options

Aesthetic Perception

Practice Have students list the techniques on page 122 and then find examples of each technique in the classroom.

Creative Expression

Student Portfolio Have pairs of students evaluate each other's portfolios using the four steps of art criticism. Remind them to share any positive comments.

Art Criticism

Activity Have students select an artwork from this unit and study it using the four steps of art criticism. (See pages 28–29 for more information about art criticism.) Have students work alone or in pairs, and present their findings aloud or in writing.

Color and Value

"The Story of Babar, the Little Elephant"
Color and value are important elements for artists. Both costume and set designers also choose a color palette when they work on a play. In the theatre production of *The Story of Babar, the Little Elephant,* the director wanted the colors to match the book illustrations that inspired the play.

What to Do Create tableaux using illustrations from a book.

Adapting a book into a play requires a lot of work. This work is done by a team of creative people, including a playwright, director, costume designer, set designer, and actors. You will work as set and costume designers for a scene in a play.

1. Choose a children's picture book.
2. Select an illustration that shows a specific setting and characters.
3. Select an emotion that captures the story's theme. Then select a palette of colors that expresses that emotion.
4. Your group will design both the set and the costumes for your scene. Divide the jobs of designing costumes and sets, but work with the same palette of colors.
5. Present your ideas to the class.

▲ Children's Theatre Company. "The Story of Babar, the Little Elephant."

 **Art Criticism**

Describe What challenges did you face in getting your group to make decisions?

Analyze What was interesting about using a specific palette of colors for both costumes and sets?

Interpret How did your palette of colors express the emotion you chose?

Decide In designing the costumes and set, did you stay true to the colors and values you chose as your palette?

Unit 3 **123**

 ## Art History and Culture

A French Children's Book

The biggest challenge in bringing a book off the page of a book and onto the stage lies in expanding two-dimensional artwork to three-dimensional artwork. In *The Story of Babar, the Little Elephant,* it was of primary importance to create the elephant and human characters on an accurate scale. The book's illustrations served as blueprints to establish these physical relationships and gave the information for color and value.

 # Color and Value in Theatre

Objective: To use an illustration in a book as a point of departure for designing costumes and sets with a specific palette of colors and values.

Materials: *The Story of Babar, the Little Elephant,"* performed by the Children's Theater Company. Running time: 3:44. Picture books, paper, paints or markers.

Focus
 Time: About 5 minutes

- Discuss the information on page 123.

 Art History and Culture

- Have students look for illustrations in books that they think will work well as inspiration for designing costumes and sets.

Teach
 Time: About 20 minutes

Aesthetic Perception

- Talk about costume and set designers.

Creative Expression

- Show illustrations from books and talk about a color palette unifying a vision.
- Divide students into small groups. Have them look through books and choose an illustration to work with.

Reflect
 Time: About 10 minutes

 **Art Criticism**

- Have students answer the four art criticism questions on page 123 aloud or in writing.
- Did students effectively design sets and costumes with a specific palette of colors and values?

Unit 4 Planning Guide

	Lesson Title	Suggested Pacing	Creative Expression Activity
Lesson 1	Formal Balance	55 minutes	Create a building drawing.
Lesson 2	Formal Balance in Masks	65 minutes	Create a papier-mâché mask.
Lesson 3	Symmetry	65 minutes	Create a symmetrical design.
Lesson 4	Approximate Symmetry	65 minutes	Create a self-portrait.
Lesson 5	Visual Texture	65 minutes	Make an outdoor scene.
Lesson 6	Tactile Texture	65 minutes	Create an appliqué banner.
ARTSOURCE	Texture and Balance in Theatre	35 minutes	Create a story about an instrument.

Materials	Program Resources	Fine Art Resources	Literature Resources
pencils, construction paper, markers, oil pastels	*Assessment,* pp. 45–46 *Home and After School Connections* *Flash Cards,* 12, 14 *Reading and Writing Test Preparation,* pp. 42–43	*Transparency,* 19 *Artist Profiles,* pp. 46, 69 *Large Prints,* 43, 44 *Animals Time Line* *Art Around The World*	*Oral History* by T. Marie Kryst *Jumping the Broom* by Courtni Wright
cardboard tubes and boxes, liquid tempera paints, paper plates, paper towels, pencils, tape, brushes of various sizes, containers of water and glue, markers, newspaper	*Assessment,* pp. 47–48 *Reading and Writing Test Preparation,* pp. 44–45	*Transparency,* 20 *Artist Profiles,* pp. 71, 77 *Large Prints,* 43, 44 *Animals Time Line* *Art Around The World*	*Masks and Mask Makers* by Kari Hunt *Masks Tell Stories* by Carol Gelber
construction paper, poster board, glue, sketch paper, black markers, scissors	*Assessment,* pp. 49–50 *Reading and Writing Test Preparation,* pp. 46–47	*Transparency,* 21 *Artist Profiles,* pp. 79, 21 *Large Prints,* 43, 44 *Animals Time Line* *Art Around The World*	*Coyote and the Fire Stick: A Pacific Northwest Indian Tale* by Barbara Diamond Goldin
flexible mirror, liquid tempera paints, paper plates for palettes, paint brushes, containers of water, pencils, paper towels, newspaper	*Assessment,* pp. 51–52 *Flash Cards,* 12–14 *Women in the Arts* *Reading and Writing Test Preparation,* pp. 48–49	*Transparency,* 22 *Artist Profiles,* pp. 75, 18 *Large Prints,* 43, 44 *Animals Time Line*	*A Place in the Sun* by Jill Rubalcaba
computer paint program	*Assessment,* pp. 53–54 *Reading and Writing Test Preparation,* pp. 50–51	*Transparency,* 23 *Artist Profiles,* pp. 9, 17 *Large Prints,* 43, 44 *Animals Time Line* *Art Around The World*	*Linnea in Monet's Garden* by Christina Bjork
felt, burlap, yarn, tapestry needles, glue, scissors, sketch paper, pencils, markers, tape	*Assessment,* pp. 55–56 *Flash Cards,* 1–6 *Reading and Writing Test Preparation,* pp. 52–53	*Transparency,* 24 *Artist Profiles,* pp. 40, 80 *Large Prints,* 43, 44 *Animals Time Line* *Art Around The World*	*A Storyteller's Story* by Rafe Martin
Voice of the Wood by Robert Faust and Eugene Friesen			

Texture and Balance

Lesson 1: Formal balance is created when equal or similar elements are placed on opposite sides of a work of art.

Lesson 2: Formal balance is created in a mask when both sides of the mask are the same. **Exaggeration** in a mask is the enlargement of elements or features beyond their normal sizes.

Lesson 3: Symmetry is a type of formal balance in which two sides of an artwork are identical.

Lesson 4: Approximate symmetry is a type of formal balance that is created when both sides of an artwork are almost exactly the same.

Lesson 5: Visual texture is how something looks as it would feel if it could be touched.

Lesson 6: Tactile texture is the way the surface of something actually feels.

Introduce Unit Concepts

"Artists use the principles of balance and texture in designing all kinds of art." "Los artistas usan los principios de equilibrio y textura en el diseño de todo tipo de arte".

Balance
■ Have students each stand perfectly still on one leg. Discuss why this is difficult to do.

■ Ask what *balance* means to students.

Texture
Vocabulary Reading
■ List a variety of objects that have pronounced textures, such as a cactus, sandpaper, and gravel roads. Have students use texture words to describe how the surface of each might feel.

Cross-Curricular Projects
■ See the *Language Arts and Reading, Mathematics, Science,* and *Social Studies Art Connections* books for activities that further develop balance and texture concepts.

Texture and Balance

Artists use **texture** and **balance** to design works of art and to show how objects may feel.

▲ **Audrey Flack.** (American). *Strawberry Tart Supreme.* 1974.
Oil over acrylic on canvas. 54 × 60 ¼ inches (137.16 × 153.04 cm). Allen Memorial Art Museum, Oberlin, Ohio.

Fine Art Prints

Display *Large Prints 43 Elephant Mask* and *44 Elizabeth of Valois, Queen of Spain*. Refer to the prints throughout the unit as students learn about texture and balance.

Large Print p. 43

Large Print p. 44

Artists can create **texture** in a work of art to show how things might feel if they were touched.

▶ What textures do you see in *Strawberry Tart Supreme*?

▶ Artists use balance in their artwork to give equal weight to both sides of a design.

▶ Are both sides of the painting exactly the same? If not, what are some differences?

In This Unit you will learn about texture and balance, and how other artists use these features in their designs. Here are the topics you will study:

▶ Formal Balance
▶ Formal Balance in Masks
▶ Symmetry
▶ Approximate Symmetry
▶ Visual Texture
▶ Tactile Texture

Audrey Flack

(1931–)

Audrey Flack always knew she wanted to be an artist. She is a native of New York City, where she attended Music and Art High School. She studied with Josef Albers at Yale and started her career as an abstract expressionist. Her desire to do realistic work brought her back to New York, where she studied at The Art Student's League and NYU.

In the mid-1960s she made paintings of famous people. During the 1970s she used photography to help her create monumental still lifes like *Strawberry Tart Supreme*. During the 1980s she created sculptures about heroic women and goddess figures.

Unit 4 125

Examine the Artwork

"Let's look closely at the painting." "Vamos a observar detalladamente la pintura".

■ Have students look at Audrey Flack's *Strawberry Tart Supreme*. Ask them to describe what they see.

■ Have students answer the questions about texture and balance on page 125.

▶ There are smooth textures in the aluminum pan, glass table, and strawberry glaze. There are rougher textures in the cake and cupcake papers.

▶ Balance is created when equal or similar elements are placed on opposite sides of a work of art.

▶ Both sides of the painting are not the same, but there is a sense of balance because of the strawberry tart in the middle and the balance of the chocolate swirl cake and chocolate frosting cupcake.

Unit Pretest

T Display *Transparency 46* as pretest. Answers: 1.C, 2.B, 3.C, 4.A, 5.A

Home Connection

■ See *Home and After-School Connections* for family newsletters and activities for this unit.

Art History and Culture NSAE 4.a; 4.b; 4.c; 5.a; 5.b

Audrey Flack

Audrey Flack (ô´drē flak)(1931–) was born to a middle-class family in New York City, where she attended the High School of Music and Art. She is considered one of the premier artists of photo-realism, although she started out as an abstract expressionist. *Kennedy Motorcade*, which she painted in 1964, is considered her first truly photo-realistic piece. During the 1970s Flack's subjects changed to artifacts. Flack also did a series of paintings, called the *Vanitas*, which were meant to encourage people to think about the purpose of life and how temporary life really is.

See pages 24–25 and 16–21 for more about art history and subject matter.

Artist Profiles, p. 20

▸ Artist Profile ◂
Audrey Flack
b. 1931

Audrey Flack (ô´ drē flak) grew up in New York City and lives there still. She earned a fine arts degree from Yale. She also studied anatomy, the structure of the human body. This helps her make her paintings more realistic. Flack is married to a musician. Early in her career she painted while raising two daughters. She has also taught at Pratt Institute and New York University.

ILLUSTRATOR PROFILE

Aliki

(1929–)

Aliki, whose full name is Aliki Liacouras Brandenberg, was raised in Philadelphia, Pennsylvania, where an observant kindergarten teacher recognized and encouraged Aliki's artistic ability. She drew constantly as a child and later earned a degree from the Philadelphia Museum College of Art.

Shortly after graduating, Aliki began working as a freelance artist, creating advertising displays, painting murals, and producing her own greeting cards. At the same time, she taught art classes to children and adults.

In 1957 Aliki married Franz Brandenberg, and they made their home in Switzerland. In that same year, Aliki published her first book, *The Story of William Tell*.

Aliki has continued to write many children's books, both fiction and nonfiction. In addition to her own works, she has illustrated more than 50 books by other children's authors, including several by her husband. Aliki's artistic style varies according to her subject matter, ranging from old-fashioned to modern.

Music

Balance in music is usually associated with symmetrical forms such as ABA—music having three sections with the middle one different from the two outer sections. *Texture* in music generally refers to combining melody and harmony to create layers of sound. Have students sing a round, such as *Frère Jacques*, and try to balance the sound between parts and demonstrate layered texture.

Literature

Show *The Forest Dwellers: Native American Arts of the Pacific Northwest* to discuss Indian masks and how students can identify balance and texture.

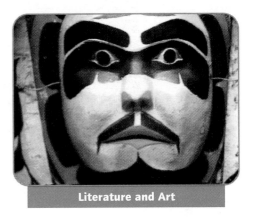

Literature and Art

Performing Arts

Show *Voice of the Wood* with Robert Faust and Eugene Friesen and discuss the elements of balance and texture in the masks, costumes, and scenery.

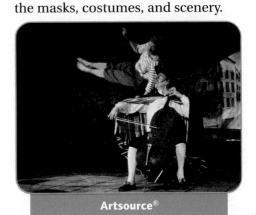

Artsource®

Lesson 1 Formal Balance

Overview

Lesson 1 introduces formal balance. Formal balance is created when equal or similar elements are placed on opposite sides of a work of art.

Objectives

 Art History and Culture

To demonstrate how artists from two different cultures use formal balance in their work NSAE 4.a; 4.b; 4.c; 5.a; 5.b

 Creative Expression

To plan and create a drawing using formal balance NSAE 1.a; 1.c; 1.d; 2.c; 3.b

 Aesthetic Perception

To identify formal balance in works of art and the environment NSAE 2.a; 2.b; 3.a

 Art Criticism

To use the four steps of art criticism to evaluate own work NSAE 1.b; 2.a; 2.b; 3.a

Vocabulary Vocabulary

Review the following vocabulary word with students before beginning the lesson.

formal balance equilibrio formal—a way of organizing the elements of an artwork so that equal or similar elements are placed on opposite sides of an imaginary, central vertical axis

See page 149B for additional vocabulary and Spanish vocabulary resources.

Art Journal: Vocabulary

Have students add this word to the Vocabulary section of their Art Journals.

Lesson Materials

- pencils
- 12" × 18" white construction paper
- colored markers
- oil pastels

Alternate Materials:
- watercolor paints
- paintbrushes

Program Resources

- *Reading and Writing Test Prep.,* pp. 42–43
- *Transparency 19*
- *Flash Cards 12, 14*
- *Artist Profiles,* pp. 46, 69
- *Animals Through History Time Line*
- *Assessment,* pp. 45–46
- *Large Prints 43* Elephant Mask and *44 Elizabeth of Valois, Queen of Spain*
- *Art Around the World*

Concept Trace
Formal Balance
Introduced: Level 1, Unit 6, Lesson 1

Reinforced: Level 4, Unit 6, Lesson 1

Lesson 1 Arts Integration

Theatre

Complete Unit 4, Lesson 1, on page 72–73 of *Theatre Arts Connections.*

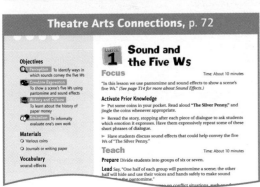

Music

 Musical forms have balance. Music in the Western tradition also has forms that create balance. Rondo form is one main musical idea over and over again with contrasting sections between. ABACADA. Listen to *Rondo* from *Rage over a Lost Penny* by Ludwig van Beethoven. How many times do you hear the A section?

Movement & Dance

Dancers show balance on the stage by how they position themselves. Create an imaginary canvas outline on the floor with string or tape. Have six students walk into the space and find a way to arrange themselves on the "canvas", being sure to observe the balance as they would in a painting. Are there too many people on one side of the canvas? Have other students give suggestions about ways to create balance.

LESSON 1 • Formal Balance **125B**

Focus

Time: About 10 minutes

Activate Prior Knowledge

"Think about looking at a butterfly. How can you describe the wings?" *"Piensen en observar una mariposa. ¿Cómo pueden decribir las alas?"*

- Discuss students' responses to the question and how a butterfly's wings look the same on both sides.

Using Literature ⭐ Reading

- Read a book illustrated by contemporary African American artist Gershom Griffith, such as T. Marie Kryst's *Oral History* or Courtni Wright's *Jumping the Broom*. Have students compare Pippin's work to Griffith's.

Thematic Connection ⭐ Reading

- **Storytelling:** Have students study the Pippin painting and create a story about the people who live in the house he painted. Encourage them to include details about character, setting, and plot.

Introduce the Art NSAE 3.a

"Let's look closely at the two works of art." *"Vamos a observar detalladamente las dos obras de arte".*

- Have students describe the subject matter in each artwork. *Victorian Parlor II* is an interior still life; *Jar* has a floral pattern.

Comparing and Contrasting ⭐ Reading

- Have students make a list of similarities and differences between the two works of art. Both works of art include floral designs, show contrasts, and have formal balance. *Victorian Parlor II* is a two-dimensional painting that includes many objects and bright colors. *Jar* is a three-dimensional container that has a floral design.

 Art History and Culture

Horace Pippin was one of the most famous African American painters of the twentieth century. He was wounded in World War I and never fully regained used of his right arm, but found a way to continue drawing and painting. NSAE 4.a; 4.b; 4.c; 5.a; 5.b

💻 **Web Connection**

Visit **www.artcyclopedia.com/artists/pippin_horace. html** for links to several museums that have works by Horace Pippin.

 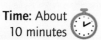 # Formal Balance

◀ **Horace Pippin.** (American). *Victorian Parlor II.* 1945.
·····················
Oil on canvas. $25\frac{1}{4} \times 30$ inches (63.5 × 76.2 cm.). The Metropolitan Museum of Art, New York.

Look at the works of art on these pages. Folk artists are self taught. *Jar* was created 700 years before *Victorian Parlor II*, yet both works make powerful use of formal balance.

 Art History and Culture

Many of Horace Pippin's works of art depict his childhood memories of war experiences, heroes, and religious experiences.

🏺 **Art History and Culture** NSAE 4.a; 4.b; 4.c; 5.a; 5.b

Horace Pippin

Horace Pippin (hôr´ əs pip´ ən) (1888–1946) was born in Pennsylvania. A self-taught artist, Pippin painted subjects from his personal experience. Pippin first began drawing at age 10, but after he was wounded in World War I, he learned to support his arm to continue drawing and painting. He often spent 17 hours a day painting. He was the first black folk painter to express his concerns about the war and social and political injustices. Most of his work shows turn-of-the-century black lifestyle.

See pages 24–25 and 16–21 for more about art history and subject matter.

Artist Profiles, p. 46

♦ Artist Profile ♦

Horace Pippin
1888–1946

Horace Pippin (här´ əs pip´ ən) was an African American artist who painted historic figures and scenes from African American culture. He was born in West Chester, Pennsylvania, and grew up in Goshen, New York, where he attended a segregated elementary school. His first drawings were biblical scenes, and at the age of 14, he created his first portrait. He enlisted in the army in 1917, but returned to West Chester in the following year with a paralyzed right arm. After spending nine years in rehabilitation, Pippin regained enough strength and dexterity to continue painting. His first solo show was in West Chester in 1937. A year later he exhibited four of his paintings at a folk art exhibition at the

Study each artwork to see balance.

▶ Draw a line down the middle of each artwork with your finger. Describe the matching objects or shapes you see on the two sides.

▶ Describe colors that are repeated in both works of art.

▶ Which areas are exactly the same on both sides of each piece?

▶ Which areas are similar but not exactly the same?

◀ **Artist Unknown.** (China). *Jar.* Northern Song Period, twelfth century.
....
Stoneware with graffito design in slip under glaze. 12 ½ inches (31.75 cm.). The Asian Society, New York, New York.

 Aesthetic Perception

Seeing Like an Artist Look for a building in the area where you live that has the same colors and forms on its left and right halves. What features are alike, but not exactly the same?

 Art History and Culture

China

Although the specific artist of *Jar* is unknown, it is representative of the incised, embossed, and modeled decoration characteristic of the pottery of this period. This jar was made during China's Northern Song dynasty, which lasted from 960–1279 A.D. Ceramics made during this time are among the most influential and revered in the world, noted for their elegant, simple shapes, lush glazes, and lively designs.

See pages 24–25 and 16–21 for more about art history and subject matter.

Artist Profiles, p. 69

◁ Artist Profile ◁
Jar
The artist who made this jar is unknown. The artist probably worked in one of the large ceramics factories located in Tz'u-hien, a province of Hopei in northeastern China.

◀ **Artist unknown.** (China). *Jar.*
Northern Song Period, twelfth century.
Stoneware with graffito design in slip under glaze.

Study

▶ Central axis: In *Victorian Parlor II*, the vase of flowers, table, wall, and rug are in the center of the painting along the central axis. In *Jar*, the curvilinear leaf shapes are on the left and right sides.

▶ Colors: In *Victorian Parlor II*, the yellow in the lamp on the left side is repeated in the books on the right side of the painting.

▶ Formal balance: In *Jar*, the curvilinear, black shapes near the top are exactly the same on both sides.

▶ Formal balance: In *Victorian Parlor II*, although the chairs are similar, they are not exactly the same. The chair on the left side is a side view, while the chair on the right side is a frontal view.

■ For more examples of Asian art, see the *Art Around the World* collection.

Art Journal: Vocabulary
Encourage students to look up the words *formal* and *balance* in a dictionary and then write sentences for the different uses of each word in the Vocabulary section of their Art Journals. Discuss how the different uses of the words still relate to the art terms.

 **Aesthetic Perception**

NSAE 2.a; 2.b; 3.a

Design Awareness Formal balance is a major element in building and furniture design. Have students identify formal balance in windows, chairs, desks, and floor patterns.

Developing Visual Literacy Invite students to consider the two different cultures represented by the works in this lesson. What are the clues about the different time periods the works were created? What are some common elements in each work, such as a focus on plants, beauty, and serenity, that demonstrate that the works were created by people with a similar theme, regardless of when the works were created?

 Web Connection
Visit **www.asiasocietymuseum.com/default.asp** to learn more about Chinese culture and history.

 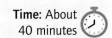
Teach

Time: About 40 minutes

- "How can you illustrate formal balance?" "¿Cómo pueden ilustrar el equilibrio formal?"

- Discuss ways to create formal balance using shapes, lines, and colors on page 128.

- Use photographs to show students examples of formal balance.

Practice

Materials: 9" × 12" white paper, pencils

Alternate Materials: markers

- Distribute the materials and have students follow the directions on page 128.

Creative Expression

Materials: 12" × 18" white construction paper, colored markers, oil pastels

Alternate Materials: watercolor paints, paintbrushes

- Distribute the materials and have students follow the directions on page 129.

- Review the Technique Tips on page 216 for visual examples of techniques using markers and oil pastels.

- See Activity Tips on page 241 for visual instructions. NSAE 1.a; 1.c; 1.d; 2.c; 3.b

 Art Journal: Brainstorming
Have students brainstorm ways they can create formal balance in a drawing. Then have students select three or four items and plan how they will show those items in their drawings for the Creative Expression activity.

Using Formal Balance

Formal balance is a way of organizing a design so that equal or similar elements are placed on opposite sides of an imaginary central dividing line. You saw examples of formal balance in the artwork on pages 126 and 127.

On a seesaw, if your partner is much bigger than you, you will stay up in the air. The seesaw is not balanced. But if your partner is your weight, the seesaw will balance. There is the same amount of weight on both sides.

A work of art can have different kinds of balance. One kind is formal balance. This is created when objects, shapes, lines, and color match on both sides of a design.

Practice

Illustrate formal balance. Use a pencil.

1. Fold a piece of paper in half and then open it again. Use a pencil to draw some geometric and free-form shapes on the left side.

2. Repeat the same design on the right side to create formal balance.

Differentiated Instruction

Reteach
Have students look around the classroom to find examples of formal balance. Ask students to list the examples and to explain how formal balance is created in each example.

Special Needs
Students may have difficulty coming up with ideas for decoration. To help ensure success, provide examples and ample time for students to generate ideas on paper.

ELL Tips
For the Practice activity, pair students to illustrate formal balance. Have one student draw a geometric or free-form shape on one side of a sheet of paper. The other student can repeat the design on the other side. Students can share their drawings and increase opportunities to practice oral language.

◀ **Keegan Faught.**
Age 9.

Think about where this student used formal balance.

Creative Expression

How do buildings show formal balance? Use formal balance in drawing.

1. Look at the artwork *Victorian Parlor II* by Horace Pippin. Think about how the outside of this house might look.

2. On a large piece of paper, draw the outside of the house. Use formal balance in your drawing.

3. Fill the house with color. Add trees and plants. Use formal balance in your landscape too.

Art Criticism

Describe What objects did you include in your drawing?

Analyze How did you create formal balance in your drawing?

Interpret How would the mood or feeling of your drawing change if you had not used formal balance?

Decide If you could redo this drawing, what would you do differently?

Reflect
Time: About 5 minutes

Review and Assess
"Were you able to create formal balance in your drawing?" "¿Pudieron crear equilibrio formal en su dibujo?"

NSAE 1.b; 2.a; 2.b

Think
In the student artwork, the house, windows, chimneys, flower boxes, and trees are organized using formal balance. The door, the clouds, and the swing do not use formal balance.

■ Use *Large Print 43 Elephant Mask* to have students identify and compare the use of formal balance in this work and the works in this lesson.

NSAE 1.b; 2.a; 2.b; 3.a; 5.c

Informal Assessment

Art Journal: Critical Thinking
Have students answer the four art criticism questions—Describe, Analyze, Interpret, and Decide—in their Art Journals. In small groups, have students discuss the use of formal balance in their drawings.

■ For standardized-format test practice using this lesson's art content, see pages 42–43 in *Reading and Writing Test Preparation.*

Art Across the Curriculum

Use these simple ideas to reinforce art concepts across the curriculum.

★ **Narrative Writing** Explain to students that in a debate, people with opposing opinions about the same issue discuss and support their opinions in a balanced argument. Have student pairs plan a debate about an issue of their choice, write opinions about an issue, and compare the points that support opposing points of view.

★ **Math** Use a double pan balance to demonstrate the mathematical concepts of balance.

★ **Science** Have students look through scientific magazines to find images that have formal balance.

★ **Social Studies** Have students study *Jar* from China and list two things people 800 years ago may have used the jar for.

★ **Technology** Have students use the paint program on a computer and select a variety of tools to design a room with formal balance. Visit **SRAonline.com** to print detailed instuctions for this activity.

NSAE 6.b

Formal Balance

Extra! For the Art Specialist

NSAE 1.a; 1.b; 1.c; 1.d; 2.a; 2.b; 2.c; 3.b

Time: About 45 minutes

Focus

Use *Transparency 19* and *Large Print 43* to discuss the ways in which artists use formal balance in works of art. Have students point out examples of formal balance in the artwork, explaining how a shape or color on one side of the artwork balances the shape or color on the other side. Tell students they are going to design a symmetrical (formal balance) building by cutting out identical shapes for doors, windows, and porches.

Teach

On chart paper, use lines, shapes, and colors to illustrate ways to create formal balance in a work of art.

Reflect

Have students use the four steps of art criticism to evaluate their work. Is the work a good reflection of formal balance? Have students present their works explaining how they used formal balance.

Alternate Activity

Materials:
- 12" × 18, 9" × 12", 6" × 9" colored construction paper
- scissors
- white glue or glue sticks
- crayons or colored pencils

1. Have students fold a 12" × 18" sheet of construction paper in half, cut out the shape of the building, and glue it onto a background sheet.

2. Using the smaller sheets of construction paper, students will fold the paper in half and cut out matching shapes for doors, windows, shutters, columns, etc. Students will glue corresponding shapes on each side of the fold (line of symmetry) to create a building with formal balance.

3. Students may add details to their buildings with crayons and/or colored pencils.

Research in Art Education

It has been shown that "elementary [art] programs establish a foundation in the arts for all students, not just for those in specialized programs or those who choose an arts course of study in high school." Providing consistent, quality instruction in the arts in elementary school also ensures that students have the time to foster skills in the arts. Many of these skills take time to develop *(Gaining the Arts Advantage: Lessons from School Districts that Value Arts Education)*. Learning about balance in art translates not only to art class, but to science and math, as well.

Assessment

Use the following rubric to evaluate the artwork students make in the Creative Expression activity and to assess students' understanding of formal balance.

	Art History and Culture	Aesthetic Perception	Creative Expression	Art Criticism
3 POINTS	The student demonstrates how artists from two cultures use balance in their work.	The student accurately identifies formal balance in works of art and the environment.	The student effectively plans and creates a drawing using formal balance.	The student evaluates his or her own work using the four steps of art criticism.
2 POINTS	The student's comparison is weak or incomplete.	The student's identification is weak or incomplete.	The student shows some awareness of how to plan and create a drawing using formal balance.	The student attempts to evaluate his or her own work but shows an incomplete understanding of evaluation criteria.
1 POINT	The student cannot compare works by artists from different cultures.	The student cannot identify formal balance in works of art.	The student shows no understanding of how to plan and create a drawing using formal balance.	The student makes no attempt to evaluate his or her own artwork.

Have students complete page 45 or 46 in their *Assessment* books.

Assessment, p. 45

Name _____ Date _____

Lesson 1 UNIT 4

Formal Balance

A. Short Answer

Use the words below to complete the sentences.

balance   formal balance

1. _____ is a design in which the important parts of a work of art are the same, or almost the same, on each half.

2. The equal arrangement of important parts in a work of art is called _____.

B. Drawing

In the space below, use crayons to draw a picture that has formal balance. Use lines, shapes, and colors in your design.

C. Identifying

Find and list four examples of formal balance.

1. _____
2. _____
3. _____
4. _____

Level 3   Unit 4 • Texture and Balance   45

Formal Balance in Masks

Lesson 2 introduces formal balance and exaggeration in masks. An artist uses formal balance to make the two sides of a mask the same and sometimes uses exaggeration to make some features or designs stand out.

Objectives

 Art History and Culture

To demonstrate knowledge of mask making by two different cultures
NSAE 4.a; 4.b; 4.c; 5.a; 5.b

 Creative Expression

To create a papier-mâché mask using formal balance NSAE 1.a; 1.c; 1.d; 2.c; 3.b

 Aesthetic Perception

To identify how artists use formal balance and exaggeration in masks
NSAE 2.a; 2.b; 3.a

 Art Criticism

To use the four steps of art criticism to evaluate own work
NSAE 1.b; 2.a; 2.b; 3.a; 5.c

Vocabulary Vocabulary

Review the following vocabulary words with students before beginning the lesson.

culture cultura—customs and beliefs that are shared by a group of people

exaggeration exageración—the enlargement of an object, figure, or feature beyond its normal size used to draw attention to it

See page 149B for additional vocabulary and Spanish vocabulary resources.

 Art Journal: Vocabulary

Have students add these words to the Vocabulary section of their Art Journals.

Lesson Materials
- newspapers
- assorted cardboard tubes and boxes
- containers of water and glue
- liquid tempera paints
- paintbrushes of various sizes
- tape
- pencils
- paper plates
- paper towels
- colored markers

Alternate Materials:
- colored tissue paper

Program Resources
- *Reading and Writing Test Prep.*, pp. 44–45
- *Transparency 20*
- *Flash Cards 12, 14*
- *Artist Profiles*, pp. 71, 77
- *Animals Through History Time Line*
- *Assessment*, pp. 47–48
- *Large Prints 43* Elephant Mask and *44* Elizabeth of Valois, Queen of Spain
- *Art Around the World*

Concept Trace
Formal Balance in Masks
Introduced: Level 1, Unit 6, Lesson 2
Reinforced: Level 4, Unit 6, Lesson 1

Lesson 2 Arts Integration

Theatre

Complete Unit 4, Lesson 2, on pages 74–75 of *Theatre Arts Connections.*

Theatre Arts Connections, p. 74

Music

 Balance in music can describe how evenly different parts are performed at the same time to make the desired blend. Listen to *Akinla*, from *African Suite*, by Fela Sowande. Discuss whether all parts are equal in dynamics at all times.

Movement & Dance

Working in groups of three, students explore balance in shape. One person stands still and creates a vertical line with his or her body. The other two people stand on each side the first person. The person on the right side designs a shape and freezes. The person on the left side designs a similar shape that creates balance on both sides. Experiment with ways this can be done. Rotate so each person gets to experience each point of view.

Focus

Activate Prior Knowledge

"Can you think of a time when you dressed in a costume and wore a mask? Describe the mask." "¿Pueden pensar en una ocasión en que se disfrazaron y usaron una mascara? Describan la máscara".

■ Discuss student responses and their experiences with masks.

Using Literature [★] Reading

■ Read *Masks and Mask Makers* by Kari Hunt or *Masks Tell Stories* by Carol Gelber. Both nonfiction books explore masks from various cultures and how they are used in ceremonies, theatre, and daily life.

Thematic Connection [★] Social Studies

■ **Being Afraid:** Have students imagine what the artists' purpose was for creating *Senufo Face Mask*. Do students think the mask was intended to frighten people, or to protect the person who was wearing the mask?

Introduce the Art

Look NSAE 3.a

"Let's take a close look at the two works of art." "Vamos a observar detalladamente las dos obras de arte".

Comparing and Contrasting [★] Reading

■ Have students list the similarities and differences between the two masks. One looks friendlier than the other and the colors are also very different. The purposes for creating the masks are different too.

NSAE 4.a; 4.b; 4.c; 5.a; 5.b

Art History and Culture

The Eskimos are the most widely dispersed group in the world still leading a partly aboriginal way of life. They live in a region that spans more than 3,500 miles, including Greenland, the northern fringe of North America, and a sector of eastern Siberia.

Eskimos are racially distinct from American Indians. In fact, the Eskimos are most closely related to the Mongolian peoples of eastern Asia. Eskimos consider themselves to be "Inuit" (The People). The Eskimo-Aleut languages are unrelated to any American Indian language groups.

Web Connection

Visit www.mama.org/masks/index.html to find out more about the history of African masks.

Lesson 2 Formal Balance in Masks

Look at the three-dimensional masks. *Senufo Face Mask* was created between the nineteenth and twentieth centuries. *Mask with Seal or Sea Otter Spirit* was created around the nineteenth century. Both artists used formal balance to design their masks.

◄ **Artist Unknown.** (Ivory Coast). *Senufo Face Mask.* Nineteenth to twentieth century.
•••••••••••••••••••••••••••••••••••
Wood, horn, fiber, cloth, feather, metal. 14 ½ inches tall (35.56 cm.). The Metropolitan Museum of Art, New York, New York.

Art History and Culture

Many Eskimos hunt for food because they have developed a widespread knowledge of animals such as the sea otter, seal, and bear.

Art History and Culture NSAE 4.a; 4.b; 4.c; 5.a; 5.b

Senufo Face Mask

Senufo Face Mask was created in the nineteenth or twentieth century by the Senufo people of the Ivory Coast in honor of the elders of the Senufo people who had died. Many of the masks that these people created were worn by special members of the tribe who performed sacred rituals. Carving such masks is a very sophisticated art. In many parts of Africa, an apprentice has to work for two or three years under a master carver and pay him for the apprenticeship. Oftentimes, the knowledge of carving is transmitted from father to son through several generations; however, sometimes a young man is selected because he has shown a special gift for carving.

See pages 24–25 and 16–21 for more about art history and subject matter.

Artist Profiles, p. 77

Senufo Face Mask

This mask was made by an unknown artist of the Senufo of the west African nation Ivory Coast. The Senufo were traditionally farmers. Today, there are approximately 600,000 Senufo in West Africa, and most of them live in villages of 50 to 2,000 people. They are known for their skills in woodcarving and brass casting and have been prolific in the creation of elaborate masks, such as the one featured here.

◄ **Artist unknown.** (Ivory Coast). *Senufo Face Mask.* Nineteenth to twentieth century.
•••••••••••••••••••••••••••••••••••
Wood, horn, fiber, cloth, feather, and metal.

◀ **Artist Unknown.**
(American). *Mask with Seal or Sea Otter Spirit.*
Nineteenth century.
....
Wood paint, gut cord, and feathers. 23 $\frac{1}{2}$ × 22 $\frac{1}{4}$ inches (59.69 × 56.52 cm.). Dallas Museum of Art, Dallas, Texas.

Study both masks to find examples of formal balance.

▶ What shapes do you see on each mask?

▶ Find shapes or objects on the left side that you also see on the right.

▶ Find areas on both sides that are exactly the same.

▶ Are any areas on either side similar, but not quite the same?

Aesthetic Perception

Seeing Like an Artist Look at posters and signs in your school to find examples of formal balance.

Art History and Culture
NSAE 4.a; 4.b; 4.c; 5.a; 5.b

Mask with Seal or Sea Otter Spirit

This mask was created around the late nineteenth century in the Yukon River area in Alaska. Because the Inuit must hunt for food, they have developed a thorough knowledge of animals such as sea otters, seals, and bears, which they depend upon for clothing. Many Inuit believe that an animal has a soul and a spirit called *inua.* It is believed that the smiling face in the center of the mask represents the spirit of the sea otter. The feathers represent stars or snowflakes. The holes in the white hands of the mask represent the doorways to the other world. The mask may also represent the harmony that can exist between humans and animals.

See pages 24–25 and 16–21 for more about art history and subject matter.

Artist Profiles, p. 71

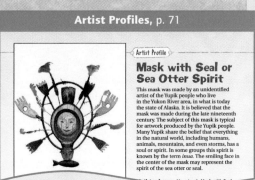

> *Artist Profile*
>
> **Mask with Seal or Sea Otter Spirit**
>
> This mask was made by an unidentified artist of the Yupik people who live in the Yukon River area, in what is today the state of Alaska. It is believed that the mask was made during the late nineteenth century. The subject of this mask is typical for artwork produced by the Yupik people. Many Yupik share the belief that everything in the natural world, including humans, animals, mountains, and even storms, has a soul or spirit. In some groups this spirit is known by the term *inua.* The smiling face in the center of the mask may represent the spirit of the sea otter or seal.
>
> Artist unknown. (American). *Mask with Seal...*

Study
NSAE 1.b; 2.a; 2.b; 3.a; 5.c

▶ Both masks have oval shapes and some rectangular shapes.

▶ Both masks represent formal balance with all of the elements on the left side repeated on the right side.

▶ In *Senufo Face Mask,* the hair, the horns, and the ears are the same. In the Inuit mask, the eyes and shapes that stick out from the face are the same.

▶ The hair and decoration at the top of the Senufo mask are not exactly the same. The feathers and the fish in the Inuit mask are not quite the same.

■ For more examples of African art, see the *Art Around the World* collection.

Art Journal: Ideas

Encourage students to design masks in the Ideas section of their Art Journals that reflect elements from favorite stories or elements from their lives. For example, they may want to create animal masks to appear friendly or strong.

Aesthetic Perception

NSAE 2.a; 2.b; 2.c

Seeing Like an Artist Encourage students to study the face of an animal and consider what makes the animal look friendly, fierce, or frightened. Have them consider the eyes and mouth, in particular. NSAE 4.a; 4.b; 4.c

Developing Visual Literacy Invite students to compare and contrast the two masks in this lesson. Consider what each mask says about the culture of the people who made it and whom or what they honor by making each mask.

Web Connection
Visit **www.tribalarts.com/feature/riordan/** to learn more about the history of Inuit masks.

Time: About two 45 minute periods

- "In what ways could you exaggerate shapes to create a special feeling in a mask? How could you use these shapes to create formal balance?" *"¿De qué maneras podrían exagerar las figuras para crear una sensación especial en una máscara? ¿Cómo pueden usar estas figuras para crear equilibrio formal?"*

- Discuss ways to create formal balance on page 132.

- Ask students how mask makers can change the normal proportions of a face. Sometimes the eyes are made large or features or raised or lowered for particular affects.

Practice   NSAE 1.a; 1.d

Materials: 9" × 12" white paper, colored markers

Alternate Materials: oil pastels

- Distribute the materials and have students follow the directions on page 142.

Creative Expression

NSAE 1.a; 1.c; 1.d; 2.c; 3.b
Materials: newspapers, assorted cardboard tubes and boxes, containers of water and glue, liquid tempera paints, paintbrushes of various sizes, tape, pencils, paper plates, paper towels

Alternate Materials: colored tissue paper

- Distribute the materials and have students follow the directions on page 133.

- Have students consider what the realistic proportions of a face are so that they can exaggerate the proportions of their masks.

- Review the Technique Tips on page 227 for visual examples of techniques.

- See Activity Tips on page 241 for visual instructions.

Art Journal: Ideas

Have students brainstorm ideas about ways to create formal balance in their Art Journals. Then have students decide how they will design their masks using papier-mâché in the Creative Expression activity.

Using Formal Balance in Masks

People in many **cultures** around the world make and use masks. Ancient hunters wore animal masks in hunting ceremonies. Storytellers and actors wear masks to portray different characters.

The features on masks are often **exaggerated,** or made larger, to show strong feelings.

The masks below have formal balance. They have the same shapes and objects on both sides of an imaginary dividing line.

Practice

Design a paper mask with exaggerated features that are formally balanced. Use colored markers.

1. Fold a piece of paper in half, and then open it to mark the middle of the mask.

2. Think of an emotion you want the mask to express. Sketch exaggerated features that express that emotion. Use free-form and geometric shapes. The features on each side of the fold should look alike in some way.

Differentiated Instruction

Reteach

Have students look through the *Student Edition* to find three different works of art that have formal balance. Ask students to list the title of each work and to describe how formal balance is used in it.

Special Needs

To ensure student success in this project, show students a variety of techniques for adding three-dimensional features to their mask.

ELL Tips

Students may find it difficult to follow a class discussion without additional visual clues. Use the illustrations provided in the *Student Edition* to demonstrate what you are talking about or to paraphrase a student response when describing the formal balance in the masks in this lesson.

◄ **Alexander Jimenez.** Age 9.

Think about how this student artist's mask shows formal balance.

 Creative Expression

Which features in a mask would show formal balance? Create a papier-mâché mask. Use formal balance.

1. Think of how you want to use your mask and what it will express. Make a few sketches until you get one you like.

2. Look at your sketch. Then cut pieces of cardboard tubes and boxes to form the features. Tape or glue them in place onto your base. Balance some of the forms formally.

3. Dip torn strips of newspaper into paste. Apply them to the mask.

 Art Criticism

Describe List the steps you followed to create your mask.

Analyze Which parts of your mask show formal balance?

Interpret What feeling does the finished mask express?

Decide Which elements of the mask do you like best? How is the finished mask different from your sketch?

 **eflect** Time: About 45 minutes

Review and Assess

■ "How can you create formal balance in a mask?" "¿Cómo pueden crear equilibrio formal en una máscara?"

Think
NSAE 1.b; 2.a; 2.b

The student artist used exaggeration by making certain parts of the mask appear larger than usual. The mask's large eye holes and teeth are exaggerated.

■ Use *Large Print 43* to have students identify and compare the use of formal balance in the print and in the artworks in this lesson.

Informal Assessment

Art Journal: Critical Thinking
Have students answer the four art criticism questions—Describe, Analyze, Interpret, and Decide—in their Art Journals. Have students discuss the uses of formal balance in their masks

■ For standardized-format test practice using this lesson's art content, see page 44–45 in *Reading and Writing Test Preparation.*

Art Across the Curriculum

Use these simple ideas to reinforce art concepts across the curriculum.

★ **Narrative Writing** Have students write sentences that include exaggeration to emphasize a feeling. Discuss how exaggeration can sometimes help communicate feelings or emotions.

★ **Math** Use a double pan balance to illustrate the concept of formal balance as it relates to mathematics. To be formal, both sides of the balance must have the same material and weigh exactly the same.

★ **Science** In science if forces are balanced, as if there are equal sides in a tug-of-war game, the net force is zero. Balanced forces produce no change in the motion of an object. Have students demonstrate balancing forces by pushing their palms together so that they do not move. Reinforce the idea that balance is equal on both sides.

★ **Social Studies** Have students each design a flag for their school, family or themselves. Have students plan which plants, animals, and/or other objects they want to use, as well as how to arrange these to create formal balance.

★ **Technology** Have students use the paint tool to create an animal using formal balance. Visit **SRAonline.com** to print detailed instuctions for this activity.

NSAE 6.b

Formal Balance in Masks

Extra! **For the Art Specialist**
NSAE 1.a; 1.b; 1.c; 1.d; 2.a; 2.b; 2.c; 3.b

Time: About 45 minutes

Focus

Use *Transparency 20* and *Large Print 43* to have students compare the uses of formal balance and exaggeration in masks.

Teach

Have students examine masks to pick out shapes on one side of the mask that are balanced by the same (or similar) shapes on the other side. Question students about times when they have worn masks (Halloween, in a play, as protection while playing a sport, etc.).

Reflect

Have students use the four steps of art criticism to evaluate their work. Did they effectively create a mask using formal balance? What are the elements that are in balance?

Alternate Activity

Materials:

- 9" × 12" colored construction paper
- white glue or glue sticks
- scissors
- feathers, yarn, beads, etc. (optional)

1. Have each student select two sheets of 9" × 12" construction paper in contrasting colors. Fold papers together in half vertically into $4\frac{1}{2}$" × 12" rectangles. Have students hold papers together on the folded edge and cut around the outside edge of the papers to make the outside shape of the mask.

2. Separate papers and cut a $1\frac{1}{2}$" slit from the top edge of one of the mask shapes. Overlap the edges of the slit and glue together to give the mask a rounded three-dimensional form.

3. Cut away areas of the second color (top layer) of construction paper to create eyes, nose, mouth, etc. Glue the top layer of construction paper to the three-dimensional base to create the mask. Have students embellish their masks.

Research in Art Education

"If perception is basic to all learning, if selective viewing is a desirable kind of behavior, and if conceptualization comes after sensory experiences, then it becomes imperative that teachers provide paths for numerous visual and tactile explorations so as to keep all of the child's senses alive and active" (Herberholz, Barbara, and Lee Hanson. *Early Childhood Art.* New York: McGraw-Hill, 1994).

Assessment

Use the following rubric to evaluate the artwork students make in the Creative Expression activity and to assess students' understanding of formal balance and exaggeration in masks.

	Art History and Culture	Aesthetic Perception	Creative Expression	Art Criticism
3 POINTS	The student demonstrates knowledge of maskmaking by two different cultures.	The student accurately identifies how artists use formal balance and exaggeration in masks.	The student effectively creates a papier-mâché mask using formal balance and exaggeration.	The student evaluates his or her work using the four steps of art criticism.
2 POINTS	The student's knowledge of works by artists from different cultures is weak or incomplete.	The student's identification is weak or incomplete.	The student shows some awareness of how to create a papier-mâché mask using formal balance and exaggeration.	The student attempts to evaluate his or her work but shows an incomplete understanding of evaluation criteria.
1 POINT	The student cannot demonstrate knowledge of works by artists from different cultures.	The student cannot identify formal balance or exaggeration in masks.	The student shows no understanding of how to create a a papier-mâché mask using formal balance or exaggeration.	The student makes no attempt to evaluate his or her artwork.

Have students complete page 47 or 48 in their *Assessment* books.

Assessment, p. 47

Name _____ Date _____ Lesson 2 UNIT 4

Formal Balance in Masks

A. Short Answer
1. What is a mask? _____
2. Masks serve many purposes. List three different ways masks are used.
3. List three different materials that can be used to make a mask.
4. List two ways that an artist can show formal balance in a mask.

B. Drawing
On the back of this paper, use crayons to draw a mask that has formal balance.

Level 3   Unit 4 • Texture and Balance   **47**

Lesson 3
Overview

Symmetry

Lesson 3 introduces symmetry. *Symmetry* is a type of formal balance in which both sides of an artwork are exactly the same, or mirror images of one another.

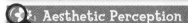
Objectives

Art History and Culture
To compare works of art from Northwest Coast and Mexican cultures
NSAE 4.a; 4.b; 4.c; 5.a; 5.b

Creative Expression
To create a three-dimensional paper sculpture illustrating symmetry
NSAE 1.a; 1.c; 1.d; 2.c; 3.b

Aesthetic Perception
To identify symmetry in three-dimensional art and the environment
NSAE 2.a; 2.b; 3.a

Art Criticism
To use the four steps of art criticism to evaluate own work
NSAE 1.b; 2.a; 2.b; 3.a; 5.c

Vocabulary ⭐ Vocabulary

Review the following vocabulary words with students before beginning the lesson.

symmetry simetría—a type of formal balance in which the two halves, or sides, of an artwork are identical

central axis eje central—an imaginary line that divides a work of art in half vertically

See page 149B for additional vocabulary and Spanish vocabulary resources.

Art Journal: Vocabulary
Have students add these words to the Vocabulary section of their Art Journals.

Lesson Materials
- construction paper
- poster board
- glue
- sketch paper
- markers

Alternate Materials:
- crayons
- brown craft paper

Program Resources
- *Reading and Writing Test Prep.*, pp. 46–47
- *Transparency 21*
- *Flash Cards 12, 14*
- *Artist Profiles*, pp. 79, 21
- *Animals Through History Time Line*
- *Assessment*, pp. 49–50
- *Large Prints 43* Elephant Mask and *44* Elizabeth of Valois, Queen of Spain
- *Art Around the World*

Concept Trace
Symmetry
Introduced: Level 2, Unit 5, Lesson 1
Reinforced: Level 4, Unit 6, Lesson 1

Lesson 3 Arts Integration

Theatre
Complete Unit 4, Lesson 3, on pages 76–77 of *Theatre Arts Connections.*

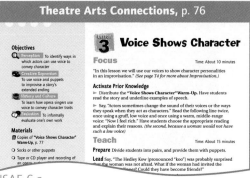
Theatre Arts Connections, p. 76

Music
 Sing or listen to *This Land is Your Land*. This song is verse and refrain, but it is in AA form. What does this say about the music in the verse as compared to the refrain?

Movement & Dance
Select a student to be the leader. Have the remaining students spread out in an open space by the leader. Using movement technique of mirroring, the leader creates slow, smooth, movement that is copied by the group in unison as if they are the leader's reflection. This reinforces the concept of symmetry. Alternate leaders.

**ocus** Time: About 10 minutes

Activate Prior Knowledge

"Think about flying a kite. What do you notice about the way most kites are designed?" "Piensen en volar un papagayo. ¿Qué les llama la atencion acerca de la manera en que se diseñan la mayoría de los papagayos?"

- Discuss students' responses and how kites are usually designed with symmetrical balance.

Using Literature Reading

- Read *Coyote and the Fire Stick: A Pacific Northwest Indian Tale* (1996) by Barbara Diamond Goldin and illustrated by Will Hillenbrand for background information about the Pacific Northwest Indians.

Thematic Connection ⭐ Social Studies

- **Holidays:** Have students look at *Candelabra* and write a short story about a celebration or holiday this piece of artwork may have been used for.

Introduce the Art

Look NSAE 3.a

"Take a close look at the two works of art." "Observen detalladamente las dos obras de arte".

Comparing and Contrasting ⭐ Reading

- Have students describe the subject matter in each artwork and make a list of the differences between the two. Both works have symmetry; however, the shapes and colors in the two works are different.

NSAE 4.a; 4.b; 4.c; 5.a; 5.b

 ## Art History and Culture

Totem poles made by Pacific Northwest Natives are made for the purpose of telling a story, not to be worshiped. Some of the stories are about the family or chief who had the pole made. Other poles tell Native American legends. These legends are often about animals that did important things. A "totem" is a symbol that each Native American family, or clan, adopts. Each clan uses a different animal as its totem. There is the Raven Clan, the Beaver Clan, and many others.

 Web Connection
Visit **www.everythingalaska.com/eta.ttp.html** for more examples of totem poles.

Look at *Totem Pole* and *Candelabra*. Both use formal balance. This totem comes from Native Americans of the Northwest Coast. A totem is a sacred symbol of one or more animals whose spirits protect a family clan. *Candelabra* was created in Mexico. It was used by a family during a religious ceremony announcing the engagement of a young couple.

◄ **Artist Unknown.** *Symmetrical View of a Totem Pole.*
....
Stanley Park, Vancouver, British Columbia, Canada.

 Art History and Culture

A totem pole was often placed in front of a home as a symbol of protection.

 Art History and Culture NSAE 4.a; 4.b; 4.c; 5.a; 5.b

Symmetrical View of a Totem Pole

Totem poles are a traditional art form in Pacific Northwest native tribal culture. Although the specific artists who created these totems are unknown, they characterize the tall, wooden carvings created in the Northwest. Totem poles used stylized creatures to tell a particular family's story. Today, totem poles serve as historical documents recording the wealth, social position, or importance of the person who commissioned them. The way a totem's eyes are made determines where it is from.

See pages 24–25 and 16–21 for more about art history and subject matter.

Artist Profiles, p. 79

Artist Profile
Symmetrical View of a Totem Pole
Totem poles are a traditional art form in Pacific Northwest native tribal cultures. The Kwakiutl and the Haida are two groups that made totem poles. The Kwakiutl and the Haida live in what is now the Canadian province of British Columbia. Western culture changed these native cultures by introducing Western beliefs, tools, ideas, and ways of life. The introduction of the beliefs of others greatly affected the mythology and belief systems of the Kwakiutl and Haida cultures.
◄ **Artist unknown.** (Canada). *Symmetrical View of a Totem Pole.*

◀ **Aurelio and Francisco Flores.**
(Mexico). *Candelabra.* c. 1980.
∙∙∙∙∙∙∙∙∙∙∙∙∙∙∙∙∙∙∙∙∙∙∙∙∙∙∙∙∙∙∙∙∙∙∙∙∙∙∙
Hand molded, fired, painted; clay, paint, wire.
42 × 26 × 8 ¼ inches (106.68 × 66.04 × 20.96
cm.). Museum of International Folk Art, Santa Fe,
New Mexico.

Study both works of
art to find examples of
symmetry.

▶ What single shape or
object do you see in
the center of each
work?

▶ Find the shapes that
are exactly the same
on both sides of the
center line.

▶ What colors are
repeated in exactly
the same place on
both sides of each
sculpture?

Aesthetic Perception

Seeing Like an Artist Look at the works of art in this book
to find other examples of symmetry.

Study   NSAE 1.b; 2.a; 2.b; 3.a; 5.c

▶ The nose is the center of the totem pole.
Three figures are on the center of
Candelabra.

▶ Shapes: The totem pole has the same
shapes on each side. In *Candelabra*, the
figures and shapes that border the
sculpture are all the same.

▶ Colors: The totem pole is dark brown in
color. *Candelabra* has red, yellow, blue,
and lavender repeated throughout it.

■ For more examples of North American art,
see the *Art Around the World* collection.

Aesthetic Perception

NSAE 2.a; 2.b; 3.a

Design Awareness Many pieces of furniture
and buildings are symmetrical with one
central object or shape, for example a three-
cushion sofa has this pattern. Have students
look around the environment for objects that
have a central axis or a line of symmetry.

Developing Visual Literacy Invite students to
look for clues in each artwork about the two
different cultures represented. Have them
consider the color and subject of each work
as well as the materials from which they were
made.   NSAE 4.a; 4.b; 4.c

Art History and Culture   NSAE 4.a; 4.b; 4.c; 5.a; 5.b

Candelabra

Candelabra is an example of Mexican folk sculpture art.
Candelabras were used throughout colonial Mexico to pay
reverence to images of saints and provide light in Catholic religious
ceremonies, such as weddings and funerals.

By the late nineteenth century, the brightly colored candelabras and
incense burners made in the state of Pueblo, Mexico, had become
well known. Many of them were made of clay and had two or three
tiers of arms. In the mid-twentieth century, the Flores family began
to make extremely large and
complex candelabras to be
placed in museums,
restaurants, and lavish homes.

See pages 24–25 and 16–21
for more about art history
and subject matter.

Artist Profiles, p. 21

› Artist Profile ‹

**Aurelio and
Francisco Flores**

Aurelio Flores (ô rēl′ yō flôr′ ās) and his son
Francisco (frən sēs′ cō) are sculpture artists
living in Izucar de Matamoros in Puebla,
Mexico. Their specialization is making large,
complex ceramic candelabras for display in
museums and restaurants. As a young man
Aurelio Flores learned how to make heavy,
ornate candelabras from his father. He
worked in his father's workshop and studied
his father's technique for creating a slightly
smaller type of candelabra made specifically
for decorating an altar at a service
announcing the engagement of a young
couple. Over time Aurelio Flores began
making more complex, multitiered
candleholders and taught the craft to his son

Web Connection

Visit **www.moifa.org** to learn more about the
Museum of International Folk Art.

Teach

Time: About 45 minutes

"How can you show perfect balance with found objects?" "¿Cómo pueden mostrar equilibrio perfecto con objetos de desperdicio?"

- Review the definition of *symmetry* on page 136.

Practice
NSAE 1.a; 1.d

Materials: double pan balance, miscellaneous objects (2 sets of each object)

Alternate Materials: ruler and pencil to create a seesaw

- Distribute the materials and have students follow the directions on page 136.

NSAE 1.a; 1.c; 1.d; 2.c; 3.b

Creative Expression

Materials: 9" × 12" inch construction paper, assorted colors, scissors, glue, black markers, pencils, sketch paper, stapler (optional)

Alternate Materials: crayons, brown craft paper

- Have students brainstorm a variety of animals they could illustrate.

- Review ways to cut symmetrical shapes from paper by putting together two pieces of paper and cutting both at the same time.

- Distribute materials and have students follow the directions on page 137.

- Review the Technique Tips on page 227 for visual examples of techniques.

- See Activity Tips on page 242 for visual instructions.

Art Journal: Ideas

Encourage students to sketch at least three different animals in their Art Journals and then indicate the central axis in each one.

Using Symmetry

These artists used symmetry to create designs on the totem pole and candleholder. **Symmetry** is a special type of formal balance in which two halves of a design are identical, or mirror images of each other. The two halves are divided by a **central axis,** which is an imaginary dividing line. Everything on one side of the central axis is balanced by the objects on the other side. Artists use symmetry when they want designs to look formal and important.

 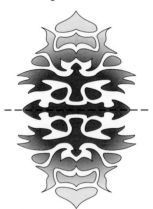

Practice

Use a balance scale to create perfect balance. Use a variety of materials.

1. Practice using formal balance by adding and taking away a variety of materials on each side of the scale.

136 Unit 4 • Lesson 3

Differentiated Instruction

Reteach

Have students look through magazines to find three examples of symmetry. Ask students to cut out examples and glue them on a sheet of paper.

Special Needs

Encourage students to extend their skills in this project by using a variety of paper cutting techniques in the execution of their totem poles.

ELL Tips

Students may have difficulty following oral directions without some kind of visual support. Consider modeling with the whole class the steps in creating a totem. To review, write the steps on the board along with quick sketches illustrating them before students complete the Creative Expression activity.

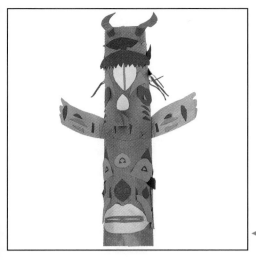

◄ **Donald Nguyen.**
Age 9.

Think about the central axis in this totem and how it runs down the center of the face.

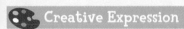 **Creative Expression**

What images would you put on a totem pole? Use symmetry to create a totem.

1. Think of a real or imaginary creature. Make several sketches.

2. Fold a sheet of paper in half. The fold will be your central axis.

3. Using small pieces of colored paper, cut out shapes to represent features such as eyes. Using symmetry, place these features on your totem. Glue the pieces into place.

4. Use symmetry to add other details.

5. Join the edges of your paper together to form a cylinder.

Art Criticism

Describe What creature did you choose for your totem? What kinds of shapes did you use?

Analyze How did you create symmetrical balance?

Interpret What kind of feeling does the formal balance give your totem?

Decide If you could create another totem, what would you do differently?

**eflect**   **Time:** About 45 minutes

Review and Assess

"What have you learned about creating symmetry?" "¿Qué han aprendido acerca de crear simetria?"

Think   NSAE 1.b; 2.a; 2.b

The central axis on this totem runs through the center of the mouths and noses and between the eyes.

- Use *Large Print 43* Elephant Mask to identify the line of symmetry or central axis.

NSAE 1.b; 2.a; 2.b; 3.a; 5.c

Informal Assessment

Art Journal: Critical Thinking
Have students answer the four art criticism question—Describe, Analyze, Interpret, and Decide—in their Art Journals. Have students discuss the use of symmetry in their sculptures.

- For standardized-format test practice using this lesson's art content, see pages 46–47 in *Reading and Writing Test Preparation.*

Art Across the Curriculum

Use these simple ideas to reinforce art concepts across the curriculum

★ **Narrative Writing** Explain to students that the creator of *Candelabra* included things of importance to him or her, just as many people include events of importance to them in their journals. Ask students to identify some events that were important to them and to explain their significance.

★ **Math** Have students draw geometric shapes that are symmetrical as well as free-form shapes that are not symmetrical. Discuss what makes a shape symmetrical.

★ **Science** Explain to students that the totem pole is made of cedar. Ask students to discuss other ways that cedar is used.

★ **Social Studies** Have students look at a map of the world or a globe. Have them point out Mexico and the Pacific Northwest.

★ **Technology** Have students use the paint tool to make a design that has symmetry. Visit **SRAonline.com** to print detailed instuctions for this activity.

Symmetry

Extra! For the Art Specialist

Time: About 45 minutes

Focus

Use *Transparency 21* and *Large Print 43* to identify the uses of symmetry.

Teach

Have students study pictures of totem poles and point out examples of symmetrical balance. Discuss the purpose of totem poles with students so they will understand that a totem stands for an animal whose spirit represents and protects a family. Explain that all Native Americans did not make totem poles. Have students name the colors that are repeated in painting the totem poles. Encourage students to make guesses about the kinds of animals depicted in the individual totems that make up the totem poles.

Reflect

Have students use the four steps of art criticism to evaluate their work. Did they effectively create a symmetrical totem pole?

Alternate Activity

Activity: Totem Pole
Materials:

- 12" × 18" construction paper in a variety of colors
- 9" × 12" construction paper in a variety of colors
- 6" × 9" construction paper in a variety of colors
- scissors
- white glue or glue sticks

1. Have students select an animal they feel represents themselves and/or their family.

2. Divide students into groups (tribes) of 5 or 6. Each student will create a totem that represents himself or herself by cutting out and gluing symmetrical shapes to a 12" × 18" horizontal sheet of construction paper to create their totem animal.

3. When students have completed their individual totems, fasten the totems together to create a totem pole.

Research in Art Education

Schools with rich in-school art programs tend to have a more positive atmosphere—children at these schools are "more likely than children in low-arts schools to have a good rapport with their teachers." This holds true across socio-economic lines. ("Learning In and Through the Arts: Curriculum Implications" in *Champions of Change*, p. 41) Learning about the artwork of different cultures can help students develop respect for people who are not like them.

Assessment

Use the following rubric to evaluate the artwork students make in the Creative Expression activity and to assess students' understanding of symmetry.

	Art History and Culture	Aesthetic Perception	Creative Expression	Art Criticism
3 POINTS	The student effectively compares works of art from Mexican and Northwest Coast cultures.	The student accurately identifies symmetry in three-dimensional art and the environment.	The student effectively plans and creates a three-dimensional paper sculpture using symmetry.	The student evaluates his or her work using the four steps of art criticism.
2 POINTS	The student's comparison is weak or incomplete.	The student shows emerging awareness of symmetry in sculptures.	The student shows some understanding of symmetry in a three-dimensional paper sculpture.	The student attempts to evaluate his or her work but shows an incomplete understanding of evaluation criteria.
1 POINT	The student cannot compare works of art from Mexican and Northwest Coast cultures.	The student cannot identify symmetry in sculptures.	The student cannot create symmetry in a three-dimensional sculpture.	The student makes no attempt to evaluate his or her artwork.

Have students complete page 49 or 50 in their *Assessment* books.

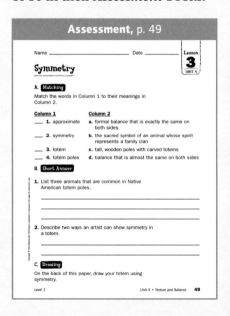

Assessment, p. 49

Lesson 4 Overview

Approximate Symmetry

Lesson 4 introduces approximate symmetry. Approximate symmetry is created when two sides of an artwork or object are almost exactly the same.

Objectives

Art History and Culture
To demonstrate knowledge of Egyptian portraits and the life and art of Philip Evergood NSAE 4.a; 4.b; 4.c; 5.a; 5.b

Creative Expression
To plan and create a self-portrait that has approximate symmetry NSAE 1.a; 1.c; 1.d; 2.c

Aesthetic Perception
To identify how artists use approximate symmetry to create portraits NSAE 2.a; 2.b; 3.a

Art Criticism
To evaluate own work using the four steps of art criticism NSAE 1.b; 2.a; 2.b; 3.a; 5.c

Vocabulary ⭐ Vocabulary

Review the following vocabulary word with students before beginning the lesson.

approximate symmetry *simetría aproximada*—a type of formal balance in which both sides of an artwork or object are almost exactly the same

See page 149B for additional vocabulary and Spanish vocabulary resources.

Art Journal: Critical Vocabulary
Have students add this word to the Vocabulary section of their Art Journals.

Lesson Materials
- 12" × 18" flexible mirror
- liquid tempera paints
- paper plates for palettes
- paintbrushes of various sizes
- containers of water
- pencils
- paper towels
- newspapers

Alternate Materials:
- oil pastels
- watercolor paints

Program Resources
- *Reading and Writing Test Prep.*, pp. 48–49
- *Transparency 22*
- *Flash Cards 12–14*
- *Artist Profiles*, pp. 75, 18
- *Animals Through History Time Line*
- *Assessment*, pp. 51–52
- *Large Prints 43* Elephant Mask and *44* Elizabeth of Valois, Queen of Spain
- *The National Museum of Women in The Arts Collection*

Concept Trace
Approximate Symmetry
Introduced: Level 3, Unit 4, Lesson 4

Reinforced: Level 5, Unit 5, Lesson 5

Lesson 4 Arts Integration

Theatre
Complete Unit 4, Lesson 4, on pages 78–79 of *Theatre Arts Connections.*

Theatre Arts Connections, p. 78

Objectives

Sound Shows Setting

Music
Listen to *Contredanse* by Jean-Phillipe Rameau. What form is this piece in? Are the beginning and ending sections exactly the same? How does the orchestration change in the middle section? The rhythm?

Movement & Dance
Divide students into groups of three. One student in each group is the central point. As the leader he or she will make a shape that the rest of the group imitates. Then each member of the group thinks of a slight variation for the shape such as facing different directions, changing level, or using different body parts. Discuss how this is appropriate symmetry.

ocus

Time: About 10 minutes

Activate Prior Knowledge

"Think about combing or brushing your hair. Is your hair arranged in exactly the same way on both sides?" *"Piensen acerca de peinarse o cepillarse el cabello en las mañanas. ¿Está arreglado su cabello igual en ambos lados?"*

- Discuss students' answers to the question and how people's heads have approximate symmetry, even if their hairstyles do not.

Using Literature ⭐ Reading

- Read Jill Rubalcaba's *A Place in the Sun* (1997) for an understanding of life in Ancient Egypt.

Thematic Connection ⭐ Social Studies

- **About Me** Have students each choose one of the paintings from this lesson and write a short story describing what they think the person in the portrait is like.

Introduce the Art

Look   NSAE 3.a

"Let's look closely at the two paintings." "Vamos a observar detalladamente las dos pinturas".

Comparing and Contrasting ⭐ Reading

- Have students describe the subject matter in each painting. Both are portraits that have approximate symmetry.

NSAE 4.a; 4.b; 4.c; 5.a; 5.b

🏺 Art History and Culture

Portrait of a Boy is typical of the multicultural, multiethnic society of Roman Egypt. It is painted in the elaborate encaustic technique, using pigments mixed with hot or cold beeswax and other ingredients such as egg, resin, and linseed oil. This allowed artists to create images that in many ways are like oil paintings in Western art.

💻 **Web Connection**

Visit **www.metmuseum.org** to see more Egyptian art.

 138 UNIT 4 • Texture and Balance

 **Lesson 4**

Approximate Symmetry

Look at the portraits on these pages. *Portrait of a Boy* is a painting from an Egyptian mummy case. It was created more than 1,800 years ago. *Her World* was painted in 1948. Both artists used approximate symmetry to create these portraits. When something is symmetrical, it is the same on both sides. *Approximate symmetry* means that something is almost the same on both sides.

◀ **Artist Unknown.** (Egypt). *Portrait of a Boy.* Second century.
....
Encaustic on wood. 15 × 7 ½ inches (38 × 19 cm.). The Metropolitan Museum of Art, New York, New York.

Art History and Culture

Encaustic paint is made by mixing color pigment with wax.

138 Unit 4 • Lesson 4

Art History and Culture   NSAE 4.a; 4.b; 4.c; 5.a; 5.b

Portrait of a Boy

The teenage boy in *Portrait of a Boy* looks almost lifelike. Egyptians painted mummy portraits on wood using the encaustic technique, which preserved the portraits for a very long time. After the death of the person portrayed, these wood pieces were placed inside his or her mummy case. Paintings of this type were often called *faiyum* which were typical of the multiethnic society of Roman Egypt. *Portrait of a Boy* was created in the Roman Empire, which included many different peoples who had their own customs, religions, and cultures.

See pages 24–25 and 16–21 for more about art history and subject matter.

Artist Profiles, p. 75

⌐ Artist Profile ⌐

Portrait of a Boy

The Egyptian artist of this painting remains unknown. *Portrait of a Boy* is an example of Fayum portraits, named for the area where most of these paintings have been found. Although the portrait resembles paintings of the Roman tradition, the funerary purpose and iconography reflect the Egyptian culture.

◀ **Artist unknown.** (Egypt). *Portrait of a Boy.* Second century.

Study each painting to find the following examples of approximate symmetry.

▶ Which features on the left side of the face are exactly the same as the ones on the right?

▶ Locate the shapes that are almost the same on both sides of the face.

▶ In which portrait is the hair the same on both sides?

◀ **Philip Evergood.** (American). *Her World.* 1948.

Oil on canvas. 48 × 35 $\frac{5}{8}$ (18.90 × 14.17 cm.). The Metropolitan Museum of Art, New York, New York.

 Aesthetic Perception

Seeing Like an Artist Look at a friend's face to find examples of approximate symmetry.

Study

▶ Symmetry: In *Portrait of a Boy*, the hair, eyebrows, and nose are the same on both sides of the face.

▶ Approximate symmetry: In *Her World*, the shapes of the eyes are almost the same on both sides of the face. In *Portrait of a Boy*, the boy's hair is almost the same on both sides.

▶ In *Portrait of a Boy* the hair is the same on both sides.

■ For more examples of portraits, see *The National Museum of Women in the Arts Collection.*

Aesthetic Perception

NSAE 2.a; 2.b; 3.a

Seeing Like an Artist Invite students to study the face of a classmate, looking for examples of approximate symmetry. NSAE 4.a; 4.b; 4.c

Developing Visual Literacy Invite students to make a list of the similarities of the subjects of the two portraits in this lesson, even though they are separated by hundreds of years.

Art History and Culture

NSAE 4.a; 4.b; 4.c; 5.a; 5.b

Philip Evergood

Philip Evergood (fil´ əp ev´ər gud) (1901–1973) was born in New York City and educated in England. His paintings varied from simple human themes to themes that were allegorical. During the Depression, he created social-protest paintings. Evergood's paintings represent his social concerns, which included isolation and prejudice. *Her World* was created when President Roosevelt's New Deal social program, which included the Works Progress Administration, provided funds to writers, artists, and theatre groups for numerous projects.

See pages 24–25 and 16–21 for more about art history and subject matter.

Artist Profiles, p. 18

◆ Artist Profile ◆

Philip Evergood
1901–1973

Philip Evergood (fi´ləp e´var go͞od) was born in New York City. His parents sent him to boarding schools in England and then to Cambridge University. He studied art briefly in Paris, France, but he taught himself to be a painter against his parents' wishes. For several years, Evergood traveled back and forth between Europe and the United States. He spent the 1930s, the years of the Great Depression, in America and used his paintings to protest against people's suffering. Evergood cared about human suffering and injustice, but he also had a temper and could be demanding and disagreeable. He married a ballet dancer, who lived with him only on weekends. He had no children, but loved his dogs

Web Connection

Visit **www.artnet.com/ag/fineartthumbnails.asp? aid=5938** to see more works of art by Philip Evergood.

Teach

"How can you show approximate symmetry in a drawing of a face?" *"¿Cómo pueden mostrar simetría aproximada en un dibujo de una cara?"*

- Discuss the use of guidelines to create facial proportions with approximate symmetry on page 140.

- Have students compare the diagram with their own facial proportions.

Practice NSAE 1.a; 1.d

Materials: 9" × 12" white paper, pencils

Alternate Materials: crayons

- Distribute the materials and have students follow the directions on page 141.

 ## Creative Expression

NSAE 1.a; 1.c; 1.d; 2.c; 3.b

Materials: 12" × 18" flexible mirror, liquid tempera paints, paper plates for palettes, paintbrushes of various sizes, containers of water, pencils, paper towels, newspapers

Alternate Materials: oil pastels and watercolor paints

- Distribute the materials and have students follow the directions on page 141.

- Have students compare the facial proportions they see in the mirror to the diagram on page 140 so their drawings have accurate facial proportions.

- Review the Technique Tips on pages 217–218 for visual examples of techniques.

- See Activity Tips on page 243 for visual instructions.

Art Journal: Ideas

Encourage students to make a list in their Art Journals of their personal traits that they would want to appear in a self-portrait.

Using Approximate Symmetry

Approximate symmetry is a special kind of formal balance that happens when both sides of a design are *almost* exactly the same. The human face has approximate symmetry. Each side is almost the same as the other.

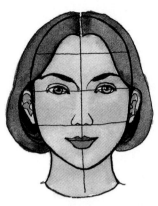

When drawing a portrait, it is helpful to draw the shape of the head first. Look at the guide lines in the face above. Notice that the eyes are placed about halfway between the top of the head and the bottom of the chin. Where are the tops of the ears? The nose? The mouth? What about your own face?

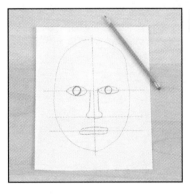

Practice

Illustrate approximate symmetry. Use a pencil.

1. Create the shape of a head by drawing a large oval shape. Draw a line *down* the middle of the shape and also *across* the middle.

2. Look at the guide lines in the diagram above to help you place the eyes, nose, mouth, and ears.

Differentiated Instruction

Reteach

Have students look through the *Student Edition* to find three different works of art that illustrate approximate symmetry. Ask students to list the title of each work and describe how approximate symmetry was created.

Special Needs

Check for student understanding of approximate or formal symmetry by having them add a background to their portrait that shows one of the types of symmetry.

ELL Tips

When asking students to create self-portraits, be sensitive to physical differences that may be present. Dealing with issues of skin color, hair type, or other physical characteristics must be handled sensitively and positively to avoid any feelings of bias or discrimination on the part of students.

Think about how this student artist created approximate symmetry.

◀ **Maribel Cardinas.**
Age 9.

 Creative Expression

What parts of your face show approximate symmetry? Use approximate symmetry in a self-portrait.

1. Look at your face in the mirror. Notice how it is almost exactly the same on both sides.

2. Use approximate symmetry to draw a self-portrait.

3. Add color.

Art Criticism

Describe What shapes did you use to create the face? What objects are included in the background?

Analyze How did you create approximate symmetry?

Interpret Give your portrait a title that expresses the emotions in the face.

Decide If you had painted this self-portrait a year ago, what objects would you have included?

 **Reflect** Time: About 🕐 45 minutes

Review and Assess

"What have you learned about approximate symmetry?" "¿Qué han aprendido sobre la simetria aproximada?"

Think NSAE 1.b; 2.a; 2.b

The student artist created lines in the background that are similar, but not exactly the same.

■ Use **Large Print 44** to have students identify and compare the uses of approximate symmetry in the print and in the artworks in this lesson.

Informal Assessment
NSAE 1.b; 2.a; 2.b; 3.a; 5.c

Art Journal: Critical Thinking
Have students answer the four art criticism questions—Describe, Analyze, Interpret, and Decide—in their Art Journals. Discuss the uses of approximate symmetry in students' self-portraits.

■ For standardized-format test practice using this lesson's art content, see pages 48–49 in **Reading and Writing Test Preparation**.

Art Across the Curriculum

Use these simple ideas to reinforce art concepts across the curriculum.

★ **Narrative Writing** Explain that ancient Egyptians used symbols of things that were important in their lives to decorate tombs. Have students write a short autobiography featuring symbols that are important to them.

★ **Math** Explain that the word *approximate* means "nearly" or "almost." Have students use a ruler to measure their hands from the tip of the longest finger to the wrist, rounding to the nearest inch.

★ **Science** Explain to students that scientists use clues to learn about people who lived many years ago. Have students look at *Portrait of a Boy* and use clues in the portrait to guess when it was created.

★ **Social Studies** Ask students to suggest ideas about how ancient Egyptian workers moved the huge stones to build the pyramids.

★ **Technology** Have students use the paint tool to draw self-portraits using approximate symmetry. Visit **SRAonline.com** to print detailed instructions for this activity.

NSAE 6.b   Art TEKS 1.A.4, 1.A.5

Approximate Symmetry

Extra! For the Art Specialist

Focus

NSAE 1.a; 1.b; 1.c; 1.d; 2.a; 2.b; 2.c; 3.b

Use *Transparency 22* and *Large Print 44* *Elizabeth of Valois, Queen of Spain* to identify uses of approximate symmetry. Have students examine the portraits in the artworks. Do they think the faces of the people are exactly symmetrical or approximately symmetrical?

Teach

Have students examine their faces in a mirror. Are their features exactly symmetrical? Explain that the differences in their features from exact symmetry are part of what makes each student unique and gives them their individual look.

Reflect

Have students use the four steps of art criticism to evaluate their work. Did they effectively create a self portrait using approximate symmetry?

Alternate Activity

Activity: **Self-Portrait**
Materials
- 12" × 18" manila paper
- colored crayons, especially a variety of tans and browns
- mirrors

1. Have students lay their hand above the middle of the drawing paper and draw around it to make an oval head shape. Have students move their hands below the head shape and draw their necks wider than their hands.

2. Have students note in the mirror how their features are almost exactly the same on each side of their face. Point out that their eyes are in the middle of their head, the tip of their nose is halfway between their eyes and their chin, and their mouth is halfway between the tip of their nose and their chin.

3. After students have drawn their facial features, have them color their portraits with crayons.

Research
in Art Education

"I argue that many of the most complex and subtle forms of thinking take place when students have an opportunity either to work meaningfully on the creation of images—whether visual, choreographic, musical, literary, or poetic—or to scrutinize them appreciatively" (Eisner, Elliot W. *The Arts and the Creation of Mind.* New Haven: Yale Univ. Press, 2002).

Assessment
Use the following rubric to evaluate the artwork students make in the Creative Expression activity and to assess students' understanding of approximate symmetry in portraits.

Have students complete page 51 or 52 in their *Assessment* books.

	Art History and Culture	Aesthetic Perception	Creative Expression	Art Criticism
3 POINTS	The student effectively demonstrates knowledge of artists from different cultures.	The student accurately identifies how artists use approximate symmetry to create portraits.	The student effectively plans and creates a self-portrait that has approximate symmetry.	The student evaluates own work using the four steps of art criticism.
2 POINTS	The student's knowledge is weak or incomplete.	The student shows emerging awareness of how artists use approximate symmetry to create portraits.	The student shows attempts to plan and create a self-portrait that has approximate symmetry.	The student attempts to evaluate own work but shows an incomplete understanding of evaluation criteria.
1 POINT	The student shows little knowledge of works of art by artists from different cultures.	The student cannot identify how artists use approximate symmetry to create portraits.	The student shows no understanding of how to plan and create a self-portrait that has approximate symmetry.	The student makes no attempt to evaluate own art work.

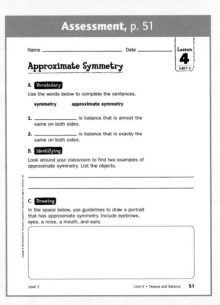

Assessment, p. 51

Name _____ Date _____

Lesson 4 UNIT 4

Approximate Symmetry

A. Vocabulary
Use the words below to complete the sentences.
symmetry   approximate symmetry

1. _____ is balance that is almost the same on both sides.
2. _____ is balance that is exactly the same on both sides.

B. Identifying
Look around your classroom to find two examples of approximate symmetry. List the objects.

C. Drawing
In the space below, use guidelines to draw a portrait that has approximate symmetry. Include eyebrows, eyes, a nose, a mouth, and ears.

Level 3   Unit 4 • Texture and Balance   51

Lesson 5 Visual Texture

Lesson 5 introduces visual texture. Visual texture is the way something looks as if it would feel if it could be touched.

Objectives

 Art History and Culture

To demonstrate knowledge of the art and life of Gustave Caillebotte and Richard Estes   NSAE 4.a; 4.b; 4.c; 5.a; 5.b

 Creative Expression

To plan and create an outdoor scene using visual texture
NSAE 1.a; 1.c; 1.d; 2.c

 Aesthetic Perception

To identify visual textures in works of art

NSAE 2.a; 2.b; 3.a

 Art Criticism

To use the four steps of art criticism to evaluate own work
NSAE 1.b; 2.a; 2.b; 3.a; 5.c

Vocabulary 🌟 Vocabulary

Review the following vocabulary words with students before beginning the lesson.

visual texture *textura visual*—the way an object looks as it would feel if it could be touched

highlights *claros*—small areas of white used to show the very brightest spots on an object

See page 149B for additional vocabulary and Spanish vocabulary resources.

 Art Journal: Critical Vocabulary

Have students add these words to the Vocabulary section of their Art Journals.

Lesson Materials
- computer paint program

Alternate Materials:
- large sheets of white paper
- crayons

Program Resources
- *Reading and Writing Test Prep.*, pp. 50–51
- *Transparency 23*
- *Flash Cards 1–6*
- *Artist Profiles*, pp. 9, 17
- *Animals Through History Time Line*
- *Assessment,* pp. 53–54
- *Large Prints 43 Elephant Mask* and *44 Elizabeth of Valois, Queen of Spain*
- *Art Around the World*

Concept Trace
Visual Texture
Introduced: Level 1, Unit 5, Lesson 2
Reinforced: Level 4, Unit 4, Lesson 4

Lesson 5 Arts Integration

Theatre

Complete Unit 4, Lesson 5, on pages 80–81 of *Theatre Arts Connections.*

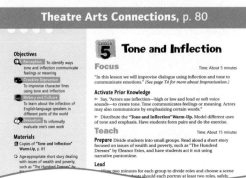

Music

 Texture in music describes whether one melody is alone or with other contrasting melodies (Polyphony), or with harmonic accompaniment. Listen to *The Moldau* by Bedrich Smetana. The Moldau is a river in his native Czechoslovakia. The piece starts with a small flow of melody from two flutes depicting two streams coming out of the mountains. Listen how the texture changes as it goes on and instruments are added.

Movement & Dance

Brainstorm a list of objects that have hard or soft textural images. Include words to describe the objects. For example: sleek cats, wrinkled leaves, rough bark, jagged rocks, splintered fences, and soft furry rabbits. Explore each of these ideas in movement. Have students select three of these movements and organize them into a sequence.

NSAE 6.a

Focus

Time: About 10 minutes

Activate Prior Knowledge

"Suppose that you are looking at a photograph of yourself. Can you actually feel the different textures of your hair and clothes?" "Vamos a suponer que están viendo una fotografía de ustedes. ¿Pueden en realidad sentir las diferentes texturas de sus cabellos y de su ropa?"

- Discuss student's answers. Point out that even though a photograph feels smooth, textures within it can be identified because of previous experiences.

Using Literature [★] Reading

- Read Christina Bjork's *Linnea in Monet's Garden* (1987) illustrated by Lena Anderson to introduce students to impressionist painters like Caillebotte and France of the late nineteenth century.

Thematic Connection [★] Reading

- **City Life and Country Life** Discuss the differences between city living as depicted in the two works in this lesson and country living.

Introduce the Art

Look NSAE 3.a

"Let's look closely at the paintings." "Vamos a observar detalladamente las pinturas".

Comparing and Contrasting [★] Reading

- Have students describe the subject matter of the two works of art. Both paintings are outdoor cityscapes but they are from different time periods. In *Paris Street, Rainy Day*, the umbrellas show a wet shininess and the clothing looks smooth and dull. *Diner* includes metal surfaces that look shiny.

NSAE 4.a; 4.b; 4.c; 5.a; 5.b

Art History and Culture

Diners, like the one in *Diner*, became a part of the American culture more than 100 years ago. The influence of diners has touched almost every aspect of American life including cooking, dining out, popular culture, design, fashion, and more. Many songs and works of art, including Edward Hopper's *Nighthawks*, have been created as a representation of this cultural icon.

Web Connection

Visit **www.artcyclopedia.com/artists/ caillebotte_gustave.html** for links to many of Caillebotte's works.

 Visual Texture

Look at the paintings on these two pages. *Paris Street Rainy Day* and *Diner* are paintings of city scenes. Both depict textures so accurately you can tell what all the surfaces would feel like if you could touch them.

▲ **Gustave Caillebotte.** (French). *Paris Street Rainy Day.* 1877.

Oil on canvas. 83 $\frac{1}{2}$ × 108 $\frac{3}{4}$ inches (210.82 × 274.32 cm.). Art Institute of Chicago, Chicago, Illinois.

Art History and Culture

Caillebotte combined the realistic style of the academics with the everyday themes and viewpoints of the Impressionists.

Art History and Culture NSAE 4.a; 4.b; 4.c; 5.a; 5.b

Gustave Caillebotte

Gustave Caillebotte (gu´ stav ka yu´ bot) (1848–1894) Gustave Caillebotte was born into a wealthy Parisian family. After serving in the Franco-Prussian War, he started painting. Early in his career he painted scenes of working-class Paris and portraits of his family and friends. Caillebotte was deeply influenced by his friends, Degas, Renoir, and Monet, famous Impressionist painters.

See pages 24–25 and 16–21 for more about art history and subject matter.

Artist Profiles, p. 9

Artist Profile

Gustave Caillebotte
1848–1894

Gustave Caillebotte (gūs´ tăv kī´ yə bŏt´) was born into a wealthy Parisian family. He earned a degree in law and was drafted into the French army. After serving in the Franco-Prussian War, he started painting. He was accepted into Paris's École des Beaux-Arts, but he decided against formal training. Caillebotte was attracted to the artistic rebels of the time, the impressionists. When the Impressionists began to disagree and the group broke up, Caillebotte moved from Paris to a French village. He continued to paint until his death, and he left his large collection of art to several museums.

Study both paintings to find visual textures.

▶ Find the textures that look smooth.

▶ Where are the shiny-looking textures?

▶ Find the bumpy textures.

▶ Do you see textures that are smooth and dull?

 Aesthetic Perception

Seeing Like an Artist Find the shiniest object in your classroom. What makes it look shiny?

▲ **Richard Estes.**
(American). *Diner.* 1971.
....
Oil on canvas. 40 × 50 inches
(102.87 × 127 cm.).
Hirshhorn Museum and Sculpture
Garden, Smithsonian Institution,
Washington, D.C.

Art History and Culture

NSAE 4.a; 4.b; 4.c; 5.a; 5.b

Richard Estes

Richard Estes (1936–) is one of the premier American photorealists, a type of realism characterized by sharp details and a photographic appearance. His works have a crisp, clean look and plenty of reflective surfaces. He uses photographs to capture the image he wants to paint because it is not possible to create his paintings from real life. Most of his works from the early 1960s are scenes of New Yorkers, but his later paintings depict glass storefronts reflecting distorted images.

See pages 24–25 and 16–21 for more about art history and subject matter.

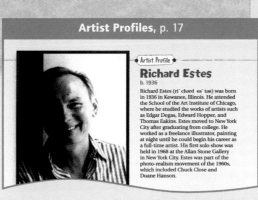

Artist Profiles, p. 17

◀ Artist Profile ▶
Richard Estes
b. 1936
Richard Estes (rī´ chard es´ tas) was born
in 1936 in Kewanee, Illinois. He attended
the School of the Art Institute of Chicago,
where he studied the works of artists such
as Edgar Degas, Edward Hopper, and
Thomas Eakins. Estes moved to New York
City after graduating from college. He
worked as a freelance illustrator, painting
at night until he could begin his career as
a full-time artist. His first solo show was
held in 1968 at the Allan Stone Gallery
in New York City. Estes was part of the
photo-realism movement of the 1960s,
which included Chuck Close and
Duane Hanson.

Study

NSAE 1.b; 2.a; 2.b; 3.a; 5.c

▶ Smooth textures: In *Rainy Day*, the street and sidewalk appear to have smooth textures. The buildings and clothing of the people also have smooth lines. In *Diner*, the booths themselves have smooth lines, as does the top portion of the diner.

▶ Shiny textures: In *Rainy Day*, the street and sidewalk have shiny textures. In *Diner*, the metal surfaces on the building and phone booths are shiny.

▶ Bumpy textures: The road in *Rainy Day* and the sidewalk in *Diner* are bumpy textures.

▶ Smooth and dull textures: The clothes in *Rainy Day* and the red in the diner and the building wall in *Diner* are examples of smooth and dull textures.

■ For more examples of European art, see the *Art Around the World Collection*.

Art Journal: Concepts
Encourage students to keep a list in their Art Journals of the following: smooth textures, shiny textures, rough textures, bumpy textures. Compare the lists in class.

NSAE 2.a; 2.b; 3.a

 Aesthetic Perception

Seeing Like an Artist Invite students to find three shiny, three smooth, and three rough textures in the classroom. Discuss what it is that makes you know what the texture is, even if you can't touch it. NSAE 4.a; 4.b; 4.c

Developing Visual Literacy Invite students to study both paintings, looking for clues as to the time period they were painted.

 Web Connection
Visit **www.thinker.org/index.asp** to learn more about Richard Estes.

Teach

Time: About 45 minutes

"How can you create visual texture of an actual object?" "¿Cómo pueden crear la textura visual de un objeto real?"

- Discuss the definition of *visual texture* on page 144.

- Discuss ways to work with watercolors to represent textures in a painting. Use a white crayon to represent a highlight and then paint over it with watercolor paint. Shake a few grains of salt into the wet watercolor paint on the paper. Experiment with watercolors to see what happens when you blot an area with a paper towel. Use a crayon to rub over a texture and then use a contrasting color of watercolor paint.

Practice   NSAE 1.a; 1.d

Materials: sheets of 9" × 12" white paper, pencils, textured objects

Alternate Materials: crayons

- Distribute the materials and have students follow the directions on page 144.

Creative Expression

NSAE 1.a; 1.c; 1.d; 2.c; 3.b
Materials: computer paint program

Alternate Materials: large sheets of white paper, crayons

- Have students follow the directions on page 145 for the computer.

- Review the Technique Tips on page 222 for visual examples of techniques.

- See Activity Tips on page 243 for visual instructions.

Art Journal: Brainstorming

Have students brainstorm ways to create outdoor scenes. Have students each make two or three sketches of different textures they see in the community in their Art Journals. Then have students decide how they will show these different textures in the Creative Expression activity.

Using Visual Texture

Visual texture is texture that you see with your eyes.

Lightly rub the surface of the pictures with your fingers. You cannot actually *feel* the different textures. You feel the smoothness of the paper instead.

If you have felt these textures before, you probably remember how they feel. Your eyes "see" the textures even though you cannot feel them. This is called visual texture.

Artists show shiny surfaces by using highlights. **Highlights** are small areas of white used to show the brightest spots on an object.

Practice

Make a rubbing of a texture to illustrate visual texture. Use a pencil.

1. Find an example of texture in your classroom.

2. Place a sheet of paper on top of the object.

3. Use the side of a pencil tip to rub the paper to create a visual texture.

Differentiated Instruction

Reteach
Have students look through the *Student Edition* to find five different works of art that illustrate visual textures. Ask students to list the title of each work and describe the textures found in each one.

Special Needs
Many students with low vision have a heightened sense of touch. Encourage all students to begin fine tuning this sense by asking them to create art that is mostly pleasing to the touch.

ELL Tips
Frequent comprehension checks can help you monitor students' abilities to follow the lesson. You can ask students for physical responses or short verbal responses to indicate their understandings.

◄ **Peter Olguin.**
Age 10.

Think about how this artist showed trees, bushes, and a sidewalk in his artwork.

Creative Expression

Think about the area outside your house and the area around it.

1. Make a few quick sketches to show what your house looks like. Include things around your house like sidewalks, bushes, trees, or fences.

2. Now use the draw tool in the paint program to draw a picture of your house and the area around it. Think about the textures that are visible, such as rough bricks, glassy windows, or prickly bushes.

3. Use the fill tool and the texture tool to add color and texture to the drawing.

Art Criticism

Describe List the steps you followed to create this picture.

Analyze Describe the texture you created with the computer.

Interpret Give your work an expressive title.

Decide Were you successful in creating a variety of textures using the computer?

 **Time:** About 45 minutes

Review and Assess

"How do artists use visual texture to create a sense of touch in their paintings?" "¿Cómo usan los artistas la textura visual para crear una sensación táctil en sus pinturas?"

■ Use **Large Print 44** to have students compare uses of visual texture in the print and in the artworks in this lesson.

Think   NSAE 1.b; 2.a; 2.b

The student artist created visual texture by using different background patterns in his computer art.

Informal Assessment
NSAE 1.b; 2.a; 2.b; 3.a; 5.c

Art Journal: Critical Thinking

Have students answer the four art criticism questions—Describe, Analyze, Interpret, and Decide. In small groups, have students discuss the uses of visual texture in their artwork.

■ For standardized-format test practice using this lesson's art content, see pages 50–51 in **Reading and Writing Test Preparation**.

Art Across the Curriculum

Use these simple ideas to reinforce art concepts across the curriculum.

★ **Narrative Writing** Have students study *Paris Street, Rainy Day* and each write a short story describing what it might have been like to live in Paris during the 1800s.

★ **Math** Have students write a list of the different geometric shapes they see in *Paris Street, Rainy Day* and *Diner*.

★ **Science** Have students compare the weather in the two different paintings. Discuss how people adapt to different types of weather.

★ **Social Studies** List the modern inventions that can be seen in *Diner* that are not seen in *Rainy Day*. Discuss how these inventions have changed city life.

★ **Technology** Have students use the paint program on a computer to create pictures of objects found in their homes. Have students use different colors and types of lines to create visual textures in the objects. Visit **SRAonline.com** to print detailed instructions for this activity.

NSAE 6.b

Visual Texture

 For the Art Specialist

NSAE 1.a; 1.b; 1.c; 1.d; 2.a; 2.b; 2.c; 3.b

Focus

Use *Transparency 23* and *Large Print 44 Elizabeth of Valois, Queen of Spain* to identify different textures.

Teach

Ask students how they can tell the artworks depict a night scene. What did the artists do to make the viewer feel it is nighttime? Explain that artists examine how light makes colors change in daylight and at sunset, on a clear day or a rainy day. How would the colors look different if the picture was in daylight rather than nighttime?

Reflect

Have students use the four steps of art criticism to evaluate their work. Did they effectively create a night scene with different textures?

Alternate Activity

Materials
- 12" × 18" manila paper
- good quality wax crayons or oil pastels
- diluted dark blue or black tempera or watercolor paint
- $\frac{1}{2}$" flat easel brushes

1. Tell students they will be drawing a picture of their neighborhood or a city at night. Be sure to have students color lights in the windows, and include street lights and the moon and stars in their pictures.

2. Students must press hard while coloring to make a thick layer of each color.

3. When the drawing is completed, students will brush the diluted paint over their pictures, in straight vertical overlapping strokes covering the drawing. The paint will resist, or pull away from, the crayon or oil pastels, creating a dark, nighttime background.

Research
in Art Education

Research has shown that "learning happens best when kids have fun, and the arts are fun for kids." It is important to remember that while the arts can act "as catalysts for learning other subject areas across the curriculum," they are also valuable in their own right ("Arts Literacy for Business" in *The Vision for Arts Education in the 21st Century*). The artwork in this lesson can inspire interesting study about a host of topics, including inventions, history, and cultural icons such as diners and telephone booths.

Assessment

Use the following rubric to evaluate the artwork students make in the Creative Expression activity and to assess students' understanding of visual texture.

Have students complete page 53 or 54 in their *Assessment* books.

	Art History and Culture	Aesthetic Perception	Creative Expression	Art Criticism
3 POINTS	The student demonstrates knowledge of the lives and cultures of both artists and how they use visual textures in their artwork.	The student accurately identifies visual textures in works of art	The student effectively plans and creates an outdoor scene displaying different textures.	The student evaluates his or her work using the four steps of art criticism.
2 POINTS	The student demonstrates no understanding of the lives and cultures of either artist and how they use visual textures in their artwork.	The student's shows emerging awareness of visual textures in works of art.	The student shows some awareness of how to plan and create an outdoor scene displaying different textures.	The student attempts to evaluate his or her work but shows an incomplete understanding of evaluation criteria.
1 POINT	The student cannot demonstrate knowledge of the lives and cultures of either artist or how they use visual textures in their artwork.	The student cannot identify visual textures in works of art.	The student shows no understanding of how to plan and create an outdoor scene displaying different textures.	The student makes no attempt to evaluate his or her artwork.

Assessment, p. 53

Name _____ Date _____
Visual Texture — Lesson 5 UNIT 4

A Matching
Match the words in Column 1 to their meanings in Column 2.

Column 1
___ 1. highlights
___ 2. visual texture

Column 2
a. the texture you see with your eyes
b. the very brightest spots on an object

B Drawing
In the boxes below, create visual texture by making a rubbing of three different surfaces. Use a pencil or a crayon.

C Short Answer
Look at the work of art *Paris Street Rainy Day* by Gustave Caillebotte. Find and describe three different visual textures created by the artist in this painting.

_____
_____
_____

Level 3   Unit 4 • Texture and Balance 53

Tactile Texture

Lesson 6 introduces tactile texture. Tactile texture is the way the surface of an object actually feels when it is touched. Artists use various media to create tactile textures in works of art, such as sculptures, weavings, and jewelry.

Objectives

 Art History and Culture

To demonstrate knowledge of North American shields and the life and art of Ayako Miyawaki   NSAE 4.a; 4.b; 4.c; 5.a; 5.b

 Creative Expression

To plan and create a fabric appliqué banner using tactile textures
NSAE 1.a; 1.c; 1.d; 2.c; 3.b

 Aesthetic Perception

To identify how artists use tactile textures in works of art and the environment
NSAE 2.a; 2.b; 3.a

 Art Criticism

To use the four steps of art criticism to evaluate own work
NSAE 1.b; 2.a; 2.b; 3.a; 5.c

Vocabulary [★] Vocabulary

Review the following vocabulary words with students before beginning the lesson.

appliqué aplicación—an art form in which cut-out fabric decorations are fastened to a larger surface to create a design

tactile texture textura táctil—the way that an object actually feels when it is touched

See page 149B for additional vocabulary and Spanish vocabulary resources.

 Art Journal: Vocabulary

Have students add these words to the Vocabulary section of their Art Journals.

Lesson Materials

- assorted pieces of colorful felt and other fabrics
- burlap
- yarn
- tapestry needles
- glue
- scissors
- sketch paper
- pencils
- markers
- tape

Alternate Materials:
- wallpaper scraps

Program Resources

- *Reading and Writing Test Prep.*, pp. 52-53
- *Transparency 24*
- *Flash Cards 1-6*
- *Artist Profiles*, pp. 40, 80
- *Animals Through History Time Line*
- *Assessment*, pp. 55–56
- *Large Prints 43* Elephant Mask and *44* Elizabeth of Valois, Queen of Spain
- *Art Around the World*

Concept Trace

Tactile Texture
Introduced: Level 1, Unit 5, Lesson 1

Reinforced: Level 4, Unit 4, Lesson 5

Lesson 6   Arts Integration

Theatre

Complete Unit 4, Lesson 6, on pages 82–83 of *Theatre Arts Connections.*

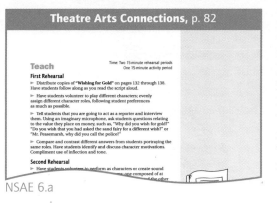

Theatre Arts Connections, p. 82

NSAE 6.a

Music

 An American composer who seemed to create sounds and textures that could be associated purely as his own was Aaron Copeland. Listen to his "Variations on Simple Gifts" from *Appalachian Spring.* He created the ballet *Appalachian Spring* for the dancer Martha Graham in 1944. His textures are open, transparent. One of the ways he creates this open sound is by grouping instruments together, such as very high instruments with low pitched instruments.

Movement & Dance

Cut egg cartons in two so you have containers that can hold six objects. Divide students into groups of six. Place six objects of different textures (such as seeds, rubber bands, cotton, wool) in each of the egg carton pockets. Have each group explore their objects through touch and create a word to describe each one. Have each student explore moving like one object for eight counts. Then have students sequence their six movements together.

 ocus

Time: About 10 minutes

Activate Prior Knowledge

"Imagine walking outside in your bare feet. Why might some textures hurt your feet when you walk on them?" *"Imagínense qué están caminando descalzos afuera. ¿Por qué algunas texturas pudieran hacerles daño a sus pies cuando caminan?"*

- Discuss student's responses to the question and the differences between touching bumpy or rough textures and smooth or silky textures.

Using Literature | Reading

- Read *A Storyteller's Story* by Rafe Martin. Have students describe how certain textures, such as the mammoth's fur, would feel.

Thematic Connection | Social Studies

- **Native Americans:** Have students each write an imaginative short story that includes a description of what they think *Thunderbird Shield* was used for.

Introduce the Art

Look   NSAE 3.a

"Let's look closely at the two works of art." *"Vamos a observar detalladamente las dos obras de arte".*

Comparing and Contrasting | Reading

- Have students describe the subject matter in each artwork. Both works are iconographic. Both include images found in nature, incorporate found materials, and contain objects stitched in place. *Various Fish* is made entirely with fibers, is intended to be displayed on a wall, and has a rectangular format. *Thunderbird Shield* includes painted areas, is functional as well as decorative, and has a circular format.

NSAE 4.a; 4.b; 4.c; 5.a; 5.b

Art History and Culture

Ayako Miyawaki created her own designs modeled after objects she observed in nature. She says she was "full of love for pieces of fabric, nature and natural objects, and full of the joy of creation."

Web Connection

Visit **www.artcyclopedia.com/nationalities/ Japanese.html** for links to works by Japanese artists.

◀ **Ayako Miyawaki.** (Japanese). *Various Fish*. 1967.
• • • • • • • • • • • • • • • •
13 × 11 ¾ inches (33.02 × 29.85 cm.). Cotton collage on burlap. The National Museum of Women in the Arts, Washington, D.C.

Look at *Thunderbird Shield* and *Various Fish*. The shield was created to wear when hunting or fighting and in special ceremonies. Both artists used a number of tactile textures in their work.

Art History and Culture

Why do you think the artist created *Various Fish*?

Art History and Culture   NSAE 4.a; 4.b; 4.c; 5.a; 5.b

Ayako Miyawaki

Ayako Miyawaki (ä ē ko mē yä wä kē) (1905–) began to make appliqué works after the end of World War II. Using the fabric from old clothes and rags, she created her own designs based on objects that she observed in nature. During World War II Miyawaki spent much of her time in bomb shelters in Japan. She began producing her appliqué works in 1945 at the age of forty, establishing an original style totally different from Western quilting. Using Japanese patterns, her textiles display an appreciation of the beauty that is all around us, in nature, in the home, and in life.

See pages 24–25 and 16–21 for more about art history and subject matter.

Artist Profiles, p. 40

Artist Profile

Ayako Miyawaki
b. 1905

During World War II Japanese artist Ayako Miyawaki (ä ē kō mē yä wä kē) spent much of her time in bomb shelters. As soon as the war ended she began to experiment with fabric art. She never attended art school. She created her first fabric picture using appliqué in 1945 at age 40. In 1950, she had her first public exhibition—in a candy store. Since then her work has become popular. It is exhibited in Japan and the United States. Her husband was a teacher and painter, and Miyawaki has several children.

◀ **Artist Unknown.** (American). *Thunderbird Shield.* c. 1830.

Buffalo-hide shield with inner cover, decorated with paintings and feathers. Smithsonian National Museum of the American Indian, New York, New York.

Study both works of art to find the tactile textures.

▶ Locate the smooth fabrics and the smooth-looking animal skin.

▶ Find the bumpy lines and dots made with string. How would they feel if you could touch them?

▶ Which artwork was made to look at, and which was made for a particular function?

Aesthetic Perception

Seeing Like an Artist Look through the works of art in this book. Find a piece that includes real textures.

NSAE 1.b; 2.a; 2.b; 3.a; 5.c

Study

▶ Smooth textures from nature: *Thunderbird Shield* is made with smooth feathers and a smooth animal skin.

▶ Bumpy stitches: In *Various Fish*, the lines and dots stitched on the fish look as if they would feel rough or bumpy to the touch.

▶ Artwork to hang: *Various Fish* Functional artwork: *Thunderbird Shield*.

■ For more examples of Asian art, see the *Art Around the World* collection.

Art Journal: Concepts

Encourage students to keep a texture glossary in their Art Journals. Have them start with twenty words that refer to all kinds of textures.

NSAE 2.a; 2.b; 3.a

Aesthetic Perception

Seeing Like an Artist Invite students to collect three objects in the classroom that have very different textures. Have them describe each texture to the class.

NSAE 4.a; 4.b; 4.c

Developing Visual Literacy Invite students to look carefully at the two works of art from two very different cultures in this lesson. What does each work say about the importance of animals in each culture?

Art History and Culture

NSAE 4.a; 4.b; 4.c; 5.a; 5.b

Thunderbird Shield

Thunderbird Shield was created by a member of the Absaroke (Crow) tribe. The Absaroke were one of the Plains cultures, enemies of the Sioux. In battle, a warrior protected himself with a shield, a personal insignia or stamp. The shield possesses individual symbolism. The owner of this shield received his personal medicine from the thunderbird. The Thunderbird was the representation of Thunder Beings in the sky. He came from the west, the direction of danger, one of the four cardinal directions. The Thunderbird had the power to cause thunder by flapping his wings and lightening by blinking his eyes, which resulted in rain. Rain was a very important commodity to the Plains Indians because drought conditions often occurred.

See pages 24–25 and 16–21 for more about art history and subject matter.

Artist Profiles, p. 80

Artist Profile

Thunderbird Shield

The Absaroke were one of the Plains cultures. They spoke the Siouan language and were called *Crow*. They lived mostly around the Yellowstone River and its territories and were a hunting culture. They were enemies of the Sioux. In battle a warrior wanted to bring as much supernatural help, or *medicine*, as possible with him. This protection was thought to be provided by the warrior's shield, facial paint, and the decorations on his garments. The shield also provided a physical defense against enemy weapons.

◀ **Artist unknown.** (United States). *Thunderbird Shield.* c. 1830.

Buffalo-hide shield with inner cover decorated with paintings and...

Web Connection

Visit **www.bbhc.org/pim/galleries.cfm** to learn more about the Plains Indians.

Teach

Time: About 45 minutes

"Find the different tactile textures in your clothing." *"Busquen las diferentes texturas táctiles en su ropa".*

- Discuss the definition of *tactile texture* on page 148.

Practice   NSAE 1.a; 1.d

Materials: objects of clothing

- Ask students to use adjectives to describe various textures.

Creative Expression

NSAE 1.a; 1.c; 1.d; 2.c; 3.b

Materials: assorted pieces of colorful felt and other fabrics, burlap, yarn, tapestry needles, glue, scissors, sketch paper, pencils, markers, tape

Alternate Materials: wallpaper scraps

- Distribute the materials and have students follow the directions on page 149.
- Review the Technique Tips on page 221 for visual examples of techniques.
- See Activity Tips on page 243 for visual instructions.

Art Journal Ideas

Have students brainstorm ways they can create tactile textures and write their ideas in their Art Journals. Then have students select three or four textures that they will use in the Creative Expression activity and plan how they will use them.

Using Tactile Texture

Tactile texture is the way the surface of an object actually feels when you touch it. It is an important element in many forms of art. Tactile textures are often the first things noticed in sculptures, jewelry, and weavings. Textured papers and fabrics make surfaces more interesting. Materials such as feathers and sand in a painting call attention to the rich variety of textures in our world.

Some artists use appliqué to create tactile texture. **Appliqué** is an art form in which cutout fabrics are attached to a larger surface.

Architects use tactile textures such as wood, brick, glass, and stone in the design of buildings.

Interior designers use tactile textures in furniture, carpets, and curtains to decorate the inside of a building. What textures are on the outside of the building where you live? What textures do you have in your bedroom or kitchen?

Practice

Look carefully at tactile textures in your clothing.

1. Find different textures in your clothing.
2. Describe how each texture feels when you touch it.

148   Unit 4 • Lesson 6

Differentiated Instruction

Reteach

Demonstrate how to create tactile textures by making a paper appliqué. Create the tactile textures by manipulating the paper; for instance, fold, pierce, crinkle, and curl it.

Special Needs

To increase student interest in this project, provide students with the opportunity to bring autobiographical textured items from home to add to their banners.

ELL Tips

Use this lesson to focus on vocabulary development for all students. Create a list that includes words that describe the textures of clothes that were mentioned in the Practice activity. Encourage English-language learners to use the chart when describing textures on their appliqué banners.

Think about this appliqué. Does the appliqué banner tell you about the student artist?

◄ **Chelsea Price.** Age 8.

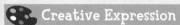 Creative Expression

What symbol would you choose to represent yourself? Design and stitch an appliqué banner.

1. Think about symbols that represent you. Make several sketches.

2. Choose your best sketch as a model. Cut out shapes from colorful fabric. Arrange them on a piece of burlap.

3. Attach shapes using glue and add details with a marker.

 Art Criticism

Describe List the symbols you put on your banner.

Analyze Describe the tactile textures in your work.

Interpret How do the symbols in the banner represent you?

Decide What do you like best about your artwork?

Reflect

Time: About 45 minutes

Review and Assess

"What kinds of textures can artists use in their works?" "¿Qué tipos de texturas pueden usar los artistas en sus obras?"

Think NSAE 1.b; 2.a; 2.b

The appliqué banner suggests that the student artist probably likes bright colors and decorations.

■ Use *Large Print 44* to have students compare tactile textures in works of art.

Informal Assessment
NSAE 1.b; 2.a; 2.b; 3.a; 5.c

Art Journal: Critical Thinking

Have students answer the four art criticism questions—Describe, Analyze, Interpret, and Decide—in their **Art Journals**. In small groups, have students discuss the uses of tactile textures in their fabric appliqués.

■ For standardized-format test practice using this lesson's art content, see pages 52–53 in *Reading and Writing Test Preparation*.

Art Across the Curriculum

Use these simple ideas to reinforce art concepts across the curriculum.

★ **Narrative Writing** Have students write a myth about the Thunderbird, the Plains Indian representation of thunder beings in the sky.

★ **Math** Discuss the math that artists, architects, and interior designers need to use to do their jobs. In designing their banners, students used the math of proportional reasoning to make sure the elements were properly places.

★ **Science** Physical properties of matter include color, taste, density, luster, and hardness. Discuss the physical properties of some of the textures students can observe.

★ **Social Studies** Have students learn where the Plains Indians who created the *Thunderbird Shield* live.

★ **Technology** Have students use the computer to create a design that looks like an appliqué. Visit **SRAonline.com** to print detailed instuctions for this activity.

NSAE 6.b

Lesson 6 Wrap-Up

Tactile Texture

Extra! For the Art Specialist

Focus

NSAE 1.a; 1.b; 1.c; 1.d; 2.a; 2.b; 2.c; 3.b

Use *Transparency 23* and *Large Print 44* *Elizabeth of Valois, Queen of Spain* to identify different textures.

Teach

Students will look at the textures in both artworks. Ask them to describe how the artist used texture in the artwork. Have students talk about how differences in size, shape, color, and texture that create interest.

Reflect

Have students use the four steps of art criticism to evaluate their work. Did they effectively use natural objects with different textures?

Alternate Activity

Materials:
- 12" × 18" light colored construction paper
- natural objects such as dried leaves, flowers, and grasses in a variety of shapes and sizes
- craft glue

1. Discuss techniques for planning and creating a design.

2. Have students experiment placing the natural objects to emphasize the textures.

3. Have students select a background paper and different natural objects with different textures.

4. Once objects are arranged, students should glue the objects in place.

Research in Art Education

"Art is a biological phenomenon that has been present as a characteristic of the human race ever since Homo sapiens emerged from prehistory. Since art is the skill man uses to give meaningful form to his intuitions and perceptions, art was one the chief agencies of man's emergence" (Herbert Read, *Education Through Art*, Random House, 1974).

Assessment

Use the following rubric to evaluate the artwork students make in the Creative Expression activity and to assess students' understanding of tactile texture.

Have students complete page 55 or 56 in their *Assessment* books.

	Art History and Culture	Aesthetic Perception	Creative Expression	Art Criticism
3 POINTS	The student identifies the similarities and differences in artwork from different cultures.	The student accurately identifies tactile textures in works of art.	The student effectively creates a fabric appliqué using tactile textures.	The student evaluates his or her work using the four steps of art criticism.
2 POINTS	The student's understanding of the differences in artwork from different cultures is weak or incomplete.	The student shows emerging awareness of tactile textures in works of art.	The student of how to create a fabric appliqué using tactile textures.	The student attempts to evaluate his or her work but shows an incomplete understanding of evaluation criteria.
1 POINT	The student cannot identify differences in artwork from different cultures.	The student cannot identify tactile textures in works of art.	The student shows no understanding of how to create a fabric appliqué using tactile textures.	The student makes no attempt to evaluate his or her artwork.

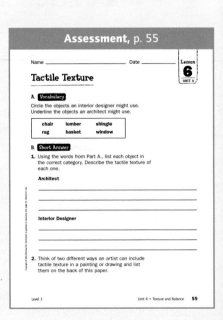

Assessment, p. 55

Name _____ Date _____

Lesson **6** UNIT 4

Tactile Texture

A. Vocabulary
Circle the objects an interior designer might use. Underline the objects an architect might use.

chair	lumber	shingle
rug	basket	window

B. Short Answer

1. Using the words from Part A., list each object in the correct category. Describe the tactile texture of each one.

   Architect
   _____
   _____

   Interior Designer
   _____
   _____

2. Think of two different ways an artist can include tactile texture in a painting or drawing and list them on the back of this paper.

Level 3   Unit 4 • Texture and Balance   55

Unit 4 Vocabulary Review

appliqué—an art form in which cut-out fabric decorations are fastened to a larger surface to create a design
aplicación—una forma artistica en que un recortado de decoracions de telas están fijadas a una superficie más grande para crear un diseño

approximate symmetry—a type of formal balance in which both sides of an artwork or object are almost exactly the same **simetría aproximada**—un tipo de equilibrio formal en que ambos lados de una obra de arte u objeto son casi iguales

architect—a person who plans and designs buildings and other structures **arquitecto**—una persona que planea y diseña edificios y otras estructuras

central axis—an imaginary line that divides a work of art in half vertically **eje central**—una línea imaginaria que divide una obra de arte en mitad verticalmente

culture—customs and beliefs that are shared by a group of people **cultura**—costumbres y creencias compartidas por un grupo de personas

exaggeration—the enlargement of an object, figure, or feature beyond its normal size used to draw attention to it **exageración**—el agrandamiento de un objeto, figura o rasgo más de lo normal usado para llamar atención

formal balance—a way of organizing the elements of an artwork so that equal or similar elements are placed on the opposite sides of an imaginary, central vertical axis **equilibrio formal**—una manera de organizar los elementos en una obra de arte para que los elementos iguales o parecidos sean colocados en lados opuestos de na eje vertical central imaginario

highlights—small areas of white used to show the very brightest spots on an object **claros**—áreas pequeñas de blanco usadas para demostrar los puntos de un objeto con más brillantez

symmetry—a type of formal balance in which the two halves, or sides, of an artwork are identical **simetría**—un tipo de equilibrio formal en que ambas mitades o lados, son idénticos en una obra de arte

tactile texture—the way that an object actually feels when it is touched **textura táctil**—la manera actual en que un objeto se siente cuando es tocado

visual texture—the way an object looks as if it would feel if it could be touched **textura visual**—la manera en que un objeto luce como si se pudiera sentir si se pudiera tocar

Vocabulary Practice

T Display *Transparency 40* to review unit vocabulary words.

Word Forms ⭐ Vocabulary
To develop vocabulary, have students say or write another form of each of the vocabulary words. For example *visual/vision, architect/architecture.* Have them use a dictionary if they need help.

Context Clues ⭐ Vocabulary
Have students write or say a sentence using context clues for five of the vocabulary words.

Antonyms and Synonyms ⭐ Vocabulary
Have students find an antonym for at least three of the vocabulary words. For example, *formal/informal, balance, inbalance.*

Texture and Balance

▲ **Henri Rousseau.** (French).
The Football Players. 1908.
Oil on canvas. 39 $\frac{1}{2}$ × 31 $\frac{5}{8}$ inches (100.33 × 81.28 cm.).
Solomon R. Guggenheim Museum, New York, New York.

Art Criticism

Critical Thinking Art criticism is an organized system for looking at and talking about art. You can criticize art without being an expert. The purpose of art criticism is to get the viewer involved in a perception process that delays judgment until all aspects of the art work have been studied.

■ See pages 28–29 for more about art criticism.

Describe

▶ Ask students to list everything they see in the credit line of the painting. Possible answers: Henri Rousseau painted *The Football Players* in 1908. He used oil paint on canvas. It is 39 $\frac{1}{2}$ inches × 31 inches and it is housed at the Guggenheim Museum in New York City.

▶ Have students discuss what they see in the painting. Possible answers: Four men are playing ball on a field. The field is bordered by trees and has a fence at one end. Two men are wearing blue and white striped shirts and shorts and the other two are wearing orange and yellow stripes. They all have on high shoes and knee-high socks. All of the men have short hair and mustaches.

Analyze

▶ Discuss with students how the work is organized.

▶ Where do they see symmetry or formal balance? Possible answers: The trunks and the leaves of the trees match on both sides of the picture.

▶ Do they see approximate symmetry? Possible answers: The men's bodies show approximate symmetry. Both sides have arms and legs, but they are in different positions. The fence at the end of the field and the trees in the distance show approximate symmetry.

Art History and Culture

Henri Rousseau

Henri Rousseau (än rē´ rū sō´) was born in a small town in France. At the age of 25 he moved to Paris, where he spent most of his life. He never attended art school. He learned to paint by practicing in gardens around the city. Because he had no formal training, he is classified as a self-taught artist.

Henri Rousseau's paintings look unlike anyone else's. In his first paintings he portrayed people and places around Paris. His paintings are known for their details. In some paintings he painted every leaf of every tree and every whisker of every animal. Many of his paintings evoke the same feelings as strange dreams.

See pages 24–25 and 16–21 for more about art history and subject matter.

Artist Profiles, p. 51

► Artist Profile ►
Henri Rousseau
1844–1910
Henri Rousseau (än rē´ rū sō´) was born in a small town in France. When he was young he played the clarinet. He also spent some time in the French army. At the age of 25 he moved to Paris, where he spent most of his life. For a long time he worked as a customs clerk. He never went to art school. He learned to paint by practicing in gardens around the city.

◀ **Henri Rousseau.** (French). *Myself* (detail). 1890.

 **Art Criticism** Critical Thinking

Describe What do you see?
▶ What does the caption tell you about this work?
▶ Describe what you see.

Analyze How is this work organized?
▶ Where do you see symmetry or formal balance?
▶ Where do you see approximate symmetry?
▶ Where do you see visual texture?
▶ How has the artist used visual texture to make the trees in the foreground different from the trees in the middle ground and background?

Interpret What is the artist trying to say?
▶ What is happening in this painting?
▶ How can you tell whether the players are enjoying themselves?
▶ Is this football as you know it? Explain.
▶ Why do you think the artist showed only four players?

Decide What do you think about the work?
▶ Is this painting successful because it is realistic, well organized, or because it has a strong message? Explain.

NSAE 1.b; 2.a; 2.b; 3.a; 4.a; 4.b; 4.c; 5.a; 5.b; 5.c

 Aesthetic Perception

Seeing Like an Artist Have students find pictures in a magazine that show sports figures. How do the pictures and the painting *The Football Players* compare?

Describe ▶ List and describe the textures and elements of balance.

Analyze ▶ Name at least three different visual textures students can see in the work.

Interpret ▶ Where do students see balance? Do they see both approximate and formal balance?

Decide ▶ Do students like the artwork? Why or why not?

▶ **Where do they see visual texture?** Possible answers: Visual texture is seen on the men's smooth clothes, the bumpy bark of the tree trunks, the prickly look of the leaves on the trees, and the fluffy clouds. We also see smooth sky, smooth skin, and a smooth-looking field.

▶ **Has the artist used visual texture to make trees in the foreground different from the trees in the middle ground and background?** Possible answers: The leaves of the closer trees have more detail and clear, sharp edges. The trees in the middle ground have less detail, and the trees in the background have very little detail.

Interpret

▶ **Discuss with students what is happening in the painting.** Possible answers: A player is about to catch the ball as he runs. The man on the left seems to have thrown it. The man in the distance is standing still while the second man in blue seems to be running toward his teammate. **Can they tell if the players are enjoying themselves?** Possible answers: Their smiling faces and active poses show they are having fun.

▶ **Is this football the way they know it?** Possible answers: This does not look like American football, but it is not soccer either because the man is catching the ball with his hands. **Why did the artist show only four players?** Possible answers: Answers will vary. Perhaps the players are friends who play together for fun. Or perhaps the artist would have had to make the players too small if the entire team was shown.

Decide

▶ **Is this painting successful because it is realistic, well organized, or because it has a strong message?** Answers will vary. Most will not say it is realistic since the figures are so stiff. Some will like the organization. Others may like it because the men are having fun.

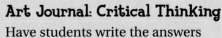 **Art Journal: Critical Thinking**
Have students write the answers to the Aesthetic Perception in their Art Journals.

"Artists use formal balance, approximate symmetry, and symmetry to create balance in all kinds of art. *Los artistas usan el equilibrio formal, la simetría aproximada y la simetría para crear equilibrio en todo tipo de arte*".

T Review unit vocabulary with students using *Transparency 40.*

Art Journal: Writing
Have students answer the questions on page 152 in their Art Journals or on a separate sheet of paper. Answers: 1. B, 2. C, 3. B, 4. A, 5. A

T For further assessment, have students complete the unit test on *Transparency 46.*

LEARNING ABOUT MUSEUMS

The Walker Art Center is housed in an award-winning building designed by architect Edward Larrabee Barnes. Internationally acclaimed for its major exhibitions of twentieth-century art, the Walker Art Center also presents vanguard music, dance, theater, and film. Initially a small, regional museum, the center has evolved into a major national and international artistic resource. Many of its exhibitions travel to major museums.

▶ In small groups, have students look through this book and identify twentieth-century artwork that could be considered for exhibition at the Walker Art Center.

"To live a creative life, we must lose our fear of being wrong."

—Joseph Chilton Pearce

Texture and Balance, continued

Show What You Know

Answer these questions on a separate sheet of paper.

1 To organize a design so equal elements are placed on each side of a central dividing line, use _____.
A. approximate symmetry
B. formal balance
C. contrast in shape

2 The kind of formal balance in which both sides of a design are exactly the same is _____.
A. emphasis
B. formal balance
C. symmetry

3 A special kind of formal balance in which both sides of a design are almost exactly the same is _____.
A. rhythm
B. approximate symmetry
C. texture

4 Texture that you see is _____.
A. visual texture
B. tactile texture
C. texture

5 The way a surface actually feels when touched is called _____.
A. tactile texture
B. visual rhythm
C. textronics

152   Unit 4

VISIT A MUSEUM
The Walker Art Center

The Walker Art Center, located in Minneapolis, Minnesota, is famous for its collection of 8,000 pieces of twentieth-century art. The collection includes paintings, sculpture, videos, prints, drawings, and photographs. The Walker Art Center also has a varied educational program that appeals to people of all ages. Beside the museum is the Minneapolis Sculpture Garden. It covers eleven acres and is one of the largest urban sculpture parks in the country. It is a popular tourist attraction.

Unit Assessment Options

Aesthetic Perception

Practice Have students select one of the concepts in the Show What You Know Section on page 152, then find examples of each concept in the classroom.

Creative Expression

Student Portfolio Have students review all the artwork they have created during this unit and select the pieces they wish to keep in their portfolios.

Art Criticism

Activity Have students select one work of art from this unit and study it using the fours steps of art criticism. (See pages 28–29 for more information about art criticism). Have students work alone or in pairs and present their findings aloud or in writing.

Texture and Balance in Music

Voice of the Wood is a play adapted from a book. The story is about a craftsman who makes a cello from the wood of an ancient tree. He searches for the one musician who can play the cello with such beautiful feelings that he or she can unlock the "voice of the wood."

What to Do Write a story about an instrument.

Think about a musical instrument you find interesting. Write a story about it. The instrument in your story can be a character or a prop. The story could be about a musician, a child searching for an instrument to play, or an instrument with a problem. Think about the characters, what they want or need, and where the story takes place. Have a clear beginning, middle, and end.

1. Write a story about an instrument.
2. Decide if the instrument is one of the characters or is a prop in the story.
3. How does your instrument sound?
4. Think of what will happen in your story. What problem will be solved?
5. What is the beginning? What happens in the middle? How does it end?
6. Share your story with a partner.

▲ Robert Faust and Eugene Friesen. "Voice of the Wood."

 Art Criticism

Describe Describe the instrument you chose.

Analyze Is your instrument a string, wind, keyboard, or percussion instrument?

Interpret What feelings do you have when you hear your instrument?

Decide Do you think you succeeded in writing a story about an instrument?

Unit 4 **153**

 Art History and Culture

About Commedia dell'Arte:

The two performers in *Voice of the Wood* use half-masks derived from the Italian theatre style, Commedia dell'Arte." It originated in Venice, Italy and flourished during the 16th and 17th centuries as a form of popular comedy. There were no scripts, but rather a short outline of the plot, within which the performers improvised. There were "stock characters" where one particular trait—greed, boastfulness, etc.—was stressed.

The book *Voice of the Wood* is written by Claude Clément. It is set in Venice, Italy. The book was adapted into a play by Robert Faust and Eugene Friesen. The cello, a member of the string family, is featured in *Voice of the Wood*. Other members of this family—the violin, viola and double bass—all evolved from ancient, plucked instruments, like the harp and the lute. The best quality string instruments are made of wood and crafted primarily by hand.

Texture and Balance in Theatre

Objective: To create a story about an instrument

Materials: *Voice of the Wood*, performed by Robert Faust and Eugene Friesen, pictures of instruments

ocus **Time:** About 5 minutes

- Discuss the information on page 153.

 Art History and Culture

- Have students brainstorm types of instruments and the materials from which they are made. Ask them to think of the sounds that instruments can make, as well as other characteristics to prepare them to write their story.

each **Time:** About 20 minutes

Aesthetic Perception

- Have students list several instruments and their characteristics.
- Review criteria for writing a story with a beginning, middle and end.

Creative Expression

- Ask students to write a short story about an instrument.
- Give them some examples of how they can get started.
- Have them share their stories with a partner.

**eflect** **Time:** About 10 minutes

Art Criticism

- Have students answer the four art criticism questions on page 153 orally or in writing.
- Did students write a story about an instrument that had a beginning, a middle and an end?

Unit 5 Planning Guide

	Lesson Title	Suggested Pacing	Creative Expression Activity
Lesson 1	Pattern and Motif	60 minutes	Create a potato print that shows random pattern.
Lesson 2	Regular Patterns	60 minutes	Use a computer to create a regular pattern.
Lesson 3	Alternating Patterns	60 minutes	Design clothing that has alternating pattern.
Lesson 4	Rhythm	60 minutes	Create a clay container that shows rhythm.
Lesson 5	Visual Rhythm	60 minutes	Draw a parade to show visual rhythm.
Lesson 6	Three-Dimensional Rhythm	60 minutes	Create a relief sculpture that shows three-dimensional rhythm.
ART SOURCE ARTSOURCE	Pattern, Rhythm, and Movement in Dance	35 minutes	Create a rhythmic sound and movement pattern.

Materials	Program Resources	Fine Art Resources	Literature Resources
12" × 18" colored construction paper, spoons, newsprint, paintbrushes, liquid tempera, halved potatoes, scissors, pencils	*Home and After-School Connections* *Reading and Writing Test Prep.*, pp. 54–55 *Assessment,* pp. 57–58	*Transparency,* 25 *Artist Profiles,* pp. 42, 66 *Animals Time Line* *Large Prints,* 45 and 46 *Women in the Arts*	*Frederick* by Leo Lionni
computer, paper	*Reading and Writing Test Prep.*, pp. 56–57 *Assessment,* pp. 59–60	*Transparency,* 26 *Artist Profiles,* pp. 36, 16 *Large Prints,* 45 and 46 *Art Around the World*	*Alex Is My Friend* by Marisabina Russo
12" × 18" construction paper, pencils, crayons, color pencils	*Reading and Writing Test Prep.*, pp. 58–59 *Assessment,* pp. 61–62	*Transparency 27* *Artist Profiles,* pp. 62, 82 *Large Prints,* 45 and 46 *Art Around the World*	*My Life with the Wave* by Catherine Cowan
clay, slip, clay tools, newspaper, found objects, kiln	*Reading and Writing Test Prep.*, pp. 60–61 *Assessment,* pp. 63–64	*Transparency,* 28 *Artist Profiles,* pp. 3, 7 *Large Prints,* 45 and 46 *Women in the Arts*	*Farewell to Shady Glade* by Bill Peet
6" × 18" white paper, crayons or oil pastels, watercolors, brushes, water, paper towels	*Reading and Writing Test Prep.*, pp. 62–63 *Assessment,* pp. 65–66	*Transparency,* 29 *Artist Profiles,* pp. 29, 33 *Large Prints,* 45 and 46 *Art Around the World*	*The Worry Stone* by Marianna Dengler
cardboard, pencils, ballpoint pens, glue, yarn, aluminum foil, crayons	*Reading and Writing Test Prep.*, pp. 64–65 *Assessment,* pp. 67–68	*Transparency,* 30 *Artist Profiles,* pp. 24, 43 *Large Prints,* 45 and 46 *Women in the Arts*	*Night in the Country* by Cynthia Rylant
Isicathulo by the African American Dance Ensemble			

Unit Overview

Pattern, Rhythm, and Movement

Lesson 1: Pattern is a design created by repeating a motif.

Lesson 2: Regular patterns repeat the same motif separated by the same amount of space.

Lesson 3: Alternating pattern occurs when two motifs (or the position of one motif) are alternated.

Lesson 4: Rhythm is created by repeating a visual beat with a rest between each beat.

Lesson 5: Visual rhythm occurs when lines, shapes, or colors repeat in an orderly manner.

Lesson 6: Three-dimensional rhythm indicates movement by repeating elements in a form.

Introduce Unit Concepts

"Artists use the principles of pattern, rhythm, and movement in designing all kinds of art."
"Los artistas usan los principios artísticos de patrón, ritmo y movimiento para diseñar todo tipo de arte".

Pattern
▪ Have students look at the clothing their classmates are wearing to find designs on their clothing that may be repeating.

Rhythm
▪ Have them beat on a tabletop two different rhythms. Have students describe what they hear and the differences between the two different rhythms.

Cross-Curricular Projects
▪ See the *Language Arts and Reading, Mathematics, Science,* and *Social Studies Art Connections* books for activities that further develop concepts of pattern, rhythm, and movement.

Pattern, Rhythm, and Movement

◀ **John James Audubon.** (American). *Great Blue Heron.* 1834.
....
Engraving, aquatint on paper. 37 ½ × 25 ½ inches (95.25 × 64.77 cm.). Orlando Museum of Art, Orlando, Florida.

Artists use pattern, rhythm, and movement to organize elements and objects in works of art.

154 Unit 5

Fine Art Prints

Display *Large Prints 45 Baby* and *46 Untitled*. Refer to the prints throughout the unit as students learn about pattern, rhythm, and movement.

Large Print 45

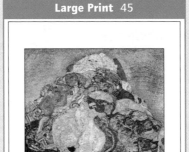

Large Print 46

Artists use **motifs** to create a **pattern** in a work of art.

▶ Artists use **rhythm** in their artwork to create a sense of visual **movement.**

▶ Where do you see patterns on the bird?

▶ Where do you see rhythms?

In This Unit you will learn about pattern, rhythm, and movement and how other artists use these methods in their designs.

Here are the topics you will study.
▶ Pattern and Motif
▶ Regular Patterns
▶ Alternating Patterns
▶ Rhythm
▶ Visual Rhythm
▶ Three-Dimensional Rhythm

John James Audubon

(1785-1851)

John James Audubon, born in Santo Domingo, was known for his fanatical interest in birds and nature. He was a self-taught artist who broke the tradition of painting birds in stiff profile. He was passionate about portraying the distinguishing characteristics of birds. In 1827 he published *Birds of America*, a set of color plates. Color plates were color images put together to create an album. The 435 plates were completed in 1839. The first edition was called the "Elephant Folio," because the album was so big.

Examine the Artwork

"Let's look closely at the painting." "Vamos a observar detalladamente la pintura".

■ Have students look at John James Audobon's *Great Blue Heron*. Ask them to describe what they see.

■ Have students answer the questions on page 155 pertaining to pattern, rhythm, and movement in the painting.

▶ Feathers on wings and tails are patterns.

▶ The repetition of curved lines is a rhythm.

National Standards for Arts Education in Visual Arts

Unit Pretest
(NSAE) 2.a, 2.b

T Display *Transparency 47* as a pretest. Answers: 1. C, 2. A, 3. A, 4. C, 5. B

Home Connection

■ See *Home and After-School Connections* for family newsletters and activities for this unit.

Art History and Culture

John James Audubon

John James Audubon (jän jāmz ô´ də bən) was born in Santo Domingo. He was raised in France by his father and his father's wife, a woman who encouraged his love of the outdoors and art. Audubon spent weeks painting day and night on some of his compositions seeking to portray every feather true to form. In 1826 he visited England with his collection of bird paintings. His paintings were so successful that portrait artist Thomas Sully personally encouraged his efforts and gave him free painting lessons. In 1843 Audubon created his final series of paintings, a study of mammals.

See pages 24–25 and 16–21 for more about art history and subject matter.

Artist Profiles, p. 5

● Artist Profile ●

John James Audubon
1785-1851

John James Audubon (jän jāmz ô´ də bən) was born in Santo Domingo, now Haiti. His mother died a few months after he was born, so he was raised in France by his father and his father's wife, a kind woman who encouraged his love of the outdoors and art. When he was 18, he left France for America to live on one of his father's plantations in Pennsylvania. Audubon drew birds only as a hobby until he and his family met with hard financial times. Audubon's successful journeys established him as a leading romantic painter and expert on ornithology. Years after his death the National Audubon Society was founded in

DIANE AND LEO DILLON

Diane and Leo Dillon were born eleven days apart in 1933, and met at the Parsons School of Design in New York. The two were intensely competitive in school, but developed system of close collaboration after their marriage. They call this collaboration the "third artist"; they pass a work back and forth, commenting and adjusting, until neither can remember who contributed what to the final piece.

The Dillons have illustrated both adult and children's books. Their work includes a wide variety of media, techniques, and styles, from drawing to crewel embroidery. They are careful to base the style of the illustrations on the story, choosing bold colors for the West African folktale *Why Mosquitoes Buzz in People's Ears* and recreating the look of Japanese wood prints for *The Tale of the Mandarin Ducks*. The Dillons are the only illustrators to win back-to-back Caldecott Medals, and Leo Dillon was the first African American to win that award.

Throughout Unit 5, share the Dillons' work with students. Discuss the use of pattern, rhythm, and movement in the artwork. How do the Dillons repeat motifs to create pattern? How do they create visual rhythm?

Music

Lead the students to notice contrasts between the straight and zigzag lines of the room and the curving, graceful lines of *Great Blue Heron*. Have them think of rhythms to match the two contrasting kinds of lines. (For example, "zigzag" melodies could have wide leaps while "curving" melodies could be more steplike.)

Literature

Show the video or DVD *Abuela* to introduce the concepts of pattern, rhythm, and movement. Pause the video and have students describe the motifs and patterns they see.

Literature and Art

Performing Arts

 Show "Isicathulo." Point out how the dancers create pattern and rhythm.

Artsource®

Lesson 1 Pattern and Motif

Overview

Lesson 1 introduces to students pattern and motif in a work of art.

Objectives

 Art History and Culture

To demonstrate knowledge of the art and life of Moulthrop and Gardner

Creative Expression

To plan and create a stamp print design in which motifs create a pattern

 Aesthetic Perception

To identify patterns and motifs in works of art

Art Criticism

To use the four steps of art criticism to evaluate their own artwork

Vocabulary Vocabulary

Review the following vocabulary words with students before beginning the lesson.

pattern patrón—design created by a repeated motif

motif motivo—a shape or an object that is repeated

random pattern patrón al azar—motifs that appear in no apparent order and have irregular spaces between them.

See page 179B for additional vocabulary and Spanish vocabulary resources.

 Art Journal: Vocabulary

Have students add these words to the Vocabulary section of their Art Journals.

Lesson Materials

- 12" × 18" colored construction paper
- spoons
- newsprint paper
- paintbrushes
- pencils
- liquid tempera
- halved potatoes
- scissors

Alternate Materials:
- markers
- liquid tempera paints

Program Resources

- *Reading and Writing Test Prep.*, pp. 54–55
- *Transparency 25*
- *Artist Profiles*, pp. 42, 66
- *Animals Through History Time Line*
- *Assessment* pp. 57–58
- *Large Prints 45 Baby and 46 Untitled*
- *The National Museum of Women in the Arts Collection*

Concept Trace

Pattern and Motif

Introduced: Level 2, Unit 4, Lesson 1

Reinforced: Level 5, Unit 2, Lesson 3

Lesson 1 Arts Integration

Theatre

Complete Unit 5, Lesson 1 on pages 90–91 of *Theatre Arts Connections.*

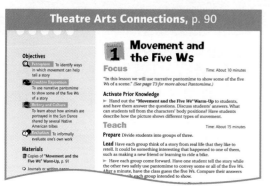

Theatre Arts Connections, p. 90

Music

 Keeping a steady pulse, clap the rhythm to *Sweet Potatoes*, a Louisiana Creole folk song. Throw your hands away from each other on the rest to create silence. Clap as you sing, then clap as you sing the words silently in your head.

Movement & Dance

Pattern arranges movement in an orderly way and is repetitive. Take four movement ideas and arrange them. For example, walk 4 counts, then bounce 4 counts, then turn 4 counts, then reach 4 counts. Repeat the pattern two more times, reducing the number of counts used for each idea (2 counts, then 1 count).

 **ocus**

Time: About 10 minutes

Activate Prior Knowledge

"Think about a design on a shirt or look at the designs on the wall of your classroom."

"Piensen en un diseño de una camisa o miren los diseños en la pared de su salón de clases".

■ Discuss student responses and explain to them that patterns do not always have a particular order.

Using Literature Reading

■ Read *Frederick* by Leo Lionni. The illustrations include random patterns in the rocks and the snow.

Thematic Connection ☆ Social Studies

■ **Perseverance:** Discuss the time and patience needed to create each work of art. Modern machinery makes Moulthrop's work easier than it would have been in the eighteenth century, when *Easy Chair* was created.

Introduce the Art NSAE 3.a

Look

"Let's look closely at the two artworks."

"Vamos a observar detalladamente las dos obras de arte".

Drawing Conclusions ☆ Reading

■ Have students discuss why these objects are considered works of art. Possible answers: They are unique and one of a kind. They are pleasant to look at. The works are well designed.

 Art History and Culture

Philip Moulthrop uses wood from the southeastern U.S., where he lives. He looks for ideas in the tree forms and leaf shapes he sees around him. Can students think of other artists they have studied who painted or sculpted works that reflected the place where they lived?

🖥 **Web Connection**

Visit **www.americanart.si.edu/collections/exhibits/whc/moulthropp.html** to learn more about Philip Moulthrop.

 Lesson 1 # Pattern and Motif

▲ **Philip Moulthrop.** (American). *White Pine Mosaic.* 1993.

$9\frac{1}{4} \times 11\frac{3}{4} \times 11\frac{3}{4}$ inches (23.50 × 27.95 × 29.85 cm.). Mint Museum of Craft, Charlotte, North Carolina.

 Look at the artwork on these pages. *Easy Chair* is made of walnut, maple, and hand stitched upholstery. *White Pine Mosaic* is made with white pine and resin. Both artists have used **motif** and **pattern** in their works of art.

 Art History and Culture

Philip Moulthrop believed in creating works of art that displayed the simple shapes and forms found in wood.

Art History and Culture

Philip Moulthrop

Philip Moulthrop (fĭl´ ip mōl´ thrəp) was born in 1947 in Atlanta, Georgia. His father, Edward Moutlthrop, is also an artist, and the two are widely known for their elegant wooden bowls. In addition to being a nationally acclaimed artist, Philip Moulthrop was also trained as a lawyer. He works from his studio in Marietta, Georgia and has work in such prestigious locations as the High Museum of Art in Atlanta, Georgia, and the Smithsonian Institution and the White House, both in Washington, D.C.

See pp. 24–25 and 16–21 for more about art history and subject matter.

Artist Profiles, p. 42

Artist Profile

Philip Moulthrop
b. 1947

Philip Moulthrop (fĭl´ ip mōl´ thrəp) was born in 1947 in Atlanta, Georgia. His father, Edward Moulthrop, is also an artist, and the two are widely known for their elegant wooden bowls. Moulthrop regards his art as a means of revealing the beauty and texture of wood and wants his viewers to enjoy his work without having to be told what it means or how it was made. In addition to being a nationally acclaimed artist, Moulthrop is also a lawyer. He works from his studio in Marietta, Georgia, and has works displayed in such prestigious locations as the High Museum of Art in Atlanta, Georgia, and the Smithsonian Institution and the White House, both in Washington D.C.

◀ **Caleb Gardner.**
(American). *Easy
Chair.* 1758.
....
Walnut, maple, and hand
stitched upholstery. 46 $\frac{3}{8}$ ×
32 $\frac{3}{8}$ × 25 $\frac{7}{8}$ inches (117.8
× 82.2 × 65.7 cm.). The
Metropolitan Museum of
Art, New York, New York.

Study both pieces of art to discover how artists use
pattern and motif.

▶ What shapes are repeated in *Easy Chair*?

▶ What shapes are the motif in *White Pine Mosaic*?

▶ How does the motif change on *Easy Chair*?

 Aesthetic Perception

Seeing Like an Artist Think about a tree or plant you
have seen. Are all the leaves on the plants or trees exactly
the same?

Art History and Culture

Caleb Gardner

Caleb Gardiner (kā´ leb gard´ nər) is the artist credited with making
this easy chair in the city of Newport, Rhode Island in the year 1758.
Very little has been documented about this individual and his work.

The style of this chair is the typical kind of easy chair made in
America during the mid-eighteenth century. It is wide, high-
backed, and heavily padded with down filler.

Easy Chair has been carefully preserved and the condition of the
fabric and wood is excellent
for an antique from this time
period.

See pages 24–25 and 16–21
for more about art history
and subject matter.

Artist Profiles, p. 66

⟨ Artist Profile ⟩

Easy Chair

Caleb Gardner is the artist credited with
making this easy chair in the city of
Newport, Rhode Island, in 1758. Very little
has been documented about this individual
and his work, but it is known that Gardner
died in 1761. This easy chair has been
carefully preserved and the condition of the
fabric and wood are excellent for an antique
from this time period.

◀ **Caleb Gardner.** (American). *Easy Chair.* 1758.
....
Walnut, maple, and hand-stitched upholstery.

Study

▶ Repeated colors and shapes: *Easy Chair:*
Diamond shape, orange and yellow colors.
White Pine Mosaic: The brown circles are
repeated.

▶ Shapes of the motif: *Easy Chair:* Diamond
shapes. *White Pine Mosaic:* Circles.

▶ Change in motif: *Easy Chair:* The shape
stays the same but the colors change in a
random manner. *White Pine Mosaic:* The
shape stays circular and the sizes of the
circles vary.

■ For more examples of utilitarian art, see
***The National Museum of Women in the
Arts Collection.***

Art Journal: Writing
Encourage students to write their
own explanations of pattern and motif in
the Concepts section of their Art Journals.
What else do they want to know about
pattern and motif?

 Aesthetic Perception

Seeing Like an Artist Discuss with students
the patterns they see in the trees and other
plants around them. What motifs are
repeated to create the patterns?

Developing Visual Literacy Invite students to
discuss how each work of art in this lesson
makes them feel. For example, does *White
Pine Mosaic* evoke thoughts of a soothing,
natural environment? What properties of the
artwork evoke that feeling?

NSAE 2.a, 2.b

 Web Connection
Visit **www.metmuseum.org/** to learn more about
The Metropolitan Museum of Art.

Teach

Time: About 45 minutes

"How can you design a motif?" "¿Cómo pueden diseñar un motivo?"

Practice

Materials: 9 × 12" paper, colored pencils

Alternate Materials: markers

- Discuss ways to design a motif on page 158.

- Distribute the materials and have students follow the directions on page 158 for creating a motif.

Creative Expression

Materials: 12" × 18" colored construction paper, spoons, newsprint paper, paintbrushes, pencils, liquid tempera, halved potatoes, scissors

Alternate Materials: markers, liquid tempera paints

- Distribute materials and have students follow the directions on page 159.

- Review the Activity Tips on page 244 for visual examples of techniques if needed.

NSAE 1.a, 1.d

Art Journal: Brainstorming

Have students brainstorm for ways they can create and design a motif. Then have students select three or four items they will make and plan how they will show those items in their drawing in the Creative Expression activity.

Using Pattern and Motif

People often use patterns to decorate objects.

A **pattern** is a repeated surface decoration. The **motif** is the unit of repetition in the pattern. The motif is made of objects or art elements.

In a **random pattern,** the motif is repeated in no particular order.

In this photograph of leaves, one leaf is the motif. The repetition of the leaves creates a random pattern of leaves.

Practice

Use color, line, and shape to design a motif.

1. Fold your sheet of paper into four sections. Using your pencil, draw a different motif in each section.

2. Using only black and white, draw one motif. Using straight lines, draw a second motif. Use a free-form shape to draw a third motif. In your fourth section, create a motif of your choice. Use colored pencils to complete your motifs.

Differentiated Instruction

Reteach
Have students look around the classroom to find examples of a motif. Ask them to list examples and explain why the design is considered a motif.

Special Needs
Encourage students to extend learning in this activity by giving them the opportunity to carve a motif design into the potato using the end of a paintbrush.

ELL Tips
ELL students will benefit from working with a peer to create a motif. For the Practice activity, have one student draw a motif on a sheet of paper. The other student can repeat the design on the other side. Students could share their drawings to practice oral language.

Think about how this student artist used pattern and motif.

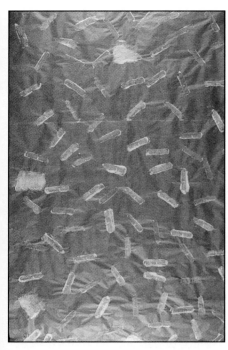

◀ **Rosemary Ankerich.**
Age 7.

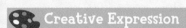
Creative Expression

Create a random print, using a potato as a stamp.

1. First cut your potato in half. On the cut side, use the pointed end of a pencil to make a design in the potato.
2. Dip the cut side of the potato into paint.
3. Randomly press the potato onto newspaper or a brown paper bag to create a pattern.
4. Use the paper as wrapping paper for a gift.

Art Criticism

Describe List the steps you followed to create your wrapping paper.

Analyze What is the motif in your pattern?

Interpret What could you wrap with your paper?

Decide If you could redo this design, what shapes would you use?

Unit 5 • Lesson 1   **159**

 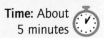

Review and Assess

"Were you able to create a motif in your drawing?" "¿Pudieron crear un motivo en su dibujo?"

Think

The artist created motifs by using a random pattern.

■ Use *Large Prints 45* Baby and *46* Untitled to have students compare the use of pattern and motif.

Informal Assessment

Art Journal: Critical Thinking
Have students answer the four art criticism questions—Describe, Analyze, Interpret, and Decide—in their Art Journals. In small groups, have students discuss the use of pattern and motif in their designs.

■ Have students work in pairs and comment on each other's artwork using the four steps of art criticism. Remind students to keep their comments positive and constructive.

■ For standardized-format test practice using this lesson's art content, see pages 54–55 in *Reading and Writing Test Preparation.*

NSAE 3.a, 3.b

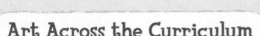
Art Across the Curriculum

Use these simple ideas to reinforce art concepts across the curriculum.

★ **Descriptive Writing** Have students write a description of a patterned utilitarian object in the classroom or in their homes.

★ **Math** Have students discuss patterns in the multiplication tables.

★ **Science** Discuss animals and insects with natural camouflage. How does pattern contribute to this camouflage?

★ **Social Studies** Discuss pattern in the U.S. flag. What motifs are repeated? What do these motifs symbolize?

★ **Technology** Have students use a paint program to create a pattern with a repeating motif. Visit **SRAonline.com** to print detailed instructions for this activity.

NSAE 6.a, 6.b

Lesson 1
Wrap-Up

Pattern and Motif

 For the Art Specialist

Time: About 45 minutes

Focus

Use *Tranparency 25* and *Large Prints 45 Baby* and *46 Untitled* to have students discuss how artists use pattern and motif in their works of art. Have students point out different kinds of lines and shapes in the works. Ask them to describe some motifs that the artist used. Have students talk about how the repetition of lines and shapes unifies the artwork.

Teach

Have students follow the directions to complete a complex pattern drawing.

Close

Have students evaluate their artwork using the four steps of art criticism.

Alternate Activity

Materials:
- 12" × 18" white drawing paper
- multicolor packs of crayons or markers

1. Have students think of different kinds of lines and shapes, both geometric and free-form.

2. Students will fold their papers in half twice horizontally and then twice vertically to divide the paper into 16 sections. Have students draw over the fold lines to separate the sections.

3. Students will decide on a type of line to draw in the first section of their papers, and then repeat the same line in each section of the paper so it is drawn sixteen times.

4. Students will select another line or a shape and repeat it sixteen times, once in each section of the paper.

5. Students will continue adding lines and shapes, repeating them in each of the 16 sections, until the complex pattern is completed.

NSAE 1.a, 1.c

Research in Art Education

" . . . the kind of deliberately designed tasks students are offered in school help define the kind of thinking they will learn to do. The kind of thinking students learn to do will influence what they come to know and the kind of cognitive skills they acquire" (Eisner, Elliot W. *The Arts and the Creation of Mind.* New Haven: Yale Univ. Press, 2002).

Assessment

Use the following rubric to evaluate the artwork students make in the Creative Expression and to assess students' understanding of pattern and motif.

Have students complete page 57 or 58 of their *Assessment* books.

	Art History and Culture	Aesthetic Perception	Creative Expression	Art Criticism
3 POINTS	The student demonstrates knowledge of the art and life of Moulthrop and Gardiner.	The student accurately identifies patterns and motif in a work of art.	The student effectively plans and creates a design using motif to create a pattern.	The student evaluates his or her own work using the four steps of art criticism.
2 POINTS	The student can demonstrate some knowledge of the life and art of Moulthrop and Gardiner.	The student shows emerging awareness of patterns and motif in a work of art.	The student shows some awareness of how to plan and create a design using motif to create a pattern.	The student attempts to evaluate his or her own work using the four steps of art criticism.
1 POINT	The student cannot demonstrate knowledge of the life or art of Moulthrop and Gardiner.	The student cannot identify patterns and motif in a work of art.	The student shows no understanding of how to plan and create a design using motif to create a pattern.	The student makes no attempt to evaluate his or her own work.

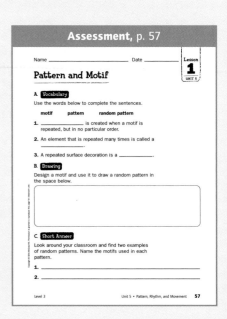

Assessment, p. 57

Name _____ Date _____ **Lesson 1 UNIT 5**

Pattern and Motif

A. Vocabulary
Use the words below to complete the sentences.

motif   pattern   random pattern

1. _____ is created when a motif is repeated, but in no particular order.
2. An element that is repeated many times is called a _____
3. A repeated surface decoration is a _____

B. Drawing
Design a motif and use it to draw a random pattern in the space below.

C. Short Answer
Look around your classroom and find two examples of random patterns. Name the motifs used in each pattern.

1. _____
2. _____

Level 3   Unit 5 • Pattern, Rhythm, and Movement **57**

Regular Patterns

Lesson 2 introduces how artists use regular pattern in their works of art.

Objectives

 Art History and Culture

To demonstrate knowledge of the life and art of Loeser and Djukulul

 Creative Expression

To use the computer to create a regular pattern

 Aesthetic Perception

To identify regular patterns in art and the environment

Art Criticism

To use the four steps of art criticism to evaluate their design

Vocabulary Vocabulary

Review the following vocabulary with students before beginning the lesson.

regular pattern *patrón regular*—visual rhythm that is achieved by repeating identical motifs, with the same interval of space between each motif

See page 179B for additional vocabulary and Spanish vocabulary resources.

Art Journal: Vocabulary

Have students add these words to the Vocabulary section of their Art Journals.

Lesson Materials
- computer
- printer
- word processing program with draw tools
- paper

Alternate Materials:
- pencils
- 9" × 12" paper

Program Resources
- *Reading and Writing Test Prep.,* pp. 56–57
- *Transparency 26*
- *Artist Profiles,* pp. 36, 16
- *Animals Through History Time Line*
- *Assessment* pp. 59–60
- *Large Prints 45* Baby and *46* Untitled
- *Art Around the World Collection*

Concept Trace
Regular Patterns

Introduced: Level 3, Unit 5, Lesson 2

Reinforced: Level 4, Unit 2, Lesson 3

Lesson 2 Arts Integration

Theatre

Complete Unit 5, Lesson 2 on pages 92–93 of *Theatre Arts Connections.*

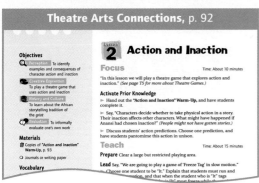

Theatre Arts Connections, p. 92

Music

Sing or listen to *Throw It Out the Window.* This song is fun to sing because of the many kinds of patterns. The rhythm has a swaying pulse. The words also have the same surprises in each verse.

Movement & Dance

Regular patterns repeat a motif to arrange movement in an orderly way. Create a sequence with a count pattern and four movement ideas. For example, walk 8 counts, bounce in place 4 counts, jump 8 counts, and melt 4 counts. Repeat the pattern four times.

 **Focus**

Time: About 10 minutes

Activate Prior Knowledge

"Look at the clothing you have on. The shoelace holes on shoes and the ribs on your socks are both examples of regular pattern."

"Miren la ropa que tienen puesta. Los agujeros de las cintas de los zapatos y los surcos de las medias son ejemplos de un patrón regular".

Using Literature ⭐ Reading

- Have students read *Alex Is My Friend* by Marisabina Russo and identify the regular patterns in the illustrations.

Thematic Connection ⭐ Reading

- **Homes:** Have students imagine the types of rooms they would put these two works of art in. For example, would they consider placing them in an office room, bedroom, dining room, or kitchen?

Introduce the Art NSAE 3.a

Look

"Let's take a close look at the two works of art." "Vamos a observar detalladamente las dos obras de arte".

Comparing and Contrasting ⭐ Reading

- Have students list the similarities and differences between these two works of art.

 Art History and Culture

Possible answer: *Four by Four* is fairly small, so it could have been used to store jewelry or small articles of clothing.

Have students compare this piece with *Easy Chair* from Lesson 1. Do they think these two pieces of furniture would go in the same room? Why or why not?

💻 **Web Connection**

Visit **www.clarkgallery.com/shows/2003/2003-11-04/show** to see more of Tom Loeser's artwork.

 Lesson 2  Regular Patterns

◀ **Tom Loeser.** (American). *Four by Four.*
....
Painted mohagany. 44 ¼ × 33 ¾ × 17 inches (112.40 × 82.73 × 43.18 cm.). Renwick Gallery, Smithsonian American Art Museum, Washington, D.C.

Look at the two works of art on these pages. *Four by Four* is a piece of decorative furniture made of mahogany. *Warnyu (flying foxes)* shows flying foxes in their coops. Each animal is the same, with each head facing the same way. Both works of art show several regular patterns.

 Art History and Culture

What do you think *Four by Four* was used for? Why?

 **Art History and Culture**

Tom Loeser

Tom Loeser (tom lō´sər) was born in Boston, Massachusetts. He first began exhibiting in 1982 and was immediately recognized by critics for a dynamic use of color in his three-dimensional sculptures.

Loeser makes many sketches and measurements of his functional furniture before preparing to carve or cut material. He cuts precise, angular shapes with tools such as tablesaws, bandsaws, and jigsaws.

See pp. 24–25 and 16–21 for more about art history and subject matter.

Artist Profiles, p. 36

> ◆ Artist Profile ◆
>
> **Tom Loeser**
> b. 1956
>
> Furniture artist Tom Loeser (tom lō´ sər) was born in 1956 in Boston, Massachusetts. He began exhibiting shortly after he graduated from college in 1982 and was immediately recognized by critics for a dynamic use of color in his three-dimensional sculptures. Among other shows, he was part of a group exhibition about resource conservation and the use of recycled materials and lesser-used wood species. This exhibit drew attention to the ways an artist can affect environmental change and maintain a healthy relationship with nature.

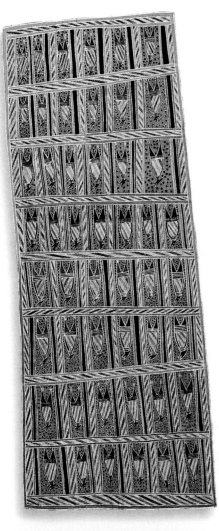

Study both works of art to find the following elements of pattern.

▶ Which work of art has patterns that are repeated?

▶ Find the objects that are repeated.

▶ How are textures used?

◀ **Dorothy Djukulul.**
(Aboriginal/Australia).
Warnyu (flying foxes).
1989. Eucalyptus bark. 106.30 × 31.89 inches (270 × 81 cm.). Kluge-Ruhe Collection of the University of Virginia, Charlottesville, Virginia.

 Aesthetic Perception

Seeing Like an Artist Look around your classroom at clothes and other fabrics. Find repeated shapes, lines, colors, and textures that are evenly spaced.

 Art History and Culture

Dorothy Djukulul

Dorothy Djukulul was born near Mulgurrum, Australia, and is a member of the Aboriginal Ganalbingu clan. When she was young, she attended a mission school, where the superintendent encouraged her to paint in the Western style. Every day after school, however, her father and uncle would teach her the traditional way of painting on bark.

Djukulul married and worked as a baker until her first husband died. She met and married Djardi Ashley, a well-known bark painter who supported her desire to paint. She has become a prominent Aboriginal artist and has participated in numerous exhibitions.

See pages 24–25 and 16–21 for more about art history and subject matter.

Artist Profiles, p. 16

◆ Artist Profile ◆
Dorothy Djukulul
b. 1942
Dorothy Djukulul was born near Mulgurrum, Australia, and is a member of the aboriginal Ganalbingu clan. When she was young she attended a Methodist mission school, where the superintendent recognized her artistic talent and encouraged her to paint in the Western style. But every day after school her father and uncle would teach her the traditional way of painting on bark. After completing school Djukulul worked on the land and helped build stockyards until she moved far from her family. She worked as a baker and then returned to her home where she met and married Djardi Ashley, a well-known bark painter who supported Djukulul's desire to paint. She has become a

Study

▶ *Repeated pattern: Four by Four:* the yellow and purple repeating pattern of lines. *Warnyu (flying foxes):* The lines are repeating boxes and the foxes are a pattern of lines.

▶ *Repeated objects: Four by Four:* the shapes of the handles. *Warnyu (flying foxes).* The foxes are all repeating.

▶ *Texture: Four by Four:* smooth textures on the sculpture. *Warnyu (flying foxes):* lines that are close together create a feeling of texture.

■ For more examples of art from Australia, see *Art Around the World.*

Art Journal: Writing
Encourage students to write their own explanations of regular patterns in the Concepts section of their Art Journals. What else do they want to know about regular patterns?

Aesthetic Perception

Seeing Like an Artist Discuss with students the regular patterns in their clothing. What makes the patterns regular?

Developing Visual Literacy Have students look again at *Warnyu (flying foxes).* What do they think the artwork "says"? Why are the foxes in coops? Bark is a traditional medium for Aboriginal art. Discuss how the artist's choice of bark, as opposed to canvas or paper, also contributes to the meaning of the piece.

NSAE 3.a, 3.b

 Web Connection
Visit **www.aboriginalart.com.au/culture/** to learn more about Australian history and culture.

Teach

Time: About 45 minutes

"How can you use regular pattern to create a design? "¿Cómo pueden usar patrón regular para crear un diseño?"

- Discuss the ways to create regular pattern on page 162.

Practice

Materials: 9 × 12" paper, pencils

Alternate Materials: colored pencils

- Distribute the materials and have students follow the directions on page 162 for creating a regular pattern.

Creative Expression

Materials: Computer, Printer, Word processing program with draw tools, paper

- Have students follow the directions on page 163.
- Review the Activity Tips on page 244 for visual examples of techniques if needed.

NSAE 1.a, 1.c, 1.d

Art Journal: Brainstorming

Have students brainstorm ideas for creating a motif in their Art Journals. Then have students decide how they will design their pattern using the computer for the Creative Expression activity.

Using Regular Patterns

Patterns are surface decorations. We see patterns on the clothes we wear. Patterns are also used in construction. Patterns are decorative and can be slightly raised.

A **regular pattern** is one kind of decorative surface design.

In a regular pattern the motif, or unit of repetition, is repeated in an even manner.

Look at the drawing to the left. Name the motif. Why is it an example of regular pattern?

Practice

1. Fold a sheet of paper into six equal boxes. In the middle of the first box, draw a large geometric shape, or write large and print a letter of the alphabet.

2. Draw exactly the same motif in each box to create regular pattern. Put equal amounts of space in between each letter or shape.

Differentiated Instruction

Reteach

Have students look through the book to find different works illustrating regular pattern. Ask them to list each of the works and describe how regular pattern is used.

Special Needs

Some students with low fine-motor skills or unstable hands may become discouraged if they are unable to recreate the same exact motif for each square. In this case, allow the student to create a template around which the student can trace within each square, providing a uniform motif.

ELL Tips

Students may feel shy or hesitant to answer the interpretive question about their artwork. You may wish to phrase the question as an either/or choice so that the vocabulary needed to answer the question is contained in the question itself.

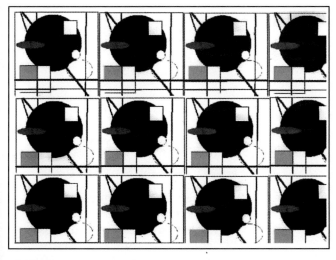

◀ **Carl Blanton.**
Age 8.

Think about how this student used regular pattern in his design.

Creative Expression

Use lines, shapes, and colors to repeat a motif, creating a design.

1. Use the auto-shape tool to create a square.
2. Use the line and auto-shape tools to create a design in the square.
3. Use the fill tool to color in the design.
4. Select the whole design and copy.
5. Paste the design several times to create a regular pattern.
6. Enlarge the completed square design.
7. Print your work.

Art Criticism

Describe What designs did you use to create your motif?

Analyze Which colors did you repeat to create your design?

Interpret How would your designs be different if you did not use the computer?

Decide If you could add one more design, what would it be?

Reflect

Time: About 5 minutes

Review and Assess

"How can you recognize regular pattern in a work of art?" "¿Cómo pueden reconocer un patrón regular en una obra de arte?"

Think

The artist used geometric shapes to create a motif in his artwork.

- Use *Large Prints 45 Baby* and *46 Untitled* to have students identify regular patterns.

Informal Assessment

Art Journal: Critical Thinking

Have students answer the four art criticism questions—Describe, Analyze, Interpret, and Decide—orally or in writing. Discuss the use of regular pattern in their computer designs.

NSAE 3.a, 3.b

- For standardized-format test practice using this lesson's art content, see pages 56–57 in *Reading and Writing Test Preparation.*

Art Across the Curriculum

Use these simple ideas to reinforce art concepts across the curriculum.

★ **Poetry** Have students write a poem with a regular rhyme scheme, such as A-B-A-B. Explain that this is similar to regular pattern in visual art.

★ **Math** As students study geometry, point out and discuss regular geometric patterns.

★ **Science** As students study energy, point out regular patterns such as sound waves.

★ **Social Studies** Discuss the regular pattern created by latitude and longitude lines on a globe.

★ **Technology** Have students use lines in a draw program to illustrate regular pattern. Visit **SRAonline.com** to print detailed instructions for this activity.

NSAE 6.a, 6.b

Regular Patterns

Extra! For the Art Specialist

Time: About 45 minutes

Focus

Use *Tranparency 25* and *Large Prints 45 Baby* and *46 Untitled* to discuss the ways that artists use regular patterns in their works of art. Have students look for repetition in the artwork that creates a regular pattern. Did the artist repeat colors, lines, or shapes in the artwork? How would the artwork look different if the artist had not used a regular pattern?

Teach

Have students follow the directions to complete their stencil prints.

Close

Have students evaluate their artwork using the four steps of art criticism.

Alternate Activity

Materials:

- 4" × 6" piece of tagboard or oaktag per student
- pencils
- scissors
- 12" × 18" sheets of lightly colored construction paper, one per student
- sponge brushes (1" × 3" pieces of sponge folded and clipped with clothespins) or stiff bristle brushes
- tempera paints in small trays or flat containers

1. Have students draw a simple shape (for example, a fish or a bird) on the tagboard. Students will cut the positive shape out of the tagboard, leaving the negative shape (background) intact.

2. Students will use the sponge brush in an up-and-down motion to print the inside of the stencil shape onto the lightly colored construction paper.

3. Students will repeat printing the stencil shape to create a regular pattern on their papers.

Research in Art Education

"Only through a multifaceted education program that develops divergent as well as convergent thinking—that encourages intuitive as well as rational thought processes—can today's young learner begin to be prepared to cope with the rapidly changing aspects of a technology-oriented world" (Herberholz, Barbara, and Lee Hanson. *Early Childhood Art.* New York: McGraw-Hill, 1994).

NSAE 1.a, 1.c

Assessment

Use the following rubric to evaluate the artwork students make in the Creative Expression activity and to assess students' understanding of regular pattern.

Have students complete page 59 or 60 of their *Assessment* books.

	Art History and Culture	Aesthetic Perception	Creative Expression	Art Criticism
3 POINTS	The student demonstrates knowledge of the art and lives of Loeser and Djukulul.	The student accurately identifies regular patterns in artwork and the environment.	The student effectively uses the computer to create a regular pattern.	The student evaluates his or her own work using the four steps of art criticism.
2 POINTS	The student demonstrates some knowledge of the art and lives of Loeser and Djukulul.	The student shows emerging awareness of regular patterns in art and the environment.	The student shows some awareness of how to use the computer to create a regular pattern.	The student attempts to evaluate his or her own work using the four steps of art criticism.
1 POINT	The student cannot demonstrate knowledge of the art and lives of Loeser and Djukulul.	The student cannot identify regular patterns in art and the environment.	The student shows no understanding of how to use the computer to create a regular pattern.	The student makes no attempt to evaluate his or her own work.

Assessment, p. 59

Name _____ Date _____

Lesson 2 UNIT 5

Regular Patterns

A. Drawing
Design a motif and use it to draw a regular pattern in the space below.

B. Writing
Study *Warnyu (flying boxes)* by Dorothy Djukulul. Write a brief paragraph describing the motif and how it is repeated.

Level 3   Unit 5 • Pattern, Rhythm, and Movement **59**

Alternating Pattern

Lesson 3 introduces how alternating pattern is used in creating designs.

Objectives

Art History and Culture
To demonstrate knowledge of the Inca and Mojave cultures

Creative Expression
To plan and create an alternating design with two personal motifs

 ### Aesthetic Perception
To identify alternating patterns in art and the environment

 ### Art Criticism
To use the four steps of art criticism to evaluate their own drawings

Vocabulary  Vocabulary

Review the following vocabulary with students.

motif *motivo*—unit that is repeated in visual rhythm or pattern. Units in a motif may or may not be an exact duplicate of the first unit.

alternating pattern *patrón alterno*—visual pattern set up by repeating motifs, but changing position or content of motifs or the spaces between them.

See page 179B for additional vocabulary and Spanish vocabulary resources.

Art Journal: Vocabulary

Have students add these words to the Vocabulary section of their Art Journals.

Lesson Materials
- 12" × 18" construction paper
- pencils
- crayons
- color pencils

Program Resources
- *Reading and Writing Test Prep.,* pp. 58–59
- *Transparency 27*
- *Flash Card 11*
- *Artist Profiles,* pp. 62, 82
- *Animals Through History Time Line*
- *Assessment* pp. 61–62
- *Large Prints 45 Baby* and *46 Untitled*
- *Art Around the World Collection*

Concept Trace
Alternating Pattern
Introduced: Level 3, Unit 5, Lesson 3

Reinforced: Level 4, Unit 2, Lesson 3

Lesson 3 Arts Integration

Theatre
Complete Unit 5, Lesson 3 on pages 94–95 of *Theatre Arts Connections.*

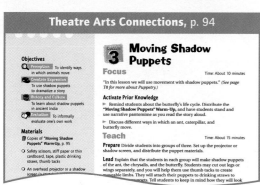

Theatre Arts Connections, p. 94

Music

Sing or listen to *Hashewie,* an Eritrean folk song. This form is "call and response." The leader sings one pattern, and the group responds with their own, different pattern. Many folk songs out of the African American tradition are this form.

Movement & Dance
Reinforce the concept of alternating pattern by combining two separate patterns into one sequence. Divide students into groups of six. The first three students do the following pattern in place: jump, jump, turn, stretch. The second three students do the following pattern, moving through the first three students: gallop, gallop, spin, lunge.

ocus

Time: About 10 minutes

Activate Prior Knowledge

"Imagine that you are playing a game of checkers. How are the squares arranged on the game board? "Imagínense que juegan un juego de damas. ¿Cómo están organizados los cuadrados en el tablero?"

▪ Discuss student responses and how the colored squares on the game board are arranged alternately.

Using Literature [★] Reading

▪ Read *My Life with the Wave* by Catherine Cowan and ask students to identify the patterns they see. Can they find alternating patterns?

Thematic Connection [★] Social Studies

▪ **About Me:** Use the artwork to discuss how the artists used motifs, colors, and patterns to illustrate things about the wearer of the art.

Introduce the Art   NSAE 3.a

Look

"Take a close look at the two artworks."
"Vamos a observar detalladamente estas dos obras de arte".

Discussing the Selection [★] Social Studies

▪ Have students discuss the region where these works of art were created. Discuss the designs each work of art and make a list of observations.

NSAE 3.a

 Art History and Culture

Possible answer: Although both works use alternating pattern, the media and styles of the artwork are very different, so they may come from different cultures. The caption information tells us that the works come from different places and times.

Web Connection

Visit **www.perutravels.net/** to learn more about Peruvian culture and history.

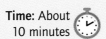 **Lesson 3**

Alternating Patterns

Look at the works of art on these two pages. *Tunic* was made between the fifteenth and sixteenth centuries. A tunic like this was probably a royal gift from the emperor to reward military achievements. *Collar* is a beadwork. It was created in the early 1900s by the Mojave people of the American Southwest region. Both works of art show alternating patterns.

◀ **Artist Unknown.** (Peru). *Tunic.* Fifteenth–sixteenth century.
··
Camel hair. 37 × 29 inches (93.99 × 73.67 cm.). The Metropolitan Museum of Art. New York, New York

 Art History and Culture

Do *Tunic* and *Collar* seem to come from the same culture?

 Art History and Culture

Inca People

Historians do not know whether this tunic was made by a particular artisan or by an ordinary Incan citizen, since cloth was designed and woven by many individuals in fifteenth- and sixteenth-century Peru. A tunic is usually a long full shirt that often serves as a kind of robe or jacket, and is worn over pants or leggings. This tunic features a grid pattern containing images of fish or birds and eight-pointed stars. The meaning or significance of these images is not known.

See pages 24–25 and 16–21 for more about art history and subject matter.

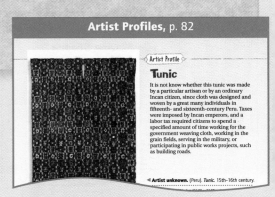

Artist Profiles, p. 82

Artist Profile

Tunic

It is not know whether this tunic was made by a particular artisan or by an ordinary Incan citizen, since cloth was designed and woven by a great many individuals in fifteenth- and sixteenth-century Peru. Taxes were imposed by Incan emperors, and a labor tax required citizens to spend a specified amount of time working for the government weaving cloth, working in the grain fields, serving in the military, or participating in public works projects, such as building roads.

◀ **Artist unknown.** (Peru). *Tunic.* 15th–16th century.

Study both works of art to find alternating patterns.

▶ Find the motifs in each work of art.

▶ In which piece is an alternating pattern harder to notice?

▶ Which piece has the most complicated pattern?

▲ **Artist Unknown.**
(Mojave/North
America). *Collar.*
1900–1925.
....
Glass beads and threads.
Birmingham Museum of
Art, Birmingham, Alabama.

 Aesthetic Perception

Seeing Like an Artist Look at the artwork in this book to find other examples of alternating patterns.

Art History and Culture

Mojave People

This beaded collar was by an unknown artist of the Mojave peoples from the southwestern United States. Mojave peoples, such as the Cahuilla group, are native to the Mojave Desert area and have adapted their lifestyle to its hot, dry environment. Before contact with nonnative peoples, Native American artists decorated their clothing with paint and porcupine-quill embroidery. Native peoples were fascinated with the beads they discovered through trade. The beadwork on this collar was done with these small seed beads.

See pages 24–25 and 16–21 for more about art history and subject matter.

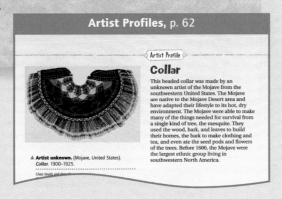

Artist Profiles, p. 62

⟨ Artist Profile ⟩

Collar

This beaded collar was made by an unknown artist of the Mojave from the southwestern United States. The Mojave are native to the Mojave Desert area and have adapted their lifestyle to its hot, dry environment. The Mojave were able to make many of the things needed for survival from a single kind of tree, the mesquite. They used the wood, bark, and leaves to build their homes, the bark to make clothing and tea, and even ate the seed pods and flowers of the trees. Before 1600, the Mojave were the largest ethnic group living in southwestern North America.

▲ **Artist unknown.** (Mojave, United States).
Collar. 1900–1925.
Glass beads and thread.

Study

▶ Motifs: *Tunic:* The eight pointed shapes and the motif with many triangles, but the variations in color make it look like many more. *Collar:* One motif at the neck is a set of triple red connected diamonds, surrounded by a double set of lines. The second motif is a set of three white diamonds—two are small and one is large.

▶ Alternating pattern: *Tunic:* Rectangle shape with a star next to rectangular shape with triangle motif. In the bottom row, notice the white star inside the green rectangles next to the green and red triangles inside the yellow rectangle. In the next row, the triangles are the same but the star is red in a green rectangle. In the third row up, the star is green on red and it changes to yellow on red. The triangles are white on green all across. *Collar:* The alternating pattern is red and white.

▪ For more examples of Latin American art, see *Art Around the World.*

Art Journal: Writing

Encourage students to write their own explanations of alternating pattern in the Concepts section of their Art Journals. What else do they want to know about alternating patterns?

Aesthetic Perception

Seeing Like an Artist Possible answers: *Child's Beaded Shirt* (p. 190) has rows of alternating pattern. *Cote d'Ivoire* (p. 87) alternates oval and rectangular shapes to create a pattern.

Developing Visual Literacy Both of these works of art are pieces of clothing. What do you think these works say about the people who wore them? Think of clothing that you have seen on television or in magazines. How are they similar to *Tunic* and *Collar*? How are they different? What do they say about the people who wear them?

NSAE 3.a

Web Connection

Visit **www.nps.gov/moja/mojahtm1.htm** to learn more about the Mojave people.

Teach

"How can you role play showing alternating pattern?" "¿Cómo pueden hacer una representación dramatica mostrando un patrón alterno?"

- Discuss and review the different ways of creating alternating pattern on page 166.

Practice

Materials: only students needed

Alternate Materials: pencils, paper

- Have students follow the directions on page 166 to demonstrate alternating pattern.

 Creative Expression

Materials: 12" × 18" construction paper, pencils, crayons, color pencils

Alternate Materials: markers

- Ask students: How can you use two motifs to create an alternating pattern?

- Have students think about motifs on clothing they have. How are the motifs arranged on the clothes?

- Distribute materials and have students follow the directions on page 167.

- Review the Activity Tips on page 245 for visual examples of techniques if needed.

NSAE 1.c, 1.d

Art Journal: Brainstorming

Have students brainstorm ideas for motifs they are going to illustrate in their Art Journals. Then have students select two or three items and plan how they will show those items in the Creative Expression activity.

Using Alternating Patterns

There are many ways to create patterns with one or more motifs. In a random pattern, the **motif,** or unit of repetition, is repeated in no particular order. In a regular pattern, the motif is repeated in an even manner. An **alternating pattern** can use one or more motifs.

Alternating patterns can be created in different ways. Using two repeated motifs that alternate in the same row can create alternating patterns. Changing the position of the motif so that one is upright and the next one is upside down is another way to create an alternating pattern.

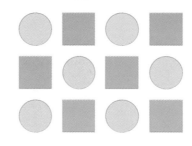 

Practice

Alternate a pattern with a group of seven students. Create an alternating pattern while role-playing.

1. Have students stand in a single-file line.

2. One student should stand upright while the next student bends down.

3. Try different ways of creating alternating patterns. What other types of patterns can you create like this?

Differentiated Instruction

Reteach
Have students look through the book to find a work of art that illustrates alternating pattern. Ask them to list the title and describe how alternating pattern was created.

Special Needs
Increase student interest in this activity by using acrylic paints to print the motifs onto shirts that the students provide.

ELL Tips
Students will benefit from working with a supportive peer to create an alternating pattern. You may wish to teach all of your students strategies for active listening and questioning that facilitate communication between people.

Think about how this student artist used an alternating pattern.

◀ **Caroline Flynn.**
Age 8.

 **Creative Expression**

Create a motif.

1. Create two motifs that you would wear on a shirt or jacket, such as cars, books, bicycles, or footballs.

2. Draw the article of clothing. Use an alternating pattern of the two motifs you created.

3. Color with crayons.

 **Art Criticism**

Describe What motif did you choose?

Analyze How did you organize your motif into a pattern?

Interpret Where would you wear this shirt?

Decide Did you use an alternating pattern successfully?

Unit 5 • Lesson 3 **167**

 **Reflect** Time: About 5 minutes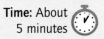

Review and Assess

"How do artists create alternating pattern?"
"¿Cómo crean los artistas un patrón alterno?"

Think

The student used two different motifs to create rows of alternating patterns.

■ Use *Large Print 46 Untitled* to have students identify regular pattern.

Informal Assessment

Art Journal: Critical Thinking
Have students answer the four art criticism questions—Describe, Analyze, Interpret, and Decide—in their Art Journals. In small groups, discuss the use of alternating pattern in their drawings.

NSAE 3.a

■ For standardized-format test practice using this lesson's art content, see pages 58–59 in *Reading and Writing Test Preparation.*

Art Across the Curriculum

Use these simple ideas to reinforce art concepts across the curriculum.

★ **Descriptive Writing** After students complete the Creative Expression activity, have them describe their motifs and explain how the motifs show something about their personalities.

★ **Math** Have students use geometric shapes to create an alternating pattern.

★ **Science** Include information about the Mojave people (found in the *Artist Profiles* book) when discussing conservation of natural resources.

★ **Social Studies** Have students compare and contrast *Collar* to the traditional clothing of other Native American peoples they are learning about in class.

★ **Technology** Have students use the computer's draw program to create an alternating pattern by rotating shapes. Visit **SRAonline.com** to print detailed instructions for this activity.

NSAE 6.a, 6.b

Alternating Pattern

Extra! For the Art Specialist

 Time: About 45 minutes

Focus

Use *Transparency 11* and *Large Print 46 Untitled* to discuss the use of alternating pattern. Have students look for the lines, shapes, or colors that create an alternating pattern in the artwork. How did the artist use them to create an alternating pattern? Have students talk about the differences in a regular and an alternating pattern. Would a different type of pattern affect the mood or feeling of the artwork?

Teach

Have students follow the directions to complete their drawings.

Reflect

Have students evaluate their works of art using the four steps of art criticism. Encourage them to locate and describe other areas of alternating pattern in paintings in the classroom or clothing of other students.

Alternate Activity

Materials:
- 12" × 18" white drawing paper
- multicolor packs of crayons or markers

1. Students will fold their papers in half twice horizontally and then twice vertically to divide the paper into sixteen sections. Have students draw lines over the fold lines to separate the sections.

2. Students will use lines and shapes to create a design in the first section of their papers. They will then create a different design in the second section of their papers.

3. Students will fill in the rest of the sixteen sections of their papers by alternately repeating the designs they created for the first and second sections to create an alternating pattern.

Research in Art Education

An overview of research concerning the arts in education shows that high-arts involvement leads to outcomes "central to the goals society typically articulates for public education-productive social membership, critical and higher-order thinking, and commitment to the skills for lifelong learning" ("Promising Signs of Positive Effects: Lessons from the Multi-Arts Studies" in *Critical Links*, p. 99).

NSAE 1.d, 3.b

Assessment
Use the following rubric to evaluate the artwork students make in the Creative Expression activity and to assess students' understanding of alternating pattern.

Have students complete page 61 or 62 of their *Assessment* books.

	Art History and Culture	Aesthetic Perception	Creative Expression	Art Criticism
3 POINTS	The student demonstrates knowledge of the Inca and Mojave cultures.	The student accurately identifies alternating pattern in art and the environment.	The student effectively plans and creates an alternating pattern with two personal motifs.	The student evaluates his or her own work using the four steps of art criticism.
2 POINTS	The student demonstrates some knowledge of the Inca and Mojave cultures.	The student shows emerging awareness of alternating pattern in art and the environment.	The student shows some awareness of how to plan and create an alternating pattern using two motifs.	The student attempts to evaluate his or her own work using the four steps of art criticism.
1 POINT	The student cannot demonstrate knowledge of the Inca and Mojave cultures.	The student cannot identify alternating pattern in art and the environment.	The student shows no understanding of how to plan and create an alternating pattern using two motifs.	The student makes no attempt to evaluate his or her own work.

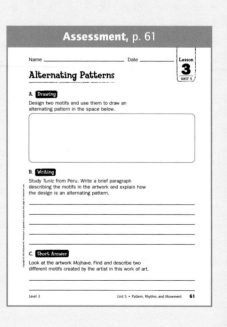

Assessment, p. 61

Name _____ Date _____
Lesson 3 UNIT 5

Alternating Patterns

A. Drawing
Design two motifs and use them to draw an alternating pattern in the space below.

B. Writing
Study *Tunic* from Peru. Write a brief paragraph describing the motifs in the artwork and explain how the design is an alternating pattern.

C. Short Answer
Look at the artwork *Mojave*. Find and describe two different motifs created by the artist in this work of art.

Level 3   Unit 5 • Pattern, Rhythm, and Movement **61**

Rhythm

Overview

Lesson 4 introduces how artists use rhythm to create a feeling of movement in their works of art.

Objectives

 Art History and Culture

To demonstrate knowledge of the art and lives of Bonheur and Abrasha

 Creative Expression

To create a functional clay container that has rhythm

 Aesthetic Perception

To identify how artists use rhythm to create feeling of movement

Art Criticism

To evaluate their own works of art using the four steps of art criticism

Lesson Materials
- clay
- slip
- clay tools
- newspaper
- kiln
- found objects

Program Resources
- *Reading and Writing Test Prep.,* pp. 60–61
- *Transparency 28*
- *Flash Cards 9* and *10*
- *Artist Profiles,* pp. 3, 7
- *Animals Through History Time Line*
- *Assessment* pp. 63–64
- *Large Prints 45 Baby* and *46 Untitled*
- *The National Museum of Women in the Arts Collection*

Concept Trace
Rhythm

Introduced: Level 2, Unit 4, Lesson 3

Reinforced: Level 4, Unit 2, Lesson 4

Vocabulary Vocabulary

Review the following vocabulary with students before beginning the lesson.

rhythm ritmo—a feeling of movement created by using the same types of lines, shapes, or colors several times in a work of art.

rest pausa—the negative space, or emptiness, between the beats in visual rhythm

See p. 179B for additional vocabulary and Spanish vocabulary resources.

 Art Journal: Vocabulary

Have students add these words to the Vocabulary section of their Art Journals.

Lesson 4 Arts Integration

Theatre

Complete Unit 5, Lesson 4 on pages 96–97 of *Theatre Arts Connections.*

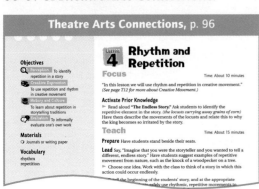

Theatre Arts Connections, p. 96

Music

 Listen to "In the Hall of the Mountain King" from *Peer Gynt Suite No.1, Op 46* by Edvard Grieg. Clap the main rhythm pattern. Notice the feeling of anticipation in the second half. What kind of mood is created by the repeated rhythm pattern in combination with the tempo (speed)?

Movement & Dance

Have students form a large circle. Have one student clap one time, then the next student, and so on around the circle, keeping the claps steady. Next have a student create a simple clapping rhythm that is repeated around the circle. Students must try to maintain the rhythm as it goes around.

**ocus**

Time: About 10 minutes

Activate Prior Knowledge

"Think about hand clapping and tapping your toes. Can rhythm be created using these movements?" "Piensen en aplaudir y zapatear. ¿Se puede crear un ritmo usando estos movimientos?"

■ Discuss students' answers.

Using Literature [★] Reading

■ Read *Farewell to Shady Glade* by Bill Peet. Discuss how the animals on the cover artwork are the beats of the rhythm, and the spaces between them are the rests.

Thematic Connection [★] Reading

■ **Imagination:** Use the artwork to discuss how each artist used imagination to create these works. Bonheur saw similar scenes, but probably did not see the exact scene she painted; Abrasha started with a traditional subject and portrayed it in a new way.

Introduce the Art   NSAE 3.a

Look

"Let's look closely at these two works of art." "Vamos a observar detalladamente las dos obras de arte".

Summarizing [★] Reading

■ Have students summarize how each work of art shows rhythm. Each work has repeated objects that are the beat of the rhythm.

 Art History and Culture

Women artists have faced the same challenges as women in the rest of society. Although there have been well-respected women artists throughout history, it was not until the twentieth century that large numbers of women entered the field and achieved recognition.

Web Connection
Visit www.ringling.org to learn more about The John and Mable Ringling Museum of Art.

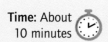 # Rhythm

▲ **Rosa Bonheur.** (French). *Plowing in Nivernais Region.* 1849.

Oil on canvas. $52\frac{1}{2} \times 102$ inches (133.35 × 259.08 cm.). The John and Mable Ringling Museum of Art, Sarasota, Florida.

Look at the works of art on these two pages. In *Plowing in Nivernais Region* the oxen are the beats of the rhythm and the spaces between them rests. *Hannukkah Menorah* is made of stainless steel, silver, and gold. There are three major beats in this sculpture. Each object is a beat, and the spaces between them are the rests.

 Art History and Culture

In 1852 Rosa Bonheur asked for permission to dress in men's clothing in order to attend a horse fair. Women at the time were not allowed into such events.

Art History and Culture

Rosa Bonheur

Rosa Bonheur (rō´ za bä nur´) was a painter and sculptor. As a woman artist of the nineteenth century, Bonheur faced many restrictions. For example, she had to obtain a police permit to wear trousers while she drew animals at a slaughterhouse.

Bonheur is known for the naturalistic manner in which she painted and sculpted images of animals. She probably did not actually witness many of the scenes she painted, but used her individual studies of landscape and animals to create her artwork.

See pages 24–25 and 16–21 for more about art history and subject matter.

Artist Profiles, p. 7

♦ Artist Profile ♦

Rosa Bonheur
1822–1899

Rosa Bonheur (rō´ za bä nur´) was a French painter and sculptor of the nineteenth century. She learned to paint from her artist father and from studying art in museums. Bonheur showed her works regularly at the Paris Salon, the principal exhibition space in France, where she won many awards. She later exhibited her art in England, where it was also very popular. She was the first female to be made an officer of the Legion of Honor—a recognition of accomplishment from the French government. As a female artist of the nineteenth century, Bonheur faced many restrictions. For example, she had to obtain a police permit to wear trousers while painting animals at a slaughterhouse.

Study each work of art to find the following elements of rhythm.

▶ Can you find three major beats in this sculpture?

▶ What other repetitions do you see in the sculpture?

▶ Which work has regular rhythm, and which one has uneven repetitions?

 Aesthetic Perception

Seeing Like an Artist Look around the classroom to find objects that are repeated. Do they create any sense of rhythm?

Art History and Culture

Abrasha

Abrasha (ə brä´ shə), who uses his first name only, was born in Holland in 1948. After apprenticing in Europe as a goldsmith for years, in 1977 he immigrated to the United States. Soon after his arrival in the United States, Abrasha began teaching jewelry making at art schools in the San Francisco Bay area. Abrasha's work is exhibited in museums and galleries throughout the country, including the Renwick Gallery at the National Museum of American Art in Washington, D.C, and the American Craft Museum in New York City.

See pages 24–25 and 16–21 for more about art history and subject matter.

Artist Profiles, p. 3

Artist Profile
Abrasha
b. 1948
The goldsmith and jewelry designer Abrasha (ə brä´ shə), who uses his first name only, was born in Holland in 1948. After apprenticing as a goldsmith for years in Europe, he immigrated to the United States in 1977. Soon after his arrival in America, Abrasha began teaching jewelry making at art schools in the San Francisco Bay area. In the many years he has lived in the Bay area, he has taught, lectured, created and exhibited artwork, and collaborated with other artists. Abrasha's work is exhibited in museums and galleries throughout the country. He is a member of the Society of North American Goldsmiths and has received numerous honors and awards in the United States and Germany.

Study

▶ Beat: *Hannukkah Menorah*. There are three major beats: the cone shaped cups, the vertical legs, and the circles in the black supports that hold the legs together. In each unit, the support that is holding the legs matches the support holding the cones. The flame is repeated nine times.

▶ Repetition: *Hannukkah Menorah* has regular repetitions. *Plowing in Nivernais Region* has uneven repetitions of the animals.

■ For more works by women artists, see *The National Museum of Women in the Arts Collection.*

Art Journal: Writing

Encourage students to write their own explanations of rhythm in the Concepts section of their Art Journals. What else do they want to know about rhythm?

Aesthetic Perception

Seeing Like an Artist Discuss with students repeated objects in the classroom, such as desks, chairs, windows, ceiling or floor tiles, and so on. Remind students that the objects are the positive spaces that create the beat of the rhythm, and the spaces between the objects are the rests.

Developing Visual Literacy Have students look through the textbook and select other works of art that are good examples of rhythm. Discuss with students how these works show rhythm.

NSAE 4.c

Web Connection
Visit **www.craftsmanshipmuseum.com/ Abrasha.htm** to view more works of art by Abrasha.

Teach

Time: About 45 minutes

"Let's look around the room for examples of rhythm." "Vamos a mirar alrededor de la habitación por ejemplos de ritmo".

■ Discuss the definition of rhythm and the elements used to create it on page 170.

Practice

Materials: round ball of clay, clay tools, newspaper

■ Distribute the materials and have students follow the directions on page 170.

Creative Expression

Materials: clay, slip, clay tools, newspaper, kiln, found objects

■ Distribute materials and have students follow directions on page 171.

■ Review the Activity Tips on page 245 for visual examples of techniques if needed.

NSAE 1.a, 1.c, 1.d

Art Journal: Brainstorming

Have students brainstorm ways they can show rhythm in making their clay pinch pots and list their ideas in their Art Journals. Then have students sketch three or four pinch pots and plan how they will arrange them in the Creative Expression activity.

Using Rhythm

Rhythm is a hand-clapping, toe-tapping musical beat. It is created by a beat and a rest between beats.

In visual art, **rhythm** is created by the repetition of a positive shape or form. That object is the beat. The negative space between the repetitions is the **rest.**

Practice

Practice joining pieces of clay. Use slip and scoring.

1. Divide a piece of clay into small balls.

2. Score the edges to be joined with a tool. Brush slip onto one surface.

3. Gently press the two scored surfaces together and smooth over the seam.

Differentiated Instruction

Reteach	Special Needs	ELL Tips
Have students clap out a beat or rhythm with their hands. Ask them to describe the sound of the rhythm and how it was achieved.	Reinforce the concept of rhythm by asking students to sound out the rhythm of the object that they created.	Students who are hesitant or not ready to speak in long sentences may find it helpful to respond physically or with one- or two-word responses to questions.

◀ **Erica Dazzle Krasle.**
Age 8.

Think about how this student artist created visual rhythm.

Creative Expression

How can you make a useful object that has visual rhythm? Make a clay container to hold different objects.

1. Make three to five pinch pots. The smallest should have a 3-inch opening.

2. Use scoring and slip to join the pots at their sides to make an interesting rhythm of round pots.

3. Smooth the places where they are joined using a clay tool or your fingers.

4. Decorate your bowls by pressing in or adding on patterns using your clay tools or found objects.

Art Criticism

Describe List three steps you followed to create your useful object.

Analyze How did you give your work a rhythmic look?

Interpret What objects would you keep in this container?

Decide Were you successful in creating an object with visual rhythm?

Reflect
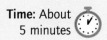 **Time:** About 5 minutes

Review and Assess

"What have you learned about rhythm?"
"¿Qué han aprendido sobre el ritmo?"

Think

The repeated pots create rhythm in the student artwork.

■ Use the *Large Print 46 Untitled* to have students identify rhythm, beat, and rest.

Informal Assessment

Art Journal: Critical Thinking
Have students answer the four art criticism questions—Describe, Analyze, Interpret, and Decide—in their Art Journals. Discuss the use of rhythm, beat and rest in their clay pots.

■ Find other works by Rosa Bonheur and share them with the class. Ask: How did Bonheur use rhythm in these works? What is the main idea? Have students discuss the works using the four steps of art criticism.

■ For standardized-format test practice using this lesson's art content, see pages 60–61 in *Reading and Writing Test Preparation.*

NSAE 3.a, 3.b

Art Across the Curriculum

Use these simple ideas to reinforce art concepts across the curriculum.

★ **Narrative Writing** Have students use *Plowing in Nivernais Region* as the setting of a one-page story.

★ **Math** Discuss how even and odd numbers can be used to create a rhythm.

★ **Science** Have students identify rhythms that occur in nature, such as the seasons and the cycles of the moon.

★ **Social Studies** Have students locate the Nivernais region of France on a world map or globe.

★ **Technology** Have students use the computer's draw program to illustrate rhythm. Visit **SRAonline.com** to print detailed instructions for this activity.

NSAE 6.a, 6.b

Rhythm

Lesson **4** Wrap-Up

 Extra! **For the Art Specialist**   **Time:** About 45 minutes

Focus

Use *Transparency 28* and *Large Print 46 Untitled* to discuss the ways that artists use rhythm in their works of art. Have students talk about how the repetition of lines and shapes unifies the artwork and gives it a sense of rhythm. Ask students how the artist's arrangement of lines and shapes leads the viewer's eye around the composition. Does the artwork have a regular or a random rhythm? How did the artist's use of space affect the rhythm of the composition?

Teach

Have students follow the directions for making a stamp print.

Close

Have students evaluate their works of art using the four steps of art criticism. Encourage them to discuss other ways of displaying rhythm beat and rest.

Alternate Activity

Materials:
- oil-based clay, 1" to 2" block per student
- gadgets for incising clay (paper clips, toothpicks, or plastic forks)
- stamp pads (tempera paint saturated paper towels in shallow trays)
- 12" × 18" white drawing or manila paper

1. Talk with students about how they can create rhythm in works of art.

2. Students will use gadgets to incise a design into their blocks of clay. They can slightly alter the shape of the clay, as long as the printing surface remains flat.

3. Students will print either a regular or a random pattern on their paper by first pressing the clay printing block onto the stamp pad and then pressing the inked block onto the paper.

Research in Art Education

One case study showed that students who were "learning disabled and who were 'reluctant' readers" were better able to engage in reading when the creation and analysis of visual art was incorporated in their discussions of stories. This suggests that combining visual art with reading may help certain readers" ("Reading *Is* Seeing: Using Visual Response to Improve the Literary Reading of Reluctant Readers" in *Critical Links*, p. 144).

NSAE 1.c, 1.d

Assessment

Use the following rubric to evaluate the artwork students make in the Creative Expression activity and to assess students' understanding of rhythm.

Have students complete page 63 or 64 in their *Assessment* books.

	Art History and Culture	Aesthetic Perception	Creative Expression	Art Criticism
3 POINTS	The student demonstrates knowledge of the art and lives of Bonheur and Abrasha.	The student accurately identifies how artists use rhythm to show movement in their works of art.	The student effectively creates several clay pinch pots that show rhythm.	The student evaluates his or her own work using the four steps of art criticism.
2 POINTS	The student demonstrates some knowledge of the art and lives of Bonheur and Abrasha.	The student shows emerging awareness of how artists use rhythm to show movement in their works of art.	The student shows some awareness of how to create several clay pinch pots that show rhythm.	The student attempts to evaluate his or her own work using the four steps of art criticism.
1 POINT	The student demonstrates no knowledge of the art and lives of Bonheur and Abrasha.	The student cannot identify how artists use rhythm to show movement in their works of art.	The student shows no understanding of how to create clay pinch pots, that show rhythm.	The student makes no attempt to evaluate his or her own work.

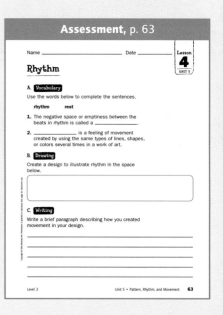

Assessment, p. 63

Name _____ Date _____ Lesson **4** UNIT 5

Rhythm

A. Vocabulary
Use the words below to complete the sentences.

rhythm   rest

1. The negative space or emptiness between the beats in rhythm is called a _____.

2. _____ is a feeling of movement created by using the same types of lines, shapes, or colors several times in a work of art.

B. Drawing
Create a design to illustrate rhythm in the space below.

C. Writing
Write a brief paragraph describing how you created movement in your design.

Level 3   Unit 5 • Pattern, Rhythm, and Movement **63**

171A UNIT 5 • Pattern, Rhythm, and Movement

Visual Rhythm

Lesson 5 introduces how artists create visual rhythm by repeating lines, shape, and color in their works of art.

Objectives

 Art History and Culture

To demonstrate knowledge of the art and lives of Lawrence and Kabotie

 Creative Expression

To create a painting of a parade using repeated lines, shapes and colors that create rhythm

 Aesthetic Perception

To identify how artists use repeated lines, shapes and colors to create rhythm in their art

Art Criticism

To use the four steps of art criticism to evaluate their own paintings

Vocabulary  Vocabulary

Review the following vocabulary word with students before beginning the lesson.

visual rhythm   *ritmo visual*—a feeling of movement created by using the same types of lines, shapes, or colors, several times in a work of art

See page 179B for additional vocabulary and Spanish vocabulary resources.

 Art Journal: Vocabulary

Have students add this word to the Vocabulary section of their Art Journals.

Lesson Materials

- 6" × 18" large white paper
- crayons or oil pastels
- watercolor paints and assorted brushes
- water
- paper towels
- pencils

Program Resources

- *Reading and Writing Test Prep.,* pp. 62–63
- *Transparency 29*
- *Flash Cards 9* and *10*
- *Artist Profiles,* pp. 29, 33
- *Animals Through History Time Line*
- *Assessment,* pp. 65–66
- *Large Prints 45* Baby and *46* Untitled
- *Art Around the World Collection*

Concept Trace
Visual Rhythm
Introduced: Level 3, Unit 5, Lesson 5

Reinforced: Level 4, Unit 2, Lesson 4

Lesson 5 Arts Integration

Theatre
Complete Unit 5, Lesson 5 on pages 98–99 of *Theatre Arts Connections.*

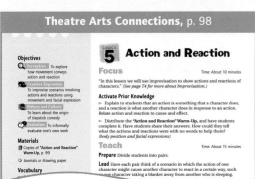

Theatre Arts Connections, p. 98

Music
 Listen to "Winter" from *The Four Seasons* by Antonio Vivaldi. Vivaldi uses rhythms and tone colors to create the feelings of the different seasons. In "Winter," we hear music suggesting freezing cold, stamping of feet, and resting somewhere warm. Imagine an event for the last exciting section.

Movement & Dance
Demonstrate the concept of visual rhythm by having students form a large circle. Begin with one person who creates two actions, such as turn (counts 1–2) and reach (counts 3–4). The next person in the circle repeats the actions; this continues around the circle. Students must try to maintain the rhythm of the movement as it goes around.

ocus

Time: About 10 minutes

Activate Prior Knowledge

"Think about patterns you have seen on different fabrics." "Piensen en patrones que hayan visto en differentes telas".

■ Discuss students' answers about various patterns they have noticed, such as stripes, dots, checkerboards, and plaids.

Using Literature ⭐ Reading

■ Read *The Worry Stone* by Marianna Dengler. The stones on the endpapers show visual rhythm.

Thematic Connection ⭐ Social Studies

■ **Communities:** Both works of art in this lesson show communities. Discuss with students how these communities are similar to or different from their own communities.

Introduce the Art   NSAE 3.a

Look

"Let's take a look closely at the paintings." "Vamos a observar detalladamente las dos pinturas".

Comparing and Contrasting ⭐ Reading

■ Have students compare and contrast the artworks. Both paintings are outdoor scenes created using different forms of visual rhythm. *Pueblo Scene Corn Dance, Hopi* uses very calm lines and all the figures are standing vertically. *Parade* is full of diagonal movement. The marchers' legs and arms are swaying. The whole picture seems to move diagonally.

 Art History and Culture

Discuss with students how artists throughout history have documented events of historical importance as well as scenes of everyday life. Discuss with students whether photography has changed the way such events are documented. Possible answer: In paintings artists can change color, proportion, or other elements of the scene to contribute to the message of the work. Photography allows events to be documented almost instantly by a large number of people.

NSAE 4.a, 4.b

🖥 **Web Connection**

Visit **www.phillipscollection.org/lawrence/** to learn more about Jacob Lawrence.

172 UNIT 5 • Pattern, Rhythm, and Movement

Lesson

Visual Rhythm

▲ **Jacob Lawrence.** (American). *Parade.*
1960. Tempera on wood. 23 ⅓ × 30 ⅜ inches (58.42 × 76.60 cm). Hirshhorn Museum, Washington, D.C.

Look at both paintings on these pages. *Parade* shows diagonal movement with the marchers' legs and arms swaying. The movement in *Pueblo Scene Corn Dance, Hopi* appears to be very calm. Both artists used visual rhythm in the design of their works of art.

 Art History and Culture

Fred Kabotie was a painter, illustrator, and writer of Hopi life, or Nakayoma, which means "day by day."

172   Unit 5 • Lesson 5

 Art History and Culture

Jacob Lawrence

Jacob Lawrence's (jā´ kəp lô´ rens) parents met on their migration to the North. His father was born in South Carolina, and his mother in Virginia. Because his mother worked all day, she enrolled Lawrence in the Harlem Art Workshop after school to keep him out of trouble. He had many excellent teachers there, including Charles Alston. During World War II he served in the U.S. Coast Guard. He created a series of paintings about his experiences, which in 1944 were exhibited by the Museum of Modern Art. Lawrence's paintings not only contribute to the art world, but they also add to our knowledge of African American history.

See pages 24–25 and 16–21 for more about art history and subject matter.

Artist Profiles, p. 33

Artist Profile
Jacob Lawrence
1917–2000

Jacob Lawrence (jā´ kəb lär´ ənz) had parents who met on their migration to the North. His father was born in South Carolina, and his mother in Virginia. Lawrence was born in Atlantic City, New Jersey, in 1917. The family finally settled in Harlem in 1929 at the end of the Harlem Renaissance. Because his mother worked all day, she enrolled Lawrence in the Harlem Art Workshop after school to keep him out of trouble. He had many excellent teachers there, including Charles Alston. Lawrence won a scholarship to the American Artists School. He taught at New York's Pratt Institute from 1958 to 1965. From 1970, he taught at the University of Washington in Seattle, where he also served as head of the

◀ **Fred Kabotie.**
(Native American).
*Pueblo Scene Corn
Dance, Hopi.* 1947.
....
Oil on canvas. 29 ½ × 25 ½
inches (74.93 × 64.77 cm).
Gilcrease Museum, Tulsa,
Oklahoma.

Study each painting to find the following elements.

▶ What are the beats that repeat to create visual
rhythm?

▶ How does the artist show a sense of calm in
Pueblo Scene Corn Dance, Hopi?

▶ Which painting shows strong diagonal movement?

▶ Find the colors that are repeated.

 Aesthetic Perception

Design Awareness Find examples of rhythm
in your classroom.

Art History and Culture

Fred Kabotie

Fred Kabotie (fred kä bō´ tē) was born in Arizona to a traditional
Hopi family. He first started drawing on rocks in his father's fields.
Later the government forced him, like other Native American
children, to attend the Santa Fe Indian School. The schools
superintendent recognized Kabotie's artistic skills and encouraged
him to become an artist. In 1920 Kabotie became the first Hopi to
be recognized nationally for his art. Kabotie often painted the
rituals and ceremonies of his people, using both oil and
watercolors. His painting
style and techniques changed
over the years and he began
to include ancient Hopi
images in his paintings,
which were more stylized
than most of his other work.

See pages 24–25 and 16–21
for more about art history
and subject matter.

Artist Profiles, p. 29

◀ Artist Profile ▶
Fred Kabotie
1900-1986
Fred Kabotie (fred kä bō´ tē) was born in
Arizona to a traditional Hopi family. He first
started drawing on rocks in his father's
fields. Later the government forced him,
like other Native American children, to
attend the Santa Fe Indian School. The
school's superintendent recognized
Kabotie's artistic skills and encouraged
him to become an artist. In 1920, Kabotie
became the first Hopi to be recognized
nationally for his art. In 1937, he returned
to his hometown and began to teach
his version of Hopi art at the new high
school. His teaching and work influenced
generations of Hopi artists. Even the French
government recognized Kabotie for his
contributions to Native American art. His

Study

▶ In the Lawrence painting the marchers in
the parade are repeated to create a visual
rhythm. In the Kabotie painting the
dancers moving in a line create the
strongest rhythmic repetition.

▶ All the figures in the parade are standing
vertically. Everything except the Koshare
clowns in the upper left corner is very
vertical. That gives the painting a calm,
dignified quality.

▶ The Lawrence painting is full of diagonal
movement. The marchers' legs and arms
are swaying. The whole picture seems to
move diagonally.

▶ In the Lawrence work each row of
marchers is wearing the same colors. In
the Kabotie painting the light blue
headdresses and the white pants are
repeated in the dance parade.

■ For more examples of art from North
America, see the *Art Around the World
Collection.*

Art Journal: Writing
Encourage students to write their
own explanation of visual rhythm in the
Concepts section of their Art Journals.

 Aesthetic Perception

Design Awareness Discuss with students
examples of visual rhythm in the classroom.
Have students identify the objects that
repeat to create the rhythm.

Developing Visual Literacy Discuss with
students the various ways artists
communicate meaning. In *Pueblo Scene Corn
Dance, Hopi*, Kabotie's subject matter
communicates information about the Hopi
people. Later in his career his paintings
became more stylized and symbolic,
communicating meaning in a different way.
In these works Kabotie used traditional
symbols of the Hopi people. Have students
think about their own life experiences. Ask
how they could symbolize these experiences
in a work of art.

NSAE 2.a, 2.b

Web Connection
Visit **www.nau.edu/library/speccoll/exhibits/
sca/collect/pubitems/index.html** to learn more
about Fred Kabotie.

Teach

Time: About 45 minutes

"How can you create visual rhythm in your work of art?" "¿Cómo pueden crear un ritmo visual en sus obras de arte?"

- Discuss the definition of visual rhythm. Discuss how the arrangement of objects in an artwork can help the viewer's eye move through the work.

Practice

Materials: 9" × 12" colored construction paper, scissors, glue

- Distribute the materials and have students follow the directions on page 174 for illustrating visual rhythm.

Creative Expression

Materials: 6" × 18" white paper, crayons or oil pastels, watercolor paints and assorted brushes, water, paper towels

- Ask students: How can you draw a parade that has visual rhythm?
- Have students brainstorm in small groups to get ideas for different objects to illustrate.
- Distribute materials and have students follow directions on page 175.
- Review the Activity Tips on page 246 for visual examples of techniques if needed.

 Art Journal: Brainstorming
Have students brainstorm ways to show a parade. Have them make two or three sketches of different objects they might see in a parade, and write them in their Art Journals. Then have students decide how they will show these different objects in the Creative Expression activity.

NSAE 2.c

Using Visual Rhythm

Visual rhythm is rhythm you see with your eyes. Visual rhythm is the feeling of movement created when an artist repeats colors, shapes, lines, and textures to pull your eyes through a work of art. Your eyes move along the artwork, following the parts that are repeated.

Practice

Demonstrate visual rhythm by creating a design.

1. Cut eight complex geometric shapes out of construction paper.
2. On another piece of construction paper, arrange the shapes to form a design that will create visual rhythm. Use your shapes to create designs that show a sense of calm or movement.
3. Remember that the shapes are *beats* in your design.

Differentiated Instruction

Reteach

Ask students to move around the classroom and then "freeze." Discuss how you might show illustrate this motion.

Special Needs

Display pictures illustrating visual rhythm for students to refer to as they complete this lesson's activity. Provide formative assessment for students by showing them the areas of their work where they are creating visual rhythm by repeating colors, shapes, and lines.

ELL Tips

To promote students' acquisition of the art terminology described in this lesson, you might ask students to check their Practice and Creative Expression works with a partner before moving to the final product. Write questions about rhythm on a chart and have students ask each other these questions.

▲ **Haley Brennan.**
Age 9.

Think about parades you have seen. What did you like about the parade?

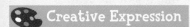 **Creative Expression**

1. Think about things you like to see in a parade. Do you like floats, marching bands, clowns, horses, elephants, and antique cars?

2. Make sketches of things you want in your parade. Draw yourself as the grand marshal or leader of the parade.

3. Select your best sketches and use chalk to transfer them to large paper.

4. Paint your parade.

 **Art Criticism**

Describe What did you include in your parade?

Analyze How did you create rhythm in your picture?

Interpret What is the occasion or holiday for your parade?

Decide Were you successful in creating visual rhythm?

Unit 5 • Lesson 5   **175**

 **Reflect** Time: About 5 minutes

Review and Assess

"Let's review what we have learned about visual rhythm." *"Vamos a repasar lo que hemos aprendido acerca de los ritmos visuales".*

Think

The artist created visual rhythm in this work by repeating the people. They make the beats of the rhythm.

- Use *Large Print 46 Untitled* to have students compare visual rhythm.

Informal Assessment

Art Journal: Critical Thinking
Have students answer the four art criticism questions—Describe, Analyze, Interpret, and Decide—in their Art Journals. In small groups, have students discuss the various objects they used to illustrate their parade. You might also have students discuss each other's work in a group session.

NSAE 3.a, 3.b

- For standardized-format test practice using this lesson's art content, see pages 62–63 in *Reading and Writing Test Preparation.*

Art Across the Curriculum

Use these simple ideas to reinforce art concepts across the curriculum.

★ **Personal Writing** Have students write invitations to parents or the principal asking them to come view the artwork created by the class.

★ **Math** Discuss how musicians use math, such as counting the beats and rests in a rhythm.

★ **Science** Discuss the relationship between energy and movement.

★ **Social Studies** Discuss the word movement as it relates to history, such as the Civil Rights Movement.

★ **Technology** Have students use the lines in the computer's draw program to illustrate visual rhythm. Visit **SRAonline.com** to print detailed instructions for this activity.

NSAE 6.a, 6.b

Visual Rhythm

Extra! For the Art Specialist

Time: About 45 minutes

Focus

Have students look at the lesson artwork and pick out patterns that make up visual rhythms. Where are different types of lines repeated? What other lines or shapes are repeated to create rhythm? Discuss how the artist used different patterns to create rhythm in the artwork. How would the artwork be affected if one of the patterns was changed?

Teach

Explain to the students that they will assemble the pre-cut geometric shapes into a composition showing rhythm.

Distribute 5" × 7" pieces of background posterboard and geometric shapes.

Close

Have students evaluate their works of art using the four steps of art criticism. Encourage them to locate and describe other areas of visual rhythm they might see in various books or magazines.

Alternate Activity

Materials:
- 5" × 7" pieces of posterboard, one per student
- pre-cut pieces of posterboard in geometric shapes, several per student
- white glue
- 9" × 12" printing papers
- brayers
- printing ink
- inking trays

1. Have students arrange the pre-cut shapes to create a design with rhythmic pattern and glue one shape at a time to the background posterboard.

2. When printing plates are dry, students will use brayers to evenly spread printing ink onto their plates.

3. Students place a sheet of 9" × 12" paper onto the inked surface and rub over the paper with their fingers to transfer the ink from the plate to the paper.

Research in Art Education

"The making of art is an essential activity for elementary children. They need and want hands-on experiences in this 'other language.' Art lessons must include cycles of experiences with basic media and techniques, allowing students to acquire and then build upon skills fundamental to creative expression" (Kay Alexander, "Art Curricula by and for Art Educators," in *Art Education: Elementary* ed. Andra Johnson [1992]).

Assessment

NSAE 1.a, 1.c, 1.d

Use the following rubric to evaluate the artwork students make in the Creative Expression activity and to assess students' understanding of visual rhythm.

Have students complete page 65 or 66 in their *Assessment* books.

	Art History and Culture	Aesthetic Perception	Creative Expression	Art Criticism
3 POINTS	The student demonstrates knowledge of the lives and art of Lawrence and Kabotie.	The student accurately identifies how artist use visual rhythm in their works of art.	The student effectively plans and creates a parade painting showing visual rhythm.	The student evaluates his or her own work using the four steps of art criticism.
2 POINTS	The student demonstrates some knowledge of the art and lives of Lawrence and Kabotie.	The student shows emerging awareness of how artist use visual rhythm in their works of art.	The student shows some awareness of how to create a parade painting showing visual rhythm.	The student attempts to evaluate his or her own work using the four steps of art criticism.
1 POINT	The student demonstrates no understanding of the lives and art of Lawrence and Kabotie.	The student cannot identify how artists use visual rhythm in their works of art.	The student shows no understanding of how to create visual rhythm in the painting.	The student makes no attempt to evaluate his or her own work using the four steps of art criticisms.

Assessment, p. 65

Name _____ Date _____

Lesson 5 UNIT 5

Visual Rhythm

A. Drawing

Decide where you want to direct your viewer's eyes and then create visual rhythm in the box below by repeating a shape, color, or type of line. On the lines below the box, explain how you created visual rhythm.

B. Writing

Look at *Pueblo Scene Corn Dance, Hopi.* Write a description to explain the visual rhythm Fred Kabotie created in this painting.

Level 3   Unit 5 • Pattern, Rhythm, and Movement   **65**

Three-Dimensional Rhythm

Lesson 6 introduces how artists use three-dimensional rhythm to create works of art.

Objectives

 Art History and Culture

To demonstrate knowledge of the life and art of John Hoover and Louise Nevelson

 Creative Expression

To plan and create a relief sculpture that shows three-dimensional rhythm

 Aesthetic Perception

To identify three-dimensional rhythm in art and the environment

 Art Criticism

To use the four steps of art criticism to evaluate their own works of art

Vocabulary ⭐ Vocabulary

Review the following vocabulary with students before beginning the lesson.

three-dimensional rhythm ritmo tridimensional—the principle of design that indicates movement by the repetition of elements in a form.

See page 179B for additional vocabulary and Spanish vocabulary resources.

 Art Journal: Vocabulary

Have students add the word to the Vocabulary section of their Art Journals.

Lesson Materials

- cardboard rectangle for background
- pencils
- ballpoint pens
- glue
- yarn
- aluminum foil, 2" longer than cardboard background on all sides
- crayons

Alternate Materials:
- heavy cord

Program Resources

- *Reading and Writing Test Prep.,* pp. 64–65
- *Transparency 30*
- *Artist Profiles,* pp. 24, 43
- *Animals Through History Time Line*
- *Assessment,* pp. 67–68
- *Large Prints 45 Baby* and *46 Untitled*
- *The National Museum of Women in the Arts Collection*

Concept Trace
Three-Dimensional Rhythm
Introduced: Level 2, Unit 4, Lesson 4
Reinforced: Level 4, Unit 2, Lesson 6

Lesson 6 Arts Integration

Theatre

Complete Unit 5, Lesson 6 on pages 100–105 of *Theatre Arts Connections.*

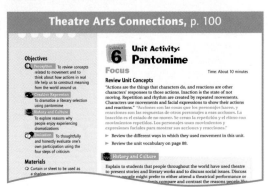

Music

 In ensemble music there may be as many rhythm patterns as there are performers. Listen to "Hunt the Squirrel" from *Suite on English Country Tunes* by Benjamin Britten. Listen for different instrumental voices playing separate rhythms, and hear how it all fits together beautifully.

Movement & Dance

Have students perform simple gestures in different directions. For example, have students reach their arms out in front, then above the head or down to the floor, then out to the sides. Discuss with students how they are moving in three dimensions (front and back, up and down, and side to side). Repeat the gestures to create rhythm.

ocus

Time: About 10 minutes

Activate Prior Knowledge

"Think of a set of building blocks. Are some of the forms the same? Where else have you seen repeating forms?" *"Piensen en un grupo de bloques de construcción. ¿Son algunas de las formas iguales? ¿Dónde han visto formas repetidas?"*

■ Discuss student responses to the questions.

Using Literature ⭐ Reading

■ Read *Night in the Country* by Cynthia Rylant. Discuss with students examples of three-dimensional rhythm in their own neighborhoods, such as fruit on trees, townhomes arranged in a row, and so on.

Thematic Connection ⭐ Science

■ **Natural Resources:** Both of the works of art in this lesson are made of wood. Discuss with students the importance of trees for ecosystems and for society.

Introduce the Art   NSAE 3.a

Look

■ "Let's look at the two works of art." *"Vamos a observar detalladamente estas dos obras de arte".*

Comparing and Contrasting ⭐ Reading

■ Have students describe the subject matter in each artwork. Both works of art are three dimensional. They both have forms that are repeated within the sculptures. *Looner Eclipse* is a representational piece of art, which displays human and animal forms. *Case with Five Baluster* is a nonobjective work. Its forms are not carved—it is assembled, and every shape was already formed and joined together to create a sculpture.

 Art History and Culture

Discuss with students how Hoover bases the subject matter of his artwork on Native Alaskan legends and stories. Occasionally he creates his own stories in the Native Alaskan tradition. Discuss with students how all artwork is a reflection of culture.

🖥 **Web Connection**
Visit **www.heard.org/exhibits-events.php** to learn more about Native American art history and culture.

  Three-Dimensional Rhythm

◄ **John Hoover.** (American). *Looner Eclipse.* 1999.
Cedar. 40 × 48 inches (101.6 × 121.92 cm.). Private Collection.

Look at the works of art on these pages. *Looner Eclipse* shows birds sitting on the moon, pushing it down. The four birds across the top of the moon create rhythm. *Case with Five Baluster* shows jumbled repetitions of triangles, rectangles, circles, and curves. If you could hear this work, it would have three movements. Both artists have used three-dimensional rhythm in their works of art.

 Art History and Culture

John Hoover, a native of Alaska, created a sculpture about the legends and stories of the native people of Alaska.

Art History and Culture

John Hoover

John Hoover (jän hōō´vər) was born in 1919 Cordova, Alaska, to an Aluet-Russian mother and a German father. His early involvement in boat building inspired his interest in sculpture. Hoover bases much of his artwork on myths and legends and creates his own artistic narratives, often including the representation of a human form in his carvings.

As one of the most respected contemporary Native American sculptors, Hoover has exhibited around the country.

See pages 24–25 and 16–21 for more about art history and subject matter.

Artist Profiles, p. 24

◆ Artist Profile ◆
John Hoover
b. 1919

John Hoover (jän hōō´vər) was born in Cordova, Alaska, to an Aleut-Russian mother and a German father. Growing up, he spent a lot of time fishing and making art, and his early involvement in boat building inspired his interest in sculpture. Hoover has always been fascinated with traditional Northwest Coast Native American carvings, and continues to reference them in his work today. As one of the most respected contemporary Native American sculptors, Hoover has exhibited around the country and continues to make art at his home in Washington.

Study both works of art. How did the artists use rhythm in their works of art?

▶ How did the artists create rhythm?

▶ Describe the shapes that are repeated.

▶ Which artwork uses a variety of different shapes?

▲ **Louise Nevelson.**
(American). *Case with Five Baluster.* 1959.

Painted wood. 27 ⅜ × 63 ⅜ × 9 ½ inches (68.58 × 160.02 × 24.13 cm.).
Walker Art Center, Minneapolis, Minnesota.

 Aesthetic Perception

Design Awareness Look around the classroom to see different shapes that repeat.

Art History and Culture

Louise Nevelson

Louise Nevelson (lū ēz´ nev´əl sən) is one of the most important and successful American sculptors of the twentieth century. She was born in Kiev, Russia. Her family re-settled in Rockland, Maine when she was five years old. While a child, she began assembling wood scraps from her father's contracting business. Her education was rich and varied, including music, theatre, dance, and visual art. She studied in New York, New York and Paris, France. Her works are found at many public sites and are in major museums and private collections throughout Europe and the United States.

See pages 24–25 and 16–21 for more about art history and subject matter.

Artist Profiles, p. 43

◆ Artist Profile ◆
Louise Nevelson
1900-1988
Louise Nevelson (lōō ēz´ ne´ val san), one of the most important and successful American sculptors of the twentieth century, was born in Kiev, Russia. Her family resettled in Rockland, Maine, when she was five years old. As a child she began assembling wood scraps from her father's contracting business. Her education was rich and varied, including music, theatre, dance, and visual art. She studied in New York, New York and Paris, France. At first she made both paintings and sculptures, but eventually concentrated on sculpture, which she exhibited irregularly from the 1930s onward. It was not until the late 1950s that she began to receive critical acclaim. Before her death, she had received more

Study

▶ Rhythm: *Looner Eclipse* and *Case with Five Baluster* show rhythm by repeating similar objects in each work.

▶ Repeated shapes: *Looner Eclipse:* The rhythm in this piece is the repetition of the four loons across the top of the moon. The turning of their heads creates a dance-like rhythm. *Case with Five Baluster:* Large beats of the curved balusters on the right and the vertically stacked cylinders on the left, and then the quicker beats of the jumbled repetitions of triangles, rectangles, circles and curves, and freeform forms near the center of the work.

▶ Various shapes: *Case with Five Baluster* has a variety of shapes.

■ For more art by Louise Nevelson, see *The National Museum of Women in the Arts Collection.*

Art Journal: Writing
Encourage students to write their own explanations of three-dimensional rhythm in the Concepts section of their Art Journals. What else do they want to know about three-dimensional rhythm?

Aesthetic Perception

Design Awareness Discuss with students the shapes and forms that repeat in the classroom to create three-dimensional rhythm.

Developing Visual Literacy *Looner Eclipse* illustrates an event from a Native Alaskan story. Discuss with students how illustrations contribute to the text of stories. How does an artist's choice of style and media contribute to the text's meaning?

NSAE 3.a

Web Connection
Visit **www.walkerart.org** to learn more about the Walker Art Center.

Teach

Time: About 45 minutes

"How can you make three-dimensional rhythmic patterns using objects found around the classroom?" "¿Cómo pueden hacer patrones rítmicos tridimensionales usando objetos del salón de clases?"

■ Read and discuss three-dimensional rhythm on page 178.

Practice

Materials: books, pencils, crayons

■ Review the definition of three-dimensional rhythm and have students follow the directions on page 178.

 ## Creative Expression

Materials: cardboard rectangle for background, pencils, ballpoint pens, glue, yarn, aluminum foil 2" longer than cardboard background on all sides, crayons

Alternate Materials: heavy cord

■ Distribute the materials and have students follow the directions on page 179.

■ Review the Activity Tips on page 246 for visual examples of techniques if needed.

Art Journal: Brainstorming

Have students brainstorm ways they can create three-dimensional rhythm and write their ideas in their Art Journals. Then have students select three or four items they will use and plan how they will show those items in the Creative Expression activity.

Using Three-Dimensional Rhythm

Three-dimensional rhythm is a principle of design that indicates movement by the repetition of elements in a form.

In three-dimensional art there are different ways an artist can create rhythm. One way is by repeating several negative spaces in a work where a number of holes are carved into it. Another way is by organizing and repeating similar forms, or by repeating textures on forms such as hair texture or fur texture.

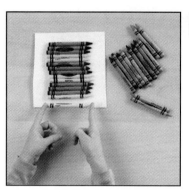

Practice

In groups of five, role-play to create a sense of rhythm.

1. Look around the classroom for three-dimensional materials, such as books on the shelf.

2. In small groups, experiment with the objects to find rhythmic patterns.

3. Place the objects in such a way that the rest of the class can identify the rhythmic pattern.

178 Unit 5 • Lesson 6

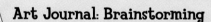

Differentiated Instruction

Reteach

Have students look through the book to find other sculptures that show rhythm.

Special Needs

Some students may have difficulty applying the right amount of pressure to the foil and may end up tearing their artwork. To avoid this, purchase high quality foil and allow each student to practice the process on a small sample piece.

ELL Tips

You may wish to use this lesson to focus on vocabulary development for all your students. Create a list to describe the objects mentioned in the Practice activity. Then make a corresponding list of descriptive words relating to those objects.

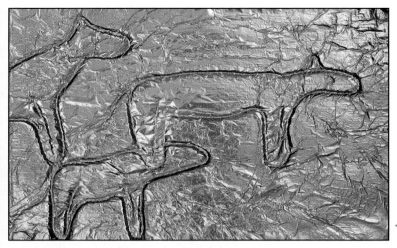

◀ **Leah Goode.**
Age 8.

Think about how the student artist used three-dimensional rhythm.

 Creative Expression

How can you create a relief sculpture of repeating animal forms?

1. Think about an animal you would like to use. Look at pictures of that animal.

2. Make sketches of the animal. Select your best sketches and draw the animal several times on the cardboard to create a rhythmic repetition of the animal.

3. Glue yarn over the outlines of your animals.

4. Cover the surface with aluminum foil. Start pressing foil near the center. As you work, gently press the foil around each raised line with your fingertips.

Art Criticism

Describe What animals did you choose for your artwork?

Analyze Describe the rhythm of the animals in your artwork.

Interpret Give your work an expressive title.

Decide Were you successful in creating an animal relief design?

Unit 5 • Lesson 6 **179**

Reflect Time: About 5 minutes

Review and Assess

"What kinds of three-dimensional rhythm can artists use in their work?" "¿Qué tipos de ritmo tridimensional pueden usar los artistas en sus obras?"

Think

The artist created three-dimensional rhythm by placing space between the animals.

Informal Assessment

Art Journal: Critical Thinking
Have students answer the four art criticism questions—Describe, Analyze, Interpret, and Decide—in their Art Journals. In small groups, have students discuss the use of three-dimensional rhythm in their works of art.

■ Collect and display works by John Hoover and other Native American artists. (For examples, see the *Art Around the World* collection.) Ask: What are the main ideas of these works? How have the artists used rhythm? Have students discuss the works using the four steps of art criticism.

■ For standardized-format test practice using this lesson's art content, see pages 64–65 in *Reading and Writing Test Preparation.*

NSAE 3.a

Art Across the Curriculum

Use these simple ideas to reinforce art concepts across the curriculum.

★ **Narrative Writing** Have students write a short story based on the artwork they made in the Creative Expression activity.

★ **Math** Have students arrange geometric solids to create three-dimensional rhythm.

★ **Science** Have students look for three-dimensional rhythm in nature.

★ **Social Studies** Discuss the stories and traditions of native peoples the students are studying in class.

★ **Technology** Have students attach their narrative story to an e-mail and send it to a friend. Visit **SRAonline.com** for detailed instructions for this activity.

NSAE 6.a, 6.b

LESSON 6 • Three-Dimensional Rhythm **179**

Lesson 6 Wrap-Up

Three-Dimensional Rhythm

Extra! For the Art Specialist

Time: About 45 minutes

Focus

Use *Transparency 30* to discuss ways that artists use three-dimensional rhythm. What did the artist use to create rhythm in the artwork? Does the artwork have tactile or visual texture? How did the artist create texture in the artwork? Does the texture help establish the three-dimensional rhythm of the artwork? Would the artwork have the same impact without the texture?

Teach

Have students follow directions on creating a community celebration collage.

Close

Have students evaluate their artwork using the four steps of art criticism.

Alternate Activity

Materials:
- 12" × 18" light-color construction paper
- 6" × 9" pieces of construction paper
- fabric scraps
- scissors
- white glue
- buttons, ribbon, rickrack, feathers, etc.
- crayons or colored markers

1. Have students think of a community event or celebration. Ask them to envision a motif that represents their selected event, such as a flag, dancers, members of a marching band, etc.

2. Explain that the students will be making a collage picture of their event, and repeating the motif they have selected to give their composition rhythm.

3. Students will make the background of their composition first, adding details with crayons or colored markers.

4. When the backgrounds are completed, students will cut multiples of their motifs that represent the selected event. The motifs will be glued to the collage to create a rhythmic design.

Research in Art Education

Case studies have indicated that students perceive "that the arts facilitate their personal and social development." It also appeared that to gain the full benefit of arts education, students should be exposed to all of the arts, including fine arts, dance, theatre, and music ("Arts Education in Secondary School: Effects and Effectiveness" in *Critical Links*, p. 76).

Assessment

Use the following rubric to evaluate the artwork students make in the Creative Expression activity and to assess students' understanding of three-dimensional rhythm.

Have students complete page 67 or 68 in their *Assessment* books.

	Art History and Culture	Aesthetic Perception	Creative Expression	Art Criticism
3 POINTS	The student demonstrates knowledge of the life and art of John Hoover and Louise Nevelson.	The student accurately identifies three-dimensional rhythm in their works of art and the environment.	The student effectively creates a relief sculpture that shows three-dimensional rhythm.	The student evaluates his or her own work using the four steps of art criticism.
2 POINTS	The student demonstrates some knowledge of the life and art of John Hoover and Louise Nevelson.	The student shows emerging awareness of three-dimensional rhythm in their works of art and the environment.	The student shows some awareness of how to create a relief sculpture that shows three-dimensional rhythm.	The student attempts to evaluate his or her own work using the four steps of art criticism.
1 POINT	The student cannot demonstrate knowledge of the life and art of John Hoover and Louise Nevelson.	The student cannot identify three-dimensional rhythm in their works of art or the environment.	The student cannot create a relief sculpture that shows three-dimensional rhythm.	The student makes no attempt to evaluate his or her own work using the four steps of art criticism.

Assessment, page. 67

Name _____ Date _____ Lesson **6** UNIT 5

Three-Dimensional Rhythm

A. Vocabulary

1. Define *three-dimensional rhythm.*

2. Explain two ways artists can create three-dimensional rhythm in forms.
   a. _____
   b. _____

B. Drawing

Draw two pictures illustrating the two ways to create three-dimensional rhythm that you explained in question 2.

C. Writing

Look at *Case with Five Baluster.* On the back of this paper, describe how Louise Nevelson created three-dimensional rhythm in her work of art.

Level 3   Unit 5 • Pattern, Rhythm, and Movement **67**

179A UNIT 5 • Pattern, Rhythm, and Movement

Unit 5 Vocabulary Review

alternating pattern—visual pattern set up by repeating motifs, but with changing position or content of motifs or spaces between them **patrón alterno**—patrón visual erigido por motivos que se repiten, pero con cambio de posicion o contenido de motivos o espacios entre ellos

motif—a unit that is repeated in visual rhythm or pattern. Units in a motif may or may not be an exact duplicate of the first unit **motivo**—una unidad que se repite en un ritmo visual o patrón. Unidades en un motivo puede o no ser copias exactas de la primera unidad

pattern—two-dimensional visual art that has no movement and may or may not have rhythm **patrón**—arte visual bidimensional que no tiene movimiento y puede o no tener ritmo

random pattern—motifs that appear in no apparent order and have irregular spaces between them **patrón al azar**—motivos que aparecen sin un orden aparente y tienen espacios irregulares entre ellos

regular pattern—visual rhythm achieved through repeating identical motifs, using the same intervals of space between them **patrón regular**—ritmo visual logrado, por medios de motivos idénticos repetidos

rest—the negative space or emptiness between the beats in visual rhythm **pausa**—el espacio negativo o el vacío entre los latidos en un ritmo visual

rhythm—a feeling of movement, created by using the same types of lines, shapes, or colors several times in a work of art **ritmo**—un sentido de movimiento creado usando los mismos tipos de líneas, figuras o colores varias vecés en una obra de arte

three-dimensional rhythm—the principle of design that indicates movement by the repetition of elements in a form **ritmo tridimensional**—el principio del diseño que indica movimiento por los elementos repetidos en una forma

visual rhythm—a feeling of movement created by using the same types of lines, shapes, or colors several times in a work of art **ritmo visual**—un sentido de movimiento creado usando los mismos tipos de líneas, figuras o colores varias veces en una obra de arte

Vocabulary Practice

T Display *Transparency 41* to review unit vocabulary words.

Reference Skills ⭐ Vocabulary

Have students practice alphabetizing. Remind students that when they are trying to locate a word in the dictionary they will often have to alphabetize the second and third letters. Have each student write down five vocabulary words that begin with same letter. Ask volunteers to put their words in alphabetical order.

Definitions: Demonstrate Meanings ⭐ Vocabulary

Display *Large Prints 45 Baby* and *46 Untitled*. Have volunteers select a vocabulary word, such as *motif,* and explain how it is shown in the works of art.

Other References ⭐ Vocabulary

Allow students to find out more about the vocabulary words by using various resources such as electronic encyclopedias, the Internet, and dictionaries.

Pattern, Rhythm, and Movement

Wrapping Up Unit 5

Pattern, Rhythm, and Movement

▲ **Mir Sayyid 'Ali.** (Persian). *Nighttime in a Palace.* c. 1539–1543.

Opaque watercolor, gold, and silver on paper. 11.26 × 7.87 inches (28.6 × 20 cm.). Arthur M. Sackler Museum, Harvard University, Cambridge, Massachusetts.

Art Criticism

Critical Thinking Art criticism is an organized system for looking at and talking about art. You can criticize art without being an expert. The purpose of art criticism is to get the viewer involved in a perception process that delays judgment until all aspects of the artwork have been studied.

■ See page 28–29 for more about art criticism.

Describe

▶ Possible answers: Brightly colored robes or tunics, some with long sleeveless coats over them. The women wear white shawls that cover their heads and shoulders. The men wear turbans of white, black or brown. People are performing many tasks in this palace. At the bottom, musicians are playing, and men are carrying trays of food. Above the musicians, someone important is sitting on a raised platform. Above him, we see a group of women.

▶ Possible answers: In the upper left corner, there is a cat. Near the top center, a white dog looks down from a roof.

Analyze

▶ Possible answers: Behind the figure in the arched doorway, there is a wall pattern of six-pointed stars.

▶ Possible answers: Regular patterns appear on the walls and the floors throughout the painting.

▶ Possible answers: In the bottom section, the figure in blue wears an alternating flower pattern.

Art History and Culture

Mir Sayyid Ali

Mir Sayyid Ali (mēr sä´yēd äl´ ē) was considered one of the great masters of Iranian Mughal painting during the Safavid Dynasty. Mughal Art is an Indo-Islamic-Persian style of painting and architecture that originated in and around India and Pakistan during the Mughal Empire. During the time that *Nighttime in a Palace* was created, Mir Sayyid Ali worked in the imperial studio of Shah Tahmasp I, a notable Safavid patron of the arts.

Nighttime in a Palace is a watercolor miniature that depicts a lively scene from the court of Bihzad Palace of the Safavid dynasty, which was located in what is today the country of Iran.

Artist Profiles, p. 4

Artist Profile

Mir Sayyid Ali

Mir Sayyid Ali (mēr sä´ yēd äl´ ē) was one of the great masters of Iranian Mughal painting during the Safavid dynasty. The Safavid dynasty, between 1499 and 1722 A.D., saw the production of some of the most ornate and exquisite mural paintings, ink drawings, illustrations, and portraits in history. Mughal art is an Indo-Islamic-Persian style of painting and architecture that originated in and around India and Pakistan during the Mughal Empire. During the time that *Nighttime in a Palace* was created, Mir Sayyid Ali worked in the imperial studio of Shah Tahmasp I, a notable Safavid patron of the arts. In 1549, Mir Sayyid Ali left the Safavid court and began to work for the Mughal emperor Humayun, who was in exile in Kabul. In

 **Art Criticism** Critical Thinking

Describe **What do you see?**

Describe the people. What are they wearing and what are they doing?
▶ What animals do you see?

Analyze **How is this work organized?**

Where do you see patterns?
▶ Where do you see regular patterns?
▶ Where do you see alternating patterns?

Interpret **What is the artist trying to say?**

What do you think is happening in this painting?
▶ Does one person seem to stand out?
▶ Look at the upper-left corner. Who do you think the elderly couple is?
▶ Is this a calm or active painting? Explain.

Decide **What do you think about the work?**

Is the work successful because it is realistic, well organized, or because it has a strong message? Explain.

Unit 5 **181**

Interpret

▶ Discuss with students what is happening in the painting. Answers will vary: Students may say there is a party going on in the palace, with music, food, visitors, and many people helping to prepare and serve food. Does it look as though one person stands out in the painting? Possible answers: The man in red seated under the arched doorway sits higher than the people in front of him. His clothing has many decorative patterns. The others in the room face him. His position near the center of the picture may also indicate that he is of higher rank.

▶ Who is the elderly couple in the upper left hand corner? Possible answers: Students may say they are the grandparents of the family who lives in the palace.

▶ Does the painting seem calm or active? Answers will vary. Students may say this painting has a festive or busy feeling because all the people seem to be moving and doing something. Some may say the busy patterns and repeating rhythms make it look busy.

Decide

▶ Is this painting successful because it is realistic, well organized, or because it has a strong message? Answers will vary: Most will talk about the storytelling aspect of the work. They may question the realism of the work because the composition is different from Western perspective.

Art Journal: Writing
Have students write answers to the Aesthetic Perception in their Art Journals.

 Aesthetic Perception

Seeing Like an Artist Think about different activities that go on in your home after dinner.

Describe ▶ List what kinds of activites people are doing in your home after dinner.

Analyze ▶ How would the activities create a visual rhythm?

Interpret ▶ Write a story about all the activities that go on in your home.

Decide ▶ Do you think other families do these activities?

"Artists often use a variety of patterns and rhythm to create a sense of movement in their works of art." *"Los artistas a menudo usan una variedad de patrones y ritmos para crear una sensación de movimiento en sus obras de arte".*

T Review unit vocabulary with students using *Transparency 41.*

> ### Art Journal: Writing
> Have students answer the questions on page 182 in their Art Journals or on a separate sheet of paper. Answers: 1. A, 2. A, 3. C, 4. C, 5. A

T For further assessment, have students complete the unit test on *Transparency 47.*

LEARNING ABOUT CAREERS IN ART
Graphic Design

▶ In small groups, have students discuss various forms of media that a graphic designer was instrumental in creating.

A graphic designer designs art and copy layouts for visual presentations. This could include designing promotional displays, marketing brochures, and developing logos for products for businesses. They use a variety of film media, print, and electronic computer software to develop new images. Graphic designers must possess strong abilities to be creative and design eye catching and effective graphics.

"Art transfigures while it transfixes—it is art that molds, remakes and preserves.

—André Malraux

Pattern, Rhythm, and Movement, continued

Show What You Know

Answer these questions on a separate sheet of paper.

1 A motif is used to create a _____.
A. pattern
B. rhythm
C. movement

2 _____ has a beat—the positive shape or form—and a rest—the negative space between the beats.
A. Visual rhythm
B. Pattern
C. Flowing rhythm

3 In _____ rhythm, there are no sudden changes in line or breaks in movement.
A. movement
B. flowing
C. visual

4 The repetition of a motif with equal amounts of space between is a/an _____.
A. alternating pattern
B. random pattern
C. regular pattern

5 Repeating motifs with changes in position or content are _____.
A. alternating patterns
B. alternating motifs
C. motifs

182 Unit 5

CAREERS IN ART
Graphic Design

Graphic Designers design magazines, ads, and promotional material. The job requires familiarity with type, color, and layout.

Audio Visual Designers develop slide presentations from a series of drawings and collages given to them by clients. A script and soundtrack are added to complete the presentation. This talent for balancing imagery and sound makes audio visual designers an important part of the presentation process.

▲ **Graphic Designer**

Unit Assessment Options

Aesthetic Perception

Practice Have students select two concepts from the Show What You Know section on page 182 and find examples of each in the classroom.

Creative Expression

Student Portfolio Have students review all the artwork they have created during this unit and select the pieces they wish to keep in their portfolio.

Art Criticism

Activity Create a class exhibition. Have students comment on the works of art using the four steps of art criticism. (See pages 28–29 for more information about Art Criticism.)

Pattern, Rhythm, and Movement in Dance

▲ African American Dance ensemble. "Isicathulo."

Isicathulo is a Zulu step dance from South Africa. Zulu dockworkers and gold miners perform clever, syncopated routines accompanied by a guitar and whistle. They create rhythmic dances by organizing their well-rehearsed patterns of movement.

What to Do Make rhythmic patterns of sounds that can be organized different ways to create dances.

1. Create a rhythmic movement that can be repeated. Include slapping your legs, stomping your feet, snapping your fingers, clapping, or hopping. Give your pattern a name.

2. Form groups of three students. Each person shares one pattern and teaches it to the others.

3. Practice all the patterns in a line formation, either shoulder-to-shoulder or in single-file, and perform in unison.

4. Choose a leader to call out the name of each pattern to be performed.

 Art Criticism

Describe What pattern names did your group learn?

Analyze Does the name of each pattern provide a clue for the movement?

Interpret Did the rhythmic patterns "feel" right? Did you change them to work better?

Decide Were you successful in making the rhythm and movements work together?

Unit 5 **183**

 Art History and Culture

Zulus of South Africa

Dr. Chuck Davis, Artistic Director of the African American Dance Ensemble, says, "To understand the culture, study the dance. To understand the dance, study the people." In 1977 he took his first trip to Africa to "sit at the feet of the elders." He returns every year to research the history of specific ethnic groups and learn how each dance is connected to the society. This popular dance is now widely performed by other African groups, as well as African Americans. It is often performed by the workers at the gold mines in Southern Africa.

Patterns, Rhythm, and Movement in Dance

Objective: To create rhythmic movement patterns that can be performed in unison

Materials: *Isicathulo*, performed by the African American Dance Ensemble. Running Time 4:37

Focus
Time: About 5 minutes

■ Discuss the information on page 183.

 **Art History and Culture**

■ Have students experiment with different rhythmic movement patterns composed of clapping, slapping, clicking and stamping.

Teach
Time: About 20 minutes

 Aesthetic Perception

■ Have students discuss *Isicathulo* and how dances change.

 Creative Expression

■ Have each student create a rhythmic sound and movement pattern. Give each pattern a name.

■ Have students work in groups to share their individual routines. Encourage students to practice each in unison. A leader calls out the name of each routine.

Reflect
Time: About 10 minutes

 **Art Criticism**

■ Have students answer the four art criticism questions on page 183 aloud or in writing.

■ Did students create original rhythmic routines which they performed in unison with groups?

Unit 6 Planning Guide

	Lesson Title	Suggested Pacing	Creative Expression Activity
Lesson 1	**Harmony**	About two 30-minute periods.	Plan and create a figural clay bowl that illustrates harmony.
Lesson 2	**Variety**	About two 30-minute periods.	Create a weaving using a variety of colors and textures.
Lesson 3	**Emphasis**	55 minutes	Create a computer drawing with an area of emphasis.
Lesson 4	**Emphasis Through Decoration**	60 minutes	Create a book cover with emphasis.
Lesson 5	**Unity Through Color**	60 minutes	Create a clay fish that is unified by color.
Lesson 6	**Unity, Repetition, and Grouping**	45 minutes	Create a crayon engraving that shows unity.
ART SOURCE ARTSOURCE	**Harmony, Variety, Emphasis, and Unity in Dance**	35 minutes	Create a dance or mime showing a variety of pioneer work movements.

Materials	Program Resources	Fine Art Resources	Literature Resources
clay, clay tools, clay mat, acrylic paint or glaze	*Reading and Writing Test Preparation,* pp. 66–67 *Flash Cards,* 17 and 18 *Assessment,* pp. 69–70 *Home and After-School Connections*	*Transparency,* 31 *Artist Profiles,* pp. 60, 70 *Large Prints,* 47 and 48 *Women in the Arts Collection*	*May'naise Sandwiches & Sunshine Tea* by Sandra Belton
9" × 12" pieces of cardboard, rulers, pencils, scissors, string, a variety of yarns and natural fibers	*Reading and Writing Test Preparation,* pp. 68–69 *Flash Cards,* 16 and 18 *Assessment,* pp. 71–72	*Transparency,* 32 *Artist Profiles,* pp. 27, 61 *Large Prints,* 47 and 48 *Art Around the World*	*Alex Is My Friend* by Marisabina Russo
computer's paint program	*Reading and Writing Test Preparation,* pp. 70–71 *Flash Card,* 15 *Assessment,* pp. 73–74	*Transparency,* 33 *Artist Profiles,* pp. 12, 84 *Large Prints,* 47 and 48 *Women in the Arts Collection*	*My Life with the Wave* by Catherine Cowan
drawing paper, construction paper, tapestry needle, watercolors, paintbrushes, water dishes, newspaper, paper towels, embroidery floss or string, medium-sized beads	*Reading and Writing Test Preparation,* pp. 72–73 *Flash Card,* 15 *Assessment,* pp. 75–76	*Transparency,* 34 *Artist Profiles,* pp. 53, 63 *Large Prints,* 47 and 48 *Art Around the World*	*The Worry Stone* by Marianna Dengler
clay, clay mat, clay tools (pencils, paper clips, toothpicks, forks), glazes	*Reading and Writing Test Preparation,* pp. 74–75 *Flash Card,* 18 *Assessment,* pp. 77–78	*Transparency,* 35 *Artist Profiles,* pp. 32, 57 *Large Prints,* 47 and 48 *Art Around the World*	*Unseen Rainbows, Silent Songs* by Susan E. Goodman
9" × 12" white paper, pencils, crayons, large paper clips, washable black ink, paintbrushes	*Reading and Writing Test Preparation,* pp. 76–77 *Flash Card,* 18 *Assessment,* pp. 79–80	*Transparency,* 36 *Artist Profiles,* pp. 13, 39 *Large Prints,* 47 and 48 *Women in the Arts Collection*	*Birds, Nests and Eggs* by Mel Boring
"Billy the Kid" performed by the Joffrey Ballet of Chicago. Running time: 8:36.			

Unit Overview

6 Harmony, Variety, Emphasis, and Unity

Lesson 1: Harmony is the peaceful look made when related elements of art are put together.

Lesson 2: Variety is using different lines, shapes, colors, and textures to make a work of art look interesting.

Lesson 3: Emphasis makes a part of an artwork stand out. Artists can create emphasis in different ways.

Lesson 4: One way an artist can create **emphasis** is **through decoration**.

Lesson 5: Unity is a feeling that everything in an artwork belongs together.

Lesson 6: Artists can create **unity** by using **repetition and grouping** in a work of art.

Introduce Unit Concepts

"Artists create harmony, variety, emphasis, and unity in their works of art." "Los artistas crean armonía, variedad, énfasis y unidad en sus obras de arte".

Harmony and Variety
- Have students suggest words or phrases that come to mind when you say the word *harmony*, such as *getting along*, or *music*. Ask students to list a *variety* of games they like to play. Discuss the similarities and differences among their responses.

Emphasis and Unity
- Repeat a sentence, putting the emphasis on a different word each time. Ask students to identify the word you emphasized each time. Discuss that the sentence has unity because all words are in the same language.

Cross-Curricular Projects
- See the *Language Arts and Reading, Mathematics, Science*, and *Social Studies Art Connections* books for activities that further develop harmony, variety, emphasis, and unity concepts.

NSAE 6.b

Harmony, Variety, Emphasis, and Unity

Artists create harmony, variety, emphasis, and unity in their works of art.

Frederic Remington's use of line, color, and texture created harmony, variety, emphasis, and unity in this form.

◀ **Frederic Remington.** (American). *Mountain Man.* 1903.
Bronze. The Carleton Collection.

184 Unit 6

Fine Art Prints

Display **Large Prints 47** *Group Portrait* and **48** *Hoosick Falls, N.Y. in Winter.* Refer to the prints throughout the unit as students learn about harmony, variety, emphasis, and unity.

Large Print 47

Large Print 48

Artists use **harmony** to make works of art look pleasing or peaceful.

► Where do you see lines in *Mountain Man* that are similar?

Artists use **variety** to create interest.

► Describe at least two different textures that you see.

Artists use **emphasis** to create a center of interest in their works.

► Which part of the artwork draws your attention most?

Harmony and variety create a feeling of **unity** in an artwork.

► What unifies this sculpture?

In This Unit you will learn and practice techniques for creating harmony, variety, and emphasis. You will also learn how harmony and variety create a feeling of unity.

Here are the topics you will study:
► Harmony
► Variety
► Emphasis
► Unity

Self-Portrait on a Horse.

Frederic Remington
(1861–1909)

Frederic Remington was born in Canton, New York, on October 1, 1861. As a young boy, he loved to draw Native Americans, cowboys, soldiers, and horses. When he was 19 years old, he left college and traveled west. He spent four years as a cowboy and a rancher and sketched everything he saw. His artwork focuses on the American West.

Unit 6 **185**

Examine the Artwork

"Let's look closely at the sculpture."
"Vamos a mirar detalladamente la escultura".

■ Have students look at Remington's sculpture *Mountain Man*. Ask them to describe what they see.

■ Have students answer the questions about harmony, variety, emphasis, and unity on page 185.

► Most of the lines in the sculpture are diagonal.

► The man's helmet and rifle have a smooth texture, while the man's hair, the horse's tail, and the rock have a rough texture.

► The man draws the viewer's attention first because he was sculpted with more detail than the horse or the rock.

► The bronze medium and the color of the *Mountain Man* unifies the sculpture.

Unit Pretest

T Display *Transparency 48* as a pretest. Answers: 1. B, 2. A, 3. A, 4. C, 5. B

Home Connection

■ See *Home and After-School Connections* for family newsletters and activities for this unit.

Art History and Culture

NSAE 4.a; 4.b; 4.c; 5.a; 5.b

Frederic Remington

Frederic Remington (fre´ drik re´ ming tən) is famous for his realistic portrayal of the American West, a subject that was the focus of his life's work. His work was first recognized in 1885, when American interest was directed to the West, and a great demand for his work resulted. He made numerous trips out West throughout his life, drawing, painting, illustrating, sculpting, and writing the drama of the land and its people.

See pages 16–21 and 24–25 for more about subject matter and art history.

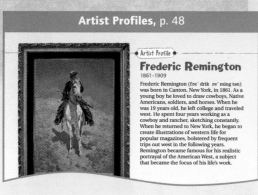

Artist Profiles, p. 48

● Artist Profile ●

Frederic Remington
1861–1909

Frederic Remington (fre´ drik re´ ming tan) was born in Canton, New York, in 1861. As a young boy he loved to draw cowboys, Native Americans, soldiers, and horses. When he was 19 years old, he left college and traveled west. He spent four years working as a cowboy and rancher, sketching constantly. When he returned to New York, he began to create illustrations of western life for popular magazines, bolstered by frequent trips out west in the following years. Remington became famous for his realistic portrayal of the American West, a subject that became the focus of his life's work.

NSAE 2.a; 2.b; 3.a

ILLUSTRATOR PROFILE
Arnold Lobel
(1933-1987)

Arnold Lobel remembered his childhood in Schenectady, New York, as mostly happy in spite of a series of childhood illnesses that required extended stays in the hospital. As an adolescent, Lobel became stronger, healthier, and determined to pursue a career in art.

Lobel studied art at the Pratt Institute in Brooklyn, where he met his wife, Anita, also an author and illustrator of children's books. Lobel illustrated his first children's book, *Red Tag Comes Back*, in 1961, and subsequently illustrated more than 60 books by other authors. *A Zoo for Mr. Muster* (1962) marked Lobel's first turn as both author and illustrator. He went on to publish many more children's books, with friendship as a recurring theme. This theme is prominent in Lobel's beloved *Frog and Toad* books.

Of his work as an illustrator, Lobel said, "I never like to use the same illustrative technique over and over, but rather use a repertory of styles as they suit the mood of the manuscript." His books include two- and three-color pencil drawings, full-color pencil drawings, as well as illustrations created with black and white pen and ink.

Music

Harmony in music refers to different pitches played or sung at the same time to produce chords. *Unity* and *variety*, created by rhythm patterns and speed, give each composition its identify and character.

Literature

Show the video or DVD *Meet Leo Lionni*. Discuss his life and how he feels about the importance of the arts.

Literature and Art

Dance

Show *Billy the Kid* and discuss how harmony, variety, emphasis, and unity are present in the ballet.

Artsource®

Lesson 1 introduces harmony, which is the peaceful look made when related elements of art are put together.

Objectives

 Art History and Culture

To compare functional pottery by Nancy Youngblood and Japanese artists
NSAE 1.a; 2.a; 3.a; 4.a; 5.a

 Creative Expression

To plan and create a figural clay bowl that illustrates harmony
NSAE 1.a; 1.c; 1.d; 2.c; 3.b

 Aesthetic Perception

To identify how artists create harmony with related colors, similar shapes, and repetition NSAE 2.a; 2.b

 **Art Criticism**

To use the four steps of art criticism to evaluate one's own work
NSAE 1.b; 2.b; 3.a; 5.c

Vocabulary ⭐ Vocabulary

Review the following vocabulary word with students before beginning the lesson.

harmony armonía—the peaceful look made when related elements of art are put together

See page 209B for additional vocabulary and Spanish vocabulary resources.

 Art Journal: Vocabulary

Have students add this word to the Vocabulary section of their Art Journals.

Lesson Materials

- 9" × 12" paper
- pencils
- markers
- clay
- clay tools (such as pencils, paper clips, or nails)
- clay mat (a square of fabric or burlap)
- acrylic paint or glaze

Alternate Materials:
- crayons
- air-drying clay

Program Resources

- *Reading and Writing Test Prep.*, pp. 66–67
- *Transparency 31*
- *Flash Cards 17* and *18*
- *Artist Profiles*, pp. 60, 70
- *Animals Through History Time Line*
- *Assessment*, pp. 69–70
- *Large Prints 47* Group Portrait and *48* Hoosick Falls, N.Y. in Winter
- *The National Museum of Women in the Arts Collection*

Concept Trace
Harmony
Introduced: Level 2, Unit 6, Lesson 1

Reinforced: Level 4, Unit 6, Lesson 4

Lesson 1 Arts Integration NSAE 6.a

Theatre

Complete Unit 6, Lesson 1, on pages 108–109 of *Theatre Arts Connections*.

Theatre Arts Connections, p. 108

Music

 The life work of Johann Sebastian Bach set down the harmonies that Western music is built upon. Listen to his *Brandenburg Concerto No. 5 last movement*. He wrote six of these concertos, named after the Margrave of Brandenburg who commissioned them.

Movement & Dance

Have three students stand in a triangle shape. One person creates smooth axial movements which are mirrored by the other two. On a cue, the first person then passes (with a movement gesture) the leadership to the next person who takes over and changes level. The group must work to maintain a sense of harmonious energy.

Focus

Time: About 10 minutes

Activate Prior Knowledge

"Think about getting dressed in the morning. Why do you choose clothes with colors that go well together?" *"Piensen en cuando se visten en la mañana. ¿Por qué escogen ropa con colores que pegan?"*

- Discuss students' responses to the question and how related colors give a feeling that things belong together.

Using Literature ⭐ Reading

- Read *May'naise Sandwiches & Sunshine Tea* by Sandra Belton. Discuss the repeated art elements that create harmony in the illustrations by Gail Gordon Carter.

Thematic Connection

- **Music:** Discuss harmony as it relates to music.

Introduce the Art

Look
NSAE 1.a; 2.a; 3.a

"Let's take a close look at the ceramic containers." *"Vamos a mirar detalladamente los envases de cerámica".*

Comparing and Contrasting ⭐ Reading

- Have students list the similarities and differences between the clay vessels. They are all forms, they all have areas of relief, and all repeat such elements as texture and shape. Youngblood's *Pottery Vessels* are in the form of spheres, are glazed, and illustrate regular rhythm. The *Jar* is in the form of a cylinder, is not glazed, and illustrates alternating rhythm.

 Art History and Culture

Possible answer: these works of art could have been used as containers, possibly to hold food or plants. They also could have been used for decoration.
NSAE 5.a

 Web Connection

Visit **www.metmuseum.org/collections/index.asp** to see more works from the Asian art collection.

186 UNIT 6 • Harmony, Variety, Emphasis, and Unity

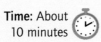

Harmony

Look at the containers on these pages. The *Jar* was created in Japan more than 4,000 years ago. The *Pottery Vessels* were crafted by Nancy Youngblood in the 1980s. All the containers were made with clay. These works contain repeated lines and textures that create harmony.

◀ **Artist Unknown.** (Japan). *Jar.* Middle Jomon period. c. 3000–2000 B.C.
·······································
Earthenware clay with applied, incised, and cord-marked decoration. 27 $\frac{1}{2}$ inches high (69.85 cm.). The Metropolitan Museum of Art, New York, New York.

 **Art History and Culture**

How do you think these containers could have been used in everyday life?

186   Unit 6 • Lesson 1

 Art History and Culture

Jar was created in Japan during the Middle Jomon period, sometime between 3000–2000 B.C. During this period, daily life consisted of hunting, gathering roots and berries, fishing, and collecting shellfish. The Jomon created a great number of ceramics in a wide variety of styles. The earliest artifacts found in Japan are pottery vessels, stone and bone tools, wooden bowls, and figurines. *Jar* is made with earthenware, which is clay fired in a kiln. *Jar* is characteristic of the low-fired pottery that was made with the coiling method. Typically, these pots were decorated with reliefs or impressions of a cord pattern.

See pages 16–21 and 24–25 for more about subject matter and art history.

Artist Profiles, p. 70

> *Artist Profile*
> ## Jar
> The artist of this piece is unknown. The jar was made during the Middle Jomon period of Japanese history. During this period daily life consisted of hunting, gathering roots and berries, fishing, and collecting shellfish. The Jomon created a great number of ceramics in a wide variety of styles.
>
> ◀ **Artist unknown.** (Japan). *Jar.* c. 3000–2000 B.C.
> Earthenware clay with applied, incised, and cord-marked decoration.

◀ **Nancy Youngblood.** (Pueblo, United States). *Pottery Vessels.* 1980–1985.

Pottery. 4 ½ × 6 inches (11.43 × 15.24 cm.). Courtesy Nancy Youngblood.

Study each ceramic piece to find examples of visual harmony.

► Which shapes are repeated?

► Which textures are repeated?

► Locate one of the motifs in each piece.

► Where do you see lines that are repeated?

Aesthetic Perception

Seeing Like an Artist Find a work of art in this book that seems peaceful to you. Which shapes, lines, or colors are repeated in it?

Unit 6 • Lesson 1   **187**

Art History and Culture

Nancy Youngblood   NSAE 4.a; 4.b; 4.c; 5.b

Nancy Youngblood (nân´ sē yəng´ blud) was born in Fort Lewis, Washington. Her mother is Native American and comes from the Tafoya family, who are well-known potters. Youngblood studied at the San Francisco Art Institute on a scholarship. At the age of 21 she had her first major exhibition at Gallery 10 in Scottsdale, Arizona. Youngblood incorporates traditional Southwest Native American styles into her work but still makes each piece distinctly hers. She began to incorporate seashell motifs in her work after a visit to St. Martin's Island in the Caribbean.

See pages 16–21 and 24–25 for more about subject matter and art history.

Artist Profiles, p. 60

◆ Artist Profile ◆

Nancy Youngblood
b. 1955

Nancy Youngblood was born in Fort Lewis, Washington. Her mother is Native American, and her father is of British descent. Her father was in the military, so they moved many times. She has lived on and off in Santa Clara, New Mexico. At a very early age, she wanted to be an artist. She went to the San Franciso Art Institute on a scholarship. Later, she worked in an art gallery, which featured Native American works. The owner, Al Packard, encouraged her to follow in her family's footsteps. She had her first major show when she was 20. Youngblood still lives in Santa Clara and has three sons. She says that each work, which she never rushes to finish, surprises and challenges her.

Study

► The free-form shell shapes are repeated on one of the pots in *Pottery Vessels*.

► The bumpy textures are repeated in *Pottery Vessels*, and the rough, rope texture is repeated in *Jar*.

► The seashells in *Pottery Vessels* are motifs. The incised, curved line at the top of *Jar* is a motif.

► The horizontal lines in *Jar* are repeated.

■ For more examples of utilitarian art see *The National Museum of Women in the Arts Collection.*

Art Journal: Writing

Encourage students to write their own explanation of harmony in the Concepts section of their Art Journals.

Aesthetic Perception

Seeing Like an Artist Have students look through the *Student Edition* to find other examples of works with harmony. Discuss how the repeated elements in each work create harmony.

Developing Visual Literacy Have students imagine they were going to place one of these containers in a room in their home. What shapes, lines, colors, or textures could they use for other decorations in the room to create harmony in the room?

Web Connection

Visit Nancy Youngblood's Web site, **www.nancyyoungbloodinc.com**, to see more of her work.

"How can you create harmony in a work of art?" "¿Cómo pueden crear armonía en una obra de arte?"

■ Discuss the definition of *harmony* and techniques for creating it on page 188.

Practice

Materials: 9" × 12" paper folded into three sections, pencils, and markers

Alternate Materials: crayons

■ Distribute the materials and have students follow the directions on page 188.

NSAE 1.a; 1.c; 1.d; 2.c; 3.b
Materials: clay, clay tools (such as pencils, paper clips, or nails), clay mat (a square of fabric or burlap), acrylic paint or glaze

Alternate Materials: air-drying clay

■ Distribute the materials and have students follow the directions on page 189.

■ Review the Technique Tips on page 225 for information about making a pinch pot.

■ See the Activity Tips on page 247 for visual examples of this lesson's activity.

Art Journal: Brainstorming

In their Art Journals, have each student write a list of things they like about the person they are honoring with their figural clay bowl. Have students make several simple sketches to plan how they will represent that person.

Using Harmony

Harmony is the peaceful look made when related elements of art are put together. Visual artists can create harmony by repeating lines, colors, shapes, textures, and objects.

Harmony can be created with colors that are related on the color wheel.

Harmony can be created with similar shapes.

Harmony can be created with similar lines.

 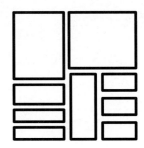 

Practice

Create harmony with color, shape, and repetition.

1. Fold a sheet of paper into three parts. Draw a simple shape in the first part using markers or crayons. Color it with three related colors.

2. In the second part, draw a geometric shape. Repeat the shape in different sizes until this part is filled.

3. In the last part, draw rows of repeating lines and shapes.

Differentiated Instruction

Reteach

Use *Flash Cards 17* and *18* to discuss harmony created by similar and repeated elements.

Special Needs

Adaptations: Use this lesson to build a sense of community in the classroom. Pair students and have each pair research information about one another. Then have each student create and present to the class a bowl design about his or her partner.

ELL Tips

Students may have difficulty following printed or oral directions without some visual support. Considering modeling with the whole class the steps in creating a clay figural pot.

◀ **Chandler Hogan.** Age 7.
◀ **Spencer Hanson.** Age 7.

Think about how these student artists created harmony in their clay bowls.

 Creative Expression

Whom do you admire? Create a figural clay bowl to honor someone you admire. Use color to create harmony in your bowl.

1. Begin by making a pinch pot. Then roll a coil to make arms that will fit halfway around the rim of your pot. Roll a sphere to make a head.

2. Using proper joining techniques, attach the arms and head to the rim of your pot. Add clay for hair. With your clay tools add details such as hands, eyes, and a mouth. Add texture to the hair.

3. Choose related colors to paint or glaze your figural pot once it has been fired.

Art Criticism

Describe Describe the steps taken to create your clay bowl.

Analyze How did you create harmony in your bowl?

Interpret How does your clay bowl represent the person you admire?

Decide What would you change if you did this project again?

Unit 6 • Lesson 1 **189**

Reflect

Time: About 5 minutes

Review and Assess

"What could you do to create harmony in your next work of art?" "¿Qué podrían hacer para crear armonía en su próxima obra de arte?"

Think

The students created harmony in their clay bowls by repeating colors and shapes.

■ Have students identify similar and repeated elements that create harmony in *Large Prints 47 Group Portrait* and *48 Hoosick Falls, N.Y. in Winter.*

Informal Assessment

Art Journal: Critical Thinking

Have students answer the four art criticism questions—Describe, Analyze, Interpret, and Decide—in their Art Journals. In small groups, have students discuss the creation of harmony in their clay bowls.
NSAE 1.b; 2.b; 3.a; 5.c

■ For standardized-format test practice using this lesson's art content, see page 66–67 in *Reading and Writing Test Preparation.*

Art Across the Curriculum

NSAE 6.b

Use these simple ideas to reinforce art concepts across the curriculum.

★ **Personal Writing** Have students use the writing process to write a letter to the person they honored in their figural clay bowls.

★ **Math** Have students create geometric shape patterns that have harmony.

★ **Science** One of the *Pottery Vessels* has a shell motif. Discuss different kinds of shells found in nature.

★ **Social Studies** Discuss the importance of compromise to create harmony between people.

★ **Technology** Have students use the computer's paint program to create a design that has harmony. Visit **SRAonline.com** to print detailed instructions for this activity.

LESSON 1 • Harmony **189**

Harmony

Extra! For the Art Specialist

Time: About 45 minutes

Focus

Use **Transparency 31** to discuss harmony. What lines, shapes, colors, or textures did the artists repeat?

Teach

Have students complete the Alternate Activity.

Reflect

Have students evaluate their works of art using the four steps of art criticism. (See pages 28–29 for more about art criticism.) Encourage students to discuss examples of harmony in nature or in the humanmade environment.

Alternate Activity

Materials:
- low-fire clay
- 12" × 14" pieces of burlap
- clay tools (such as pencils, plastic forks, paper clips)

1. Distribute a piece of burlap and two 2" diameter balls of clay to each student. Have students make a pinch pot from each ball of clay.

2. Have students join the pots together, rim to rim, by scoring, applying slip, and smoothing.

3. Have students form the joined pots into an interesting shape by gently pushing them or rolling them on the table. Have students gently push a finger into the clay at the top to make the hole of the vase.

4. Have students use the clay tools to create a harmonious design on the vase.

Research in Art Education

It has been shown that "elementary [art] programs establish a foundation in the arts for all students, not just for those in specialized programs or those who choose an arts course of study in high school." Providing consistent, quality instruction in the arts in elementary school also ensures that students have the time to foster skills in the arts. Many of these skills take time to develop *(Gaining the Arts Advantage: Lessons from School Districts that Value Arts Education).*

Assessment

Use the following rubric to evaluate the artwork students make in the Creative Expression activity and to assess students' understanding of harmony.

Have students complete page 69 or 70 in their **Assessment** books.

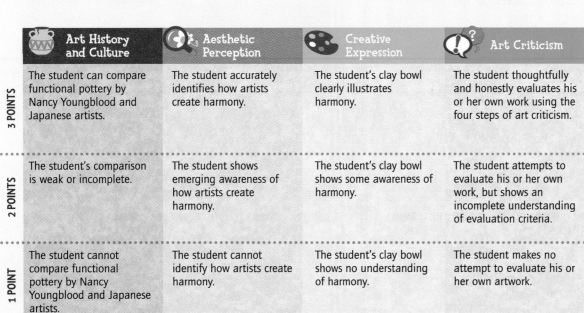

	Art History and Culture	Aesthetic Perception	Creative Expression	Art Criticism
3 POINTS	The student can compare functional pottery by Nancy Youngblood and Japanese artists.	The student accurately identifies how artists create harmony.	The student's clay bowl clearly illustrates harmony.	The student thoughtfully and honestly evaluates his or her own work using the four steps of art criticism.
2 POINTS	The student's comparison is weak or incomplete.	The student shows emerging awareness of how artists create harmony.	The student's clay bowl shows some awareness of harmony.	The student attempts to evaluate his or her own work, but shows an incomplete understanding of evaluation criteria.
1 POINT	The student cannot compare functional pottery by Nancy Youngblood and Japanese artists.	The student cannot identify how artists create harmony.	The student's clay bowl shows no understanding of harmony.	The student makes no attempt to evaluate his or her own artwork.

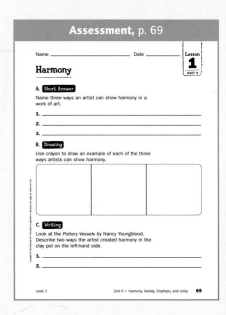

Assessment, p. 69

Name _____ Date _____

Lesson 1 UNIT 6

Harmony

A. Short Answer
Name three ways an artist can show harmony in a work of art.

1. _____
2. _____
3. _____

B. Drawing
Use crayon to draw an example of each of the three ways artists can show harmony.

C. Writing
Look at the *Pottery Vessels* by Nancy Youngblood. Describe two ways the artist created harmony in the clay pot on the left-hand side.

1. _____
2. _____

Level 3   Unit 6 • Harmony, Variety, Emphasis, and Unity **69**

Lesson 2 Variety

Overview

Lesson 2 introduces variety, which is using different lines, shapes, colors, and textures to make a work of art look interesting.

Objectives

Art History and Culture

To describe the materials used by artists from two Native American cultures
NSAE 4.a; 4.b; 4.c

Creative Expression

To create a weaving using a variety of colors and textures
NSAE 1.a; 1.c; 1.d

Aesthetic Perception

To identify how artists use variety to create interest in a work of art
NSAE 2.b

Art Criticism

To use the four steps of art criticism to evaluate one's own work
NSAE 1.b; 2.b; 3.a; 5.c

Vocabulary Vocabulary

Review the following vocabulary word with students before beginning the lesson.

variety variedad—using different lines, shapes, colors, and textures to make a work of art interesting.

See page 209B for additional vocabulary and Spanish vocabulary resources.

 Art Journal: Vocabulary

Have students add this word to the Vocabulary section of their Art Journals.

Lesson Materials

- 9" × 12" paper
- pencils
- markers
- 9" × 12" cardboard
- rulers
- scissors
- a variety of yarns and natural fibers

Alternate Materials:
- crayons
- paper weaving

Program Resources

- *Reading and Writing Test Prep.*, pp. 68–69
- *Transparency 32*
- *Flash Cards 16* and *18*
- *Artist Profiles*, pp. 27, 61
- *Animals Through History Time Line*
- *Assessment*, pp. 71–72
- *Large Prints 47* Group Portrait and *48* Hoosick Falls, N.Y. in Winter
- *Art Around the World Collection*

Concept Trace

Variety
Introduced: Level 2, Unit 6, Lesson 3
Reinforced: Level 4, Unit 6, Lesson 5

Lesson 2 Arts Integration NSAE 6.a

Theatre

Complete Unit 6, Lesson 2, on pages 110–111 of *Theatre Arts Connections*.

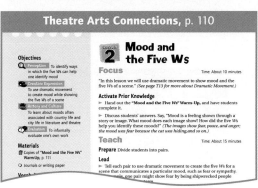

Music

Listen to "Variations on Simple Gifts" from *Appalachian Spring* by Aaron Copeland. He created the ballet *Appalachian Spring* for the dancer Martha Graham in 1944. *Simple Gifts* is a Shaker hymn, and something changes each time it repeats. Is the tune ever varied to the point you can't recognize it?

Movement & Dance

Repetition can exhaust our attention, so by adding a little contrast, a feeling of variety can be created. Have students work in groups of three and stand in a triangle shape, with adequate space between them. One person begins as the leader, the other two mirror the axial movements as accurately as possible. As each person passes the leadership to the next person, there must be a change of level used by the new leader. A sense of variety must be maintained.

Focus

Activate Prior Knowledge

"Think about eating a slice of bread. What if you had to eat a plain slice of bread every day? What would make it taste better and more fun to eat?" "Piensen en comer una rebanada de pan. ¿Qué pasaría si tuvieran que comer una rebanada de pan sin nada todos los días? ¿Qué haría que supiera mejor y que fuera más divertido comerlo?"

▪ Discuss students' responses to the question and how variety creates interest.

Using Literature Reading

▪ Read *Alex Is My Friend* by Marisabina Russo. Discuss the variety of lines, shapes, colors, and patterns found in the illustrations.

Thematic Connection Science

▪ **Animals:** Discuss variety in animals. For instance, there are many different breeds of dogs.

Introduce the Art

Look   NSAE 3.a

"Let's take a close look at the two works of art." "Vamos a mirar detalladamente las dos obras de arte".

Summarizing Reading

▪ Have students identify the subject matter in each textile. *Child's Beaded Shirt* is iconographic. It depicts symbols. *Pictorial Weaving* is a narrative landscape. This type of weaving portrays scenes from everyday life on the Navajo Reservation.

 Art History and Culture

Possible answer: Both artists chose to use natural materials (such as buffalo hide) as well as humanmade materials (such as glass beads). The artists might have tried to use all parts of the animals or plants they used for food, as well as using humanmade materials that were available to them.
NSAE 4.c; 5.a; 5.b

💻 **Web Connection**
Visit the Web site of the Dallas Museum of Art at **www.dm-art.org**.

 Lesson 2 Variety

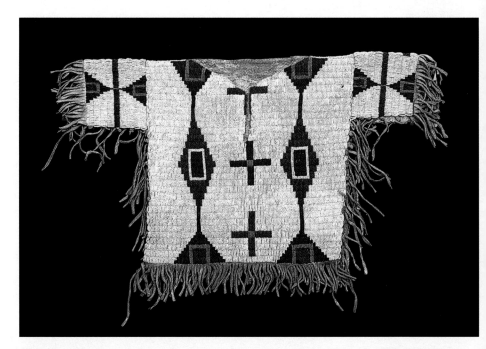

Look at the textile art on these pages. A Central Plains woman made *Child's Beaded Shirt* around 1865. It is decorated with a variety of textures, colors, and materials. Navajo artist Isabel John created *Pictorial Tapestry* more than 100 years later with a variety of shapes and colors. Both artists used variety in their designs to create interest.

▲ **Artist Unknown.**
(Northern Cheyenne or Teton Dakota, United States). *Child's Beaded Shirt.* c. 1865.
....
Buffalo hide, glass seed beads. 13 3/16 × 23 inches (33.5 × 58.5 cm.). Dallas Museum of Art, Dallas, Texas.

🏺 **Art History and Culture**

Compare the materials used to make each work of art. Why do you think the artists chose these materials?

🏺 **Art History and Culture**

The *Child's Beaded Shirt* is representative of the beadwork done by the Plains Native American women. They usually made clothing for members of their family. Before contact with non-natives, Plains people decorated most clothing with paint and porcupine quill embroidery. By the 1850s, Plains people could acquire glass seed beads (like the ones used in this shirt) through trade. Based on earlier quill work designs, the beadwork patterns are not only decorative but have symbolic and spiritual meanings.

See pages 16–21 and 24–25 for more about subject matter and art history.

Artist Profiles, p. 61

Artist Profile

Child's Beaded Shirt

Most native Plains women made clothing for members of their families. Their designs were usually abstract and geometric. The patterns in these designs were often balanced. This shirt was probably made by an individual of the northern Cheyenne or Teton Dakota culture.

▲ **Artist unknown.** (Northern Cheyenne or Teton Dakota/United States).
Child's Beaded Shirt. c. 1865.

▲ **Isabel John.**
(Navajo, United States). *Pictorial Tapestry.* Mid-1980s.
. . . .
Wool, commercial, and natural dyes. 44 × 77 $\frac{1}{2}$ inches (111.76 × 196.85 cm.). Birmingham Museum of Art, Birmingham, Alabama.

Study both works of art to find examples of variety.

▶ Find different geometric and free-form shapes in the same artwork.

▶ Find shapes of different sizes in each piece.

▶ Locate places where you see different textures.

▶ Which work seems to have more variety?

Aesthetic Perception

Seeing Like an Artist Choose an element of art, such as line, color, shape, or texture. How many different varieties can you find in your classroom?

Art History and Culture

Isabel John

Isabel John (i´ zə bel´ jän) is a Navajo. The Navajos are one of the largest Native American groups in the United States. The Navajo women are well known for their weavings. John shears sheep and spins and dyes her own wool to use in her weavings. She weaves by hand on an upright loom. *Pictorial Weaving* is a landscape pictorial. This style became popular in the 1970s. These weavings show landscapes but also portray scenes from everyday Navajo life.

See pages 16–21 and 24–25 for more about subject matter and art history.

Artist Profiles, p. 27

◆ Artist Profile ◆

Isabel John

Isabel John (i´ za bel´ jän) is the best-known weaver of Navajo pictorial rugs today. John probably learned how to weave from an aunt or grandmother because this skill is traditionally passed down from mother to daughter. She has been weaving for many years and is now teaching this skill to others. She lives on the Navajo reservation in the northeastern Arizona city of Many Farms.

Study

▶ *Child's Beaded Shirt* has many different geometric shapes including rectangles, squares, triangles, and diamonds. The pieces of fringe are free-form shapes. *Pictorial Weaving* has geometric shapes, including rectangles and squares. It has many free-form shapes, such as the animals and the clouds.

▶ The shapes on the sleeves in *Child's Beaded Shirt* are small, while the shapes on the front of the shirt are larger. The animals in the background of *Pictorial Weaving* are smaller than the weaving and the person.

▶ In *Child's Beaded Shirt*, the beads look like they have a bumpy texture, and the buffalo hide fringe looks smooth.

▶ *Pictorial Weaving* seems to have more variety because there are more differences in the types of shapes and sizes of the shapes.

■ For more examples of art from North America see *Art Around the World Collection.*

Art Journal: Writing
Encourage students to write their own explanation of variety in the Concepts section of their Art Journals.

Aesthetic Perception

Seeing Like an Artist Students will notice that there are many variations of the art elements found in the classroom. You might want to have students chart their findings.

Developing Visual Literacy Have students look at *Pictorial Weaving.* Do they think it would take longer to paint this scene or to weave it? Why?

Web Connection
Have students share their ideas about works they view at the Web site of the Birmingham Museum of Art, www.artsbma.org/index.htm.

Teach

Time: About two 30-minute periods

"How can you create variety in a work of art?"
"¿Cómo pueden crear variedad en una obra de arte?"

■ Discuss the definition of *variety* and techniques for creating it on page 192.

Practice

Materials: 9" × 12" paper, pencils or crayons

Alternate Materials: oil pastels

■ Distribute the materials and have students follow the directions on page 192.

■ When students have completed their designs, discuss the techniques used to add variety, and whether students feel they were successful in making an interesting design.

Creative Expression

NSAE 1.a; 1.c; 1.d
Materials: 9" × 12" piece of cardboard, rulers, pencils, scissors, string, a variety of yarns and natural fibers

Alternate Materials: paper weaving

■ Distribute the materials and have students follow the directions on page 193.

■ See the Activity Tips on page 247 for visual examples of this lesson's activity.

■ After notching the cardboard, string the warp by starting at the top left notch. Bring the string down to the bottom left notch, pull it behind this notch, and then bring it back up again to the next notch. Keep going until the cardboard is completely strung with an uneven number of threads.

■ Begin weaving by leaving 1 inch of fabric sticking out. Be sure to leave loops of the weaving fabric on the side so that the warp won't be pulled too tight.

Art Journal: Brainstorming

In their Art Journals, have each student plan how they will change colors and textures to create variety in their weavings.

Using Variety

Variety is using different lines, shapes, colors, and textures to make a work of art interesting.

Too much of the same color, line, or shape in an artwork can be boring. Adding something different or unexpected can break up the repetition. Using a variety of colors or lines can give people more to think about.

What has been changed to add variety to the designs below?

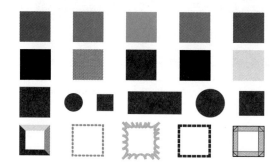

Practice

Create a design that has variety. Use pencil and one other medium.

1. Draw a geometric or free-form shape on your paper with a pencil. Repeat the shape in the same size until your paper is filled.

2. Add a different element to your design to create variety. For example, you might add different colors, lines, or textures.

Differentiated Instruction

Reteach
Use *Flash Cards 16* and *18* to discuss variety created by different lines, shapes, and colors.

Special Needs
Adaptations: Increase interest in this project by allowing students to bring materials from home (perhaps representing their different family members) to incorporate into their weaving.

ELL Tips
During the Seeing Like an Artist activity, pair students with fluent English-speaking peers. Encourage pairs to share with others to maximize opportunities for students to engage in discussions.

◀ Joseph Fernandez. Age 9.

Think about how this student created variety in his weaving.

 Creative Expression

What different ways can you use a weaving? Make a weaving with a variety of colors and textures.

1. Think about how you will use your weaving. Select a variety of ribbons, natural fibers, and yarn for your weaving.

2. Cut out a piece of cardboard, and notch it on the top and the bottom. Then, string the warp thread on it.

3. Weave your fibers to create variety.

Art Criticism

Describe What materials did you use in your weaving?

Analyze Which colors and textures did you repeat? Where did you create variety?

Interpret How would the interest of your weaving change if you had used only one color and one texture?

Decide If you could add other colors and textures, what would you choose?

 **eflect**   **Time:** About 5 minutes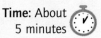

Review and Assess

"What do artists do to create variety in their works of art?" "¿Qué hacen los artistas para crear variedad en sus obras de arte?"

Think

The student created variety in his weaving by using materials of different colors and textures. He also varied the widths of the vertical stripes.

■ Have students identify examples of variety in *Large Prints 47* Group Portrait and **48** *Hoosick Falls, N.Y. in Winter*.

Informal Assessment

Art Journal: Critical Thinking

Have students answer the four art criticism questions—Describe, Analyze, Interpret, and Decide—in their Art Journals. In small groups, have students discuss the use of variety in their weavings. NSAE 1.b; 2.b; 3.a; 5c

■ For standardized-format test practice using this lesson's art content, see pages 68–69 in *Reading and Writing Test Preparation*.

Art Across the Curriculum   NSAE 6.b

Use these simple ideas to reinforce art concepts across the curriculum.

★ **Narrative Writing** Have each student write a short story from simple ideas you have provided about who, what, where, when, why, and how. Discuss the variety of stories made from the same ideas.

★ **Math** Discuss a variety of ways to express a math sentence, such as $5 \times 3 = 15$ and $5 + 5 + 5 = 15$.

★ **Science** The weavings were made from a variety of fibers. Discuss the characteristics of natural fibers.

★ **Social Studies** Learn more about the weaving traditions of Native American cultures.

★ **Technology** Use the computer's paint program to design a tapestry using a variety of lines. Visit **SRAonline.com** to print detailed instructions for this activity.

Extra! For the Art Specialist

Time: About 45 minutes

Focus

Use **Transparency 32** to discuss how artists can create variety. What lines, shapes, or colors are different? Would the works of art be as interesting if all of the lines, shapes, or colors were the same?

Teach

Have students complete the Alternate Activity.

Reflect

Have students evaluate their works of art using the four steps of art criticism. (See pages 28–29 for more about art criticism.) Encourage students to discuss examples of variety in nature or in the humanmade environment.

Alternate Activity

Materials:
- plastic straws
- masking tape
- precut 36" strands of yarn
- various colors of yarn

1. Give each student four plastic straws. Have students insert one strand of precut yarn into each straw and let 1-inch of yarn protrude from the end. Fold the yarn and tape it to the straw using a 1-inch piece of tape.

2. When yarn has been taped to one end of each straw, hold the four straws side by side and tape them together using a 3-inch piece of tape at the opposite end from the previously taped yarn. Tie the four ends of yarn together in an overhand knot.

3. Weave 4-feet to 5-feet pieces of yarn on the straw loom. When the weaving fills the straws, push the yarn towards the knot all the way off the straws, cut them off, and tie a knot to hold the weaving together.

Research in Art Education

An overview of research concerning the arts in education shows that high-arts involvement leads to outcomes "central to the goals society typically articulates for public education—productive social membership, critical and higher-order thinking, and commitment to the skills for lifelong learning" ("Promising Signs of Positive Effects: Lessons from the Multi-Arts Studies" in *Critical Links,* p. 99).

Assessment

Use the following rubric to evaluate the artwork students make in the Creative Expression activity and to assess students' understanding of variety.

Have students complete page 71 or 72 in their **Assessment** books.

	Art History and Culture	Aesthetic Perception	Creative Expression	Art Criticism
3 POINTS	The student successfully discusses the materials used by the Native American artists.	The student accurately identifies how artists create variety.	The student's weaving clearly illustrates variety.	The student thoughtfully and honestly evaluates his or her own work using the four steps of art criticism.
2 POINTS	The student's discussion is incomplete.	The student shows emerging awareness of how artists create variety.	]The student's weaving shows some awareness of variety.	The student attempts to evaluate his or her own work, but shows an incomplete understanding of evaluation criteria.
1 POINT	The student cannot discuss the materials used by the Native American artists.	The student cannot identify how artists create variety.	The student's weaving shows no understanding of variety.	The student makes no attempt to evaluate his or her own artwork.

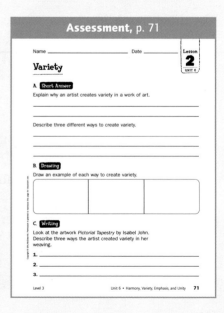

Assessment, p. 71

Name _____ Date _____

Variety

A. Short Answer
Explain why an artist creates variety in a work of art.

Describe three different ways to create variety.

B. Drawing
Draw an example of each way to create variety.

C. Writing
Look at the artwork *Pictorial Tapestry* by Isabel John. Describe three ways the artist created variety in her weaving.
1. _____
2. _____
3. _____

Level 3   Unit 6 • Harmony, Variety, Emphasis, and Unity 71

Lesson 3 Emphasis
Overview

Lesson 3 introduces emphasis. Artists create emphasis to make a part of an artwork stand out. Artists can create emphasis in different ways.

Objectives

Art History and Culture
To identify that content in works of art can document history
NSAE 4.a; 4.b; 4.c

Creative Expression
To create a computer drawing with an area of emphasis
NSAE 1.a; 1.c; 1.d

Aesthetic Perception
To describe how artists use emphasis to create a center of interest in a work of art
NSAE 2.b

Art Criticism
To use the four steps of art criticism to evaluate one's own work
NSAE 1.b; 2.b; 3.a; 5.c

Vocabulary Vocabulary
Review the following vocabulary words with students.

contrast contraste—to set in opposition in order to show or emphasize a difference

emphasis énfasis—the principle of design that stresses one element or area in a work of art over another

focal point punto focal—the area of a work of art to which the viewer's eyes are drawn

See page 209B for additional vocabulary and Spanish vocabulary resources.

Art Journal: Vocabulary
Have students add these words to the Vocabulary section of their Art Journals.

Lesson Materials
- 9" × 12" paper
- pencils
- black crayons
- computer's paint program

Alternate Materials:
- collage of light-colored shapes on dark paper
- white paper, markers

Program Resources
- *Reading and Writing Test Prep.*, pp. 70–71
- *Transparency 33*
- *Flash Card 15*
- *Artist Profiles*, pp. 12, 84
- *Animals Through History Time Line*
- *Assessment*, pp. 73–74
- *Large Prints 47* Group Portrait and *48* Hoosick Falls, N.Y. in Winter
- *The National Museum of Women in the Arts Collection*

Concept Trace
Emphasis
Introduced: Level 2, Unit 5, Lesson 3
Reinforced: Level 4, Unit 4, Lesson 6

Lesson 3 Arts Integration NSAE 6.a

Theatre
Complete Unit 6, Lesson 3, on pages 112–113 of *Theatre Arts Connections*.

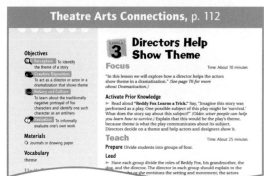

Theatre Arts Connections, p. 112

Music
 The most famous example of emphasis by dynamics, or "accent" is in *The Surprise Symphony No. 94* by Franz Joseph Haydn. When Haydn was frustrated that his audiences were getting sleepy during his after dinner entertainment he added the famous accents to wake them up.

Movement & Dance
Have students walk in the room, weaving in and around each other as they move to the beat of a drum or other percussion instrument. Students emphasize a part of the body by leading with it as they walk through the space. This changes the emphasis of weight and position of body parts.

Focus

Activate Prior Knowledge

"Think about sitting in a dark movie theater. Why does the movie screen catch your attention?" *"Piensen en sentarse en un cine oscuro. ¿Por qué la pantalla del cine llama su atencion?"*

■ Discuss students' responses to the question and how a light area attracts attention when surrounded by a dark area.

Using Literature Reading

■ Read *My Life with the Wave* by Catherine Cowan. Ask students what they notice first in each illustration.

Thematic Connection Social Studies

■ **Safety:** Discuss ways to emphasize safety, such as by painting a crosswalk.

Introduce the Art

Look NSAE 3.a

"Let's take a close look at the two works of art." *"Vamos a mirar detalladamente las dos obras de arte".*

Main Idea and Details Reading

■ Have students identify the subject matter in each work of art. Then have students look more closely and identify details about each picture. *Hairdresser's Window* is a genre painting. It shows a hairdresser at work and the people on the street. *Jane's Remington* is a still life. It shows a typewriter. Details of *Hairdresser's Window* include the signs surrounding the window and the appearance of the passers-by. Details of *Jane's Remington* include the shadow in the background and the appearance of the typewriter's individual parts.

 Art History and Culture

Possible answers: *Hairdresser's Window* shows the type of clothing and hairstyles worn and the appearance of buildings and signs. *Jane's Remington* records what this type of typewriter looked like.
NSAE 4.a; 4.b; 4.c

 Web Connection

More information about The Eight can be found at **www.sohoart.com/ashcan.htm.**

 **Lesson 3 Emphasis**

◄ **John Sloan.** (American). *Hairdresser's Window.* 1907.
Oil on canvas. 32 × 25 ⅛ inches (81 × 66 cm.). Wadsworth Atheneum Museum of Art, Hartford, Connecticut.

Look at the works of art on these pages. Both are oil paintings. *Hairdresser's Window* is a genre painting. It shows a scene of American life from the time it was painted. *Jane's Remington* is a still life. It shows an inanimate object. Each painting has an area of emphasis.

 Art History and Culture

Works of art can be a record of history. What does each of these paintings show about the past?

Art History and Culture

John Sloan

John Sloan (jän slōn) (1871–1951) was born in Pennsylvania. He left school at age 16 to help support his family. However he taught himself to draw and attended evening classes at the Pennsylvania Academy. There he became friends with another artist named Robert Henri. Sloan joined with Henri in a group of painters called The Eight. This group often painted New York city street scenes. They believed it was important to depict subjects as they truly appeared rather than idealizing them.

See pages 16–21 and 24–25 for more about subject matter and art history.

Artist Profiles, p. 84

John Sloan
1871–1951

John Sloan (jän slōn) was born in Lock Haven, Pennsylvania, in 1871. He grew up a classmate of painter William Glackens and the modern art advocate Albert C. Barnes. At the age of 16, Sloan left school to support his family. He was an avid reader and taught himself how to draw and create etchings, eventually acquiring a job as an illustrator for the *Philadelphia Inquirer* in 1892. He attended evening classes at the Pennsylvania Academy, where he became friends with Robert Henri. He soon joined Henri in an avant-garde group of young painters called The Eight, also known as the Ash Can School. Sloan exhibited with The Eight throughout his career, and although he was never able to make a living selling his

◀ **Robert Cottingham.**
(American). *Jane's
Remington.* 2000.
••••••••••••••••••••••••••
Oil on canvas. 84 × 74 inches
(213.36 × 187.96 cm.). Forum
Gallery, New York, New York.

Study the works of art to find the areas of emphasis.

▶ Which people and objects do you see in the paintings?

▶ How are the people and objects arranged?

▶ What part of each picture attracts your eye?

 Aesthetic Perception

Design Awareness If important information is on the board,
what can your teacher do to draw attention to it?

Art History and Culture

Robert Cottingham

Robert Cottingham (räb´ ərt côt´ ting hem) (1935–   ) was born in
Brooklyn, New York. He studied art at the Pratt Institute and
became an art director for an advertising company. In 1968 he quit
his job to become a fulltime artist. Cottingham's style is called
photorealism. This means his paintings are so detailed and realistic
that they look like photographs. Cottingham often paints common
objects from American life, such as typewriters or cameras.

See pages 16–21 and 24–25 for more about subject matter and art
history.

Artist Profiles, p. 12

◀ Artist Profile ▶
Robert Cottingham
b. 1935

Neon signs, storefronts, and shop awnings
are only a few of the many subjects Robert
Cottingham (räb´ côt´ ting hem) uses
in his photorealistic artwork. Born in
Brooklyn, New York, Cottingham grew
up with an appreciation for the urban
environment. He studied art at the Pratt
Institute and worked as an art director for
advertising companies in New York and Los
Angeles. In 1968, he quit his job to become
a full-time artist and began painting the
buildings of Los Angeles. As he worked,
he began to look higher and higher and
realized that there was a world of familiar
commercial imagery right above his head.
This realization led to Cottingham's
successful career as a photorealist and

Study   NSAE 2.b

▶ *Hairdresser's Window* shows a building.
Three people are seen through the second
story window: one woman is sitting with
her back to the viewer and the other two
are combing her hair. On the street below
are eight other people. *Jane's Remington*
shows one object: a typewriter.

▶ In *Hairdresser's Window* the three people
in the window are located at the top
center of the painting. The other people
are along the bottom of the painting. The
typewriter in *Jane's Remington* takes up
almost the entire painting.

▶ In *Hairdresser's Window* the people in the
window draw the viewer's eye first because
everyone else in the painting is looking at
them. In *Jane's Remington* the lines of the
typebars draw the viewer's eye to the
center of the typewriter.

■ For more examples of genre paintings, see
***The National Museum of Women in the
Arts Collection***.

Art Journal: Writing
Encourage students to write their
own explanation of emphasis in the
Concepts section of their Art Journals.

Aesthetic Perception

Design Awareness Discuss with students
methods they have seen for drawing
attention to important text written on the
board in the classroom. Possible answers
include: circling the text, writing it in a
different color, or writing it larger than other
text.

Developing Visual Literacy Discuss with
students what they think may have been the
artist's purpose in creating emphasis in each
work of art. What was important about each
area of emphasis?
NSAE 5.a

Web Connection
See more work by Robert Cottingham at the Forum
Gallery's Web site, **www.forumgallery.com/index2.
html**.

Teach

Time: About 40 minutes

"How do artists create *emphasis* in their works of art?" "¿Cómo los artistas crean énfasis en sus obras de arte?"

- Discuss the definition of *emphasis* and techniques for creating it on page 196.

Practice

Materials: 9 " × 12 " paper, pencils, black crayons

Alternate Materials: collage of light-colored shapes on dark paper

- Distribute the materials and have students follow the directions on page 196.
- When students have completed their designs, ask which shape attracts their attention first. Why?

Creative Expression

NSAE 1.a; 1.c; 1.d

Materials: computer's paint program

Alternate Materials: white paper, markers

- Distribute the materials and have students follow the directions on page 197.
- Review the Activity Tips on page 248 for visual examples of this activity's techniques.
- If the paint program has a pattern tool, students may add patterns to the gray areas around the circle.

Art Journal: Brainstorming

Have students make sketches to plan their designs in their Art Journals.

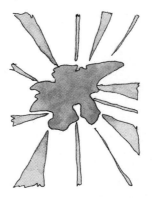

Using Emphasis

Sometimes an artist wants you to look immediately at a certain area in a work of art. This area is the center of interest, or the **focal point.** An artist uses **emphasis** to draw your attention there. Emphasis makes a part of an artwork stand out.

One way to create emphasis is to have everyone in the picture look at one person or thing, like in *Hairdresser's Window.* That becomes the focal point.

Another way to create emphasis in a design is to have lines lead the viewer's eyes to the focal point, as in *Jane's Remington.*

A third way to create emphasis is to use **contrast.** Artists create contrast by making one object different from the rest of the artwork. A bright color stands out from dark colors. A rough texture stands out from a smooth texture.

Practice

Contrast values to create emphasis. Use pencil and black crayon.

1. Draw a shape several times until a small piece of paper is filled. Keep the shapes about the same size.
2. Pick one to be the center of interest. Color it with black crayon, leaving the rest of the shapes uncolored to create emphasis.

196 Unit 6 • Lesson 3

Differentiated Instruction

Reteach
Use *Flash Card 15*. Discuss what was done to create an area of emphasis.

Special Needs
Adaptations: Encourage students to extend their knowledge in this activity by allowing them to take digital images of scenes that have obvious focal points. The color and values in these digital images can then be altered in an attempt to over-emphasize the focal point.

ELL Tips
Students may be hesitant to answer interpretive questions about their artwork. You may wish to phrase questions as an either/or choice so the vocabulary needed to answer the question is contained in the question itself.

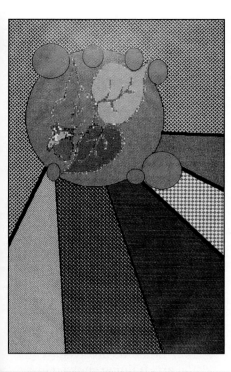

Think about how this student created an area of emphasis.

◄ **Carl Blanton.**
Age 8.

 Creative Expression

What object in nature would you like to emphasize? Make a computer design with that object as the focal point.

1. Use the ellipse tool to draw a circle. Use the draw tool to draw something from nature within the circle.

2. Use the line tool to draw diagonal lines that connect to the circle. Use the fill tool to fill the sections around the circle with shades of gray.

3. Use the brush tool to paint the design inside the circle. Make it colorful.

 **Art Criticism**

Describe List the procedures you used to make this work.

Analyze How did you create a focal point?

Interpret Give your work a creative title.

Decide Were you successful in creating a design with emphasis?

Unit 6 • Lesson 3 **197**

 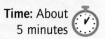 **Time:** About 5 minutes

Review and Assess

"What are some ways you could create a center of interest in your works of art?"
"¿Cuáles son algunas maneras en que podrían crear un centro de interés en sus obras de arte?"

Think

The student emphasized the circle by using bright colors within the circle and darker colors around it. The lines going from the edge of the artwork to the circle draw the viewer's eyes to it.

■ Discuss with students what they feel the areas of emphasis are in *Large Prints 47 Group Portrait* and *48 Hoosick Falls, N.Y. in Winter.*

Informal Assessment

Art Journal: Critical Thinking
Have students answer the four art criticism questions—Describe, Analyze, Interpret, and Decide—in their Art Journals. In small groups, have students discuss the use of variety in their weavings.
NSAE 1.b; 2.b; 3.a; 5.c

■ For standardized-format test practice using this lesson's art content, see pages 70–71 in *Reading and Writing Test Preparation.*

● **Art Across the Curriculum** ●   NSAE 6.b

Use these simple ideas to reinforce art concepts across the curriculum.

★ **Descriptive Writing** Discuss with students that they can emphasize a character in a story by writing more descriptively about that character than about others

★ **Math** Artists can create emphasis by making a shape larger than the rest. Discuss relative sizes of objects.

★ **Science** Discuss examples of emphasis in nature, such as colorful fruit on a tree.

★ **Social Studies** Discuss how holiday celebrations can create emphasis on a particular day of the year.

★ **Technology** Have students manipulate a digital photo to create emphasis. Visit **SRAonline.com** to print detailed instructions for this activity.

 For the Art Specialist

 Time: About 45 minutes

Focus

Use *Transparency 33* to discuss emphasis. What is the most important part of each work of art? Have students explain what the artists did to draw the viewer's eyes to that area.

Teach

Have students complete the Alternate Activity. Discuss other ways students could have created emphasis on their mosaic masks.

Reflect

Have students evaluate their works of art using the four steps of art criticism. (See pages 28–29 for more about art criticism.) Have students look for areas of emphasis in the classroom.

Alternate Activity

Materials:
- 9" × 11" pieces of posterboard
- 1" wide craft sticks
- white glue or glue sticks
- 1" × 12" strips of colored construction paper
- scissors

1. Have each student cut a piece of posterboard into a mask shape. Have students cut the strips of construction paper into 1" squares to make mosaic pieces.

2. Have students glue the mosaic pieces onto the mask shape. Students begin by making facial features and then filling in the open areas with contrasting colors to emphasis the facial features. Have students continue until the entire mask is covered with mosaic pieces.

3. When the mask is completed, have students glue a craft stick handle to the back of the mask.

Research in Art Education

Research has shown that the "looking and reasoning skills" learned during visual art training can also be applied to scientific images ("Investigating the Educational Impact and Potential of the Museum of Modern Art's Visual Thinking Curriculum" in *Critical Links*, p. 142). Students involved in visual arts training showed less circular reasoning and more evidential reasoning when evaluating both fine art images and scientific images.

Assessment

Use the following rubric to evaluate the artwork students make in the Creative Expression activity and to assess students' understanding of emphasis.

Have students complete page 73 or 74 in their *Assessment* books.

	Art History and Culture	Aesthetic Perception	Creative Expression	Art Criticism
3 POINTS	The student successfully identifies how works of art can document history.	The student accurately describes how artists create emphasis.	The student's computer drawing clearly has an area of emphasis.	The student thoughtfully and honestly evaluates his or her own work using the four steps of art criticism.
2 POINTS	The student's discussion is incomplete.	The student shows emerging awareness of how artists create emphasis.	The student's computer drawing shows some awareness of emphasis.	The student attempts to evaluate his or her own work, but shows an incomplete understanding of evaluation criteria.
1 POINT	The student cannot identify how works of art can document history.	The student cannot identify how artists create emphasis.	The student's computer drawing shows no understanding of emphasis.	The student makes no attempt to evaluate his or her own artwork.

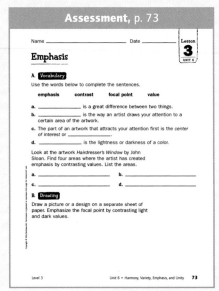

Assessment, p. 73

Name _____ Date _____ Lesson **3** UNIT 6

Emphasis

A. Vocabulary
Use the words below to complete the sentences.

emphasis   contrast   focal point   value

a. _____ is a great difference between two things.
b. _____ is the way an artist draws your attention to a certain area of the artwork.
c. The part of an artwork that attracts your attention first is the center of interest or _____.
d. _____ is the lightness or darkness of a color.

Look at the artwork *Hairdresser's Window* by John Sloan. Find four areas where the artist has created emphasis by contrasting values. List the areas.

a. _____   b. _____
c. _____   d. _____

B. Drawing
Draw a picture or a design on a separate sheet of paper. Emphasize the focal point by contrasting light and dark values.

Level 3   Unit 6 • Harmony, Variety, Emphasis, and Unity   **73**

Lesson 4 Overview
Emphasis Through Decoration

Lesson 4 continues teaching emphasis. One way an artist can create emphasis is by decorating an area to draw attention to it.

Objectives

Art History and Culture
To compare covers of books from different times
NSAE 3.a; 4.a; 4.b; 4.c

Creative Expression
To create a book cover with emphasis
NSAE1.a; 1.c; 1.d; 2.c; 3.b

Aesthetic Perception
To describe how artists use emphasis to create interest in book covers
NSAE 2.a; 2.b; 3.a

Art Criticism
To use the four steps of art criticism to evaluate one's own work
NSAE 1.b; 2.b; 3.a; 5.c

Vocabulary Vocabulary

Review the following vocabulary word with students before beginning the lesson.

emphasis énfasis—the principle of design that stresses one element or area in a work of art over another

See page 209B for additional Spanish vocabulary resources.

Art Journal: Vocabulary
Have students add this word to the Vocabulary section of their Art Journals.

Lesson Materials
- pencils
- crayons
- $4\frac{1}{2}$" × 9" heavy white drawing paper
- $4\frac{1}{2}$" × 6" construction paper in various colors
- scissors
- glue
- tapestry needle
- embroidery floss or string
- medium sized beads (optional)
- watercolors and brushes
- water dishes
- newspaper
- paper towels

Alternate Materials:
- sketch paper
- yarn for binding

Program Resources
- *Reading and Writing Test Prep.*, pp. 72–73
- *Transparency 34*
- *Flash Card 15*
- *Artist Profiles*, pp. 53, 63
- *Animals Through History Time Line*
- *Assessment*, pp. 75–76
- *Large Prints 47* Group Portrait and *48* Hoosick Falls, N.Y. in Winter
- *Art Around the World Collection*

Concept Trace
Emphasis Through Decoration
Introduced: Level 2, Unit 5, Lesson 3
Reinforced: Level 4, Unit 6, Lesson 5

Lesson 4 Arts Integration NSAE 6.a

Theatre
Complete Unit 6, Lesson 4 on pages 114–115 of *Theatre Arts Connections*.

Theatre Arts Connections, p. 115

Name _____ Date _____
Characters Show Theme
The pictures below tell the fable of the ant and the grasshopper. Look at the subject below. Write this story's theme.

Music
Vocal soloists have subtle ways of decorating a melody in their performances. Listen to *Summertime*, from *Porgy and Bess*, by George Gershwin. Listen to the flexibility in the soprano's voice and how it contributes to her expression.

Movement & Dance
Have students walk through the room, weaving in and around each other to the beat of a drum or other percussive instrument. Have them explore ways to decorate their walk by moving specific body parts as they walk, such as circling their shoulders.

 **Focus**

Activate Prior Knowledge

"Think about parts of a book. Why is the cover important?" *"Piensen en las partes de un libro. ¿Por qué es importante la portada?"*

■ Discuss students' responses. Talk about how the cover is important because it holds the pages together and can give information about what is contained inside. Since most books are similarly shaped, the covers can help us distinguish between them at a glance.

Using Literature ⭐ Reading

■ Read *The Worry Stone* by Marianna Dengler. Discuss how the book cover has emphasis.

Thematic Connection

■ **Colors:** Discuss how emphasis can be created by contrasting colors.

Introduce the Art

Look   NSAE 3.a

"Let's take a close look at the two books."
"Vamos a mirar detalladamente los dos libros".

Comparing and Contrasting ⭐ Reading

■ Have students list the similarities and differences between the books. Both books have decorative covers. Both covers have metal on them. *Cover of Armenian Book* shows a narrative scene surrounded by a colorful border, while the cover of *British Museum Memoir* just has a decorative pattern in one color. Only the cover of *Cover of Armenian Book* is visible, but *British Museum Memoir* is opened and the pages are visible in the background.

🏺 Art History and Culture

Possible answers: Students will probably guess that someone rich or important owned *Cover of Armenian Book* since it is covered with jewels and precious metals. They may also guess that a religious person owned the book since it is decorated with images of Christianity. NSAE 4.a; 4.b; 4.c

💻 Web Connection

Students can learn more about Armenia by doing a country study at the Library of Congress's Web site, lcweb2.loc.gov/frd/cs/.

Emphasis Through Decoration

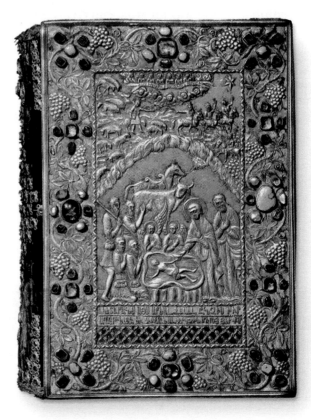

Look at the books on these pages. *Cover of Armenian Book* was made by hand during the thirteenth century. The pages of the book contain prayers and illustrations. *British Museum Memoir* was also made by hand about 700 years later. The pages contain private writings and drawings. Each artist decorated the cover to create emphasis.

◀ **Artist Unknown.** (Armenia).
Cover of Armenian Book.
Thirteenth century.
Carved and hammered silver, gilded and enameled, and set with jewels, and rubricated vellum. $10\frac{1}{4} \times 7\frac{3}{8}$ inches (26.04 × 18.73 cm.). The Metropolitan Museum of Art, New York, New York.

🏺 Art History and Culture

Whom do you think owned the *Cover of Armenian Book?* Why?

🏺 Art History and Culture

Christianity became the official religion of Armenia during the fourth century. Armenian artists used scenes from the Gospel and images of Christianity to decorate their churches and illustrate their manuscripts. Existing illustrated Armenian manuscripts date from the ninth to the seventeenth centuries. Like other illustrations of this period, this book cover contains floral, geometric, and animal patterns.

See pages 16–21 and 24–25 for more about subject matter and art history.

Artist Profiles, p. 63

Artist Profile

Cover of an Armenian Book

This cover was made in 1691 in the Armenian city of Kayseri, Turkey, the home of skilled silversmiths and goldsmiths. The illustrations inside were completed by artists from the city of Cilicia who were known for their painting skills. The words in the book were written by a scribe named Gregor. He gilded some letters in the first part of the book.

◀ **Artist Unknown.** (Armenia).
Cover of Armenian Book. Thirteenth century.
Carved and hammered silver, gilded and enameled, and set with

Study the books to find examples of emphasis.

▶ Which colors and textures do you see in each work?

▶ What part of *British Museum Memoir* draws your attention first?

▶ What do you think the artist felt was the most important area of *Cover of Armenian Book*?

 Aesthetic Perception

Design Awareness Have you ever chosen a book just because you liked the cover? What about the cover drew you to it?

▲ **Pamela Spitzmueller.** (American). *British Museum Memoir.* 1997.
· ·
Small grid graph paper, colored pencil, copper sheet, and copper wire. 11 × 47 inches (27.94 × 119.38 cm.). National Museum of Women in the Arts, Washington, D.C.

Study NSAE 2.a; 2.b; 3.a

▶ *Cover of Armenian Book* has the colors green, blue, and gold repeated throughout. It has bumpy textures created by the jewels and hammered metal. The tops of the jewels and metal look smooth. The cover of *British Museum Memoir* is a copper cover. It looks bumpy and rough.

▶ The cover of *British Museum Memoir* draws the viewer's attention first because it is more prominent and more decorated than the pages in the background.

▶ The artist probably felt the scene in the center of *Cover of Armenian Book* was the most important area because it is surrounded by jewels.

■ For more examples of art from Europe see *Art Around the World.*

Art Journal: Writing
Encourage students to list ways they could create emphasis through decoration in the Concepts section of their Art Journals.

 **Aesthetic Perception**

Design Awareness Discuss student responses. Talk about art elements that may have drawn students to book covers, such as interesting shapes or colors.

Developing Visual Literacy Ask students if they have ever heard the idiom "You can't judge a book by its cover." Explain that it means you can't know what is on the inside of something or someone when you have only seen the surface. Discuss with students whether they can tell anything about the inside of these books from what they see on the covers.

 **Art History and Culture**

Pamela Spitzmueller

Pamela Spitzmueller (pâm´ ə lə spiz´ myū lər) is a book artist and a conservator. Book artists make books that are meant to be looked at as art and not necessarily meant to be read. Conservators study and preserve old books. Spitzmueller has worked as a conservator for many libraries including the Library of Congress and Harvard University. Since 1991, she has been a co-director of the Paper and Book Intensive, which holds programs to teach students about book arts.

See pages 16–21 and 24–25 for more about subject matter and art history.

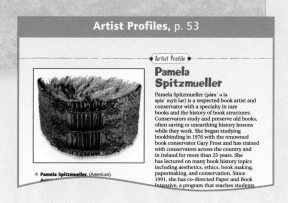

Artist Profiles, p. 53

◆ Artist Profile ◆
Pamela Spitzmueller
Pamela Spitzmueller (pâm´ ə lə spiz´ myū lər) is a respected book artist and conservator with a specialty in rare books and the history of book structures. Conservators study and preserve old books, often saving or unearthing history lessons while they work. She began studying bookbinding in 1976 with the renowned book conservator Gary Frost and has trained with conservators across the country and in Ireland for more than 25 years. She has lectured on many book history topics including aesthetics, ethics, book making, papermaking, and conservation. Since 1991, she has co-directed Paper and Book Intensive, a program that teaches students

▲ **Pamela Spitzmueller.** (American).

 Web Connection
Visit **www.bostonbookarts.org** to see more work by Pamela Spitzmueller and other book artists.

LESSON 4 • Emphasis Through Decoration 199

 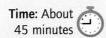
"How can artists emphasize one part of a plain design?" *"¿Cómo pueden los artistas enfatizar una parte de un diseño sencillo?"*

- Remind students what they have learned about *emphasis* and techniques for creating it. Discuss the technique on page 200.

Practice

Materials: Art Journals, pencils, crayons

Alternate Materials: sketch paper, markers

- Distribute the materials and have students follow the directions on page 200

- When students have completed their drawings, discuss whether they successfully emphasized themselves.

Creative Expression

NSAE 1.a; 1.c; 1.d; 2.c; 3.b

Materials: $4\frac{1}{2}$" × 9" heavy white drawing paper, $4\frac{1}{2}$" × 6" construction paper in various colors, scissors, glue, tapestry needle, embroidery floss or string, medium sized beads (optional), watercolors and brushes, water dishes, newspaper, paper towels

Alternate Materials: yarn for binding

- Distribute the materials and have students follow the directions on page 201.

- Review the Technique Tips on page 231 for information about sewing a book.

- See the Activity Tips on page 248 for visual examples of this lesson's activity.

Art Journal: Brainstorming

If students are unhappy with the drawings they made in the Practice activity, have them create new sketches in their Art Journals and choose one to use for the Creative Expression activity.

200 UNIT 6 • Harmony, Variety, Emphasis, and Unity

Using Emphasis Through Decoration

When you add decoration to one area of an otherwise plain design, you emphasize that area of the design.

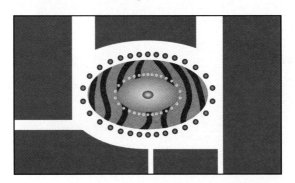

Practice

Create emphasis in a drawing of your favorite activity.

1. Think of an activity you like to do, such as roller skating, painting, or playing an instrument. Draw a sketch of yourself doing your favorite activity. Draw the background.

2. Color just you doing the activity. Leave the rest of the drawing plain.

3. Do you look like the most important thing in your drawing?

200   Unit 6 • Lesson 4

Differentiated Instruction

Reteach

Discuss how emphasis was created on covers of books found in the classroom.

Special Needs

Adaptations: Encourage students to further emphasize their picture by allowing them to incorporate mixed media materials.

ELL Tips

Students may have difficulty following oral directions without some kind of visual support. Consider modeling the steps with the whole class.

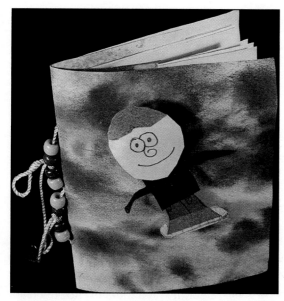

Think about how this student created emphasis on his book cover.

◀ **Josh Nelms.**
Age 9.

 Creative Expression

Can you create a book using emphasis on your cover?

1. Use a sheet of paper for the cover. Use a wash of warm or cool colors on the sheet. Let it dry.

2. On a sheet of construction paper, re-create your drawing from the Practice activity. Cut the image out. Glue a paper ring to the back.

3. Stack three sheets of paper on top of your cover. Fold it in half so that the cover is on the outside. Stitch your pages together. Glue the paper ring to the cover so the image is raised from the surface.

 **Art Criticism**

Describe What activity did you portray yourself doing?

Analyze Which contrasting colors did you use for your cover? How did you create emphasis?

Interpret If you had to put a title on your book cover, what would it be?

Decide What would you change if you did this project again?

**Reflect**   Time: About 5 minutes

Review and Assess

"How do artists create emphasis on book covers?" "¿Cómo los artistas crean énfasis en las portadas de libros?"

Think

The student artist creates emphasis by using bright, solid colors for the figure and by raising the figure off the cover.

■ Discuss with students whether there are any areas of emphasis created by decoration in *Large Prints 47 Group Portrait* and *48 Hoosick Falls, N.Y. in Winter*.

Informal Assessment

> **Art Journal: Critical Thinking**
> Have students answer the four art criticism questions—Describe, Analyze, Interpret, and Decide—in their Art Journals. In small groups, have students discuss the use of variety in their weavings.
> NSAE 1.b; 2.b; 3.a; 5.c

■ For standardized-format test practice using this lesson's art content, see pages 72–73 in *Reading and Writing Test Preparation*.

Art Across the Curriculum   NSAE 6.b

Use these simple ideas to reinforce art concepts across the curriculum.

★ **Expository Writing** Have students use the writing process to write an explanation of the steps completed in the Creative Expression activity.

★ **Math** Have students draw several shapes, decorating a few to emphasize them. Then have students use fractions to describe the emphasized shapes as part of a set.

★ **Science** Discuss examples of emphasis on animals' bodies, such as a peacock's feathers.

★ **Social Studies** Have students color a map of the United States and decorate their state with images of state symbols to emphasize it.

★ **Technology** Have students use the computer's word processing program to type stories or poems that could be included in the books from the Creative Expression activity. Visit **SRAonline.com** to print detailed instructions for this activity.

Emphasis Through Decoration

Extra! For the Art Specialist

Time: About two 30-minute sessions

Focus

Use *Transparency 34* to discuss emphasis through decoration. What is the center of interest of each form? How did the artist make that part of the artwork the most important?

Teach

Have students complete the Alternate Activity. What other ideas do students have for creating emphasis on a book cover?

Reflect

Have students evaluate their works of art using the four steps of art criticism. (See pages 28–29 for more about art criticism.) Have students look for examples of emphasis on covers of books in the classroom.

Alternate Activity

Materials:
- newspapers
- construction paper
- water containers
- old blender
- pieces of window screening stapled to old picture frames
- paper towels

1. Tear the paper into dime-sized pieces. Soak the pieces of paper in containers of water overnight. Keep the different colors of paper separate.

2. Fill a blender with water and one color of the paper pieces and blend until the paper is pulped.

3. Pour pulp mixture through a piece of window screen to separate pulp from water. Press extra water from pulp with paper towels, and remove hand-made paper from screening onto a paper towel to dry. Designs can be added to the paper with the colored paper pulp. When the paper is dry, it can be used as the cover of a hand-made book.

Research in Art Education

A pilot project evaluating the effects of arts education showed that "when students spend additional time in arts programs their performance in other schools subjects does *not* decline." Teachers do not need to be afraid that devoting class time to arts education will hurt students' studies in other curricula areas ("The Arts in the Basic Curriculum Project: Looking at the Past and Preparing for the Future" in *Critical Links*, p. 90).

Assessment

Use the following rubric to evaluate the artwork students make in the Creative Expression activity and to assess students' understanding of emphasis through decoration.

Have students complete page 75 or 76 in their *Assessment* books.

	Art History and Culture	Aesthetic Perception	Creative Expression	Art Criticism
3 POINTS	The student successfully compares books from different times.	The student accurately describes how artists create emphasis on book covers.	The student's book cover clearly has an area of emphasis.	The student thoughtfully and honestly evaluates his or her own work using the four steps of art criticism.
2 POINTS	The student's discussion is incomplete.	The student shows emerging awareness of how artists create emphasis on book covers.	The student's book cover shows some awareness of emphasis.	The student attempts to evaluate his or her own work, but shows an incomplete understanding of evaluation criteria.
1 POINT	The student cannot compare books from different times.	The student cannot identify how artists create emphasis on book covers.	The student's book cover shows no understanding of emphasis.	The student makes no attempt to evaluate his or her own artwork.

Unity Through Color

Lesson 5 introduces unity, which is a feeling in a work of art that everything belongs together. Artists can create unity by making everything the same color.

Objectives

 Art History and Culture

To identify a few facts about the jobs of professional artists
NSAE 5.a

 Creative Expression

To create a clay fish that is unified by color
NSAE 1.a; 1.c; 1.d

 Aesthetic Perception

To identify that artists use similar colors to create unity in an artwork
NSAE 2.b

 Art Criticism

To use the four steps of art criticism to evaluate one's own work
NSAE 1.b; 2.b; 3.a; 5.c

Vocabulary Vocabulary

Review the following vocabulary words with students before beginning the lesson.

simplicity simplicidad—unity created by using a single color, texture, or shape

unity unidad—the feeling of wholeness in a work of art

See page 209B for additional vocabulary and Spanish vocabulary resources.

 Art Journal: Vocabulary

Have students add these words to the Vocabulary section of their Art Journals.

Lesson Materials

- construction paper
- pencils
- crayons
- clay
- clay mat
- clay tools (pencils, paper clips, toothpicks, forks)
- glazes (or 3 parts tempera mixed with 1 part floor wax)

Alternate Materials:
- air-drying clay

Program Resources

- *Reading and Writing Test Prep.*, pp. 74–75
- *Transparency 35*
- *Flash Card 18*
- *Artist Profiles*, pp. 32, 57
- *Animals Through History Time Line*
- *Assessment*, pp. 77–78
- *Large Prints 47* Group Portrait and *48* Hoosick Falls, N.Y. in Winter
- *Art Around the World Collection*

Concept Trace
Unity Through Color
Introduced: Level 2, Unit 6, Lesson 5

Reinforced: Level 4, Unit 6, Lesson 6

Lesson 5 Arts Integration NSAE 6.a

Theatre

Complete Unit 6, Lesson 5 on pages 116–117 of *Theatre Arts Connections.*

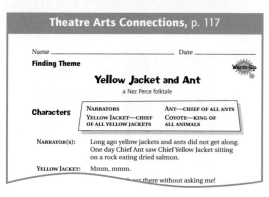

Music

 An instrumental color can by used in an entire piece to express a feeling. Listen to *Humming Chorus* from *Madame Butterfly* by Giacomo Puccini. The tone color does not change throughout the composition. This music was used in the opera when Madame Butterfly was waiting for a loved one. How does this calm stability portray her confidence her loved one will arrive?

Movement & Dance

Students form a large circle. One person creates a flowing movement (like cursive writing) that is passed to the next person. That person picks up the movement from where it left off, turns it into something else, and then passes it on. This pattern will go completely around the circle. Students must maintain the sense of flow and rhythm in the circle.

Focus

Time: About 10 minutes

Activate Prior Knowledge

"Think about a cat. What different body parts does a cat have? What do those parts have in common?" *"Piensen en un gato. ¿Cuáles son las diferentes partes del cuerpo de un gato? ¿Qué tienen en común esas partes?"*

- Discuss the different parts that make up a cat's body, such as legs, paws, a tail, a head, and ears. Talk about how the parts are different shapes, but they are unified because they are all covered in soft fur. Discuss how a single texture or color creates unity.

Using Literature ☆ Reading

- Read *Unseen Rainbows, Silent Songs* by Susan E. Goodman. Discuss how the pages are unified by repeated colors.

Thematic Connection ☆ Science

- **Environment:** Discuss how color creates unity in the natural environment.

Introduce the Art

Look   NSAE 3.a

"Let's take a close look at the two works of art." *"Vamos a mirar detalladamente las dos obras de arte".*

Summarizing ☆ Reading

- Have students describe what they see in each work of art. *Flowers* is a two-dimensional work of art. It shows four similar flowers on a background of grass. *Gin Matsuba* is a sculpture. It shows a fish.

 Art History and Culture

Share with students the information about each artist's profession from the Art History and Culture sections on pages 202 and 203. Discuss that Lundin Kudo often sculpts koi, and her customers can choose how they want their fish to appear when they commission a koi sculpture.
NSAE 5.a

🖥 **Web Connection**

Students can make their own silk screen at the Andy Warhol Museum's Web site, **www.warhol.org**.

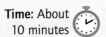 Unity Through Color

Look at the works of art on these pages. Andy Warhol made a series of silkscreens of these flowers. Each print was painted in different colors. The fish in *Gin Matsuba* is a type of Japanese fish called koi. Lundin Kudo makes sculptures of koi. Each artist used one color throughout these works of art.

◄ **Andy Warhol.** (American). *Flowers.* 1967.
· ·
Silk screen ink and synthetic polymer paint on canvas. 115 ½ × 115 ½ inches (293.4 × 293.4 cm). Museum of Contemporary Art, San Diego, California.

 Art History and Culture

Koi are like a living work of art! They are popular ornamental pond fish that are sometimes called "living jewels" or "swimming flowers."

202   Unit 6 • Lesson 5

 Art History and Culture

Andy Warhol

Andy Warhol (an´ dē wôr´ hōl) (1928–1987) was born in Pennsylvania. He attended the Carnegie Institute of Technology and moved to New York after he graduated. He became a successful commercial artist and illustrator. His illustrations were published in many magazines. Warhol was very interested in popular culture and often painted celebrities and images from advertisements. The technique of silk-screening allowed him to produce many copies of a single image, which he would then paint in different colors.

See pages 16–21 and 24–25 for more about subject matter and art history.

 **Artist Profiles, p. 57**

✦ Artist Profile ✦
Andy Warhol
1928–1987
Andy Warhol (an´ dē wôr´ hōl) was born Andrew Warhola in Pittsburgh, Pennsylvania. After graduating from the Carnegie Institute of Technology, he moved to New York and became a successful commercial artist and illustrator. Fascinated with consumer culture, the media, and fame, his photography and silkscreen paintings were often critiqued as both an ingenious expression of American culture or a base representation of low, common imagery.

▲ **Lundin Kudo.**
(American).
Gin Matsuba.
....
19 × 7 × 9 inches (48.26
× 17.78 × 22.86 cm.).
Private Collection.

Study the works of art to find unity.

▶ Which repeated shapes create harmony in
Flowers?

▶ Which different lines and textures create variety in
Gin Matsuba?

▶ What colors do you see in each work of art?

Aesthetic Perception

Seeing Like an Artist Where do you see examples of unity
in your classroom?

Art History and Culture

Lundin Kudo

Lundin Kudo (lun´ dēn kōō´ dō) studied art at a private studio in
Spain and earned a degree from the University of Michigan. She
has a studio in Florida where she makes clay sculptures. Kudo
created her own business to sell her artwork. Kudo works on
commission, meaning her customers hire her to create the art
they want.

See pages 16–21 and 24–25 for more about subject matter and art
history.

Artist Profiles, p. 32

◆ Artist Profile ◆

Lundin Kudo

Lundin Kudo (lun´ dēn kōō´ dō) creates pear
sculptures so realistic that a viewer might
not realize they are made of clay and take a
bite. Kudo uses the pear shape in much of
her work, and she explores the different
textures, shapes, and colors of everyday
objects through her art. She also uses color
and texture to explore subjects, such as her
life-size sculptures of middle-aged women.

Study NSAE 2.b

▶ *Flowers* has harmony because of the
repeated grass and flower shapes.

▶ *Gin Matsuba* has variety because of the
different textures. The fins and tail have
straight lines and a slightly rough texture,
while the body has curved lines and a
somewhat bumpy texture. The front of the
fish's head has a smooth texture.

▶ *Flowers* has black and blue. *Gin Matsuba*
has a warm pearly color.

■ For more examples of art from North
America see ***Art Around the World.***

Art Journal: Writing

Encourage students to write their
own definitions of unity in the Concepts
section of their Art Journals.

Aesthetic Perception

Seeing Like an Artist Discuss with students
where they see examples of unity in the
classroom because of a single texture or
color. Possibilities include: the four walls,
floor tiles, the desks, books on a bookshelf.

Developing Visual Literacy Discuss how the
artists' choices of elements affected students'
reactions to each artwork. Would students
feel differently about *Flowers* if each flower
had been a different color? What if the fish in
Gin Matsuba had a single texture but
different colors?
NSAE 2.b; 5.c

Web Connection

Visit **www.lundinkudo.com** to see more work by
Lundin Kudo. Have students identify main ideas
about her work.

Teach

"How can artists create unity in their works of art?" "¿Cómo pueden los artistas crear unidad en sus obras de arte?"

■ Read and discuss the information about unity and simplicity on page 204.

Practice

Materials: construction paper, pencils, crayons

Alternate Materials: sketch paper, markers

■ Distribute the materials and have students follow the directions on page 204.

■ When students have completed their drawings, discuss whether they successfully created unity.

Creative Expression

NASE 1.a; 1.c; 1.d

Materials: clay, clay mat, clay tools (pencils, paper clips, toothpicks, forks), glazes (or 3 parts tempera mixed with 1 part floor wax)

Alternate Materials: air-drying clay

■ Distribute the materials and have students follow the directions on page 205.

■ Review the Technique Tips on pages 225–226 for information about working with clay.

■ See the Activity Tips on page 249 for visual examples of this lesson's activity.

■ Create a class exhibition of students' finished works. Have students discuss each others' use of unity.

Art Journal: Brainstorming

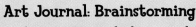

In their Art Journals, have students plan the textures they will show on the clay fish.

Using Unity

Unity is the "invisible glue" that makes different parts look as if they belong together. It helps you see a work of art as a whole instead of as separate parts.

Harmony is created by using similar lines, shapes, colors, or textures. Variety is created by using different lines, shapes, colors, or textures. Works of art that have harmony or variety can also have unity. One way an artist can create unity is by making everything in a work one color, texture, or shape. This is called **simplicity**.

Practice

Create and color a design that illustrates unity. Use a crayon.

1. Draw a variety of geometric and free-form shapes to create a design.

2. Color all of the shapes with the same color.

Differentiated Instruction

Reteach

Use *Flash Card 18*. Discuss how the repetition of the red-orange color somewhere on each child creates unity.

Special Needs

Adaptations: To ensure success in this project, provide students with a practice piece of clay. Have them produce a variety of clay textures they can use in their project.

ELL Tips

Students may have difficulty following oral directions without some kind of visual support. Consider modeling the steps of the Creative Expression activity with the whole class.

◄ **Will Collier.**
Age 9.

Think about how this student created unity in his fish.

 Creative Expression

Have you ever seen a fish with interesting textures on its body? Create a clay fish with unity.

1. Flatten a palm-sized ball of clay until it is about as thick as your little finger. Fold the clay like a taco. Score the edges and seal it along the top.

2. Shape clay into fins and eyes. Attach by scoring, applying slip, and smoothing. Pinch a tail.

3. Use clay tools to create scales. Make interesting textures on your fish.

4. After the fish is fired, glaze or paint it with one color.

 Art Criticism

Describe List the steps you followed to create your clay fish.

Analyze How did you give your work a variety of textures? How did you create unity?

Interpret Give your clay fish a name that sums up its expressive quality.

Decide Were you able to successfully create unity in your ceramic sculpture?

 **Time:** About 5 minutes

Review and Assess

"How can artists use color to create unity in a work of art?" "¿Cómo pueden los artistas usar el color para crear unidad en una obra de arte?"

Think

The student created unity in his fish by glazing the fish's body with black glaze.

■ Discuss with students whether there are any examples of unity through color in **Large Prints 47** Group Portrait and **48** Hoosick Falls, N.Y. in Winter.

Informal Assessment

Art Journal: Critical Thinking
Have students answer the four art criticism questions—Describe, Analyze, Interpret, and Decide—in their Art Journals. In small groups, have students discuss the use of variety in their weavings.
NSAE 1.b; 2.b; 3.a; 5.c

■ For standardized-format test practice using this lesson's art content, see pages 74–75 in **Reading and Writing Test Preparation**.

● **Art Across the Curriculum** ●   NSAE 6.b

Use these simple ideas to reinforce art concepts across the curriculum.

★ **Persuasive Writing** Have students decide which work of art is a better example of unity, and then write a persuasive paragraph explaining their choice.

★ **Math** Discuss measuring the dimensions of the works of art in this lesson.

★ **Science** Have students look for examples of unity in nature.

★ **Social Studies** Have students identify national and state monuments and discuss how they have unity.

★ **Technology** Have students look for unity in the pieces of technology equipment, such as a computer keyboard. Visit **SRAonline.com** to print detailed instructions for this activity.

Unity Through Color

Extra! For the Art Specialist

Time: About 45 minutes

Focus

Use **Transparency 35** to discuss unity through color. How else did the artists create unity in the works of art? Have students look for repetition of other elements, such as line, shape, or texture.

Teach

Have students complete the Alternate Activity. Did students successfully create unity in their works of art?

Reflect

Have students evaluate their works of art using the four steps of art criticism. (See pages 28–29 for more about art criticism.) Have students look for examples of unity in the classroom.

Alternate Activity

Materials:
- shoebox lids
- small found objects (such as buttons or scrap wood pieces)
- white glue
- acrylic paint or spray paint (for teacher use only)
- paint brushes

1. Have students select several found objects to begin their assemblage inside the shoebox lid. Encourage students to rearrange their assemblages a few times to get the most pleasing composition.

2. After students have completed their compositions, distribute white glue so they can adhere the objects to the container lid. Sculptures can either be painted one color with acrylic paint, or taken outside to be spray painted by the teacher.

Research in Art Education

One large study demonstrated that students involved with the arts were "less likely to drop out of school, watched fewer hours of television, were less likely to report boredom in school, had a more positive self-concept, and were more involved in community service." These social and practical outcomes show the need to give all students a chance at arts involvement ("Involvement in the Arts and Success in Secondary School" in *Critical Links*, p. 68).

Assessment
Use the following rubric to evaluate the artwork students make in the Creative Expression activity and to assess students' understanding of unity through color.

Have students complete page 77 or 78 in their *Assessment* books.

	Art History and Culture	Aesthetic Perception	Creative Expression	Art Criticism
3 POINTS	The student successfully identifies a few facts about the jobs of professional artists.	The student accurately describes how artists use color to create unity in an artwork.	The student's clay fish is unified by color.	The student thoughtfully and honestly evaluates his or her own work using the four steps of art criticism.
2 POINTS	The student's identification is weak or incomplete.	The student shows emerging awareness of how artists use color to create unity in an artwork.	The student's clay fish shows some awareness of unity through color.	The student attempts to evaluate his or her own work, but shows an incomplete understanding of evaluation criteria.
1 POINT	The student cannot identify facts about the jobs of professional artists.	The student cannot identify how artists use color to create unity in an artwork.	The student's clay fish shows no understanding of unity through color.	The student makes no attempt to evaluate his or her own artwork.

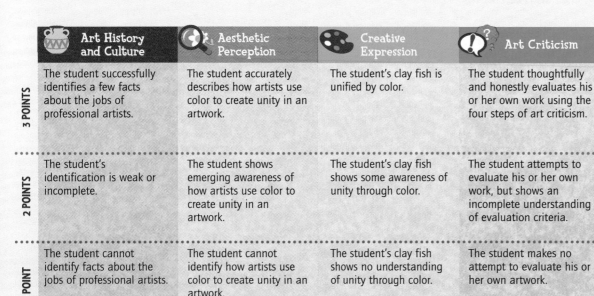

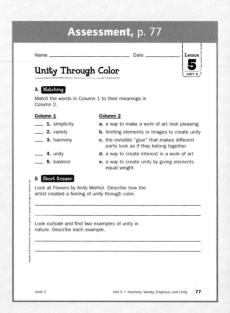

Assessment, p. 77

Name _____ Date _____

Lesson 5 UNIT 6

Unity Through Color

A. Matching
Match the words in Column 1 to their meanings in Column 2.

Column 1
___ 1. simplicity
___ 2. variety
___ 3. harmony
___ 4. unity
___ 5. balance

Column 2
a. a way to make a work of art look pleasing
b. limiting elements or images to create unity
c. the invisible "glue" that makes different parts look as if they belong together
d. a way to create interest in a work of art
e. a way to create unity by giving elements equal weight

B. Short Answer
Look at *Flowers* by Andy Warhol. Describe how the artist created a feeling of unity through color.

Look outside and find two examples of unity in nature. Describe each example.

Level 3   Unit 6 • Harmony, Variety, Emphasis, and Unity   77

Unity, Repetition, and Grouping

Lesson 6 continues teaching unity. Artists can create unity by repeating lines, shapes, colors, or textures, or by grouping different objects together with a similar background.

Objectives

Art History and Culture

To discuss some facts about the life and art of Davis and Matisse
NSAE 4.a

Creative Expression

To create a crayon engraving that shows unity
NSAE 1.a; 1.c; 1.d

Aesthetic Perception

To identify how repetition and grouping create unity in a work of art
NSAE 2.a; 2.b

Art Criticism

To use the four steps of art criticism to evaluate one's own work
NSAE 1.b; 2.b; 3.a; 5.c

Vocabulary ★ Vocabulary

Review the following vocabulary words with students before beginning the lesson.

repetition repetición—a technique for creating rhythm and unity in which a motif or single element appears again and again

unity unidad—the feeling of wholeness in a work of art

See page 209B for additional vocabulary and Spanish vocabulary resources.

Art Journal: Vocabulary

Have students add these words to the Vocabulary section of their Art Journals.

Lesson Materials

- construction paper
- 9" × 12" white paper
- pencils
- crayons
- large paper clips
- washable black ink
- paintbrushes

Alternate Materials:
- sketch paper, markers
- oil pastels

Program Resources

- *Reading and Writing Test Prep.*, pp. 76–77
- *Transparency 36*
- *Flash Card 18*
- *Artist Profiles*, pp. 13, 39
- *Animals Through History Time Line*
- *Assessment*, pp. 79-80
- *Large Prints 47 Group Portrait and 48 Hoosick Falls, N.Y. in Winter*
- *The National Museum of Women in the Arts Collection*

Concept Trace

Unity, Repetition, and Grouping
Introduced: Level 2, Unit 6, Lesson 6

Reinforced: Level 4, Unit 6, Lesson 6

Lesson 6 Arts Integration NSAE 6.a

Theatre

Complete Unit 6, Lesson 6, on pages 118–123 of *Theatre Arts Connections*.

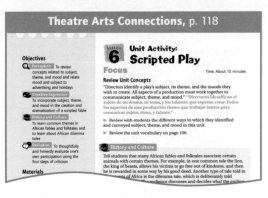

Music

Music from movies often portrays the mood of a scene before anyone speaks. In the movie *Fantasia,* Mickey Mouse gets in over his head to the music of Paul Dukas. Listen to *Sorcerer's Apprentice* by Paul Dukas. The melodic pattern that belongs to the broom never changes. What contributes to the mood changes in the music?

Movement & Dance

Divide students into groups of five. Write down four different movement ideas, such as turns, jumps, or stretches, on pieces of paper and put them up around the classroom, assigning a specific activity to an area of room. Each group begins in one area and takes eight counts to explore the activity before rotating to the next area.

Focus

Time: About 10 minutes

Activate Prior Knowledge

"Imagine that you are looking into a fishbowl. What are some different objects that you see? How does the bowl give a feeling of unity to all these different objects?" *"Imagínense que miran una pecera. ¿Cuáles son algunos de los diferentes objetos que observan? ¿Cómo da la pecera una sensación de unidad a todos estos objetos?"*

■ Discuss students' answers to the questions and the fact that the fishbowl brings objects close together in a small area.

Using Literature ☆ Reading

■ Read *Birds, Nests and Eggs* by Mel Boring. Discuss unity in the illustrations created by repetition and grouping.

Thematic Connection ☆ Social Studies

■ **Neighborhoods/Communities:** Discuss how unity can be created in a neighborhood or community.

Introduce the Art

Look
NSAE 3.a

"Let's take a close look at the two works of art." *"Vamos a mirar detalladamente las dos obras de arte".*

Comparing and Contrasting ☆ Reading

■ Have students list the similarities and differences in the works of art. Both works have lines engraved into a background color. Both works repeat limited colors. *Woman in Blue* shows shallow space, has bright colors, and repeats lines throughout. *Ancestral Spirit Dance* shows flat space, has contrasting colors, and repeats lines in a contained space.

Art History and Culture

Answers may vary. Share with students the information from the Art History and Culture sections on pages 206 and 207. Discuss that artists have many reasons for making their works of art. Davis makes art to celebrate his heritage.
NSAE 5.a; 5.b

 Web Connection
Have students explore the Kids Wing of the Museum of Web Art at **www.mowa.org/kids/**.

206 UNIT 6 • Harmony, Variety, Emphasis, and Unity

Unity, Repetition, and Grouping

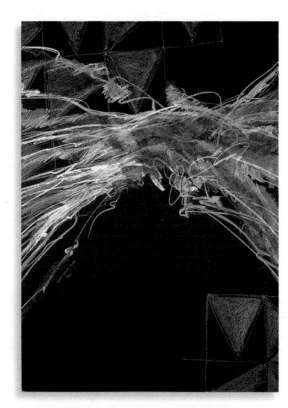

Look at the paintings on these pages. Henri Matisse painted *Woman in Blue* in France. About 50 years later, Willis "Bing Davis" painted *Ancestral Spirit Dance Series,* an abstract design based on memories of African dancers. Both artists have created unity to give their work a feeling of wholeness.

◀ **Willis "Bing" Davis.** (American). *Ancestral Spirit Dance Series.* 1990.
Oil pastel. 60 × 40 inches (152.4 × 101.6 cm.). Collection of Willis Bing Davis.

Art History and Culture

Why do you think the artists created these works of art?

206 Unit 6 • Lesson 6

Art History and Culture

Willis "Bing" Davis

Willis "Bing" Davis (wil´əs bing dā´vəs) (1937–   ) was born in Dayton, Ohio. He had talents in both art and sports. He won an athletic scholarship to DePauw University and he earned a degree in Art Education. Davis had a fellowship in Nigeria, where he explored the heritage of his African ancestors. Most of Davis's works are created as an inquiry or reflection of his heritage.

See pages 16–21 and 24–25 for more about subject matter and art history.

Artist Profiles, p. 13

Artist Profile

Willis "Bing" Davis
b. 1937

Bing Davis (bing dā´vəs) was born in Dayton, Ohio. He was a student with many talents and gifts, including those for athletics and the arts. Because he excelled in sports, he was awarded a scholarship to DePauw University in Indiana, where he earned a degree in art education. He continued to study and earned his master's degree from Miami University in Oxford, Ohio. Davis has pioneered such projects as the Dayton-based, now nationwide, program Artists in the Schools. Davis has had more than 50 one-man exhibitions since 1959.

Study both works of art to find examples of unity.

▶ Where do you see geometric shapes combined with wild zigzag lines?

▶ Name the colors in each work. How many are there in each?

▶ Locate the thin lines repeated throughout *Woman in Blue*.

◀ **Henri Matisse.** (French). *Woman in Blue.* 1937.

. . . .
Oil on canvas. 36½ × 29 inches (92.71 × 73.66 cm.). Philadelphia Museum of Art, Philadelphia, Pennsylvania.

Aesthetic Perception

Seeing Like an Artist Look outdoors. Find objects in nature that are surrounded by a single color.

Art History and Culture

Henri Matisse

Henri Matisse (än´ rē ma tēs´) (1869–1954) was born in France. He studied for a career in law, but in 1890 became ill with appendicitis and was bedridden. While he was recovering from his illness, he began to paint to relieve his boredom. After he recovered, Matisse gave up law and decided to study art. Matisse was the leader of an art movement called fauvism. The name fauve means "wild beast" in French and was given to these artists because of their wild use of bright colors.

See pages 16–21 and 24–25 for more about subject matter and art history.

Artist Profiles, p. 39

◆ Artist Profile ◆

Henri Matisse
1869-1954

Henri Matisse (än´ rē ma tēs´) was the son of a middle-class couple in the north of France. He was not interested in art while he was in school. After high school his father sent him to law school in Paris. When he was 21 an appendicitis attack changed his life. Because he had to spend a long time in the hospital, his mother brought him a paint box to help him pass the time. Matisse eventually convinced his father to let him drop out of law school and study art. Matisse married and started a family soon after. His paintings were not selling, so he worked for a decorator and his wife opened a hat shop. During the last years of his life he suffered from arthritis. Unable to hold a brush in his hands, he devoted his efforts to

Study

▶ *Ancestral Spirit Dance* has triangles combined with zigzag lines.

▶ *Woman in Blue* contains the primary colors (red, yellow, blue), black, and white. Ancestral Spirit Dance contains black, white, pink, and blue.

▶ Thin, crisscrossed lines are found throughout the background.

■ For more examples of portraits see *The National Museum of Women in the Arts Collection*.

Art Journal: Writing

Encourage students to list ways they could create unity in the Concepts section of their Art Journals.

Aesthetic Perception

Seeing Like an Artist Discuss that the sky or the ground can often unify different objects outdoors.

Developing Visual Literacy Have students look at *Ancestral Spirit Dance Series*. How does the title reflect what they see in the work of art?

Web Connection

Visit the Philadelphia Museum of Art's Web site, **www.philamuseum.org**

**each** Time: About 30 minutes

"How can artists use repetition and grouping to create unity?" "¿Cómo pueden los artistas usar repetición y agrupación para crear unidad?"

■ Remind students what they learned in Unit 6, Lesson 5, about *unity* and techniques for creating it. Discuss the other techniques on page 208.

Practice

Materials: construction paper, pencils, crayons

Alternate Materials: sketch paper, markers

■ Distribute the materials and have students follow the directions on page 208.

■ When students have completed their drawings, discuss whether they successfully created unity.

Creative Expression

NSAE 1.a; 1.c; 1.d
Materials: 9" × 12" white paper, pencils, crayons, large paper clips, washable black ink, paintbrushes

Alternate Materials: oil pastels

■ Distribute the materials and have students follow the directions on page 209.

■ See the Activity Tips on page 249 for visual examples of this lesson's activity.

Art Journal: Brainstorming

Have students make sketches in their Art Journals to plan the creatures they will use for their crayon engraving.

Using Repetition and Grouping to Create Unity

Unity is the feeling of wholeness in a work of art. Artists use repetition and grouping to show that different parts of a work belong together.

Repetition is when an artist repeats lines, shapes, colors, or textures. An architect, for example, might repeat colors and textures on the outside of a house.

Objects that are grouped together are unified by what surrounds them. Seashells arranged on a beach are a good example of unity. They are usually different shapes and sizes, but the sand in the background unifies them.

Practice

Illustrate unity. Use pencil and crayon.

1. Draw a large free-form shape. Fill it with a variety of smaller geometric shapes.

2. Use pencil to darken the spaces between the geometric shapes. Use crayon to color the whole area outside the free-form shape one color.

208 Unit 6 • Lesson 6

Differentiated Instruction

Reteach

Have students look through the book to find other works of art that have unity created by repetition and grouping. Discuss how unity was created in each work of art.

Special Needs

Adaptations: Consider providing fossilized rocks for students to examine as motivation for this activity. The many animal textures found there can inspire the content or arrangement of their works of art.

ELL Tips

Students may feel hesitant about answering the interpretive question concerning their artwork. You may wish to phrase the question as an either/or choice so the vocabulary needed to answer the question is contained in the question itself.

◄ **Toni Thompson.**
Age 8.

Think about how this student showed unity in her design.

 Creative Expression

How can you use creatures to show unity? Create a crayon engraving.

1. Use crayons to cover a sheet of paper with many different colors. Then, paint the whole surface with thinned black ink until you can no longer see the color.

2. While the ink is drying, sketch a few creatures on scratch paper. Choose some to draw.

3. Engrave the creatures by scratching lines and line patterns in the black background with the pointed end of a paper clip. Add detail and texture.

 **Art Criticism**

Describe What creatures did you draw?

Analyze How did you create unity in your engraving?

Interpret How would the mood of your picture change if you had not covered the surface with black ink?

Decide Can you think of another theme to use for this art project?

Unit 6 • Lesson 6   **209**

R**eflect** 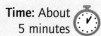 Time: About 5 minutes

Review and Assess
"What are some ways artists can create unity in their works of art?" "¿Cuáles son algunas maneras en que los artistas pueden crear unidad en sus obras de arte?"

Think

The student's artwork has unity because of repeated lines of similar widths. The artwork is also unified by the single background color.

■ Discuss with students whether there are any areas of unity created by repetition or grouping in *Large Prints 47* Group Portrait and *48 Hoosick Falls, N.Y. in Winter*.

Informal Assessment

Art Journal: Critical Thinking
Have students answer the four art criticism questions—Describe, Analyze, Interpret, and Decide—in their Art Journals. In small groups, have students discuss the use of variety in their weavings.
NSAE 1.b; 2.b; 3.a; 5.c

■ For standardized-format test practice using this lesson's art content, see pages 76–77 in *Reading and Writing Test Preparation*.

Art Across the Curriculum

NSAE 6.b

Use these simple ideas to reinforce art concepts across the curriculum.

★ **Poetry Writing** Discuss how poems have unity created by repetition of rhyming sounds and grouping of sentences. Have students write a poem that has unity.

★ **Math** Discuss how math uses repetition and grouping to solve problems.

★ **Science** Discuss machines or systems that have unity among parts, such as cars.

★ **Social Studies** Discuss the concept of unity within families or communities.

★ **Technology** Have students use the computer's paint program to create an artwork that has unity through repetition and grouping. Visit **SRAonline.com** to print detailed instructions for this activity.

Unity, Repetition, and Grouping

Extra! For the Art Specialist

 Time: About 45 minutes

Focus

Use *Transparency 36* to discuss unity through repetition and grouping. What objects in each work are the same? What objects are different? How did the artists' use of materials create a feeling of unity?

Teach

Have students complete the animal sculpture Alternate Activity.

Reflect

Have students evaluate their work using the four steps of art criticism. (See pages 28–29 for more about art criticism.)

Alternate Activity

Materials:
- various small containers and boxes, cardboard tubes, container lids, and egg cartons
- 4" × 6" pieces of posterboard
- scissors
- glue
- masking tape
- shoe box lids
- hot glue gun and glue sticks (teacher use only)
- tempera paints
- paintbrushes
- water containers

1. Ask students to select three or four geometric forms from the collected items, plus other materials, to create an animal sculpture.

2. Have students glue and tape the forms together. Once the students have completed the animal sculptures, the teacher can hot glue the sculpture to the shoe-box lid.

3. Students can paint their animal sculptures with tempera paint.

Research in Art Education

Research has shown that "the relevancy of activities [in arts education], respectful climate, and opportunities for learners to take responsibility . . . [provide] a context for learner risk-taking and increased motivation and engagement." Studies also have demonstrated that "these desirable processes and teaching characteristics are inherent to dynamic, multiple-arts teaching environments" ("Promising Signs of Positive Effects: Lessons from the Multi-Arts Studies" in *Critical Links*, p. 99).

Assessment
Use the following rubric to evaluate the artwork students make in the Creative Expression activity and to assess students' understanding of unity, repetition, and grouping.

Have students complete page 79 or 80 in their *Assessment* books.

	Art History and Culture	Aesthetic Perception	Creative Expression	Art Criticism
3 POINTS	The student successfully discusses some facts about the life and art of Davis and Matisse	The student accurately describes how repetition and grouping create unity in a work of art.	The student's crayon engraving clearly shows unity.	The student thoughtfully and honestly evaluates his or her own work using the four steps of art criticism.
2 POINTS	The student's discussion is incomplete.	The student shows emerging awareness of how repetition and grouping create unity in a work of art.	The student's crayon engraving shows some awareness of unity.	The student attempts to evaluate his or her own work, but shows an incomplete understanding of evaluation criteria.
1 POINT	The student cannot discuss some facts about the life and art of Davis and Matisse	The student cannot identify how repetition and grouping create unity in a work of art.	The student's crayon engraving shows no unity.	The student makes no attempt to evaluate his or her own artwork.

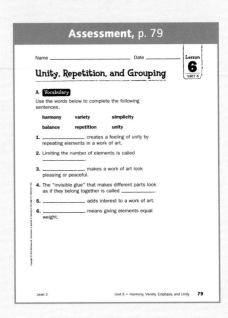

Assessment, p. 79

Name _____ Date _____ Lesson **6** UNIT 6

Unity, Repetition, and Grouping

A. Vocabulary
Use the words below to complete the following sentences.

harmony	variety	simplicity
balance	repetition	unity

1. _____ creates a feeling of unity by repeating elements in a work of art.
2. Limiting the number of elements is called _____.
3. _____ makes a work of art look pleasing or peaceful.
4. The "invisible glue" that makes different parts look as if they belong together is called _____.
5. _____ adds interest to a work of art.
6. _____ means giving elements equal weight.

Level 3   Unit 6 • Harmony, Variety, Emphasis, and Unity   **79**

Unit 6 Vocabulary Review

contrast—to set in opposition in order to show or emphasize a difference **contraste**—poner en oposición para mostrar o enfatizar una diferencia

emphasis—the principle of design that stresses one element or area in a work of art over another **énfasis**—el principio del diseño que destaca un elemento o área en una obra de arte sobre otra

focal point—the area of a work of art to which the viewer's eyes are drawn **punto focal**—el área de una obra de arte hacia la cual se atrae la vista del espectador

harmony—the peaceful look made when related elements of art are put together **armonía**—la apariencia serena que se logra cuando se reúnen elementos relacionados de arte

repetition—a technique for creating rhythm and unity in which a motif or single element appears again and again **repetición**—una técnica para crear ritmo y unidad en la cual aparece un motivo o un solo elemento una y otra vez

simplicity—unity created by using a single color, texture, or shape **simplicidad**—unidad creada al usar un solo color, textura o figura

unity—the feeling of wholeness in a work of art **unidad**—la sensación de totalidad en una obra de arte

variety—using different lines, shapes, colors, and textures to make a work of art interesting **variedad**—usar diferentes líneas, figuras, colores y texturas para hacer una obra de arte interesante

---

Vocabulary Practice

T Display *Transparency 42* to review unit vocabulary words.

Definitions:
Brief Definitions ⭐ Vocabulary
Give a brief definition of *contrast*. Have students identify the unit vocabulary word you defined. Repeat for each unit vocabulary word.

Examples ⭐ Vocabulary
Display *Large Prints 47* and *48*. Have students select a unit vocabulary word and find an example of that word in one of the works of art.

Answering Questions ⭐ Vocabulary
Have students practice critical thinking skills by answering questions using unit vocabulary words. For instance, "Can an artwork have emphasis and unity?"

Wrapping Up Unit 6

Harmony, Variety, Emphasis, and Unity

Harmony, Variety, Emphasis, and Unity

Art Criticism

Critical Thinking Art criticism is an organized system for looking at and talking about art. You can criticize art without being an expert. The purpose of art criticism is to get the viewer involved in a perception process that delays judgment until all aspects of the artwork have been studied.

- See page 28–29 for more about art criticism.

Describe

▶ Ask students to examine the credit line of the artwork and identify the information it provides.

▶ Ask students to describe the people in the artwork. Student answers will vary. There are eight African-American women well known in history: (from left) Madame C. J. Walker , Sojourner Truth, Ida B. Wells, Fannie Lou Hamer, Harriet Tubman, Rosa Parks, Mary McLeod Bethune, and Ella Baker. There is one man—the artist Vincent van Gogh. The women wear clothing from their time period in history. All but two of them wear clothing with patterns. Vincent van Gogh has a red beard and wears a blue shirt, black pants, and a yellow straw hat. The women are seated around a large quilt frame. They are sewing a quilt. Van Gogh stands slightly behind them, holding a vase of sunflowers.

▶ Ask students to describe what else they see in the artwork. Behind and around the women is a field of sunflowers. In the background there are houses and trees. Above and below the picture is a strip of printed words. There is a border of flowered quilt squares around the edge.

Analyze

▶ Ask students where harmony is created by similar colors and shapes. Harmony is created by three colors that are related on

▲ **Faith Ringgold.** (American). *The Sunflower Quilting Bee at Arles.* 1991.

Acrylic on canvas, printed and tie-dyed fabric. 74 × 80 inches (187.96 × 203.2 cm.). Private Collection.

Art History and Culture

Faith Ringgold

Faith Ringgold (fāth ring´gōld) (1930–   ) was born in New York. As a child, Ringgold learned sewing and quilt making from her mother and grandmother. She graduated from the City College of New York and became an art teacher. Ringgold uses her artwork to draw attention to the challenges faced by African Americans, especially women. Her quilts tell stories, with and without words.

See pages 16–21 and 24–25 for more about subject matter and art history.

Artist Profiles, p. 49

Artist Profile

Faith Ringgold
b. 1930

Faith Ringgold (fāth ring´gōld) grew up in Harlem in New York City. As a child her asthma often kept her home from school. To pass the time her mother taught her how to draw and sew. After high school Ringgold wanted to become an artist, but at the time the City College of New York did not allow women to study liberal arts. Instead Ringgold became an art teacher and taught for almost 20 years. She used her own artwork to draw attention to the challenges faced by African Americans, especially women.

 **Art Criticism** Critical Thinking

Describe **What do you see?**

During this step you will collect information about the work.

► What does the credit line tell us about this work?

► Describe the people.

Analyze **How is this work organized?**

Think about how the artist has used the elements and principles of art.

► Where do you see harmony created by similar colors and shapes?

► Where do you see variety created by difference?

Interpret **What is the artist trying to say?**

Use the clues you discovered during your analysis to find the message the artist is trying to show.

► What do you think the women are talking about?

► Why do you think van Gogh is in the painting?

Decide **What do you think about the work?**

Use all the information you have gathered to decide whether this is a successful work of art.

► Is the work successful because it is realistic, because it is well-organized, or because it has a strong message?

Unit 6 **211**

 Aesthetic Perception

Seeing Like an Artist Have students think about another quilt they have seen. How does it compare with *The Sunflower Quilting Bee at Arles*? Discuss the following questions with students.

Describe ► What does the quilt look like?

Analyze ► How does the quilt have harmony?
► Does it have variety?
► How does the quilt have unity?

Interpret ► Was the quilt made to tell a story, or for another purpose?

Decide ► Did the artist create a successful work?

the color wheel: yellow, yellow-green, and green. The yellows and greens are repeated throughout the work of art. Harmony is created by the similar shapes of the sunflowers. The similar shapes of the buildings also create harmony. The women sit in similar positions.

► Ask students where they see variety created by difference. The free-form shapes of the people contrast with the geometric shapes of the sunflowers and the buildings. The flowered rectangles around the border of the quilt add variety because they are different from the sunflowers. All the people are wearing different colors and styles of clothing.

► Ask students what the focal point of the artwork is. The focal point is the group of women. The artist created emphasis by making the women's clothing contrast with the flowers and buildings.

► Ask students what gives the artwork unity. The repeated shape of the sunflowers on the women's quilt and in the field around them creates unity. The repeated colors appear in the picture and the border. Small red shapes appear throughout the artwork.

Interpret

► Ask students what they think the women in the artwork are talking about. Answers will vary. Students may say they are talking about their quilt, or perhaps their lives.

► Ask students why they think van Gogh is in the painting. Answers will vary. Students may know that his sunflower paintings are very famous. Some may say van Gogh is bringing them some more sunflowers to use in their artwork, or that he is bringing the sunflowers as a gift. Some may say van Gogh is telling them how beautiful their quilt is, or that he just came to watch them work.

Decide

► Ask students if they feel the work is successful because it is realistic, because it is well-organized, or because it has a strong message. Answers will vary.

Art Journal: Writing
Have students write the answers to the Aesthetic Perception questions in their Art Journals.

"Artists create works of art that have harmony, variety, emphasis, and unity." "Los artistas crean obras de arte que tienen armonía, variedad, énfasis y unidad".

T Review unit vocabulary with students using *Transparency 42*.

Art Journal: Writing
Have students answer the questions on page 212. Answers: 1. B, 2. A, 3. A, 4. C, 5. B

T For further assessment, have students complete the unit test on *Transparency 48*.

VISIT A MUSEUM
The Philadelphia Museum of Art

▶ Visitors to the Philadelphia Museum of Art feel as if they are taking a walk through time. Due to the vision of Fiske Kimball, the museum's architectural historian, curators were sent to all parts of the world to find architectural interiors that were well preserved. As museum-goers move from gallery to gallery, they pass through an Indian temple, a Chinese palace hall, and a Japanese teahouse.

"Art is a technique of communication. The image is the most complete technique of communication."
    —Claes Oldenburg

Show What You Know

Answer these questions on a separate sheet of paper.

❶ _____ is using different lines, shapes, colors, and textures to make a work look interesting.
A. Harmony
B. Variety
C. Focal point

❷ Artists create _____ to make an object look different from the rest of an artwork.
A. contrast
B. unity
C. harmony

❸ _____ is the peaceful look made when related elements of art are put together.
A. Harmony
B. Variety
C. Emphasis

❹ Which is not an example of unity?
A. Simplicity
B. Grouping
C. Contrast

❺ An artist uses emphasis to draw your attention to the _____.
A. repetition
B. focal point
C. unity

212 Unit 6

VISIT A MUSEUM
The Philadelphia Museum of Art

The Philadelphia Museum of Art was established in Philadelphia, Pennsylvania, in 1875. There are over 300,000 objects in the museum's collection. The Asian collection has artwork dating from 500 B.C. to the present. The European collections have sculpture, stained glass, and paintings. The American collections have paintings, furniture, silver, and Pennsylvania German art. In addition, the museum offers many programs for people of all ages. These include school tours, workshops, and performances for families.

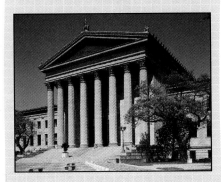

Unit Assessment Options

 Aesthetic Perception

Have students look for examples of harmony, variety, emphasis, and unity in the classroom.

Creative Expression

Student Portfolio Have students review the works of art they have created during this unit and select the pieces they wish to keep in their portfolios. Have students share their portfolios and discuss each others use of harmony, variety, emphasis, and unity.

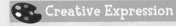 Art Criticism

Have students select their favorite work of art from this unit and study it using the four steps of art criticism. (See pages 28–29 for more about art criticism.)

Harmony, Variety, Emphasis, and Unity in Dance

This is a photo of a dancer playing a famous outlaw named "Billy the Kid." The ballet about his life and the Westward Movement shows the chores pioneers did to survive. It was choreographed by Eugene Loring. Aaron Copland composed the music with musical themes based on old cowboy songs.

What to Do Create a dance or mime showing a variety of pioneer work movements.

1. Select a few ideas to show. Some choices include chopping wood or pushing a plow. Experiment by exaggerating the movement and giving it a rhythm.
2. Find three ways to vary each work action. Suggestions are changing the direction or doing it in slow motion.
3. Select two different actions and build a mime or movement sequence.
4. Share with a partner. Combine all four ideas and show a perspective of pioneer work life as you perform them together.

▲ Eugene Loring. "Billy the Kid."

 Art Criticism

Describe Describe the way you and your partner worked together.

Analyze What things did you do to create harmony, variety, emphasis, and unity?

Interpret How did it feel to perform the work of pioneers?

Decide Were you successful in creating a pioneer work dance or mime?

Unit 6   **213**

 **Art History and Culture**

Billy the Kid

Billy the Kid is a ballet that has been preserved as an historical piece. It was choreographed in 1938 in America. It was the first ballet featuring American themes, music, and movement motifs. Eugene Loring began choreographing by organizing the events of Billy's life onto a storyboard. He placed events sequentially into scenes and then determined their dramatic impact and length. These plans were sent to Aaron Copland in Paris, who used them to create his musical score, based on themes from cowboy songs.

Harmony, Variety, Emphasis, and Unity in Dance

Objective: To create a dance or mime showing a variety of pioneer work movements

Materials: *Billy the Kid* performed by the Joffrey Ballet of Chicago. Running time: 8:36.

Focus
Time: About 5 minutes

- Discuss the information on page 213.

 **Art History and Culture**

- Have students brainstorm and list types of work done by the pioneers during the Westward Movement.

Teach
Time: About 20 minutes

 Aesthetic Perception

- Have students watch *Billy the Kid*. Discuss examples of harmony, variety, emphasis, and unity in the dance.

Creative Expression

- Have students follow the directions on page 213. Direct students to mime a variety of different work movements from the list. Encourage them to find ways to vary their movements using levels and rhythm. Ask students to select two work actions and create a movement sequence. Divide students into pairs and have each learn the partner's movements. Combine and perform them.

- **Informal Assessment** Comment positively on students' interpretations.

Reflect
Time: About 10 minutes

 **Art Criticism**

- Have students answer the four art criticism questions on page 213 orally or in writing.

- Did students successfully create a dance or mime showing a variety of pioneer work movements?

Drawing

It is important to allow the students to experiment with the drawing media. Use gentle guidance to show them how to properly hold the drawing media. Prior to use, demonstrate the techniques as they are illustrated here. Proper handling and use will increase success and establish good habits for the future. It will also make the media last longer.

Pencil

- Primary pencils with medium-soft lead should be used.

- When making thin lines, the students should hold the pencil as in writing.

- For thick lines, hold the pencil on its side near the point between the thumb and fingertips.

Colored Pencils

- When blending colors with colored pencils, it is important to color the lighter color before the darker one. A color can be darkened easily, but it is almost impossible to lighten a color.

- To create shadows, blend complementary colors. This will create browns and darker colors.

Technique Tips

Drawing

Pencil Basics

For darker values, use the side of your pencil lead, press harder, and go over areas more than once. You can add form to your objects using shading.

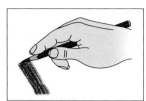
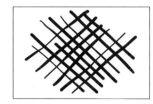

Colored Pencils

You can blend colors with colored pencils. Color with the lighter hue first. Gently go over the light hue with the darker hue until you get the hue you want.

You can create shadows by blending complementary colors.

Technique Tips

Crayon Basics

Crayons can be used to make thick and thin lines and dots. You can use both ends of a crayon.

You can color in large areas by using the long side of a crayon.

Marker Basics

You can use the point of a marker to create thin lines and small dots.

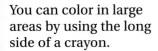

You can use the side of a marker tip to make thick lines.

Always replace the cap of a marker when you are finished using it.

Crayon

- Thin lines and small dots can be created with the sharpened end of the crayon.

- Thick lines and large dots can be made with the flat end. Large areas can be colored in with the side of an unwrapped crayon.

- Students may become concerned over broken crayons. Reassure them that these pieces are still useful for drawing and coloring in areas.

Marker

- To avoid damage, students should not press hard on the marker tip. Tell them to handle the marker gently for better control.

- For thin lines and dots, a conical-tipped marker can be used.

- The side of the tip can be used to make wider lines and color in areas.

- Remind students to replace the cap to prevent drying.

Oil Pastels

- Oil pastels are pigments that are mixed with oil and compressed into sticks. They are used like crayons. By pressing with gentle force and coloring over an area several times, students can create the effect of paint.

- Students can create lines by drawing with the tip. Textures can be created by making marks such as dots and lines. Textures can also be made by layering colors and scratching though with a paper clip straightened out at one end.

- Colors can be mixed or blended by smearing them with a paper towel wrapped around a finger.

- Oil pastels break easily. Reassure the students that these pieces can still be used like new ones. If the oil pastels become dirty from use, instruct the students to mark on a paper towel until the colors are clean again.

Colored Chalk

- Colored chalks are used to make colorful, soft designs. The use of dustless chalk is recommended for elementary classroom. The tip of the chalk is used much like an oil pastel to make lines. To fill a space or shape with solid color, use gentle force and color over an area more than once.

- Colors can be mixed or blended by smearing them together with a paper towel wrapped around a finger.

- Like oil pastels, colored chalks break easily. Reassure the students that these pieces can still be used like new ones. Colored chalks also become dirty from use. Instruct students to mark on a paper towel until the colors are clean.

Technique Tips

Oil Pastels

Oil pastels can be used like crayons. When you press down hard on oil pastels, your picture will look painted. Oil pastels are soft and break easily. They can also be messy. Wash your hands with soap and water after using them.

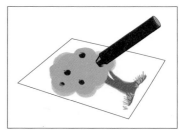

Colors can be mixed or blended by smearing them using a tissue or your finger.

You can use oil pastels to draw over other media, such as tempera and crayon.

Colored Chalk

Colored chalks can be used to make colorful, soft designs. Colored chalk is soft and breaks easily. Reuse broken pieces.

Make bolder colors by going over an area more than once.

Blend colors by using a soft tissue or your finger.

Technique Tips

Painting

Brush Care

Rinse your brush in water between colors.
Blot the brush dry on a paper towel.

Clean the brush when you are finished painting.

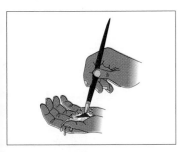

1. Rinse the brush in clean water. Wash the brush with soap.

2. Rinse the brush well again and blot it dry.

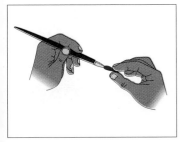

3. Shape the bristles.

4. Store brushes with bristles up.

Painting

Brush Care

- Taking proper care of a paintbrush will increase its time in use. By teaching students the rules for proper care, good habits will be established in the beginning.

- Students should always thoroughly rinse their brush tips between colors of paint. Next, they should gently blot the brush on a paper towel to test for missed paint. If paint appears on the towel, it should be rinsed and tested again. Sometimes paint gets deep inside the bristles and the brush needs more rinsing.

- To properly wash and store the brush when finished, students should:

  1. Rinse the brush under gently flowing water. Do not use hot water. Place a small amount of soap in the palm of one hand. Gently rub the bristles of the brush in their soapy palms. This will remove stubborn paint from deep inside the bristles.

  2. Rinse the brush under gently running water to remove all of the soap.

  3. Reshape the bristles into a point.

  4. Store the brushes in a container with the bristles up so their shape will be kept when the brush dries.

- When these habits are established early in the school year, the students will be more likely to respect the importance of proper care of the art media and tools.

Tempera

- For best results, it is recommended that quality liquid tempera paint is used.

- To remove excess water from the brush, gently wipe the end of the brush on the inside edge of the container. This will allow the water to run back into the container. Discourage students from tapping their brushes on the rim of the container. This will prevent paint splatters.

- When mixing paints on a palette, always mix the darker color into the lighter color a little at a time until the desired color is reached. This reduces wasted paint. Paper plates work well as palettes and reduce cleanup.

- Use a thin brush for details.

- Use a wide brush for large spaces.

Technique Tips

Tempera

Wet your brush in a water container. Wipe off extra water using the inside wall of the container and blot the brush on a paper towel.

Mix colors on a palette. Put some of each color that you want to mix on the palette. Add darker colors a little at a time to lighter colors. To create a tint, mix a small amount of a hue into white. To create a shade, mix a small amount of black into a hue.

Use a thin, pointed brush to paint thin lines and details.

Use a wide brush to paint large areas.

Technique Tips

Watercolors

Wet your brush in a water container. Wipe off extra water using the inside wall of the container and blot the brush on a paper towel. Add a drop of water to each watercolor cake. Rinse your brush between colors.

Mix colors on a palette. Put some of each color that you want to mix on the palette. Add darker colors a little at a time to lighter colors. To create a tint, add more water to a hue. To create a shade, mix a small amount of black into a hue.

Paint on damp paper to create soft lines and edges. Tape your paper to the table, brush clean water over the paper, and allow the water to soak in.

Paint on dry paper and use very little water to create sharp lines and shapes.

Watercolors

- School watercolors come in semimoist cakes. Moisten each cake that is going to be used by dripping a little water from the brush onto the cake and gently stirring the water on the surface of the paint.

- Create thick lines by gently pressing down on the brush.

- Create thin lines by lightly touching the surface of the paper with the tip of the brush.

Watercolor Resists

▪ By drawing on the paper first with crayons and/or oil pastels, students can achieve a resist effect. Because of their waxy or oily compositions, crayons and oil pastels show through watercolors. Best results are achieved when cool-colored drawings are painted over with warm colors, or vice versa.

Collage

Scissors

▪ It is important to teach students safety when they use scissors. They should always cut away from their bodies. Of course they should never point their scissors at others, spin them on the table, or walk around the room with them.

▪ There are scissors specially made to spring open for students who are physically challenged, or who are not yet developmentally ready to use standard school scissors. Many scissors on the market today can be used with the right or left hand. If these are not available, keep a supply of "lefty" scissors for students who need them.

▪ To cut thick yarn or fabric, encourage students to work in pairs. While one cuts, the other can stretch the yarn or fabric. This makes cutting easier and encourages cooperation.

Watercolor Resists

Certain materials will show through watercolors. Crayons and oil pastels both show through watercolors. To make a watercolor resist, make a drawing using crayons or oil pastels. Then paint over the drawing using watercolors. The watercolors will cover the blank parts of the paper. The watercolors will not be visible on the parts of the paper covered with crayon or oil pastels.

Collage

Scissors

Always cut away from your body.

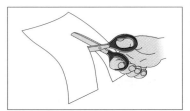

Ask a classmate to stretch yarn or fabric as you cut.

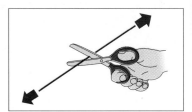

Use folded paper to cut symmetrical shapes. Fold a sheet of paper in half. Cut a shape using the folded edge as the axis.

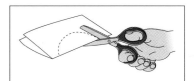

Technique Tips

Arranging a Design

When creating a collage, it is important to plan your design. Take into consideration the size of shapes and spaces, placement of shapes and spaces, color schemes, and textures. When you have made an arrangement you like, glue the shapes in place.

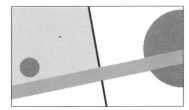

Glue

Squeeze a line of glue onto the paper. You can smooth the line with the tip of the glue bottle.

Close the glue bottle and clean the top when you are finished using it.

Arranging a Design

- Provide a variety of textured and colored papers, yarns, fabrics, and found objects for students to use. Hard-to-cut materials should be precut for students.

- When using paper, students may choose to tear and/or cut their shapes.

- Encourage students to arrange the design first. They should pay as much attention to the negative spaces as the positive ones.

- Glue only after the final colors, shapes, and textures have been chosen and arranged. White glue will attach most porous items to the background surface.

Glue

- To attach two pieces of fabric or paper, use only a few drops of glue and smooth them with the tip of the bottle.

- When finished, students should wipe the bottle clean with a paper towel, close the top, and store upright.

Texture Rubbing

- When rubbing textures have the student hold the uncovered crayon so that he is rubbing with the side and not the tip.

- With one hand hold the paper and the edges of the material being rubbed. Then rub away from the holding hand for every stroke. If the student rubs back and forth the paper will wrinkle up and a smooth rubbing will not be made.

- Rubbings can be made with the side of a pencil point, an uncovered wax crayon, or an uncovered oil pastel.

- It is better to use dark colors to make the rubbing so that the texture impression shows up. Red, green, blue, and violet are good colors to use.

- Some materials that make good rubbings are burlap, lace, weeds, shoe bottoms, and commercial rubbing plates.

Technique Tips

Texture Rubbing

Place a texture plate or textured surface underneath your paper.

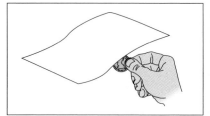

Hold the paper and object down firmly so they do not slip.

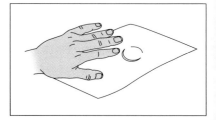

Use the long side of your crayon and rub away from you only. Do not move the crayon back and forth.

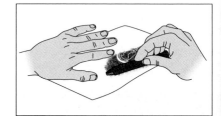

Technique Tips

Printmaking
Making Stamps

You can cut sponges into shapes to make stamps.

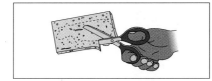

You can carve shapes into potatoes to make stamps.

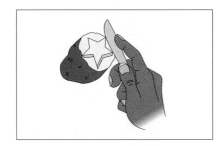

Making a Sponge Print

Use a different sponge for each color. Dip a sponge into paint. Press the sponge onto paper.

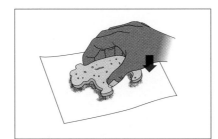

Printmaking

Making Stamps

- If students wish to cut a sponge into a specific shape, use thin sponges. Draw the shape on the sponge with a marker and use scissors to cut it out.

- To make a potato print the teacher should pre-cut potatoes in half with a sharp knife to make sure that the printing surface is smooth. To keep the potatoes for any length of time put them in a container of water. When you are ready to use them be sure to blot them dry.

  1. Have the students use a pencil or ballpoint pen to draw a shape on the potato surface.

  2. Then using a plastic knife or a metal spoon, the child can outline the shape first and then carve away the area that is not to be printed. Remember that the print will be the opposite of the stamp. If the child is making a letter of the alphabet the letter must be backwards on the potato so that it will be correct in the print.

  3. The best way to apply paint to the stamp is to brush on tempera using a flat, broad brush making sure that the paint is only applied to the raised surface. The potato can be rinsed in water and blotted so that another color can be used.

- Oil-based modeling clay can also be used to make a stamp. This is done by drawing or sculpting a design on a flat piece of modeling clay. There are a variety of tools manufactured for carving clay. Some classroom items that will work just as well include plastic eating utensils, craft sticks, and paper clips. The straightened end of a paper clip can be used to draw in the clay. The rounded end can be used as a gouge to carve clay away. To create a raised stamp, simply add pieces of clay to the bottom of the clay stamp.

Printing a Sponge Print

- Dispense colors onto individual palettes, or spread out on a surface large enough to avoid mixing. Lightly press the sponge into the paint, being careful not to get too much paint on it. Lift the sponge and lightly press it into place on the paper. The sponge should be thoroughly rinsed between colors.

More about Making Prints

▪ Below is the procedure for using a brayer, which is a soft roller, to make prints.

1. Pour a small amount of water-based printing ink or paint onto a flat, solid surface. Roll the brayer in the ink or paint until there is an even coating on the surface and brayer.

2. Roll the brayer over the top of the stamp. The ink should cover the stamp evenly without getting into the grooves of the design.

3. Apply the stamp carefully to the paper, rubbing the back of the stamp with the side of the fist.

4. Peel the paper and stamp apart.

5. Reink the stamp as needed if you wish to make more than one print.

6. When finished, wash the brayer, surface, and stamp.

▪ Another method for making prints calls for a paintbrush to apply the ink or paint. This method works better than the brayer with a raised stamp that the brayer would flatten out. Brush the ink or paint onto the stamping surface. Then follow the steps above, ending with thoroughly cleaning the brush.

Technique Tips

Printing Stamps

Put a small amount of ink or paint on a flat solid surface. Roll a brayer back and forth in the ink until there is an even coating of ink on the surface and the brayer.

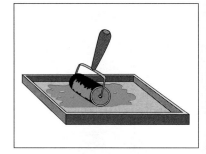

Roll the brayer over your stamp.

Apply the stamp carefully to your paper.

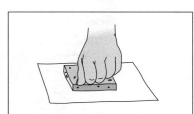

Technique Tips

Sculpture

Clay Basics

Clay can be pinched, pulled, and squeezed into the desired shape.

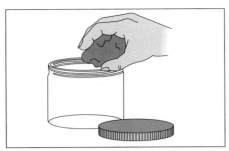

Store clay in an airtight container to keep it from drying out.

Pinch Pots

Push your thumb into your clay up to the first joint. Turn the clay on your thumb to create an opening.

Keeping your thumb in the hole, place your fingers on the outside of the clay and gently squeeze as you turn. Repeat until you have formed a bowl.

Gently tap the bottom of your bowl on your table so that it sits flat.

Sculpting

Working with Clay

- Always protect the work area with a cloth or newspaper. Clay dust is messy. Always wash the tables after working with clay.

- To help prevent earth clay from drying and cracking, students should not overhandle the clay. Keep damp paper towels nearby for students to keep their hands moist.

- The following steps are for modeling a person or animal from clay:
  1. Roll the piece of clay into an oval-shaped form. Describe this to the students as a "potato" shape.
  2. Pinch a head shape on one end.
  3. Pinch and pull out arms and legs.
  4. Leave some, but not too much, clay for the body.
  5. Squeeze the head, arms, legs, and body into the desired shapes.

- Clay is often sold in 25 pound bags. The bags are usually strong enough to keep the clay damp, but be sure to close the bag tightly with a twist tie or some other device to keep it sealed. It is a good idea to place the bag inside a second bag, like a heavy duty garbage bag, for long time storage.

Making a Pinch Pot

- It is important that the students gently squeeze the clay to form the pot. If they pinch the clay quickly the walls will be uneven. If they pinch the clay too hard they might make a hole in the wall of the bowl. If a student makes a hole, you might have him or her start over, or you can repair the hole by adding a small piece of clay using slip and scoring.

- The walls of the pinch pot should be the same width all around the bowl. To do this, have students hold their bowls with one thumb inside the bowl and their fingers held flat on the outside of the bowl. Then have students squeeze gently while constantly turning the bowl with their other hand. As the bowl opens up, both hands can be used to shape the walls.

- If the students are going to press designs into the walls of the bowl make sure that they have their fingers together inside the bowl to keep the bowl from collapsing.

Joining Clay

- Clay is joined by using **slip,** a creamy mixture of clay and water. Slip can be made by putting a few dry pieces of clay in a container and covering them with water. When the clay dissolves, stir to achieve a creamy consistency.

- Joining clay also requires a scoring tool such as a straightened paper clip. The steps below are called the four S's–score, slip, smooth, and squeeze.

  1. **Score** the two pieces to be joined.
  2. Apply **slip** to one of the surfaces.
  3. **Smooth** the seam.
  4. **Squeeze** the two surfaces together.

Carving Clay

There are a variety of tools manufactured for carving clay. Some classroom items that will work just as well are plastic eating utensils, craft sticks, and paper clips. The straightened end of a paper clip can be used to draw in the clay. The rounded end can be used as a gouge to carve clay away.

Painting Clay

- Once clay has been properly fired in a kiln it can be painted with tempera or acrylic paints. It can be glazed and refired.

- The biggest problem with firing student work is that the clay must be thoroughly dried before firing. This can be achieved in an old kiln by stacking everything that is ready to be fired in the kiln and then leaving the lid cracked open. Turn on only one heating coil to dry out the ware for a few hours before closing the lid and firing it up to the desired temperature.

Technique Tips

Joining Clay

Two pieces of clay can be joined together by using slip and scoring.

Score both pieces to help them stick together.

Apply slip to one of the pieces using a brush.

Squeeze together the two pieces of clay. Smooth the edges where they are joined.

Painting Clay

Clay can be painted and decorated with glazes once it is dry or fired.

Technique Tips

Paper Sculpture

You can curl, fold, and bend paper strips to make paper sculptures.

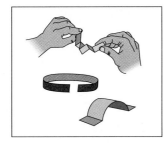
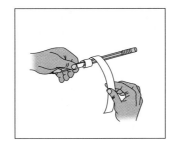

Papier-Mâché

Create a supporting form, if needed. Forms can be made of almost anything. Masking tape can be used to hold the form together.

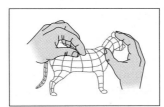

Tear paper into strips. Dip the strips into paste, or rub the paste onto the strips using your fingers. Use wide strips for wide forms and small strips for small forms.

Apply several layers of strips, applying each layer in a different direction. Smooth over rough edges with your fingers. When your sculpture dries, you can paint it.

Paper Sculpture

Making Strip Forms

Paper strips can be folded, curved, twisted, and then glued to create many different forms. A few basic forms are described here. Students will create many more.

1. Prepare by precutting enough paper strips for class use. This can be done on a paper cutter. The strips should be one to three inches wide in a variety of lengths.

2. Make a circle by curving the strip around to its beginning and gluing the ends together.

3. Make a box by folding a strip into four equal sections, leaving a small section for a tab. Bend the tab over its matching end and glue.

4. Make a triangle form by folding a strip into three sections plus a tab. Glue together.

5. Make a cone by cutting out a circle, cutting along its radius, overlapping the side of the cut, and gluing into a cone shape.

Papier-Mâché

Papier-Mâché is a French term that means "mashed paper." It refers to sculpting methods that use paper and liquid paste. The wet paper and paste material is molded over supporting structures such as wadded dry paper or crumpled foil. The molded paper dries to a hard finish.

- Below are three common papier-mâché solutions:

  1. Mix one part white glue to one part water by adding one half the amount of water to a glue bottle that is half full. Close the lid. Shake vigorously. Add second half of the water. Close the lid and shake until mixed.

  2. Make a creamy mixture of wheat paste and water. To mix wheat paste, wear a dust mask and pour dry paste into a large mixing bowl. Add water and stir until the mixture is creamy. Mash lumps with a spoon or your hands.

  3. Use liquid starch.

Aluminum Foil

- Before making a finished product, give students a small piece of foil to experiment with so that they can see how the foil holds its shape.

- Use thin foil so that it can be easily manipulated.

- To add something like a tail, use a pencil to poke a hole into a form, insert the tail, and then press the foil form around the tail to hold it in place.

- Two separate pieces can be joined by wrapping them with thin strips of foil which are then pressed into the form to make them "disappear."

Building with Forms

- To join two cardboard forms it is best to put the tape on one piece and the place it against the second before pressing the tape firmly in place.

- Tacky glue can also be used to join two forms. Apply a small amount of tacky glue to one surface, spread it thin with the bottle tip, and then gently press the two pieces together and hold them for a count of ten.

Technique Tips

Aluminum Foil

Foil can be pinched and squeezed to make sculptures.

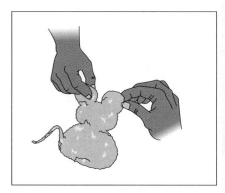

Building with Forms

To make sculptures with paper or cardboard forms, place the forms together and use masking tape to join them.

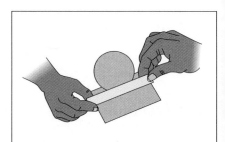

Technique Tips

Puppets

Cut out the pieces for your puppet from paper.

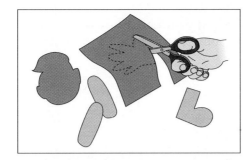

Use a hole punch to make holes at the joints where two pieces go together.

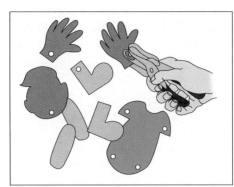

Use a brad to join the pieces. Stick a brad through both holes, and then unfold the metal clamps.

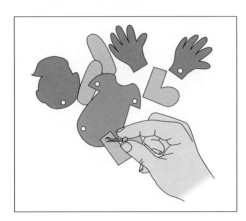

Puppets

- Have students draw the parts of the puppet before they cut them out. Check to make sure the arms and legs are wide enough to have holes punched in them.

- Use poster board or tag board to make the puppets so that the parts are strong enough to work together without tearing.

Needlework

- Large tapestry needles purchased at fabric stores, craft shops, or from art supply catalogs are appropriate for embroidery. They have blunt points and large eyes for easier threading.

- For threading the needle, discourage students from moistening the end of the yarn or thread. It doesn't work and spreads germs. Below are two alternate methods. Either of them will require some patience to master.

  1. Demonstrate twisting the end of the yarn or thread to make a point. Then push it through the eye of the needle.

  2. Another method is to bend the end of the yarn or thread back against itself and then push the looped end through the eye of the needle. This method keeps the frayed end from blocking the opening of the eye of the needle.

- Pull about one fourth of the length of the yarn or thread through the needle. The students can grasp this in their stitching hand as they embroider to keep the yarn or thread from pulling out of the needle. Do not encourage them to tie knots.

- The running stitch is made by simply pulling the needle and yarn or thread up through the fabric and pushing it back through the front in a path. When finished, let the loose ends hang out the back. Trim them.

Technique Tips
Needlework

Thread your needle, or get help threading your needle. Tie a knot in the end of the thread.

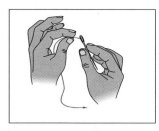

Carefully push the needle up from the bottom through the fabric where you want your stitch to start. Pull the needle through until the knot catches.

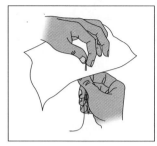

Carefully push the needle down through the fabric where you want your stitch to end. Repeat.

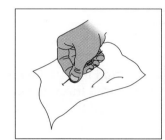

Technique Tips

Sewing a Book

1. Find the center of the fold and make a mark. Measure 1″ above and below the center mark.

2. Use a tapestry needle and poke holes through your marks.

3. Thread your needle and go through the top hole from the outside of your book and back through the center hole. Cut your thread so that you can tie both ends together.

4. Repeat for the bottom of your book.

Sewing a Book

- Choose a strong yarn or embroidery thread for sewing a book.

Activity Tips

Expressive Lines

Creative Expression

1. Think about the different kinds of weather where you live. What mood does each create?

2. Select the type of weather condition you would like to draw. Make a rough sketch to plan the scene. Experiment with different kinds of lines. Decide which lines will best express the mood you wish to create.

3. Draw your scene. Be sure to use the right kinds of lines to create a calm or active feeling.

Unit 1 · Lesson 2 **Line Variations**

Creative Expression

1. Think about a room you would like to decorate. Is it your classroom, your bedroom, or some other room?

2. Draw the room showing the floor, walls, and furniture, inside a shoebox.

3. Make some sketches of the kind of face that you would like to see in that room. Select your favorite idea to transfer into the box.

4. Using a variety of lines, draw the face in the box. Use black markers to complete the drawing.

Activity Tips

Shapes

 Creative Expression

1. Arrange five objects of different shapes and sizes in a variety of ways. Select the best arrangement.

2. Which object captures your attention most? Outline the shape of that object on your paper. In the same way, add the shapes of the other objects.

3. Begin to fill your shapes with different colors. Use one color at a time in several places on your picture. Continue to do this until your paper is filled with color.

Complex Geometric Shapes

 Creative Expression

1. Imagine a design you can create with complex geometric shapes.

2. Use your imagination to make a design using simple and complex geometric shapes.

3. Use your scrap paper to design a frame or border for your art.

Activity Tips

Shapes in Architecture

 Creative Expression

1. Walk outside and choose an area of your school building that you would like to draw.

2. Point out all the geometric shapes you see. Then look for the free-form shapes.

3. Draw the area of the school building you selected. Make sure you include all the geometric and free-form shapes you see.

Shapes of People

 Creative Expression

1. Ask a classmate to be your model. Select some objects from the classroom to use as props. Have your model use these props as they pose for you.

2. Look carefully at your model. Find the geometric and free-form shapes.

3. Use chalk to draw your model and the props. Use lines to create the geometric and free-form shapes you see. Fill the shapes with oil pastels.

Activity Tips

Positive and Negative Space

 Creative Expression

1. Study *Sleeveless Shirt* and *Tree of Life*.

2. Choose a light color, full-size sheet of construction paper. Choose a contrasting color for the half sheet.

3. Lay the half sheet on top of the left side of the full sheet of construction paper.

4. When all pieces are positioned in the correct location, glue them into place.

Creating Depth

 Creative Expression

1. Think about a place where there are lots of animals.

2. Make a rough sketch of the animals and other objects you want in your scene. Show depth by drawing animals and objects larger in the foreground and smaller in the background.

3. Fill your scene with color.

Activity Tips

Unit 2 · Lesson 3   Overlapping

 **Creative Expression**

1. Think about the different parts of a tree. How do the branches look? Sketch some, using different kinds of lines.

2. Draw some trees, making each tree's branches and leaves overlap to create a feeling of depth.

3. Fill your page, and touch all edges of the paper with your lines and shapes.

Unit 2 · Lesson 4   Form

Creative Expression

1. Have you ever seen a sculpture shaped like an animal form?

2. Notice the sculptures *The Walking Flower* and *Sun God*. What are the similarities and differences?

3. Find objects outdoors to be used to create an animal.

4. Use a rectangular box or juice can for the body. Use pieces of cardboard for the legs. You can draw texture on your animal sculpture.

Activity Tips

Relief Sculpture

 Creative Expression

1. Describe what is happening in both of the relief works. Do some of the areas appear to stick out more than others?

2. If you could make a relief sculpture that told a story about you, what would you put on the relief?

3. Roll out a slab of clay and create a relief of objects or a picture of a person who is important to you.

4. With a pencil, draw the design into the clay. Press lightly so as not to cut through the clay.

Three-Dimensional Art to Wear

 Creative Expression

1. Think about small objects that have interesting shapes.

2. Cut a piece of cardboard into a geometric shape. Arrange objects on top of the cardboard in different ways. Glue your favorite arrangement to the cardboard.

3. When dry, cover the surface with foil.

4. Punch a hole at the top of your design. Pass a piece of yarn or ribbon through the hole, and tie the ends to make a necklace.

Activity Tips

Unit 3 · Lesson 1   Looking at Color

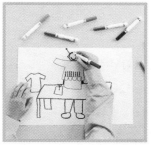

 Creative Expression

1. Think of ways that you, your family, and friends celebrate special events. Choose one event for your drawing. What colors will you need to include? What colors will you use to show the mood of this event?

2. Draw the event or occasion with colored markers on white construction paper.

3. Fill your paper with color.

Unit 3 · Lesson 2   Intermediate Colors

 Creative Expression

1. The colors must be in the correct order.

2. Use primary paint colors to mix secondary and intermediate colors.

3. The wheel does not have to be round, or even a circle.

4. Plan and decide on a way to indicate the difference between primary, secondary, and intermediate colors.

Activity Tips

Color Wheel

 **Creative Expression**

1. Think about an amusement ride you can make using all the colors from a color wheel in order.

2. Be creative. Remember that the colors have to follow the order of the color wheel.

Cool Colors

 Creative Expression

1. Think of ideas dealing with your environment, such as an animal habitat or a playground in the year 3001. Choose an idea and then sketch a few things you would find there.

2. Select several pieces of cool-colored paper. Choose one piece for the base. Outline objects you want in your environment on the other sheets of paper and cut them out. Add detail with oil pastels in cool colors. Attach the objects to your base.

Activity Tips **239**

Activity Tips

Unit 3 · Lesson 5 — Warm Colors

 Creative Expression

1. Use your imagination to create a fantasy landscape that includes three unrelated items such as a matchstick, a bowling pin, and a pair of sunglasses. Make a rough sketch of your idea.

2. Use lines to draw your idea on a sheet of white paper with warm-colored oil pastels.

3. Mix a variety of warm values with watercolor paint. Paint your scene. Remember that the values will get lighter as you add more water to your paint.

Unit 3 · Lesson 6 — Color Contrast

 Creative Expression

1. In a small group, make a list of underwater creatures. Draw the creatures on sheets of warm-colored construction paper. Use warm-colored oil pastels to add color and detail.

2. As a team, paint an underwater scene on a large sheet of paper. Mix cool colors to create water and plant life.

3. When the paint is dry, arrange and glue the sea creatures in place.

240   Activity Tips

Activity Tips

Formal Balance

 Creative Expression

1. Look at the artwork *Victorian Parlor II* by Horace Pippin. Think about how the outside of this house might look.

2. On a large piece of paper, draw the outside of the house. Use formal balance in your drawing.

3. Fill the house with color. Add trees and plants. Use formal balance in your landscape too.

Formal Balance in Masks

 Creative Expression

1. Think of how you want to use your mask and what it will express. Make a few sketches until you get one you like.

2. Look at your sketch. Then cut pieces of cardboard tubes and boxes to form the features. Tape or glue them in place onto your base. Balance some of the forms formally.

3. Dip torn strips of newspaper into paste. Apply them to the mask.

Activity Tips

Unit 4 · Lesson 3   Symmetry

Creative Expression

1. Think of a real or imaginary creature. Make several sketches.
2. Fold a sheet of paper in half. The fold will be your central axis.
3. Using small pieces of colored paper, cut out shapes to represent features such as eyes. Using symmetry, place these features on your totem. Glue the pieces into place.
4. Use symmetry to add other details.
5. Join the edges of your paper together to form a cylinder.

Unit 4 · Lesson 4   Approximate Symmetry

Creative Expression

1. Look at your face in the mirror. Notice how it is almost exactly the same on both sides.
2. Use approximate symmetry to draw a self-portrait.
3. In the spaces around your portrait, draw objects that are important to you.
4. Add color.

Activity Tips

Visual Texture

 **Creative Expression**

1. Make a few quick sketches to show what your house looks like. Include things around your house like sidewalks or bushes.

2. Now use the draw tool to draw a picture of your house and the area around it. Think about the textures that are visible, like bricks.

3. Use the fill and texture tools to add color and texture to the drawing.

Tactile Texture

 Creative Expression

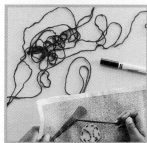

1. Think about symbols that represent you. Make several sketches.

2. Choose your best sketch as a model. Cut out shapes from colorful fabric. Arrange them on a piece of burlap.

3. Attach shapes using glue. Stitch around the edges of each shape and add details with a marker.

Activity Tips

Unit 5 · Lesson 1 — Pattern and Motif

Creative Expression

1. First, cut your potato in half. On the cut side, use the pointed side of a pencil to make a design in the potato.

2. Dip the cut side of the potato in paint.

3. Randomly press the potato onto newspaper or a brown paper bag to create a pattern.

4. Use the paper as wrapping paper for a gift.

Unit 5 · Lesson 2 — Regular Patterns

Creative Expression

1. Use the auto-shape tool to create a square.

2. Use the line and auto-shape tools to create a design in the square.

3. Use the fill tool to color in the design.

4. Select the whole design and copy.

5. Paste the design over several times, to create a regular pattern.

6. Enlarge the completed square design.

7. Print your work.

244 Activity Tips

Activity Tips

Alternating Patterns

 Creative Expression

1. Create two motifs that you would wear on a shirt or jacket, such as cars, books, bicycles, or footballs.

2. Draw the article of clothing. Use an alternating pattern of the two motifs you created.

3. Color with crayons.

- -

Rhythm

 Creative Expression

1. Make three to five pinch pots. The smallest should have a 3″ opening.

2. Use scoring and slip to join the pots at their sides to make an interesting rhythm of round pots.

3. Smooth the places where they are joined using a clay tool or your fingers.

4. Decorate your bowls by pressing in or adding on patterns using clay tools or found objects.

Activity Tips

Visual Rhythm

🎨 Creative Expression

1. Think about things you like to see in a parade. Do you like floats, marching bands, clowns, horses, elephants, or antique cars?

2. Make sketches of things you want in your parade. Draw yourself as the grand marshal or leader of the parade.

3. Select your best sketches and use chalk to transfer them to large paper.

4. Paint your parade.

Three-Dimensional Rhythm

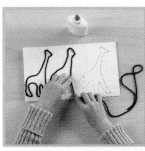

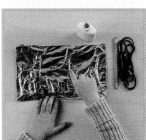

🎨 Creative Expression

1. Think about an animal you would like to use. Look at pictures of that animal.

2. Make sketches of the animal. Select your best sketches and draw the animal several times on the cardboard to create a rhythmic repetition of the animal.

3. Glue yarn over the outlines of your animals.

4. Cover the surface with aluminum foil. Start pressing foil near the center. As you work, gently press the foil around each raised line with your fingertips.

Activity Tips

 Unit 6 · Lesson 1 **Harmony**

 Creative Expression

1. Begin by making a pinch pot. Then roll a coil to make arms that will fit halfway around the rim of your pot. Roll a sphere to make a head.

2. Using proper joining techniques, attach the arms and head to the rim of your pot. Add clay for hair. With your clay tools add details such as hands, eyes, and a mouth. Add texture to the hair.

3. Choose related colors to paint or glaze your figural pot once it has been fired.

Unit 6 · Lesson 2 **Variety**

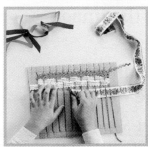

Creative Expression

1. Think about how you will use your weaving. Select a variety of ribbons, natural fibers, and yarn for your weaving.

2. Cut out a piece of cardboard, and notch it on the top and the bottom. Then string the warp thread on it.

3. Weave your fibers to create variety.

Activity Tips

Unit 6 · Lesson 3 Emphasis

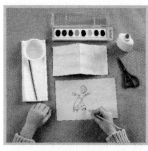

 Creative Expression

1. Use the ellipse tool to draw a circle. Use the draw tool to draw something from nature within the circle.

2. Use the line tool to draw diagonal lines that connect to the circle. Use the fill tool to fill the sections around the circle with shades of gray.

3. Use the brush tool to paint the design inside the circle. Make it colorful.

Unit 6 · Lesson 4 Emphasis Through Decoration

 Creative Expression

1. Use a sheet of paper for the cover. Wet the paper with water. Use a wash of warm or cool colors. Let it dry.

2. On a sheet of construction paper, recreate your drawing from the Practice activity. Cut the image out. Glue a paper ring to the back.

3. Stack three sheets of paper on top of your cover. Fold it in half so that the cover is on the outside. Stitch your pages together. Glue the paper ring to the cover so the image is raised from the surface.

Activity Tips

Unit 6 · Lesson 5   Unity Through Color

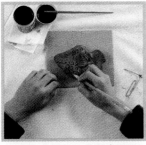

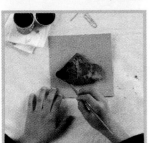

 **Creative Expression**

1. Flatten a palm-sized ball of clay until it is about as thick as your little finger. Fold the clay like a taco. Score the edges and seal it along the top.

2. Shape clay into fins and eyes. Attach by scoring, applying slip, and smoothing. Pinch a tail.

3. Use clay tools to create scales. Make interesting textures on your fish.

4. After the fish is fired, glaze or paint it with one color to unify all the texture and parts.

Unit 6 · Lesson 6   Unity, Repetition, and Grouping

Creative Expression

1. Think about insects and reptiles with interesting shapes. Use crayons to cover a sheet of paper with many different colors. Then paint the whole surface with thinned black ink until you can no longer see the color.

2. While the ink is drying, sketch a few real or imaginary reptiles and insects on scratch paper. Choose some to draw.

3. Engrave the creatures by scratching lines and line patterns in the black background with a paper clip. Add detail and texture.

Activity Tips   **249**

Visual Index

Artist Unknown
Jar
2000–3000 B.C.
(page 186)

Artist Unknown
*Hunting Scene on Handle
from a large bowl*
2nd century. A.D. (page 83)

Artist Unknown
Portrait of a Boy
2nd century.
(page 138)

Artist Unknown
*Hat: Birds and
Geometric Patterns*
c. 700–1000.
(page 100)

Artist Unknown
*Presentation of Captives
to a Maya Ruler*
c. 785. (page 82)

Artist Unknown
Jar
12th century.
(page 127)

Artist Unknown
Cover of Armenian Book
13th century. (page 198)

Artist Unknown
Mihrab
1354. (page 49)

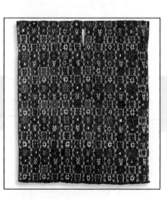

Artist Unknown
Tunic
15th–16th century.
(page 164)

Artist Unknown
Sleeveless Shirt
(Two Cats)
c. 1438–1532.
(page 66)

Artist Unknown
Covered Jar
c. 1522 –1566.
(page 117)

Mir Sayyid Ali
Nighttime in the Palace
c. 1539–1543. (page 180)

Giovanni Antonio Canal
The Clock Tower in the Piazza
San Marco
c. 1730. (page 53)

Caleb Gardner
Easy Chair
1758. (page 157)

Thomas Gainsborough
Jonathan Buttall: The
Blue Boy
c. 1770. (page 57)

Artist Unknown
Washington's Headquarters
1780
c. 1876. (page 70)

Artist Unknown
Mask with Seal or Sea
Otter Spirit
19th century. (page 131)

Artist Unknown
Senufo Face Mask
19th–20th century.
(page 130)

Joseph Mallord William Turner
Mortlake Terrace
1826. (page 71)

Artist Unknown
Thunderbird Shield
c. 1830. (page 147)

John James Audubon
Great Blue Heron
1834. (page 154)

Rosa Bonheur
*Ploughing in the
Nivernais Region*
1849. (page 168)

Artist Unknown
Child's Beaded Shirt
c. 1865. (page 190)

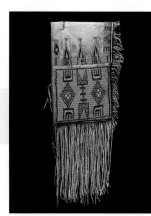

Artist Unknown
Double Saddlebag
1875. (page 48)

Gustave Caillebotte
Paris Street Rainy Day
1877. (page 142)

Edgar Degas
*Little Dancer, Aged
Fourteen*
c. 1881. (page 64)

Claude Monet
Japanese Bridge over a Pool of Water Lilies
1899. (page 36)

Lundin Kudo
Gin Matsuba
20th century.
(page 203)

Artist Unknown
Necklace
20th century.
(page 86)

Artist Unknown
Symmetrical View of a Totem Pole
20th century. (page 134)

Artist Unknown
Cote d'Ivoire
1900. (page 87)

Frederic Remington
Mountain Man
1903. (page 184)

Artist Unknown
Collar
c. 1900–1925. (page 165)

John Sloan
Hairdresser's Window
1907. (page 194)

Henri Rousseau
The Football Players
1908. (page 150)

Wassily Kandinsky
Improvisation No. 27
1912. (page 40)

Allen E. Cole
Silas Johnson
1920s. (page 56)

Arthur Lismer
September Gale,
Georgian Bay
1921. (page 37)

Pablo Picasso
Mother and Child
1922. (page 34)

Georgia O'Keeffe
Red Canna
1925-1928. (page 113)

Edward Hopper
The City
1927. (page 52)

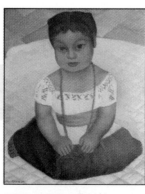

Diego Rivera
Kneeling Child on Yellow
Background
1927. (page 94)

Paul Klee
Rotes Haus
1929. (page 112)

Vaclav Vytlacil
Composition
1931. (page 45)

Shirley Ximena Hopper Russell
Boy's Day
1935. (page 96)

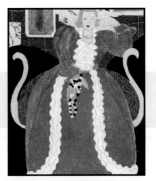

Henri Matisse
Women in Blue
1937. (page 207)

Man Ray
La Fortune
1938. (page 104)

Horace Pippin
Victorian Parlor II
1945. (page 126)

Fred Kabotie
Pueblo Scene Corn Dance, Hopi
1947. (page 173)

Philip Evergood
Her World
1948. (page 139)

Calvin Jones
Brilliant as the Sun upon the World
c. 1950 (page 105)

Fernand Leger
The Walking Flower
1951. (page 78)

Milton Avery
Sea Grasses and Blue Sea
1958. (page 109)

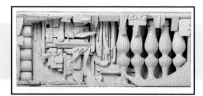

Louise Nevelson
Case with Five Balusters
1959. (page 177)

Jacob Lawrence
Parade
1960. (page 172)

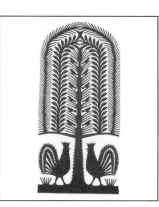

Stanistawa Bakula
Tree of Life
1962. (page 67)

René Magritte
*Carte Blanche
(The Blank Signature)*
1965. (page 90)

Ayako Miyawaki
Various Fish
1967. (page 146)

Andy Warhol
Flowers
1967. (page 202)

Richard Estes
Diner
1971. (page 143)

Joseph Jean-Gilles
Haitian Landscape
1973. (page 75)

Audrey Flack
Strawberry Tart Supreme
1974. (page 124)

Jacob Lawrence
Builders No. 1
1971. (page 60)

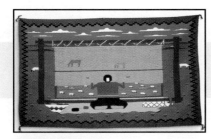

Isabel John
Pictorial Tapestry
1980s. (page 191)

Aurelio and Francisco Flores
Candelabra
c. 1980. (page 135)

Jonathan Borofsky
Self Portrait with Big Ears Learning to Be Free
1980–1984. (page 41)

Nancy Youngblood
Pottery Vessels
1980–1985. (page 187)

Al Held
Piero's Piazza
1982. (page 97)

Niki de Saint Phalle
Sun God
1983. (page 79)

William T. Wiley
*Remedial
Archaeology and
the Like*
1986. (page 101)

Wayne Thiebaud
Lighted City
1987. (page 108)

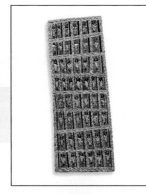

Dorothy Djukulul
Warrnyu (Flying Foxes)
1989. (page 161)

Wayne Thiebaud
Display Rows
1989. (page 120)

Idelle Weber
Pistia Kew
1989. (page 116)

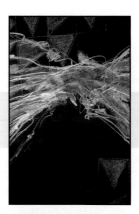

Willis Bing Davis
*Ancestral Spirit
Dance*
1990. (page 206)

Sylvia Plimack Mangold
*The Locust Trees with
Maple*
1990. (page 75)

Faith Ringgold
The Sunflower Quilting
Bee at Arles
1991. (page 210)

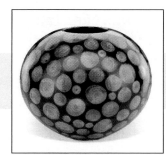

Philip Moulthrop
White Pine Mosaic
1993. (page 156)

Tom Loeser
Four by Four
1994. (page 160)

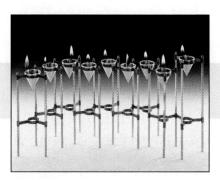

Abrasha
Hannukkah Menorah
1995. (page 169)

Janet Fish
Yellow Pad
1997. (page 44)

Pamela Spitzmueller
British Museum Memoir
1997. (page 199)

John Hoover
Looner Eclipse
1999. (page 176)

Robert Cottingham
Jane's Remington
2000. (page 195)

A

alternating pattern (ôl' tər nāt ing pat' ərn), *noun*   A pattern in which one motif is repeated after a second, different motif

appliqué (ap' li kā), *noun*   An art form in which cutout fabrics are attached to a larger surface

approximate symmetry (ə 'präk sə mət sim' i trē), *noun* A special kind of formal balance where both sides of a design are almost exactly the same. One example is the human face: each side is almost the same as the other.

architect (är' kə tekt), *noun* The artist who plans and designs buildings

architecture (är' kə tek' chər), *noun*   The art of designing and planning buildings

C

central axis (sen' trəl ak' sis), *noun* An imaginary dividing line

color spectrum (kul' ər spek' trum), *noun*   The range of colors that comes from light. Rainbows are the most famous display of this spectrum in nature.

color wheel (kul' ər 'wēl), *noun* The spectrum that artists use bent into the shape of a circle

complex geometric shapes (kom' pleks jē' ə met' rik shāps), *noun* Shapes made by combining simple geometric shapes such as triangles, squares, and rectangles. Some examples of complex geometric shapes are diamonds, pentagons, trapezoids, hexagons, parallelograms, and octagons.

contrast (kon' trast), *noun* Showing differences between things

cool colors (kül kul' erz), *noun* Blue, green, and violet. These are colors that remind us of cool objects like grass, water, and ice. These colors can create a sense of depth because they seem to move away from the viewer.

culture (kəl chər), *noun* Another word for *custom*

curved (kûrvd), *adj.* Lines that bend and change direction slowly. They give a feeling of graceful movement.

D

depth (depth), *noun* 1. The appearance of distance; 2. How far something extends toward or away from the viewer

diagonal (dī ag' ə nəl), *noun (adj.)* Lines that are slanted. They look as if they are falling or rising. They make things look active.

E

emphasis (em' fə sis), *noun* The way an artist makes something in a work of art stand out

exaggerate (eg zaj' ə rā' te), *verb* To make much larger than actual size

F

formal balance (fôr' mel bal' əns), *noun* Organization of elements where equal objects are on opposite sides of the artwork

forms (formz), *noun* Three-dimensional objects that can be measured in three ways: height, width, and depth. Some examples of simple forms are spheres, cones, pyramids, and cylinders.

free-form shapes (frē' fôrm' shāps), *noun* Uneven and irregular shapes. Puddles, clouds, and flowers are examples of free-form shapes found in nature.

freestanding forms (frē stan' ding formz), *noun* Forms that can be seen from all around

G

geometric shapes (je' ə met' rik shāps), *noun* A math shape such as a circle, triangle, or rectangle that is usually found in objects that are made by people. Buildings, furniture, and road signs are some examples of geometric shapes.

H

harmony (här' mə nē), *noun*
The peaceful look made when related elements of art are put together. Artists create harmony by repeating lines, colors, shapes, textures, and objects.

highlight (hī līt'), *noun* Small areas of white used to show the brightest spots on an object

horizontal (hôr' ə zon təl), *adj.* Lines that move straight across from side to side. They give a feeling of calm peace.

hue (hū), *noun* Another word for color

I

interior designers (in tîr' ē ər di zī' nər), *noun* Artists who decorate the inside of a building

intermediate colors (in' tər mē' dē it kul' ərs), *noun* Colors made by mixing a primary color and a secondary color. There are six intermediate colors—red-orange, yellow-orange, yellow-green, blue-green, blue-violet, and red-violet.

J

jeweler (jü' ə lər), *noun* An artist who designs and makes jewelry

jewelry (jü' əl rē), *noun* Three-dimensional artwork that is made for people to wear

L

lines (līnz), *noun* Marks drawn by a tool such as a pencil, pen, or paintbrush as it moves across a surface

line variety (līn və rī' ə tē), *noun* The different possibilities in the character of lines. For example, lines can be long or short, thick or thin, rough or smooth, and broken or solid.

M

mask (mask), *noun* A three-dimensional art form of sculpted faces

motif (mō tēf), *noun* The unit of repetition in the pattern. The motif is made of objects or art elements.

N

negative space (neg' ə tiv spas'), *noun*   Empty space in an artwork

O

overlapping (o' vər lap ing), *verb* One object covers part of another object. Overlapping makes the object in front seem closer to the viewer.

P

pattern (pat' ərn), *noun* A repeated surface decoration

positive space (poz' i tiv spas'), *noun*   The area that shapes and objects fill

primary colors (pri' mer ē kul' erz), *noun*   Red, yellow, and blue. They cannot be made by mixing colors.

R

random pattern (ran' dəm pat' ərn), *noun* A pattern in which the motif is repeated in no particular order

regular pattern (reg' yə lər pat' ərn), *noun* A pattern in which the motif is repeated in an even manner

relief sculptures (ri lēf' skulp' chər), *noun*   Forms that stand out from a flat surface, like coins

repetition (rep' i tish' ən), *noun* Lines, shapes, colors, or textures that are repeated throughout an artwork

rest (rest), *noun*   The negative space between repetitions of the motif

rhythm (rith' əm), *noun* A feeling created by the repetition of a positive shape or form. That object is the beat. The negative space between the repetitions is the rest.

S

sculpture (skulp' chər), *noun* Three-dimensional art

secondary colors (sek' ən der' ē kul' erz), *noun* Orange, green, and violet. These colors are made by mixing two primary colors.

shade (shād), *noun*   Darker values of a color

shape (shāp) *noun* Flat, two-dimensional areas that are geometric or free-form. They can be measured in only two ways: height and width.

spectral colors (spek' trəl kul' ər) *noun* The colors of the light spectrum: red, orange, yellow, green, blue, and violet

symmetry (sim' i trē), *noun* Two halves of a design are identical, mirror images of each other. The two halves are divided by the central axis. Everything on one side of the central axis is balanced by the objects on the other side.

T

tactile texture (tak' təl teks' chər), *noun* Texture that can be felt

three-dimensional rhythm (thrē di men' shə nəl rith' əm), *noun* A principle of design that indicates movement by the repetition of elements in a form

tint (tint), *noun* Lighter values of a color

two-dimensional (tü' di men' shə nəl), *adj.* flat and can be measured by length and width

U

unity (ū' ni tē), *noun* The feeling of wholeness in a work of art. Artists use repetition and grouping to show that different parts of a work belong together.

V

value (val' ū), *noun* The lightness or darkness of a color.

variety (və ri' ə tē), *noun* Different lines, shapes, colors, and textures to make a work of art interesting.

vertical lines (vür tə kəl līnz), *noun* Lines that move straight up and down. They make things look tall, steady, and calm.

visual rhythm (vizh' ü əl rith' əm), *noun* The feeling of movement created when artists repeat colors, shapes, lines, and textures to lead the viewer's eyes through a work of art

visual texture (vizh' ü əl teks' chər), *noun* Texture that you see

W

warm colors (wōrm′ kul′ ərz), *noun* Yellow, orange, and red. These colors remind the viewer of a sense of warmth in a work of art. These colors often are the first to attract the viewer's attention.

Z

zigzag (zig′ zag) *noun (adj.)* Diagonal lines that connect. They give a feeling of excitement.

Index

A

Abrasha, 169
abstract art, 96, 97
advertisers, 62
'Ali, Mir Sayyid, 180
alternating pattern, 164–167
Ancestral Spirit Dance (Davis), 206
animals, 63
animation, 93
appliqué, 66, 148
approximate symmetry, 138–141
architects, 54, 92, 148
architectural graphic designers, 182
architectural renderer, 182
architecture, 52–55
art directors, 62
Audubon, John James, 154, 155
Avery, Milton, 108, 109
axis, 136

B

background, 72
Bakula, Stanistawa, 67
balance, 124–129, 134–137
The Blank Signature (Carte Blance) (Magritte), 90
Bonheur, Rosa, 168
Borofsky, Jonathan, 41
Boy's Day (Russell), 96
Brilliant as the Sun Upon the World (Jones), 105
British Museum Memoir (Spitzmueller), 198, 199

Builders No. 1 (Lawrence), 60
buildings, 52–55

C

Caillebotte, Gustave, 142
Canal, Giovanni Antonio, 53
Candelabra (Flores), 134, 135
careers, 54, 62, 88, 92, 148, 182
Case with Five Balusters (Nevelson), 176, 177
central axis, 136
Child's Beaded Shirt (Unknown), 190
circle, 46
The City (Hopper), 52
city planners, 92
The Clock Tower in the Piazza San Marco (Canaletto), 53
Cole, Allen E., 56
Collar (Unknown), 164, 165
colors
    and balance, 127
    and contrast, 116–119
    cool, 108–111, 118
    and harmony, 188
    intermediate, 100–103, 118
    primary, 98, 102
    secondary, 98, 102
    spectrum, 106
    and unity, 202–205
    and value, 94–95, 123
    and variety, 192
    warm, 112–115, 118
color wheel, 102, 104–107

Acknowledgments

Grateful acknowledgment is given to the following publishers and copyright owners for permissions granted to reprint selections from their publications. All possible care has been taken to trace ownership and secure permission for each selection included. In case of any errors or omissions, the Publisher will be pleased to make suitable acknowledgments in future editions. From GRANDPA'S FACE by Eloise Greenfield, illustrated by Floyd Cooper, copyright © 1988 by Floyd Cooper. Used by permission of Philomel Books for young Readers, A Division of Penguin Young Readers Group, A Member of Penguin Group (USA) Inc., 345 Hudson Street, New York, NY 10014. All rights reserved. From DREAMS by Ezra Jack Keats, copyright © 1974 by Ezra Jack Keats. Used by permission of Viking Penguin, A Division of Penguin Young Readers Group, A Member of Penguin Group (USA) Inc., 345 Hudson Street, New York, NY 10014. All rights reserved. WILD AND WOOLY MAMMOTHS-REVISED EDITION by ALIKI. COPYRIGHT © 1977 BY ALIKI BRANDENBERG. Used by permission of HarperCollins Publishers. FROG AND TOAD ARE FRIENDS by ARNOLD LOBEL. Cover art copyright © 1970 Arnold Lobel. Used by permision of HarperCollins Publishers. Cover from ASHANTI TO ZULU: AFRICAN TRADITIONS by Margaret Musgrove, pictures by Leo and Diane Dillon, copyright © 1976 by Leo and Diane Dillon, pictures. Used by permission of Dial Books for Young Readers, A Division of Penguin Young Readers Group, A Member of Penguin Group (USA) Inc., 345 Hudson Street, New York, NY 10014. All rights reserved. From WILL YOU SIGN HERE, JOHN HANCOCK? By Jean Fritz, pictures by Trina Schart Hyman, copyright © 1976 by Trina Schart Hyman, illustrations. Used by permission of Coward-McCann, A Division of Penguin Young Readers Group, A Member of Penguin Group (USA) Inc., 345 Hudson Street, New York, NY 10014. All rights reserved.

Photo Credits

Cover National Gallery of Art, Washington, D.C. Collection of Mr. and Mrs. Paul Mellon, Image © 2003 Board of Trustees, National Gallery of Art, Washington. © 2004 C. Herscovici, Brussels/Artists Rights Society (ARS), New York; 5 The Baltimore Museum of Art: The Cone Collection formed by Dr. Claribel Cone and Miss Etta Cone of Baltimore, Maryland. © 2004 Estate of Pablo Picasso/Artists Rights Society (ARS), New York; 6 (c) The Metropolitan Museum of Art, H.O. Havemeyer Collection, Bequest of Mrs. H.O. Havemeyer, 1929. Photograph © The Metropolitan Museum of Art; 07 San Francisco Museum of Modern Art, Bequest of Elise S. Hass. Photo by Ben Blackwell; 8 © Allen Memorial Art Museum, Oberlin College, National Endowment for the Arts Museum Purchase Plan and Fund for Contemporary Art 1974; 9 Collection of the Orlando Museum of Art, Gift of Council of 101 and Mr. and Mrs. William duPont, III; 10 The Carleton Collection; 12 (tl) Collection of Whitney Museum of American Art, New York. Photography Copyright © 1998: Whitney Museum of American Art, New York, (tr) The Baltimore Museum of Art: The Cone Collection formed by Dr. Claribel Cone and Miss Etta Cone of Baltimore, Maryland. © 2004 Estate of Pablo Picasso/Artists Rights Society (ARS), New York; (bl) Home and Away Gallery; 13 (tl) National Museum of Women in the Arts. Gift of Wallace and Wilhelmina Holladay, (tr) Schmidt Bingham Gallery. New York, New York., (bl) Photography by Ansel Adams. Used with permission of the Trustees of the Ansel Adams Publishing Rights Trust. All Rights Reserved. © Digital Image © The Museum of Modern Art/Licensed by SCALA/Art Resource, NY, (br) The Metropolitan Museum of Art, the Michael C. Rockefeller Collection, Purchase, Nelson A. Rockefeller Gift, 1964. (1978.412.489) Photograph by Schecter Lee. Photograph © 1986 The Metropolitan Museum of Art; 15 (tl) Photograph Oliver Folk Art, (bl) © Digital Image © The Museum of Modern Art/Licensed by SCALA/Art Resource, NY. © Henry Moore Foundation, (br) The Metropolitan Museum of Art, Gift of Mrs. J. Insley Blair, 1950. Photograph © 1981 The Metropolitan Museum of Art; 16 Image © The Museum of Modern Art/Licensed by SCALA/Art Resource, NY; 17 The Metropolitan Museum of Art, H.O. Havemeyer Collection, Bequest of Mrs. H.O. Havemeyer, 1929. (29.100.113) Photograph © 1996 The Metropolitan Museum of Art; 18 © Jacob and Gwendolyn Lawrence Foundation. Photograph Courtesy of Gwendolyn Knight Lawrence/Art Resource, NY; 19 Collection of The Newark Museum, Newark, New Jersey. Purchased 1937 Felix Fund Bequest Fund; 20 San Francisco Museum of Modern Art, Bequest of Elise S. Hass. Photo by Ben Blackwell; 21 The Metropolitan Museum of Art, New York, New York; 22 (t, tcl, tcr, br, bcr) © Photodisc/Getty Images, Inc, (bcl, bl) © Digital Vision/Getty Images, Inc; 23 (t) © Corbis, (tcl, tcr, bl, bcl, bc) © Photodisc/Getty Images, Inc, (br) © Index Stock; 24, 26, 28, 30 The Metropolitan Museum of Art, Arthur Hoppock Hearn Fund, 1958. (58.26) Photograph © 1992 The Metropolitan Museum of Art; 32-33 © Aaron Haupt; 34 The Baltimore Museum of Art: The Cone Collection formed by Dr. Claribel Cone and Miss Etta Cone of Baltimore, Maryland. © 2004 Estate of Pablo Picasso/Artists Rights Society (ARS), New York; 35 © Bettmann/Corbis; 36 The Metropolitan Museum of Art, H.O. Havemeyer Collection, Bequest of Mrs. H.O. Havemeyer, 1929. (29.100.113) Photograph © 1996 The Metropolitan Museum of Art; 37 © National Gallery of Canada. Purchased 1926; 38 © Eclipse Studios; 39 Frank Fortune; 40 The Metropolitan Museum of Art, The Alfred Stieglitz Collection, 1949. (49.70.1). Photograph © 1987 The Metropolitan Museum of Art. © 2004 Artists Rights Society (ARS), New York/ADAGP, Paris; 41 Collection of the Modern Art Museum of Fort Worth, Museum Purchase; 42 © Eclipse Studios; 43 Randy Ellett; 44 Collection of the Columbus Museum, Columbus, GA; Museum purchase made possible by Norman S. Rothschild in honor of his parents Aleen and Irwin B. Rothschild. © Janet Fish/Licensed by VAGA, New York, NY; 45 Norton Museum of Art, West Palm Beach, Florida, Gift of the Estate of Vaclav Vytlacil, 99.104; 46 © Eclipse Studios; 47 Randy Ellett; 48 Detroit Institute of Arts, Detroit, Michigan; 49 The Metropolitan Museum of Art, Harris Brisbane Dick Fund, 1939. (39.20) Photograph © 1982 The Metropolitan Museum of Art; 50 © Eclipse Studios; 51 Photo by Ko Yoshida; 52 Collection of The University of Arizona Museum of Art, Tucson, Gift of C. Leonard Pfeiffer x45.9.23; 53 The Nelson-Atkins Museum of Art, Kansas City, Missouri (Gift of Byron and Eileen Cohen) F85-17/1 A-D photograph by Mel McLean; 54 (tl) Jodi Cobb/National Geographic Society/Getty Images, Inc, (tcl) Digital Vision/Getty Images, Inc, (tcr, bl, bcl, bcr) Photodisc/Getty Images, Inc, (tr) Michael Melford/The Image Bank/Getty Images, Inc, (b) © Eclipse Studios, (br) Alfredo Maiquez/Lonely Planet Images/Getty Images, Inc; 55 Frank Fortune; 56 Western Reserve Historical Society; 57 © SuperStock; 58 (tl) Digital Vision/Getty Images, Inc, (tr, cr) Photodisc/Getty Images, Inc, (b) © Eclipse Studios, (cl) SRA photo, (cr) Photodisc/Getty Images, Inc; 59 Frank Fortune; 60 © Jacob and Gwendolyn Lawrence Foundation; 62 Taxi/Getty Images, Inc; 63 Don Perdue; 64 The Metropolitan Museum of Art, H.O. Havemeyer Collection, Bequest of Mrs. H.O. Havemeyer, 1929. Photograph © The Metropolitan Museum of Art; 65 © Francis G. Mayer/Corbis; 66 The Metropolitan Museum of Art, The Michael C. Rockefeller Memorial Collection, Bequest of Nelson A. Rockefeller, 1979. (1979.206.1131) Photograph © 1981 The Metropolitan Museum of Art; 67 From the Girard Foundation Collection, in the Museum of International Folk Art, a unit of the Museum of New Mexico, Santa Fe, New Mexico; 68 © Eclipse Studios; 69 Randy Ellett; 70 Smithsonian American Art Museum/Art Resource, NY; 71 National Gallery of Art, Washington, DC. Andrew W. Mellon Collection, Image © 2003 Board of Trustees, National Gallery of Art, Washington; 72 © Eclipse Studios; 73 Randy Ellett; 74 Brooke Alexander Gallery; 75 Collections of the Art Museum of the Americas - Organization of American States; 76 © Eclipse Studios; 77 Randy Ellett; 78 Albright-Knox Art Gallery. © 2004 Artists Rights Society (ARS), New York/ADAGP, Paris; 79 Photograph © Becky Cohen. © 2004 Artists Rights Society (ARS), New York; 80 © Eclipse Studios; 81 Randy Ellett; 82 Copyright © 2003 Kimbell Art Museum; 83 The Metropolitan Museum of Art, Fletcher Fund, 1934 (34.33) Photograph © 1995 The Metropolitan Museum of Art; 84 © Eclipse Studios; 85 Randy Ellett; 87 Museum of Fine Arts, Houston, Texas. Photograph The Bridgeman Art Library; 88 (t) ThinkStock LLC/Index Stock Imagery, (b) © Eclipse Studios; 89 Randy Ellett; 90 National Gallery of Art, Washington, D.C. Collection of Mr. and Mrs. Paul Mellon, Image © 2003 Board of Trustees, National Gallery of Art, Washington. © 2004 C. Herscovici, Brussels/Artists Rights Society (ARS), New York; 92 © Andreas Pollok/Getty Images, Inc; 93 Craig Schwartz © 1998; 94 San Francisco Museum of Modern Art, Bequest of Elise S. Hass. Photo by Ben Blackwell; 95 © Corbis; 96 Honolulu Academy

Table of Contents

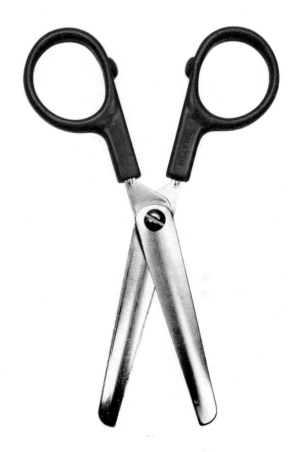

The Elementary Art Curriculum

Rosalind Ragans, Ph.D., Associate Professor Emerita, Georgia Southern University

Art education is for all students. It provides learning opportunities for the artistically talented few, as well as the many students who may never produce art outside the classroom.

A strong elementary visual arts curriculum teaches students that they can communicate a variety of ideas and emotions in many different ways. Students learn that some problems have many different solutions, and they will not be afraid to use divergent-thinking strategies. They will learn concepts and techniques that will give them control of the visual images they produce.

A strong elementary art curriculum also enables students to expand their perceptive, interpretive, and analytical abilities. They learn to find meaning in visual images, and they learn to identify aesthetic qualities in a variety of works of art and in the environment. They begin to develop the ability to make aesthetic judgments.

The visual arts have always been an integral component in the history of humanity, and through the study of art history, students will develop a better understanding of beliefs and ideas that are different from their own.

The four components of a quality art program are Aesthetic Perception, Art Criticism, Art History and Culture, and Art Production and Creative Expression.

Aesthetic Perception

Aesthetics is a branch of philosophy. In visual art, aesthetics becomes the study of the nature of beauty and art. Aesthetics is concerned with the question "What is art?" In the past, aesthetics was defined as the study of beauty because the creation of beauty was thought to be the purpose of art. Today, some aestheticians still believe that the purpose of art is to create beauty or beautifully organized arrangements of the elements of art. Some believe that art must imitate reality. Others think of art as a strong means to communicate ideas and emotions.

Aesthetic concepts are the core of the *Art Connections* curriculum. They are the framework upon which all aspects of art learning are constructed. The **About Aesthetic Perception** section in the *Student Edition* and *Teacher Edition* offers concrete methods for introducing students to aesthetics.

 Art Criticism

Works of art are the focus of every lesson. Art criticism is the sequential process used in this textbook to guide students through the procedures needed to learn from these works of art. Art criticism enables students to learn from works of art that have been created by artists from many cultures and time periods. Art criticism also provides a procedure that students can use to objectively study their own art products.

The four-step process of art criticism will help students expand their perceptive, analytical, interpretive, and aesthetic valuing abilities. The sequential steps of art criticism are similar to those used in the scientific method. During the first two steps, **Describe** and **Analyze,** students are asked to collect data objectively. During the third step, **Interpret,** students speculate about the meaning of the work based on the data collected: they make a hypothesis abut the idea, emotion, or mood expressed by the artist. During the fourth step, **Decide,** or aesthetic judgment, the students offer their conclusions about the work of art.

Art criticism helps students study a work of art before making an aesthetic judgment. Too often, beginners look at a work of art briefly and immediately make a value judgment. The sequential procedures in art criticism force the students to postpone judgment while becoming immersed in the image.

In this program art criticism is used as a higher-level method of thinking about the concepts taught in each unit. One work of art has been selected that emphasizes the elements or principles that were the focus of the lesson. Art criticism is also used to help students make a personal assessment of the artwork produced during the Creative Expression activities. The questions offered are neutral and avoid judgments involving likes and dislikes. This avoids embarrassing moments when discussing works in front of peers.

Art History and Culture

Art Connections is not an art history text, but any study of art should begin with learning something about the history of world art and the people who created it. Information about art history related to the featured work of art in each lesson is provided for the students throughout the text. The **About Art History and Culture** section provides an overview of how to include art history information in classroom instruction. Additional information is provided for the teacher in each lesson and in ancillary materials such as the *Artist Profiles* books and on the backs of the *Large Prints.* The *Art Around the World* collection and *The National Museum of Women in the Arts Collection* contain works of art from many countries and provide additional historical and cultural information.

Art Production and

 Creative Expression

Each lesson includes an art production activity identified as **Practice** and **Creative Expression** in the *Student Edition.* This is the place for each student to creatively explore the lesson concept. Hands-on activities are often the most enjoyable aspect of art learning. The student integrates and internalizes the verbal and visual concepts of the lesson during the creative manipulation of art materials. While every component in the art program is equally important, every component does not need equal time. Art production requires the longest amount of time.

Do not skip the self-assessment section of the lesson. Most students would be embarrassed to offer subjective statements about their own work or the work of classmates. The four steps of art criticism offer an objective procedure for thinking about the concepts and technical procedures used during the creation of art.

Art Magazine Resources for Teachers

American Artist	*ARTnews*	*Crayola Kids*
Art Education	*Arts and Activities*	*Scholastic Art*
Art to Zoo	*Arts Education Policy Review*	*School Arts*

About Aesthetic Perception

Richard W. Burrows , Executive Director, Institute for Arts Education, San Diego, California

The Association of Institutes for Aesthetic Education promotes and fosters aesthetic education principles and practices through professional and institutional development. The Association provides policy and program leadership to the arts and education field at the national, state, and local levels.

Aesthetics has been defined as the branch of philosophy that focuses on the nature of beauty, the nature and value of art, and the inquiry processes and human responses associated with those topics.

Aesthetic perception can be most simply defined as an educational approach designed to enhance understanding of artistic expression. Aesthetic perception requires two primary elements to exist: a work of art and a viewer to perceive it. An aesthetic perception approach to viewing works of art is predicated on the belief that the arts can be studied in an active, experiential way. The focus is on developing skills of perception by using works of art as a "textbook" or a focus for study. The instruction delivered by teachers is in partnership with the work of art.

Aesthetic perception provides opportunities to heighten perception and understanding through direct encounters with a broad spectrum of works of art. Students and teachers become actively involved with the artwork—observing, listening to and discussing works of art, and exploring their perceptions of these works through participatory activities. The focus is on developing skills of perception through greater understanding of art forms, of how artists make aesthetic choices, and of how these understandings relate to other aspects of life.

Misconceptions About Aesthetic Perception

As aesthetic perception approaches have become more widely used, a number of misconceptions have developed about the purpose of aesthetic perception education in the understanding of works of art.

Multidisciplinary Versus Interdisciplinary

The purpose of aesthetic perception is not to explore the commonalities among works of art. Each work of art must be studied separately first; connections should be made after an in-depth understanding of that particular work. Every work of art has a separate intention and different meaning. If aesthetic perception is to develop a thinking- or meaning-based understanding of the work of art, then activities must reflect that point of view.

You Cannot Teach What You Do Not Like

A strong "personal" negative reaction to a work of art does not invalidate it as an object of study for students.

Arts Integration

While arts experiences must integrate with all other areas of the curriculum, it is important to understand the separate language that the arts have and acknowledge the connections with other cross-curricular areas as they arise.

The Therapeutic Value of Aesthetic Perception

Very often students and teachers will comment on the therapeutic value of aesthetic perception—it seems separate from the actual art-making processes. This is often a side effect of active engagement in artistic creation and perception. This is not the purpose of aesthetic perception, which should be seen as an alternative way of viewing the work of art and the world in which it is created.

Using Aesthetic Perception

Below are some guidelines for using an aesthetic-perception approach to education.

Deciding What to Teach

It would not be appropriate to teach the same elements over and over in connection with each work of art. Instead, knowledge of all of the elements within a given art discipline should provide the background knowledge for making a decision about what aesthetic perception experiences to design. These decisions should be based on the most predominant elements in the work of art—the responses and the backgrounds of the students.

Creating a Safe Space and Adopting a Critical Stance

It is important to create a working and learning environment with both students and teachers in which they feel comfortable taking risks and trying out new ideas. This does not mean, however, that everything that occurs in aesthetic perception has to be met with uncritical approval. Instead, experiences can be structured so that participants receive feedback on their aesthetic choices and are given an opportunity to revise and improve their solutions to problems.

Documenting the Experience

Various types of documentation serve as a way of recording the aesthetic perception events as they occur or are revisited. This documentation should include written observations, interviews, journals, and student projects. It is important in any case to record this work in order to be able to see the "habits of mind" that reveal themselves in this complex and rich way of thinking and knowing.

Aesthetic perception is a long-term undertaking and requires a patient conviction that the arts and aesthetic perception should be a part of the learning experience of young people. It requires flexibility, stamina, ingenuity, and perseverance. The rewards are astronomical in terms of student response, content understanding, and classroom relationships.

Introduction to Art History

Gene A. Mittler, Ph.D., Professor Emeritus, Texas Tech University

> *"The art of the Greeks, of the Egyptians, of the great painters who lived in other times, is not an art of the past; perhaps it is more alive today than it ever was. Art does not evolve by itself; the ideas of people change and with them their mode of expression."* —Pablo Picasso

One of the primary goals of education in the visual arts is to prepare students to make and support intelligent and sensitive decisions about works of art. In order to make those kinds of decisions students can employ two ways of examining and responding knowledgeably to visual art forms. One of these ways, art criticism, involves them in learning *from* works of art. Another approach is art history, which enables students to learn *about* works of art and the artists who created them.

The Art History Approach to Learning about Art and Artists

Art historians contend that no work of art can be fully understood unless it is viewed in relation to the circumstances in which it was created. Every artwork is created in a particular place at a particular time in history and to some degree is bound to reflect the prevailing conditions of that time and place. For example, an art history approach to the study of a painting by Rembrandt would include an examination of seventeenth century Holland—the time and place in which that particular artist lived and worked. Adhering to this approach would require that students focus attention on the social, religious, and economic conditions that existed in the republic at that time in history before focusing attention on the painter and his work. All these conditions would have impacted Rembrandt's choice of subject matter, medium, his way of handling materials, and the visual language he chose to use in expressing his ideas and feelings.

Art history, then, involves a study of the visual arts in relation to the times and places from which they sprang. This study will provide students with a richer, broader, and deeper understanding of the specific art objects selected for study and the world as it existed when those art objects were created. However, to determine the significance of the place of a particular work, such as a picture by Rembrandt, involves more than just an examination of the world conditions at the time that artist lived. It also requires a study of what went on in the world *before* and *after* Rembrandt painted his picture. A study of this kind will show students that Rembrandt, like all artists, took into account the works of other artists, selecting some ideas and techniques to use in his own painting while rejecting other ideas and techniques. This is a valuable lesson that students can apply to their own efforts to create art.

Consequently, a historical examination of a painting by Rembrandt would include the identification of any artists who may have influenced his style of painting. The most important of these artists was the Italian painter Caravaggio, whose paintings Rembrandt never saw, but without which his own work would not have taken on certain stylistic innovations. However, to understand Caravaggio, students would have to become acquainted with the artists *he* admired as well as the ones he rejected while arriving at his own revolutionary painting style. Thus, students adhering to an art history approach will find themselves involved in a fascinating learning process not unlike a game of dominoes, in which an entire row of game pieces is seen to collapse by upsetting the first domino in that row. The very last "domino" to fall in this comparison of art history to dominoes would be the very first visual image ever created—perhaps an image scratched on the rough wall of a cave by the very first prehistoric artist.

The Use of Historical Periods

For convenience, art historians divide the history of art into more or less artificial periods such as Medieval, Renaissance, Baroque, and Rococo. Doing so does no harm as long as students are reminded that the changes in art history identified by these labels, like changes of the seasons, are gradual. Each historical period passes into the next as smoothly as spring passes into summer.

If it can be assumed that an understanding of the present can be illuminated by a study of the past, then a chronological ordering of art history periods can be most helpful. By beginning at the beginning and observing the changes in art created from one year, decade, or century to the next, students will find it easier to understand how the art produced today has its roots in the art produced in the past. If students are to gain an understanding of art history, they should be afforded opportunities to see and learn about art examples from every corner of the world representing every historical period, not just those created by Western artists.

In every art history period students will encounter artists whose works preserve the traditional values of earlier artists, artists who chose to build upon current art trends, and still other artists who opted to explore revolutionary ways of expressing themselves through their art. Art history is filled with the stories of artists who accepted or rejected, endorsed or protested, conformed or reformed, contrasted or destroyed, dreamed of the past or conjured up visions of the future—but every one of those artists did so from the springboard of his or her own time and place, be that tenth-century China or twentieth-century America.

Art History as a Means of Understanding Each Other

Through art history students learn that a painting, a statue, or a temple is a consequence of how imaginative, sensitive members of any given society viewed and responded to the world around them. Art history also encourages students to regard works of art as more than objects that are pleasing to the eye, more than splendid and original products of human skill and inventiveness. Works of art also represent springboards for learning, revealing how differently people thought and acted at different times and in different geographical locations throughout the long history of humankind. A work of art reveals not only the customs, social habits, architecture, and technical achievements of its time and place; it also reflects the prevailing fears, beliefs, superstitions, desires, and values of people living in different ages at different geographic locations. Art history, then, is a vital part of the history of the human race.

Art History and Changing Tastes

As they study art history, students will discover that, over time, works of art do not always look the same to the people viewing them. This happens because people from different times and places look at art from different points of view. Cultures vary and change and so do tastes. Take any great artist or any great work of art from a bygone era and note how there have been periods in which that artist or work has been highly regarded, treated with indifference, or even ridiculed. For example, few today would venture a negative judgment of a painting created by Rembrandt, who is universally regarded as one of the greatest artists of all time. Yet, over the years, this Dutch master has not always been understood or appreciated. Indeed, when Italian artists first viewed a painting by Rembrandt they were puzzled and disappointed. They failed to understand why this artist was so highly regarded. His style, they concluded, was most peculiar because it made use of large areas of dark values and made no use of outlines favored by Italian artists.

Students must learn that art is a two-way process involving *both* artist and viewer. If students are to grasp more than the superficial appearance of a work of art, they must be prepared to learn its purpose, its *contemporary* meaning within the society in which it was produced, and its place in the historical process. No work of art is created in a vacuum. If students are to share in the ideas and feelings that contributed to the creation of a work of art, they must recognize the concepts, desires, and expectations of the person expressing those ideas and feelings at a particular point in time. This will result in a richer, broader, deeper understanding of both the artwork and the culture that witnessed its creation.

The Art History Operations

The study of art history is made easier for students if a plan of action is offered. One such plan makes use of four steps, or operations, that bear the same labels used to describe the four steps used in art criticism. These operations are description, analysis, interpretation, and decision. However, while these operations enable students to gain information from works of art during art criticism, they also are used to help students gather information about those works during art history. Briefly, the four art history operations are:

Description During this first operation, students seek to discover when, where, and by whom the work was created. In other words, they determine the period in which the work was created, the place where the artist lived, and, assuming it is known, the name of the artist.

Analysis This operation requires students to identify the unique features in a work of art that determine its artistic style. In the visual arts, style has come to mean the personal and unique way in which the artist uses the elements and principles of art to express ideas and feelings. For example, one artist may choose to delineate shapes in his painting by surrounding them with a heavy dark outline. Another painter might ignore the use of an outline and suggest shapes by creating areas of bright hues that contrast with the dull hues surrounding them.

> "Art historians contend that no work of art can be fully understood unless it is viewed in relation to the circumstances in which it was created."

Interpretation When interpreting a work of art, students take into account the impact of time and place upon the artist. It is during this operation that they learn that pictures of the same subject painted at the same time but in different geographic locations typically differ in appearance because they reflect different traditions and values. A landscape painted in fifteenth-century Italy will differ dramatically from a landscape painted at the same time in Japan. Moreover, a work of art created in the same country but at different times may also bear few stylistic similarities. A landscape painted by a French artist living and working in the late nineteenth century would have little in common with a landscape done by a French artist living and working at the beginning of the same century.

In an effort to express themselves in visual terms, artists make use of the materials and processes placed in their hands by the circumstances of time and place. Thus, a nineteenth-century African artist might have carved a figure from a piece of wood to serve as a dwelling place for a departed spirit, while a seventeenth-century artist applied his brush to canvas to paint a lifelike portrait of his king. In the spotlight of history, the efforts of both artists are magnified or diminished, honored or dismissed by forces that neither could predict or control but that had little to do with the values the artists sought to express in their work. It is the desire to discover those values that motivates students when interpreting artists' works.

Decision The final art history operation requires that students make a decision about the historical importance of a work of art. They will discover that some works are more important than others because they were the first examples of a new, revolutionary style. Others are found to be significant because they are the most accomplished and successful examples of a particular style. As their knowledge and understanding of art grows, students will find themselves liking a great many more works of art than they thought possible at the start. Gradually they will gain confidence in their historical judgments and exercise skill in defending those judgments.

Art history is a fascinating, provocative learning experience affording students the opportunity to travel through time and space. It provides them with access to the inner lives of many kinds of people and offers clues to where we come from and who we are. Finally, art history reveals that artists and their art have succeeded in helping people communicate with each other in a manner we cannot express in any other way.

Art Criticism

Rosalind Ragans, Ph.D., Associate Professor Emerita, Georgia Southern University

Art criticism is organized discussion about art. The art criticism procedures used in this program were developed by Edmund B. Feldman based on his analysis of the writings of professional art critics. He organized the elaborate procedures followed by critics and summarized them into four steps. The purpose of these four steps is to delay impulse judgments of visual images and to involve the viewer in a complex interaction with the image that can result in a truly aesthetic experience.

Art criticism involves the use of high-level thinking skills. The viewer translates the visual language of the image created by an artist into everyday words. To have a truly aesthetic experience the viewer must go beyond simple identification and recognition to the types of thinking required to analyze, interpret, and judge visual clues.

Anyone can do art criticism. All that is needed are eyes to see the image and a brain to think about what is seen. Art criticism gives a viewer of any age the confidence to discuss a work of art without worrying about what other people have said about it. One does not need to know anything about the artist, the style, or the time when the work was made to get involved with the work. After the steps of art criticism have been followed in a school setting, students are usually so interested in the art that they want to know more about the who, what, where, when, and how of the work. In other words, the students are ready to learn about art history and culture.

Description

The first step of art criticism is a clue-collecting step. The purpose of this step is to get to know the work as intimately and deeply as one can. All the information from the credit line should be noted. It is important for the viewer to know whether the artwork is 20 × 30 inches or 20 × 30 feet. The medium with which the work is made is also important. Whether a piece of sculpture is modeled with clay or carved from stone affects the viewer's impression. Then the observer names everything that is seen in the image. During description the observer must remain objective. All the descriptive terms must be neutral, value-free words.

Analysis

This is an advanced form of description. It is also an objective, clue-collecting step. During this stage the viewer studies the elements of art and the principles that have been used to organize those elements. It is during this step that the viewer begins to discover how the artist has organized the formal qualities of the work to create the content or meaning. In this program you will see how the art criticism lesson at the end of each unit is used to reinforce the concepts taught during each unit. Works of art have been selected that will help the student comprehend the artist's use of the specific elements or principles that were introduced in that unit.

Interpretation

This is the most important part of art criticism. It is during this step that the viewer pulls together all the descriptive and analytical observations to make sense of the work. The viewer makes inferences about the mood, meaning, or message being conveyed by the work. This step goes beyond narration to a generalization about life. The viewer makes guesses, but these ideas must be supported by the clues collected during the first two steps. This can be the most difficult step because it requires imagination and courage. Every interpretation can be different because each is based on the feelings and life experiences of the viewer. No one individual has done or seen exactly the same things as the next person. The viewer may see ideas in a work of art that were never dreamed of by the artist. That is not wrong. It simply means that the work is so powerful that it carries special meanings for everyone.

A good interpretation goes beyond answering "What is happening?" to answering "What does it mean?"

Decision (Judgment)

This is the step where a professional critic will decide the quality of a work. Is this as good as the rest of the works by this artist? How does it measure up to the works of other artists in the same group? The students who are using this program do not have enough experience to make that level of decision, so the works of art in *Art Connections* have been selected because they have already been judged to be outstanding examples of art.

The students are asked to make personal decisions. There are two levels of judgment to be made. The first is "Do you like the work?" This opinion may be embarrassing for students to share in front of classmates, and it is best left unspoken. No one can ever tell someone else what they should like or dislike.

The second level of judgment is also subjective. We ask the student to decide why the work is successful, and we use aesthetic theories to help each individual make decisions about the work. The three aesthetic theories that we employ are the most common theories: imitationalism/realism, formalism/composition, and emotionalism/expressionism. More than one theory can be used to judge a work of art.

- Some critics think the most important thing about a work of art is the realistic presentations of the subject matter. People with this point of view think that an artwork should imitate life. This theory, called **imitationalism** or **realism**, focuses on realistic representation.
- Other critics think that composition is the most important factor in a work of art. This aesthetic theory, called **formalism** or **composition**, places emphasis on the design qualities, the arrangement of the elements of art using the principles of art.
- **Emotionalism** or **expressionism** is the theory concerned with the content or meaning of the work. This theory requires that a work of art convey a message. It must arouse a response of feelings, moods, or emotions in the viewer.

In this program we provide leading questions to help the teacher and student delve into a work of art by using the steps of art criticism. These are not all the questions that can be addressed in viewing a work, and teachers are encouraged to go beyond what is presented on the pages of these books.

Meeting National and State Standards for Art Education

Nan Yoshida

Art Connections has been carefully designed to help educators meet the standards of state and national art curriculum guidelines.

The *National Standards for Arts Education* are part of Goals 2000, the overarching plan for improving American education. Approved by the United States Congress in 1994, the standards describe what every young American student should know and be able to do in the arts.

In addition to the national standards, individual states have curriculum documents that set forth guidelines and requirements in subject areas. For example, both the *Texas Essential Knowledge and Skills for Art* and the *Visual and Performing Arts Framework for California Public Schools, Kindergarten through Grade Twelve* discuss four components of visual arts education common to most other state guidelines.

Placing the national standards side by side with the Texas and California standards, one can readily see that the documents match in their expectations of what students should know and be able to do in the visual arts.

Art Connections has been developed with these national and state expectations in mind. Every lesson in the program was designed to address the components of art education in Aesthetic Perception, Art History and Culture, Creative Expression, and Art Criticism.

Aesthetic Perception
(Artistic Perception)

Each lesson begins with Activate Prior Knowledge, which asks students to recall and visualize an image from personal experience that will help them take a purposeful look at the artwork.

Introduce the Art focuses students' attention on specific attributes of the artwork, design elements and principles, underlying structures, and functions. As students answer the questions about the work of art, they develop critical *observation* skills.

Aesthetic Perception directs students to extend their artistic perception to their environment and objects in the environment. The transition is made to use keen visual and tactile perception of formal art objects in everyday life (lifelong learning).

> "In **Art Connections** students are exposed to a variety of types and styles of art from many cultures and historical periods."

Art History and Culture
(Cultural Context)

In *Art Connections* students are exposed to a variety of types and styles of art from many cultures and historical periods. Students study art from Africa; Asia; Australia; Europe; and North, Central, and South America. They learn about the role of the artist in societies. They develop appreciation for paintings, drawings, prints, photographs, sculptures, textiles, and architecture. They relate to folk, decorative, functional, and formal arts.

While information about the works of art and the artist is necessarily brief in the *Student Edition*, teachers are encouraged to use the Art History and Culture feature of the *Teacher Edition* and the *Artist Profiles* books to provide students with enriching information about the artists, the periods of art history, and cultural perspectives.

Creative Expression
(Art Production)

Creative expression is fundamental to every art lesson. The Practice activity provides a structure for students to apply lesson concepts in meaningful practice. In the Creative Expression activity, students refine their new knowledge and skills by producing original artwork based on their personal visions. The lessons throughout the program introduce a variety of art media and techniques.

Art Criticism
(Aesthetic Valuing)

Reflection and self-assessment are inherent in the art-making process. Upon completion of the Creative Expression activity, students

evaluate their own work using the four steps of art criticism: Describe, Analyze, Interpret, and Decide. These four steps of art criticism are a method for making an informed critique of others' artwork as well.

Arts Integration

In addition to the high priority placed on teaching the visual arts as a unique discipline, both national and state standards recommend the appropriate integration or interrelation of the visual arts with the other arts disciplines of music, dance, and theatre. Toward this goal, every unit in *Art Connections* culminates with a lesson integrating one of these performing arts. In addition, connections are made to music and movement/dance in every lesson of the *Teacher Edition*.

Curriculum Integration

The *Teacher Edition* has an Art Across the Curriculum section that ties art concepts to other curriculum areas. Every lesson has a connection to Reading/Language Arts, Math, Science, Social Studies, and Technology.

National Standards for Arts Education © 1994

1. Understand and apply media, techniques, and processes.
2. Use knowledge of structures and functions.
3. Choose and evaluate a range of subject matter, symbols, and ideas.
4. Understand the visual arts in relation to history and cultures.
5. Reflect upon and assess the characteristics and merits of their work and the work of others.
6. Make connections between the visual arts and other disciplines.

The Development of Children's Art

Rosalind Ragans, Ph.D.

A child's ability to make and understand art develops along with his or her cognitive, social, emotional, and physical development. In 1947 Victor Lowenfeld was the first to identify and label the sequential stages that students move through as they create images. Since then many others have continued to study the development of children's visual images.

Understanding these stages will help you recognize what your students are doing; however, you must also understand that these stages describe untutored progression through the making of images. There are many outside influences on students, and these will show in their work. A well-meaning adult might teach a child to make stick figures, and because they are so easy to make, the child adopts this symbol.

Just as reading levels vary widely within one class, so do art abilities. Just as you teach students to appreciate differences in ability in other subject areas, you must help them understand that not everyone will have the same art abilities at the same time.

There are many different versions of the developmental stages; here we present a three-step version of art development. The stages of artistic development are useful norms that can help you, but they are **not** rules that must be followed.

The Manipulative Stage

Ages 2–5 (Grade K)

This has been called the scribble stage, and it is usually seen in children from two to five years old. During the early part of this stage, the child makes random, disordered scribbles. Making art at this stage is such a sensory experience that the child may hold crayons in both hands. Children who have opportunities to scribble produce a wide variety of lines, marks, dots, and shapes. The child who develops a variety of graphic marks during the scribble years will use them to produce complex symbolic drawings as he or she matures. Children who rarely scribble will have a more limited range of expression, and they will need a great deal of encouragement to continue drawing.

As the random scribbles become more controlled, the child starts to pull the marks into circular patterns until a mandala, or rough circle, is created. Rhoda Kellogg, who studied thousands of children's drawings from all over the world, found that the mandala appears as the final stage between random scribbling and representation. This controlled scribble becomes a named scribble. Expressive concepts develop as children recognize the relationship between their marks and the visual outcome.

The Symbol-Making Stage

Ages 4–9 (Grades 1–4)

When a child makes the connection between images and an idea, a shape becomes a symbol. During this stage children develop a series of distinct images that stand for objects in their experiences. These symbols are eventually related to an environment within the drawing. The first representation of a person is a mandala. This can represent anyone the child wants it to be. Although this shape appears to be just a head, it represents the entire person. Soon the child adds a line and two marks, which represent a person with a mouth and two eyes. Then two lines are added to the shape to represent legs, two lines for arms, and a scribble for hair. The child is drawing what he or she knows, not what he or she sees. As children develop from the early symbolic stage into the symbol-making stage, they start to add more details and develop a symbol that includes all the body parts.

At first, space is not a consideration, and the size of symbols in a work is related to importance. Objects and people seem to float. Eventually the child wants to make people and objects stand up and will line things up on the bottom of the paper or on a baseline. Along with a baseline, the child starts to represent the sky with a strip of color across the top of the paper that includes a round symbol with radiating lines for the sun. As far as the child is concerned, the space between the sky and the baseline is air. The sky will not touch the earth until the child develops a more mature sense of perception, usually the result of sensitive art instruction.

Another spatial problem is overlap. Children realize that two objects cannot occupy the same space at the same time, and they avoid overlapping. As the environments they depict become more complex, children may use a bird's-eye view, a foldover view, or multiple views to represent space.

Children in this stage develop their own schema, or image, that resembles an actual object. Once a schema has been invented it will be used over and over. As the child continues to make art, the schema will become more detailed and sophisticated.

Giving a child this age coloring books may lead to self-doubt because of the conflict between the child's schema and the adult image. After coloring a seated dog in a coloring book, the child may become frustrated when his or her own drawing of a dog does not measure up to his or her memory of the adult image. Because children are exposed to so many adult images, many of which have low artistic quality, it is helpful for the teacher to expose children to the many high-quality works of art available in this program.

The Preadolescent Stage

Ages 8–13 (Grades 3–8)

Preadolescent children are still naturally inquisitive and creative, but they have learned to be more cautious. They have become very sensitive to peer opinion. They have reached a "crisis of confidence" regarding the images they make. If a work doesn't look exactly the way they think it should, or if it looks childlike, they reject the art product. This is the time when many children become frustrated and stop making art.

This is a critical time in students' visual development. They need to be taught to work slowly and with patience. They need to be taught drawing skills such as perspective and human proportions. They need to master the language of art and the use of design principles. They need the technical skills to master the various media such as painting, printmaking, ceramics, and sculpture.

Students need to see how different artists in the past have solved problems, and to observe what contemporary artists are doing today. Artists solve problems differently, and young people need to be exposed to many different ideas as they try to create their own solutions to visual problems.

The strong art teacher will lead students over this perilous bridge of doubt by gently stretching their minds to help them see more so that they can do more. At every stage in the child's visual development, a strong, understanding teacher can help the child move forward.

Brain-Based Learning

Jamye Ivey, K–12 Art Supervisor, Dougherty County School System, Georgia

At the end of the school day, teachers often face many unanswered questions concerning the young people whose education is their responsibility. Educators cannot help but wonder why students fail to respond to instructional strategies that were successful in their own experiences. Why is today's student so different?

Brain Research

Neuroscientists are now able to supply some of the answers that have plagued educators for years. The amazing, constantly changing world of technology has unlocked for researchers a new realm of understanding of the human brain. With the aid of advanced medical techniques and strategies using equipment such as MRI, FMRI, CAT, and PET scans, the working brain can be observed. Translating these new and often startling medical findings into the educational arena has provided the classroom teacher with practical methodologies and a better understanding of how, why, and when students learn best.

The brain is the most powerful organ in the body. Researchers have discovered that today's brains grow better in the real world than in artificial learning environments. Students must be able to connect their learning to previous experience in order for new learning to occur. For years teachers have designed and taught units with the activities culminating in field trips. When we consider these recent findings, we realize this procedure should be reversed. The field trip provides the student relevance that would facilitate learning. Without a related experience in the memory bank of past experiences, the learner finds no significance in the new material.

It is also important to note that synapses in the brain are formed, strengthened, and maintained by interaction with experience. The stronger the synapses, the faster the messaging travels and the greater the number of neural pathways that are created in the brain. This enables a person to be capable of creating more flexible thought processing and better memory.

Research confirms that environments shape brains. Teachers should create an environment that provides the best opportunities for this generation of young people to learn. Students of today need to move, talk, and touch more than previous learners did. Eric Jensen explains that the part of the brain that processes movement is the same part that processes learning. Thus, there needs to be movement in the classroom.

Today, we know that lecturing is the poorest way to present new learning. Only about fifty percent of the audience is actively listening in any given oral presentation. Students learn the most at the beginning of a presentation, the second-most at the end, and the least in the middle. Learners need breaks during teacher talk sessions. The attention span of a preadolescent is ten to twelve minutes.

This generation of children has more trouble organizing thoughts and learns on a more global scale. Expect students to want to understand the big picture before dealing with the details. One way to accomplish this is to let the class spend a few minutes looking through the whole chapter before focusing on the first page.

We know now that students cannot learn if they feel threatened or stressed. If a teacher shouts at a student, it takes fifteen minutes for the adrenaline levels to subside in all the students in the class. The glucose needed for cognitive functioning is redirected to combat stress, so all learning is governed to some extent by emotions. The constant threat of failure needs to be removed and recognition should be placed on individual performance, experience, and interest. Pressure, tension, and stress slow down or eliminate learning.

Brain-Based Learning and the Arts

Art teachers are known for using creative methods to capture the imaginations of their students. Need, novelty, meaning, and emotion are four ways to gain a student's attention, and using humor during instruction increases attention by fifty percent. A happy classroom is a more brain-compatible classroom.

The arts are an important part of effective teaching and an essential component of brain-compatible instruction. There is evidence that art-making has been around for over one million years. Brain research documents the arts as basic to the brain. Every culture in human history has one common thread: all had the arts. Stable art, music, and dance experiences not only enhance the aesthetic life of the learner, but they also provide important activity for the growing neurological system.

For both teacher and student, the most encouraging summation from recent research is that we continue to grow brain cells regardless of our age. Noted neuroscientist

Marion Diamond explains that it is best to keep the brain curious and active. In her opinion the most significant finding of her career has been that the brain can learn at any age. Be a lifelong learner and engage in physical activitities, which also helps build brain cells. Stay curious and stay active. How affirming this is for art educators because the successful teaching of art daily demands both creative curiosity and physical endurance.

References

Sousa, David A. (2002). *How the Brain Learns, Second Edition.* Corwin Press.

Sylwester, Robert (1995). *A Celebration of Neurons, an Educator's Guide to the Brain.* Alexandria, VA: Association for Supervision and Curriculum Development.

Eric Jensen (2001). *Arts With the Brain in Mind.* Alexandria, VA: Association for Supervision and Curriculum Development.

Sprenger, Marilee (1999). *Learning & Memory-The Brain in Action.* Alexandria, VA: Association for Supervision and Curriculum Development.

Armstrong, Thomas (1987). *In Their Own Way.* G.P. Putnam's Sons.

Armstrong, Thomas (1991). *Awakening Your Child's Natural Genius.* G.P. Putnam's Sons.

Classroom Management and Motivation Strategies for Teaching Elementary Art

Bunyan Morris, Art Teacher, Effingham County School System, Georgia

While motivating students to express themselves visually through creative means, the elementary art teacher is challenged with the task of maintaining proper classroom management. The purpose of this article is to provide some practical methods of motivating creative thought and action under the guidance of successful classroom management. Combine these methods with your own to give students the best learning experience possible.

Be Prepared. Begin the lesson excited and ready. Students will pick up on your mood the moment they walk into the room. If you set the tone at the beginning and grasp immediate control, it will be much easier to keep it throughout the lesson. It is important to have art prints and demonstration materials ready and in place for the initial focus. Practice an activity before demonstrating it if it is the first time that it has been taught. Something might happen that could not be foreseen; prepare for the best and the worst. Also, it might be a good idea to practice a concept or an activity that has not been taught in a long time. Even classroom veterans forget things.

Focus. For the initial focus of the lesson, gather the students into a group on the floor, in chairs, or on benches in an area of the room that is ready for discussion and demonstration. By gathering the students into a compact group, it is easier to make eye contact and to keep the attention of all learners. If there is no room for a separate demonstration and discussion spot, gather the tables or desks into a closer group so that no one is "out of reach."

Introduce the Art. Always introduce a lesson with a work of art that relates to what the students will be learning. Students get excited playing detective. Finding clues and ideas in a painting or sculpture allows them to make their own interpretations and assessments about art. They will in turn learn to apply this to their own work. The students don't have to know that this activity has a lofty term called *art criticism* to gain from its purpose. Encouraging them to ask questions and share ideas about a master work will give the students motivation and fresh ideas to take into the Creative Expression portion of the lesson.

Moving to Art Production. Always control the manner in which students move to the Creative Expression area from the Demonstration/Discussion center. Release students in a manner that will keep order but not quell their enthusiasm about the lesson. Use positive reinforcement by complimenting those who are sitting quietly, and send them first. It will not take long for the others to catch on. After time most of the students will become conditioned to this expectation. Even if they've been involved in a lively discussion, they will automatically become settled as this transitional period approaches.

Classroom Design. Not only should the students be orderly, but the classroom must also be organized and conducive to the movement of the teacher and students. The Creative Expression stations should have enough space between them for the teacher to reach every student. There should be enough space in traffic areas for student movement. Children need easy access to supply shelves and sinks, and should be able to move from one Creative Expression station to another unencumbered. The supplies should be organized on leveled shelves so that the students will return them to their proper places. If the teacher keeps the room and supplies organized, hopefully the students will too.

As well as keeping the room and supplies organized, the rest of the room should be visually pleasing. Display student art with master prints. This builds self-esteem. When possible, display every child's work. Make learning centers organized and interesting. Keep interesting objects around the room for visual reference. These objects might include plants, pottery, old bottles, discarded sports equipment, old toys, or anything that might capture the attention and interest of your students. Use these objects in still lifes and as objects of visual reference for lines, shapes, and other elements and principles of art.

When moving about the room assisting students, it is important to keep the senses alive and be aware of what is happening with the other students. See and hear what they think you can't.

Closing the Lesson. Normally one should try to close the class with a review of the lesson's objectives. This should be short and interesting. This is also the time to reward the students for good behavior. The art teacher must set the criteria for earning the award. Do not give the award if it is not earned. Of course, the students must be aware of the opportunity to earn an award ahead of time.

One method that works is to award the students with a "Super Behavior Card." This is simply a colorful card that can be given to the class to take back to their classroom teacher for having good behavior during art. This requires the cooperation of the classroom teacher to award the students in some manner for collecting a certain number of Super Behavior Cards. Awards might include a popcorn party or extra time at recess. If the classroom teacher is unwilling, you will have to provide the award in your class. Awarding of the Super Behavior Card can be coordinated with cleanup at the end of the period. Choose one student at the table who cleans up most thoroughly and quietly to carry the Super Behavior Card back to the classroom teacher. The students at each table will work together to earn the Super Behavior Card.

Hopefully these ideas and suggestions will reduce the challenge of maintaining classroom control and motivating students. The individual teacher must decide what works best for each situation. All of the motivation and management techniques suggested here have been tried and have been proven to work. Combined with each teacher's individual strategies, they will increase the probability of success in the art classroom.

A Sampling of Art Games for Home or School

Art Lotto: National Gallery of Art. Safari Limited, Miami, Florida.

ARTDECK. Aristoplay, Ann Arbor, Michigan.

The Fine Art Game. Piatnik, Wiener Spielkartenfabrik, Ferd. PIATNIK & Söhne.

Where Art Thou? WJ Fantasy, Inc., Bridgeport, Connecticut.

Art Instruction for Students with Disabilities

Mandy Yeager, Art Educator, Ph.D. Student, The University of North Texas, Denton, Texas

Art education empowers all students to look at, respond to, create, and enjoy works of art. Students who are disabled are no exception to this privilege. The arts have often been understood as an equalizing force in the education of students with disabilities; often these students experience discrimination from peers and adults because of their disability. This discrimination often manifests itself in avoidance of or lowered expectations for these students. Stereotypes of persons with disabilities cast them as helpless, unintelligent, dangerous, or contemptible. These stereotypes are maintained by a lack of knowledge or personal experiences with persons who are disabled.

The visual arts, because they use images to express ideas about the human experience, play a vital role in challenging and eliminating many of these stereotypes. The current emphasis of art education upon visual literacy allows students to examine and transform stereotypes that exist in the media regarding all types of differences (including age, race, class, gender, and ability). Artists throughout time have engaged in this process of recording and seeking to transform societal injustices through visual imagery.

The benefits of art for students with disabilities cannot be underestimated. The skills gained in visual arts often result in increased confidence and ability in other academic subjects. Arts-based learning is often effective because of the ways it engages the multiple senses and abilities of students.

The arts also give students opportunities to explore, express, and celebrate their identities. Teachers who include the work of artists with disabilities in their art curriculum help all students realize that disability is a part of the human experience and does not prevent anyone from being a creator of art.

Resources to Assist Art Educators

The first step to developing competence is to develop an understanding of the child's disability. There are a number of resources to assist the art teacher in this regard.

Resources at the School Level

Resources at the school level include special-education staff and related service providers who have contact with the child such as occupational and physical therapists. All of these staff members can provide the art teacher with insight into the child's learning strengths and needs and his or her physical and emotional development. They can also provide helpful suggestions for how a particular art medium or tool can be made accessible to a particular student.

Another valuable resource for the art teacher is the student's Individualized Education Plan (IEP). This plan exists for every student receiving special education services and provides information about learning styles, needs, and modifications. The *Individuals with Disabilities Education Act* (IDEA) requires that all regular education teachers of students with disabilities have access to the child's IEP and are provided support in implementing modifications to the general curriculum.

Art educators can design their art curricula to meet students' annual IEP goals. For instance, art criticism activities have the potential to enhance students' expressive language skills. Cooperative learning activities such as mural painting can foster social skills. Art production often produces self-efficacy in students with disabilities as they learn to trust their ability to achieve success. Art teachers who engage in this process of reviewing a child's IEP and delineating the ways that art curricula can address annual goals become more confident in their abilities to successfully instruct students with disabilities.

Art Education and Disability Organizations

VSA arts has been designated by the U.S. Congress as the National Coordinating Agency of Arts in Learning for Persons with Disabilities. The agency fulfills this role through a vast network of state affiliates. VSA arts produces art and disability awareness curricula and showcases the work of students with disabilities by regularly sponsoring national calls for art. It also provides access to the work of artists with disabilities.

The Special Needs Interest Group of the National Art Education Association (NAEA) meets annually at the NAEA convention to discuss best practices in art education and disability. This group publishes a column in the bimonthly publication *NAEA News*.

Adapting the Art Experience for Students with Disabilities

It is often necessary to adapt some aspect of the art experience for students with disabilities. Adaptations ensure that learning is accessible to every child; as such, adaptation is a principle of good instruction.

Adapting the art experience is essentially a creative activity, as many different combinations of students, media, and processes coalesce in one semester of art instruction. Accordingly, effective adaptations are individualized and begin with knowledge of a particular student's learning strengths and needs. Teachers may choose to adapt art media, instructional strategies, and/or physical space, depending upon the situation. This process of adaptation often begins by observation of students in an introductory art-making experience. If a student is having difficulty with an art task, try to determine the source of the difficulty. Consult with other school staff and use some of the resources listed below to determine what is most appropriate for the student and situation.

The adaptations accompanying every lesson in this text are provided as suggestions only, because learning needs and strengths vary with each child, medium, and project. It is hoped that art educators, upon reading this article, will feel equipped to utilize available resources to design and implement empowering learning experiences for all students.

Resources

Disability Education Organizations

National Dissemination Center for Children with Disabilities (NICHCY), www.nichy.org/index.html

The Council for Exceptional Children, www.cec.sped.org/

ERIC Clearinghouse on Disability and Gifted Education, http://ericec.org

Art and Disability Organizations and Resources

VSA arts, www.vsarts.org

Art, Disability and Expression Online Exhibit, www.vsarts.org/showcase/exhibits/disability/index.html

The National Art Education Association Special Needs Interest Group

EDGE: Education for Disability and Gender Equity, www.disabilityhistory.org/dwa/edge/curriculum/index-netscape.htm

National Arts and Disability Center (NADC), http://nadc.ucla.edu/

Safe Use of Art Materials

Mary Ann Boykin, Director, The Art School for Children and Young Adults
University of Houston—Clear Lake, Texas

Elementary art teachers need to be aware of safety issues that can affect the well-being of the children they teach, as well as themselves. Follow the guidelines established by the Center for Safety in the Arts to assure that neither students nor teachers are injured by the unsafe use of art materials.

Elementary teachers should do two things to prevent problems. The first is to keep all toxic and hazardous substances out of the classroom. The second is to know how to use the materials safely, because any materials can become hazardous when used inappropriately.

Toxic Substances

A toxic substance is defined by the Center for Occupational Hazards as "a poison which can damage your body's organ systems when you are overexposed to it." This harm can be immediate or can be the result of repeated exposure over time. Toxic substances can enter the body in three ways:

1. absorption through the skin
2. inhalation through the nose or mouth
3. ingestion through eating or drinking in the area where toxic materials are being used

It is up to the teacher to make sure toxic substances do not enter the classroom and that all materials are used safely to avoid problems.

Pregnant women and those who are nursing must be especially careful to prevent exposure to toxic substances. Fumes, sprays, dusts, and powders present a real hazard to the fetus, can be transferred to the infant through the mother's milk, and can be carried home to the infant or young child through dusts and residue picked up by clothing and hair. The safe path is to completely avoid exposure to any toxin by carefully reading labels and applying common sense to the situation. For example, if you plan to mix powdered tempera paint or work with chalks or clay, the safe method would include use of a respirator mask, which would prevent inhalation of these substances.

Children and Safe Art Materials

Preschool and elementary children are particularly vulnerable to unsafe art materials for a variety of reasons. Their lower body weight allows a toxic substance to become more concentrated in their bodies. Because children have a more rapid metabolism than adults, toxic substances are more quickly absorbed into their bodies. Children also tend to have more hand-to-mouth contact than adults, which allows ingestion of toxic materials. Furthermore, children are easily distracted from safety warnings regarding materials as they become involved in the art process. The tendency of children to have cuts and scratches also allows for ready entry of toxins into their bodies.

What the Labels Mean

Since 1990 our government has required the labeling of all hazardous materials. Any product labeled as hazardous is totally inappropriate for the elementary school. Safe art materials carry the statement that the material "Conforms to ASTMD-4236." A simple "nontoxic" statement on a product is not adequate.

The Arts and Crafts Materials institute developed a voluntary program to provide a safe standard for materials used by children. Products bearing the labels AP (Approved Product) or CP (Certified Product) have been tested by toxicologists in major universities and have been deemed safe for children to use. The HL (Health Label) on art products indicates that these products are appropriate to use with children 12 years old or older under the supervision of an art teacher. Products with HL labels are not safe for elementary children.

Safe Art Materials

The following are guidelines for choosing and using basic art materials in a safe manner.

Drawing Materials

- Use only water-soluble AP- or CP-designated markers. Permanent markers are extremely dangerous and can cause lung and liver damage if inhaled. Never use permanent markers in the elementary classroom.
- Do not use scented markers. This teaches children to sniff or smell materials.
- Use only dustless chalk. The amount of dust created in a classroom by twenty children wiping and blowing chalk can be irritating to those who suffer from allergies, asthma, and other respiratory problems.
- Use oil pastels; the colors are richer than crayons and the satisfaction is greater! Crayons should also bear the AP or CP label to ensure that no lead is present in these materials.

Painting Materials

- Use only liquid tempera and/or watercolor paints. If you must use powdered tempera paints, mix these outside and have the paints ready before children enter the classroom. Avoid inhaling the powders of tempera paints.
- Do not use any spray paints or fixatives. These are extremely dangerous.

Printmaking Materials

- Use only water-soluble printers' inks. Do not use any solvent-based inks.
- Use pencils to carve into unused foam trays for printing blocks. Do not use mat knives or other sharp instruments.

Collage Materials

- Sharp scissors should not be used by young children; blunt points are safe. Fourth- and fifth-graders may use rounded points with teacher supervision.
- Use only school paste or white glue for adhering papers. Do not use rubber cement unless it bears the AP or CP label. Do not use any solvent-based glues.

Sculpture and Three-Dimensional Materials

- Use premixed, moist clay for sculpture and pottery. Do not allow students to take home any unfired clay.
- Remind students to wash their hands thoroughly after using clay. The residual dust can be harmful and irritating if inhaled.
- Paint clay pieces with tempera or watercolor paints. Do not use glazes. Some have the approved labels, but they are not recommended for elementary use.
- Use pencils, craft sticks, or other blunt tools to carve clay. Soapstone should not be used for carving in a closed environment.
- Read labels carefully on pastes used for papier-mâché, because some pastes contain pesticides or preservatives that are extremely harmful.

Stitchery, Weaving, and Fiber Materials

- Use blunt plastic needles and loosely woven fabrics such as burlap for stitchery. Blunt metal tapestry needles are safe if their use is supervised.
- Young children will have trouble cutting fabric and yarn with their scissors. Precut lengths of fabric and yarn prior to introducing a task.

Art Assessments

Assessment in art can be problematic for a variety of reasons. Many educators are reluctant to evaluate a student's creative expression as good or bad. Because there are often no right or wrong answers, students and their parents could challenge a teacher's subjective opinion of a work if it is reflected in a letter grade. Furthermore, many teachers without a strong art background do not feel qualified to grade student artwork. In addition, teachers do not want to discourage creative expression by giving a low grade or an undeserved grade. Many people also often feel that talented students have the advantage in art class and that students should not be evaluated on how talented they are, but rather on how much effort they put into their work and how much progress they make.

All of these assessment difficulties stem from the focus on art production in the art classroom, rather than a reflection of art history and culture, aesthetics, or art criticism. A broader focus in the art classroom and a variety of assessment options may help in more effective art assessment.

Assessment of Lesson Objectives

Instead of subjective opinions of whether or not one likes a student's artwork, students can be evaluated on whether or not they meet the art lesson objectives or demonstrate the knowledge and skills introduced in the lesson. In a quality art program, there are objectives for aesthetic perception, art history, and art criticism, as well as for demonstrating understanding of the elements and principles of art in art production.

In *Art Connections,* every lesson has four clear, measurable objectives. At the end of each lesson, a rubric provides evaluation criteria for each objective.

Art Production: Evaluating Student Artwork

Art teachers frequently evaluate student artwork on the basis of how well it reflects the elements and principles of art that are being stressed in the lesson and how well the student meets the criteria for the artwork. Some teachers can construct rubrics or standards for the artwork beforehand and tell students how their work will be evaluated at the time it is assigned. Other teachers use

written or mental checklists of their standards as they look at student artwork. Teachers may use this form of evaluation as an opportunity to discuss the work with a student and find out whether the student thought he or she met the objectives for the artwork.

In *Art Connections,* teachers can also use the Assessment Masters in the *Assessment* book to get an idea of whether a student understands the elements or principle of art for a lesson.

Art Criticism and Aesthetic Perception: Self- and Peer-Assessment

The four-step process of art criticism (Describe, Analyze, Interpret, Decide) provides a procedure that students can use to objectively study their own art products, as well as the works of others. The sequential steps of art criticism are similar to those used in the scientific method. During the first two steps, Describe and Analyze, students are asked to collect data objectively. During the third step, Interpret, students speculate about the meaning of the work based on the data collected: they make a hypothesis about the idea, emotion, or mood expressed by the artist. During the fourth step, Decide, students offer their aesthetic judgment about the work of art. The sequential procedures in art criticism force students to postpone judgment while becoming immersed in the image. It forces them to have a fully funded visual experience before drawing conclusions about a work.

Art Connections includes art criticism questions for every Creative Expression activity. Additionally, the Aesthetic Perception feature in every lesson of the *Student Edition* provides students with an opportunity to evaluate their developing aesthetic perception.

Art History and Culture

Art is a visual record of history and diverse cultures. The goals for elementary art education are that students understand and appreciate different historical periods, cultures, and artistic styles and develop respect for the traditions and contributions of diverse societies.

In *Art Connections* every lesson introduces a work of art from a particular culture, time, and style. In the Introduce the Art strategies, teachers are encouraged to compare, contrast,

and share the Art History and Culture information as well as the information provided in *Artist Profiles* to help students develop an understanding of the visual arts in relation to history and cultures. Through discussion and elements in students' own artwork, teachers can evaluate students' awareness in this area.

Portfolio Assessment

Art educators could claim to have inspired the growing use of portfolio assessment in other subject areas. Many art teachers collect the best examples of a student's work and look at the progress over time. They display it and discuss it with students and parents. Student art journals with ideas, drawings, and sketches also provide an opportunity for portfolio assessment.

In *Art Connections* students are encouraged to keep their best work in a Student Portfolio and to maintain an Art Journal. Reminders of these types of portfolio assessments appear in the *Teacher Edition.*

Performance Assessment

Unlike other subject areas, art education has a long tradition of performance assessment. In art class students make things to demonstrate what they can do. In quality art programs, teachers use performance descriptions not only for art production, but also for art criticism, art history and culture, and aesthetic perception to aid them in evaluating student demonstrations of their knowledge and skills in art.

In *Art Connections,* every work of art a student produces can be considered for performance assessment of the lesson concept. Performance assessments can also involve discussions about the works of art to introduce the lesson concept and art criticism questions.

Art not only enables teachers to evaluate student knowledge and skills in art each year, but it also provides a wonderful opportunity to assess students' growth and development over time. Students and parents are often reluctant to discard artwork and fondly review it from time to time to see how children's ideas and skills have changed. Schools often keep examples of student artwork in student portfolios from year to year.

A thoughtful and fair art assessment program enables teachers to really see how much their students are capable of accomplishing.

Art and Cross-Curricular Connections

Tina Farrell

The study and production of artwork enhances learning in all areas of the curriculum. When teachers and students connect art to other subjects, learning occurs in the natural and interrelated way that it exists in the real world. We know from experience that learning is most meaningful when it is interconnected, not isolated. Therefore, making the natural connections that exist within each discipline of study, art including, enhances total understanding and brings meaning to fragmented information.

Below are a few of the ways that art education can impact the study of other subjects.

Reading/Language Arts In the viewing and analysis of a work of art, students develop oral and written communication skills. Teachers can enhance the language process by writing art terms and concepts on the board, having students generate lists of adjectives and adverbs to describe works of art, encouraging reflective inquiry into art, having students read about art and artists, and having students use works of art as stimuli for all forms of writing.

Mathematics Mathematics concepts are enhanced through art. When math concepts are presented or expressed in a visual or manipulative manner, students can more easily grasp them. The comparison and development of shapes and forms, visual-spatial relationships, measurement, proportion, estimation, and grids and graphs, for example, all are best explained through art.

> "We know from experience that learning is most meaningful when it is interconnected—not isolated."

Science In the art-making process, children learn that multiple ways to solve problems exist. They learn to discover, imagine, try new materials and techniques, experiment, develop and test hypotheses, and observe and record visual data. These are many of the skills, objectives, and habits of mind taught in science.

Social Studies The history of the world is reflected in the functional and aesthetic works of art produced by the peoples of the world. Children can gain great insights about near and distant cultures through the study of art, artifacts, and architecture.

The Arts The arts all complement each other in the skills, elements, principles, and beliefs that are emphasized in each one. Each discipline presents a unique way to express ideas and transform emotions into song, dance, interactions, words, or images. Visual artists research, develop rough drafts (sketches), plan, develop ideas, produce completed visual ideas, and sign and title their works. These are the processes that authors, writers, dancers, composers, actors, and poets also employ.

Life Skills In art, children develop craftsmanship, self-discipline, dedication to a task, skills for working both individually and cooperatively, and pride in one's work. These skills are necessary for success in all areas of their lives.

Critical-Thinking Skills Studying the visual arts develops higher-level thinking skills as studenst analyze, compare, interpret, synthesize, and make inferences and judgments about works of art.

Art is a great integrating subject because art, first and foremost, is a form of human communication. Art is one of the first forms of communication for children. Children often express complex ideas through visual symbols that represent their beginning language systems. Art is a vehicle for children to learn about the world around them and to organize the information in a comprehensive format. As young children draw, they take textures, shapes, and colors from a complex world and form them into coherent visual images. This visual cognition, a powerful way for children to process information, is the basis for learning in and through art.

A Sampling of Art Program Resources for Schools

The California Arts Project
    (http://www.ucop.edu/tcap/aeol.html)
Getty Education Institute for the Arts
    (http://www.artsednet.getty.edu)
The Kennedy Center ArtsEdge
    (http://artsedge.kennedy-center.org)

The Metropolitan Museum of Art
    (http://www.metmuseum.org/explore/index.asp)
The Educator's Reference Desk
    (http://www.eduref.org/cgi-bin/res.cgi/Subjects/Arts)

Integrating the Four Art Forms

Susan Cambigue-Tracey, Education Division, The Music Center of Los Angeles County

Albert Einstein said, "Imagination is more important than knowledge." Without exercising the imagination, knowledge is stored in the individual containers of the mind, but connections are not made. When students are taught to use the elements, skills, and content of the visual and performing arts the possibilities for synthesizing and applying what they know are multiplied. Teachers need to ensure that imagination and creativity are always nourishing the roots of learning.

The importance of artistic activity for all students goes beyond the intrinsic value of each art form in itself. Real arts investigation requires the rigor of being able to focus, make decisions, develop discipline, promote originality, and undertake research, study, and practice. Helping students to experience new ways of thinking and seeing allows them to construct personal meaning from what they experience and to build confidence and motivation.

Each art form is a discrete discipline with its own elements, vocabulary, and strategies. However, it is interesting to see connections among them where there are fundamental concepts shared across the arts and other subjects. For example, lines in art are the marks used to create images. Line in dance is the path of gestures and traveling movements, as well as body design. Line in music is a melody and also the lyrics of a song, while lines in theatre are the words that the actors speak.

A common core of knowledge is built through the arts. The principles of visual art, such as emphasis, variety, harmony, unity, and contrast, are the underlying principles used to creating anything—an architectural structure, a musical composition, a piece of literature, a dance, or a play.

It is easy to find ways to integrate one or more of the art forms and still make connections that are viable and authentic. For example, when viewing and discussing a work of art from a particular time period or culture, select music from that same time period or culture. Aztec art will have more relevance when Aztec-inspired music is played or students can view an Aztec dance and see the colors and design of the costumes. A style of music might also inspire art. Matisse did a jazz series that begs for jazz music and dance. Students can then see and hear the structural and improvisational aspects of this style in three different art forms.

When viewing or painting family scenes in art, challenge students to think of family activities that can be portrayed in a tableau, or live,

frozen picture. When viewing or creating sculpture, pair students and have one person become the "clay" and the other the "sculptor" who shapes the clay with respect and cooperation. This can extend into dance by directing the sculpted person (clay) to develop a movement idea lasting eight counts that starts and ends with the sculpted pose or form. Two people in contrasting sculptural poses can have eight counts to slowly transform from one into the other.

Three-dimensional forms in art can inspire counterbalanced (push, pull, leaning) designs made by small groups. A story, such as "The Two Skyscrapers Who Wanted to Have a Child" by Carl Sandburg, could be retold using story theatre or be portrayed in tableaux or as dramatized scenes. Students could also research musical selections to accompany their work.

> "Imagination is more important than Knowledge."
> —Albert Einstein

Students will be better able to express emotions in their visual artwork if they first work with them through drama, music, and dance. Students can begin by showing a variety of emotions in the face, hands, and feet and then move toward portraying these emotions in postures such as sitting, standing, and walking. Everyday activities such as cooking or brushing teeth can be done with different emotional motivations. Students can also create short musical pieces depicting an emotion or mood or find music that expresses specific feelings or moods.

All four performing arts can become a powerful component of integrated learning. For example, during a fifth-grade project focused on the Lewis and Clark expedition, students did research in books and on the Internet to collect historical, scientific, geographical, and cultural content. This information served as the basis for group projects in music, dance, theatre, visual arts, technology, and language.

Challenged by well-designed tasks, students discussed what they knew and selected different aspects to explore through dance, music, theatre, and visual art. They learned songs of the times, listened to traditional fiddle music, and learned a rhythmic chant that was used to measure the depth of rivers. In dances, they captured the sense of traveling through "boundless space"; portrayed animals encountered during the expedition; created weather conditions such as storms; and showed the struggles in navigating rivers, waterfalls, and mountains. In theatre, students drew upon the historical characters, interpreted various scenarios, and read journal entries of Lewis and Clark. Visual art classes focused on observation drawings of plants and wild animals.

Students also created journals in which they recorded their feelings, observations, sketches, and discoveries. They were able to make connections between their own journeys and that of the Corps of Discovery. Finally, the students shared what they had learned about this epic journey in a multi-arts culmination.

The arts bring accessibility and vitality to learning, empowering students to construct meaning that has relevance for their lives. When children learn to draw, they learn to see. When children learn to act, they learn how it feels to be in different roles, cultures, and circumstances. When children learn to dance, they learn to feel comfortable in their bodies and to use movement expressively. When children learn to play an instrument, they learn perseverance and the rewards of expression through music. When children learn to sing, they release their voices and are empowered to harmonize. When children learn to write a play, they learn to observe life by thinking, reflecting, and writing. When creativity and imagination are nurtured, children learn how to use all of their resources to solve problems, to dream, and build on the ideas of others.

The Creative Process and Problem Solving

Bunyan Morris, Art Teacher, Effingham County School System, Georgia

There is great reward in watching the artistic growth of a child. Simply providing the media and the time for creating is not enough. The student's natural curiosity and desire to create must be nurtured, encouraged, and challenged. Even the brightest and most talented students need a teacher's guidance in developing the critical-thinking skills necessary for creative problem solving. The intention of this article is to provide ideas and methods for fostering creativity by developing and encouraging divergent problem solving and critical-thinking skills in elementary school art students.

Classroom Management

Fostering creativity in the art classroom is possibly an art teacher's most important skill. In order to encourage creativity, a teacher must be able to relate to students at their thinking level and then guide them to a higher level of cognitive reasoning. Classroom and behavior management are essential. There cannot be an atmosphere of creativity in a room with chaos. That is not to say that one must be a firm authoritarian. A good art teacher will learn how to walk the fine line between maintaining order and maximizing creative energy among students. Although some may not admit it, all students prefer an educational environment that is free from annoying distractions created by other students. Therefore, good behavior management is a must for maintaining a creative environment.

Visual References

Introducing a lesson with a work of art and going through the art criticism process is a tried and true method of encouraging creativity. It is important to discuss works of art that are related to the objectives of the lesson. Working strictly from imagination and memory is usually not effective. Students must have visual references from which to gather ideas.

Picture files, reference books, and the Internet are just a few sources for visual images. Photographs of people and various natural and humanmade objects provide ideas and references for drawing. Images can be collected from magazines and calendars or unwanted photographs. The image file should be organized according to subject matter or theme.

Reference books filled with images related to the lesson should be available to students. They may be checked out of the media center and kept in the room, or they may belong to the classroom. Some media specialists are willing to search for and reserve books that a teacher may need for an upcoming lesson.

An image search on the Internet is one method to help students access a visual reference that may not be available in the classroom's image file, reference books, or the school's media center.

Art Journals

Students who keep art journals maintain handy reference tools. An art journal is the best way to record ideas through sketching and writing. If art journals and writing tools are kept handy, students can jot down ideas or make sketches to save for future use. Ideas can come to mind any place or any time such as in the cafeteria, on the playground, or at the bus stop. The method or tool doesn't really matter that much. It is just important that students have a way of practicing and recording creative ideas.

Exercising the Brain

Reading should be encouraged. Students who like to read perform better in all subjects. Descriptive language stimulates the imagination. Reading a passage about the beauty of a tree or the sound of a waterfall creates a visual image in the brain. This visual image can be stored in the sketchbook and later rendered as a sculpture, painting, or drawing. Encouraging reading encourages creativity. Teachers and schools should encourage parents to limit their children's time watching television because this takes away from reading and creative play time.

Resting the Brain

Teachers should be tolerant of students taking small breaks. Sometimes students need down time to regenerate their mental energy. This down time can take the form of daydreaming or play. Both are important to the creative process. Common sense and good judgment is used to determine when a student is using time for thinking as opposed to just wasting time. Students should be reminded to get a

> "Fostering creativity in the art classroom is possibly an art teacher's most important skill."

good night's sleep every night. This is not something teachers can control, but it should be encouraged. We all know that brains function better after a good night's rest.

Enriching Observation Skills

Enriched observation skills lead to more focused experimentation in art. Artists are naturally observant, but teachers know that most students are not born with natural talent. Through practice, all students can enrich their observation and critical-thinking skills. It is important to get students to slow down and see what they might not otherwise observe. One way to do this is to play an observation game. With the students' help, the teacher can set up a still life in the room. A fun game similar to "I Spy" can be played once the still life is ready. The students describe textures, lines, shapes, colors, and other elements and principles of art found within the real-life objects. The teacher writes the observations and descriptions on the board. Once the game is over and students move to the project portion of the lesson, they will be better equipped with enriched observation skills and more focused critical-thinking skills as they create.

In order to gain more focused and creative experimentation from students, an important goal of every art teacher should be to encourage creativity and divergent problem solving and critical thinking. Hopefully, teachers will find value in the ideas shared in this article and combine them with their own ideas to encourage creativity in their students.

Using Writing to Enhance Your Art Curriculum

Mary Lazzari, Ed.S., Elementary Art Teacher, Clarke County School District, Athens, Georgia

In recent decades, art teachers have expanded their area of expertise from art production to lessons that include art criticism, art history, and aesthetics. Art is being used as a vehicle not only for increasing creativity but also for developing thinking skills. One way to broaden the art experience and enhance these skills is through guided, interactive writing techniques. Writing about art is an essential component of a well-rounded art curriculum because it provides students with the opportunity to transform thoughts and feelings into words and images. It can also provide the art teacher a more personalized format for communicating with a large student population and assist art teachers in meeting the increased demand to qualify and quantify their students' learning.

> "Art is being used as a vehicle not only for increasing creativity but also for developing thinking skills."

A visual arts curriculum rich in written language activities can facilitate the development of higher-order thinking skills, such as the ability to analyze, defend, and interpret. The use of written statements can help students slow down and refine their thoughts about their own art and the art of others. Words can become the voice for a shy or inarticulate student. With writing as a means of self-expression, art educators can be more in tune with their students' inner thoughts. Some art teachers may be reluctant to incorporate writing into their curriculum because they fear a less than enthusiastic response from their students. Here are a variety of suggestions that can help motivate elementary students to write about art.

Journals

Whether it is a few sheets of paper stapled together or a spiral notebook, students enjoy having a place to write their private thoughts and feelings. Journals can be used to record the thought process from the beginning to the end of a project. It can also be a place to brainstorm ideas or vent frustrations. Art teachers can give written feedback and encouragement to each student in his or her journal.

Titles

Materials: Selected works of art, pencil and paper

At the completion of a project, students can write descriptive titles for their works of art. A title can inform, challenge, or even surprise a viewer. Younger children or students with a language deficit can dictate the title as the teacher writes. Include the student's title when displaying the artwork. Students can also think of a new title for a famous work of art. Compare it to the artist's original title and discuss the similarities and differences.

Acrostic Poems

Materials: Selected works of art, pencil and paper (for individual writings), or dry/wipe board (for group writing)

Select an artist's name or art topic and write the letters vertically. Instruct students to think of words that describe the artist or topic. Students should think of a decriptive word for each letter in the artist's name or art topic. Descriptive words can start, end, or have the letter anywhere in the selected word. Display acrostic poems with the art work that inspired them.

Venn Diagrams

Materials: Individual sheets of Venn diagrams (or draw a large diagram on the board for a whole group discussion); a set of art postcards

Place an image in each of the two outer circles of the Venn diagram. Students describe qualities they see in each of the two works of art. Qualities that are unique to each image are written in the circle that contains the image. Qualities that they have in common are written in the center of the diagram where the two circles overlap. Invite individuals or groups to share their observations. Mount and display Venn diagrams with student artwork.

Artist Statements

Materials: Pencil and paper

Direct students to write three to five sentences about their artwork. Have the students consider these questions: What did I study? What did I create? What did I learn? Display the artist statements with the completed artwork.

Writing Buddies

If you have students who are reluctant or unmotivated to write during art class, have them work in groups. Ask for a student volunteer to be the group secretary. This student is responsible for writing down the group's thoughts and ideas. Students who are not strong in written expression will still feel success in sharing their ideas and opinions.

Brainstorming Ideas

Incorporate writing at the beginning of a lesson by having students use writing devices such as webs. The main topic is placed on the center of the page and ideas that support or expand it are written on the sides.

Vocabulary

Incorporate vocabulary into the art room. Post the "Word of the Day" on a chart or bulletin board display. Build a "Word Wall" with art vocabulary that is added throughout the year. Use word labels on art materials and equipment around the room. Create art flash cards with art words or concepts printed on them. Use the flash cards to find elements such as line, shape, and color in works of art or to review these concepts at the beginning or end of a lesson.

Try writing yourself!

Post statements about projects when displaying your students' works of art. Describe the learning objects and concepts in your statement. Use the display to inform parents, teachers and administrators about the rich and interesting learning that is taking place in your art class. Include articles about lessons, projects, and student achievements in your school or district newsletter.

Writing is an important means of creative expression. It is as valid and essential to the art curriculum as drawing or painting. Using writing to augment the art curriculum not only improves the students' ability to express ideas, it helps the art teacher communicate more effectively with every student. When art teachers integrate art instruction and writing about art, the entire curriculum is enhanced. By pairing art production, a realization of students' thoughts and ideas, with writing, a reflective way to understand and validate their opinions and feelings, art teachers can broaden the scope of the art experience. At the same time, the art teacher will develop a critical means to record and assess student learning.

The Importance of Cultural Diversity Through Art in the Elementary Classroom

Jane Rhoades Hudak, Ph.D., Professor of Art, Georgia Southern University

Culture is learned. People acquire information about the world and how to deal with it as members of a society. Individuals do not learn about their culture by themselves. Children learn about the art of their own culture and other cultures through family and friends, through the mass media, and through the Internet. The information learned this way is often valuable, but it cannot be relied upon to always give adequate and correct information. Schools are often the most effective place for giving students the opportunity to learn about the art of their culture and other cultures.

Our view of the nature of the world and our place in it is expressed and communicated culturally. Every society has institutions that teach culture—family and school are two of the best examples in our society. All societies have religions, which are bodies of cultural knowledge and practices. We also have rituals for birth and death. All cultures have objects that are used for everyday living. We express our world and views through dance, drama, music, and art. We decorate our world and our bodies. We paint our faces and the walls of our houses. We make music with instruments and our voices. All this activity is shaped by our participation in a cultural tradition.

A quality elementary art program provides a wonderful opportunity for teachers to expose students to a variety of cultures as well as their own and to help them to become culturally aware. Following are several of the areas such a program can enhance.

Art Promotes Intracultural Understanding

Through a culturally diverse art program, students begin to understand the role and function that art and artists play in society. Through learning about the art of other cultures, they have the opportunity to identify similarities and differences among their culture and others. They learn that art reflects the religion, politics, economics, and other aspects of a culture.

Through a quality art program, students can address issues of ethnocentrism, bias, stereotyping, prejudice, discrimination, and racism. Students can learn that no one racial, cultural, or national group is superior to another and that no one group's art is better than another.

Art Teaches Self-Esteem Through Diversity

Through a quality art program, students learn to recognize, acknowledge, and celebrate racial and cultural diversity through art within their own society. A good program helps promote the enhancement and affirmation of their self-esteem and encourages pride in their heritage. Personal expression is encouraged, and the result is often a statement in visual form that is both inventive and filled with personal meaning.

Art Teaches Effective Communication

When a quality art program is implemented, students are encouraged to increase their visual literacy skills. Students begin to understand that artists transmit information that cannot be disclosed through other modes of communication. Students learn visual literacy by looking, understanding, talking, writing, and making images. They learn that each society has its own way of communicating through image. Through a culturally sensitive art program, students will be able to discuss and compare art from other societies.

Art Teaches about the Past

Through a quality art program, students develop sensitivity and understanding for the history of humankind. For many periods in history, it is only through visual remains or material culture that societies' cultures can be pieced together. Experiences that students have with these art objects from the past teach them respect for others, challenge their minds, and stimulate not only their intellect but also their imagination.

Art Teaches Critical Thinking

A culturally sensitive art program encourages a variety of critical thinking skills. When students look at art from other cultures, they make critical judgments and develop their own opinions. Students are asked to identify and recall information; to organize selected facts and ideas; to use particular facts, rules, and principles; to figure out component parts or to classify; and to combine ideas and form a new whole.

Art Teaches Perceptual Sensitivity and Aesthetic Awareness

As a result of a quality art program, students develop a keen sense of awareness and an appreciation for beauty. They learn that each culture has its own criteria for beauty. Art experiences help cultivate an aesthetic sensitivity and respect for the natural and humanmade environment. Art classes are the only place in the school curriculum where students learn about what constitutes quality visual design—about harmony, order, organization, and specific design qualities such as balance, movement, and unity.

Art Teaches Creativity

When a culturally sensitive art program is implemented, creativity in all students is stimulated and nurtured. Students learn to solve problems creatively. They learn that every society has some form of creative expression. In some societies, no one special person is called an artist—everyone in the culture makes "art" objects.

Teachers can help prevent students from having a simplistic view of other cultures and help them understand the cultural context of how and why works of art are created. *Art Connections* has been carefully constructed so that students will be exposed to works of art that represent a wide variety of cultures. Questions and strategies are designed to help teachers put art in a cultural context for students. The Art History and Culture feature in the *Teacher Edition* and the *Artist Profiles* book provide additional information about the works of art and the artists.

As a teacher, you are a cultural transmitter. A quality art program taught by a culturally sensitive teacher benefits every student. When educators teach in a systematic, meaningful way, students acquire knowledge about art and cultures that will benefit them throughout their lives.

Museum Education

Marilyn J.S. Goodman, Director of Education, Solomon R. Guggenheim Museum

Museums are truly magnificent places. In recent years, these bastions of culture have taken tremendous strides toward making their collections accessible to a broader audience. Museum educators are usually eager to share new information and ideas and are delighted to assist school educators with programs and materials that can easily be incorporated into the classroom. Museums contain a wealth of treasures that offer extraordinary resources for teachers and students, and which will undoubtedly enrich the overall classroom experience.

Getting acquainted with museums in your region can be a real eye-opener. Museums collect objects that document human achievement, both in our own and in other cultures. A local historical society or farm museum might contain a variety of clothing and tools that can bring history to life. A science museum may offer interactive exhibits about phenomena in the natural or physical sciences, sensory perception, new technologies, or space exploration. A children's museum will offer hands-on displays specially designed to motivate young children to learn by doing. Art museums contain visually stunning works that reflect the diversity of human thought and experience.

Museums do not supplant classroom instruction. They enhance and reinforce what is taught by providing raw materials in the forms of objects, artifacts, and exhibits. Museums give students the chance to see and sometimes handle the real thing. It is one thing to talk about Egypt's role in the history of civilization; it is another thing entirely to see the wrappings on a cat mummy, discover hieroglyphs on a sarcophagus, or be overwhelmed by the power and grandeur of large stone sculptures of kings and queens.

When students have the chance to look at portraits, still lifes, landscapes, genre scenes, furniture, clothing, and artifacts, they learn more than by just seeing a picture of a person, place, or thing. They learn how to "read" a culture. Perhaps more importantly, they learn to develop their own process of investigation and critical inquiry. What was this person's life really like? What can one learn about the class structure of this society? What can we tell about craftspeople, available materials, or the objects this society valued? What does the clothing tell us about the climate of the region? What can we learn about the geography, topography, and vegetation? What did people eat? How did they spend leisure time? What were their

religious beliefs? Is there any evidence of trade and communication with other regions? What scientific inventions were present at the time? Can one tell if they communicated through language or by writing? Because children are naturally curious, objects will motivate them to think, research, and learn.

> "A visit to a museum will make the curriculum come alive as students begin to explore objects and learn about their meanings."

A visit to a museum will make the curriculum come alive as students begin to explore objects and learn about their meanings. Museum objects give us information in a way that is very different from reading about the objects. Students must think critically to determine both the questions and answers for themselves. A first-hand, visual investigation of an object's style, material, subject matter, and physical characteristics offers preliminary clues to deciphering its meaning. When the exploration is combined with other knowledge, such as the geography and natural resources of a region; the historical context; the social, political, and economic structure of a culture; or even advances in science and technology, students can be engaged in a type of learning that is truly multidisciplinary and may lead them into other areas of study. Moreover, methods for gathering information go far beyond what people see. Exploring objects and works of art allows students to use all of their senses, combining intellect with intuition. The

opportunity for experiential, emotional, and intellectual learning is always present.

Museum objects present different historical and cultural perspectives. Students can gather information about people, culture, belief systems, values, and the ways people lived in the past. Museum visits encourage students to see things from broader global and intellectual points of view, developing respect for the work, lives, and points of view of others. Students are encouraged to respond in a variety of ways and on different levels. Most importantly, students are invited to formulate and express their ideas and then discuss them with others.

To learn about museum resources, teachers can contact the education departments of museums in their region. If teachers explain the level of their students, the subjects they are studying, and the specific aspects of the curriculum they would like to supplement, the museum's education department can help to tailor the resources to the class. In addition to guided tours and workshops, the museum education department may offer materials for loan, including slides, pamphlets, posters, postcards, kits, and other printed materials. Some museums have teacher resource rooms filled with books, films, videos, CD-ROMs, and computer databases geared toward educators. Trained staff is available to answer questions or to help teachers develop a complete learning unit that can integrate museum objects with classroom studies.

Using museums is an excellent way to enrich and enliven the classroom experience. Educators can take the first step by learning all they can about the rich and diverse resources available to them and their students.

U.S. MuSeum ReSourceS

Alabama

1 Birmingham Museum of Art
*2000 8th Avenue North,
Birmingham*
http://www.ARTSbma.org

2 Mobile Museum of Art
4850 Museum Drive, Mobile
http://www.mobilemuseum
ofart.com

3 Montgomery Museum
of Fine Arts
1 Museum Drive, Montgomery
http://www.mmfa.org

Alaska

4 Alaska State Museum
395 Whittier Street, Juneau
http://www.museums.
state.ak.us/asmhome.html

5 Anchorage Heritage Library
Museum
*301 West Northern Lights
Boulevard, Anchorage*
http://www.wellsfargohistory.
com/museums/alaska.ht

6 Anchorage Museum
of History and Art
*121 West 7th Avenue,
Anchorage*
http://www.anchorage
museum.org

Arizona

7 Heard Museum
2301 N Central Avenue, Phoenix
http://www.heard.org/

8 Phoenix Art Museum
*1625 North Central Avenue,
Phoenix*
http://www.phxart.org

9 Scottsdale Museum
of Contemporary Art - (SMOCA)
7380 E 2nd St, Scottsdale
http://www.scottsdalearts.org

Arkansas

10 Arkansas State
University Museum
Jonesboro, AR 72467
http://museumastate.edu

11 Historic Arkansas Museum
*200 East 3rd Street,
Little Rock*
http://www.arkansashistory.
com/

12 Old State House Museum
*300 West Markham Street,
Little Rock*
http://www.oldstatehouse.com

California

13 Asian Art Museum
of San Francisco
Golden Gate Park, San Francisco
http://www.asianart.org

14 Berkeley Art Museum
and Pacific Film Archive
2625 Durant Avenue, Berkeley
http://www.bampfa.berkeley.
edu

15 El Museo Mexicano -
Mexican Museum
*Fort Mason Center,
Building D, San Francisco*
http://www.mexican
museum.org

16 J Paul Getty
Center Museum
*1200 Getty Center Drive,
Los Angeles, CA*
http://www.getty.edu

17 Japanese American
National Museum
*369 East 1st Street,
Los Angeles*
http://www.janm.org

18 Korean American Museum
*3780 Wilshire Boulevard
220, Los Angeles*
http://www.kamuseum.org

19 L A County Museum
of Art
*5905 Wilshire Boulevard,
Los Angeles*
http://www.lacma.org

20 San Francisco Museum
of Modern Art
*151 3rd Street Building A,
San Francisco*
http://www.sfmoma.org/

21 Santa Barbara
Museum of Art
1130 State Street, Santa Barbara
http://www.sbmuseart.org

22 Southwest Museum
234 Museum Drive, Los Angeles
http://www.southwest
museum.org/

Colorado

23 Aspen Art Museum
590 North Mill Street, Aspen
http://www.aspenart
museum.org

24 Boulder Museum
of Contemporary Art
1750 Thirteenth Street, Boulder
http://www.bmoca.org/

25 Denver Art Museum
100 West 14th Avenue, Denver
http://www.denverart
museum.org

Connecticut

26 New Britain Museum
of American Art
*56 Lexington Street,
New Britain*
http://www.nbmaa.org

27 Norwalk Museum
41 North Main Street, Norwalk
http://www.norwalkct.org/
norwalkmuseum/index.htm

28 Wadsworth Atheneum
Museum of Art
600 Main Street, Hartford
http://www.wadsworth
atheneum.org/

Delaware

29 Delaware Art Museum
*800 S Madison Street
Suite B, Wilmington*
http://www.delart.org

30 Sewell C Biggs Museum
of American Art
406 Federal Street, Dover
http://www.biggsmuseum.
org

31 Winterthur Museum
Route 52, Winterthur
http://www.winterthur.org/

Florida

32 Bass Museum of Art
2121 Park Ave, Miami
http://www.bassmuseum.org/

33 Key West Art and
Historical Society
281 Front Street, Key West
http://www.kwahs.com

34 Lowe Art Museum
1301 Stanford Drive, Miami
http://www.lowemuseum.
com/

35 Miami Art Museum
101 West Flagler Street, Miami
http://www.miamiart
museum.org/

36 Museum of Fine Arts,
St Petersburg
*255 Beach Drive Northeast, St
Petersburg*
http://www.fine-arts.org

37 Salvador Dali Museum
*1000 3rd Street South,
St Petersburg*
http://www.salvadordali
museum.org

Georgia

38 Albany Museum of Art
311 Meadowlark Drive, Albany
http://www.albany
museum.com/

39 High Museum of Art
*1280 Peachtree Street
Northeast, Atlanta, GA*
http://www.high.org

40 Morris Museum of Art
1 10th Street, Augusta
http://www.themorris.org

Hawaii

41 Contemporary Museum,
Honolulu
*2411 Makiki Heights Drive,
Honolulu*
http://www.tcmhi.org

42 Kauai Museum
4428 Rice Street, Lihue
http://www.kauaimuseum.org

43 University of Hawaii
at Manoa Art Gallery
*University of Hawaii at Manoa,
Honolulu*
http://www.hawaii.edu/
artgallery

Idaho

44 Boise Art Museum
670 Julia Davis Drive, Boise
http://www.boiseart
museum.org

45 Eagle Rock Art Museum
and Education Center, Inc.
*300 S Capital Avenue,
Idaho Falls*
http://www.eaglerockart
museum.org

Illinois

46 Art Institute of Chicago
*111 South Michigan Avenue,
Chicago*
http://www.artic.edu/aic/

47 Krannert Art Museum
*500 East Peabody Drive,
Champaign*
http://www.kam.uiuc.edu

48 Martin D'Arcy
Museum of Art
*6525 N Sheridan Road,
Chicago*
http://darcy.luc.edu

49 Mitchell Museum
of the American Indian
*2600 Central Park Ave,
Evanston*
http://www.mitchell
museum.org/

50 Museum of
Contemporary Art
*220 East Chicago Avenue,
Chicago*
http://www.mcachicago.org

51 Smart Museum of Art
*5550 South Greenwood Avenue,
Chicago*
http://smartmuseum.
uchicago.edu/

Indiana

52 Brauer Museum of Art
*Valparaiso University Center
for the Arts, Valparaiso*
http://wwwstage.valpo.edu/
artmuseum/index.html

53 Eiteljorg Museum
of American Indian
and Western Art
*500 West Washington Street,
Indianapolis*
http://www.eiteljorg.org

54 Indianapolis
Museum of Art
*1200 West 38th Street,
Indianapolis*
http://www.ima-art.org

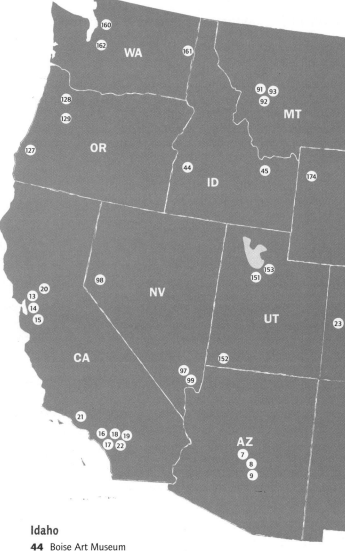

U.S. Museum Resources (continued)

Iowa

55 Cedar Rapids
Museum of Art
*410 3rd Avenue Southeast,
Cedar Rapids*
http://www.crma.org

56 Davenport Museum of Art
*1737 West 12th Street,
Davenport*
http://www.art-dma.org

57 Dubuque Museum of Art
36 East 8th Street, Dubuque
http://www.dbqart.com

Kansas

58 Coutts Memorial Museum
*110 North Main Street,
El Dorado*
http://skyways.lib.ks.us/
kansas/museums/coutts/ind

59 Spencer Museum of Art
*1301 Mississippi Street,
Lawrence*
http://www.ukans.edu/~sma/

60 Wichita Art Museum
*West Museum Boulevard,
Wichita*
http://www.wichitaart
museum.org

Kentucky

61 Kentucky Museum
of Arts + Design
609 West Main Street, Louisville
http://www.kentuckycrafts.org

62 Speed Art Museum, the
2035 South Third St., Louisville
http://www.speedmuseum.org

63 University of Kentucky
Art Museum
*Rose and Euclid Avenue,
Lexington*
http://www.uky.edu/Art
Museum/

Louisiana

64 African-American Museum
*125 New Market Street,
St Martinville*
http://stmartinparish-
la.org/tourism_africanmuseum

65 Louisiana State Museum
751 Chartres Street, New Orleans
http://lsm.crt.state.la.us/

66 New Orleans
Museum of Art
*City Park 1 Collins Diboll Circle,
New Orleans*
http://www.noma.org

Maine

67 Farnsworth Art Museum
*352 Main Street, Box 466,
Rockland*
http://farnsworthmuseum.org/

68 Ogunquit Museum
of American Art
Shore Road, Ogunquit
http://www.ogunquit
museum.org

69 Portland
Museum of Art
7 Congress Square, Portland
http://www.portlandmuseum.
org

Maryland

70 African Art
Museum of Maryland
*5430 Vantage Point Road,
Columbia*
http://www.Africanart
museum.org

71 Baltimore
Museum of Art
10 Art Museum Drive, Baltimore
http://www.artbma.org/

72 Walters Art Museum
*600 North Charles Street,
Baltimore*
http://www.thewalters.org

Massachusetts

73 Harvard University
Art Museums
32 Quincy Street, Cambridge
http://www.artmuseums.
harvard.edu/

74 Institute of Contemporary
Art
955 Boylston Street, Boston
http://www.icaboston.org

75 MASS MoCA -
Massachusetts Museum
of Contemporary Art
87 Marshall Street, North Adams
http://www.massmoca.org

76 Mead Art Museum
*Amherst College, PO Box 5000,
Amherst*
http://www.amherst.edu/
~mead/

77 Museum of Fine Arts
Boston
465 Huntington Avenue, Boston
http://www.mfa.org/

78 Worcester Art Museum
55 Salisbury Street, Worcester
http://www.worcesterart.org

Michigan

79 Cranbrook Art Museum
*39221 Woodward Avenue,
PO Box 801, Bloomfield Hills*
http://www.cranbrook.
edu/art/museum/

80 Detroit Institute of Arts
*5200 Woodward Avenue,
Detroit*
http://www.dia.org

81 Grand Rapids
Art Museum
55 Division Ave N, Grand Rapids
http://www.gramonline.org

Minnesota

82 Frederick R Weisman
Art Museum
*333 East River Road # 200,
Minneapolis*
http://hudson.acad.umn.edu/

83 Minnesota Museum
of American Art
*Landmark Center 75 West 5th
Street West, St Paul*
http://www.mmaa.org

84 Walker Art Center
*725 Vineland Place,
Minneapolis*
http://www.walkerart.org

Mississippi

85 Lauren Rogers
Museum of Art
*5th Avenue and 7th Street,
Laurel*
http://www.lrma.org/

86 Mississippi Museum
of Art
*201 E Pascagoula St
Ste 103, Jackson*
http://www.msmuseumart.
org/

87 Walter Anderson
Museum of Art
*510 Washington Avenue,
Ocean Springs*
http://www.walteranderson
museum.org/

Missouri

88 Albrecht-Kemper Art Museum
2818 Frederick Avenue, St Joseph
http://www.albrecht-
kemper.org/

89 Nelson-Atkins
Museum of Art
4525 Oak Street, Kansas City
http://www.nelson-
atkins.org/

90 St Louis Art Museum
1 Fine Arts Drive, St Louis
http://www.slam.org

Montana

91 Art Museum of Missoula
*335 North Pattee Street,
Missoula*
http://www.artmissoula.org/

92 Hockaday Museum
of Art
*2nd Avenue East at
Third Street, Kalispell*
http://www.hockadayart
museum.org/

93 Montana Museum
of Art and Culture
University of Montana, Missoula
http://www.umt.edu/partv/
famus/

Nebraska

94 Joslyn Art Museum
2200 Dodge St., Omaha
http://www.joslyn.org

95 Museum of Nebraska Art
(MONA)
2401 Central Avenue, Kearney
http://monet.unk.edu/mona/

96 Sheldon Memorial
Art Gallery and
Sculpture Garden
*University of Nebraska-Lincoln,
12th and R Streets, Lincoln*
http://sheldon.unl.edu/

Nevada

97 Las Vegas Art Museum
*9600 West Sahara Avenue,
Las Vegas*
http://www.lvam.com

98 Nevada Museum of Art
160 West Liberty Street, Reno
http://www.nevadaart.org

99 Walker African-American
Museum and Research Center
*705 W Van Buren Ave,
Las Vegas*
http://members.aol.com/
Bigbrwnsis/

New Hampshire

100 Currier Museum of Art
201 Myrtle Way, Manchester
http://www.currier.org

101 Hood Museum of Art
Wheelock Street, Hanover
http://web.dartmouth.
edu/~hood/

102 Mariposa Museum
26 Main Street, Peterborough
http://www.mariposa
museum.org

New Jersey

103 Jane Voorhees
Zimmerli Art Museum
*71 Hamilton St, Rutgers
University, New Brunswick*
http://www.zimmerlimuseum.
rutgers.edu

104 Jersey City Museum
*350 Montgomery Street,
Jersey City*
http://www.jerseycity
museum.org/

105 Princeton University
Art Museum
Princeton University, Princeton
http://www.princetonart
museum.org/

New Mexico

106 Georgia O'Keeffe Museum
217 Johnson Street, Santa Fe
http://www.okeeffe
museum.org

107 Harwood Museum of Art
*238 Ledoux Street, 4080
NDCBU, Taos*
http://www.harwood
museum.org

108 Institute of American
Indian Arts Museum
Cathedral Place, Santa Fe
http://www.iaiancad.org

New York

109 Albright-Knox
Art Gallery
1285 Elmwood Avenue, Buffalo
http://www.albrightknox.org

110 Metropolitan Museum
of Art
*6626 Metropolitan Avenue
FL 2, Flushing*
http://www.Metmuseum.org/

111 Museum of Modern Art
MoMA
11 West 53 Street , New York
http://www.moma.org/

112 New Museum
of Contemporary Art
583 Broadway, New York
http://www.newmuseum.org/

113 Solomon R Guggenheim
Museum, New York
1071 5th Ave at 89th, New York
http://www.guggenheim.org
/new_york_index.html

114 Whitney Museum
of American Art
*945 Madison Avenue FL 5,
New York*
http://www.whitney.org

North Carolina

115 Ackland Art Museum
*Columbia and Franklin Street,
Chapel Hill*
http://www.ackland.org

116 Duke University
Museum of Art
*Buchanan Blvd-Trinity Avenue,
Durham*
http://www.duke.edu/web/
duma/

117 North Carolina Museum
of Art
2110 Blue Ridge Road, Raleigh
http://www.ncartmuseum.org/

North Dakota

118 *North Heritage Center of
the State Historical Society of
North Dakota, Bismarck*
http://www.state.nd.us/hist/
index.html

119 North Dakota
Museum of Art
Centennial Drive, Grand Forks
http://www.ndmoa.com

120 Plains Art Museum
219 7th Street South, Fargo
http://www.plainsart.org/

Ohio

121 Cincinnati Art Museum
953 Eden Park Drive, Cincinnati
http://www.cincinnatiart
museum.com/

122 Cleveland Museum of Art
11150 East Boulevard, Cleveland
http://www.clemusart.com/

123 Columbus Museum of Art
480 East Broad Street, Columbus
http://www.columbusmuseum.
org

Oklahoma

124 Fred Jones Jr
Museum of Art
410 West Boyd Street,
University of Oklahoma, Norman
http://www.ou.edu/fjjma/

125 Oklahoma City
Art Museum
3113 Pershing Boulevard,
Oklahoma City
http://www.okcartmuseum.
com/

126 Philbrook Museum of Art
2727 South Rockford Road,
Tulsa, OK
http://www.philbrook.org/

Oregon

127 Coos Art Museum
235 Anderson Avenue, Coos Bay
http://www.coosart.org

128 Portland Art Museum
1219 SW Park Ave., Portland
http://www.pam.org

129 University of Oregon
Museum of Art
1223 University of Oregon,
Eugene
http://uoma.uoregon.edu/

Pennsylvania

130 The Andy Warhol
Museum
117 Sandusky Street, Pittsburgh
http://www.clpgh.org/warhol/

131 The Palmer
Museum of Art
Curtin Rd, The Pennsylvania
State University, University Park
http://www.psu.edu/dept/
palmermuseum/

132 Philadelphia
Museum of Art
26th Street and the Benjamin
Franklin Parkway, Philadelphia
http://pma.libertynet.org/

Rhode Island

133 Museum of Art,
Rhode Island School of Design
224 Benefit Street, Providence
http://www.risd.edu/

134 Museum Of Primitive
Art & Culture
1058 Kingstown Road,
South Kingstown

135 National Museum
of American Illustration
Vernon Court 492 Bellevue
Avenue , Newport
http://www.american
illustration.org

South Carolina

136 Gibbes Museum of Art
135 Meeting Street, Charleston
http://www.gibbes.com/

137 Columbia Museum of Art
Main and Hampton Streets,
Columbia
http://www.colmusart.org/

138 The Spartanburg County
Museum of Art
385 S Spring St., Spartanburg
http://www.sparklenet.com/
museumofart

South Dakota

139 Journey Museum
222 New York Street, Rapid City
http://www.journeymuseum.org

140 Oscar Howe Art Center
and Middle Border Museum
1300 E University Street P.O
Box 1071 Mitchell
http://www.oscarhowe.com/
index.htm

141 South Dakota Art Museum
P.O Box 2250, Brookings
http://web.sdstate.edu/sites/
artmuseum/

Tennessee

142 Hunter Museum of Art
10 Bluff View, Chattanooga
http://www.huntermuseum.
org/

143 Institute of Egyptian
Art and Archaeology
The University of Memphis,
Memphis
http://www.memst.edu/
egypt/about.html

144 Knoxville Museum of Art
1050 Worlds Fair Park Drive,
Knoxville
http://www.knoxart.org

Texas

145 Dallas Museum of Art
1717 North Harwood, Dallas
http://dm-art.org/

146 Kimbell Art Museum
3333 Camp Bowie Blvd.,
Fort Worth
http://kimbellart.org/

147 Mexic-Arte Museum
419 Congress Avenue, Austin
http://www.mexic-arte
museum.org

148 The Museum of Fine Arts
1001 Bissonnet, Houston
http://mfah.org/

149 Panhandle-Plains
Historical Museum,
West Texas A&M University
2401 4th Ave., Canyon
http://www.wtamu.edu/
museum/

150 San Antonio Museum
of Art
200 West Jones Avenue,
San Antonio
http://www.sa-museum.org

Utah

151 BYU Museum of Art
Brigham Young University,
Provo
http://www.byu.edu/moa/

152 St George Art Museum
175 East 200 North, St George
http://www.ci.st-george.ut.us/
arts/artmuseum.php

153 Utah Museum of Fine
Arts, University of Utah
370 South 1530 East
University of Utah , Salt Lake City
http://www.utah.edu/umfa/

Vermont

154 The Bennington Museum
West Main St., Bennington
http://www.bennington
museum.com

155 Robert Hull
Fleming Museum
Colchester Avenue, Burlington
http://www.uvm.edu/
~fleming/home/

156 Shelburne Museum
US Route 7, PO Box 10,
Shelburne
http://www.shelburne
museum.org

Virginia

157 Chrysler Museum of Art
245 West Olney Rd., Norfolk
http://www.chrysler.org/

158 Maier Museum of Art
2500 Rivermont Avenue,
Lynchburg
http://www.rmwc.edu/
Maier/

159 Virginia Museum
of Fine Arts
2800 Grove Ave., Richmond
http://www.vmfa.state.va.us/

Washington

160 Frye Art Museum
704 Terry Ave., Seattle
http://fryeart.org/

161 Jundt Art Museum
502 East Boone Avenue,
Spokane
http://www.gonzaga.edu/
Campus+Resources/Museums
+an

162 Seattle Art Museum
100 University St., Seattle
http://seattleartmuseum.
org/

Washington, D.C.

163 Arthur M Sackler Gallery
and the Freer Gallery of Art
1050 Independence Avenue, SW
http://www.asia.si.edu/
default.htm

164 Corcoran Gallery of Art
500 17th Street Northwest
http://www.corcoran.org/

165 Hirshhorn Museum
and Sculpture Garden
Independence Avenue
and 7th Street Southwest
http://hirshhorn.si.edu/

166 National Gallery of Art
http://www.nga.gov/

167 The National Museum
of Women in the Arts
1250 New York Ave., NW
http://www.nmwa.org/

168 Smithsonian Museums
Smithsonian Institution
http://www.si.edu/

West Virginia

169 Huntington Museum
of Art
2033 McCoy Rd., Huntington
http://www.hmoa.org/

170 Oglebay Institute:
Mansion Museum and
Glass Museum
Burton Center, Wheeling
http://www.oionline.com/

Wisconsin

171 Elvehjem Museum of Art
800 University Avenue,
Madison
http://www.lvm.wisc.edu

172 Leigh Yawkey Woodson
Art Museum
700 North Twelfth St, Wausau
http://www.lywam.org/

173 Milwaukee Art Museum
750 North Lincoln Memorial
Dr., Milwaukee
http://www.mam.org/

Wyoming

174 National Museum
of Wildlife Art
2820 Rungius Road, Jackson
http://www.wildlifeart.org

175 University of Wyoming
Art Museum
2111 Willett Dr., Laramie
http://uwadmnweb.uwyo.
edu/artmuseum/

World Museum Resources

Argentina

1 Fundacion Federico Klemm
Buenos Aires, Argentina
www.fundacionfjklemm.org

Australia

2 Art Gallery of New South Wales
Sydney, Australia
www.artgallery.nsw.gov.au/

3 Australian National Art Gallery
Canberra, Australia
www.nga.gov.au/Home/index.cfm

4 Museum of Contemporary Art
Sydney, Australia
www.mca.com.au/

Austria

5 Kunsthistorisches Museum Wien
Vienna, Austria
www.khm.at/

Bahrain

6 Al Hayat Museum
Manama, Bahrain
www.beitalquran.com/

Brazil

7 Museu Historico Nacional
Rio de Janeiro, Brazil
www.museuhistoriconacional.com.br/ingles/index.htm

Canada

8 Art Gallery of Calgary
Calgary, Canada
www.artgallerycalgary.com/

9 Morris and Helen Belkin Art Gallery, University of British Columbia
Vancouver, Canada
www.belkin-gallery.ubc.ca/

10 Art Gallery of Newfoundland and Labrador
St. Johns, Canada
www.mun.ca/agnl/main.html

11 Art Gallery of Nova Scotia
Halifax, Canada
www.agns.gov.ns.ca/

12 Art Gallery of Ontario
Toronto, Canada
www.ago.net/navigation/flash/index.cfm

13 National Gallery of Canada
Ottawa, Canada
www.national.gallery.ca/

14 The Montreal Museum of Fine Arts
Quebec, Canada
www.mmfa.qc.ca/en/index.html

15 McMichael Canadian Art Collection
Toronto, Canada
www.mcmichael.com/

16 Winnipeg Art Gallery
Winnipeg, Canada
www.wag.mb.ca/

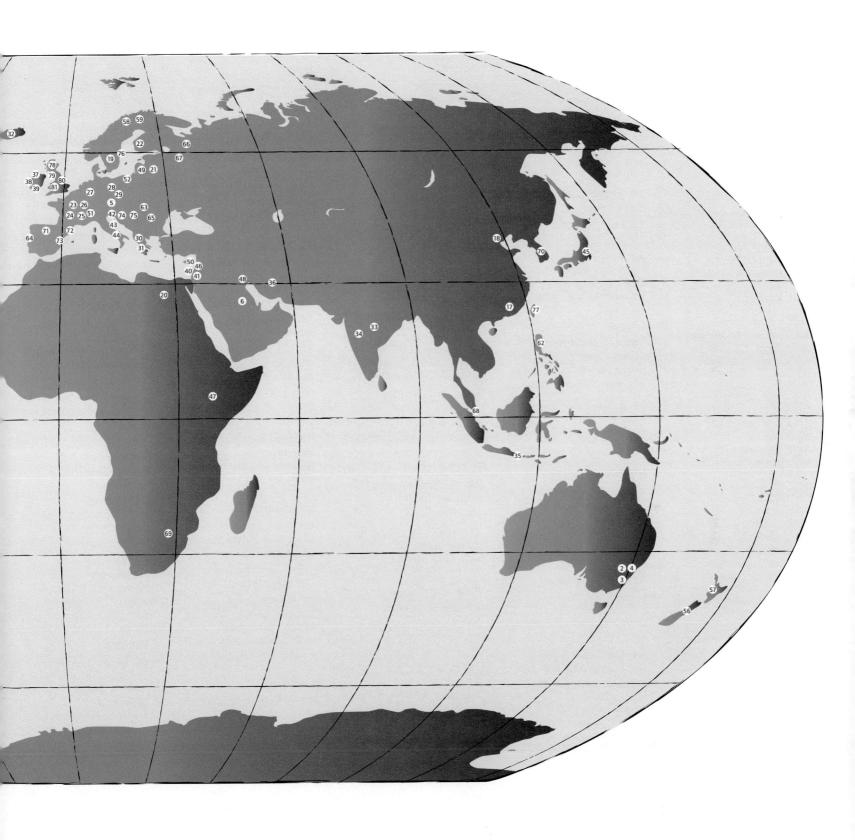

World Museum Resources

China

17 Hong Kong
Museum of Art
Hong Kong, China
www.lcsd.gov.hk/CE/Mus
eum/Arts/english/intro/
eintro.html

18 Palace Museum
Beijing, China
www.dpm.org.cn/

Denmark

19 National Museum
Copenhagen, Denmark
www.natmus.dk/sw1413.
asp

Egypt

20 The Egyptian Museum
Cairo, Egypt
www.egyptianmuseum.
gov.eg/

Estonia

21 Estonian National
Museum
Tartu, Estonia
www.erm.ee/?lang=ENG

Finland

22 The Finnish
National Gallery
Helsinki, Finland
www.fng.fi/fng/rootnew/
en/vtm/etusivu.htm

France

23 The Louvre
Paris, France
www.louvre.fr/louvrea.htm

24 Musee d'Orsay,
Paris, France
www.musee-orsay.fr/

25 Centre Georges
Pompidou
Paris, France
www.cnac-gp.fr/Pompidou/
Accueil.nsf/tunnel?
OpenForm

Germany

26 Neues Museum
Nuremberg, Germany
www.nmn.de/

27 Hamburg Kunsthalle
Hamburg, Germany
www.hamburger-
kunsthalle.de/

28 Alte National Galerie
Berlin, Germany
www.alte-nationalgalerie.
de/

29 Bauhaus Archiv
Museum of Design
Berlin, Germany
www.bauhaus.de/english/

Greece

30 Acropolis Museum
Athens, Greece
www.culture.gr/2/21/211/
21101m/e211am01.html

31 Benaki Museum
Athens, Greece
www.benaki.gr/index-
en.htm

Iceland

32 Living Art Museum
Reykjavik, Iceland
www.nylo.is/English/
index.html

India

33 National Museum
of India
New Delhi, India
www.nationalmuseumindia
.org/index.html

34 Chhatrapati Shivaji
Maharaj Vastu Sangrahalaya
(Formerly the Prince of Wales
Museum of
Western India)
Mumbai (Bombay), India
www.bombaymuseum.org/

Indonesia

35 Agung Rai
Museum of Art
Ubud, Bali, Indonesia
www.nusantara.com/
arma/

Iran

36 National
Museum of Iran
Tehran, Iran
www.nationalmuseumofira
n.com/

Ireland

37 Hunt Museum
Limerick, Ireland
www.huntmuseum.com/

38 Irish Museum
of Modern Art
Dublin, Ireland
www.modernart.ie/

39 National Gallery
of Ireland
Dublin, Ireland
www.nationalgallery.ie/

Israel

40 The Israel Museum
Jerusalem, Israel
www.imj.org.il/

41 Tel Aviv Museum of Art
Tel Aviv, Israel
www.tamuseum.com/

Italy

42 Uffizi Gallery
Florence, Italy
www.uffizi.firenze.it/
welcomeE.html

43 Museo di Roma
Rome, Italy
www.museodiroma.comune
.roma.it/PalazzoBraschi/
inizio.mostra

44 Vatican Museum
Vatican City
http://mv.vatican.va/
3_EN/pages/MV_Home.
html

Japan

45 Kyoto National Museum
Tokyo, Japan
www.kyohaku.go.jp/index
e.htm

Jordan

46 Darat al Funun
Home for the Arts
Amman, Jordan
www.daratalfunun.org/

Kenya

47 National Museum
of Kenya
Nairobi, Kenya
www.museums.or.ke/

Kuwait

48 Kuwait National
Museum
Kuwait City, Kuwait
www.kmia.org.kw

Latvia

49 State Museum of Art
Riga, Latvia
www.vmm.lv/en/muzejs.
html

Lebanon

50 American University of
Beirut Archaeology Museum
Beirut, Lebanon

Liechtenstein

51 Kunstmuseum
Liechtenstein
Vaduz, Liechtenstein
www.kunstmuseum.li/web
2306e/index.html

Lithuania

52 Lithuanian Art Museum
Vilnius, Lithuania
www.ldm.lt/ldm_en.htm

Mexico

53 Museo de
Arte Moderno
Mexico City, Mexico
www.arts-history.mx/
museos/mam/home2.html

54 National Museum
of Anthropology
Mexico City, Mexico
www.mna.inah.gob.mx/

55 Museo de Arte
Contemporaneo de Oaxaca
Oaxaca, Mexico
www.arts-history.mx/
museos/maco/home.html

New Zealand

56 Centre of
Contemporary Art
Christchurch, New Zealand
www.coca.org.nz/

57 Auckland Art Gallery
Auckland, New Zealand
www.aucklandartgallery.
govt.nz/

Norway

58 National Gallery
of Norway
Oslo, Norway
www.museumsnett.no/
nasjonalgalleriet/flash_
versjon_engelsk/

59 Lillehammer
Art Museum
Lillehammer, Norway
www.lillehammerart
museum.com/

Panama

60 Museo de Arte
Contemporaneo de Panama
*Panama, Republic
of Panama*
www.macpanama.org/

Peru

61 Museo Arqueologico
Rafael Larco Herrera
Lima, Peru
museolarco.perucultural.
org.pe/

Philippines

62 Philippine National
Museum
Manila, Philippines
http://nmuseum.tripod.
com/

Poland

63 Polish National Museum
Warsaw, Poland
www.mnw.art.pl/

Portugal

64 Museu Calouste
Gulbenkian
Lisbon, Portugal
www.gulbenkian.pt/

Romania

65 The National Museum
of Art of Romania
Bucharest, Romania
http://art.museum.ro/
museum.html

Russia

66 The State Hermitage
Museum
St. Petersburg, Russia
www.hermitagemuseum.
org/

67 Pushkin Museum
of Fine Arts
Moscow, Russia
www.museum.ru/gmii/

Singapore

68 Singapore Art Museum
*Singapore, Republic of
Singapore*
www.nhb.gov.sg/SAM/
sam.shtml

South Africa

69 Pretoria Art Museum
Pretoria, South Africa
www.pretoriaartmuseum.
co.za/

South Korea

70 Seoul Metropolitan
Museum of Art
Seoul, South Korea
www.metro.seoul.kr/
muse/eng/

Spain

71 Guggenheim
Bilbao Museum
Bilbao, Spain
www.guggenheim-
bilbao.es/idioma.htm

72 Museu d'Art
Contemporani
Barcelona, Spain
www.macba.es/home.php

73 Valencian Institute
of Modern Art
Valencia, Spain
www.ivam.es/

Switzerland

74 Kunstmuseum Basel
Basel, Switzerland
www.kunstmuseumbasel.
ch/de/

75 Kunsthaus
Zurich, Switzerland
www.kunsthaus.ch/

Sweden

76 National Museum
Stockholm, Sweden
www.nationalmuseum.se/

Taiwan

77 National Palace Museum
T'aipei, Taiwan
www.npm.gov.tw/english/
index-e.htm

United Kingdom

78 National Gallery
of London
London, England
www.nationalgallery.
org.uk/

79 British Museum
London, England
www.thebritishmuseum.
ac.uk/

80 Tate Gallery
London, England
www.tate.org.uk/home/
default.htm

81 Victoria and
Albert Museum
London, England
www.vam.ac.uk/

Uruguay

82 Museo Nacianal
de Artes Visuales
Montevideo, Uruguay
www.mnav.gub.uy/

Elements and Principles of Art

Scope and Sequence

Elements of Art	Level K						Level 1						Level 2						Level 3					
	U1	U2	U3	U4	U5	U6	U1	U2	U3	U4	U5	U6	U1	U2	U3	U4	U5	U6	U1	U2	U3	U4	U5	U6
Line	1-6						1-6	1					1-4						1-2					
Shape		1-6			6			1-6		1			5-6					2, 4	3-6					
Color			1-6						1-6						1-3			1, 3				1-6		
Value																4-6						1		
Space				1, 3						2, 5, 6				5-6							1-3			
Form			2-6		5					1-4		4	1-4					2, 4		4-6				
Texture					1-6						1-3							5-6					5-6	

Principles of Art	Level K						Level 1						Level 2						Level 3					
	U1	U2	U3	U4	U5	U6	U1	U2	U3	U4	U5	U6	U1	U2	U3	U4	U5	U6	U1	U2	U3	U4	U5	U6
Pattern						1				4-5					1-2								1-3	
Rhythm						2					6				3-6								4-6	
Balance				3-4								1-2				1-2						1-4		
Proportion																								
Emphasis											3-4					3-4								3-4
Variety																		3-4						2
Harmony																		1-2						1
Unity						5-6						5-6						5-6						5-6

*Numbers indicate lesson numbers within a given unit.

Level 4						Level 5						Level 6						Level 7	Level 8
U1	U2	U3	U4	U5	U6	U1	U2	U3	U4	U5	U6	U1	U2	U3	U4	U5	U6	Exploring Art	Understanding Art
1-6							1-2						1					Chapter 2, 6, 7, 8, 9, 10, 11	Chapter 2, 6, 8, 9, 12, 15, 16
	1-2						3	1					2					Chapter 2, 6, 8, 9, 10, 11	Chapter 2, 3, 5, 8, 9, 13, 14, 16, 17
		1-4						1-4					1-4					Chapter 2, 4, 8, 9, 11, 13	Chapter 2, 3, 4, 8, 11, 12, 14-17
		5-6					4-6						2-3					Chapter 14	Chapter 13, 14, 15
			1-3				1-3							5-6				Chapter 2, 4, 10, 12	Chapter 6, 7, 13, 15
			1-3					4-6						3-4				Chapter 2, 6, 11, 12, 13	Chapter 6, 14, 15
				4-5						1				5-6				Chapter 2, 14	Chapter 3, 5, 6, 11-16

Level 4						Level 5						Level 6						Level 7	Level 8
U1	U2	U3	U4	U5	U6	U1	U2	U3	U4	U5	U6	U1	U2	U3	U4	U5	U6	Exploring Art	Understanding Art
	3						5-6						1-3					Chapter 3, 6	Chapter 7, 8, 10, 15, 17
	4-6							2-3					4-6					Chapter 3, 4, 7	
			1-3					4-6							1-4			Chapter 3, 11, 12	Chapter 5, 7, 9, 10, 11, 13
			4-6					1-6							1-6			Chapter 3, 11, 14	Chapter 5, 11, 12
			6		5				3-4						5-6			Chapter 3, 11	Chapter 5, 10, 11, 12, 16
					5				2								1-2	Chapter 3, 6, 13	Chapter 3, 4, 5, 10, 15
					4				1								3-4	Chapter 3, 6, 7	Chapter 4, 5, 7, 12, 16
					6				5-6								5-6	Chapter 3	Chapter 7

Media

Scope and Sequence

Media	Level K						Level 1						Level 2						Level 3					
	U1	U2	U3	U4	U5	U6	U1	U2	U3	U4	U5	U6	U1	U2	U3	U4	U5	U6	U1	U2	U3	U4	U5	U6
Collage	6	2	2, 3		1	3	3		5			3, 4	5	5						4				
Drawing	2, 4, 5	4, 5	1, 4, 5	1	2	1, 2	1	1–3, 5	1, 4		2, 6	1, 5				2, 3	2–4, 6	4	1, 2, 5, 6	3	1	1	3, 5	6
Fiber Arts				4, 6							5						5					6		2
Mixed Media		6		3, 4	3				5			5	1	2	2, 6	2	2, 3	6		6	4, 6			4
Painting	1		6				1, 2, 4	4	3, 6	6			3, 4	6	1, 4–6		1, 3		3	2	2, 3, 5	4		
Photography																								
Printmaking		3									4				1					1			1	
Three-Dimensional Forms				2, 5, 6	5	4, 6				1–4	3	6	1	1, 3, 4		4	1	5		4, 5		2, 3	4, 6	1, 5
Technology	3	1				5	6	6	2							5		2, 6				5	2	3

*Numbers indicate lesson numbers within a given unit.

Level 4						Level 5						Level 6						Level 7 Exploring Art	Level 8 Understanding Art
U1	U2	U3	U4	U5	U6	U1	U2	U3	U4	U5	U6	U1	U2	U3	U4	U5	U6		
	6	3				1		4	2			5	6				1	Chapter 1, 6, 10	Chapter 10
1–6	3, 4	2		1, 2, 4, 5		2, 4, 5	1, 4	1, 5	1, 4	3	2	1	3	1, 2, 4	3–5	1, 2, 5		Chapter 2, 7, 11, 14	Chapter 3, 15, 16
					3, 6	3, 6								2	4	2	3, 5	Chapter 1, 2, 3, 13	Chapter 7, 8, 10, 12
	1, 5		4, 5			1, 4				1			6			6	4	Chapter 5, 13	Chapter 2, 3
		4–6				2, 5	2, 3	3	3	4, 5	1	5	1, 2, 4	5	1			Chapter 2, 3, 4, 5, 6, 9, 11, 14	Chapter 1–8, 10, 11, 13–17
			3			6											2	Chapter 10	Chapter 1, 17
																3		Chapter 3, 4, 8	Chapter 1, 3, 6, 8, 14–17
		1–3					5, 6	6	5, 6		6	3, 4		3, 6	6	3	6	Chapter 2, 3, 4, 5, 7, 12, 13	Chapter 1, 2, 3, 5–13, 15–17
	2	1		6	6	3		2			6		5		2	4		Chapter 4, 11, 15	Chapter 3, 17

Program Glossary

A

active lines *noun* Lines that show action and add energy and movement to a work of art. Diagonal, zigzag, and curved lines are examples of active lines.

additive sculpture *noun* When something is added to either relief or freestanding sculpture

alternating pattern *noun* Can repeat a motif, but change position; alter spacing between motifs or add a second motif

analogous color scheme *noun* Uses colors that are side by side on the color wheel and have a common color

analogous colors *noun* Colors that sit side by side on the color wheel and have a common hue. Violet, blue-violet, blue, blue-green are examples of analogous colors.

angle *noun* A shape formed when two lines extend in different directions from the same point

animal forms *noun* A three-dimensional representation of an animal

ant's view *noun* Viewers feel they are looking up, toward an object or figure.

appliqué *noun* An art form in which cutout fabrics are attached to a larger surface

approximate symmetry *noun* A special kind of formal balance where both sides of a design are almost exactly the same. One example is the human face: each side is almost the same as the other.

arc *noun* Any portion of a curved line from a circle

architects *noun* Artists who design buildings, cities, and bridges using three-dimensional forms

architecture *noun* The art of designing and planning buildings, cities, and bridges

armature *noun* A framework for supporting material used in sculpting

art form *noun* A type of art

assemblage *noun* A sculpture technique in which a variety of objects is assembled to create one complete piece

asymmetrical balance *noun* Another name for informal balance

asymmetry *noun* Another name for informal balance. Something asymmetrical looks balanced even if it is not the same on both sides.

atmospheric perspective *noun* The effects air and light have on how we perceive an object

axis *noun* A real or imaginary line across the center of a work of art

B

background *noun* The area of the picture plane farthest from the viewer

balance *noun* The principle of design that deals with visual weight in an artwork

bird's-eye view *noun* Or aerial view; viewers feel they are looking down on a scene.

black ■

blending *noun* A shading technique that creates a gradual change from light to dark or dark to light

blind contour drawing *noun* A drawing that is made by looking at the object being drawn, not at the paper.

blob *noun* A type of free-form shape

body forms *noun* Three-dimensional representations of a person

body proportions *noun* The size relationship of one part of the body to another

brass *noun* A metal made by combining copper and zinc

bright colors *noun* colors that appear to reflect light

broken (line) *noun* A line that is made of a series of dashes, not solid

building *noun* a structure where we live, work, meet, or play

C

calm lines *noun* Lines that give a work of art a quiet and peaceful mood. Horizontal and vertical lines are calm lines.

carving *noun* Art made by cutting into the surface of the medium.

central axis *noun* A real or imaginary dividing line that can run in two directions, vertically and horizontally

circle *noun* A round, geometric shape made when all points are placed the same distance from a center point.

close-up view *noun* Viewers feel they are right next to an object, or are a part of the action in a picture.

coil *noun* A long roll of clay joined into a circle or spiral. Clay coils are used to make pottery.

collage *noun* A two-dimensional work of art made up of pieces of paper and/or fabric to create the image.

collograph *noun* A printmaking technique where cut papers or thin boards are arranged to create an image on a stiff printing plate.

color *noun* 1. The art element that is created from reflected light; 2. In balance: a brighter color has more visual weight than a dull color; 3. In perspective: bright-colored objects seem closer, while dull or pale objects appear farther away.

color intensity *noun* The brightness or dullness of a color

color scheme *noun* A plan for organizing the colors used in an artwork

color spectrum *noun* The effect that occurs when light passes through a prism and separates into a band of colors in the order of red, orange, yellow, green, blue, and violet.

color wheel *noun* Shows the color spectrum bent into a circle

column *noun* A supporting pillar on a building

complementary color scheme *noun* Uses one set of complementary colors; for example, red and green, blue and orange, and yellow and violet

complementary colors *noun* Colors that are opposite each other on the color wheel

complex geometric shapes *noun* Shapes made by combining simple geometric shapes such as triangles, squares, and rectangles. Some examples of complex geometric shapes are diamonds, pentagons, trapezoids, hexagons, parallelograms, and octagons.

contour *noun* The edges and surface ridges of an object

contour hatching *noun* A shading technique that follows the form of an object

contour lines *noun* Continuous, unbroken lines that show the edges and surface ridges of an object or figure

contrast *noun* 1. A technique for creating a focal point or area of interest in a work of art using differences in elements; 2. In emphasis: contrast occurs when one element stands out from the rest of the work; 3. showing differences between things

converging *adj.* (*verb*) Coming together at one point or place

converging lines *noun* One of the six perspective techniques. Parallel lines seem to converge or move toward the same point as they move away from you.

cool colors *noun* Green, violet, and blue. They suggest coolness and move away from the viewer.

cool hues *noun* Blue, green, and violet. Cool hues are associated with cool things like snow, water, and grass.

cross-hatching *noun* A shading technique created when sets of parallel lines cross or intersect

culture *noun* Another word for custom

curling *verb* Hold one end of a long strip of paper. Grip the middle of the paper strip next to the side of a pencil. With a quick motion, pull the strip firmly across the pencil.

curved *adj.* Lines that bend and change gradually or turn inward to form spirals

curved (line) *noun* A line that changes directions slowly and bends in arcs

curving movement *verb* Using curved lines to move the viewer's eyes through a work of art and make the viewer feel that objects in the work of art are moving along curves

D

dark lines *noun* Created by using less water for watercolor paints

dark value *noun* A value that has more black added to it

decorative *adj.* Serving to make more beautiful; to adorn with ornaments

depth *noun* 1. The appearance of distance; 2. How far something extends toward or away from the viewer.

detail *noun* One of the six perspective techniques. Objects with fuzzy, blurred edges appear farther away than those with clear sharp edges.

diagonal *noun* (*adj.*) Lines that are slanted. They look as if they are falling or rising. They make things look active.

diagonal movement *verb* Using diagonal lines to move the viewer's eyes through a work of art and make the viewer feel that objects in the work of art are moving along diagonals

dimension *noun* A measurement of the amount of space an object takes up in one direction

diorama *noun* A display of a scene using sculpted, miniature figurines

directional lines *noun* How a line moves: diagonally, vertically, or horizontally

distortion *noun* A deviation from normal or expected proportions

dominant *noun* (*adj.*) The part of the work of art that seems more important to the viewer. Dominant elements have been emphasized.

dominant element *noun* The element in a work of art that is noticed first.

dull colors Colors that are not bright

E

earthenware *noun* Ceramics made out of clay and fired at a low heat

elongate *verb* To stretch out or make long

embroidery *noun* The art of decorating designs with needle and thread

emphasis *noun* The principle of design that stresses one area in an art work over another area

even balance *adj.* Both halves are equal. Left side and right side are the same.

exaggerate *verb* To make much larger than actual size

exaggeration *noun* To increase or enlarge beyond what is expected or normal

F

facial proportions *noun* The relationship of one feature of a face to another feature

faraway view *noun* Or eye-level view; viewers feel they are standing far away from the scene.

fiber *noun* A material used to make baskets and cloth. Grass, yarn, and straw are kinds of fibers.

flowing lines *noun* Create a feeling of calm and gracefulness. Flowing lines are fluid; they change direction and size.

flowing rhythm *noun* Created when curved lines or shapes are repeated

focal point *noun* The point where the receding lines meet. It is the first part of a composition to attract the viewer's attention.

foreground *noun* The area of the picture plane that is closest to the viewer

form *noun* A three-dimensional object that is measured by height, width, and depth

formal balance *noun* Occurs when equal or similar elements are placed on opposite sides of a central axis

Program Glossary (continued)

free-form forms *noun* Three-dimensional forms with irregular edges often found in nature

free-form shapes *noun* Two-dimensional images made of straight or curved lines or a combination of both

freestanding *noun* Forms that can be seen from all around

freestanding sculpture *noun* A three-dimensional work of art that can be viewed on all sides because it is surrounded by space

fringing *verb* Make parallel straight cuts along the edge of a piece of paper to create a ruffled look.

frontal proportions *noun* A front view of the head that is divided by three horizontal lines across the central axis

futurists *noun* A group of Italian artists during the early twentieth-century who repeated and overlapped shapes and lines to create the illusion of movement

G

geometric forms *noun* Mathematically precise forms based on geometric shapes

geometric shapes *noun* Mathematically precise shapes: circle, square, and triangle

gesture *noun* An expressive movement

gesture drawings *noun* Quick drawings used to capture the position or pose of the body

gesture lines *noun* Lines drawn to capture the movement of a person, an animal, or an object in a painting or drawing

gesture sketch *noun* Quick drawings used to capture the position or movement of the body

guide lines *noun* Lines used by artists to create both full-face and profile portraits more accurately

H

hand tools *noun* Simple instruments for carving or sculpting

harmony *noun* The principle of art that creates unity by stressing similarities of separate but related parts

hatching *noun* A shading technique that looks like a series of parallel lines

height *noun* A vertical measurement, or how tall something is

high-intensity color *noun* A pure hue such as red

highlights *noun* Small areas of white or light value to show the brightest spots

horizon line *noun* The point at which the earth and sky meet. The horizon line is always at the viewer's eye level.

horizontal *noun* (*adj.*) A line that moves from side to side

hues *noun* The spectral colors, or colors of the rainbow. Hues do not include black or white. Hues are red, orange, yellow, green, blue, and violet.

I

informal balance *noun* A way of organizing parts of a design so that unlike objects have equal visual weight

installation *noun* An artwork that was created for a specific place, such as a gallery or outdoor location

intensity *noun* The brightness or dullness of a color

interior designers *noun* Artists who decorate the inside of a building

intermediate colors *noun* Colors made by mixing a primary color and a secondary color. There are six intermediate colors—red-orange, yellow-orange, yellow-green, blue-green, blue-violet, and red-violet.

intermediate hues *noun* Yellow-green, red-orange, blue-green, made by combining a primary hue with either of the secondary hues that are adjacent on the color wheel

invented texture *noun* Created when an artist uses lines or other elements to make a textural look without any specific texture in mind

irregular *adj.* Does not follow a rule or pattern

isolation *noun* An object is emphasized by its placement apart from other objects.

J

jeweler *noun* An artist who designs and makes jewelry

jewelry *noun* Three-dimensional artwork that is made for people to wear

K

kinetic movement *noun* Actual or real movement

kinetic sculpture *noun* A three-dimensional form that actually moves in space

L

landscape *noun* a picture of the outdoors

light lines *noun* Created by adding more water to watercolor paints

light value *noun* A value that has more white added to it

line *noun* A mark drawn by a tool such as a pencil, pen, or paintbrush as it moves across a surface

line variety *noun* The different possibilities in the character of lines. For example, lines can be long or short, thick or thin, rough or smooth, and broken or solid.

linear perspective *noun* A system used to create the illusion of depth on a flat surface

lines *noun* One of the six perspective techniques. Parallel lines seem to converge or move toward the same point as they move away from the viewer.

location *noun* Artists can emphasize an object by placing it closer to the center of the piece.

low-intensity color *noun* A dull hue made by mixing a color with its complement

M

mandala *noun* A radial design divided into sections or wedges, each of which contains a different image

maquette *noun* A small model for a larger sculpture

mask *noun* A three-dimensional art form of sculpted faces

matte *noun* A dull, sometimes rough finish

medium *noun* The supply an artist uses to create art. Some media are clay, paint, or wood.

middle ground *noun* The area of the picture plane that is usually toward the center

minimal details *noun* Used in gesture sketches to complete the drawing

mix a neutral color *verb* Mix a neutral color with another color to change its value

mixed-media *noun* An art object that has been created from an assortment of media or materials

mobile *noun* A moving sculpture in which shapes are balanced and arranged on wire arms and suspended from the ceiling to move freely in the air currents

monochromatic *adj.* A color scheme that is made up of one color and the tints and shade of that color

monochromatic color scheme *noun* Uses only one color and the values of that color

monotonous *adj.* Lack of variety; boring

monumental sculptures *noun* Sculptures that are larger than human forms

motif *noun* A unit that is made up of objects or art elements that can be repeated

movement *noun* The principle of art that leads a viewer's eyes throughout a work of art

mural *noun* A painting done on a wall

N

negative space *noun* The empty space that surrounds objects, shapes, and forms

neon *noun* A special kind of light that can be made to be many bright colors

neutral color scheme *noun* Uses black, white, and a variety of grays

neutral colors *noun* Black, white, and gray; give hues a range of values

nonobjective *adj.* Art that has no recognizable subject matter

O

one-point linear perspective *noun* A system used to create the illusion of depth on a flat surface where all receding lines meet at one point

opaque *adj.* Does not let light through

outline *noun* a line drawn around the edge of an object

overlap *verb* To place one object on top of another object and partially cover the first object up

overlapping *noun* 1. One object covers a portion of another object. 2. In perspective: one of the six perspective techniques; the object covering another will appear closer to the viewer, creating a feeling of depth.

P

painting *noun* An art form using paint on a flat surface

paper sculpting techniques *noun* Six different techniques used to create paper sculptures: scoring a straight line, scoring a curve, pleating, curling, fringing, tab and slot.

parallel lines *noun* Lines that move in the same direction and always stay the same distance apart

pattern *noun* A repeated surface decoration

perception drawing *verb* Looking at something carefully and thinking deeply about what you see as you draw

perspective *noun* The method used to create the illusion of depth in two-dimensional art: overlapping, size, placement, detail, color, converging lines

perspective techniques *noun* The six techniques an artist uses to create the illusion of depth in two-dimensional art: overlapping, size, placement, detail, color, converging lines

photograph *noun* A picture taken using light-sensitive film and a camera

picture plane *noun* The surface of a drawing or painting

placement *noun* One of the six perspective techniques. Objects placed lower in the picture appear to be closer than those placed near eye level. There are three areas on a picture plane: foreground, middle ground, and background.

pleating *verb* Fold piece of paper from edge to edge. Then fold the same amount of paper in the other direction. Continue folding the paper back and forth in this manner.

point of view *noun* The angle at which the viewer sees an object

portrait *noun* A two- or three-dimensional artwork created in the image of a person or animal

posed *verb* Arranged in a special way

position *noun* In balance: a larger, positive shape and a small, negative space can be balanced by a small, positive shape and a large, negative space.

positive space *noun* Refers to any object, shape, or form in two- and three-dimensional art

primary colors *noun* Red, yellow, and blue. They cannot be made by mixing colors.

primary hues *noun* Red, yellow, and blue, used to mix the other hues on the color wheel

print *noun* An image created by using a stamp or printing plate. When artists make prints, they can make many identical images.

printing *verb* Pressing a shape from one thing to another many times

printing plate *noun* A plate that holds the image that will be used to create a print

prism *noun* A wedge-shaped piece of glass that bends light as it passes through

profile *noun* A side view of a person or animal

profile proportions *noun* A side view of the head that is divided by three horizontal lines

proportion *noun* The principle of art that is concerned with the size relationship of one part to another

Program Glossary (continued)

R

radial balance *noun* A type of balance that occurs when the art elements come out, or radiate, from a central point

rainbow *noun* An arc of spectral colors, usually identified as red, orange, yellow, green, blue, indigo, and violet, that appears in the sky opposite the sun

random pattern *noun* Occurs when the motif is repeated in no apparent order

ratio *noun* A comparison of size between two things

real texture *noun* Texture you can feel

realistic scale *noun* When an artist creates a work of art where everything fits together and makes sense in size relation

rectangle *noun* A four-sided geometric shape made of all right angles and whose opposite sides are equal in length.

regular pattern *noun* Occurs when identical motifs are repeated with an equal amount of space between them

relief *noun* A type of sculpture where forms project from a flat background

relief sculpture *noun* A sculpture in which objects stick out from a flat surface

repeated lines *noun* Used to give the feeling of movement or motion in a gesture drawing

repetition *noun* Lines, shapes, colors, or textures that are repeated throughout an artwork

rest *noun* The negative space between repetitions of the motif

rhythm *noun* The principle of design that organizes the elements in a work of art by repeating elements and/or objects

rough *noun* (*adj.*) A surface that has ridges; not smooth

rough (line) *noun* A line that has jagged, uneven edges

S

sail *noun* A type of free-form shape

scale *noun* Size as measured against a standard reference

score *verb* The repeated scratching of the clay surface at the area that another scored piece will be attached

scoring a curve *verb* Gradually cut bending curves in the paper with the point of the scissors

scoring a straight line *verb* Hold a ruler in the center of a piece of paper. Run the point of the scissors along the edge of the ruler to cut the paper in a straight line.

sculpture *noun* Three-dimensional art

sculpture model *noun* The study or detailed example of what the sculpture will look like when completed

secondary colors *noun* Orange, green, and violet. These colors are made by mixing two primary colors.

secondary hues *noun* Orange, green, and violet; the result of mixing two primary hues

self-portrait *noun* A two- or three-dimensional artwork that an artist makes of him or herself

sets of complementary colors *noun* There are three sets on the color wheel: red and green, blue and orange, and yellow and violet.

shade *noun* Any hue blended with black

shading *noun* A technique for creating dark values or darkening an area by repeating marks such as lines or dots

shadows *noun* Shaded areas in a painting or drawing

shape *noun* A two-dimensional area that is measured by height and width

shape reversal *noun* Occurs when an object, shape, or form is positive space in one image and then in another image becomes negative space

shiny *noun* Bright from reflected light

silhouette *noun* The shape of a shadow

simulated texture *noun* Imitates real texture, see also visual texture

size *noun* 1. in perspective: objects that are closer look larger than objects that are farther away; 2. In balance: a large shape or form will appear to be heavier than a small shape, and several small shapes can balance one large shape.

slip *noun* A mixture of clay and water that is creamy to the touch and is used to attach two scored pieces of clay together

smooth *noun* A surface free from roughness; even

smooth (line) *noun* A line that has even edges

solid (line) *noun* A line that has no breaks, gaps, or holes

space *noun* The art element that refers to the areas above, below, between, within, and around an object

spectral color scheme *noun* Uses all the colors of the rainbow: red, orange, yellow, green, blue, and violet

spectral colors *noun* The colors of the light spectrum: red, orange, yellow, green, blue, and violet

spectrum *noun* The range of colors that it is possible to see; the rainbow

splash *noun* A type of free-form shape

square *noun* A four-sided geometric shape where all sides are the same length and all angles are right angles

statue *noun* Three-dimensional art that is a body form

still life *noun* The arrangement of common inanimate objects from which artists draw or paint

stippling *noun* A shading technique using dots to show value

stitchery *noun* Art made with yarn on cloth

storyteller doll *noun* A Native American sculpture that shows one person relating the history of the culture to many children

style *noun* A unique quality of an object

subordinate *noun* The parts of the artwork that seem less important. Subordinate objects are not emphasized.

subtractive sculpture *noun* When an artist carves pieces away from a form

surrealism *noun* An art movement that emphasized art in which dreams, fantasy, and the subconscious served as inspiration for artists

symmetrical When two sides of a work of art are mirror images of each other

symmetry *noun* A type of formal balance in which two halves of a balanced artwork are identical, mirror images of each other

T

tactile texture *noun* The texture that can be felt

texture *noun* 1. The art element that refers to the way something feels; 2. In balance: a rough texture has an uneven pattern of highlights and shadows. For this reason, a rough surface attracts the viewer's eyes more easily than a smooth, even surface.

thick (line) *adj.* Wide

thick line *noun* Created by beginning with a thin line and gradually pressing the brush down

thin (line) *adj.* Narrow

thin line *noun* Created when a brush is held vertically to paper and touched lightly with the tip of the brush

three-dimensional *adj.* Has measurements in three directions: height, width, and depth

three-dimensional patterns *noun* Patterns that have depth and are formed on the surface of a sculptural form

three-dimensional rhythm *noun* A principle of design that indicates movement by the repetition of elements in a form

tint *noun* Any hue blended with white

transparent *adj.* Allows light to pass through so objects on the other side can be seen

triangle *noun* A three-sided geometric shape

two-dimensional *adj.* Shapes that are flat and can be measured by length and width

two-dimensional decoration *noun* Flat decoration produced on the surface of a work of art

U

unity *noun* The feeling of wholeness in a work of art. Artists use repetition and grouping to show that different parts of a work belong together.

unrealistic scale *noun* When an artist makes size relationships that do not make sense

V

value *noun* The lightness or darkness of a hue

value contrast *noun* The lightness or darkness stands out from the value that surrounds it

vanishing point *noun* The point on the horizon line where all parallel receding lines meet

variety *noun* The principle of art which is concerned with difference or contrast

vertical *noun* (*adj.*) Lines that move straight up and down. They make things look tall, steady, and calm.

visual movement *noun* Occurs when the eye is pulled through a work of art by a rhythm of beats and rests

visual rhythm *noun* The feeling of movement created when artists repeat colors, shapes, lines, and textures to lead the viewer's eyes through a work of art

visual texture *noun* Or simulated texture, imitates real texture. It is the illusion of a three-dimensional surface.

visual weight *noun* cannot be measured on a scale; it is measured by which objects the viewer's eyes see first.

W

warm colors *noun* Red, yellow, and orange. They suggest warmth and come toward the viewer.

warm hues *noun* Red, orange, and yellow. Warm hues are associated with warm things such as fire or sunshine.

weave *verb* To interlace or interweave strips or strands of material

width *noun* A horizontal measurement, or how long across something is

Z

zigzag *noun* (*adj.*) A line that is made by joining diagonal lines

Program Index

Program Index (continued)

Program Index (continued)

Program Index (continued)

Program Index (continued)